# G·L·O·B·A·L  S·T·U·D·I·E·S

THE MIDDLE EAST

NINTH EDITION

**Dr. William Spencer**

## OTHER BOOKS IN THE GLOBAL STUDIES SERIES
- Africa
- China
- Europe
- India and South Asia
- Japan and the Pacific Rim
- Latin America
- Russia, the Eurasian Republics, and
  Central/Eastern Europe

**McGraw-Hill/Dushkin**
**530 Old Whitfield Street, Guilford, Connecticut 06437**
**Visit us on the Internet—http://www.dushkin.com**

# STAFF

| | |
|---|---|
| **Ian A. Nielsen** | Publisher |
| **Brenda S. Filley** | Director of Production |
| **Lisa M. Clyde** | Developmental Editor |
| **Roberta Monaco** | Editor |
| **Charles Vitelli** | Designer |
| **Robin Zarnetske** | Permissions Editor |
| **Lisa Holmes-Doebrick** | Senior Program Coordinator |
| **Marie Lazauskas** | Permissions Assistant |
| **Michael Campbell** | Production Coordinator |
| **Laura Levine** | Graphics |
| **Tom Goddard** | Graphics |
| **Eldis Lima** | Graphics |
| **Nancy Norton** | Graphics |
| **Juliana Arbo** | Typesetting Supervisor |
| **Cynthia Vets** | Typesetter |

Cataloging in Publication Data
Main Entry under title: Global Studies: Middle East. 9/E.
        1. Middle East—History. 2. Arab countries—History. 3. Israel—History.
I. Title: Middle East. II. Spencer, William, *comp.*
ISBN 0-07-250575-3        954        94-071561        ISSN 1056-6848

Ninth Edition

We would like to thank Digital Wisdom Incorporated for allowing us to use their Mountain High Maps cartography software. This
software was used to create the relief maps in this edition.

Printed in the United States of America        234567890BAHBAH543        Printed on Recycled Paper

# The Middle East

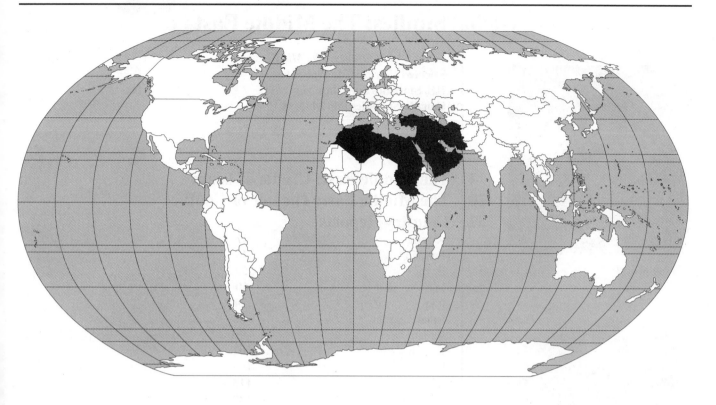

## AUTHOR/EDITOR

### Dr. William Spencer

The author/editor for *Global Studies: The Middle East* was formerly professor of history at Florida State University and has specialized in Middle East/North African affairs for more than 40 years. He is the author of many books on the region and, in addition to his university teaching, has traveled extensively on research, U.S. government, and United Nations assignments. Since retiring from Florida State, Dr. Spencer has continued to be active in his field, serving as visiting professor at various colleges and universities. In his teaching and service as a curriculum consultant, particularly to school systems and community colleges, Dr. Spencer has made his life's work helping U.S. educators develop a better understanding of this volatile region of the world.

## CONSULTANT
### Elizabeth Bouvier Spencer

Elizabeth Spencer is an artist and teacher who has traveled with her husband, Dr. William Spencer, to the Middle East on many research trips. She is responsible for much of the material in this book on home and family life, architecture, and housing, aside from her contributions as grammarian and amanuensis extraordinary.

## SERIES CONSULTANT
### H. Thomas Collins
Washington, D.C.

# Contents

## Global Studies: The Middle East

Islamic World      Page 12

Egypt      Page 52

Israel      Page 87

Kuwait                    Page 104

Syria                     Page 148

# Using Global Studies: The Middle East

## THE GLOBAL STUDIES SERIES

The Global Studies series was created to help readers acquire a basic knowledge and understanding of the regions and countries in the world. Each volume provides a foundation of information—geographic, cultural, economic, political, historical, artistic, and religious—that will allow readers to better assess the current and future problems within these countries and regions and to comprehend how events there might affect their own well-being. In short, these volumes present the background information necessary to respond to the realities of our global age.

Each of the volumes in the Global Studies series is crafted under the careful direction of an author/editor—an expert in the area under study. The author/editors teach and conduct research and have traveled extensively through the regions about which they are writing.

In *Global Studies: The Middle East,* the author/editor has written several regional essays and country reports for each of the countries included.

## MAJOR FEATURES OF
## THE GLOBAL STUDIES SERIES

The Global Studies volumes are organized to provide concise information on the regions and countries within those areas under study. The major sections and features of the books are described here.

### Regional Essays

For *Global Studies: The Middle East,* the author/editor has written several essays focusing on the religious, cultural, sociopolitical, and economic differences and similarities of the countries and peoples in the various regions of the Middle East. Regional maps accompany the essays.

### Country Reports

Concise reports are written for each of the countries within the region under study. These reports are the heart of each Global Studies volume. *Global Studies: The Middle East, Ninth Edition,* contains 20 country reports.

The country reports are composed of five standard elements. Each report contains a detailed map visually positioning the country among its neighboring states; a summary of statistical information; a current essay providing important historical, geographical, political, cultural, and economic information; a historical timeline, offering a convenient visual survey of a few key historical events; and four "graphic indicators," with summary statements about the country in terms of development, freedom, health/welfare, and achievements.

### A Note on the Statistical Reports

The statistical information provided for each country has been drawn from a wide range of sources. (The most frequently referenced are listed on page 234.) Every effort has been made to provide the most current and accurate information available. However, sometimes the information cited by these sources differs to some extent; and, all too often, the most current information available for some countries is somewhat dated.

Aside from these occasional difficulties, the statistical summary of each country is generally quite complete and up to date. Care should be taken, however, in using these statistics (or, for that matter, any published statistics) in making hard comparisons among countries. We have also provided comparable statistics for the United States and Canada, which can be found on pages viii and ix.

### World Press Articles

Within each Global Studies volume is reprinted a number of articles carefully selected by our editorial staff and the author/editor from a broad range of international periodicals and newspapers. The articles have been chosen for currency, interest, and their differing perspectives on the subject countries. There are 12 articles in *Global Studies: The Middle East, Ninth Edition.*

The articles section is preceded by an annotated table of contents providing a brief summary of each article.

### WWW Sites

An extensive annotated list of selected World Wide Web sites can be found on the facing page (vii) in this edition of *Global Studies: The Middle East.* In addition, the URL addresses for country-specific Web sites are provided on the statistics page of most countries, as space permits. All of the Web site addresses were correct and operational at press time. Instructors and students alike are urged to refer to those sites often to enhance their understanding of the region and to keep up with current events.

### Glossary, Bibliography, Index

At the back of each Global Studies volume, readers will find a glossary of terms and abbreviations, which provides a quick reference to the specialized vocabulary of the area under study and to the standard abbreviations used throughout the volume.

Following the glossary is a bibliography, which lists general works, national histories, and current-events publications and periodicals that provide regular coverage on the Middle East.

The index at the end of the volume is an accurate reference to the contents of the volume. Readers seeking specific information and citations should consult this standard index.

### Currency and Usefulness

*Global Studies: The Middle East,* like the other Global Studies volumes, is intended to provide the most current and useful information available necessary to understand the events that are shaping the cultures of the region today.

This volume is revised on a regular basis. The statistics are updated, regional essays and country reports revised, and world press articles replaced. In order to accomplish this task, we turn to our author/editor, our advisory boards, and—hopefully—to you, the users of this volume. Your comments are more than welcome. If you have an idea that you think will make the next edition more useful, an article or bit of information that will make it more current, or a general comment on its organization, content, or features that you would like to share with us, please send it in for serious consideration.

# Selected World Wide Web Sites for The Middle East

**All of these Web sites are hot-linked through the *Global Studies* home page:**
***http://www.dushkin.com/globalstudies* (just click on a book).**

Some Web sites are continually changing their structure and content, so the information listed may not always be available.

## General Sites

BBC News—**http://news.bbc.co.uk/hi/english/world/middle_east/ default.stm**—Access current Middle East news from this BBC site.

CNN Interactive—World Regions: Middle East—**http://www.cnn. com/WORLD/#mideast**—This 24-hour news channel often focuses on the Middle East and is updated every few hours.

C-SPAN Online—**http://www.c-span.org**—See especially C-SPAN International on the Web for International Programming Highlights and archived C-SPAN programs.

Library of Congress—**http://www.loc.gov**—An invaluable resource for facts and analysis of 100 countries' political, economic, social, and national-security systems and installations.

ReliefWeb—**http://www.reliefweb.int/w/rwb.nsf**—UN's Department of Humanitarian Affairs clearinghouse for international humanitarian emergencies. It has daily updates, including Reuters and Voice of America.

United Nations—**http://www.unsystem.org**—The official Web site for the United Nations system of organizations. Everything is listed alphabetically, and data on UNICC and Food and Agriculture Organization are available.

UN Development Programme (UNDP)—**http://www.undp.org**—Publications and current information on world poverty, Mission Statement, UN Development Fund for Women, and much more. Be sure to see the Poverty Clock.

UN Environmental Programme (UNEP)—**http://www.unep.org**—Official site of UNEP with information on UN environmental programs, products, services, events, and a search engine.

U.S. Central Intelligence Agency Home Page—**http://www.cia. gov/ index.html**—This site includes publications of the CIA, such as the World Factbook, Factbook on Intelligence, Handbook of International Economic Statistics, CIA Maps and Publications, and much more.

U.S. Department of State Home Page—**http://www.state.gov/ www/ind.html**—Organized alphabetically (i.e., Country Reports, Human Rights, International Organizations, and more).

World Health Organization (WHO)—**http://www.who.ch**—Maintained by WHO's headquarters in Geneva, Switzerland, the site uses Excite search engine to conduct keyword searches.

## Middle East Sites

Access to Arabia—**http://www.accessme.com**—Extensive information about traveling and working in the Arab world is presented on this Web site.

ArabNet—**http://www.arab.net**—This site is an extensive online resource for the Arab world in the Middle East and North Africa. There are links to every country in the region, covering current news, history, geography, culture, government, and business topics.

Arabia.On.Line—**http://www.arabia.com**—Discussions of Arab news, business, and culture are available at this site.

Camera Media Report—**http://world.std.com/~camera/**—This site is run by the Committee for Accuracy in Middle East Reporting in America, and it is devoted to fair and accurate coverage of Israel and the Middle East.

Center for Middle Eastern Studies—**http://w3.arizona.edu/~cmesua/**—This Web site is maintained by the University of Arizona Center for Middle Eastern Studies. The Center's mission is to further understanding and knowledge of the Middle East through education.

Center for Middle Eastern and Islamic Studies—**http://www.dur. ac.uk/~dme0www/**—The University of Durham in England maintains this site. It offers links to the University's extensive library of Middle East information; the Sudan Archive is the largest collection of documentation outside of Sudan itself.

The Middle East Institute—**http://www.mideasti.org**—The Middle East Institute is dedicated to educating Americans about the Middle East. The site offers links to publications, media resources, and other links of interest.

Middle East Internet Pages—**http://www.middle-east-pages. com**—A large amount of information on specific countries in the Middle East can be obtained on this site. Their engine allows you to browse through virtually every aspect of Middle East culture, politics, and current information.

Middle East Policy Council—**http://www.mepc.org**—The purpose of the Middle East Policy Council's Web site is to expand public discussion and understanding of issues affecting U.S. policy in the Middle East.

Middle East Times—**http://metimes.com**—The *Middle East Times* is a source for independent analysis of politics, business, religion, and culture in the Middle East.

Middle Eastern and Arab Resources—**http://www.ionet.net/ ~usarch/WTB-Site.shtml**—This omnibus site offers extensive information on each of the Middle Eastern countries. Scroll to their flags.

## Israel Sites

The Abraham Fund—**http://www.coexistence.org**—The goal of peaceful coexistence between Jews and Arabs is the theme of this site. Information to various projects and links to related sites are offered.

Zionist Archives—**http://www.wzo.org.il/cza**—This site is the official historical archives of the World Zionist Organization, the Jewish Agency, the Jewish National Fund, Karen Hayesod, and the World Jewish Congress.

---

**We highly recommend that you review our Web site for expanded information and our other product lines. We are continually updating and adding links to our Web site in order to offer you the most usable and useful information that will support and expand the value of your book. You can reach us at: *http://www.dushkin.com*.**

# The United States (United States of America)

## GEOGRAPHY

*Area in Square Miles (Kilometers):* 3,717,792 (9,629,091) (about ½ the size of Russia)

*Capital (Population):* Washington, DC (568,000)

*Environmental Concerns:* air and water pollution; limited freshwater resources, desertification; loss of habitat; waste disposal

*Geographical Features:* vast central plain, mountains in the west, hills and low mountains in the east; rugged mountains and broad river valleys in Alaska; volcanic topography in Hawaii.

*Climate:* mostly temperate

## PEOPLE

### Population

*Total:* 276,000,000

*Annual Growth Rate:* 0.91%

*Rural/Urban Population Ratio:* 24/76

*Major Languages:* predominantly English; a sizable Spanish-speaking minority; many others

*Ethnic Makeup:* 83.5% white; 12.4% black; 3.3% Asian; 0.8% Amerindian

*Religions:* 56% Protestant; 28% Roman Catholic; 2% Jewish; 4% others; 10% none or unaffiliated

## Health

*Life Expectancy at Birth:* 74 years (male); 80 years (female)

*Infant Mortality Rate (Ratio):* 6.82/1,000

*Physicians Available (Ratio):* 1/365

### Education

*Adult Literacy Rate:* 97% (official; estimates vary widely)

*Compulsory (Ages):* 7–16; free

## COMMUNICATION

*Telephones:* 173,000,000 main lines

*Daily Newspaper Circulation:* 238 per 1,000 people

*Televisions:* 776 per 1,000 people

*Internet Service Providers:* 7,800 (2001 est.)

## TRANSPORTATION

*Highways in Miles (Kilometers):* 3,906,960 (6,261,154)

*Railroads in Miles (Kilometers):* 149,161 (240,000)

*Usable Airfields:* 13,387

*Motor Vehicles in Use:* 206,000,000

## GOVERNMENT

*Type:* federal republic

*Independence Date:* July 4, 1776

*Head of State:* President George W. Bush

*Political Parties:* Democratic Party; Republican Party; others of minor political significance

*Suffrage:* universal at 18

## MILITARY

*Military Expenditures (% of GDP):* 3.8%

*Current Disputes:* none

## ECONOMY

*Per Capita Income/GDP:* $33,900/$9.25 trillion

*GDP Growth Rate:* 4.1%

*Inflation Rate:* 2.2%

*Unemployment Rate:* 4.2%

*Labor Force:* 139,430,000

*Natural Resources:* minerals; previous metals; petroleum; coal; copper; timber; arable land

*Agriculture:* food grains; feed crops; fruits and vegetables; oil-bearing crops; livestock; dairy products

*Industry:* diversified in both capital- and consumer-goods industries

*Exports:* $663 billion (primary partners Canada, Mexico, Japan)

*Imports:* $912 billion (primary partners Canada, Japan, Mexico)

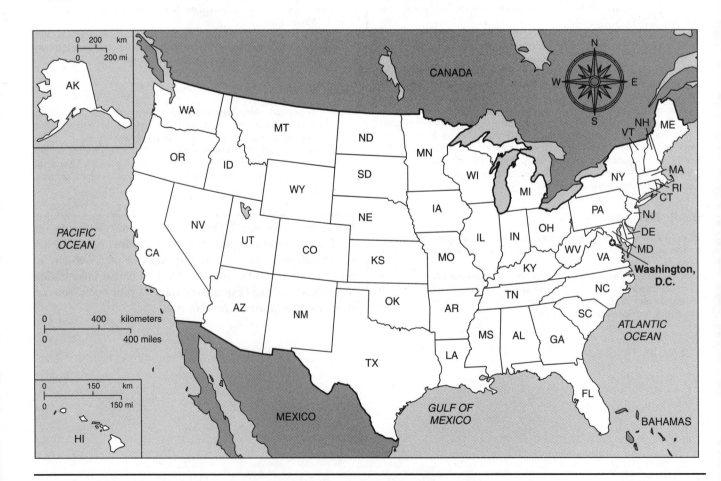

# Canada

## GEOGRAPHY

*Area in Square Miles (Kilometers):* 3,850,790 (9,976,140) (slightly larger than the United States)

*Capital (Population):* Ottawa (1,000,000)

*Environmental Concerns:* air pollution and resulting acid rain severely affecting lakes and damaging forests; water pollution; industrial damage to agriculture and forest productivity

*Geographical Features:* permafrost in the north hinders development, mountains in the west, central plains, and a maritime culture in the east

*Climate:* from temperate in south to subarctic and arctic in north

## PEOPLE

### Population

*Total:* 31,300,000

*Annual Growth Rate:* 1.02%

*Rural/Urban Population Ratio:* 23/77

*Major Languages:* both English and French are official

*Ethnic Makeup:* 28% British Isles origin; 23% French origin; 15% other European; 6% others; 2% indigenous; 26% mixed

*Religions:* 46% Roman Catholic; 16% United Church; 10% Anglican; 28% others

### Health

*Life Expectancy at Birth:* 76 years (male); 83 years (female)

*Infant Mortality Rate (Ratio):* 5.08/1,000

*Physicians Available (Ratio):* 1/534

### Education

*Adult Literacy Rate:* 97%

*Compulsory (Ages):* primary school

### COMMUNICATION

*Telephones:* 18,500,000 main lines

*Daily Newspaper Circulation:* 215 per 1,000 people

*Televisions:* 647 per 1,000 people

*Internet Service Providers:* 760 (2001 est.)

### TRANSPORTATION

*Highways in Miles (Kilometers):* 559,240 (902,000)

*Railroads in Miles (Kilometers):* 22,320 (36,000)

*Usable Airfields:* 1,411

*Motor Vehicles in Use:* 16,800,000

### GOVERNMENT

*Type:* confederation with parliamentary democracy

*Independence Date:* July 1, 1867

*Head of State/Government:* Queen Elizabeth II; Prime Minister Jean Chrétien

*Political Parties:* Progressive Conservative Party; Liberal Party; New Democratic Party; Reform Party; Bloc Québécois

*Suffrage:* universal at 18

### MILITARY

*Military Expenditures (% of GDP):* 1.2%

*Current Disputes:* none

### ECONOMY

*Currency ($U.S. Equivalent):* 1.53 Canadian dollars = $1

*Per Capita Income/GDP:* $23,300/$722.3 billion

*GDP Growth Rate:* 3.6%

*Inflation Rate:* 1.7%

*Labor Force:* 15.1 million

*Natural Resources:* petroleum; natural gas; fish; minerals; cement; forestry products; wildlife; hydropower

*Agriculture:* grains; livestock; dairy products; potatoes; hogs; poultry and eggs; tobacco; fruits and vegetables

*Industry:* oil production and refining; natural-gas development; fish products; wood and paper products; chemicals; transportation equipment

*Exports:* $277 billion (primary partners United States, Japan, United Kingdom)

*Imports:* $259.3 billion (primary partners United States, Japan, United Kingdom)

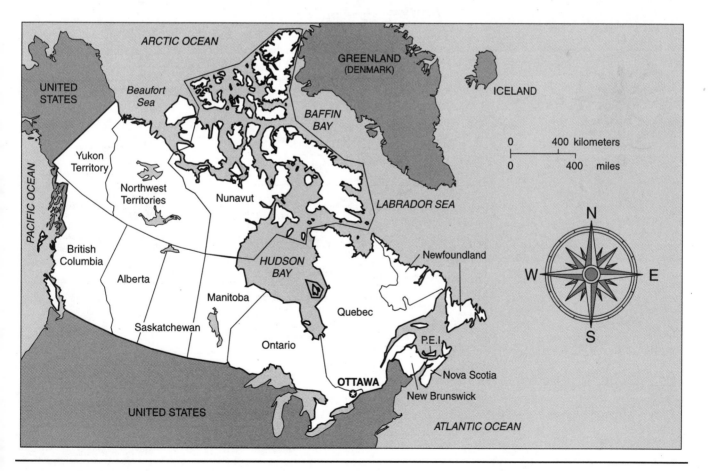

This map is provided to give you a graphic picture of where the countries of the world are located, the relationships they have with their region and neighbors, and their positions relative to major powers and power blocs. We have focused on certain areas to illustrate these crowded regions more clearly.

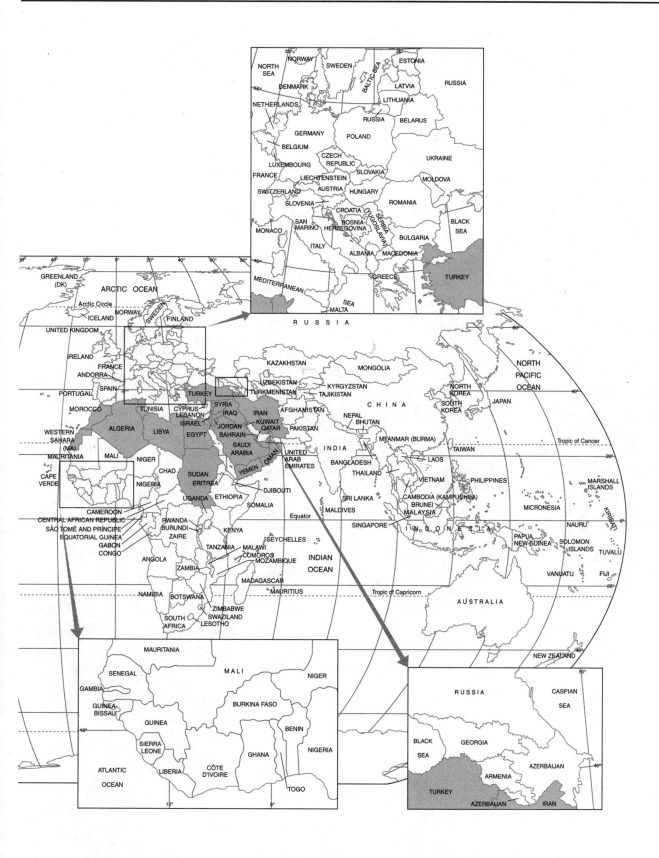

# The Middle East

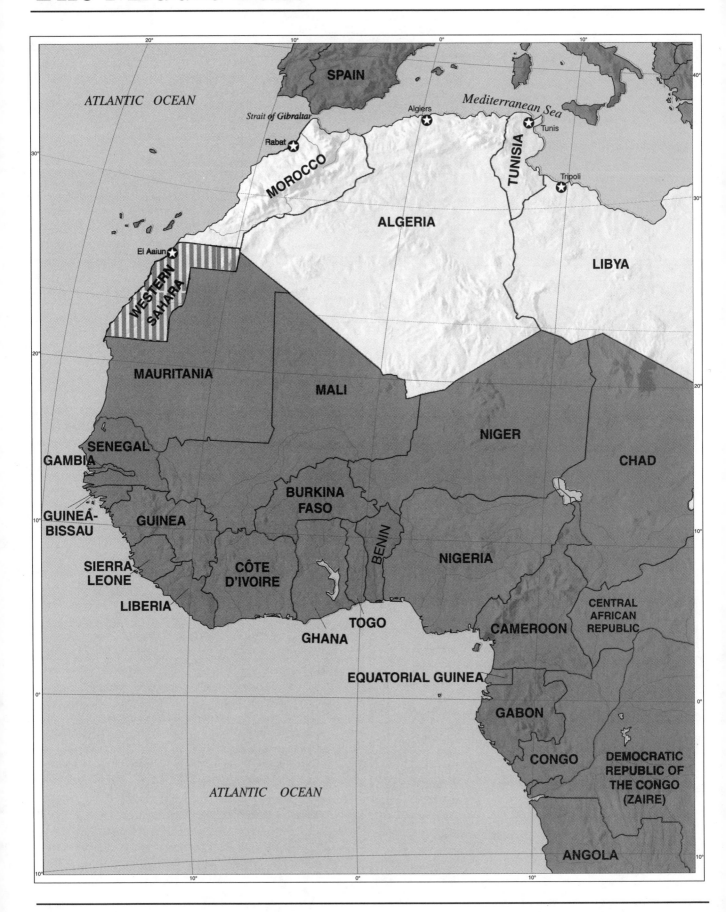

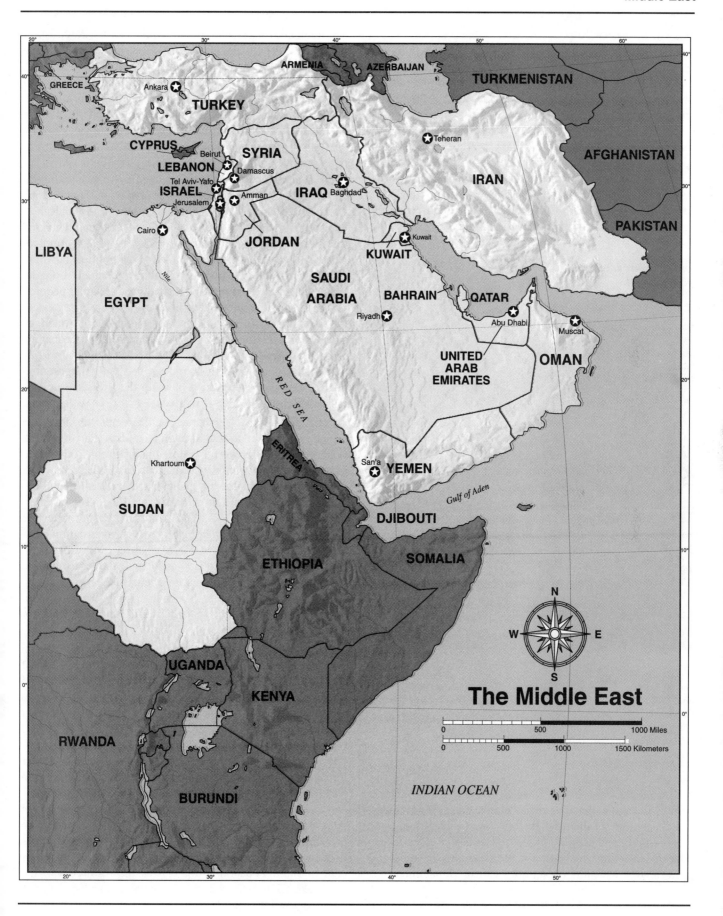

The Middle East

# The Middle East: Cradle of Islam

## ISLAM IN FERMENT

Until quite recently, the world of Islam, centered in the Middle East, was a remote grey area to most Americans. To many of those who passed through the area en route to the invasions of occupied Europe in World War II, it was a hot, dusty place, peopled by men dressed in what appeared to be bed sheets, who sat in fly-blown cafés at the outskirts of military bases drinking endless glasses of hot sweet tea and speaking an incomprehensible language. This naive stereotype changed little in the intervening years, except for the addition of the State of Israel, whose Jewish peoples made the desert bloom and more than stood their ground militarily against the children of those men in "bed sheets."

(UN photo)

The Middle East did not make a real impact on the American consciousness until 1979, when the followers of the Ayatollah Khomeini seized the U.S. Embassy in Teheran and held its occupants hostage for more than a year. The extent to which fundamentalist Shia Muslims would follow Khomeini, pictured on the placard displayed above, was little recognized before this event.

Seen against the strong image of Israel, that country's Middle Eastern neighbors seemed unimportant. Most Americans knew little of their rich histories or of their struggles to attain dignity and stability in the new world of independent states. Many people had only a vague awareness of a religious group called Muslims (mistakenly called Mohammedans), who inhabited the Middle East in large numbers and practiced a religion known as Islam. But in political terms, the Muslims seemed powerless, disorganized, always on the brink of conflict. With the exception of Israel—often perceived as an extension of the United States—the predictability that Americans had come to expect of governments like their own was not to be found among the quarrelsome leaders of these Middle Eastern states. Thus the thunderous impact of Islam on the United States came with little advance warning or preparation.

The American public abruptly came face to face with militant Islam in 1979, when the U.S. Embassy in Teheran, Iran, was seized by supporters of religious leader Ayatollah Ruhollah Khomeini and its occupants held hostage. Their detention for more than a year made yellow ribbons a symbol of America's captivity to Islam and led to the political downfall of President Jimmy Carter, but produced relatively little development in Americans' understanding of Islamic peoples. Later, misreading of their motivations by the Reagan administration led to the disastrous assignment of American marines to Lebanon as part of a multinational peacekeeping force after the 1982 Israeli invasion of that country. In 1983, a truck carrying what was later described as the largest nonnuclear bomb ever exploded blew up the U.S. Marine barracks in Beirut, killing 241 marines.

In the mid-1980s, the Islamic Jihad, a secret Lebanese Shia organization linked to Iran through Hizbullah (Party of God), Lebanon's most powerful Shia Muslim group, initiated a campaign of kidnappings of Americans and other foreigners in Beirut. Other shadowy organizations, such as Revolutionary Justice and Islamic Holy War for the Liberation of Palestine, followed suit. U.S. involvement in Lebanon after the Israeli invasion and revelations of the Reagan administration's secret arms deals with Iran shifted the kidnappers' focus to one of revenge for U.S. and Israeli actions against the "sacred Islamic soil" of Lebanon, whereas the original reason for the hostage taking had been to obtain the release of "Islamic brothers" held in Israeli and European jails for terrorist activities.

Altogether, more than a dozen Americans, plus Briton Terry Waite (the personal representative of the archbishop of Canterbury) and a number of British, French, German, and Italian citizens, were held hostage for periods of up to seven years. The longest-held was Associated Press Middle East bureau chief Terry Anderson. Between 1986 and 1990, there were no hostage releases; but in 1990–1991, protracted negotiations by United Nations (UN) secretary-general Javier Perez de Cuellar and his mediators, through intermediaries in Iran (the protective umbrella for Lebanese Shia organizations and essentially the only outside force capable of influencing the kidnappers), led finally to the resolution of the "hostage problem." One contributing factor in the complex negotiations was the release by Israel of Shia Lebanese prisoners held in south Lebanon. Another was the resolution of the Lebanese Civil War and establishment of de facto Syrian control over most of that country. However, Islamic Jihad's release of Anderson in December 1991 was accompanied by a statement emphasizing both the political and the Islamic aspects of the long-running hostage issue. It stated, in part: "The confrontation created by the kidnappings made the world listen to the voice of oppressed people and unmasked the ugly American and Israeli faces ... but after finishing several stages we decided to free our last captive, thus folding this page in the hostage file before glorious Christmas."

These and other shocks since 1979, particularly the terrorist attacks in the United States on September 11, 2001, have brought the United States face to face with what appears to be a recent phenomenon of confrontation in the Middle East between Muslims and Westerners. To give the phenomenon a name, we call it "Islam in ferment."

What has caused this ferment? What does it consist of, and why is it directed so violently against the United States in particular? Is it a new phenomenon, or is it a natural progression for Islam, arising out of the circumstances in which Muslims find themselves in the world today? What are the elements that play a role in the Islamic ferment? We address these questions in this report.

## THE CONCEPT OF JIHAD

Jihad is one of the most important elements in the Islamic ferment. It may be defined as "sacred struggle," "striving" (i.e., of the individual to carry out God's will), or, when exercised against the enemies of Islam, "holy war." The Afghan *mujahideen* (resistance fighters) who fought during the 1980s to expel Soviet forces from their homeland characterized their struggle as a jihad, as did Iranian Revolutionary Guards challenging U.S. forces in the Persian Gulf, to give just two of many examples.

But jihad can also be directed against apostates or weak believers *within* the House of Islam. In 1979, Muslims who seized the Great Mosque in Mecca, Saudi Arabia, argued that the Saudi government should be replaced, on these grounds: Islam does not allow secular kings or dynasties, and the Saudi government had deviated from "true" Islamic law and principles. And during the trial of those arrested for the 1981 assassination of Egyptian president Anwar al-Sadat, their leader argued that there were three reasons for the justness of their act: the incompatibility of Egypt's laws with Islamic law, Sadat's peace with Israel, and the sufferings of "good" Muslims under the regime.[1]

Another form of jihad-inspired violence within Islamic society has developed out of the religious division of Islam into Sunni and Shia groups. The Muslim Brotherhood, to give an example, is a Sunni Muslim organization, spread throughout the Islamic world, that seeks the replacement of all existing regimes by a universal Islamic state faithful to the ideals and practices of the original community of believers founded by Muhammad. As a result, it has at times been banned, proscribed, and ruthlessly repressed by those regimes. In

(Aramco Photo)

One of the Five Pillars of Islam, or five basic duties of Muslims, is to go on a pilgrimage to Mecca in Saudi Arabia once in their lifetime. There they circle seven times around the Black Box (the Ka'ba, pictured above), kiss the Black Stone, drink from the well of Zam Zam, and perform other sacred rites.

Syria, the Brotherhood represented the principal opposition to the Alawi Shia minority government of President Hafez al-Assad. The Brotherhood's main power base was once the city of Hama, home of a conservative Sunni population. Brotherhood members carried out a series of assassinations of Alawi officials from Hama and made two attempts on the life of the Syrian president. They called Assad an "enemy of Allah" and a Maronite (Lebanese Christian). In 1982, after the discovery of an Air Force plot to overthrow him that was linked to the Brotherhood, Assad ordered his troops into Hama and all but obliterated the city in the process of crushing his opposition.[2]

These militant events have not occurred in isolation. They are part of the struggle of Muslim peoples to come to terms with the modern world and to define an appropriate role for Islam in that world.

The difficulty for fundamentalist Muslims in defining such a role stems from the fact that their religion operates under very specific divine rules of conduct. These rules were laid down in the A.D. 600s by Muhammad the Messenger, who received them as revelations from God. The sum total of these

## THE KORAN: THE HOLY BOOK OF ISLAM

Muslims believe that the Koran is the literal Word of God and that Muhammad was chosen to receive God's Word through the Angel Gabriel as a *rasul* (messenger). But the Koran does not cancel out the Bible and Torah, which preceded it. The Koran is viewed, rather, as providing a corrective set of revelations for these previous revelations from God, which Muslims believe have been distorted or not followed correctly. To carry out God's Word, as set down in the Koran, requires a constant effort to create the ideal Islamic society, one "that is imbued with Islamic ideals and reflects as perfectly as possible the presence of God in His creation."*

The Koran was revealed to Muhammad over the 22-year period of his ministry (A.D. 610–632). The revelations were of varying lengths and were originally meant to be committed to memory and recited on various occasions, in particular the daily prayers. Even today, correct Koranic practice requires memorization and recitation; during the fasting month of Ramadan, one section per day should be recited aloud.

In its original form, the Koran was either committed to memory by Muhammad's listeners or written down by one or more literate scribes, depending upon who was present at the revelation. The scribes used whatever materials were at hand: "paper, leather, parchment, stones, wooden tablets, the shoulder-blades of oxen or the breasts of men."** The first authoritative version was compiled in the time of the third caliph, Uthman, presumably on parchment. Since then, the Holy Book has been translated into many other languages as Islam has spread to include non-Arab peoples.

All translations stem from Uthman's text. It was organized into 114 *suras* (chapters), with the longest at the beginning and the shortest at the end. (The actual order of the revelations was probably the reverse, since the longer ones came mostly during Muhammad's period in Medina, when he was trying to establish guidelines for the community.)***

Many of the revelations provide specific guides to conduct or social relationships:

*When ye have performed the act of worship, remember Allah sitting, standing and reclining. . . . Worship at fixed times hath been enjoined on the believers. . . .*
(*Sura IV,* 103)

*Establish worship at the going down of the sun until the dark of night, and at dawn. Lo! The recital of the Koran at dawn is ever witnessed.*
(*Sura XVII,* 78–79)

*Make contracts with your slaves and spend of your own wealth that God has given you upon them. . . .*
(*Sura XXIV,* 33)

*If you fear that you will be dishonest in regard to these orphan girls, then you may marry from among them one, two, three or four. But if you fear you will not be able to do justice among them, marry only one.*
(*Sura IV,* 3)

Much of the content of the Koran is related to the ethical and moral. It is an Arab Koran, given to Arabs "in clear Arabic tongue" (*Sura XLI,* 44) and characterized by a quality of style and language that is essentially untranslatable. Muslim children, regardless of where they live, learn it in Arabic, and only then may they read it in their own language, and then always accompanied by the original Arabic version. Recitals of selections from the Koran are a feature of births, marriages, funerals, festivals, and other special events and are extraordinarily effective, whether or not the listener understands Arabic.****

* Peter Awn, "Faith and Practice," in Marjorie Kelly, ed., *Islam: The Religious and Political Life of a World Community* (New York: Praeger, 1984), pp. 2–7.
** *The Qur'an, The First American Version,* Translation and Commentary by T.B. Irving (Brattleboro, VT: Amana Books, 1985), Introduction, XXVII.
*** On this topic, see Fazlur Rahman, *Major Themes of the Qur'an* (Chicago: Bibliotheca Islamica, 1980), *passim.*
**** "The old preacher sat with his waxen hands in his lap and uttered the first Surah, full of the soft warm coloring of a familiar understanding. . . . His listeners followed the notation of the verses with care and rapture, gradually seeking their way together . . . like a school of fish following a leader, out into the deep sea." Lawrence Durrell, *Mountolive* (London: Faber and Faber, 1958), p. 265.

revelations is the Koran, the Holy Book of Islam. Because Muslims believe that the Koran is the literal Word of God, they also believe that it is not subject to change but only to interpretation—and that to within a narrow range. Until very recently, Muslim's acceptance of the Koran as God's Word, perfect and immutable, precluded research into its possible historical origins and development. Questions about its authenticity as a text were considered an attack against Islam itself. However, the discovery in Yemen in 1972 of a cache of parchment pages and fragments from damaged copies of the Koran, dating back to the first two centuries of Islam (seventh–eighth centuries A.D.), which contain variations from the standard version, suggests that rather than the immutable Word of God, His Holy Book has its own developmental history.

Differing views as to the Koran's authenticity as text may develop in the future in the Islamic world to divide Muslims just as the Reformation divided Christian society in the 1600s. But the ferment in Islamic society today derives from different interpretations of *jihad.*

Conflict over interpretation of the term has had a great impact on Muslims the world over. For example, members of the organization Islamic Jihad believe that their interpretation of *jihad* as a holy war against the enemies of Islam is the correct one. The holy-war definition of *jihad* is the one most familiar to non-Muslims. Muslims have always believed that God intended them to struggle to establish Islam as a universal religion, although conversion of other monotheists (Jews and Christians) would not be required as long as these communities recognized the superiority of Islam. The military interpretation of *jihad* has led to the division of the world into the Dar al-Islam ("House of Islam") and the Dar al-Harb ("House of Dissidence"), the area yet to be brought into the House of Islam.[3]

Other Muslim groups, notably the Nakshbandi, a dervish order based in Bukhara (modern Uzbekistan) that dates back to the fourteenth century, reject the warlike view of *jihad*. Instead, they follow a policy of peace, tolerance, and cooperation with all faiths.

Another definition of *jihad,* the striving of the individual for justice, is perhaps the most controversial. Islam teaches that if rulers—whether elected or appointed over some Islamic territory—become unjust, their subjects should bear the injustices with fortitude; God will, in due course, reward their patience. Some Muslims interpret this injunction to mean that they should strive to help the leaders to see the error of their ways—by whatever action deemed necessary. Centuries ago, a secret society, the Hashishin ("Assassins"; so named because they reportedly were users of hashish), carried out many assassinations of prominent officials and rulers, claiming that God had inspired them to rid Islamic society of tyrants. Since Islam emphasizes the direct relationship of people to God—and therefore people's responsibility to do right in the eyes of God and to struggle to help other believers follow the same, correct path—it becomes most dangerous when individuals feel that they do not need to subject themselves to the collective will but, rather, to impose their own concepts of justice on others.

In our own day, jihad is often associated with the struggle of Shia Muslims for social, political, and economic rights within Islamic states. Inspired by the example of Iran, some seek to establish a true Islamic government in the House of Islam. But Iranian Muslims are not only militant, they are also strongly nationalistic. In this respect, they differ sharply in their approach to Islamic reform from the approaches of other militant Islamic groups, notably the Muslim Brotherhood. Its founder, Hassan al-Banna, stressed peaceful and gradual change in Islamic governments.: "The Brotherhood stands ready to assist [these] governments in the improvement of society through basic Islamification of beliefs, moral codes, and institutions." [4] Osama bin Laden's al Qaeda terrorist network, in contrast, seeks the overthrow of these governments by violence, considering them unrepresentative and therefore un-Islamic.

No such strictures affect Iranians' view of jihad. An important element in their belief system derives from their special relationship with their religious leaders, particularly the late Ayatollah Khomeini. In his writings and sermons, Khomeini stressed the need for violent resistance to unjust authorities.

A strong example of "internal" Islamic jihad in recent years developed during the annual *Hajj* ("Great Pilgrimage") to Mecca in August 1987. Iranian pilgrims, taking literally Khomeini's injunction that the Hajj is the ideal forum for demonstration of the "proper use of Islam in politics," staged a political rally after midday prayer services. Demonstrators carrying posters of Khomeini shouted, "Death to America! Death to the Soviet Union! Death to Israel!" Saudi police attempting to control them were attacked, and the demonstra-

tion swiftly grew into a riot. When it was over, more than 400 people had been killed, including 85 policemen, and 650 people had been injured. "To take revenge for the sacred bloodshed is to free the holy shrines from the wicked Wahhabi," an Iranian government official told a crowd in Teheran.[5]

## ISLAMIC ORIGINS

Some negative views of Islam by Westerners are the result of the Crusades, highly colored by generations of Sunday-school textbooks. However, Islam developed among a particular people, the Arabs; was built on earlier foundations of Christianity and Judaism; and was primarily concerned with the transmission of the spiritual message of God to humankind as a corrective measure. It is an article of faith among Arab nationalists and Muslim Arab scholars that the Arabs were chosen as a people to receive God's revelations because they were cousins of the Jews through Abraham and therefore were included in the Judeo–Christian tradition. But they did not have scriptures of their own.

Islam was founded in the seventh century A.D. by Muhammad, a merchant in the small town of Mecca in southwestern Arabia. Muslims believe that Muhammad's religious teachings came from revelations that he received orally from God via the Angel Gabriel. After Muhammad's death, these revelations were put into book form in the *Koran* ("Recitation"), the Holy Book of Islam.

During Muhammad's lifetime, the various revelations he received were used to guide his followers along the "Way" of conduct (*Shari'a,* in Arabic) acceptable to God. The Arabs followed traditional religions in Muhammad's time, worshipping many gods. Muhammad taught belief in one God—Allah—and in the Word of God sent down to him as messenger. For this reason, Muhammad is considered the Prophet of Islam.

Muhammad's received revelations plus his own teachings issued to instruct his followers make up the formal religious system known as Islam. The word *Islam* is Arabic and has been translated variously as "submission," "surrender" (i.e., to God's will), and the fatalistic "acceptance." A better translation might be "receptiveness." Those who receive and accept the Word of God as transmitted to Muhammad and set down in the Koran are called Muslims.

Islam is essentially a simple faith. Five basic duties are required of the believer; they are often called the Five Pillars because they are the foundations of the House of Islam. They are:

1. The confession of faith: "I testify that there is no God but God, and Muhammad is the Messenger of God."
2. Prayer, required five times daily, facing in the direction of Mecca, the holy city.
3. Fasting during the daylight hours in the month of Ramadan, the month of Muhammad's first revelations.
4. Alms giving, a tax or gift of not less than $2\frac{1}{2}$ percent of one's income, to the community for the help of the poor.

## THE ISLAMIC CALENDAR

The Islamic calendar is a lunar calendar. It has 354 days in all, divided into 7 months of 30 days, 4 months of 29 days, and 1 month of 28 days. The first year of the calendar, A.H. 1 (*Anno Hegira,* the year of Muhammad's "emigration" to Medina to escape persecution in Mecca), corresponds to A.D. 622.

In the Islamic calendar, the months rotate with the Moon, coming at different times from year to year. It takes an Islamic month 33 years to make the complete circuit of the seasons. The fasting month of Ramadan moves with the seasons and is most difficult for Muslims when it takes place in high summer.

5. Pilgrimage, required at least once in one's lifetime, to the House of God in Mecca.

It is apparent from the above description that Islam has many points in common with Judaism and Christianity. All three are monotheistic religions, having a fundamental belief in one God. Muslims believe that Muhammad was the "seal of the Prophets," the last messenger and recipient of revelations. But they also believe that God revealed Himself to other inspired prophets, from Abraham, Moses, and other Old Testament (Hebrew Bible) figures down through history, including Jesus Christ. However, Muslims part company with Christians over the divinity of Jesus as the Son of God; the Resurrection of Jesus; and the tripartite division into Father, Son, and Holy Ghost or Spirit.

Although Muhammad is in no way regarded as divine by Muslims, his life is considered a model for their own lives. His *hadith* ("teachings" or "sayings") that were used to supplement Koranic revelations (or to deal with specific situations when no revelation was forthcoming) have served as guides to Muslim conduct since the early days of Islam. The Koran and hadith together form the *Sunna* (translated literally as "Beaten Path"), which provides an Islamic code of conduct for the believers.

The importance of Muhammad's role in Islam cannot be overemphasized. Among Muslims, his name is used frequently in conversation or written communication, always followed by "Peace Be Unto Him" (PBUH). A death sentence imposed on the writer Salman Rushdie by Iran's revolutionary leader Ayatollah Khomeini resulted from an unflattering portrait of Muhammad in Rushdie's novel *The Satanic Verses* (1988). And an Israeli woman's depiction of Muhammad as a pig writing in the Koran, on a poster displayed in Hebron, roused a storm of protest throughout the Muslim world. She was arrested by Israeli police and given a 21-year jail sentence for "harming religious sensibilities."[6]

## ISLAMIC DIVISIONS: SUNNIS AND SHIAS

The great majority (90 percent) of Muslims are called Sunnis, because they follow the Sunna, observe the Five Pillars, and practice the rituals of the faith. They also interpret as correct the history of Islam as it developed after Muhammad's death, under a line of successors termed *caliphs* ("agents" or "deputies") who held spiritual and political authority over the Islamic community. However, a minority, while accepting the precepts and rituals of the faith, reject this historical process as contrary to what Muhammad intended for the community of believers. These Muslims are called Shias (commonly, but incorrectly, Shiites). The split between Sunnis and Shias dates back to Muhammad's death in A.D. 632.

Muhammad left no instructions as to a successor. Since he had said that there would be no more revelations after him, a majority of his followers favored the election of a caliph who would hold the community together and carry on his work. But a minority felt that Muhammad had intended to name his closest male blood relative, Ali, as his successor. Supporters of Ali declared that the succession to Muhammad was a divine right inherited by his direct descendants. Hence they are known as Shias ("Partisans") of Ali.

The first three caliphs—Abu Bakr, Umar, and Uthman— were chosen by majority vote by the Mecca community. Under their leadership, Arab armies expanded Islam's territory far outside Arabia, changing what had been essentially a religious community into a political power through the conversion of non-Arab peoples to Islam and the imposition of rule by Islamic caliphs. These conquests compounded Sunni–Shia differences.

Ali was eventually elected as the fourth caliph; but by that time, the divisions were so deep that his election was disputed. The Kharijites, an extremist group, who felt that Muhammad's original purpose in founding the Islamic community had been distorted, decided to assassinate Ali and his major rival, on the grounds that Ali had accepted arbitration in his dispute with this rival over the election. The Kharijites argued that the office of caliph could not be bartered away; it was a sacred trust transmitted from God to Muhammad. One of them murdered Ali outside a mosque in A.D. 661.

Ali's younger son and designated successor, Husayn, was ambushed and killed in A.D. 680 by the army of Yazid, the son of the fourth caliph's major rival, near the town of Karbala (in modern Iraq). This event led to the founding of a hereditary dynasty, the Umayyads. The Umayyad caliphs moved the Islamic capital from Mecca to Damascus. But the intrigues and rivalries of Muslim leaders continued to hamper political stability. A century and a half later, a rival group overthrew the Umayyads and established a third caliphate, the Abbasids. The caliphal capital was moved eastward, to Baghdad, where it endured for 500 years and developed the distinctive features of *Islamic* civilization, the successor in many respects of Greek and Roman civilizations and precursor of European civilization.

The Abbasid caliphs were Sunnis, and Shia resistance to them as presumed usurpers of the rightful heritage of Ali and his descendants resulted in much persecution. Shia rebellions were put down with bloody massacres by the ruling Sunnis.

Forced to go underground, the Shia Muslims began to practice *taqiya* ("dissimulation" or "concealment"). Outwardly, they bowed to the authority of Sunni rulers; secretly, however, they continued to believe in the divine right of Ali's descendants to rule the Islamic world.

Most Shia Muslims recognize a line of 12 direct descendants of Muhammad, through Ali and Husayn, as their Imams, or spiritual leaders. When the 12th Imam died, a number of Shia religious leaders declared that he was not dead but hidden (alive, present in this world, but invisible) and would return at the end of time to pronounce the Day of Judgment. Until the Hidden Imam returned, the religious leaders would provide leadership and interpretation of God's will and make decisions on behalf of the Shia community. This doctrine gave the Shia religious leaders more authority over Shia Muslims than Sunni religious leaders have over Sunni Muslims. This helps to explain the tremendous power and prestige that Ayatollah Khomeini, leader of the revolution that established an Islamic republic in Iran, held among his people.

With one exception, Shia Muslims remained a minority in Islamic lands and did not acquire political power. The exception was Iran. In the early 1500s, Shaykh Safi, the leader of a religious brotherhood in northern Iran, preached a jihad against the Ottoman Turks, accusing them of unjust practices and discrimination against the non-Turkish subjects of their empire. His successor, as head of the brotherhood, claimed to be descended from Ali, which entitled him to act on behalf of the Hidden Imam. In order to obtain further sanction for his wars with the Ottomans, the successor reached an agreement with Shia religious leaders whereby they would recognize him as ruler of Iran in return for a commitment to establish Shia Islam as the majority there.

Since then, Shia Islam has been the strongest bond linking the Iranian people; it transcends ethnic, linguistic, and social differences. The generally tolerant policies of Iran's rulers, dating back to the emperor Cyrus's return of the Jews to their ancestral homeland, has, however, one notable exception, that of the Bahais. The Bahai faith developed in Iran out of Islam in the late-nineteenth century. It was founded originally by Baha Ullah (Glory of God) within Islam. Baha Ullah, however, preached the unity of all religions and the oneness of humanity. For this reason he incurred the enmity of Iran's Shia religious leaders. The Bahais were protected and tolerated under the monarchy of Shah Mohammed Reza Pahlavi, but the overthrow of the last shah and the establishment of a theocratic republic in Iran destroyed the centuries-old balance between rulers and religious leaders that had enabled non-Islamic religious groups to survive unmolested.

## SHIA MUSLIMS AND MARTYRDOM
The murder of Husayn, far more than that of his father Ali, provided the Shia community with a martyr figure. This is due to the circumstances surrounding Husayn's death—the lingering image of Muhammad's grandson, with a small band of followers, surrounded in the waterless desert, to be cut down by the vastly superior forces of Yazid, has exerted a powerful influence on Shias. As a result, Shias often identify themselves with Husayn, a heroic martyr fighting against hopeless odds. For example, an important factor in the success of Iran in repelling the invasion of Iraqi forces in the bitter 1980–1988 Iran–Iraq War was the Basijis, teenage volunteers led into battle by chanters, in the firm belief that death at the hands of the Sunni Iraqi enemy was a holy action worthy of martyrdom.[7]

## ISLAM AND EUROPE: CHANGING ROLES
The early centuries of Islam were marked by many brilliant achievements. An extensive network of trade routes linked the cities of the Islamic world. It was a high-fashion world in which the rich wore silks from Damascus ("damask"), slept on fine sheets from Mosul ("muslin"), sat on couches of Morocco leather, and carried swords and daggers of Toledo steel. Islamic merchants developed many institutions and practices used in modern economic systems, such as banks, letters of credit, checks and receipts, and bookkeeping. Islamic agriculture, based on sophisticated irrigation systems developed in the arid Middle East, brought to Spain, in particular, a number of previously unknown food crops that include oranges, lemons, eggplant, radishes, and sugar. (The very names of these foods are Arabic in origin.) Successful agriculture, along with fine libraries, magnificent mosques, such as the Great Mosque in Cordoba, and citadel-palaces like the Alhambra in Granada, remain as monuments to

---

### 'ASHURA

A special Shia Muslim festival not observed by Sunnis commemorates the 10 days of 'Ashura, the anniversary of the death of Husayn. Shia Muslims mark the occasion with a series of ritual dramas that may be compared to the Christian Passion Play, except that they may be performed at other times during the year. Particularly in Iran, the ritual, called Ta'ziyeh, is presented by strolling troupes of actors who travel from village to village to dramatize the story with songs, poetry, and sword dances. Ta'ziyeh also takes place in street parades in cities, featuring penitents who lash themselves with whips or slash their bodies with swords. Freya Stark, the great English travel writer, describes one such procession in her book *Baghdad Sketches*:

All is represented, every incident on the fateful day of Karbala, and the procession stops at intervals to act one episode or another. One can hear it coming from far away by the thud of beaters beating their naked chests, a mighty sound like the beating of carpets, or see the blood pour down the backs of those who acquire merit with flails made of knotted chains with which they lacerate their shoulders; and finally the slain body comes, headless, carried under a bloodstained sheet through wailing crowds.

Spain's 700 years of high-Islamic civilization. During the European "dark" and Middle Ages, Islamic Spain and its capital, Cordoba, were the center of high civilization, one in which Muslims, Christians, and Jews lived in harmony.

Islamic medical technology reached a level of excellence in diagnosis and treatment unequaled in Europe until the nineteenth century. Muslim mathematics gave Europeans Arabic numerals and the concept of zero. Muslim navigators made possible Columbus's voyages, through their knowledge of seamanship and inventions such as the sextant and the compass. Their libraries were the most extensive in existence at that time.

The level of achievements of Islamic civilization from roughly 750 to 1200 was far superior to that of Europe. The first Europeans to come in direct contact with Islamic society were Crusader knights, Christians who invaded the Middle East in order to recapture Jerusalem from its Muslim rulers. The Crusaders marveled at what they saw, even though they were the sworn enemies of Islam. This Christian occupation of the Holy Land, while short-lived (1099–1187), contributed significantly to the mutual hostility that has marked Christian–Muslim relations throughout their coexistence. (A retired German diplomat who became a Muslim in 1980 expressed the difference between Christianity and Islam in social terms: "The alternative to an increasingly amoral lifestyle in the West is Islam, but an Islam rigorously practiced and free from fanaticism, brutality, violence, violation of human rights and other practices erroneously associated in the Western mind with the religion.")[8]

The hostility between Muslims and Christians generated by the Crusades was intensified by the rise of the Ottoman Turks, one of the many newly converted Islamic peoples, to power in the Islamic world. By the 1400s, they had established a powerful Islamic military state. In 1453, the Ottomans captured Constantinople (present-day Istanbul), capital of the East Roman (Byzantine) Empire, and soon controlled most of Central/Eastern Europe.

During the centuries of Ottoman rule, many people from the Christian European provinces became converts to Islam. Islamic peoples from other parts of the empire also migrated there, drawn by opportunities for land or other inducements, and Ottoman soldiers were often given land grants in return for service to the state. Muslims in Central/Eastern Europe remained there after countries such as Yugoslavia, Romania, Bulgaria, and Albania gained their independence from the sultan. Not until recently did their governments interfere substantially with the personal lives of their Muslim subjects. However, the wave of nationalism that swept over Central/Eastern Europe in the late 1980s in the wake of Soviet efforts under Mikhail Gorbachev to revitalize the Communist system led at least one government—that of Bulgaria—to begin a forcible assimilation of its Muslim minority.

The Ottoman state not only ruled Central/Eastern Europe for nearly four centuries but also dominated such emerging European nations as Russia, Austria, France, and England. These nations were struggling to limit the powers of absolute monarchs, develop effective military technology, and build systems of representative government. The Ottomans and the various Islamic peoples they governed did not think that any of these things were necessary. The Ottoman sultan was also the caliph of Islam. He was convinced that God had given him the right to rule and to know what was best for the people. Ottoman military success against Europe seemed to prove that God had given the Islamic world a stronger army, superior military technology, and a more effective way of life. The Ottomans were so sure of the superiority of Islam over anything that could be devised in the Christian West that they allowed Christian and Jewish communities under their control to practice their beliefs and rituals freely under their own leaders, in return for payment of a special tax and admission of their inferior military and political status, in exchange for Ottoman protection.

Gradually, these roles were reversed. The first reversal came with the defeats of Ottoman armies by various European powers. The Ottoman sultans were forced to sign treaties with rulers they deemed inferior. Worse yet, they lost territories with each defeat. In the early nineteenth century, European powers seized control of Egypt; in Central/Eastern Europe, meanwhile, the Greeks, Romanians, Serbs, and other subject peoples won their independence with European support. The defeat in Egypt was particularly shocking to Ottoman leaders, because Egypt had been part of the Islamic heartland for a thousand years.

An even greater shock came with the discovery by Muslims that the despised Europeans had developed a relatively advanced technology. Upper-class Muslim visitors to European lands in the late nineteenth century were astonished by this technology. Electric lights, railroads, broad boulevards sweeping through cities, telegraph lines, factories, and a long list of labor-saving inventions were all new to the Muslims. Most Islamic peoples were still living much as their ancestors had lived for centuries. When this apparent superiority in technology was added to European military dominance, it seemed to thoughtful Muslims that something had gone wrong.

The question was, What had gone wrong? How had it happened that the Islamic world had fallen behind Europe? Some Muslims believed that all one could do was to await the inevitable; God Himself had decided that it was time to bring the world to an end, and, therefore, the decline of Islam was a logical consequence. Other Muslims believed that the problem had developed because they had not been true to their religion or observed correctly the obligations of the faith. A third group of Muslims were convinced that Islam itself had to be "changed, modified, adapted or reformed to suit modern conditions . . . so as to overcome Western domination."[9]

The contrast between the second and third approaches to Islamic reform has been important in forming the Middle Eastern states of today. Two states, Saudi Arabia and, more

The mosque at Khan El Khalili, Egypt.

recently, Iran, developed out of a movement to reestablish the Islamic community of Muhammad in its original form, basing their campaign on calls for strict adherence to the Koran and the Sunna. The other Middle Eastern states developed on an ad hoc basis through Western tutelage and gradual acceptance of Western methods and technology.

## ISLAMIC FUNDAMENTALISM

The fundamentalism that appears to pervade the Islamic world today has its roots in earlier, nineteenth-century movements that sought to revitalize Islam through internal reform, thus enabling Islamic societies to resist foreign control. Some of these movements sought peaceful change; others were more militant. The most prominent of the militant groups was the Wahhabi movement, which laid the basis for the Saudi Arabian state—a pure Islamic state in form, law, and practice. Another was the Sanusiya, founded by a prominent scholar who sought to unite the nomadic and seminomadic peoples of Libya into a brotherhood. The Sanusiya movement was

also based on strict interpretation and application of the Koran. A third movement, Mahdism, developed in Sudan; its purpose was not only to purify Sudanese Islam but also to drive out the British who had invaded Sudan from Egypt. The aims of these three movements were essentially parochial and territorial, either to expel foreigners from Islamic soil or to impose a "purification" on their tribal neighbors.

More recent reform movements, emerging in the twentieth century, such as the Muslim Brotherhood, have concentrated their efforts on removal of secular Islamic governments, which, in their view, do not conform to the principles of the true faith and therefore are illegitimate. Islamic reform on the scale of the Christian Protestant Reformation has yet to be attempted, and the establishment of fixed national boundaries by Islamic governments bent on preserving their legitimacy makes it unlikely that a global Islamic state will emerge in the foreseeable future.

*Fundamentalism* is a somewhat incomplete term to apply to these recent Islamic movements, because it suggests to Westerners a religious view that is antimodernist, literal in interpretation, and with a strong emphasis on traditional ethics. Some fundamentalists would reestablish Islamic society peacefully through internal change, but others would revolutionize Islam in the manner of Marxist or other European revolutionary movements. Shia Muslim factions in Lebanon, such as the Hizbullah, view the revolutionary struggle as one aimed at expelling foreign influences first and achieving social justice second. This revolutionary movement, once centered around Khomeini in Iran, is committed to the rule of the religious leaders; while Libya's Muammar al-Qadhafi would eliminate the influence of the religious leaders entirely, substituting rule by "people's committees." The only common ground for these movements and groups is their fundamental opposition to the onslaught of materialistic Western culture. Their desire is to reassert a distinct Islamic identity for the societies they claim to represent.

The great danger to Islam is that rather than being a true revival of the religion, these movements may have altered its nature. Some of them would modernize Islam by grafting onto the religion negative and spiritually devastating ideas borrowed from the West. In the name of religious fervor, they close the door to the kind of open dialogue that could produce general agreement or understanding of what form Islam should take.

A common concern among Muslims is how to achieve *Islamic modernization,* meaning a future wherein political and social development and economic progress appropriate for the realities of the modern era are firmly rooted in Islamic history and values. The struggle between "modernizers" and "fundamentalists" for social control of Islamic peoples became, in the latter part of the twentieth century, a contest for political control of governments, because they were considered to be non-Islamic. In the modern Islamic states, the contest has varied in level of intensity and degree of violence. In Egypt and Jordan, the Muslim Brotherhood operates as a

(UN photo/John Isaac)

A common concern among Muslims is how to achieve Islamic modernization, wherein social development considers the realities of the current era. This dichotomy is illustrated by these Egyptian women in traditional dress waiting for a bus, a modern convenience.

quasi-legitimate political organization. It rejects violence and consequently finds itself aligned with their governments against extremists.

Elsewhere in the Middle East and North Africa, the Islamists (a more accurate term than fundamentalists) have had varying degrees of success. The Islamic Salvation Front (FIS) in Algeria, for example, was declared illegal after winning elections in 1991 for the country's first multiparty National Assembly. Annulment of the elections by military commanders and the arrest of key FIS leaders triggered a conflict between the military regime and militants of the Armed Islamic Group (GIA). The conflict soon turned to civil war, with the Algerian people caught between the Islamists and the army. Since then there have been periods of calm, interspersed with murderous violence that has caused more than 120,000 deaths. Although the current regime has announced an amnesty for members of the GIA in return for surrender of their arms, few have done so, and there is little indication that the conflict will end in the near future.

Turkey provides another example of a secular Islamic state that has been adversely affected by the contest between secularists and Islamists. In 1995, the Islamic Welfare Party (Refah) won control of the government in national elections and became the first Islamic-oriented party to do so since the founding of the Turkish republic. However, Refah's leader, Prime Minister Necmettin Erbakan, was forced to resign by the country's military leaders (who viewed themselves as guardians of the secular state founded by Ataturk). Subsequently, Refah was outlawed by a Turkish court as a subversive organization, and it was reformed under another name, Virtue. However, the party ran a poor third in the 1999

elections for the GNA. Up to now, the determination of miltary leaders to preserve the secular state, as guardians of Ataturk's legacy, have thwarted increased Islamist participation in the political process.

It should be noted that the long interaction between the West and the Islamic Middle East has resulted in the development of a large number of Western-oriented, if not Western-educated, leaders and professionals. Even the structure of the Middle East's Islamic regimes is modeled on Western institutions. Bernard Lewis reminds us that the Islamic Republic of Iran—the prototype for putative Islamic regimes—has an elected Assembly and a written Constitution, "for which there is no precedent in the Islamic past."[10] Modern secularist Muslims and fundamentalists alike view Islam as a divinely ordained alternative to both communism and Western free-market capitalism. Where they differ is that secularists would incorporate Western principles of law and political practice into Islamic society, blending them with a leaven of Islamic law. The fundamentalists, in contrast, would exclude these principles and turn to Islam as the sole controlling principle in society.

At various times fundamentalists groups have briefly seized control of Islamic governments, notably the Taliban in Afghanistan and the National Islamic Front in Sudan. Elsewhere, especially in Algeria and Egypt, they remain a threat to the government and create social instability, but they have failed to achieve political success.

Muslims today, in the Middle East as elsewhere, are searching for ways to reassert their Islamic identity while reconciling a traditional Islamic way of life with the demands of the contemporary world. The commonality of the faith, its overarching cultural and social norms, is easily grasped and appeals to Muslims irrespective of their different backgrounds. One positive result of the fundamentalist movement is that it enables Muslims to take pride in their heritage. They no longer have to defend or apologize for their beliefs or practices. Islam, regardless of what often seems to be a bad press, has not only matured but also stands as a valid, legitimate institution, one that can be respected by adherents and non-adherents alike.

## ISLAMIC SOCIETY IN TRANSITION

I have come, I know not where,
   but I have come.
And I have seen a road before me,
   and have taken it.[11]

Most Muslims inhabit a world still dominated by Islamic law, custom, spirituality, and belief, despite the waves of violence, puritanical reaction, revolution, ideological conflict, and power struggles among leaders that have threatened it. Islam is not only the bond that unites diverse peoples over a vast

## MUSLIM HOUSING IN THE MIDDLE EAST: FORM FOLLOWS FUNCTION

Muslim families in the Middle East live in many different kinds of houses. A common feature is the suitability of the traditional Islamic residence to the surrounding environment. Nomads in the desert live in woven goat-hair tents, easily dismantled when ready to break camp. In Syria and Turkey, one finds the cone-shaped beehive house, built of mud brick, which can be put up easily by unskilled labor and costs little in the way of materials. The high dome of the house collects the hot, dry air and releases it through narrow openings, while the dome shape sheds rainfall before the mud brick can absorb moisture and crumble. The construction provides natural air conditioning; interior temperatures remain in the 75°F–85°F range, while the outside temperatures may reach 140°F. The beehive house illustrates Frank Lloyd Wright's dictum that "form follows function."

Further illustrations of ingenious designs to suit the harsh climate are the cave houses in southern Tunisia. Caves have been hollowed out from a central shaft below the desert floor. (The movie *Star Wars* was filmed here.) Most residences on the Persian/Arab Gulf, where strong winds blow, have open-sided towers above the rooftops to catch any wind and funnel it into the rooms below. Many city residences are built with tiny windows and are joined together and covered by deep overhangs to provide shade for passersby.

In San'a, Yemen, houses are several stories high, are gaily decorated, and are painted with slatted overhangs for women to look out of without being seen. Some farmers in northern Tunisia utilize hay to construct their houses. These hay houses are sometimes elaborate and contain windows and wooden doors.

Mud brick, cut and sun-dried, has been a common building material in the Middle East for 8,000 years. Today, with the increased use of air conditioning and reinforced concrete, steel, and other prefabricated building materials, Middle Eastern cities have begun to take on the look of cities everywhere. Not only have most Middle Eastern cities lost their distinctive look, but widespread use of cement instead of the traditional

(UN photo/W. Graham)

This cave house in the Matmata Mountains suits the harsh climate of southern Tunisia.

and easily available building materials has had more dire consequences. To raise the cash to buy cement for housing in rural areas, someone must often leave the village, thus disrupting family and community life.

---

territory; it also brings equilibrium to counterbalance the visible disruptions that increasingly affect daily life.

One element of Islam that brings Muslims together in a ritual that transcends differences is the Hajj, the Great Pilgrimage to Mecca and Medina, the sacred shrines of the faith. It is the fifth of the Five Pillars and thus an obligation for believers. One may make a pilgrimage at any time, but the Great Hajj takes place only once a year, under the direct sponsorship of the Saudi Arabian government in its capacity as "Guardian of the Holy Places." Although it is intended to bring Muslims from all over the world in a spirit of harmony and reverence, the Hajj has become a vehicle for social and political protest in recent years.

Yet, for the *hajjis* ("pilgrims"), the Pilgrimage is still the ultimate religious experience. The Imam of the Muslim community of Toledo, Ohio, vividly described its impact: "You feel the weight of all the history. And everyone dresses identically in the *ihram* [the white seamless robe of the pilgrim] and sandals. You see the equality of all people before God:

rich people, poor, women and men, kings and janitors, black and white, all in the same uniform, all together."[12]

A major challenge to traditional Islam comes from globalization. The Internet, satellite dishes, cultural and social interchanges, and the immediacy of media images have linked Islamic societies with the larger world. These changes have also made Muslims aware of their dependence on Western technology, the model being that of the United States. While the "clash of civilizations" predicted by Samuel Huntington between Western and Islamic civilizations overstates the case, Osama bin Laden's stance against the United States as the main impediment to Middle Eastern peace, and his angry opposition to Islamic leaders for their failure to improve the lives of their citizens, strikes a chord with many Muslims. Even many totally secularized, Western-oriented Muslim believers hold a range of grievances against Western intrusion and political domination.

However, Islam's political weakness is matched to some extent by its cultural strength. The faith provides a cultural

(UN photo/J. Isaac)

Privacy is emphasized in the communities of the Middle East. The nondescript walls near this child in Morocco may very well surround beautiful courtyards decorated with fruit trees, flowers, and fountains.

conformity in its overarching cultural and social norms. These are easily grasped and appeal to Muslims irrespective of their different backgrounds. One result of the fundamentalist movement is that it enables Muslims to take pride in their heritage. They no longer feel that they have to defend or apologize for their beliefs and practices. For example, it has brought a new consciousness among American Muslims of their dual identities. Pride in their religious identity is shared with Muslims in the Middle East and elsewhere in the world.

Another area of modern technology that has reduced the cultural isolation of Islam is broadcasting. Al Jazeerah, a freewheeling news station based in Qatar but broadcasting across the Arab world, often presents programs critical of Arab regimes. Yet it provides further evidence of the common cultural order that binds these regimes together despite their political differences. This cultural order has many components. Some of them are the importance of the family as the central social unit, distrust of centralized governments, tribalism as the norm, bargaining as a necessary social practice, and in recent years the rejection of Western cultural importations.

## ARCHITECTURE: AN EXPRESSION OF RELIGIOUS FAITH

Islamic architecture is centered on the mosque, the house of worship. The first mosque was a simple structure of palm branches laid over a frame of tree trunks to provide shade from the desert sun for worshippers. As time passed, Muslim architects built more magnificent structures, dedicating their work to the glory of God, much as medieval Christian artisans did with the great cathedrals of Europe. The engineer–architect Sinan (1497–1588), who served as chief of the Imperial Architects under three sultans, designed and built 477 such structures, including mosques, royal tombs, public baths, and inns for travelers. His architectural genius is visible in many Turkish cities even today.

Along with mosques and other public buildings, which were usually decorated with elaborate designs in calligraphy and stonework, Islamic cities developed a distinct spatial order that made them functionally useful to their residents. Their outer limits were encircled by massive walls pierced by heavy iron gates that were closed at night or upon threat of invasion. Within the walls were residential and commercial quarters, adjoined; suburbia beyond the walls lay far in the future for these genuinely urban communities. At the city's heart were the ruler's palace and the main mosque, the center of government.

The classic example of this urban configuration was the "round city" of Baghdad, probably the world's first completely planned urban structure. Its core held the Great Mosque, the caliph's palace, and other public buildings. Nearby was the vast *suq* (market), with its cottage industries of potters, tinsmiths, woodworkers, and other artisans; its spice-sellers with their burlap sacks of spices of all varieties;

its tiny shops of tailors, cloth merchants, and jewelers; its tanners, dyers and weavers, and carpet-sellers.

One can still see examples of this traditional Islamic Middle Eastern city in such places as Fez, Morocco, and San'a, Yemen, both designated as world Historic Landmarks by UNESCO; and even in an overcrowded, traffic-burdened city such as Cairo, street life predominates. But large-scale rural–urban migration, the proliferation of Western-style skyscrapers and high-rise housing blocks, and the omnipresent automobile have destroyed to a great extent the uniqueness of Islamic cities. Most of them suffer from the same traffic jams, air and noise pollution, overcrowding, and other unfavorable elements of modern urban life elsewhere in the world.

Islamic architecture has benefited greatly from the work of contemporary architects such as Hassan Fathy of Egypt. His use of the "sacred design," linking faith with the physical setting, may be seen in a low-income housing project in the desert near Cairo, as well as in places as far away as Abiquiu, New Mexico, where the adobe architecture of the Dar al-Islam community blends perfectly into the arid landscape. Similarly, in 1998 the Aga Khan awards for architecture went to the Tuwaiq Palace, a curvilinear building enclosing lush gardens on a barren limestone plateau near Saudi Arabia's capital, Riyadh.

### HOME AND FAMILY LIFE

Within the residential quarters of Islamic cities there existed, and in large measure still exists, a kinship arrangement very different from that of the typical American subdivision. The households of each quarter claim either a kinship relation or close personal ties to one another. Everyone knows everyone else, and most households are related in some way. In one residential quarter of the town of Boujad, Morocco, the great majority of households claim descent from a common ancestor, the founder of the group from which they descended patrilineally. Other households regard themselves as being under the protection of that group.

The resulting cooperation establishes what anthropologists call the notion of closeness (*qaraba*), which defines the social organization of the quarter. Closeness is essential to the proper functioning of society. Christine Eickelman describes the *hayyan* (family cluster) in inner Oman as an essential support network for village women. The hayyan consists of those women (some of them relatives, others not related) whom each woman regards as her confidantes and to whom she will confide matters that she may not reveal even to her own husband or immediate family. Visits among hayyan members are made on a daily basis, aside from the support provided in stressful situations such as birth, marriage, or death. Hayyan members also provide mutual protection and even share housework and child care.[13]

Within the Islamic family, the father has the final say on all matters, which gives him, in theory, absolute authority. However, the role of women in family life is crucial to its continu-

ation. Women in Muslim families not only ensure successive generations but are also responsible for the discipline and informal education of the young. Mothers hold the family together through the transmission of cultural and religious traditions and values learned from *their* mothers. A tragic result of the turmoil in Lebanon and the Palestinian resistance movement in Israeli-occupied territories has been the breakup of the family, the loss of parental authority, and the substitution of war and violence for traditional family values among Lebanese and Palestinian youth.

Communities in the Middle East emphasize the private over the public life of residents. It is not possible for someone walking along a town or city residential street to know much about the economic or social circumstances of those who live there. Many homes have blank, windowless walls facing the street; entry is usually achieved through a massive studded door set in the wall, a brass hand serving as a knocker. Inside, one may find, in a wealthier home, low-ceilinged rooms furnished with rich carpets, banquettes, and ottomans in lieu of chairs and sofas (though this is disappearing), and in the center an open courtyard with flowers, fruit trees, and a plashing fountain.

### FAMILY CELEBRATIONS

In the Islamic countries of the Middle East, as well as in Israel, the family has traditionally been the central social unit. This is true even today. To a considerable degree the family overrides the nation and its laws. Middle Eastern rulers such as the late kings Hussein of Jordan and Hassan II of Morocco referred to themselves in public utterances as heads of families rather than leaders of nations. In Saddam Hussain's Iraq, the ties between ruler and family were important well before his accession to total power, and have continued to be essential to him, especially after the Gulf War and U.S. efforts to remove him from office.[14]

Most celebrations and holidays in the Middle East are related to religion; although such holidays as No-Ruz (New Year) in Iran pre-date Islam and celebrate the onset of spring. Most modern Middle Eastern states observe a "national day" marking their independence from colonial rule. But the majority of festivals still spring essentially out of religious observances. Thus the most solemn festival in Judaism is collectively the "Days of Awe" or "High Holy Days," beginning each year with Rosh Hashanah (the Jewish New Year) and ending with Yom Kippur (the Day of Atonement). On that day, Jews are enjoined to pray, reflect on their lives, and avoid all customary activities; in Israel, even the buses do not run. Other festivals are more joyous, helping to bind families together in a closer relationship. Thus families join in building the thatched hut outdoors on Sukkot, celebrating the time when their ancestors wandered in the wilderness of Sinai. Similarly, Hanukkah, the Festival of Lights, marks the victory of the Maccabees over the Syrian forces of the Emperor Antiochus more than 2,000 years ago. Purim, one of the most joyous holidays on the Jewish calendar, recalls the story of Esther, the Jewish queen of King Ahasuerus of Persia, who saved her people from death after the king had been persuaded by his chief minister, Haman, that they were disloyal and should be killed on a day chosen by the drawing of lots (*purim,* in Hebrew). Esther offered herself as a sacrifice, and, convinced by her honesty, King Ahasuerus changed his mind. This "day of deliverance" is celebrated with a multicourse feast, the giving of homemade sweets to relatives and friends, and triangular pastries called *oznei Haman* (Haman's ears). Similarly, the Hanukkah gelt themselves—gold-foil–covered chocolate "coins" hidden in households for children to find—symbolize the new coins minted long ago by Judas Maccabaeus to mark Jewish independence from religious and political persecution.

Muslim households observe a similar pattern. Ramadan, the ninth month of the Muslim year, is observed as a fasting month to mark Allah's first revelations to Muhammad. In principle, Muslim families go without food or nourishment of any kind from sunrise to sunset during the month. Increasingly, even in secular Muslim countries such as Turkey, the fast is being observed, as fundamentalism spreads across the Islamic world. The *iftar*—the "Breaking of the Fast," the evening meal that ends the day's fasting—follows, with special dishes and spices reserved for the occasion. It was interesting to note that U.S. president George W. Bush, in seeking the support and participation of Muslim states in the global anti-terrorism coalition, invited all 50 of their Muslim ambassadors to Washington to attend an iftar at the White House.

Equally important among Islamic festivals is Mouloud, the Prophet Muhammad's birthday. Similar to the custom in Jewish festivals, Mouloud features a special dish called zematta, made of durum wheat cooked slowly for two days, then mixed with melted butter, nutmeg, gum Arabic, honey, cinnamon, sesame seeds, and toasted almonds.

## A CUISINE SUITED TO THE ENVIRONMENT

Middle Eastern cooking largely transcends political, linguistic, religious, and other differences. It is a highly varied cuisine that makes much use of natural, unprocessed foods. The pungent smells of lamb roasting over charcoal, stuffed eggplant and roasted sweet peppers, tiny cups of thick coffee and hot, sweet tea are common across national boundaries. The basics of Middle Eastern cooking originated in ancient Persia (modern Iran) and have been continually refined, with subtle differences developing from country to country.

Beef is relatively scarce in the region due to the aridity and lack of pasture, although this is changing with the introduction of Texas cattle and other breeds suited to the arid climate. There is abundant lamb and chicken, and people eat a great variety of seafood. Because of the lack of cattle, more olive oil is used in cooking than butter, and goat and sheep cheeses are more common than cheese made from cows' milk. Yogurt is a staple dessert but is also used in soups and sauces.

Potatoes are seldom used, but rice pilaf made with chicken broth, onions, and currants is popular. There is an almost limitless variety of herbs and spices.

Little milk is drunk. Fresh orange juice and guava juice are common, along with other fruit juices. Desserts are usually fruit, and sometimes cheese. Middle Easterners are also fond of rich, sweet pastries such as baklava and cakes, which are reserved for holidays and special occasions.

Coffee beans were first discovered growing wild in Ethiopia and were probably brought to Yemen by Ethiopian invaders. From there coffee spread throughout the Middle East as a popular beverage, the Port of Mocha becoming synonymous with export of the crop. Early Islamic religious authorities tried to ban its use because of its presumed narcotic properties, even driving coffee vendors from the precincts of the Great Mosque in Mecca, under the argument that coffee drinking interfered with the services. But in the end, public preference triumphed over religious zeal. The beverage was brought to Europe by the Ottoman Turks, probably during the Siege of Vienna. Perhaps as a result, the heavily sweetened drink taken after dinner as a demitasse is often referred to as "Turkish coffee," although no coffee is grown in Turkey. In the Arab world, coffee is the universal symbol of hospitality, whether in a Bedouin tent, a princely palace, or a modest private residence. It is offered in demitasse cups, thick and strong and usually flavored with cardamom.[15]

Mint tea is also very popular in the Middle East, particularly in Morocco, where it is heavily laced with sugar and drunk from small glasses. The elaborate tea-making ceremony is an important part of a formal meal.

Each Middle Eastern country has its special dishes that serve as symbols of the cultural heritage of its people. In Israel and among Jewish communities elsewhere, for example, the *haroseth* ("clay," in Hebrew) has become an essential component of the Seder, the traditional formal Passover meal. Haroseth, small mashed balls of fruit and nuts in various combinations, are eaten during the Seder to remind Jewish families of the wanderings of their ancestors over the centuries of Jewish dispersion.

Couscous, a dish of steamed semolina (hard wheat) made into a stew with vegetables and sometimes meat, is a staple of Muslim family meals in the Maghrib (North Africa), the "sunset land" of Islam. It is the centerpiece of the Friday meal that follows the community prayer service in the local mosque. In the Maghrib, couscous is often associated with special events in family life, such as reunions, circumcision and marriage ceremonies, and even funerals. At these gatherings and meals, there is a couscous "ritual" in which the diner puts a small mound into a bowl, adds a spoonful of hot harissa sauce and picks out bits of marga, meat, and semolina with the fingers. In rural areas, couscous preparation is still a group effort, involving the women and children of several families as they sift, steam, and stir.

Turkish cuisine is another "mosaic of culture." The six centuries of Ottoman domination in the Middle East resulted in a number of dishes that are now standard in other culinary systems. They include shish kebabs, dolmas (stuffed grape leaves), and yogurt. Some Turkish specialties, often hawked by street vendors, are simits (crescent-shaped rolls dusted with sesame seeds), pekmez (pomegranate-based molasses), and kirmizi bibir, a rich, hot chili powder. Most Turkish meals begin with meze, which features such dishes as white bean salad with garlic, roasted red peppers, stuffed mussels, grilled octopus, and pureed eggplant.[16] Iran also has a distinctive cuisine, with dishes such as *khoresh-e-bademjan*, an eggplant, lamb, and potato stew; *tajin-e-mergh,* chicken baked with rice and spices, and a special flat bread shaped like a large pizza and baked until golden brown and bumpy on top.[17]

As is true elsewhere in the world, in the Middle East, the traditional distinctive culinary arts and specialties are giving way to a homogenized "international" cuisine, just as shoes and plastic sandals now adorn many Middle Easterners' feet. Labor-saving devices such as microwave ovens and refrigerators simplify the task of meal preparation in Middle Eastern homes, and McDonald's and Kentucky Fried Chicken stores have introduced a fast-food wedge into Middle Eastern life. But a strong undercurrent of traditionalism pervades Islamic society in the region. This undercurrent has been strengthened by the relative success of Khomeini's revolution in Iran and the appeal of this revolution to Muslims as a force independent of both the United States and the former Soviet Union. Traditions die hard anyway; and the more isolated Muslims become—by their own choice—from Western thought, behavior, and practice, the more likely it is that all elements in their social system that reflect preferences and values, including those related to food, will remain appropriate to that system.

## CHALLENGES TO THE MUSLIM FAMILY

The Muslim family in the Middle East today is subject to many of the same strains and stresses as those that affect families everywhere, but they have somewhat greater impact on Muslim families because of their suddenness in the region. The Middle East did not have the lengthy period of conditioning and preparation that Europe and the United States had due to the Industrial Revolution. The story is told that when some Turkish villagers saw their first automobile, early in the 1940s, they could not believe that it ran on its own power. Where is the donkey that will pull it? they wondered. Similarly, King Ibn Saud, a former ruler of Saudi Arabia, was faced with angry opposition by the religious leaders of the kingdom when he wished to install a radio network to link the far-flung cities and towns of his realm. He satisfied the religious leaders by having the Koran read over a radio hookup between Mecca and Riyadh, his capital, pointing out to them that if the machine could carry the Word of God, then God must have approved its use.

One of the challenges to family solidarity in the contemporary Middle East is "Western" secular education, which separates parents from their children who have been educated to acquire university degrees and enter the world of modern technology. Until recently, this education had to be obtained abroad. As a result, a generation of young Muslim men (and, increasingly, women) trained and educated in Western countries have returned to take up leadership positions in their own countries. Particularly in the 1970s and early 1980s, oil-producing Arab countries channeled oil revenues into education, setting up universities, medical centers, and technical institutes of high quality, staffed initially by expatriates but, in the 1990s, largely by indigenous personnel.

A more difficult challenge to the Muslim family, and to the economy and society in general, has been posed by labor emigration. In the 1970s and early 1980s, several million Turks, Yemenis, Moroccans, Tunisians, Egyptians, and others emigrated either to Europe or to Arab oil-prospecting states on work contracts. Although their work was seldom of a highly skilled nature, the pay differential was enormous. Remittances from expatriate labor were important to the home economies, particularly of oil-less Islamic states. The 1980s recession and drop in world oil prices, followed by the 1991 Gulf War, brought significant efforts by the Gulf states to reduce their dependence on foreign workers. Many of these workers came from poor countries, not only from Pakistan, the Philippines, and other Asian countries, but also from neighboring Middle Eastern countries such as Yemen. The resulting expulsion has not only affected the economies of these less fortunate countries but also required some difficult social adjustments, as long-absent fathers known primarily for their remittances are suddenly brought home, unemployed and sometimes penniless.

In terms of the traditional Muslim family, perhaps the thorniest issue today involves the position and rights of women. The Koran would seem to confirm a degree of subservience of women to men (e.g., *Suras II,* 32 and *IV,* 34). But other revelations stipulate only that women dress modestly and conduct themselves decently in public. It should be noted also that Muhammad was an Arab, a member of a tribal society governed by men and emphasizing traditional patriarchal values and beliefs. While Muhammad's message was universal in its intent, in terms of practical implementation, Islam took root in a patriarchal society and has always taken a patriarchal family structure to be the norm.

The emergence of Islamic states committed to nation-building has put a new spin on women's rights and obligations in Islamic societies. Secular leaders such as Mustafa Kemal Atatürk in Turkey and Habib Bourguiba in Tunisia recognized early that women could make significant contributions to national development and that they needed to be trained, educated, and emancipated in order to do so. These leaders viewed the patriarchal "dead hand of Islam" as an obstacle to the enhancement of women's rights and status. Under their leadership, laws were passed to provide legal safeguards and rights for women, notably in the areas of voting rights, personal relations, education, and work opportunities. Other Islamic leaders continued the emancipation process. Thus Reza Shah, Iran's new ruler after World War I, literally "tore the veil" from women's faces, outlawing its use in his zeal to modernize his country.

Education for women, which was previously nonexistent in Muslim lands, became possible with the establishment of Western-type educational institutions such as the American Universities of Beirut and Cairo, Beirut College for Women, and the American College for Girls in Istanbul. U.S. church-supported secondary schools were also established in various Ottoman provinces and as far away as Tehran and Tabriz, Iran. They were staffed by missionary teachers, and, as a result, women began to enter the labor force as skilled professionals in law, medicine, teaching, the sciences, and the arts.

The 1979 Iranian Revolution reversed the process, as Islamic clerics imposed their interpretations of Islamic dress codes and behavior on what had become under the shah an open, Western-oriented society. The new codes are enforced by *komitehs,* "Neighborhood morals squads," who regulate every aspect of public dress and behavior, from stray hairs outside a woman's headscarf to unrelated men and women walking together. Women in Sudan, until very recently, were similarly confined, not allowed to appear in public without the all-enveloping chador and limited to daytime jobs outside the home. Algerian professional women have been particular targets of the Armed Islamic Group; during the 1990s, some 400 women—doctors, nurses, journalists, editors, and television personalities—were murdered there.

During the period of Taliban rule in Afghanistan (1996–2001), the "government" pursued policies that were not only extreme but offensive to most Muslims. Their harshest restrictions were reserved for women. Women were required to wear shapeless black robes called *burqas* in public, their faces covered and with slits for eyes. Cosmetics were prohibited as were Adidas or Nikes and white socks, as these would arouse the lust of men. Women were forbidden to work outside the home, the only exceptions being health practitioners, and these were severely restricted in their movements and practice. Education for girls was not allowed. Infractions of these "rules" were punished, usually by beatings with a heavy cable or truncheon. In the Taliban view, the restrictions were needed because of the "rescuing nature" of Islam as a religion, respecting women and protecting them from the cruelty of men. But after five years of Taliban control, almost all of Afghanistan's female population had been deprived of education at all levels, to say nothing of the loss of the nurses, doctors, teachers, and other professionals urgently needed to restore that war-ravaged country.

In other parts of the Middle East, there has been some progress in bringing women into politics and other areas of national life. The first taxi service with women as drivers opened for business in the United Arab Emirates in May 2000, encouraged by husbands who felt more comfortable having their wives transported by other women. In Kuwait, the government approved a soccer tournament for teams from girls' high schools, despite howls of protest from conservatives who declared that it would "bring the wrath of God down on society." (Needless to say, it did not do so.)

In the political sphere, Qatari women not only voted in the 1999 elections for municipal councils, but several ran for office, albeit unsuccessfully. The sultan of Oman appointed two women to the country's newly expanded *Majlis al-Shura* (Advisory Council). Bahrain named its first female ambassador; and in Saudi Arabia, a royal princess was named assistant undersecretary for education, a subcabinet post.

In some areas of Middle Eastern Islamic life, women's rights are still circumscribed, both by custom and interpretation of law. Women are now allowed to file for divorce in Egypt under a new Assembly law. However, the Egyptian courts are so overburdened with cases that only a handful have been granted, and delays by obstructionist husbands may take years before they are adjudicated.

Under long-established tradition in these patriarchal societies, the practice of "honor killings" of wives or female relatives by men, on the grounds that the women's behavior has brought dishonor to the family, has until recently brought no more than a judicial-system "slap on the wrist" for men who carry them out. But in at least one Islamic society, Jordan's, a new law prescribes much heavier sentences. The law was passed following one such killing, in doubtful circumstances and under protest from Jordanian as well as international human-rights and feminist organizations.

## PROSPECTS FOR ISLAM

The success of the Taliban in Afghanistan in gaining control of most of the country, and the imposition of its draconian version of Islamic law on the Afghan people without more than murmurs of protest from the rest of the Islamic world, might suggest that extremist Islamic fundamentalist movements elsewhere in the Middle East can succeed by using similar tactics. Certainly the ideal of an Islamic community replicating that of the original one founded by Muhammad remains valid. However, the unique nature of the Taliban itself, and the special conditions that made its success possible, do not exist in North Africa or the rest of the Middle East. The Taliban's membership was recruited from Afghan refugee camps in Pakistan or remote villages within Afghanistan. Members, nearly all of them illiterate, were given only the rudiments of Koranic instruction, given by semiliterate *mullahs,* in so-called religious schools (*madrasas*) set up on a temporary basis in the camps or towns controlled by the organization. When they had completed this "education," they became *talibs* ("students"—hence the name) and were sent in a body to take part in a jihad in Afghanistan intended to restore law and order. Most Taliban members' exposure to the outside world—even the larger Islamic world—was nonexistent, and as a result they had no experience or model to turn to in their relation to women, to other cultures, or in state-building. Actions such as the destruction of ancient Buddhist statues, denial of women's rights, and then the requirement that non-Muslims, particularly Hindus, must wear identifying badges and clothing, brought international condemnation. But it was the condemnation of other Middle Eastern Islamic states that finally underscored the isolation of the Taliban.

At the dawn of the millennium, Muslims everywhere are struggling to come to terms with a world increasingly globalized. Borders are no longer barriers; they are easily crossed by technology, with nations connected by instant communications. Within the Middle East, there are great political and economic inequalities among the various Islamic states. The Iranian model of an "Islamic republic," a theocratic state, is not only not exportable but also is no longer accepted in its current form by the majority of its people. In the last analysis, given these uncertainties, the most likely model for Islamic growth may well be found in the Arab Gulf states. There, at least, a combination of economic wealth, social stability, gradual democratization and wise leadership may be providing the basis for nation-building in an Islamic context.

## NOTES

1. R. Hrair Dekmejian, *Islam in Revolution* (Syracuse, NY: Syracuse University Press, 1985), p. 99.

2. Emmanuel Sivan, *Radical Islam: Medieval Theology and Modern Politics* (New Haven, CT: Yale University Press, 1985), reports the comment of an imprisoned Brotherhood member that underscores this violence: "These regimes are animated by vicious hatred of Islam; no dialogue with them is possible, for their sole answer is repression" (p. 41). Thomas L. Friedman, in *From Beirut to Jerusalem* (New York: Farrar Straus Giroux, 1989), devotes a chapter to "Hama Rules" to describe the uses of power by secular rulers in Islamic nation-states.

3. Peter Awn, "Faith and Practice," in Marjorie Kelly, ed., *Islam: The Religious and Political Life of a World Community* (New York: Praeger, 1984), p. 26.

4. Tareq Y. Ismael and Jacqueline S. Ismael, *Government and Politics in Islam* (New York: St. Martin's Press, 1985), pp. 64–67.

5. *Time* (August 17, 1987). The Koran, *Sura II,* verse 197, enjoins: "Anyone who undertakes the Pilgrimage should not engage in . . . any immorality or wrangling."

6. Reported in *The Los Angeles Times* (July 3, 1997). Muslims follow Jewish dietary laws in regarding pigs as unclean animals, and Muslim scholars called her action "a declaration of war against Islam."

7. V. S. Naipaul, "After the Revolution," *The New Yorker* (May 26, 1997), pp. 46–70. The Basijis were reminded of "the unequal battle of Karbala, where the Prophet's grandson and his followers were massacred by Iraqis—the Shia tragedy and passion, unendingly rehearsed" (p. 68).

8. Stephen King, in *The New York Times* (April 13, 1997).

9. Seyyed Hossein Nasr, "Islam in the West Today, an Overview," in C. K. Pullapilly, ed., *Islam in the Contemporary World* (Notre Dame, IN: Cross Roads Books, 1980), p. 7.

10. Bernard Lewis, "The Roots of Muslim Rage," in *The Atlantic Monthly* (September 1990), p. 60.

11. Eliya Abu Madi, quoted in Michael Asher, *In Search of the Forty Days' Road* (London: Longman, 1984), p. 132.

12. Rebekah Scott, in *The Toledo Blade* (June 8, 1997). American Muslim leader Malcolm X wrote of his Hajj experience in his autobiography: "I lay awake among sleeping Muslim brothers and I learned that pilgrims from every land—snored in the same language" (p. 344).

13. Christine Eickelman, *Women and Community in Oman* (New York: New York University Press, 1984) pp. 80–111.

14. "Fearing U.S. intentions, Saddam became almost totally dependent for his and his regime's survival on his own family and clan. A plethora of half-brothers, sons, cousins and other relatives occupied powerful cabinet portfolios and critical security positions." Adeed Dawisha, "Identity and Political Survival in Saddam's Iraq," *Middle East Journal,* 53, 4 (Autumn 1999), p. 566.

15. Cardamom, an aromatic spice ground from pods of a tall, palm-like plant, came originally from India. Today, the bulk of the crop is grown at high altitudes in Guatemala and exported to the Arab countries, which do not grow any. See Larry Luxner, "The Cardamom Connection," *Aramco World,* Vol. 48, No. 2 (March–April 1997).

16. Florence Fabricant, "America Discovers the Turkish Mosaic," *The New York Times* (November 10, 1999).

17. Christine Bird, *Neither East Nor West* (New York: Pocket Books/Simon & Schuster, 2001), p. 24. Bird comments that "eating is a constant pastime in Iran" (p. 63).

# The Middle East: Theater of Conflict

As defined here, the Middle East, a region approximately equal in size to the continental United States and slightly larger in population, extends from the Atlantic coast of Morocco, in North Africa, to the mountains of Afghanistan, where the Indian subcontinent begins. The Middle East is thus intercontinental rather than continental, with the diversity of topography, climate, and physical and social environments characteristic of the two continents, Africa and Asia, that define its territory. Geography and location have dictated a significant role in world affairs for the Middle East throughout recorded history; humankind's earliest cities, governments, organized societies, and state conflicts were probably located there. In the twentieth century, this traditional role has been confirmed by the exploitation of mineral resources vital to the global economy and by the rivalries of nations that regard the Middle East as strategically important to their national interests.

The nations of the contemporary Middle East are very different, however, from their predecessors of 100 or 200 years ago. One important difference is political. When the United States became independent of England, there were three more or less "sovereign" Middle Eastern nation-states and empires: the Sherifian Sultanate of Morocco; the Otto-man Turkish Empire; and Iran, reunited by force under the new Qajar Dynasty, which would remain in power until it was succeeded by the Pahlavi Dynasty in the 1920s. These three states were still in place late in the nineteenth century, but European influence and control over their rulers had effectively robbed them of most of their independence. Since then—a process accelerated since World War II—the Middle Eastern map has been redrawn many times. The result of the redrawing process is the contemporary Middle East, 20 independent states with diverse political systems overlaying a pastiche of ethnic groups, languages, customs, and traditions.

The diversity of these states is compensated for, in part, by the cohesion provided by various unifying factors. One of these factors is geography. The predominance of deserts, with areas suitable for agriculture compressed into small spaces where water was available in dependable flow, produced the *oasis-village* type of social organization and agricultural life. Beyond the oases evolved a second type of social organization suited to desert life, a less settled lifestyle termed *nomadism.* Another type of village settlement evolved in plateau and mountain regions, wherever the topography afforded physical protection for the defense of the community. In Egypt, and to a lesser extent in the Tigris and Euphrates

(UN photo)

Humankind's earliest governments, cities, and organized societies were probably located in what is known today as the Middle East. The remnants of the ancient Roman town of Timgad, Algeria, pictured above, testify to people's continued attempts over many centuries to live in the arid expanses of this part of the world.

River Valleys, *villages* were established to take advantage of a dependable water supply for crop irrigation. Peoples living in the region mirrored these lifestyles, with the Middle Eastern city developing as an urban refinement of the same traditions.

The broad set of values, traditions, historical experiences, kinship structures, and so on, usually defined as "culture," is a second cohesive factor for the Middle East's peoples. Islam, for example, is either the official state religion or the leading religion in all but one (Israel) of the states. The Arabic language, due to its identification with Islam, is a bond even for those peoples who use another spoken and/or written language (such as Turkish, Hebrew, or Farsi); and, in any case, the social order of Islam is another unifying force.

A third unifying factor, while it is intangible and difficult to define, is a common historical experience. Without exception, the states of the Middle East are the products of twentieth-century international politics and the conflict of interests of outside powers. Clashing national interests and external involvement in regional affairs have set the tone for the internal and regional conflicts of Middle Eastern states. Thus, the intercommunal violence in modern Lebanon has its roots in foreign (French and British) support for various communal groups in the 1860s, setting the groups against one another under the guise of protecting them from the Ottoman government and its misrule. But Lebanon is only one example of a broad historical process. Throughout Middle Eastern history, invaders and counterinvaders have rolled across the region, advancing, conquering, and being conquered; below the surface of conflict, meanwhile, other peoples have crisscrossed the land in peace, building homes, establishing cities, forming the bedrock of settlement and social development.

## THE LAND ISLAND

Until recently, the Middle East was compartmentalized. Its peoples had little awareness of one another and even less of the outside world. Months of arduous travel were needed for a directive from the caliph in Baghdad—the chief personage of the theocratic Islamic state—to reach his viceroy in far-off Morocco. Communications within the region were relatively poor; residents of one village often would know nothing of what was going on in other nearby villages—that is, if they were at peace and not feuding. Travel for caravans between cities was uncertain and often dangerous; the Tuareg of the Western Sahara Desert, a nomadic society, made a good living by charging tolls and providing mounted escorts for merchants crossing the desert.

Consequently, the combination of vast distances, poor communications, and geographical isolation brought about the early development of subregions within the larger Middle East. As early as the tenth century A.D., three such subregions had been defined: North Africa, the Arab lands traditionally known to Europeans as the Near East, and the highland plateaus of Turkey and Iran. In the twentieth century, these

(UN photo/Kata Bader)

Life in the Sahara Desert is often perceived as nomadic, with the people living in tents and riding camels. To some extent this is still true, but there are many towns that offer a more settled way of life, such as this town in the Algerian Sahara.

three areas were further separated from one another by foreign political control—the French in North Africa, the French and British jointly in the Arab lands, with Turkey and Iran nominally independent but subject to pressures from various outside powers. Alan Taylor's phrase "the Arab balance of power," referring to the "patterns of equilibrium, dislocation and readjustment that unfolded among the Arab states," applies equally well to the interaction of peoples and nations within the subregions.[1]

Many years ago, naval historian Alfred Thayer Mahan defined the Middle East as a central part of the "land island" or heartland whose possession would enable some powerful nation to dominate the world. Mahan's definition stemmed from his view of naval power as an element in geopolitics; he saw the United States, as a growing naval power, and Russia, expanding across Asia, as the competitors for world domination in the twentieth century.

Mahan's definition derived from observation of the nineteenth-century conflict between England and Tsarist Russia, the superpowers of that period, for domination of Central Asia. Their conflict is often described as the "Great Game," or "Tournament of Shadows," since it involved venturing into unknown areas and conducting warfare by proxies in order to control those areas. The British sought to advance their sphere of interest northward to protect India, their imperial prize, from a perceived Russian expansionist threat, while, at the same time, the Russians were expanding their land empire inexorably southward to bring civilization to Asian peoples. Each power felt that its national interest lay far from home—on the bleak plateau of Tibet, the Pamir Mountains, and the wind-swept steppes of the Saian heartland. As a "Victorian predecessor of the cold war between the United States and the Soviet Union," the Great Game expended vast efforts in an essentially unwinnable contest for power.[2]

The Ronald Reagan administration's commitment to a strongly anti-Communist policy revived the Great Game in new locations in the 1980s. Thus President Reagan insisted in 1983–1984 that American marines were in Lebanon to defend vital U.S. interests. In 1987, the United States accepted a request from Kuwait to "reflag" Kuwaiti tankers in the Persian Gulf and provide them with naval protection, ostensibly to thwart Iran but also to forestall a Soviet move into the region. Reagan had warned Iran and Iraq earlier that any attempt to close the Strait of Hormuz to oil-tanker traffic would be regarded as a threat to the free world's access to Middle East oil and therefore to American national interests. Before its disintegration in 1991, the Soviet Union from time to time made equally strong pronouncements.[3]

## SUBREGIONAL CONFLICTS

The periodic outbreak of local or subregional conflicts characteristic of Middle Eastern societies, which stem from their tribal or ethnic origins, has brought the region to the forefront of world affairs in recent years. Although such conflicts as the Lebanese Civil War, the Iran–Iraq War, the Gulf War, the Arab–Israeli conflict, Palestinian self-rule, and Morocco's absorption of the Western Sahara against the opposition of Saharan nationalists have from time to time drawn in outside powers, they have also developed an internal rhythm that resists negotiated solutions.

Although thus far these Middle Eastern conflicts have been confined to their areas of origin or mediated by outside powers to reduce tension levels, some government policy-makers continue to fear that they might spread and involve other nations in a wider war, possibly proving or at least demonstrating the effectiveness of the "domino theory" often invoked as a guide to modern international relations. The domino theory holds that tensions or unresolved disputes between two nations will widen as neighboring nations are drawn inevitably into the dispute, even without taking sides. The uninvolved nations will then become involved, as the

## IRANIANS AND ARABS

Iranians (or Persians) and Arabs are nearly all Muslims. But they have very different ethnic origins, linguistic and geographical backgrounds, and histories.

The Iranians were a loosely organized nomadic people from Central Asia who migrated into the Iranian plateau some 3,000 years ago, settling in the province of Parsa (hence the name Persian) as sedentary farmers and herders. They gradually expanded their territory at the expense of the earlier inhabitants, and in about 600 B.C. they joined forces with the Medes, another tribal people, under the leadership of the Persian chief Cyrus. In a few years they conquered other Near Eastern peoples to form the world's first true empire, in the sense of many different peoples ruled by a single ruler. His successors, the Achaemenian Dynasty, expanded Iranian territory east to the Indus River and westward to the edge of Asia on the Mediterranean Sea. Iranians have retained a lofty sense of their many important contributions to civilization beginning with this period. Except in Iraq and the Persian Gulf states, where there are significant Iranian communities, Iranians have largely remained in their country of origin.

The Arabs, whose lanquage is different in origin and roots from the Iranian languages, as are their culture and tribal identity, were originally the principal inhabitants of the Arabian Peninsula. They were loosely organized into various tribal groups, the majority desert nomads but with a small urban element. Unlike the Iranians, Arabs derive their sense of unity and distinctiveness as people from Islam. Islam was brought to them by the Prophet Muhammad in the seventh century A.D. After his death, they expanded into other areas of the Middle East, first as conquerors, and then as settlers. Arabs form the majority in the broad area stretching from Morocco on the west, across North Africa, eastward to Egypt, Sudan, the "Arab states" and Arabia proper. There are also large Arab minorities in Iran and Israel.

particular dispute becomes buried in the rivalries of competing national interests. At some point, a specific incident ignites a general war, as nation after nation falls like a domino into the widening conflict. The classic example of the theory is World War I.

While the applicability of the domino theory to the Middle East has yet to be proven, regional conflict there thus far has not affected long-term global commerce or national survival, and international terrorist acts identified with Middle Eastern governments remain sporadic and uncoordinated. But there are very real limits to involvement or effective management, even by the superpowers. President Reagan recognized these limits implicitly by withdrawing American marines from Lebanon; and when Egypt's President Anwar al-Sadat ordered the withdrawal of all Soviet military advisers from his country some years ago, home they went.

A final point about these conflicts is that they are all direct results of European intervention in the Middle East. For much of its history, the Middle East was a region without defined

(Gamma-Liaison/François Lochon)

These young Iranians, taken prisoner by Iraq, were typical of those fighting in the Iran–Iraq War. The Iranians' patriotic fervor produced thousands of volunteers, some barely in their teens.

borders, other than the intangible limits fixed for Muslims by their religion. Even the Ottoman Empire, the major power in the region for more than five centuries, did not mark off its territories into provinces with precise boundaries until well into the 1800s. But the European powers brought a different set of rules into the area. They laid down fixed borders sanctified by treaties, played ruler against ruler, divided and conquered. It was this European ascendancy, building on old animosities while creating new ones, that laid the groundwork for today's conflicts.

## THE IRAN–IRAQ WAR:
## BATTLE OF ISLAMIC BROTHERS

The Iran–Iraq War broke out in September 1980, when Iraqi forces invaded Iran and occupied large portions of Khuzestan Province. This measure was in retaliation for Iranian artillery attacks across the border and efforts by Iranian agents to subvert the Iraqi Shia Muslim population, along with propaganda broadcasts urging Iraqis to overthrow the Iraqi regime of Saddam Hussain. But, as is the case with most Middle Eastern conflicts, the causes of the war are complex.

One factor is the ancient animosity between Iranians and Arabs, which dates back to the seventh century A.D., when invading Arab armies overran the once powerful Sassanid Empire of Iran, defeating the Iranian Army at the famous Battle of Qadisiya in 637. The Iranians were converted to Islam with relative ease, yet they looked down on the Arabs as uncivilized nomads who needed to be taught the arts of

government and refined social behavior. The Arabs, in turn, despised the Iranians for what they considered their effeminateness—their love of gardens and flowers, their appreciation of wine and fine banquets. These attitudes have never entirely disappeared.[4] After the 1980 invasion, Iraq's government-controlled press praised ·it as Saddam Hussain's Qadisiya, reminding readers of the earlier Arab success.

Iran and Iraq have been at swords' points over a number of issues in recent years. One is occupation of three small islands at the mouth of the Persian Gulf. The British had included these islands in their protectorate over eastern Arabia and transferred them to the United Arab Emirates after that country became independent. But Shah Mohammed Reza Pahlavi, then the leader of Iran, contested the transfer, on the grounds that historically they had belonged to Iran. In 1971, an Iranian commando force seized the islands. Although the islands had never belonged to Iraq, the Iraqis denounced the occupation as a violation of *Arab* sovereignty and mounted a campaign among the predominantly Arab population of Iran's Khuzestan Province, adjacent to the border, to encourage them to revolt against the central government.

Another issue was the shah's support for Kurdish guerrillas who had been fighting the Iraqi government for years to obtain autonomy for their mountain region. The shah also resented Iraq's grant of asylum to the Ayatollah Khomeini in 1963, because of the religious leader's continued anti-shah activities and propaganda broadcasts into Iran.

These disagreements intensified after the overthrow of the shah in 1979. Iraq accused the Khomeini regime of mistreatment of Khuzestan Arabs and of sending agents to incite its own Shia Muslim population to rebel. Iraqi governments have been dominated by the Sunni Muslim population since independence, although more than half of the population are Shia. The regime of Saddam Hussain, like its predecessors, is paranoid about opposition in general, but about Shia opposition in particular.[5]

The personal hatred between Saddam and Khomeini certainly contributed to the war. The two had been bitter enemies since 1978, when Saddam ordered Khomeini expelled from Iraq and accused him of working with Iraqi Shia Muslim leaders to undermine the regime. But differences in their views on the nature of authority and of social development also set the two leaders in opposition. For Saddam Hussain, the development of Islamic society to the fullest is best achieved by a secular Socialist party (e.g., the Ba'th); Islam is tangential. Khomeini, in the republic that he fashioned for Iran based on his Islamic political philosophy, argued for authority to be vested in religious leaders like himself, since they are qualified by wisdom, moral uprightness, and insight to know what is best for the Islamic community.

One issue often overlooked as a cause of the war is a territorial dispute, dating back many centuries, that has been aggravated by European intervention in the Middle East. The dispute concerns the Shatt al-Arab, the 127-mile waterway from the junction of the Tigris and Euphrates Rivers south to the Persian Gulf. The waterway was a bone of contention between the Ottoman and Iranian Empires for centuries, due to its importance as a trade outlet to the Gulf. It came entirely under Ottoman control in the nineteenth century. But with the collapse of the Ottoman Empire in World War I, the new kingdom of Iraq, set up by Britain, came in conflict with a revitalized Iran over navigation and ownership rights. Iran demanded ownership of half the Shatt al-Arab under international law, which would mean to mid-channel at the deepest point. Iraq claimed the entire waterway across to the Iranian side. Conflict intensified as both countries built up their oil exports in the 1960s and 1970s. In 1969, the shah of Iran threatened to occupy Iran's side of the waterway with gunboats, and he began a program of military support to Kurdish (Sunni Muslim) rebels fighting the Iraqi government.

Iran was much wealthier and militarily stronger than Iraq at that time, and Iraq could do little about Iranian support for the Kurds. But the Iraqis did have the Shatt al-Arab as a bargaining chip, in that their rights to it were embodied in several treaties. In 1975, after lengthy negotiations, Houari Boumedienne, then the president of Algeria, interrupted an oil ministers' conference in Algiers to announce that "our fraternal countries Iran and Iraq have reached agreement on their differences."[6] Iraq agreed to recognize Iranian ownership of the Shatt from bank to mid-channel, and Iran agreed to stop supporting Kurdish rebels in Iraq.

The advantage to Iraq of bringing an end to the Kurdish rebellion was offset by the humiliation felt by Iraqi leaders because they had bartered away a part of the sacred Arab territory. Hussain considered the agreement a personal humiliation because he had been the chief negotiator. When he became president, he said that he had negotiated it under duress and that Iraq would one day be strong enough to revoke it.[7]

The fall of Shah Reza Pahlavi, followed by the internal upheaval in Iran let loose by the 1979 Revolution, seemed to Saddam Hussain to be an excellent opportunity to reverse Iraq's humiliation. In September 1980, he announced that the 1975 treaty was null and void, and he demanded Iran's recognition of Iraqi sovereignty over the entire Shatt al-Arab. He also called for the return of the three islands seized by the shah's forces in 1971 and the transfer of predominantly Arab areas of Khuzestan to Iraqi control. Although the two countries were roughly equal in military strength at the time, purges in Iranian Army leadership, low morale, and lack of spare parts for weapons due to the U.S. economic boycott convinced Saddam that a limited attack on Iran would almost certainly succeed.

However, the quick and easy victory anticipated by the Iraqis did not materialize. Political expectations proved equally erroneous. Iraq had expected the Arabs of Khuzestan to support the invasion, but they remained loyal to Iran's Khomeini regime. The Iraqi forces failed to capitalize on their early successes and were stopped by determined Iranian resistance. The war quickly turned into a stalemate.

In 1981–1982, the momentum shifted strongly in Iran's favor. The war became a patriotic undertaking as thousands of volunteers, some barely teenagers, headed for the front. An Iranian operation, appropriately code-named Undeniable Victory, routed three Iraqi divisions. Iran's blockade of Iraqi oil exports put a severe strain on the Iraqi economy. After the defeat, Saddam withdrew all Iraqi forces from Iranian territory and asked for a cease-fire. But Iran refused; Khomeini set the ouster of "the traitor Saddam" as a precondition for peace.

Iraqi forces fared better on their own soil and threw back a number of large-scale Iranian assaults, with huge casualties. Subsequent Soviet deliveries of missiles and new aircraft gave Iraq total air superiority. In early 1985, the Iraqis launched a campaign of "total war, total peace," combining air raids on Iranian ports and cities with an all-out effort to bring international pressure on Iran to reach a settlement.

In March 1985, Iranian forces launched another major offensive toward Basra from their forward bases in the Majnoon Islands, deep in the marshes, which they had captured by surprise in 1984. Although they were driven back with heavy losses, a year later, the Iranian forces captured the Fao (Faw) Peninsula southeast of Basra in another surprise attack and moved to within artillery range of Iraq's second city.

With the ground war stalemated, conflict shifted in 1986 and 1987 to the sky and sea lanes. Iraq's vast air superiority enabled the country to carry the war deep into Iranian territory, with almost daily bombing raids on Iranian cities, industrial plants, and oil installations.

But the most dangerous aspect of the conflict stemmed from Iraqi efforts to interdict Iranian oil supplies in order to throttle its enemy's economy. The war had had a high-risk potential for broader regional conflict from the start, and in 1984, Iraqi missile attacks on tanker traffic in the Persian Gulf came close to involving other states in the region in active participation.

The internationalization of the war, which had been predicted by many analysts, became a reality in its seventh year, like a plague of locusts. The secret dealings with the United States (revealed in the 1987 Iran–Contra hearings) had immeasurably strengthened Iran's air power and defenses; Iraq lost one fifth of its aircraft in a series of battles in the marshes. Iranian arms dealers were successful in purchasing weaponry from many sources. One of their major suppliers was China, from which they purchased a number of Silkworm missiles, which were installed at secret launching sites along the coast facing the Strait of Hormuz and the Fao Peninsula. At the same time, Iranian Revolutionary Guards established bases in various small harbors from whence they could mount missile and grenade attacks in fast patrol boats against ships passing in the Gulf. The government warned that tankers bound for

Kuwait and other Gulf ports would be attacked if Iraq continued its air raids.

The direct cause of the internationalization of the war, however, was an Iraqi air raid on the U.S. naval frigate *Stark* on May 17, 1987. Thirty-seven American sailors were killed in the raid. (Although more than 200 ships had been attacked by Iraq or Iran since 1984, the *Stark* was the first warship attacked, and it suffered the heaviest casualties.) Saddam apologized, calling the attack a "tragic mistake." The United States drastically increased its naval forces in the Gulf and, in the following month, accepted a request from Kuwait for tanker protection under the American flag, along with naval escorts. In June 1987, the first convoy of "reflagged" Kuwaiti tankers traversed the Gulf without incident, escorted by U.S. warships and overflying jets from the aircraft carrier *Constellation.*

Predictably, Iran's threat to make the Gulf "safe for every one or no one," following the U.S. buildup in the region, affected nearby countries as well as international shipping. Saboteurs blew up oil installations and factories in the United Arab Emirates, Bahrain, and Saudi Arabia. Revolutionary Guardsmen carried out their earlier threats with hit-and-run strafing and grenade attacks on passing tankers. But the most serious danger came from floating mines strewn at random in shipping lanes. After a number of tankers had been damaged, the United States and several European countries previously uninvolved in the conflict, notably Italy, began sending minesweepers to the area.

With the Gulf in a state of high tension, the United Nations (UN) Security Council mounted a major effort to end the war. In July 1987, the Security Council unanimously approved *Resolution 598.* It called for an immediate cease-fire, the withdrawal of all forces to within recognized international boundaries, repatriation of all prisoners, and negotiations under UN auspices for a permanent peace settlement. Iraq accepted the resolution, but Iran temporized. Its president, Ali Khamenei, told the UN General Assembly: "The Security Council's stance in relation to the war imposed on us has not changed up to this moment."[8]

A year later, though, Iran accepted *Resolution 598,* in an abrupt about-face. A number of factors combined to bring about this change, but the principal one was probably Iraqi success on the battlefield. Early in 1988, Republican Guard units specially trained in chemical warfare recaptured Fao in a massive assault, using nerve gases such as tabun and sarin along with mustard gas to thwart counterattacks. These chemical weapons worked with deadly effectiveness against the "human wave" tactics of teenage Iranian volunteers. Meanwhile, Saddam Hussain's crash program of development of long-range missiles enabled his forces to hit cities and military installations deep inside Iran and bring a further drop in Iranian morale.

Khomeini's death in June 1989 removed a major obstacle to peace negotiations. He had been persuaded only with great difficulty to approve the cease-fire, and his uncompromising hatred of Saddam Hussain was not shared by many of his associates.

A real peace settlement would enable both regimes to turn their full attention to the enormous problems of reconstruction. Unfortunately, their diametrically opposed positions on war gains worked against dialogue. Iran insisted on the withdrawal of Iraqi troops from its territory as a first step, while Iraq demanded that prisoner exchanges and clearing of the Shatt al-Arab should precede withdrawal.

The 1990 Iraqi invasion of Kuwait brought about an important change in the relationship. Urgently in need of allies, Saddam Hussain abruptly agreed to the original peace terms set by the United States and accepted by Iran. These terms required Iraqi troop withdrawal from occupied Iranian territory along with prisoner exchanges and clearance of mines and other obstacles from the Shatt al-Arab. Iran stayed neutral during the Gulf War and provided sanctuary for Iraqi pilots fleeing Allied air attacks, although it impounded their aircraft, which as of this writing have yet to be returned.

A formal peace treaty has yet to be signed between these long-time hostile neighbors, although they have reestablished diplomatic relations and exchanged some prisoners. Iran released 2,939 Iraqi POWs in May 2000; most of them had been held since the early days of the war. But the main reason for the delay in formalizing peace is the support each gives to opposition groups. Iraq provides bases and financial support for Mujahideen-I-Khalq, which seeks the overthrow of Iran's clerical regime; while Iran supports Al-Badr, the Shia "brigade" that organized the Shia uprising in southern Iraq after the Gulf War and escaped when the revolt was crushed by the Iraqi Army.

## THE GULF WAR AND ITS AFTERMATH

On August 2, 1990, the Iraqi Army, which had been mobilized along the border, invaded and occupied Kuwait, quickly overcoming light resistance as the ruling Kuwaiti emir and his family escaped into exile. The invasion climaxed a long dispute between the two Arab neighbors over oil-production quotas, division of output from the oil fields of the jointly controlled Neutral Zone along the border, and repayment of Iraqi debts to Kuwait from the war with Iran. Saddam Hussain had criticized Kuwait for producing more than its quota as allotted by the Organization of Petroleum Exporting Countries (OPEC), thus driving down the price per barrel and costing Iraq $7 billion to $8 billion in lost revenues. The Iraqi leader also charged Kuwait with taking more than its share of the output of the Neutral Zone. The Iraqi charges found considerable support from other Arab states, most of which consider the Kuwaitis to be stingy and arrogant. However, an Arab League summit meeting of oil ministers failed to resolve the dispute. Kuwait agreed only to a month-long adherence to its OPEC quota and continued to press for repayment of Iraqi war debts.

What had been initially an inter-Arab conflict was globalized by the invasion. Although Iraq called its occupation a recovery of part of the Arab homeland, which had been "stolen" from the Arabs by the British and given its independence under false premises, the action was viewed as aggression by nearly all the countries in the world. The UN Security Council on August 6 approved *Resolution 660*, calling for an immediate withdrawal of Iraqi forces from Kuwait and restoration of the country's legitimate government. Pending withdrawal, a worldwide embargo would be imposed on Iraq, covering both exports and imports and including medical and food supplies as well as military equipment. A similar resolution approved by the League of Arab States denounced Iraq's aggression against the "brotherly Arab state of Kuwait" and demanded immediate Iraqi withdrawal and restoration of Kuwaiti independence.

The invasion divided the Arab states, as several, notably Yemen and Sudan, agreed with Iraq's contention that Kuwait was historically part of Iraq and that Kuwaiti arrogance was partly responsible for the conflict. Others took the opposite view. Egyptian president Hosni Mubarak accused Saddam Hussein of breaking a solemn pledge not to invade Kuwait. Saudi Arabia, fearing that it might be Iraq's next victim, requested U.S. help under the bilateral defense treaty to protect its territory. U.S. president George Bush and Soviet president Mikhail Gorbachev issued a joint pledge for action to expel Iraqi forces from Kuwait. A massive military buildup followed, largely made up of U.S. forces, but with contingents from a number of other countries, including several Arab states. Although led by U.S. military commanders, the collective force operated under the terms of UN *Resolution 660* and was responsible ultimately to the Security Council as a military coalition.

The UN embargo continued in effect for six months but failed to generate an Iraqi withdrawal from Kuwait, despite its severe impact on the civilian population. (The only concession made by Saddam Hussein during that period was the release of foreign technicians who had been working in Kuwait at the time of the invasion). As a result, the coalition forces launched the so-called Operation Desert Storm on January 16, 1991. With their total air superiority and superior military technology, they made short work of Iraq's army, as thousands of Iraqi soldiers fled or surrendered. On the express orders of George Bush, the campaign was halted on February 7, after Iraqi forces had been expelled from Kuwait. Yet Saddam remained in power, and uprisings of the Kurdish and Shia populations in Iraq were ruthlessly crushed by the reorganized Iraqi Army, which remained loyal to its leader. Although the Bush administration was unwilling to commit American forces to assist these populations and presumably risk significant casualties in unfamiliar territory, the United States and other members of the UN Security Council established "no-fly zones" north of the 36th parallel and south of the 33rd parallel of longitude, which would be off limits to

Iraqi forces. The zones effectively limited Iraq's sovereignty to approximately two thirds of its own territory.

Saddam Hussein's running battle with the United Nations kept world attention focused on Iraq in 1992–1993. Despite his country's sound defeat in the Gulf War, the Iraqi dictator had gained the support not only of some other Arab states but also of many developing-world leaders, for what appeared to them to have been an infringement on Iraq's sovereignty by the United Nations in its zeal to destroy Iraq's weapons of mass destruction. But for the United Nations and the United States, the main issue involved Iraq's noncompliance with UN resolutions. Thus *Resolution 687* directed the country to destroy all its long-range ballistic missiles and dismantle its chemical- and nuclear-weapons facilities, while *Resolution 715* would establish a permanent UN monitoring system, with surveillance cameras, for all missile test sites and installations as well as nuclear facilities. Iraq's compliance with these resolutions would end the embargo imposed after the invasion of Kuwait and would enable Iraq to sell $1.6 billion in oil to finance imports of badly needed medicines, medical supplies, and foodstuffs. Iraqi representatives argued that their country had complied with *Resolution 687* by demolishing under international supervision the al-Atheer nuclear complex outside Baghdad and by opening all missile sites to UN inspectors. But they said that *Resolution 715* was illegal under international law, since it infringed on national sovereignty.

Since then, Iraq and the United Nations (along with the United States) have been deadlocked over the issue of inspections in a potentially deadly cat-and-mouse game played with consummate skill by Saddam. In 1996, the Iraqi government accepted UN terms to allow it to sell $2 billion worth of oil every six months, in return for opening all missile-testing sites and biological- and chemical-weapons facilities to inspectors. The oil revenues would be used for purchases of critically needed food, medicines, and children's supplies. However, the UN Security Council was divided, with the United States insisting on Iraq's adherence to all its obligations specified in *Resolution 715*, while other Council members argued that the embargo was hurting the most vulnerable groups in the population without affecting the leadership.

The standoff hardened in late 1997, when Saddam ordered the American members of the inspection team to leave his country, saying that they were spies. The Bill Clinton administration threatened to use force to compel their return and beefed up U.S. military strength in the Persian Gulf. A UN-sponsored mediation effort temporarily averted the threat.

Since then, Iraq has refused consistently to allow the inspectors to return. The regime claims that it has met its obligation to dismantle its weapons program, and that a continuation of the inspections would violate Iraq's sovereignty and control over its internal affairs. In extending the oil-for-food program in 1999, the Security Council replaced the Special Commission on Iraq with a new body, the UN

Monitoring, Verification and Inspection Commission (UN-MOVIC). However, the new team, recruited from various member states as weapons experts, has yet to set foot on Iraqi soil. In 2000, its first two directors resigned, along with the director of the World Food Program in Iraq, to protest the hardships imposed on the Iraqi people by the UN sanctions.

Iraq's adamant refusal to accept renewed inspections along with the patrolling by U.S. and British aircraft of the "no-fly zones" led to increased attacks on the aircraft by Iraqi gunners. The United States and Britain, in response, began bombing military targets within the country, aimed particularly at Iraqi air-defense and communications targets. The conflict escalated in December 1998, when some 100 such installations were either damaged or destroyed. The bombings were justified not only in response, but also to destroy installations used allegedly to produce weapons of mass destruction. In 2001, the attacks were scaled back. By that time Iraqi gunners were firing surface-to-air missiles (SAMS) at the aircraft, but thus far, in more than 200,000 sorties, none has been hit. The closest call came on July 25, when a missile exploded near a high-altitude U-2 spy plane.

In August 2001, the overflights and Iraqi gunner responses increased significantly, as U.S. and British aircrafts struck at Iraq anti-aircraft sites, communications facilities, and other elements in the country's air-defense system. Overall there were 370 Iraqi violations of the no-fly zone in 2001, compared with 221 in 2000.

Saddam Hussain's continued insistence on the removal of UN sanctions and eliminations of the no-fly zones as preconditions for the return of UNMOVIC inspectors remains as the major obstacle to Iraq's reintegration into the world community of nations as a sovereign entity. Eliminating the no-fly zones will be more difficult than suspending sanctions, since the former are not UN–backed. The countries that have reestablished diplomatic and trade relations with Iraq would have to persuade the United States and Britain to suspend the overflights. Although proof that the country had actually resumed weapons production was lacking, its refusal to re-admit the inspectors remained an obstacle to the removal of the sanctions. In December 2001, the Security Council renewed them for an additional six months. Under a compromise resolution backed by the United States and Britain, the existing oil-for-food program would be revised to establish a "goods review list" for supplies and materials that could be used either for military or civilian purposes. These would have to be approved separately by all Security Council member states. All goods not on the list would not require Council approval.

A by-product of the September 11, 2001, attacks on the United States has been renewed attention by the George W. Bush administration to Iraq as part of what he unfortunately termed the "evil axis" of alleged state sponsors of terrorism. Although evidence of any Iraqi connection with the attacks or with Osama bin Laden's al-Qaeda network was lacking, some administration officials early in 2002 pressed for a military campaign to oust Saddam Hussain as "phase two" in the war against terrorism. However, others, along with the media and numerous scholars and area experts, warned that such a campaign would result in high casualties and would unravel the global coalition formed by President Bush to invade Afghanistan.

## THE ARAB–ISRAELI CONFLICT

Until very recently, the Arab–Israeli conflict involved two peoples: those grouped into the modern Arab states, for the most part products of European colonialism, and the modern State of Israel. Israel's military superiority over its Arab neighbors seemed to remove the likelihood of a sixth Arab–Israeli war, and the peace treaties with Jordan and Egypt were further deterrents to renewal of armed conflict. However, with the spiraling cycle of violence between Israelis and Palestinians in 2001 and 2002, the Arab states have refocused on Israel as their long-term enemy.

In its essentials the conflict stems from opposing views of land ownership. The land in question is Palestine, ancient Judea and Samaria for Jews, claimed by modern Israel on historical, emotional, and symbolic grounds. The Jewish claim to possession is to fulfill God's original covenant with Abraham, patriarch of the ancient Jewish tribes. To the Jews, it is a sacred homeland. The modern Israelis are the returned Jews, immigrants from many lands, plus the small Jewish community that remained there during the centuries of dispersion (diaspora). The Palestinians, mostly descendants of peoples who settled there over the centuries, were formerly 80 percent Muslim and 20 percent Christian, but emigration and displacement under the Jewish state in its wars have reduced the latter to 2 percent of the population. For most of its history the territory was ruled by outside powers—Persians, Syrians, Rome, the Byzantine Empire, and from the 1400s to 1917 by sultans of the Ottoman Turkish Empire. Under Ottoman rule it was divided into two *vilayets* (provinces) plus the separate Sanjak of Jerusalem (a more or less self-governing district). When Britain was given the League of Nations mandate over the southern vilayet, named Acre from its principal town, the British named the territory "Palestine," possibly from biblical associations with the ancient Philistine inhabitants.

In the twentieth century, the question of a Palestine homeland was given form and impetus by two nationalist movements: Zionism and Arab nationalism. *Zionism,* the first to develop political activism in implementation of a national ideal, organized large-scale immigration of Jews into Palestine. These immigrants, few of them skilled in agriculture or the vocations needed to build a new nation in a strange land, nevertheless succeeded in changing the face of Palestine. In a relatively short time, a region of undeveloped sand dunes near the coast evolved into the bustling city of Tel Aviv, and

## ZIONISM

*Zionism* may be defined as the collective expression of the will of a dispersed people, the Jews, to recover their ancestral homeland. This idealized longing was given concrete form by European Jews in the nineteenth century.

In 1882, a Jewish law student, Leon Pinsker, published *Auto-Emancipation,* a book that called on Jews, who were being pressed at the time between the twin dangers of anti-Semitism and assimilation into European society, to resist by establishing a Jewish homeland *somewhere.* Subsequently, a Viennese journalist, Theodor Herzl, published *Der Judenstaat (The Jewish State)* in 1896. Herzl argued that Jews could never hope to be fully accepted into the societies of nations where they lived; anti-Semitism was too deeply rooted. The only solution would be a homeland for immigrant Jews as a secular commonwealth of farmers, artisans, traders, and shopkeepers. In time, he said, it would become a model for all nations through its restoration of the ancient Jewish nation formed under a covenant with God.

Herzl's vision of the Zionist state would give equal rights and protection to people of other nationalities who came there. This secular view generated conflict with Orthodox Jews, who felt that only God could ordain a Jewish state and that, therefore, Zionism would have to observe the rules and practices of Judaism in establishing such a state.

---

previously unproductive marshland was transformed into profitable farms and kibbutz settlements.

*Arab nationalism,* slower to develop, grew out of the contacts of Arab subject peoples in the Ottoman Empire with Europeans, particularly missionary-educators sent by their various churches to work with the Christian Arab communities. It developed political overtones during World War I, when British agents such as T. E. Lawrence encouraged the Arabs to revolt against the Turks, their "Islamic brothers." In return, the Arabs were given to understand that Britain would support the establishment of an independent Arab state in the Arab lands of the empire. An Anglo–Arab army entered Jerusalem in triumph in 1917 and Damascus in 1918, where an independent Arab kingdom was proclaimed, headed by the Emir Faisal, the leader of the revolt.

The Arab population of Palestine took relatively little part in these events. But European rivalries and conflicting commitments for disposition of the provinces of the defeated Ottoman Empire soon involved them directly in conflict over Palestine. The most important document affecting the conflict was the Balfour Declaration, a statement of British support for a Jewish homeland in Palestine in the form of a letter from Foreign Secretary Arthur Balfour to Lord Rothschild, a prominent Jewish banker and leader of the Zionist Organization.

Although the Zionists interpreted the statement as permission to proceed with their plans for a Jewish National Home in Palestine, neither they nor the Arabs were fully satisfied

with the World War I peace settlement, in terms of the disposition of territories. The results soon justified their pessimism. The Arab kingdom of Syria was dismantled by the French, who then established a mandate over Syria under the League of Nations. The British set up a mandate over Palestine, attempting to balance support for Jewish aspirations with a commitment to develop self-government for the Arab population, in accordance with the terms of the mandate as approved by the League of Nations. It seemed an impossible task; and in 1948, the British gave up, handing the "Palestine problem" back to the United Nations, the successor to the League of Nations. The United Nations had approved a partition plan for Palestine in November 1947; and, after the termination of the mandate, the Zionists proclaimed the establishment of the State of Israel.

Most state-to-state disputes are susceptible to arbitration and outside mediation, particularly when they involve borders or territory. But Palestine is a special case. Its location astride communication links between the eastern and western sections of the Arab world made it essential to the building of a unified Arab nation, the goal of Arab leaders since World War I. Its importance to Muslims as the site of one of their holiest shrines, the Dome of the Rock in Jerusalem, is underscored by Jewish control—a control made possible, in the Arab Muslim view, by the "imperialist enemies of Islam," and reinforced by the relatively lenient treatment given by an Israeli court to Jewish terrorists arrested for trying to blow up the shrines on the Dome and build a new temple on the site. Also, since they lack an outside patron, both the dispersed Palestinians and those remaining in Israel look to the Arab states as the natural champions of their cause.

Yet the Arab states have never been able to develop a coherent, unified policy toward Israel in support of the Palestinian cause. There are several reasons for this failure. One is the historic rivalry of Arab leaders—a competitiveness that has evolved from ancient origins, strong individualism, and family pride. Other reasons include the overall immaturity of the modern Arab political system and the difficulty of distinguishing between rhetoric and fact. The Arabic language lends itself more to the former than the latter. Thus the repeated declarations of Arab leaders that with God's help "we will drive the Jews into the sea. . . " are not meant to be taken literally. But because rhetoric urges them to subscribe to the ideal of a single Arab nation, they are torn between the ideal of this nation and the reality of separate nations. With the exception of Egypt, they lack the collective maturity that would enable them to negotiate on a firm basis with Israel. This lack of political maturity has been amply demonstrated in the past, as opportunities to make some sort of durable peace, even on somewhat unfavorable terms, were squandered regularly. The Arab states are thus probably more of a liability than an asset to the Palestinian cause.

Another reason for Arab disunity stems from the relationship of the Arab states with the Palestinians. During the

British mandate, the Arab Higher Committee—the nexus of what became the Palestine national movement—aroused the anger of Arab leaders in neighboring countries by refusing to accept their authority over the committee's policies in return for financial support. After the 1948 Arab–Israeli War, the dispersal of Palestinians into Arab lands caused further friction; the Palestinians, often better educated than their reluctant hosts and possessed of greater political skills, seemed to threaten the authority of some Arab leaders and to dominate some Arab economies. Finally, the performance of the Arab states in the wars with Israel was a bitter disillusionment to the Palestinians. Constantine Zurayk of the American University of Beirut expressed their shame in his book *The Meaning of Disaster:*

> Seven Arab states declare war on Zionism, stop impotent before it and turn on their heels.... Declarations fall like bombs from the mouths of officials at meetings of the Arab League, but when action becomes necessary, the fire is still and quiet.[9]

Without the interference of Arab state rhetoric and instances of inept Arab military intervention, it is possible that the Palestinians might have come to terms with their Jewish neighbors long ago. As early as the 1930s, some Jews sought accommodation with Palestinian leaders. Chaim Weizmann, later the first president of Israel, wrote to an American friend: "Palestine is to be shared by two nations.... Palestine must be built without violating [by] one iota the legitimate rights of the Arabs."[10] Martin Buber, a distinguished Jewish philosopher and theologian, argued tirelessly for Jewish–Arab harmony. In 1947, on the eve of the UN partition resolution, he warned: "What is really needed by each of the two peoples... in Palestine is self-determination, autonomy... but this most certainly does not mean that each is in need of a state in which it will be the sovereign."[11]

More recently, Uri Avnery, a prominent Zionist and Knesset (Israeli Parliament) member, writing in the afterglow of Israel's triumph over the Arab states in the 1967 Six-Day War, said, "The government [should] offer the Palestine Arabs assistance in setting up a national republic of their own. . . . [which] will become the natural bridge between Israel and the Arab world."[12]

The effort to distinguish between a rightful Jewish "homeland" and the occupied territories gained momentum in 1977 with the formation of Peace Now, a movement initiated by army officers who felt that the government of Menachem Begin should not miss the opportunity to negotiate peace with Egypt. Peace Now gradually became the engine of the Israeli peace movement, leading public opposition to invasion of Lebanon and establishment of Jewish settlements in the occupied territories. (With Labor's return to power in Israel in the 1992 election, Peace Now's policy of "exchanging land for peace and the ethical rights of Palestinians to national self-expression" became official government policy.)[13]

Domestic political pressures, the broad sympathy of Americans for Israel, and support for the country as a dependable ally in the Middle East have been passed along from one U.S. administration to another. This innate preference has not been helped by the position taken on the issue by the Palestine Liberation Organization (PLO), the international exponent organization of the Palestinian cause, which has sometimes resorted to terrorism. The PLO, upon its founding in 1964, issued a charter calling for the destruction of Israel and the establishment of a sovereign Palestinian Arab state. The PLO until recently was also ambivalent about its acceptance of UN *Resolutions 242* and *338,* which call for Israeli withdrawal from the West Bank and Gaza Strip as a prelude to peace negotiations.

During the 34-year Israeli occupation of the territories, the Palestinians there undertook few initiatives on their own to challenge the occupation. An entire generation grew up under Israeli control, living in squalid refugee camps or towns little changed since Ottoman times and deprived of even the elemental human rights supposedly guaranteed to an occupied population under international law. In December 1987, a series of minor clashes between Palestinian youths and Israeli security forces escalated into a full-scale revolt, or uprising, against the occupying power. This single event, called in Arabic the *intifada* (literally, "resurgence"), has changed the context of the Israeli–Palestinian conflict more decisively than any other in recent history.

The intifada caught not only the Israelis but also the PLO by surprise. Having lost their Beirut base due to the Israeli invasion of 1982, PLO leaders found themselves in an unusual situation, identified internationally with a conflict from which they were physically separated and could not control directly or even influence to any great degree. As more and more Palestinians in the territories were caught up in the rhythm of struggle, the routine of stone-throwings, waving of forbidden Palestinian flags, demonstrations, and cat-and-mouse games with Israeli troops, the PLO seemed increasingly irrelevant to the Palestinian cause.

## THE BALFOUR DECLARATION

The text of the Balfour Declaration is as follows: "I have much pleasure in conveying to you on behalf of His Majesty's Government the following declaration of sympathy with Jewish Zionist aspirations which has been submitted to and approved by the Cabinet:

"His Majesty's Government view with favor the establishment in Palestine of a National Home for the Jewish people and will use their best endeavors to facilitate the achievement of this project, it being clearly understood that nothing shall be done which may prejudice the civil and religious rights of existing non-Jewish communities in Palestine or the rights and political status enjoyed by Jews in any other country."

(Israeli Government Tourism Administration)

The Dome of the Rock in Jerusalem is the site of one of the holiest Muslim shrines. The Israeli control of Jerusalem is one of the reasons why the Palestinian Muslims turn to the Arab states for assistance in regaining control of the area.

Yet this organization, particularly its leader Yassir Arafat, had a talent for theater, for dramatic moves that not only kept the cause in the international spotlight but also provided hope for several million Palestinians that an apparently unwinnable conflict might someday be won. This talent was amply demonstrated in December 1988, the first anniversary of the intifada. Arafat concluded a meeting of the PLO National Council, the organization's executive body, in Tunis, Tunisia, with the historic statement that, in addition to formal acceptance of *Resolutions 242* and *338* as the basis for peace negotiations, the PLO would recognize Israel's right to exist. Arafat amplified the statement at a special UN General Assembly session in Geneva, Switzerland, formally accepting Israeli sovereignty over its own territory and renouncing the use of terrorism by the PLO.

The evidence of five wars and innumerable smaller conflicts suggests that the Arab–Israeli conflict will remain localized. Israel's invasion of Lebanon, like its predecessors, remained localized once the United States had intervened, and it proved only a temporary setback for the PLO, a displacement. The Arab states continue to be haunted by the Palestinians, an exiled, dispersed people who refuse to be assimilated into other populations or to give up their hard-won identity. Mohammed Shadid contends that "Palestine is the conscience of the Arab world and a pulsating vein of the Islamic world . . . perhaps the only issue where Arab nationalism and Islamic revivalism are joined."[14] In 1995, Libya's leader, Muammar al-Qadhafi, the Arab world's most fervent advocate of Arab unity since Gamal Abdel Nasser of Egypt, abruptly expelled 1,500 Palestinian workers long resident in his country. He did so, he said, to protest the Palestinian–Israeli peace agreements, which he called a sellout of Arab interests.

Libya is not the only Arab state affected by the Palestinians and their goal of return to their homeland. Israel's 1982 invasion of Lebanon, led by former general (and current prime minister) Ariel Sharon, was intended to drive the PLO leadership out of Beirut. It succeeeded in that goal but led to the collapse of the Begin government after Christian militiamen, supposedly allied with Israelis, massacred Palestinians in the Sabra and Shatila refugee camps. An internal committee of inquiry placed the blame for the massacre on Sharon, because he had not prevented it. The other unintended result was the emergence in southern Lebanon of an anti-Israeli guerrilla force, Hizbullah, which eventually forced the Israelis to withdraw.

The Arab states that surround Israel, although politically new, are heirs to a proud and ancient tradition, reaching back to the period when Islamic–Arab civilization was far superior to that of the Western world. This tradition and the self-proclaimed commitment to Arab brotherhood, however, have yet to bring them together in a united front toward Israel. A major obstacle to Arab unity is the variety of political systems that exist in the individual Arab states. These range from patriarchal absolute rule in Saudi Arabia by a ruling family to the multiparty system of Lebanon. Other Arab states reflect a variety of political systems—constitutional and patriarchal monarchies, authoritarian single-party governments, and regimes dependent on a single individual, to name a few examples. The United Arab Emirates provides one model of successful unification, mainly because the individual emirates are patriarchally ruled; in addition, aside from large expatriate workforces their populations are ethnically and linguistically unified. The Yemen Arab Republic, the other successful example, resulted from unification of the Marxist People's Republic of Yemen (South Yemen) and the tribal Arab Republic of Yemen (North Yemen). Their unification nearly collapsed in 1994 due to civil war, but the triumph of northern over southern forces and subsequent coalition government, confirmed by national elections, seem to have assured its survival.

Aside from the immediate success of the Gulf War in its limited objectives, the one accomplishment of the George Bush administration vis-à-vis the Middle East political situation was the launching of direct peace talks among Arab,

Israeli, and Palestinian representatives to establish a "total Middle East peace." These talks, begun in Madrid, Spain, in 1991, were continued at various locations for nearly a dozen rounds, but without much progress toward a solution.

A major breakthrough, however, took place in September 1993, as negotiations conducted in secret by Palestinian and Israeli negotiators in Norway, a neutral country, resulted in a historic agreement. The agreement, although it fell far short of Palestinian objectives of an independent state, provided for Israeli recognition of Palestinian territorial rights and acceptance of a Palestinian "mini-state" in the Gaza Strip and an area around the West Bank city of Jericho, which would be its capital. It would be governed by an elected Council and would have limited self-rule for a five-year transitional period, after which discussions would begin on its permanent status.

After many false starts and delays that were caused by extremist violence on both sides, Israel and the PLO reached an interim agreement for additional land transfers to Palestinian self-rule in 1995. However, the election of Benjamin Netanyahu as Israel's prime minister in that year put a hold on the process. Netanyahu did meet with Arafat at the Wye River Plantation in Maryland in October 1998, with President Bill Clinton and Jordan's King Hussein as mediators. Arafat and Netanyahu signed the "Wye Agreement," which provided for three more land transfers and a "safe passage route" for Palestinians between the Gaza Strip and the West Bank. In addition, 750 Palestinian prisoners held in Israel were released, bringing the number to 7,000 since 1993. Netanyahu later put a moratorium on the implementation of these provisions.

Ehud Barak's election as Israeli prime minister in May 1999 breathed new life into the peace process after a long hiatus under Netanyahu. In January 2000, Barak met with Syrian foreign minister Farouk al-Atassi in Sheperdstown, West Virginia, in a renewed effort to bring about a Syrian–Israeli peace treaty. President Clinton served as moderator and mediator. However, Israel and Syria remained far apart on issues of mutual concern, notably ownership of the Golan Heights, and the talks adjourned without agreement. The renewal of violent Israeli–Palestinian confrontation in 2000 made any further moves toward peace between Israel and its last hostile state neighbor impossible.

Barak brought partial peace with Lebanon by ordering the withdrawal of Israeli forces from their self-declared "security zone" just inside the Lebanese border in April 2000, ahead of schedule. Peacekeeping units of the United Nations Interim Force in Lebanon (UNIFIL) then moved up to the border. As a result, the occupied West Bank and Gaza Strip remained the only part of "Arab land" still under foreign control.

## ISRAEL AND THE PALESTINIANS

With Israeli–Arab relations in a state of temporary peace, the focus of Middle East conflict centered on the Palestinian population of the occupied West Bank and Gaza Strip. Following Barak's election, several steps were taken to implement the 1993 Oslo Agreement. Another 12 percent of the West Bank was turned over to the Palestine National Authority in late 1999 and early 2000. In the summer of 2000, Barak met with PNA head Yassir Arafat at Camp David, Maryland, with President Clinton again serving as moderator. In what seemed at the time to be a generous proposal, Barak offered to turn over 94 percent of the West Bank, along with administrative control over the Dome of the Rock (exclusive of the Wailing Wall) and the Old City of Jerusalem, with its separate Jewish, Muslim, Christian, and Armenian quarters. Arafat, for his part, agreed that Jewish settlements outside of Jerusalem built illegally on Palestinian land would be exempt from Palestinian control. However, he insisted that the "right of return" of dispossessed Palestinians to their former homes and villages in what is now Israel be included in the agreement. This right of return has been an article of faith for them since the establishment of the Israeli state.

In retrospect, it seems doubtful that Barak's proposals would have been acceptable to the Israeli public and given the necessary approval by a bitterly divided Knesset. But in any case, they were doomed by Arafat's insistence on the right of refugee return. Subsequently, in 2001, Barak was defeated in elections for the office of prime minister, called prematurely after several no-confidence votes in the Knesset. His successor, former general Ariel Sharon, said he would not be bound by the proposals and would consider only interim agreements with the PNA, with no additional transfers of land to the Palestinians.

## Intifada II

In September 2000, Sharon had made an unexpected but widely publicized visit to the Islamic shrines of the Dome of the Rock, accompanied by journalists and a body of security guards. He said that his visit was peaceful and was intended to emphasize Israel's right to sovereignty over its entire territory. But predictably, the visit enraged the Palestinians. It seemed to many of them that Israel had no intention of complying with the Oslo agreements and was simply using them as a means for further expansion of its control over Palestinian territory.

"Intifada II," which broke out that fall, is in some respects different from its predecessor. The first intifada sought to call attention to the cause of an essentially powerless people, and to remind the world that their rights as a conquered people under international law were being ignored. The second intifada evolved in a similar manner. But rather than from Palestinian powerlessness, it sprang from Palestinian feelings of despair, reflecting frustration at lack of jobs, and charges of indignities imposed on them by Israel.

The second intifada has evolved into something close to civil war. The only difference is that the Palestinians are an occupied population rather than internal dissidents. Increased

Palestinian use of mortars and other heavy weapons—including frequent suicide bombers who blow themselves up in crowded places, killing many civilians—is being countered by Israeli tanks, helicopter gunships, and even missiles. West Bank cities as well as parts of Gaza are occupied periodically by Israeli forces in their pursuit of militants. Another Israeli tactic has been the demolition of Palestinian homes, in the belief that they harbor gunmen.

As of late spring 2002 Palestinians and Israelis were literally at war, with a total breakdown of trust on both sides. Palestinian suicide bombers increasingly attacked targets within Israel; in response, Israeli tanks blockaded Arafat's headquarters and re-occupied West Bank cities. In May, the Bush administration injected itself directly into the conflict, fearing that it would undermine the war against terrorism. But shuttle missions of various high-level U.S. negotiators, including Secretary of State Colin Powell, have yet to produce results beyond temporary Israeli withdrawal from the disputed territory.

## SEPTEMBER 11, 2001

On September 11, 2001, a band of hijackers seized control of two U.S. commercial aircraft in flight and flew them deliberately into the twin towers of the World Trade Center in New York City. A third aircraft was hijacked and smashed into one side of the Pentagon near Washington, D.C.; while a fourth, perhaps intended for the U.S. Capitol Building, crashed in a field in Pennsylvania, well short of its objective. The hijackings not only caused significant loss of civilian lives and huge losses in property damages; they also brought global terrorism to American soil. For almost the first time in their history, Americans were rendered vulnerable by unknown, faceless enemies preaching a doctrine of hate.

The hijackings were a wake-up call for a nation that had always assumed that it was safe from the violence that had become a way of life elsewhere, notably Israel, parts of Russia, Algeria, and various countries in sub-Saharan Africa, among others. The Bush administration launched a concerted effort, first to identify the hijackers and the network behind them and thereafter to bring those responsible to justice. Preliminary investigation indicated that the hijackers were Arabs from several Middle Eastern countries, mainly Egypt, Saudi Arabia, Sudan, and Yemen. They formed part of a terrorist network identified as *al-Qaeda* ("The Base" in Arabic).

Al-Qaeda's leader and founder is Osama bin Laden, a multimillionaire member of a prominent Saudi Arabian family originally from the Hadhramaut, in southern Yemen. The family migrated to Saudi Arabia when he was young, and the senior bin Laden developed an enormously successful contracting business. Eventually the business became an international conglomerate, with interests and subsidiaries in many countries. But along the way, young Osama seemed to have developed an undying hatred of the United States and everything it stands for. He broke with his family, and, although an elitist by Saudi Arabian (for that matter universal) standards, chose first to join the mujahideen ("resistance" or "freedom fighters") in Afghanistan fighting the Soviet invasion, and then used that experience to build a secret terrorist network to carry out attacks on various perceived enemies. One end product was the September 11 terrorist attacks.

Aside from the Middle East origins of al-Qaeda and its leadership (bin Laden's chief associates were two Egyptians) and his Afghan base, the Middle East "connection" with the events of September 11 is an important one because it helps us understand the "why" of the attacks. Why is there so much hatred of the United States as to cause young men to take their own lives in suicide attacks against America? Why is it that members of prominent and prosperous Middle Eastern families become convinced that America is the enemy of their peoples, and particularly of Islam? From a Middle Eastern perspective, one explanation is that the United States supports Israel against the internationally approved right of the Palestinian people to their own nation-state. Also, the presence of American military forces in Saudi Arabia, the "sacred soil" of Islam, has angered millions of Muslims in the region who feel that, although invited by the Saudi government, the Americans are there as rulers, protectors of U.S. interests, rather than defenders of the Saudi people from outside threats such as those from Iraq.

There is, of course, some resentment among Middle Easterners of U.S. power and wealth in a world of increasing scarcity. Predictably, but nonetheless sincerely, Islamic fundamentalist groups such as the Muslim Brotherhood argue that without the U.S. support for unrepresentative regimes such as Egypt's, these regimes would collapse and be replaced by ones governed by true Islamic law.

Reaction in the Middle East to the September 11 attacks has varied from country to country. Most national leaders have condemned them as un-Islamic and contrary to the rules of jihad. Thus Saudi Arabia's highest-ranking legal scholar stated categorically that suicide bombers would not die as martyrs but, rather, as simple suicides, an action forbidden by the Koran. An emergency meeting of the 56-nation Organization of the Islamic Conference (OIC) criticized the Taliban regime in Afghanistan for sheltering the "heretic" bin Laden but warned against the "targeting of any Islamic or Arab state under the pretext of fighting terrorism." And the emir of Qatar told the conference that "we assert our utter rejection of these attacks and assert that those confronting them must not touch innocent civilians and must not extend beyond those who carry out those attacks."

Backing for the U.S.–led coalition against terrorism has varied widely. Britain and France promptly committed troops to the campaign in Afghanistan. Other European countries, notably Germany, Spain, and Italy, arrested numbers of members and alleged members of al-Qaeda. Indonesia, Malaysia, and Yemen, among other countries, pursued a roundup of militants and former "Afghan Arabs," returned veterans of the Soviet–Afghan War. In Yemen, a favorite hideout of anti–U.S. terrorism due to its geographical isolation and bin Laden's family background, American special forces were invited by the government in February 2002 to proceed there and train the Yemeni Army in counterterrorism.

On the political side, in October 2001, Saudi Arabia and United Arab Emirates withdrew their recognition of the Taliban as the Afghan government. Iran closed its border with Afghanistan and provided arms to the Northern Alliance, while Iranian mediators in Germany helped unite the various Afghan warlords into an interim government for that war-torn country. But with bin Laden and leaders of his network possibly having escaped to Pakistan and with the technology available to al-Qaeda, the probability was that U.S. military success in Afghanistan was at best a first step in the long struggle to eliminate global terrorism.[15]

## WATER: A REGIONAL PROBLEM

War over water—it is an obscenity yet it is conceivable.

Queen Noor (Jordan)

The Middle East is becoming slowly a desert

Foreign Minister Shimon Peres (Israel)

Underlying the territorial, ethnic, religious, and other conflicts and disputes over land ownership in the region are the crucial issue of water sharing and control over water resources. In recent years, this issue has literally spilled over into regional politics. Turkey's Great Anatolia Project (GAP), a series of dams on the Euphrates centered on the giant Ataturk Dam, will irrigate 4.2 million acres of farmland in the country's impoverished southeastern provinces when it is completed in 2005. But the diversion of Euphrates, has the potential to irrigate 1.6 million acres of agricultural land. However, the anticipated reduction of 40 percent in Euphrates, water has already sparked controversy with its downstream neighbors Syria and Iraq. Syria's recently completed Taqba Dam, also on the Euphrates, has the potentional to irrigate 1.6 million acres of agricultural land. However, the anticipated reduction of 40 percent in Euphrates water available to Syria threatens the success of a project badly needed to support the growing Syrian population. At present, 85 percent of Syrian water comes from the Euphrates, while GAP provides 50 percent of Turkey's electricity needs.

As a World Bank study reported in 1994, "Population and development have overwhelmed traditional water management practices." A 1999 report from the U.S. Academy of Sciences noted that the draining of aquifers and diversion of water for intensive irrigation of tropical agriculture crops was the main reason for Israel's serious water shortage.

Unfortunately, cooperation in water use has fared poorly. Israel, with 12,148 cubic feet per capita, is the largest water user, compared with 3,284 cubic feet per capita for Palestinians. The 1994 Israeli–Jordanian peace treaty guarantees Jordan 7.5 billion cubic feet annually from the Jordan and Yarmuk Rivers, but thus far Jordan has received less than half its allotment. Recently a three-year drought, the worst in 58 years, not only affected Jordan's water allotment from these rivers but seriously depleted Israel's main water source, the Sea of Galilee. The Dead Sea, important to both countries for its deposits of potash and bromine, had shrunk from 47 to 34 miles in length by 2000, due to drought as well as mining and resort development along its shoreline. Some residents of Amman, Jordan's capital, have access to water only once a week. Water is also rationed in Syria, due not only to shortages of supply but also to the country's inadequate, antiquated water system. With their populations expected to double in several decades at current growth rates, both countries face critical water problems.

Water sharing between Israel and the Palestinian population of the occupied West Bank and Gaza Strip is equally contentious. Prime Minister Yitzhak Rabin recognized Palestinian water "rights" in the 1995 peace negotiations that followed the 1993 Oslo agreements. His successors have yet to implement those rights. Israel contends that its advanced economy requires greater water resources than those of the Palestinians, with their largely agricultural economy. But Israel's water use is mostly at Palestinian expense. The 170,000 Israeli settlers in the West Bank use water at the rate of 74 gallons daily per capita. (The World Health Organization, or WHO, estimates that 26.5 gallons per day are required to meet minimum health and sanitation standards; Palestinian consumption is 18.5 gallons per day.) The imbalance is more striking in the Gaza Strip. Israeli settlers there use 75 percent of ground water from aquifers already polluted by sewage and threatened by advancing sea water. Due to the fact that Israel controls water resources in the West Bank, some 215,000 Palestinians live in villages that are connected to the Israeli water network but lack a supply of potable water; the water is used up before it can reach them.

In any case, water overuse in the region has reached a critical stage. Overall per capita access to water dropped from 123,599 cubic feet annually in 1960, to 44,142 cubic feet in 1996. About 90 percent of Yemenis have access to 3,150 cubic feet annually; their capital of San'a is currently using water from its aquifer at a rate four times greater than its recharge capability. The only countries in the region with a per capita water supply above WHO minimum standards are Iraq and Turkey.

The overuse of groundwater, contamination of water sources by fertilizers and pesticides, mismanagement, and diversion of water to tropical crops at the expense of those less water-intensive have brought this largely rainless region to the crisis point in water availability and use.

The crisis has forced a number of governments to take politically unpopular but economically necessary steps. Algeria passed a law in 1996 prohibiting use of water at night. Also in 1996, United Arab Emirates completed two new desalinization plants, at enormous expense, in order to be able to meet the needs of its growing population; the rapid depletion of its underground water resources left it no alternative. Two new water-desalinization plants are under contruction in Israel, but they will meet only 5 percent of annual water needs when they are completed in 2004. Saudi Arabia, the world's leader in the practice, draws 70 percent of its potable water from desalinization, making possible extensive cultivation of wheat and other crops not normally grown in the desert.

Can the water crisis be headed off before it reaches major conflict levels? In 1997, the World Bank proposed a 20-year "action plan" to member states. The plan has several specific targets: a 40 percent reduction in water losses due to inefficiency, a 10 percent reduction in the use of water for irrigation, and a 50 percent increase in water for domestic and industrial use that could result from these savings. Achievement of these targets, the World Bank noted, would depend on the full support of states in the region.

In the new century, there has been little progress toward the multinational cooperation needed to meet these goals. The establishment in 1997 of the Middle East Desalination Center, based in Oman, was a first step in this direction. The center's goal is to encourage water-short Middle Eastern countries to fund new desalinization plants, using reverse osmosis (a process of applying pressure to sea water to force it through a membrane so that the salt is left behind). This process is far cheaper than the current large-scale desalinization technique, costing $2 per 988 gallons. Water has become a major factor in Arab–Israeli relations. What is needed, according to former U.S. senator Paul Simon, is some sort of international system of measuring and analyzing water flow and draw-down of aquifers and similar technical questions, backed by an international "water court" similar to the International Court of Justice and with comparable powers of arbitration.

One positive step toward resolving the region's water crisis without resort to war is Turkey's "water for peace" program. In April 2001, the project got off the ground (or the water) through an agreement with Israel. Turkey agreed to provide Israel with 50 million cubic meters of water annually from the Seyhan and Ceyhan Rivers, which flow south from the Anatolian interior to the Mediterranean. Other countries in the region have not as yet taken advantage of the offer, although Turkey has been supplying water to drought-stricken northern Cyprus by tugboat for the past two years.

## THE WESTERN SAHARA: WHOSE DESERT?

It is a fearsome place, swept by sand-laden winds that sting through layers of clothing, scorched by 120°F temperatures, its flat, monotonous landscape broken occasionally by dried-up *wadis* (river beds). The Spanish called it Rio de Oro, "River of Gold," in a bitter jest, for it has neither. Rainfall averages

(UN photo/Y. Nagata)

The Western Sahara region is flat and very hot. At this time, it appears that this land eventually will be integrated with Morocco.

two to eight inches a year in a territory the size of Colorado. The population is largely nomadic. Before the twentieth century, this region, which we know today as the Western Sahara, was outside the control of any central authority. Other than a brief period of importance as the headquarters of the Almoravids, a dynasty that ruled most of North Africa for about a century, the Western Sahara was a backwater.

As a political entity, the Western Sahara resulted from European colonization in Africa in the late nineteenth century. Britain and France had a head start in establishing colonies. Spain was a latecomer. By the time the Spanish joined the race for colonies, little was left for them in Africa. Since they already controlled the Canary Islands, off the West African coast, it was natural for them to claim Rio de Oro, the nearest area on the coast.

In 1884, Spain announced a protectorate over Rio de Oro. The other European powers accepted the Spanish claim, under the principle that "occupation of a territory's coast entitled a colonial power to control over the interior."[17] But Spanish rights to the Saharan interior clashed with French claims to Mauritania and French efforts to control the independent Sultanate of Morocco to the north. After the establishment of a joint Franco–Spanish protectorate over Morocco in 1912, the boundaries of the Spanish colony were fixed, with Mauritania on the south and east and Morocco to the north. The nomads of the Western Sahara now found themselves living within fixed boundaries defined by outsiders.

The Spanish moved very slowly into the interior. The entire Western Sahara was not "pacified" until 1934. Spain invested heavily in development of the important Western Sahara phosphate deposits but did little else to develop the colony. The Spanish population was essentially a garrison community, living apart from the Sahrawis, the indigenous Saharan population, in towns or military posts. A few Sahrawis went to Spain or other European countries, where they received a modern education; upon their return, they began to organize a Saharan nationalist movement. Other Sahrawis traveled to Egypt and returned with ideas of organizing a Saharan Arab independent state. But a real sense of either a Spanish Saharan or an independent Sahrawi identity was slow to emerge.[16]

Serious conflict over the Spanish Sahara developed in the 1960s. By that time, both Morocco and Mauritania had become independent. Algeria, the third African territory involved in the conflict, won its independence after a bloody civil war. All three new states were highly nationalistic and were opposed to the continuation of colonial rule over any African people, but particularly Muslim peoples. They encouraged the Sahrawis to fight for liberation from Spain, giving arms and money to guerrilla groups and keeping their borders open.

However, the three states had different motives. Morocco claimed the Western Sahara on the basis of historical ties dating back to the Almoravids, plus the oath of allegiance sworn to Moroccan sultans by Saharan chiefs in the nineteenth and twentieth centuries. Kinship was also a factor; several important Saharan families have branches in Morocco, and both the mother and the first wife of the founder of Morocco's current ruling dynasty, Mulay Ismail, were from Sahrawi families.

The Mauritanian claim to the Spanish Sahara was based not on historical sovereignty but on kinship. Sahrawis have close ethnic ties with the Moors, the majority of the population of Mauritania. Also, Mauritania feared Moroccan expansion, since its territory had once been included in the Almoravid state. A Saharan buffer state between Mauritania and Morocco would serve as protection for the Mauritanians.

Algeria's interest in Spanish Sahara was largely a matter of support for a national liberation movement against a colonial power. The Algerians made no territorial claim to the colony. But Algerian foreign policy has rested on two pillars since independence: the right to self-determination of subject peoples and the principle of self-determination through referendum. Algeria consistently maintains that the Saharan people should have these rights.

In the 1960s, Spain came under pressure from the United Nations to give up its colonies. After much hesitation, the Spanish announced in August 1974 that a referendum would be held under UN supervision to decide the colony's future.

The Spanish action brought the conflict to a head. King Hassan declared that 1975 would mark the restoration of Moroccan sovereignty over the territory. The main opposition to this claim came from Polisario (an acronym for the Popular Front for the Liberation of Saguia al-Hamra and Rio de Oro, the two divisions of the Spanish colony). This organization, formed by Saharan exiles based initially in Mauritania, issued a declaration of independence, and Polisario guerrillas began attacking Spanish garrisons, increasing the pressure on Spain to withdraw. In October 1975, Hassan announced that he would lead a massive, peaceful march of civilians, "armed" only with Korans, into the Spanish Sahara to recover sacred Moroccan territory. This "Green March" of half a million unarmed Moroccan volunteers into Spanish territory seemed an unusual, even risky, method of validating a territorial claim, but it worked. In 1976, Spain reached agreement with Morocco and Mauritania to partition the territory into two zones, one third going to Mauritania and two thirds to Morocco. The Moroccan Zone included the important phosphate deposits.

Polisario rejected the partition agreement. It announced formation of the Sahrawi Arab Democratic Republic (S.A.D.R.), "a free, independent, sovereign state ruled by an Arab democratic system of progressive unionist orientation and of Islamic religion."[17]

Polisario tactics of swift-striking attacks from hidden bases in the vast desert were highly effective in the early stages. Mauritania withdrew from the war in 1978, when a military coup overthrew its government. The new Mauritanian rulers signed a peace treaty in Algiers with Polisario representatives. Morocco, not to be outdone, promptly annexed the Mauritanian share of the territory and beefed up its military forces. A fortified "Sand Wall," which was built in stages from the former border with Rio de Oro down to the Moroccan–Mauritanian border and in 1987 extended about 350 miles to the Atlantic Ocean, provided the Moroccan Army with a strong defensive base from which to launch punitive raids against its elusive foe. The new segment also cut off the Polisario's access to the sea; Polisario raiders had begun to intercept and board fishing vessels in attempts to disrupt development of that important Moroccan resource and to bring pressure on foreign countries (such as Spain) that use the fishing grounds to push Morocco toward a settlement.

Although a large number of member states of the Organization of African Unity (OAU) subsequently recognized the Sahrawi Republic, Morocco blocked its admission to the OAU, on the grounds that it was part of Moroccan territory. However, the drain on Moroccan resources of indefinitely maintaining a 100,000-man army in the desert led King Hassan II to soften his obduracy, particularly in relation to Algeria. With both countries affected by severe economic problems and some political instability, a rapprochement became possible in the late 1980s. Diplomatic relations were restored in 1988; and in 1989, Morocco joined Algeria, Libya, Tunisia, and Mauritania in the Arab Maghrib Union (AMU). The AMU charter binds member states not to support resistance movements in one another's territory. As a result, Algeria withdrew its backing for S.A.D.R. and closed Polisario offices in Algiers.

Algeria's preoccupation with internal affairs and the withdrawal of Algerian and Libyan financial aid placed Polisario in a difficult position. Two of its founders, Omar Hadrami and Noureddine Belali, defected in 1989 and acknowledged Moroccan sovereignty over the territory. A 1990 amnesty offer by King Hassan for all Polisario members and Saharan exiles was accepted by nearly 1,000 persons; these included S.A.D.R.'s foreign minister, Brahim Hakim.

In 1983, Polisario leaders reached agreement in principle with the king to settle the dispute by referendum. Participants in the referendum would be limited to the original inhabitants of the territory. But with the Moroccan Army entrenched behind its Sand Wall and the Polisario in control of the open desert, there was little incentive on either side toward implementation of the referendum.

UN mediation produced a formal cease-fire in 1991. A UN observer force, the Mission for the Referendum in the Western Sahara (MINURSO), proceeded to the territory to supervise voter registration. By that time, thousands of Moroccan settlers had moved there to take advantage of free land, housing, and other inducements offered by the government to help "Moroccanize" the country's newest province. The new residents changed the population balance, thereby complicating registration procedures. Morocco insisted that they should be eligible to vote in the referendum. A further complication arose from the fact that some 140,000 of the original inhabitants included in the 1974 Spanish census were now refugees in Algeria.

In May 1995, the UN Security Council, prodded by Algeria and Sahrawi activists, approved *Resolution 995*, which called for prompt registration of voters in the territory under the supervision of MINURSO. By December 1998, 147,000 voters had been registered. However, the Moroccan government insisted that 85,000 others, belonging to three Sahran tribes resident there in the past, should be included in the registration rolls. Former U.S. secretary of state James Baker was appointed as a "high-profile" envoy to mediate between Morocco and the Polisario to resolve the registration deadlock and promote a final settlement for the territory.

After several unproductive efforts at mediation, Baker submitted a proposal to Moroccan and Polisario representatives to break the deadlock. The "Baker Plan" would postpone the referendum until 2006. In the interim, the resident Sahrawi population would elect an autonomous governing body with powers limited to local and provincial affairs. Although well short of independence, the plan seemed the best that the Polisario could expect out of their long struggle. Increasingly, international support has veered toward acceptance of Moroccan rule. French president Jacques Chirac visited the country in December and praised Morocco for the development of its southern provinces. Subsequently, King Muhammad VI traveled to the territory to receive a royal welcome from its settler-dominated population. The king also approved concessions for oil exploration offshore in Western Saharan waters, and he released prominent Sahrawi political prisoners. As a result, S.A.D.R. sovereignty remained limited to four small refugee camps in a sliver of desert between Algeria and Morocco.

## NOTES

1. Alan R. Taylor, *The Arab Balance of Power* (Syracuse, NY: Syracuse University Press, 1982), Preface, XIII.

2. Karl Meyer and Shareen Blair Brysac, *Tournament of Shadows: The Great Game and the Race for Central Asia.* (Washington, D.C.: Counterpoint Press, 1999), p. xiii. The term was coined by Count Nesselrode.

3. Soviet leader Leonid Brezhnev argued that "the Soviet action in Afghanistan was made necessary by the real threat of seeing the country transformed into an imperialist military platform on the Southern frontier of the U.S.S.R."

4. Terence O'Donnell, *Garden of the Brave in War* (New York: Ticknor and Fields, 1980), p. 19, states that in visits to remote Iranian villages, he was told by informants that the Arabs never washed, went around naked, and ate lizards.

5. Daniel Pipes, "A Border Adrift: Origins of the Conflict," in Shirin Tahir-Kheli and Shaheen Ayubi, eds., *The Iran-Iraq War: New Weapons, Old Conflicts* (New York: Praeger, 1983), pp. 10–13.

6. *Ibid.,* quoted on p. 20.

7. Stephen R. Grummon, *The Iran-Iraq War: Islam Embattled,* The Washington Papers/92, Vol. X (New York: Praeger, 1982), p. 10.

8. *The Christian Science Monitor* (September 23, 1987).

9. Quoted in Barry Rubin, *The Arab States and the Palestine Conflict* (Syracuse, NY: Syracuse University Press, 1981), p. 7.

10. Letter to James Marshall, January 17, 1930, in Camilo Dresner, ed., *The Letters and Papers of Chaim Weizmann,* Vol. 14 (New Brunswick, NJ: Rutgers University Press, 1979), pp. 208–211.

11. Martin Buber, in *Land of Two Peoples,* Paul Mendes-Flohr, ed. (New York: Oxford University Press, 1983), p. 199.

12. Uri Avnery, *Israel Without Zionists* (New York: Macmillan, 1968), pp. 187 and 189.

13. Yaron Ezrahi, *Rubber Bullets: Power and Conscience in Modern Israel* (New York: Farrar, Straus & Giroux, 1997), p. 220.

14. Mohammed Shadid, *The United States and the Palestinians* (New York: St. Martin's Press, 1981), p. 195.

15. For details on bin Laden and al-Qaeda, see Peter Bergen, *Holy War Inc.: Inside the Secret World of Osama bin Laden* (New York: Free Press, 2001); also *World Press Review* (February 2002), *passim.*

16. John Damis, *Conflict in Northwest Africa: The Western Sahara Dispute* (Palo Alto, CA: Hoover Institution Press, 1983), p. 110.

17. *Ibid,* p. 13, notes that a tribal assembly (Jama'a) was formed in 1967 for the Sahrawis but that its 43 members were all tribal chiefs or their representatives; it had only advisory powers.

# Algeria (Democratic and Popular Republic of Algeria)

## GEOGRAPHY

*Area in Square Miles (Kilometers):* 919,352 (2,381,740) (about 3½ times the size of Texas)

*Capital (Population):* Algiers (3,705,000)

*Environmental Concerns:* soil erosion; desertification; water pollution; inadequate potable water

*Geographical Features:* mostly high plateau and desert; some mountains; narrow, discontinuous coastal plain

*Climate:* arid to semiarid; mild winters and hot summers on coastal plain; less rain and cold winters on high plateau; considerable temperature variation in desert

## PEOPLE

### Population
*Total:* 31,736,000
*Annual Growth Rate:* 1.7%
*Rural/Urban Population Ratio:* 44/56
*Major Languages:* Arabic; Berber dialects; Ahaggar (Tuareg); French
*Ethnic Makeup:* 99% Arab-Berber; less than 1% European
*Religions:* 99% Sunni Muslim (Islam is the state religion); 1% Shia Muslim, Christian, and Jewish

### Health
*Life Expectancy at Birth:* 69 years (male); 71 years (female)
*Infant Mortality Rate (Ratio):* 40.5/1,000
*Physicians Available (Ratio):* 1/1,066

### Education
*Adult Literacy Rate:* 61.6%
*Compulsory (Ages):* 6–15

## COMMUNICATION
*Telephones:* 1,600,000 main lines
*Daily Newspaper Circulation:* 52 per 1,000 people
*Televisions:* 71 per 1,000 people
*Internet Service Providers:* 2 (2000)

## TRANSPORTATION
*Highways in Miles (Kilometers):* 63,605 (102,424)
*Railroads in Miles (Kilometers):* 2,963 (4,772)
*Usable Airfields:* 135
*Motor Vehicles in Use:* 920,000

## GOVERNMENT
*Type:* republic
*Independence Date:* July 5, 1962 (from France)

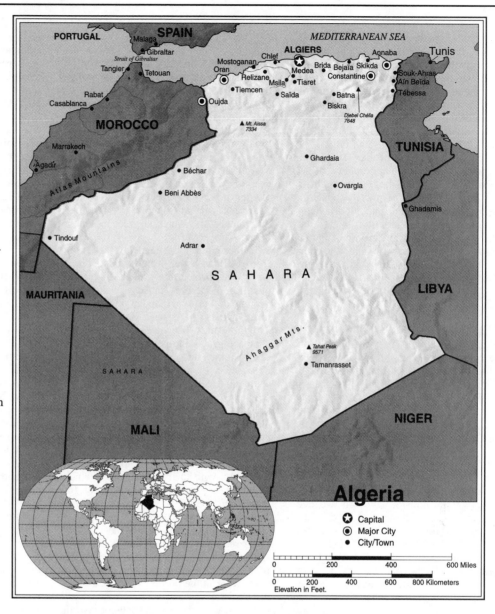

*Head of State/Government:* President Abdelaziz Bouteflika; Prime Minister Ali Benfis; real power rests with military leaders serving as Higher Council of State

*Political Parties:* Democratic National Rally; National Liberation Front; Socialist Forces Front; Rally for Culture and Democracy; Algerian Renewal Party; Islamic Salvation Front (outlawed); others

*Suffrage:* universal at 18

## MILITARY
*Military Expenditures (% of GDP):* 4.1%
*Current Disputes:* territorial disputes with Morocco and Libya; civil war

## ECONOMY
*Currency ($ U.S. Equivalent):* 83.29 dinars = $1
*Per Capita Income/GDP:* $5,500/$171 billion
*GDP Growth Rate:* 5%
*Inflation Rate:* 2%
*Unemployment Rate:* 30%
*Labor Force:* 9,100,000
*Natural Resources:* petroleum; natural gas; iron ore; phosphates; uranium; lead; zinc
*Agriculture:* wheat; barley; oats; grapes; olives; citrus fruits; sheep; cattle
*Industry:* petroleum; natural gas; light industries; mining; electrical; petrochemicals; food processing
*Exports:* $19.6 billion (primary partners Italy, United States, France)
*Imports:* $9.2 billion (primary partners France, Italy, Germany)

## ALGERIA

The modern state of Algeria occupies the central part of North Africa, a geographically distinctive and separate region of Africa that includes Morocco and Tunisia. The name of the country comes from the Arabic word *al-Jaza'ir,* "the islands," because of the rocky islets along this part of the Mediterranean coast. The name of the capital, Algiers, has the same origin.

The official name of the state is the Democratic and Popular Republic of Algeria. It is the second-largest nation in Africa (after Sudan). The overall population density is low, but the population is concentrated in the northern third of the country. The vast stretches of the Algerian Sahara are largely unpopulated. The country had an extremely high birth rate prior to 1988, but government-sponsored family-planning programs have significantly reduced the rate.

## GEOGRAPHY

Algeria's geography is a formidable obstacle to broad economic and social development. About 80 percent of the land is uncultivable desert, and only 12 percent is arable without irrigation. Most of the population live in a narrow coastal plain and in a fertile, hilly inland region called the Tell (Arabic for "hillock"). The four Saharan provinces have only 3 percent of the population but comprise more than half the land area.

The mineral resources that made possible Algeria's transformation in two decades from a land devastated by civil war to one of the developing world's success stories are all located in the Sahara. Economic growth, however, has been uneven, generally affecting the rural and lower-class urban populations unfavorably. The large-scale exodus of rural families into the cities, with consequent neglect of agriculture, has resulted in a vast increase in urban slums. Economic disparities were a major cause of riots in 1988, that led to political reforms and the dismantling of the socialist system responsible for Algerian development since independence.

Algeria is unique among newly independent Middle Eastern countries in that it gained its independence through a civil war. For more than 130 years (1830–1962), it was occupied by France and became a French department (similar to a U.S. state). With free movement from mainland France to Algeria and vice versa, the country was settled by large numbers of Europeans, who became the politically dominant group in the population although they were a minority. The modern Algerian nation is the product of the interaction of native Muslim Algerians with the European settlers, who also considered Algeria home.

Algeria's geography is a key to the country's past disunity. In addition to its vast Saharan territory, Algeria is broken up into discontinuous regions by a number of rugged mountain ranges. The Mediterranean coastline is narrow and is backed throughout its length by mountains, notably the imposing Kabyle range. The Algerian Atlas range, a continuation of the Moroccan Atlas, is a complex system of deep valleys, high plateaux, and peaks ranging up to 6,000 feet. In southeastern Algeria is the most impressive range in the country, the Aurès, a great mountain block.

The original inhabitants of the entire North African region were Berbers, a people of unknown origin grouped into various tribes. Berbers make up about 30 percent of the total population. The majority live in the eastern Kabylia region and the Aures (Chaouia), with a small, compact group in the five cities of the Mzab, in the Algerian Sahara. The Tuareg, a nomadic Berber people spread across southern Algeria, Mali, and Niger, are the only ones with a written script, called Tifinagh. In the past, they were literally "lords of the desert," patrolling the caravan routes on their swift camels and collecting tolls for safe passage as guides for caravaneers. They were a colorful sight in their tents with their indigo robes (which tinted their skin blue, hence the name for them, the "Blue Men"). But Saharan droughts, motorized transport, and the development of the oil industry have largely destroyed their traditional role and lifestyle. Today, Tuareg are more likely to be found pumping gas in cities or doing low-wage work in the oil fields than patrolling the desert.

The Arabs, who brought Islam to North Africa in the seventh century A.D., converted the Algerian Berbers after a fierce resistance. The Arabs brought their language as a unifying feature, and religion linked the Algerians with the larger Islamic world. Today, most follow Sunni Islam, but a significant minority, about 100,000, are Shia Muslims. They refer to themselves as *Ibadis,* from their observance of an ancient Shia rite, and live in five "holy cities" clustered in a remote Saharan valley where centuries ago they took refuge from Sunni rulers of northern Algeria. Their valley, the Mzab, has always maintained religious autonomy from Algerian central governments. The much larger Berber population of Kabylia has also resisted central authority, whether Islamic or French, throughout Algerian history. One of many pressures on the government today is that of an organized Kabyle movement, which seeks greater autonomy for the region and an emphasis on Berber language in schools, along with the revitalization of Kabyle culture.

## HISTORY

### The Corsair Regency

The foundations of the modern Algerian state were laid in the sixteenth century, with the establishment of the Regency of Algiers, an outlying province of the Ottoman Empire. Algiers in particular, due to its natural harbor, was developed for use by the Ottomans as a naval base for wars against European fleets in the Mediterranean. The Algerian coast was the farthest westward extent of Ottoman power. Consequently, Algiers and Oran, the two major ports, were exposed to constant threats of attack by Spanish and other European fleets. They could not easily be supported, or governed directly, by the Ottomans. The regency, from its beginnings, was a state geared for war.

The regency was established by two Greek-born Muslim sea captains, Aruj and Khayr al-Din (called Barbarossa by his European opponents because of his flaming red beard). The brothers obtained commissions from the Ottoman sultan for expeditions against the Spanish. They made their principal base at Algiers, then a small port, which Khayr al-Din expanded into a powerful fortress and naval base. His government consisted of a garrison of Ottoman soldiers sent by the sultan to keep order, along with a naval force called the corsairs.

Corsairing or piracy (the choice of term depended upon one's viewpoint) was a common practice in the Mediterranean, but the rise to power of the Algerine corsairs converted it into a more or less respectable profession.[1] The cities of Tetuan, Tunis, Salé (Morocco), and Tripoli (Libya) also had corsair fleets, but the Algerian corsairs were so effective against European shipping that for 300 years (1500–1800), European rulers called them the "scourge of the Mediterranean." One factor in their success was their ability to attract outstanding sea captains from various European countries. Renegades from Italy, Greece, Holland, France, and Britain joined the Algerian fleet, converted to Islam, and took Muslim names as a symbol of their new status. Some rose to high rank.

Government in Algiers passed through several stages and eventually became a system of deys. The deys were elected by the Divan, a council of the captains of the Ottoman garrison. Deys were elected for

(UN/UNDP Photo 155705/Ruth Massey)

Agriculture is important in raising the living standards of Algeria. These farmers are harvesting forage peas, which will be used for animal feed.

life, but most of them never fulfilled their tenure due to constant intrigue, military coups, and assassinations. Yet the system provided considerable stability, security for the population, and wealth and prestige for the regency. These factors probably account for its durability; the line of deys governed uninterruptedly from the late 1600s to 1830.

Outside of Algiers and its hinterland, authority was delegated to local chiefs and religious leaders, who were responsible for tax collection and remittances to the dey's treasury. The chiefs were kept in line with generous subsidies. It was a system well adapted to the fragmented society of Algeria and one that enabled a small military group to rule a large territory at relatively little cost.[2]

### The French Conquest
In 1827, the dey of Algiers, enraged at the French government's refusal to pay an old debt incurred during Napoleon's wars, struck the French consul on the shoulder with a fly-whisk in the course of an interview. The king of France, Charles X, demanded an apology for the "insult" to his representative. None was forthcoming, so the French blockaded the port of Algiers in retaliation. But the dey continued to keep silent. In 1830, a French army landed on the coast west of the city, marched

overland, and entered it with almost no resistance. The dey surrendered and went into exile.[3]

The French, who had been looking for an excuse to expand their interests in North Africa, now were not sure what to do with Algiers. The overthrow of the despotic Charles X in favor of a constitutional monarchy in France confused the situation even further. But the Algerians considered the French worse than the Turks, who were at least fellow Muslims. In the 1830s, they rallied behind their first national leader, Emir Abd al-Qadir.

Abd al-Qadir was the son of a prominent religious leader and, more important, was a descendant of the Prophet Muhammad. Abd al-Qadir had unusual qualities of leadership, military skill, and physical courage. From 1830 to 1847, he carried on guerrilla warfare against a French army of more than 100,000 men with such success that at one point the French signed a formal treaty recognizing him as head of an Algerian nation in the interior. Abd al-Qadir described his strategy in a prophetic letter to the king of France:

France will march forward, and we shall retire. But France will find it necessary to retire, and we shall return. We shall weary and harry you, and our climate will do the rest.[4]

In order to defeat Abd al-Qadir, the French commander used "total war" tactics, burning villages, destroying crops, killing livestock, and levying fines on peoples who continued to support the emir. These measures, called "pacification" by France, finally succeeded. In 1847, Abd al-Qadir surrendered to French authorities. He was imprisoned for several years, in violation of a solemn commitment, and was then released by Emperor Napoleon III. He spent the rest of his life in exile.

Although he did not succeed in his quest, Abd al-Qadir is venerated as the first Algerian nationalist, able by his leadership and Islamic prestige to unite warring groups in a struggle for independence from foreign control. Abd al-Qadir's green and white flag was raised again by the Algerian nationalists during the second war of independence (1954–1962), and it is the flag of the republic today.

### Algérie Française
After the defeat of Abd al-Qadir, the French gradually brought all of present-day Algerian territory under their control. The Kabyles, living in the rugged mountain region east of Algiers, were the last to submit. The Kabyles had submitted in 1857, but they rebelled in 1871 after a series of decrees by the French government had made all Algerian Muslims subjects

but not citizens, giving them a status inferior to French and other European settlers.

The Kabyle rebellion had terrible results, not only for the Kabyles but for all Algerian Muslims. More than a million acres of Muslim lands were confiscated by French authorities and sold to European settlers. A special code of laws was enacted to treat Algerian Muslims differently from Europeans, with severe fines and sentences for such "infractions" as insulting a European or wearing shoes in public. (It was assumed that a Muslim caught wearing shoes had stolen them.)

In 1871, Algeria legally became a French department. But in terms of exploitation of natives by settlers, it may as well have remained a colony. One author notes that "the desire to make a settlement colony out of an already populated area led to a policy of driving the indigenous people out of the best arable lands."[5] Land confiscation was only part of the exploitation of Algeria by the *colons* (French settlers). They developed a modern Algerian agriculture integrated into the French economy, providing France with much of its wine, citrus, olives, and vegetables. Colons owned 30 percent of the arable land and 90 percent of the best farmland. Special taxes were imposed on the Algerian Muslims; the colons were exempted from paying most taxes.

The political structure of Algeria was even more favorable to the European minority. The colons were well represented in the French National Assembly, and their representatives made sure that any reforms or laws intended to improve the living conditions or rights of the Algerian Muslim population would be blocked.

In fairness to the colons, it must be pointed out that many of them had come to Algeria as poor immigrants and worked hard to improve their lot and to develop the country. By 1930, the centenary of the French conquest, many colon families had lived in Algiers for two generations or more. Colons had drained malarial swamps south of Algiers and developed the Mitidja, the country's most fertile region. A fine road and rail system linked all parts of the country, and French public schools served all cities and towns. Algiers even had its own university, a branch of the Sorbonne. It is not surprising that to the colons, Algeria was their country, "Algérie Française." Throughout Algeria they rebaptized Algerian cities with names like Orléansville and Philippeville, with paved French streets, cafes, bakeries, and little squares with flower gardens and benches where old men in berets dozed in the hot sun.

Jules Cambon, governor general of Algeria in the 1890s, once described the country as having "only a dust of people left her." What he meant was that the ruthless treatment of the Algerians by the French during the pacification had deprived them of their natural leaders. A group of leaders developed slowly in Algeria, but it was made up largely of *evolués*—persons who had received French educations, spoke French better than Arabic, and accepted French citizenship as the price of status.[6]

Other Algerians, several hundred thousand of them, served in the French Army in the two world wars. Many of them became aware of the political rights that they were supposed to have but did not. Still others, religious leaders and teachers, were influenced by the Arab nationalist movement for independence from foreign control in Egypt and other parts of the Middle East.

Until the 1940s, the majority of the evolués and other Algerian leaders did not want independence. They wanted full assimilation with France and Muslim equality with the colons. Ferhat Abbas, a French-trained pharmacist who was the spokesman for the evolués, said in 1936 that he did not believe that there was such a thing as an Algerian nation separate from France.

Abbas and his associates changed their minds after World War II. In 1943, they had presented to the French government a manifesto demanding full political and legal equality for Muslims with the colons. It was blocked by colon leaders, who feared that they would be drowned in a Muslim sea. On May 8, 1945, the date of the Allied victory over Nazi Germany, a parade of Muslims celebrating the event but also demanding equality led to violence in the city of Sétif. Several colons were killed; in retaliation, army troops and groups of colon vigilantes swept through Muslim neighborhoods, burning houses and slaughtering thousands of Muslims. From then on, Muslim leaders believed that independence through armed struggle was the only choice left to them.

### The War for Independence

November 1 is an important holiday in France. It is called Toussaint (All Saints' Day). On that day, French people remember and honor all the many saints in the pantheon of French Catholicism. It is a day devoted to reflection and staying at home.

In the years after the Sétif massacre, there had been scattered outbreaks of violence in Algeria, some of them created by the so-called Secret Organization (OS), which had developed an extensive network of cells in preparation for armed insurrection. In 1952, French police accidentally uncovered the network and jailed most of its leaders. One of them, a former French Army sergeant named Ahmed Ben Bella, subsequently escaped and went to Cairo, Egypt.

As the day of Toussaint 1954 neared, Algeria seemed calm. But appearances were deceptive. Earlier in the year, nine former members of the OS had laid plans in secret for armed revolution. They divided Algeria into six *wilayas* (departments), each with a military commander. They also planned a series of coordinated attacks for the early morning hours of November 1, when the French population would be asleep and the police preparing for a holiday. Bombs exploded at French Army barracks, police stations, storage warehouses, telephone offices, and government buildings. The revolutionaries circulated leaflets in the name of the National Liberation Front (FLN), warning the French that they had acted to liberate Algeria from the colonialist yoke and calling on Algerian Muslims to join in the struggle to rebuild Algeria as a free Islamic state.

There were very few casualties as a result of the Toussaint attacks; for some time the French did not realize that they had a revolution on their hands. But as violence continued, regular army troops were sent to Algeria to help the hard-pressed police and the colons. Eventually there were 400,000 French troops in Algeria, as opposed to just 6,000 guerrillas. But the French consistently refused to consider the situation in Algeria a war. They called it a "police action." Others called it the "war without a name."[7] Despite their great numerical superiority, they were unable to defeat the FLN.

Elsewhere the French tried various tactics. They divided the country into small sectors, with permanent garrisons for each sector. They organized mobile units to track down the guerrillas in caves and hideouts. About 2 million villagers were moved into barbed-wire "regroupment camps," with a complete dislocation of their way of life, in order to deny the guerrillas the support of the population.

The war was settled not by military action but by political negotiations. The French people and government, worn down by the effects of World War II and their involvement in Indochina, grew sick of the slaughter, the plastic bombs exploding in public places (in France as well as Algeria), and the brutality of the army in dealing with guerrilla prisoners. A French newspaper editor expressed the general feeling: "Algeria is ruining the spring.

This land of sun and earth has never been so near us. It invades our hearts and torments our minds."[8]

The colons and a number of senior French Army officers were the last to give up their dream of an Algeria that would be forever French. Together the colons and the army forced a change in the French government. General Charles de Gaulle, the French wartime resistance hero, returned to power after a dozen years in retirement. But de Gaulle, a realist, had no intention of keeping Algeria forever French. He began secret negotiations with FLN leaders for Algerian independence.

By 1961 the battlefield had extended into metropolitan France, with plastic bombs set off in cafés and other public places, killing hundreds of people. On its side, the French military routinely used torture and gang-style executions without trial to crush the rebellion. Some 3,000 of those arrested simply disappeared.[9] Clashes between FLN fighters and those of its rival, the Algerian Nationalist Movement, caused further disruptions. In October, the shooting of Paris police officers led to the deaths of several hundred Algerians by the police during a peaceful protest march (an error not revealed by the French government until its archives for the period were opened in 1999).

Subsequently, colon and dissident military leaders united in a last effort to keep Algeria French. They staged an uprising against de Gaulle in Algiers, seizing government buildings and demanding his removal from office. But the bulk of the French Army remained loyal to him.

An attempted assassination of the French president in 1962 was unsuccessful. The colon–military alliance, calling itself the Secret Army Organization (OAS), then launched a savage campaign of violence against the Muslim population, gunning down people or shooting them at random on streets and in public markets. The OAS expected that the FLN would break the cease-fire in order to protect its own people. But it did not do so.

## THE AGONY OF INDEPENDENCE

With the collapse of the OAS campaign against the FLN as well as its own government, the way was clear for Algeria to become an independent nation for the first time in its history. This became a reality on July 5, 1962, with the signing of a treaty with France. However, few modern nations have become self-governing with so many handicaps. Several hundred thousand people—French, Algerian Muslims, men, women, and children—were casualties of the conflict. An even more painful loss was the departure of the entire Euro-

pean community. Panicked colons and their families boarded overcrowded ships to cross the Mediterranean, most of them to France, a land they knew only as visitors. Nearly all of the skilled workers, managers, landowners, and professionals in all fields were French, and they had done little to train Algerian counterparts.

The new Algerian government was also affected by factional rivalries among its leaders. The French writer Alexis de Tocqueville once wrote, "In rebellion, as in a novel, the most difficult part to invent is the end." The FLN revolutionaries had to invent a new system, one that would bring dignity and hope to people dehumanized by 130 years of French occupation and eight years of savage war.

The first leader to emerge from intraparty struggle to lead the nation was Ah-

med Ben Bella, who had spent the war in exile in Egypt but had great prestige as the political brains behind the FLN. Ben Bella laid the groundwork for an Algerian political system centered on the FLN as a single legal political party, and in September 1963, he was elected president. Ben Bella introduced a system of *autogestion* (workers' self-management), by which tenant farmers took over the management of farms abandoned by their colon owners and restored them to production as cooperatives. Autogestion became the basis for Algerian socialism—the foundation of development for decades.

Ben Bella did little else for Algeria, and he alienated most of his former associates with his ambitions for personal power. In June 1965, he was overthrown in a military coup headed by the defense minister,

(UN photo/Kata Bader)

The rapid growth in the population of Algeria, coupled with urban migration, has created a serious housing shortage, as this crowded apartment building in Algiers testifies.

Colonel Houari Boumedienne. Ben Bella was sentenced to house arrest for 15 years; he was pardoned and exiled in 1980. While in exile, he founded the Movement for a Democratic Algeria, in opposition to the regime. In 1990, he returned to Algeria and announced plans to lead a broad-based opposition party in the framework of the multiparty system. He retired from political and public life in 1997, and the Movement was dissolved.

Boumedienne declared that the coup was a "corrective revolution, intended to reestablish authentic socialism and put an end to internal divisions and personal rule."[10] The government was reorganized under a Council of the Revolution, all military men, headed by Boumedienne, who subsequently became president of the republic. After a long period of preparation and gradual assumption of power by the reclusive and taciturn Boumedienne, a National Charter (Constitution) was approved by voters in 1976. The Charter defined Algeria as a socialist state with Islam as the state religion, basic citizens' rights guaranteed, and leadership by the FLN as the only legal political party. A National Popular Assembly (the first elected in 1977) was responsible for legislation.

In theory, the Algerian president had no more constitutional powers than the U.S. president. However, in practice, Boumedienne was the ruler of the state, being president, prime minister, and commander of the armed forces rolled into one. In November 1978, he became ill from a rare blood disease; he died in December. For a time, it appeared that factional rivalries would again split the FLN, especially as Boumedienne had named neither a vice-president nor a prime minister, nor had he suggested a successor.

The Algeria of 1978 was a very different nation from that of 1962. The scars of war had mostly healed. The FLN closed ranks and named Colonel Chadli Bendjedid to succeed Boumedienne as president for a five-year term. In 1984, Bendjedid was reelected. But the process of ordered socialist development was abruptly and forcibly interrupted in October 1988. A new generation of Algerians, who had come of age long after the war for independence, took to the streets, protesting high prices, lack of jobs, inept leadership, a bloated bureaucracy, and other grievances.

The riots accelerated the process of Algeria's "second revolution" toward political pluralism and dismantling of the single-party socialist system. President Bendjedid initially declared a state of emergency; and for the first time since independence, the army was called in to restore order. Some 500 people were killed in the rioting, most of them jobless youths. But the president moved swiftly to mobilize the nation in the wake of the violence. In a national referendum, voters approved changes in the governing system to allow political parties to form outside the FLN. Another constitutional change, also effective in 1989, made the cabinet and prime minister responsible to the National Assembly.

The president retained his popularity during the upheaval and was reelected for a third term, winning 81 percent of the votes. A number of new parties were formed in 1989 to contest future Assembly elections. They represented a variety of political and social positions. Thus, the People's Movement for Algerian Renewal advocated a "democratic Algeria, representative of moderate Islam," while the National Algerian Party, more fundamentalist in its views, had a platform of full enforcement of Islamic law and the creation of 2 million new jobs. The Socialist Forces Front (FFS), founded many years earlier by exiled FLN leader Hocine Ait Ahmed, resurfaced with a manifesto urging Algerians to support "the irreversible process of democracy."

For its part, the government sought to revitalize the FLN as a genuine mass party on the order of the Tunisian Destour, while insisting that it would not duplicate its neighbor country's *democratie de façade* but would instead embark on real political reforms. Recruitment of new members was extended to rural areas. Although press freedom was confirmed in the constitutional changes approved by the voters, control of the major newspapers and media was shifted from the government to the FLN, to provide greater exposure.

## FOREIGN POLICY

During the first decade of independence, Algeria's foreign policy was strongly nationalistic and anti-Western. Having won their independence from one colonial power, the Algerians were vocally hostile toward the United States and its allies, calling them enemies of popular liberation. Algeria supported revolutionary movements all over the world, providing funds, arms, and training. The Palestine Liberation Organization, rebels against Portuguese colonial rule in Mozambique, Muslim guerrillas fighting the Christian Ethiopian government in Eritrea—all benefited from active Algerian support.

The government broke diplomatic relations with the United States in 1967, due to American support for Israel, and did not restore them for a decade. In the mid-1970s, Algeria moderated its anti-Western stance in favor of nonalignment and good relations with both East and West. Relations improved thereafter to such a point that Algerian mediators were instrumental in resolving the 1979–1980 American hostage crisis in Iran, since Iran regarded Algeria as a suitable mediator—Islamic yet nonaligned. However, Algeria's subsequent alignment with Iraq (in sympathy for Iraq as a fellow-Arab state) during the Iran–Iraq War caused a break in diplomatic relations with the Islamic Republic. They were not restored until 2000.

Until recently, Algeria's relations with Morocco were marked by suspicion, hostility, and periodic conflict. The two countries clashed briefly in 1963 over ownership of iron mines near Tindouf, on the border. Algeria also supported the Western Saharan nationalist movement fighting for independence for the former Spanish colony against Moroccan occupation. After Morocco annexed the territory, Algeria provided bases, sanctuary, funds, and weapons to the Polisario Front, the military wing of the movement. The Bendjedid government recognized the self-declared Sahrawi Arab Democratic Republic in 1980 and sponsored SADR membership in the Organization for African Unity.

However, Algeria's own economic problems, along with moves to open the political system to multiparty activity, sharply reduced Algerian support for the Polisario in the 1980s. Polisario offices in Algiers were closed, and relations with Morocco improved after meetings between Benjedid and Hassan II, in which the latter accepted "in principle" a UN–sponsored referendum on the disputed territory.

The success of Algerian mediators in resolving international disputes has been duplicated in recent years in conflicts involving its other neighbors. In 1987, they succeeded in influencing Libyan leader Muammar al-Qadhafi to provide compensation for Tunisian workers expelled from Libya. A 1989 peace treaty between Libya and Chad also resulted from Algerian mediation.

## THE ECONOMY

Algeria's oil and gas resources were developed by the French. Commercial production and exports began in 1958 and continued through the war for independence; they were not affected, since the Sahara was governed under a separate military administration. The oil fields were turned over to Algeria after independence but continued to be managed by French technicians until 1970, when the industry was nationalized.

Today, the hydrocarbons sector provides the bulk of government revenues and 90 percent of exports. New oil discoveries in 1996 and 2001 are expected to increase oil production, currently 852,000 barrels per day. Algeria provides 29 percent of the liquefied natural gas (LNG) imported by European countries, much of it through undersea pipelines to Italy and Spain.

During President Boumedienne's period in office, all sectors of the Algerian economy were governed under the 1976 National Charter. This document set forth provisions for national development under a uniquely Algerian form of state socialism. However, persistent economic difficulties caused by a combination of lower oil prices and global oversupply led the Bendjedid government to scrap the Charter. Since then, Algeria has borrowed heavily and regularly from international lenders to pay for continued industrial growth.

After a number of years of negative economic growth, the government initiated an austerity program in 1992. Imports of luxury products were prohibited and several new taxes introduced. The program was approved by the International Monetary Fund, Algeria's main source of external financing. In 1995, the IMF loaned $1.8 billion to cover government borrowing up to 60 percent under the approved austerity program to make the required "structural adjustment." In August of that year, the Paris Club—the international consortium that manages most of Algeria's foreign indebtedness—rescheduled $7 billion of the country's foreign debts due in 1996–1997, including interest payments, to ease the strain on the economy.

The agricultural sector employs 47 percent of the labor force and accounts for 12 percent of gross domestic product. But inasmuch as Algeria must import 70 percent of its food, better agricultural production is essential to overall economic development. Overall agricultural production growth has averaged 5 percent annually since 1990. The autogestion system introduced as a stopgap measure after independence and enshrined later in FLN economic practice, when it seemed to work, was totally abandoned. In 1988, some 3,500 state farms were converted to collective farms, with individuals holding title to lands.

Privatization of state-owned enterprises is a key feature of the government's plan to attract foreign investment. The telecommunications sector was privatized in August 2000, and some 200 other public enterprises were in process of transfer to private ownership.

## THE FUNDAMENTALIST CHALLENGE

Despite the growing appeal of Islamic fundamentalism in numerous Arab countries in recent years, Algeria until very recently seemed an unlikely site for the rise of a strong fundamentalist movement. The country's long association with France, its lack of historic Islamic identity as a nation, and several decades of single-party socialism militated against such a development. But the failure of successive Algerian governments to resolve severe economic problems, plus the lack of representative political institutions nurtured within the ruling FLN, brought about the rise of fundamentalism as a political force during the 1990s. Fundamentalists took an active part in the 1988 riots; and with the establishment of a multiparty system, they organized a political party, the Islamic Salvation Front (FIS). It soon claimed 3 million adherents among the then 25 million Algerians.

FIS candidates won 55 percent of urban mayoral and council seats in the 1989 local and municipal elections. The FLN conversely managed to hold on to power largely in the rural areas. Fears that FIS success might draw army intervention and spark another round of revolutionary violence led the government to postpone for six months the scheduled June 1991 elections for an enlarged 430-member National People's Assembly. An interim government, under the technocrat prime minister Sid Ahmed Ghozali, was formed to oversee the transition process.

In accordance with President Bendjedid's commitment to multiparty democracy, the first stage of Assembly elections took place on December 26, 1991, with FIS candidates winning 188 out of 231 contested seats. But before the second stage could take place, the army stepped in. FIS leaders were arrested, and the elections were postponed indefinitely. President Bendjedid resigned on January 17, 1992, well ahead of the expiration (in 1993) of his third five-year term. He said that he did so as a sacrifice in the interest of restoring stability to the nation and preserving democracy. Mohammed Boudiaf, one of the nine historic chiefs of the Revolution, returned from years of exile in Morocco to become head of the Higher Council of State, set up by military leaders after the abortive elections and resignation of President Bendjedid. FIS headquarters was closed and the party declared illegal by a court in Algiers. Local councils and provincial assemblies formed by the FIS after the elections were dissolved and replaced by "executive delegations" appointed by the Higher Council.

Subsequently, Boudiaf named a 60-member Consultative Council to work with the various political factions to reach a consensus on reforms. However, the refusal of such leaders as former president Ben Bella and Socialist Forces Front (FFS) leader Hocine Ait Ahmed to participate limited its effectiveness. Boudiaf was also suspected of using it to build a personal power base. On June 29, 1992, he was assassinated, reportedly by a member of his own presidential guard.

With Boudiaf gone, Algeria's generals turned to their own ranks for new leadership. In 1994, General Liamine Zeroual, the real strongman of the regime, was named head of state by the Higher Council. Zeroual pledged that elections for president would be held in November 1995 as a first step toward the restoration of parliamentary government. He also released from prison two top FIS leaders, Abbasi Madani and Ali Belhaj, confining them to house arrest on the assumption that in return for dialogue, they would call a halt to the spiraling violence.

However, the dialogue proved inconclusive, and Zeroual declared that the presidential elections would be held on schedule. Earlier, leaders of the FIS, FFS, FLN, and several smaller parties had met in Rome, Italy, under the sponsorship of Sant-Egidio, a Catholic service agency, and announced a "National Contract." It called for the restoration of FIS political rights in return for an end to violence, multiparty democracy, and exclusion of the military from government. The Algerian "personality" was defined in the Contract as Islamic, Arab, and Berber.

Military leaders rejected the National Contract out of hand, due to the FIS's participation. However, the November 1995 presidential election was held as scheduled, albeit under massive army protection—soldiers were stationed within 65 feet of every polling place. Zeroual won handily, as expected, garnering 61 percent of the votes. But the fact that the election was held at all, despite a boycott call by several party leaders and threats of violence from the Armed Islamic Group (GIA), was impressive.[11]

## THE KILLING FIELDS

Algeria's modern history has been well described as one of excesses. Thus "the colonial period was unusually harsh, the war for independence particularly costly... the insistence on one-party rule initially unwavering and the projects for industrialization overly ambitious," as specialists on the country have noted.[12] Extremes of violence are nothing new in Algerian life. But in addition to horrifying violence, the real tragedy of the conflict has been to pit "an inflexible regime and a fanatical opposition" against "innocent victims doomed by their secular lifestyle or their piety."[13]

Shortly before the 1995 election, Ahmed Ben Bella, Algeria's first president and the leader of the now-dissolved Movement for a Democratic Algeria, wrote a thoughtful analysis of the "dialogue at Rome" in which he had participated and that produced the National Contract. He noted: "A mad escalation of violence is the hallmark of everyday life. Nobody is safe: journalists, intellectuals, women, children and old people are all equally threatened. Yet the use of force, the recourse to violence, will not allow any of the protagonists to solve the problem to their advantage, and the solution must be a political one." The dialogue at Rome, he added, "was meant to lead to a consensus that would bring together everyone—including the regime in power—within the framework of the current Constitution, which stipulates political pluralism, democracy, respect for all human rights and freedoms."[14]

The conflict between the armed wing of the FIS, the Armed Islamic Group (GIA), and the military regime reached a level of violence in the period after the 1995 "election" that left no room for compromise. The GIA targeted not only the army and police but also writers, journalists, government officials and other public figures, professional women, even doctors and dentists. Ironically, one of its victims was the head of the Algerian League for Human Rights, which had protested the detention without trial of some 9,000 FIS members in roofless prisons deep in the Sahara.

As the violence continued, the GIA also attacked foreigners, killing among others seven Trappist monks and the bishop of Oran. Rural villages were a favorite target since they lacked police or army protection. Men, women, and children in these villages were massacred under conditions of appalling brutality. A UN Human Rights subcommittee visited the country in 2000 and reported that the GIA and government troops were almost equally responsible for the casualties. By 2001, it was estimated that more than 120,000 people had been killed.

The violence tapered off in 2001, due in part to newly elected president Bouteflikas's amnesty plan, withdrawal of popular support for the GIA, and loss of its main base in the Algiers Casbah. Unfortunately, few GIA fighters responded to the amnesty offer, as it would have required them to surrender their weapons. Violence broke out again in the coastal provinces. The amnesty offer expired in 2001, and with 5,000 guerrillas at large, the prospects for peace in Algeria seemed more remote than ever. In the first half of the year, there were more casualties (2,500) than in all of 1999.

## WHAT PRICE DIALOGUE?

Algerians have been described as having one of two personality types: those "tolerant in matters of religion and way of life, multicultural in languages and traditions, open to the diversities of location at the great hub of the Mediterranean world" and those "secretive, violent, enemies of Islamic secularism, irreverence (toward Islam) and modernism." The establishment of the first group in control of the nation resulted largely from Zeroual's efforts. After his election in 1995, he ordered a referendum on key revisions to the Constitution. These included a ban on religious, linguistic, regional, and gender-based political parties; a five-year, two-term limit for presidents; and commitments to Islam as the state religion and Arabic as its official language. Another revision established a bicameral Legislature with an appointed upper house (the Council of the Nation) and a lower house, the National Assembly, popularly elected under a system of proportional representation. The revisions were approved in November by 85.8 percent of eligible voters.

Zeroual next set June 5, 1997, for elections to the 380-member Assembly, the first national election since the abortive 1992 one. Despite a meager 65.5 percent voter turnout due to fears of violence, Zeroual's newly formed party, the National Democratic Rally, won 115 seats. Along with the FLN's 64 seats, the results gave the regime a slim majority.

Two "moderate" Islamist parties (so called because they rejected violence) also participated in the elections. The Movement for a Peaceful Society ran second to the government party, with 69 seats; and An-Nahdah won 34 seats, giving at least a semblance of opposition in the Assembly. The first local and municipal elections in Algeria's modern history were held in 1997 as well, continuing the trend as government-backed candidates won the majority of offices.

In 1999, Zeroual resigned and scheduled open presidential elections for April. Seven candidates filed; they included former foreign minister Abdelaziz Bouteflika, who had lived in Switzerland for many years. Subsequently all the other candidates withdrew, citing irregularities in the election process. But the election went off as scheduled, and Bouteflika was declared the winner, with 74 percent of the vote. The names of the other candidates remained on the ballot (the two "moderate" Islamist candidates received 17 percent of the vote).

Since then, and to his credit, President Bouteflika has made a great effort to restore the multiparty system that had prevailed before the 1991 military takover. In January 2001, elections were held for the Senate, the upper house of the Legislature. Its 144 seats are two-thirds elected and one-third appointed by the president. Suffrage was limited to the 15,000 members of communal and provincial popular assemblies elected in 1997. The National Rally for Democracy (RND), which holds a majority of seats in the lower house, won 78 Senate seats, to 31 for its main opposition, the Movement for a Peaceful Society (MSP).

Bouteflika's good intentions and early success became mired in 2000 and 2001, however, in a power struggle with military leaders. And with neither the campaign against the GIA nor moves toward reconciliation with the Islamists yielding much in the way of results, the Algerian people have become more disillusioned than ever.

Recent riots in Kabylia have compounded Bouteflika's difficulties. The Berber people of that region have chafed since independence against Arab political and economic domination, and have fought to preserve their culture and language. The death of a young Berber while in police custody sparked riots during April and May 2001, which soon spread over the whole country. Rioters clashed with police in Bejaia and Tizi Ouzou, the

**Civil war, ending with Algerian independence
1954–1962**

**Ben Bella is overthrown by Boumedienne
1965**

**The National Charter commits Algeria to revolutionary socialist development
1976**

**President Boumedienne dies
1978**

**Land reform is resumed with the breakup of 200 large farms into smaller units; Arabization campaign
1980s**

**President Bendjedid steps down; the Islamic Salvation Front becomes a force and eventually is banned; the economy undergoes an austerity program; civil war
1990s**

**2000s**

Efforts to restore the multiparty system

Continued civil conflict

regional capitals, after heavy-handed police actions had killed some 80 people. The crackdown generated public criticism abroad, particularly in France, where a government spokesman condemned "the violence of the repression" and urged a peaceful dialogue with the Berber population.

Another blow to the embattled regime came with the walkout from the Assembly of members of the Rally for Culture and Democracy (RCD), the main Berber party represented in the ruling coalition. Its leaders cited government failure to address Berber demands for official recognition of their language, affordable housing and job opportunities for youth as the main reasons for their withdrawal. Such issues as these, notably those of housing and jobs, affect the entire population. And it seemed to more and more Algerians that Bouteflika was not "on the right track" either to resolve these problems or to restore democracy. Along with most Algerians, they said that Le Pouvoir, the small clique of military leaders and politicians around Bouteflika, was the major obstacle to economic and political progress in Algeria. An opposition member in the Assembly put the problem in simple terms: "There is no one to talk to the young rebels with the necessary credentials. The divorce between regime and society is total."

## NOTES

1. See William Spencer, *Algiers in the Age of the Corsairs* (Norman, OK: University of Oklahoma Press, 1976), Centers of Civilization Series. "The corsair, if brought to justice in maritime courts, identified himself as *corsale* or *Korsan,* never as fugitive or criminal; his occupation was as clearly identifiable as that of tanner, goldsmith, potter or tailor," p. 47.

2. Raphael Danziger, *Abd al-Qadir and the Algerians* (New York: Holmes and Meier, 1977), notes that Turkish intrigue kept the tribes in a state of near-constant tribal warfare, thereby preventing them from forming dangerous coalitions, p. 24.

3. The usual explanation for the quick collapse of the regency after 300 years is that its forces were prepared for naval warfare but not for attack by land. *Ibid.,* pp. 36–38.

4. Quoted in Harold D. Nelson, *Algeria, A Country Study* (Washington, D.C.: American University, Foreign Area Studies, 1979), p. 31.

5. Marnia Lazreg, *The Emergence of Classes in Algeria* (Boulder, CO: Westview Press, 1976), p. 53.

6. For Algerian Muslims to become French citizens meant giving up their religion, for all practical purposes, since Islam recognizes only Islamic law and to be a French citizen means accepting French laws. Fewer than 3,000 Algerians became French citizens during the period of French rule. Nelson, *op. cit.,* pp. 34–35.

7. John E. Talbott, *The War Without a Name: France in Algeria, 1954–1962* (New York: Alfred A. Knopf, 1980).

8. Georges Suffert, in *Esprit,* 25 (1957), p. 819.

9. The opening of French historical archives in 1999 and recent interviews with leading generals in Algiers at the time, such as Jacques Massu, have reopened debate in France about the conduct of the war. In December 2000, members of the French Communist Party, which had backed the FLN, urged formation of a special commission to investigate charges of torture and provide compensation for victims' families. Suzanne Daley, in *The New York Times* (December 30, 2000). Retired general Paul Aussarress was fined $6,500 in 2001 for his 1999

book, *Algeria Special Forces 1955–1957,* in which he admitted the torture and execution of many Algerians and the disappearance of some 3,000 suspects while in custody; he was charged with "trying to justify war."

10. Nelson, *op. cit.,* p. 68.

11. Robert Mortimer, "Algeria: The Dialectic of Elections and Violence," *Current History* (May 1997), p. 232.

12. Frank Ruddy, who was assigned to Tindouf by the United Nations as a member of the observer group monitoring the referendum in the Western Sahara, comments on the town's natural-history museum, "the one cultural attraction." However, "most of its space is devoted to especially grisly photos of terrible things the French did to Algerians during the Algerian war of independence." *The World & I* (August 1997), p. 138.

13. Robert Fisk, in *The Independent* (London) (March 16, 1995).

14. Ahmed Ben Bella, "A Time for Peace in Algeria," *The World Today* (November 1995), p. 209.

## DEVELOPMENT

Algeria's oil industry is a major supplier of oil and gas to Europe, especially to France, Italy, and Spain. Oil production, currently 852,000 barrels per day, will be increased to 1.2 million b/d, and new discoveries have increased recoverable reserves to 1.2 billion barrels. Algeria is the world's 8th-largest natural-gas producer, supplying markets as far away as Boston.

## FREEDOM

The country's gradual return to civilian government was marked in 1997 by election of a legislative Popular Assembly and in 2001 by election of two thirds of the 144 members of an upper house, the Senate. The latter were chosen by those elected to communal and provincial assemblies, in the country's first such election in history.

## HEALTH/WELFARE

The 1984 Family Law improved women's rights in marriage and educational and work opportunities. But professional women and, more recently, rural women and their children have become special targets of Islamic violence. Some 400 professional women were murdered in 1995 and more than 400 were killed in a one-day rampage in January 1998.

## ACHIEVEMENTS

A new pipeline from the vast Hassi Berkine oil field, the African continent's largest, went into production in 1998, with export of 300,000 barrels per day. Increased foreign investment due to expansion of the hydrocarbons sector, privatization of state-owned enterprises, and favorable terms for foreign companies increased GDP growth to 5% in 2001.

# Bahrain (State of Bahrain)

## GEOGRAPHY
*Area in Square Miles (Kilometers):*
266 (688) (about 3½ times the
size of Washington, D.C.)
*Capital (Population):* Manama
(166,200)
*Environmental Concerns:*
desertification; coastal
degradation resulting from
oil spills and discharges from
ships and industry; no
natural freshwater
*Geographical Features:* mostly low
desert plain, rising gently to low
central escarpment
*Climate:* hot and humid summers;
temperate winters

## PEOPLE

### Population
*Total:* 646,000
*Annual Growth Rate:* 1.73%
*Rural/Urban Population Ratio:* 9/91
*Major Languages:* Arabic; English
*Ethnic Makeup:* 63% Bahraini; 19%
Asian; 10% other Arab; 8% Iranian
*Religions:* 70% Shia Muslim; 15%
Sunni Muslim; 15% Bahai,
Christian, and others

### Health
*Life Expectancy at Birth:* 71 years
(male); 76 years (female)
*Infant Mortality Rate (Ratio):*
19.7/1,000
*Physicians Available (Ratio):* 1/1,115

### Education
*Adult Literacy Rate:* 85.2%
*Compulsory (Ages):* 6–17; free

## COMMUNICATION
*Telephones:* 153,000 main lines
*Daily Newspaper Circulation:* 128
per 1,000 people
*Televisions:* 442 per 1,000 people
*Internet Service Provider:* 1 (2000)

## TRANSPORTATION
*Highways in Miles (Kilometers):* 1,927
(3,103)
*Railroads in Miles (Kilometers):* none
*Usable Airfields:* 3
*Motor Vehicles in Use:* 172,000

## GOVERNMENT
*Type:* constitutional monarchy as of 2001
*Independence Date:* August 15, 1971
(from the United Kingdom)
*Head of State/Government:* Emir Hamad
bin Isa al-Khalifa; Prime Minister
Khalifa bin Salman al-Khalifa

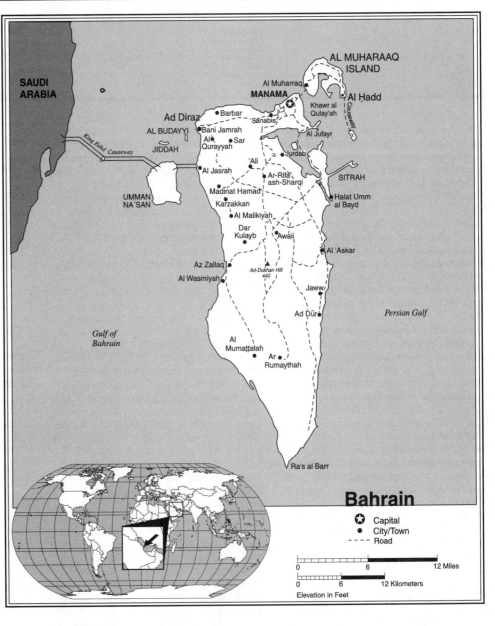

*Political Parties:* none, but elections by
direct ballot for a new parliament, including women, are scheduled for
October 2002
*Suffrage:* scheduled for 2004

## MILITARY
*Military Expenditures (% of GDP):* 5.2%
*Current Disputes:* none; dispute with
Qatar resolved in 2001

## ECONOMY
*Currency ($ U.S. Equivalent):* 0.377
dinar = $1 (fixed rate)
*Per Capita Income/GDP:* $15,900/$10.1
billion
*GDP Growth Rate:* 5%
*Inflation Rate:* 2%

*Unemployment Rate:* 15%
*Labor Force:* 150,000
*Natural Resources:* oil; associated and
nonassociated natural gas; fish
*Agriculture:* fruits; vegetables; poultry;
dairy products; shrimp; fish
*Industry:* petroleum processing and
refining; aluminum smelting; offshore
banking; ship repairing; tourism
*Exports:* $5.8 billion (primary partners
India, United States, Saudi Arabia)
*Imports:* $4.2 billion (primary partners
France, United States, United Kingdom)

http://lcweb2.loc.gov/frd/cs/bhtoc.html
http://www.usembassy.com.bh

# BAHRAIN

Bahrain is the smallest Arab state. It is also the only Arab island state, consisting of an archipelago of 33 islands, just five of them inhabited. The largest island, also named Bahrain (from the Arabic *bahrayn,* or "two seas"), has an area of 216 square miles.

Although it is separated from the Arabian mainland, Bahrain is not far away; it is just 15 miles from Qatar and the same distance from Saudi Arabia. A causeway linking Bahrain with mainland Saudi Arabia opened in 1986, technically ending its insular status. Improvements to the causeway in 2001 link the country even closer to its larger neighbor, as Saudis pour across the border to enjoy the movies, bars, and shopping boutiques of the freer Bahraini society.

Bahrain is unusual among the Persian Gulf states in that it started to diversify its economy early. Oil was discovered there in 1932. Its head start in the exportation of oil enabled the government to build up an industrial base over a long period and to develop a large, indigenous, skilled labor force. As a result, today about two thirds of the population are native-born Bahrainis.

## HISTORY

Excavations by archaeologists indicate that roughly 5,000 years ago, Bahrain was the legendary *Dilmun,* "home of the gods" and the land of immortality in the Mesopotamian Epic of Gilgamesh. It had a fully urbanized society and was the center of a far-flung trade network between Mesopotamia, Oman, the Arabian Gulf, and the Indus Valley cities farther east.

During the centuries of Islamic rule in the Middle East, Bahrain (it was renamed by Arab geographers) became wealthy from the pearl-fishing industry. By the fourteenth century A.D., it had 300 villages. Bahraini merchants grew rich from profits on their large, lustrous, high-quality pearls. Bahraini sea captains and pearl merchants built lofty palaces and other stately buildings on the islands.

The Portuguese were the first Europeans to land on Bahrain, which they seized in the early sixteenth century as one of a string of fortresses along the coast to protect their monopoly over the spice trade. They ruled by the sword in Bahrain for nearly a century before they were ousted by Iranian invaders. The Iranians, in turn, were defeated by the al-Khalifas, a clan of the powerful Anaizas. In 1782, the clan leader, Shaykh Ahmad al-Khalifa, established control over Bahrain and founded the dynasty that rules the state today. (The al-Khalifas belong to the same clan as the

(UN photo/Ian Steele)

Bahrain may be the first of the Gulf states to get out of the oil business, due to its dwindling reserves. Other income-generating industries are being explored, and diversification of the economy along with political stability make Bahrain a stable regional business center. The need for an effective educational system to supply an informed labor force is paramount, as these children and their teacher at a nursery school near Manama attest.

al-Sabahs, the rulers of Kuwait, and are distantly related to the Saudi Arabian royal family.)

## A British Protectorate

In the 1800s, Bahrain came under British protection in the same way as other Gulf states. The ruler Shaykh Isa, whose reign was one of the world's longest (1869–1932), signed an agreement making Britain responsible for Bahrain's defense and foreign policy. He also agreed not to give any concessions for oil exploration without British approval. The agreement was important because the British were already developing oil fields in Iran. Control

of oil in another area would give them an added source of fuel for the new weaponry of tanks and oil-powered warships of World War I. The early development of Bahrain's oil fields and the guidance of British political advisers helped prepare the country for independence.

## INDEPENDENCE

Bahrain became fully independent in 1971. The British encouraged Bahrain to join with Qatar and seven small British-protected Gulf states, the Trucial States, in a federation. However, Bahrain and Qatar felt that they were more advanced economically, politically, and socially than were the Trucial States and therefore did not need to federate.

A mild threat to Bahrain's independence came from Iran. In 1970, Shah Mohammed Reza Pahlavi of Iran claimed Bahrain, on the basis of Iran's sixteenth-century occupation, plus the fact that a large number of Bahrainis were descended from Iranian emigrants. The United Nations discussed the issue and recommended that Bahrain be given its independence, on the grounds that "the people of Bahrain wish to gain recognition of their identity in a fully independent and sovereign state."[1] The shah accepted the resolution, and Iran made no further claims on Bahrain during his lifetime.

The gradual development of democracy in Bahrain reached a peak after independence. Shaykh Khalifa (now called emir) approved a new Constitution and a law establishing an elected National Assembly of 30 members. The Assembly met for the first time in 1973; but it was dissolved by the emir only two years later.

### What Had Happened?

Bahrain is an example of a problem common in the Middle East: the conflict between traditional authority and popular democracy. Fuad Khuri describes the problem as one of a "tribally controlled government that rules by historical right, opposed to a community-based urban population seeking to participate in government through elections. The first believes and acts as if government is an earned right, the other seeks to modify government and subject it to a public vote."[2]

Governmental authority in Bahrain is defined as hereditary in the al-Khalifa family, according to the 1973 Constitution. The succession passes from the ruling emir to his eldest son. Since Bahrain has no tradition of representative government or political parties, the National Assembly was set up to broaden the political process without going through the lengthy period of conditioning necessary to establish a multiparty system. Members were expected to debate laws prepared by the Council of Ministers and to assist with budget preparation. But as things turned out, Assembly members spent their time arguing with one another or criticizing the ruler instead of dealing with issues. When the emir dissolved the Assembly, he said that it was preventing the government from doing what it was supposed to do.

Since that time, government in Bahrain has reverted to its traditional patriarchal-authority structure. However, Shia demands for reinstatement of the Assembly, a multiparty system with national elections, and greater representation for Shias in government have been met in part through changes in the governing structure. In 1993, the emir appointed a 30-member *Shura* (Council), composed of business and industry leaders along with members of the ruling family.

In December 2000, the Shura was enlarged to 40 members, including for the first time women and representatives of the Shia majority community. Shaykh Hamad, who had succeeded his father in 1999 after the latter's sudden death, also approved a "National Action Charter" as the starting point for gradual democratization. It was approved in February 2001 by 80 percent of eligible voters. Previously he had freed all political prisoners, abolished state-security courts, and annulled a 1974 law allowing imprisonment without trial or appeal for political crimes. A leading Shia cleric was released and acquitted of antigovernment disturbances.

### FOREIGN RELATIONS

The U.S. involvement in Bahrain dates back over a century, to the establishment of the American Hospital in Manama in 1893. American missionaries subsequently founded a number of schools, including the Bahrain-American School, which is still in existence. In recent years, Bahrain has become a key factor in U.S. Middle Eastern policy, due to its strategic location in the Persian Gulf. During the Iran–Iraq War, Bahrain's British-built naval base was a staging point for U.S. convoy escort vessels in the Gulf. Then, in the aftermath of the 1991 Gulf War, Bahrain became a "front-line state" in the American containment strategy toward Iraq. It is the permanent headquarters for the new U.S. Fifth Fleet, under a mutual-defense agreement, with some 1,000 American military and naval personnel stationed there. Following the September 11, 2001, terrorist attacks in the United States, Bahrain strongly supported the international coalition against terrorism and granted use of its base for U.S. air strikes in Afghanistan.

Bahrain's only serious foreign-policy problem since its independence has involved neighboring Qatar. In 1992, the Qatari ruler unilaterally extended Qatar's territorial waters to include the islands of Hawar and Fishat al-Duble, which had been controlled by Bahrain since the 1930s, when both nations were British protectorates. Bahrain in turn demanded that Qatar recognize Bahrain's sovereignty over the al-Zeyara coastal strip, which adjoins Bahraini territorial waters. After considerable wrangling, the two countries agreed to take their dispute before the International Court of Justice (ICJ). In 2001, it confirmed Qatari sovereignty over Zabarah and Janan Islands. Bahrain was awarded sovereignty over Hawar and Qit'at Jaradeh Islands. The boundary between their maritime zones is to be drawn in accordance with the Court's decision.

In 1981, concern over threats by its more powerful neighbors led Bahrain to join with other Gulf states in forming the Gulf Cooperation Council, a regional mutual-defense organization. The other members are Kuwait, Oman, Qatar, Saudi Arabia, and the United Arab Emirates. In 2001, the members signed a formal defense pact, sponsored by the United States. The pact expanded the rapid-deployment force of 5,000 soldiers to 22,000, with members contributing troops in accordance with the size of their armed forces. The United States agreed to provide a $70 million early warning system to identify any chemical or biological weapons used by belligerent forces in an attack on GCC member states.

### THREATS TO NATIONAL SECURITY

The 1979 Revolution in Iran caused much concern in Bahrain. The new Iranian government revived the old territorial claim, and a Teheran-based Islamic Front for the Liberation of Bahrain called on Shia Muslims in Bahrain to overthrow the Sunni regime of the emir. In 1981, the government arrested a group of Shia Bahrainis and others, charging them with a plot against the state, backed by Iran. The plotters had expected support from the Shia population, but this did not materialize. After seeing the results of the Iranian Revolution, few Bahraini Shia Muslims wanted the Iranian form of fundamentalist Islamic government. In 1982, 73 defendants were given prison sentences ranging from seven years to life. Bahrain's prime minister told a local newspaper that the plot didn't represent a real danger, "but we are not used to this sort of thing so we had to take strong action."[3]

Until the 1990s, the Shia community was politically inactive, and as a result, 100 Shia activists were pardoned by the emir and allowed to return from exile. However, the increase in fundamentalist activities against Middle Eastern regimes elsewhere has destabilized the island nation to some extent. Between 1994 and 1999, a low-level campaign of antigovernment violence claimed 30 lives and resulted in a number of sabotage incidents. In 1996, eight opposition leaders were arrested; they included Shaykh Abdul-Ameer al-Jamri, allegedly the head of the opposition movement. In July 1999, he was given a 10-year jail sentence and

| Periodic occupation of Bahrain by Iran after the Portuguese ouster **1602–1782** ● | The al-Khalifa family seizes power over other families and groups **1783** ● | Bahrain becomes a British protectorate **1880** ● | Independence **1971** ● | The new Constitution establishes a Constituent Assembly, but the ruler dissolves it shortly thereafter **1973–1975** ● | Bahrain takes aggressive steps to revive and diversify its economy **1990s** ● |

**2000s**

Territorial disputes with Qatar resolved

Important changes in representation and participation in government

fined $14.5 million for having spied for a foreign power (unnamed), for inciting unrest, and for continuing to agitate illegally for political reform. But he was released the day after his sentencing, partly due to his ill health, but also due to criticism from the United States and other countries of Bahrain's failure to observe his civil and legal rights. The government also released some 320 other detainees.

## AN OIL-LESS ECONOMY?

Bahrain was an early entrant in the oil business and may be the first Gulf state to face an oil-less future. Current production from its own oil fields is 42,000 barrels per day. The Bahrain Petroleum Company (Bapco) controls all aspects of production, refining, and export. However, Bapco must import 70,000 b/d from Saudi Arabia to keep its refinery operating efficiently.

In the past, Bahrain's economic development was characterized by conservative management. This policy changed radically with the accession of the current ruler. A January 2001 decree allows foreign companies to buy and own property, particularly for non-oil investment projects. (Oil currently accounts for 80 percent of exports and 60 percent of revenues.)

The slow decline in oil production in recent years has been balanced by expansion of the liquefied natural gas (LNG) sector. Current production is 170 million cubic feet per day. But with 9 billion cubic feet of proven reserves, production of LNG will long outlast oil production.

Aluminium Bahrain (ALBA), which accounts for 60 percent of Bahrain's non-oil exports, expanded its production in 2001 to become the world's largest aluminium smelter, with an annual output of 750,000 tons. Some 450,000 of this is exported. A

seawater-desalination plant was completed in 1999. It uses waste heat from the smelter to provide potable water for local needs.

## INTERNATIONAL FINANCE

During the Lebanese Civil War, Bahrain encouraged the establishment of "Offshore Banking Units" in order to replace Lebanon as a regional finance center. OBUs are set up to attract deposits from governments or large financial organizations such as the World Bank as well as to make loans for development projects. OBUs are "offshore" in the sense that a Bahraini cannot open a checking account or borrow money. However, OBUs bring funds into Bahrain without interfering with local growth or undercutting local banks.

The drop in world oil prices in the 1980s and the Iraqi occupation of Kuwait seriously disrupted the OBU system, and a number of offshore banks were closed. Increased oil production and higher world prices have revitalized the system, both for offshore and in-shore banks. In 2001, BNP Paribas, the sixth largest bank in the world, relocated its Middle East operations office to Bahrain, as did Turkey's Islamic Bank, an emerging giant in the Islamic banking system.

Bahrain's economic recovery has been enhanced by the Systems Development Council, a government body set up in 2000 to oversee development. The Bahrain Stock Exchange, opened in 1992, has revised its regulations to require foreign firms to employ 60 percent local labor, which strengthens Bahrainis' participation in the development of the emirate.

## THE FUTURE

One key to Bahrain's future may be found in a Koranic verse (*Sura XIII, II*):

*Lo! Allah changeth not the condition of a people until they first change what is in their hearts.*

For a brief time after independence, the state experimented with representative government. But the hurly-burly of politics, with its factional rivalries, trade-offs, and compromises found in many Western democratic systems, did not suit the Bahraini temperament or experience. Democracy takes time to mature. Emile Nakhleh reminds us that "any serious attempt to democratize the regime will ultimately set tribal legitimacy and popular sovereignty on a collision course."[4]

The emir demonstrated his commitment to gradual democratization in 2000, issuing an edict, confirmed in a national referendum, that defines Bahrain as a constitutional monarchy ruled by a king. He scheduled elections for municipal councils for May 2002 and parliamentary elections for October.

## NOTES

1. UN Security Council *Resolution 287,* 1970. Quoted from Emile Nakhleh, *Bahrain* (Lexington, KY: Lexington Books, 1976), p. 9.

2. Fuad I. Khuri, *Tribe and State in Bahrain* (Chicago: University of Chicago Press, 1981), p. 219.

3. *Gulf Daily News* (May 15, 1982).

4. Nakhleh, *op. cit.*, p. 11.

---

**DEVELOPMENT**

The 2001–2002 budget sets revenues at $3 billion and expenditures at $4 billion, the increase due largely to new development projects. Its goal is to encourage foreign investment and improve health and housing services while continuing to diversify the economy. In 2001, Bahrain was ranked 1st for the 7th consecutive year among Middle Eastern countries in economic freedom by the Heritage Foundation.

**FREEDOM**

Although the 1973 Constitution and the National Assembly that it created remain suspended, Bahrain's ruler is moving systematically toward representative government. In 2002, he issued a new National Charter. Among other provisions, it allows women to run for office in local elections. He also scheduled elections for a new National Assembly, for October 2002.

**HEALTH/WELFARE**

A 1993 labor law allows unions to organize and bargain with their employers and guarantees equal pay for all workers, male and female alike. The requirement that new industries, both foreign- and locally owned, must employ 60% local labor should strengthen the job market and with it the sense of participation by Bahrainis in national development. Unemployment has hit hardest in the Shia community.

**ACHIEVEMENTS**

In August 2000, a high-speed ferry service was inaugurated linking Bahrain with the Iranian ports of Bushehr and Bandar Abbas, Umm Qasr in Iraq, and with ports in other Gulf states. A women's swim team from Bahrain was the first from any Gulf state to compete in the 2000 Sydney Summer Olympics. It included a 12-year-old swimmer.

# Egypt (Arab Republic of Egypt)

## GEOGRAPHY

*Area in Square Miles (Kilometers):*
386,258 (1,001,258) (about
3 times the size of New Mexico)

*Capital (Population):* Cairo
(6,800,000)

*Environmental Concerns:* loss of
agricultural land; increasing soil
salinization; desertification; oil
pollution threatening coral reefs
and marine habitats; other water
pollution; rapid population growth

*Geographical Features:* a vast desert
plateau interrupted by the Nile
Valley and Delta

*Climate:* desert; dry, hot summers;
moderate winters

## PEOPLE

### Population

*Total:* 69,600,000

*Annual Growth Rate:* 1.7%

*Rural/Urban Population Ratio:* 55/45

*Major Languages:* Arabic; English;
French

*Ethnic Makeup:* 99% Eastern Hamitic
(Egyptian, Bedouin, Arab, Nubian);
1% others

*Religions:* 94% Muslim (mostly
Sunni); 6% Coptic Christian and
others

### Health

*Life Expectancy at Birth:* 62 years
(male); 66 years (female)

*Infant Mortality Rate (Ratio):*
60.4/1,000

*Physicians Available (Ratio):* 1/472

### Education

*Adult Literacy Rate:* 51.4%

*Compulsory (Ages):* for 5 years
between 6 and 13

## COMMUNICATION

*Telephones:* 3,972,000 main lines

*Daily Newspaper Circulation:* 43 per
1,000 people

*Televisions:* 110 per 1,000 people

*Internet Service Providers:* 50 (2000)

## TRANSPORTATION

*Highways in Miles (Kilometers):* 39,744
(64,000)

*Railroads in Miles (Kilometers):* 2,973
(4,955)

*Usable Airfields:* 90

*Motor Vehicles in Use:* 1,703,000

## GOVERNMENT

*Type:* republic

*Independence Date:* July 23, 1952, for
the republic; February 28, 1922, marking the end of British rule

*Head of State/Government:* President
Mohammed Hosni Mubarak; Prime
Minister Atef Obeid

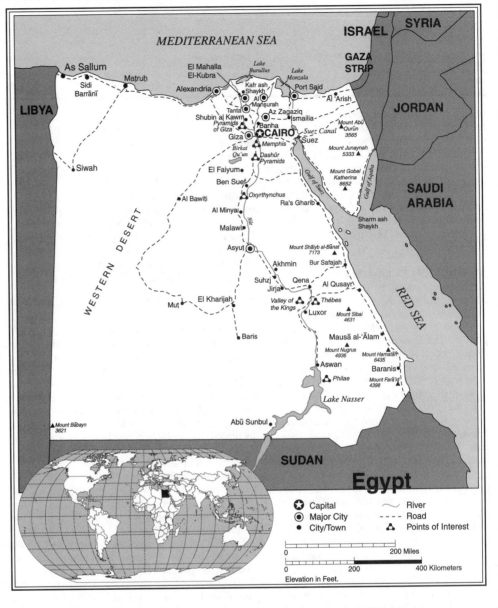

Egypt

*Political Parties:* National Democratic
Party; Socialist Liberal Party; New
Wafd Party; National Progressive Union-
ist Grouping of Tagammu; Democratic
Union Party; Nasserist Arab Democratic
Party or Nasserists; others

*Suffrage:* universal and compulsory at 18

## MILITARY

*Military Expenditures (% of GDP):* 4.4%

*Current Disputes:* territorial dispute with
Sudan over the Hala'ib Triangle

## ECONOMY

*Currency ($ U.S. Equivalent):* 4.65
pounds = $1

*Per Capita Income/GDP:* $3,600/$247
billion

*GDP Growth Rate:* 5%

*Inflation Rate:* 3%

*Unemployment Rate:* 11.5%

*Labor Force:* 19,500,000

*Natural Resources:* petroleum; natural gas;
iron ore; phosphates; manganese; limestone; gypsum; talc; asbestos; lead; zinc

*Agriculture:* cotton; sugarcane; rice; corn;
wheat; beans; fruits; vegetables;
livestock; fish

*Industry:* textiles; food processing;
tourism; chemicals; petroleum; construction; cement; metals

*Exports:* $7.3 billion (primary partners
European Union, Middle East, Afro-
Asian countries)

*Imports:* $17 billion (primary partners
European Union, United States, Afro-
Asian countries)

 http://lcweb2.loc.gov/frd/cs/egtoc.htm

# EGYPT

The Arab Republic of Egypt is located at the extreme northeastern corner of Africa, with part of its territory—the Sinai Peninsula—serving as a land bridge to Southwest Asia. The country's total land area is approximately 386,000 square miles. However, 96 percent of this is uninhabitable desert. Except for a few scattered oases, the only settled and cultivable area is a narrow strip along the Nile River. The vast majority of Egypt's population is concentrated in this strip, resulting in high population density. Migration from rural areas to cities has intensified urban density; Cairo's population is currently 6.8 million, with millions more in the greater metropolitan area. It is a city that is literally "bursting at the seams."

Egypt today identifies itself as an Arab nation and is a founding member of the League of Arab States (which has its headquarters in Cairo). But its "Arab" identity is relatively new. It was first defined by the late president Gamal Abdel Nasser, who as a schoolboy became aware of his "Arabness" in response to British imperialism and particularly Britain's establishment of a national home for Jews in Arab Palestine. But Egypt's incredibly long history as a distinct society has given its people a separate Egyptian identity and a sense of superiority over other peoples, notably desert people such as the Arabs of old.[1] Also, its development under British tutelage gave the country a headstart over other Arab countries or societies. Despite its people's overall low level of adult literacy, Egypt has more highly skilled professionals than do other Arab countries.

## HISTORY

Although Egypt is a modern nation in terms of independence from foreign control, it has a distinct national identity and a rich culture that date back thousands of years. The modern Egyptians take great pride in their brilliant past; this sense of the past gives them patience and a certain fatalism that enable them to withstand misfortunes that would crush most peoples. The Egyptian peasants, the *fellahin,* are as stoic and enduring as the water buffaloes they use to do their plowing. Since the time of the pharaohs, Egypt has been invaded many times, and it was under foreign control for most of its history. When Nasser, the first president of the new Egyptian republic, came to power in 1954, he said that he was the first native Egyptian to rule the country in nearly 3,000 years.

It is often said that Egypt is the "gift of the Nile." The mighty river, flowing north to the Mediterranean with an enormous annual spate that deposited rich silt along its banks, attracted nomadic peoples to settle there as early as 6000 B.C. They developed a productive agriculture based on the river's seasonal floods. They lived in plastered mud huts in small, compact villages. Their villages were not too different from those one sees today in parts of the Nile Delta.

Each village had its "headman," the head of some family more prosperous or industrious (or both) than the others. The arrival of other nomadic desert peoples gradually brought about the evolution of an organized system of government. Since the Egyptian villagers did not have nearby mountains or wild forests to retreat into, they were easily governable.

The institution of kingship was well established in Egypt by 2000 B.C., and in the time of Ramses II (1300–1233 B.C.), Egyptian monarchs extended their power over a large part of the Middle East. All Egyptian rulers were called pharaohs, although there was no hereditary system of descent and many different dynasties ruled during the country's first 2,000 years of existence. The pharaohs had their capital at Thebes, but they built other important cities on the banks of the Nile. Recent research by Egyptologists indicate that the ancient Egyptians had an amazingly accurate knowledge of astronomy. The Pyramids of Giza, for example, were built so as to be aligned with true north. Lacking modern instruments, their builders apparently used two stars, Thaban and Draconis, in the Big Dipper, for their alignment, with a point equidistant from them to mark their approximation of true north. Only centuries later was the North Star identified as such. The pyramids and Sphinx were built with Egyptian labor and without more than rudimentary machinery. They underline the engineering expertise of this ancient people. The world's

(UN photo/John Isaac)

These pyramids at Giza are among the most famous mementos of Egypt's past.

(UN Photo/152,385/Jeffrey Foxx)

Two young Egyptian boys gaze in wonder at the language of their ancestors, Karnak.

oldest irrigation canal, its base paved with limestone blocks, was unearthed near Giza in 1996; and in 1999, a 2,000-year-old cemetery, discovered by chance in Bahariya Oasis, was found to contain rows of mummified men, women, and children along with wall murals showing funeral ceremonies, all in a remarkable state of preservation. The recent discovery of the bones of the second-largest dinosaur ever identified, in the same area, indicates that 90 million years ago, long before the pharaohs, Bahariya was a swampy tropical region similar to the Florida Everglades.

Another important discovery, in November 1999, was that of inscriptions on the walls of *Wadi Hoi* ("Valley of Terror") that may well be the world's oldest written language, predating the cuneiform letters developed by the Sumerians in Mesopotamia.

In the first century B.C., Egypt became part of the Roman Empire. The city of Alexandria, founded by Alexander the Great, became a center of Greek and Roman learning and culture. Later, it became a center of Christianity. The Egyptian Coptic Church was one of the earliest organized churches. The Copts, direct descendants of the early Egyptians, are the principal minority group in Egypt today. (The name Copt comes from *aigyptos,* Greek for "Egyptian.") The Copts welcomed the Arab invaders who brought Islam to Egypt, preferring them to their oppressive Byzantine Christian rulers. Muslim rulers over the centuries usually protected the Copts as "Peoples of the Book," leaving authority over them to their religious leaders, in return for allegiance and payment of a small tax. But in recent years, the rise of Islamic fundamentalism has made life more difficult for Egypt's Christians. As a minority group, they are caught between the fundamentalists and government forces seeking to destroy them.

Egypt also had, until very recently, a small but long-established Jewish community that held a similar position under various Muslim rulers. Most of the Jews emigrated to Israel after 1948.

## THE INFLUENCE OF ISLAM

Islam was the major formative influence in the development of modern Egyptian society. Islamic armies from Arabia invaded Egypt in the seventh century A.D. Large numbers of nomadic Arabs followed, settling the Nile Valley until, over time, they became the majority in the population. Egypt was under the rule of the caliphs ("successors" of the Prophet Muhammad) until the tenth century, when a Shia group broke away and formed a separate government. The leaders of this group also called themselves caliphs. To show their independence, they founded a new capital in the desert south of Alexandria. The name they chose for their new capital was prophetic: *al-Qahira*—"City of War"—the modern city of Cairo.

In the sixteenth century, Egypt became a province of the Ottoman Empire. It was then under the rule of the Mamluks, originally slaves or prisoners of war who were converted to Islam. Many Mamluk leaders had been freed and then acquired their own slaves. They formed a military aristocracy, constantly fighting with one another for land and power. The Ottomans found it simpler to leave Egypt under Mamluk control, merely requiring periodic tribute and taxes.

## EGYPT ENTERS THE MODERN WORLD

At the end of the eighteenth century, rivalry between Britain and France for control of trade in the Mediterranean and the sea routes to India involved Egypt. The French general Napoleon Bonaparte led an expedition to Egypt in 1798. However, the British, in cooperation with Ottoman forces, drove the French from Egypt. A confused struggle for power followed. The victor was Muhammad Ali, an Albanian officer in the Ottoman garrison at Cairo. In 1805, the Ottoman sultan appointed him governor of Egypt.

Although he was not an Egyptian, Muhammad Ali had a vision of Egypt under his rule as a rich and powerful country. He began by forming a new army consisting of native Egyptians instead of mercenaries or slave-soldiers. This army was trained by European advisers and gave a good account of itself in campaigns, performing better than the regular Ottoman armies.[2] His successor, Ismail, went a step further by hiring some 50 demobilized veterans of the American Civil War, both Yankees and rebels, who brought discipline and military experience to the training of Egyptian recruits. These mercenaries remained in Egypt after the end of the campaigns of Ismail and his successors in the Middle East, and when they died they were buried in the long-forgotten and neglected American cemetery in a corner of Cairo.

Muhammad Ali set up an organized, efficient tax-collection system. He suppressed the Mamluks and confiscated all the lands that they had seized from Egyptian peasants over the years, lifting a heavy tax burden from peasant backs. He took personal charge of all Egypt's exports. Cotton, a new crop, became the major Egyptian export and became known the world over for its high quality. Dams and irrigation canals were dug to improve cultivation and expand arable land. Although Muhammad Ali grew rich in the process of carrying out these policies, he was concerned for the welfare of the peasantry. He once said, "One must guide this people as one guides children; to leave them to their own devices would be to render them subject to all the disorders from which I have saved them."[3]

Muhammad Ali's successors were named *khedives* ("viceroys"), in that they ruled Egypt in theory on behalf of their superior, the sultan. In practice, they acted as independent rulers. Under the khedives, Egypt was again drawn into European power politics, with unfortunate results. Khedive Ismail, the most ambitious of Muhammad Ali's descendants, was determined to make Egypt the equal of Western European nations. His major project was the Suez Canal, built by a European company and opened in 1869. The Italian composer Verdi was invited to compose the opera *Aida* for its inauguration. He refused to do so at first, saying that Egypt was a country whose civilization he did not admire. Eventually he was persuaded (with the help of the then-princely bonus of $20,000!) and set to music the ancient Egyptian legend of imperialism and grand passion. Verdi's task was eased by the fact that Auguste Mariette, the preeminent Egyptologist of the period, wrote the libretto and designed sets and costumes with absolute fidelity to pharaonic times.

However, the expense of this and other grandiose projects bankrupted the country.

(UN photo)

In 1952, the Free Officers organization persuaded Egypt's King Farouk to abdicate. The monarchy was formally abolished in 1954, when Gamal Abdel Nasser (pictured above) became Egypt's president, prime minister, and head of the Revolutionary Command Council.

Ismail was forced to sell Egypt's shares in the Suez Canal Company—to the British government!—and his successors were forced to accept British control over Egyptian finances. In 1882, a revolt of army officers threatened to overthrow the khedive. The British intervened and established a de facto protectorate, keeping the khedive in office in order to avoid conflict with the Ottomans.

## EGYPTIAN NATIONALISM
The British protectorate lasted from 1882 to 1956. An Egyptian nationalist movement gradually developed in the early 1900s, inspired by the teachings of religious leaders and Western-educated officials in the khedives' government. They advocated a revival of Islam and its strengthening to enable Egypt and other Islamic lands to resist European control.

During World War I, Egypt was a major base for British campaigns against the Ottoman Empire. The British formally declared their protectorate over Egypt in order to "defend" the country, since legally it was still an Ottoman province. The British worked with Arab nationalist leaders against the Turks and promised to help them form an independent Arab nation after the war. Egyptian nationalists were active in the Arab cause, and although at that time they did not particularly care about being a part of a new Arab nation, they wanted independence from Britain.

At the end of World War I, Egyptian nationalist leaders organized the *Wafd* (Arabic for "delegation"). In 1918, the Wafd presented demands to the British for the complete independence of Egypt. The British rejected the demands, saying that Egypt was not ready for self-government. The Wafd then turned to violence, organizing boycotts, strikes, and terrorist attacks on British soldiers and on Egyptians accused of cooperating with the British.

Under pressure, the British finally abolished the protectorate in 1922. But they retained control over Egyptian foreign policy, defense, and communications as well as the protection of minorities and foreign residents and of Sudan, which had been part of Egypt since the 1880s. Thus, Egypt's "independence" was a hollow shell.

Egypt did regain control over internal affairs. The government was set up as a constitutional monarchy under a new king, Fuad. Political parties were allowed, and in elections for a Parliament in 1923, the Wafd emerged as the dominant party. But neither Fuad nor the son who succeeded him, Farouk, trusted Wafd leaders. They feared that the Wafd was working to establish a republic. For their part, the Wafd leaders did not believe that the rulers were seriously interested in the good of the country. So Egypt waddled along for two decades with little progress.

## THE EGYPTIAN REVOLUTION
During the years of the monarchy, the Egyptian Army gradually developed a corps of professional officers, most of them from lower- or middle-class Egyptian backgrounds. They were strongly patriotic and resented what they perceived to be British cultural snobbery as well as Britain's continual influence over Egyptian affairs.

The training school for these young officers was the Egyptian Military Academy, founded in 1936. Among them was Gamal Abdel Nasser, the eldest son of a village postal clerk. Nasser and his fellow officers were already active in anti-British demonstrations by the time they entered the academy. During World War II, the British, fearing a German takeover of Egypt, reinstated the protectorate. Egypt became the main British military base in the Middle East. This action galvanized the officers into forming a revolutionary movement. Nasser said at the time that it roused in him the seeds of revolt. "It made [us] realize that there is a dignity to be retrieved and defended."[4]

When Jewish leaders in Palestine organized Israel in May 1948, Egypt, along with other nearby Arab countries, sent troops to destroy the new state. Nasser and several of his fellow officers were sent to the front. The Egyptian Army was defeated; Nasser himself was trapped with his unit, was wounded, and was rescued only by an armistice. Even more shocking to the young officers was the evident corruption and weakness of their own government. The weapons that they received were inferior and often defective, battle orders were inaccurate, and their superiors proved to be incompetent in strategy and tactics.

Nasser and his fellow officers attributed their defeat not to their own weaknesses but to their government's failures. When they returned to Egypt, they were determined to overthrow the monarchy. They formed a secret organization, the Free Officers. It was not the only organization dedicated to the overthrow of the monarchy, but it was the best disciplined and had the general support of the army.

On July 23, 1952, the Free Officers launched their revolution. It came six months after "Black Saturday," the burning of Cairo by mobs protesting the continued presence of British troops in Egypt. The Free Officers persuaded King Farouk to abdicate, and they declared Egypt a republic. A nine-member Revolutionary Command Council (RCC) was established to govern the country.

### EGYPT UNDER NASSER

In his self-analytical book *The Philosophy of the Revolution,* Nasser wrote, " I always imagine that in this region in which we live there is a role wandering aimlessly about in search of an actor to play it."[5] Nasser saw himself as playing that role. Previously, he had operated behind the scenes, but always as the leader to whom the other Free Officers looked up. By 1954, Nasser had emerged as Egypt's leader. When the monarchy was formally abolished in 1954, he became president, prime minister, and head of the RCC. Cynics said that Nasser came along when Egypt was ready for another king; the Egyptians could not function without one!

Nasser came to power determined to restore dignity and status to Egypt, to eliminate foreign control, and to make his country the leader of a united Arab world. It was an ambitious set of goals, and Nasser was only partly successful in attaining them. But in his struggles to achieve these goals, he brought considerable status to Egypt. The country became a leader of the "Third World" of Africa and Asia, developing nations newly freed from foreign control.

Nasser was successful in removing the last vestiges of British rule from Egypt.

British troops were withdrawn from the Suez Canal Zone, and Nasser nationalized the canal in 1956, taking over the management from the private foreign company that had operated it since 1869. That action made the British furious, since the British government had a majority interest in the company. The British worked out a secret plan with the French and the Israelis, neither of whom liked Nasser, to invade Egypt and overthrow him. British and French paratroopers seized the canal in October 1956, but the United States and the Soviet Union, in an unusual display of cooperation, forced them to withdraw. It was the first of several occasions when Nasser turned military defeat into political victory. It was also one of the few times when Nasser and the United States were on the same side of an issue.

Between 1956 and 1967, Nasser developed a close alliance with the Soviet Union—at least, it seemed that way to the United States. Nasser's pet economic project was the building of a dam at Aswan, on the upper Nile, to regulate the annual flow of river water and thus enable Egypt to reclaim new land and develop its agriculture. He applied for aid from the United States through the World Bank to finance the project, but he was turned down, largely due to his publicly expressed hostility toward Israel. Again Nasser turned defeat into a victory of sorts. The Soviet Union agreed to finance the dam, which was completed in 1971, and subsequently to equip and train the Egyptian Army. Thousands of Soviet advisers poured into Egypt, and it seemed to U.S. and Israeli leaders that Egypt had become a dependency of the Soviet Union.

The lowest point in Nasser's career came in June 1967. Israel invaded Egypt and defeated his Soviet-trained army, along with those of Jordan and Syria, and occupied the Sinai Peninsula in a lightning six-day war. The Israelis were restrained from marching on Cairo only by a United Nations cease-fire. Nasser took personal responsibility for the defeat, calling it *al-Nakba* ("The Catastrophe"). He announced his resignation, but the Egyptian people refused to accept it. The public outcry was so great that he agreed to continue in office. One observer wrote, "The irony was that Nasser had led the country to defeat, but Egypt without Nasser was unthinkable."[6]

Nasser had little success in his efforts to unify the Arab world. One attempt, for example, was a union of Egypt and Syria, which lasted barely three years (1958–1961). Egyptian forces were sent to support a new republican government in Yemen after the overthrow of that coun-

(UN photo/Muldoon)

Nasser died in 1970 and was succeeded by Vice-President Anwar al-Sadat. Sadat, initially virtually unknown by the Egyptian people, took many bold steps in cementing his role as leader of Egypt.

try's autocratic ruler, but they became bogged down in a civil war there and had to be withdrawn. Other efforts to unify the Arab world also failed. Arab leaders respected Nasser but were unwilling to play second fiddle to him in an organized Arab state. In 1967, after the Arab defeat, Nasser lashed out bitterly at the other Arab leaders. He said, "You issue statements, but we have to fight. If you want to liberate [Palestine] then get in line in front of us."[7]

Inside Egypt, the results of Nasser's 18-year rule were also mixed. Although he talked about developing representative government, Nasser distrusted political parties and remembered the destructive rivalries under the monarchy that had kept Egypt divided and weak. The Wafd and all other political parties were declared illegal. Nasser set up his own political organization to replace them, called the Arab Socialist Union (ASU). It was a mass party, but it had no real power. Nasser and a few close associates ran the government and controlled the ASU. The associates took their orders directly from Nasser; they called him *El-Rais*—"The Boss."

As he grew older, Nasser, plagued by health problems, became more dictatorial, secretive, and suspicious. The Boss tolerated no opposition and ensured tight control over Egypt with a large police force and a secret service that monitored activities in every village and town.

Nasser died in 1970. Ironically, his death came on the heels of a major policy success: the arranging of a truce between the Palestine Liberation Organization and the government of Jordan. Despite his health problems, Nasser had seemed indestructible, and his death came as a shock. Millions of Egyptians followed his funeral cortege through the streets of Cairo, weeping and wailing over the loss of their beloved Rais.

## ANWAR AL-SADAT

Nasser was succeeded by his vice-president, Anwar al-Sadat, in accordance with constitutional procedure. Sadat had been one of the original Free Officers and had worked with Nasser since their early days at the Military Academy. In the Nasser years, Sadat had come to be regarded as a lightweight, always ready to do whatever The Boss wanted.

Many Egyptians did not even know what Sadat looked like. A popular story was told of an Egyptian peasant in from the country to visit his cousin, a taxi driver. As they drove around Cairo, they passed a large poster of Nasser and Sadat shaking hands. "I know our beloved leader, but who is the man with him?" asked the peasant. "I think he owns that café across the street," replied his cousin.

When Sadat became president, however, it did not take long for the Egyptian people to learn what he looked like. Sadat introduced a "revolution of rectification," which he said was needed to correct the errors of his predecessor.[8] These included too much dependence on the Soviet Union, too much government interference in the economy, and failure to develop an effective Arab policy against Israel. He was a master of timing, taking bold action at unexpected times to advance Egypt's international and regional prestige. Thus, in 1972 he abruptly ordered the 15,000 Soviet advisers in Egypt to leave the country, despite the fact that they were training his army and supplying all his military equipment. His purpose was to reduce Egypt's dependence on one foreign power, and as he had calculated, the United States now came to his aid.

A year later, in October 1973, Egyptian forces crossed the Suez Canal in a surprise attack and broke through Israeli defense lines in occupied Sinai. The attack was coordinated with Syrian forces invading Israel from the east, through the Golan Heights. The Israelis were driven back with heavy casualties on both fronts, and although they eventually regrouped and won back most of the lost ground, Sadat felt he had won a moral and psychological victory. After the war, Egyptians believed that they had held their own with the Israelis and had demonstrated Arab ability to handle the sophisticated weaponry of modern warfare. On the 25th anniversary of the 1973 October War, Egypt held its first military parade in 17 years, and 250 young couples were married in a mass public wedding ceremony at the Pyramids to remind the new generation—a third of the population are under age 15—of Egypt's great "victory."

Anwar al-Sadat's most spectacular action took place in 1977. It seemed to him that the Arab–Israeli conflict was at a stalemate. Neither side would budge from its position, and the Egyptian people were angry at having so little to show for the 1973 success. In November, he addressed a hushed meeting of the People's Assembly and said, "Israel will be astonished when it hears me saying . . . that I am ready to go to their own house, to the Knesset itself, to talk to them."[9] And he did so, becoming for a second time the "Hero of the Crossing,"[10] but this time to the very citadel of Egypt's enemy.

Sadat's successes in foreign policy, culminating in the 1979 peace treaty with Israel, gave him great prestige internationally. Receipt of the Nobel Peace Prize, jointly with Israeli prime minister Menachem Begin, confirmed his status as a peacemaker. His pipe-smoking affability and sartorial elegance endeared him to U.S. policymakers.

The view that more and more Egyptians held of their world-famous leader was less flattering. Religious leaders and conservative Muslims objected to Sadat's luxurious style of living. The poor resented having to pay more for basic necessities. The educated classes were angry about Sadat's claim that the political system had become more open and democratic when, in fact, it had not. The Arab Socialist Union was abolished and several new political parties were allowed to organize. But the ASU's top leaders merely formed their own party, the National Democratic Party, headed by Sadat. For all practical purposes, Egypt under Sadat was even more of a single-party state under an authoritarian leader than it had been in Nasser's time.

Sadat's economic policies also worked to his disadvantage. In 1974, he announced a new program for postwar recovery, *Infitah* ("Opening"). It would be an open-door policy, bringing an end to Nasser's state-run socialist system. Foreign investors would be encouraged to invest in Egypt, and foreign experts would bring their technological knowledge to help develop industries. Infitah, properly applied, would bring an economic miracle to Egypt.

Rather than spur economic growth, however, Infitah made fortunes for just a few, leaving the great majority of Egyptians no better off than before. Chief among those who profited were members of the Sadat family. Corruption among the small ruling class, many of its members newly rich contractors, aroused anger on the part of the Egyptian people. In 1977, the economy was in such bad shape that the government increased bread prices. Riots broke out, and Sadat was forced to cancel the increase.

On October 6, 1981, President Sadat and government leaders were reviewing an armed-forces parade in Cairo to mark the eighth anniversary of the Crossing. Suddenly, a volley of shots rang out from one of the trucks in the parade. Sadat fell, mortally wounded. The assassins, most of them young military men, were immediately arrested. They belonged to *Al Takfir Wal Hijra* ("Repentance and Flight from Sin"), a secret group that advocated the reestablishment of a pure Islamic society in Egypt—by violence, if necessary. Their leader declared that the killing of Sadat was an essential first step in this process.

Islamic fundamentalism developed rapidly in the Middle East after the 1979 Iranian Revolution. The success of that revolution was a spur to Egyptian fundamentalists. They accused Sadat of favoring Western capitalism through his Infitah policy, of making peace with the "enemy of Islam" (Israel), and of not being a good Muslim. At their trial, Sadat's assassins said that they had acted to rid Egypt of an unjust ruler, a proper action under the laws of Islam.

Sadat may have contributed to his early death (he was 63) by a series of actions taken earlier in the year. About 1,600 people were arrested in September 1981 in a massive crackdown on religious unrest. They included not only religious leaders but also journalists, lawyers, intellectuals, provincial governors, and leaders of the country's small but growing opposition parties. Many of them were not connected with any fundamentalist Islamic organization. It seemed to most Egyptians that Sadat had overreacted, and at that point, he lost the support of the nation. In contrast to Nasser's funeral, few tears were shed at Sadat's. His funeral was attended mostly by foreign dignitaries. One of them said that Sadat had been buried without the people and without the army.

## MUBARAK IN POWER

Vice-President Hosni Mubarak, former Air Force commander and designer of Egypt's 1973 success against Israel, succeeded Sadat without incident. Mubarak dealt firmly with Islamic fundamentalism at the beginning of his regime. He was given emergency powers and approved death sentences for five of Sadat's assassins in 1982. But he moved cautiously in other areas of national life, in an effort to disassociate himself from some of Sadat's more unpopular policies. The economic policy of Infitah, which had led to widespread graft and corruption, was abandoned; stiff sentences were handed out to a number of entrepreneurs and capitalists, including Sadat's brother-in-law and several associates of the late president.

Mubarak also began rebuilding bridges with other Arab states that had been damaged after the peace treaty with Israel. Egypt was readmitted to membership in the Islamic Conference, the Islamic Development Bank, the Arab League, and other Arab regional organizations. In 1990, the Arab League headquarters was moved from Tunis back to Cairo, its original location. Egypt backed Iraq with arms and advisers in its war with Iran, but Mubarak broke with Saddam Hussain after the invasion of Kuwait, accusing the Iraqi leader of perfidy. Some 35,000 Egyptian troops served with the UN–U.S. coalition during the Gulf War; and as a result of these efforts, the country resumed its accustomed role as the focal point of Arab politics.

Despite the peace treaty, relations with Israel continued to be difficult. One bone of contention was removed in 1989 with the return of the Israeli-held enclave of Taba, in the Sinai Peninsula, to Egyptian control. It had been operated as an Israeli beach resort.

The return of Taba strengthened the government's claim that the 10-year-old peace treaty had been valuable overall in advancing Egypt's interests. The sequence of agreements between the Palestine Liberation Organization and Israel for a sovereign Palestinian entity, along with Israel's improved relations with its other Arab neighbors, contributed to a substantial thaw in the Egyptian "cold peace" with its former enemy. In March 1995, a delegation from Israel's Knesset arrived in Cairo, the first such parliamentary group to visit Egypt since the peace treaty.

But relations worsened after the election in 1996 of Benjamin Netanyahu as head of a new Israeli government. Egypt had strongly supported the Oslo accords for a Palestinian state, and it had set up a free zone for transit of Palestinian products in 1995. The Egyptian view that Netanyahu was not adhering to the accords led to a "war of words" between the two countries. Israeli tourists were discouraged from visiting Egypt or received hostile treatment when visiting Egyptian monuments, and almost no Egyptians opted for visits to Israel. The

newspaper *Al-Ahram* even stopped carrying cartoons by a popular Israeli-American cartoonist because he had served in the Israeli Army. The two governments cooperated briefly in the return of a small Bedouin tribe, the Azazma, to its Egyptian home area in the Sinai. The tribe had fled into Israel following a dispute with another tribe that turned into open conflict.

Ehud Barak's election as Israeli prime minister and his overtures for peace with the Palestinians were well received in Egypt. However, his resounding defeat in the 2000 elections by Ariel Sharon reinstituted the deep freeze in relations. The Israeli–Palestinian conflict has generated a great increase in anti-Israeli sentiments among the Egyptians. In part to counter these sentiments, but also to provide Israelis with a better understanding of the Arab world, a new government television station began broadcasting in Hebrew in December 2001.

## Internal Politics

Although Mubarak's unostentatious lifestyle and firm leadership encouraged confidence among the Egyptian regime, the system that he inherited from his predecessors remained largely impervious to change. The first free multiparty national elections held since the 1952 Revolution took place in 1984—although they were not entirely free, because a law requiring political parties to win at least 8 percent of the popular vote limited party participation. Mubarak was reelected easily for a full six-year term (he was the only candidate), and his ruling National Democratic Party won 73 percent of seats in the Assembly. The New Wafd Party was the only party able to meet the 8 percent requirement.

New elections for the Assembly in 1987 indicated how far Egypt's embryonic democracy had progressed under Mubarak. This time, four opposition parties aside from his own party presented candidates. Although the National Democratic Party's plurality was still a hefty 69.6 percent, 17 percent of the electorate voted for opposition candidates. The New Wafd increased its percentage of the popular vote to 10.9 percent, and a number of Muslim Brotherhood members were elected as independents. The National Progressive Unionist Group, the most leftist of the parties, failed to win a seat.

Mubarak was elected to a fourth six-year term in September 1999, making him Egypt's longest-serving head of state in the country's independent history. His victory margin was 94 percent, two points less than in 1993, when as per usual he was the only candidate. Some 79 percent

of Egypt's 24 million registered voters cast their ballots.

The January 2001 elections provided more evidence of public disaffection with Mubarak and the ruling party. The elections were held in stages beginning in October 2000. In the first stage, NDP candidates won only 38 of 118 seats. In the second and third stages, they won 179 of the Assembly's 454 seats. Some 218 seats were won by self-declared independents, and the rest by various minority parties. The independents subsequently aligned with NDP members to give the ruling party an 85 percent majority in the Legislature. However, barely 50 percent of eligible voters cast their ballots, emphasizing public disillusionment with the government.

## AT WAR WITH FUNDAMENTALISM

Egypt's seemingly intractable social problems—high unemployment, an inadequate job market flooded annually by new additions to the labor force, chronic budgetary deficits, and a bloated and inefficient bureaucracy, to name a few—have played into the hands of Islamic fundamentalists, those who would build a new Egyptian state based on the laws of Islam. Although they form part of a larger fundamentalist movement in the Islamic world, one that would replace existing secular regimes with regimes that adhere completely to spiritual law and custom (*Shari'a*), Egypt's fundamentalists do not harbor expansionist goals. Their goal is to replace the Mubarak regime with a more purely "Islamic" one, faithful to the laws and principles of the religion and dominated by religious leaders.

Egypt's fundamentalists are broadly grouped under the organizational name al-Gamaa al-Islamiya, with the more militant ones forming subgroups such as the Vanguard of Islam and Islamic Jihad, itself an outgrowth of al-Takfir wal-Hijra, which had been responsible for the assassination of Anwar Sadat. Ironically, Sadat had formed Al-Gamaa to counter leftist political groups. However, it differs from its parent organization, the Muslim Brotherhood, in advocating the overthrow of the government by violence in order to establish a regime ruled under Islamic law. During Mubarak's first term, he kept a tight lid on violence. But in the 1990s, the increasing strength of the Islamists and their popularity with the large number of educated but unemployed youth led to an increase in violence and destablized the nation.

Violence was initially aimed at government security forces, but starting in 1992, the fundamentalists' strategy shifted to vulnerable targets such as foreign tourists and the Coptic Christian minority. A number of Copts were killed and many Copt business owners were forced to pay "protection money" to al-Gamaa in order to continue in operation. Subsequently the Copts' situation improved somewhat, as stringent security measures were put in place to contain Islamic fundamentalist violence. Gun battles in 1999 between Muslim and Copt villagers in southern Egypt resulted in 200 Christian deaths and the arrests of a number of Muslims as well as Copts. Some 96 Muslims were charged with violence before a state-security court, but only four were convicted, and to short jail terms. However, Muslim–Coptic relations remained unstable. Early in 2002, two Coptic weekly newspapers, *Al Nabaa* and *Akbar Nabaa*, were shut down after the Superior Press Council, a quasi-government body, filed a lawsuit charging them with "offending Egyptians and undermining national unity."

Islamic Jihad, the major fundamentalist organization and the one responsible for Sadat's assassination, subsequently shifted its locale and objectives in order to evade the repression of the Mubarak government. Many of its members joined the fighters in Afghanistan who were resisting the Soviet occupation of that country. After the Soviet withdrawal in 1989, some 300 of them remained, forming the core of the Taliban force that eventually won control of 90 percent of Afghanistan. In that capacity, they became associated with Osama bin Laden and his al-Qaeda international terror network. Two of their leaders, Dr. Ayman al-Zawahiri (a surgeon) and Muhammad Atif, are believed to have planned the September 11, 2001, terrorist bombings in the United States. However, Islamic Jihad's chief aim is the overthrow of the Mubarak government and its replacement by an Islamic one. Its hostility to the United States stems from American support for that government and for the U.S. alliance with Israel against the Palestinians.

In targeting tourism in their campaign to overthrow the regime, fundamentalists have attacked tourist buses. Four tourists were killed in the lobby of a plush Cairo hotel in 1993. In November 1997, 64 tourists were gunned down in a grisly massacre at the Temple of Hatshepsut near Luxor, in the Valley of the Kings, one of Egypt's prize tourist attractions. Aftershocks from the terrorist attacks on the United States have decimated the tourist industry, which is Egypt's largest source of income ($4.3 billion in 2000, with 5.4 million visitors in that year). Egyptair, the national airline, lost $56 million in October 2001 alone; and cancellations of package tours, foreign-airline bookings, and hotel reservations led to a 45 percent drop in tourist revenues.

One important reason for the rise in fundamentalist violence stems from the government's ineptness in meeting social crises. After the disastrous earthquake of October 1992, Islamic fundamentalist groups were first to provide aid to the victims, distributing $1,000 to each family made homeless, while the cumbersome, multilayered government bureaucracy took weeks to respond to the crisis. Similarly, al-Gamaa established a network of Islamic schools, hospitals, clinics, daycare centers, and even small industries in poor districts such as Cairo's Imbaba quarter.

The Mubarak government's response to rising violence has been one of extreme repression. The death penalty may be imposed for "antistate terrorism." The state of emergency that was established after Anwar Sadat's assassination in 1981 has been renewed regularly, most recently in 2001 for a three-year extension, over the vehement protests of opposition deputies in the Assembly. Some 770 members of the Vanguard of Islam were tried and convicted of subversion in 1993. The crackdown left Egypt almost free from violence for several years. But in 1996, al-Gamaa and two other hitherto unknown Islamic militant groups, Assiut Terrorist Organization and Kotbion (named for a Muslim Brotherhood leader executed in 1966 for an attempt to kill President Nasser), resumed terrorist activities. Eighteen Greek tourists were murdered in April, and the State Security Court sentenced five Assiut members to death for killing police and civilians in a murderous rampage. At their trial they chanted "God make a staircase of our skulls to Your glory," waving Korans in their cage, in an eerie replay of the trials of Sadat's assassins.

An unfortunate result of government repression of the militants is that Egypt, traditionally an open, tolerant, and largely nonviolent society, has taken on many of the features of a totalitarian state. Human rights are routinely suspended, the prime offenders being officers of the dreaded State Security Investigation (SSI). Indefinite detention without charges is a common practice, and torture is used extensively to extract "confessions" from suspects or their relatives. All of al-Gamaa's leaders are either in prison, in exile, or dead; and with 20,000 suspected Islamists also jailed, the government could claim with some justification that it had broken the back of the 1990s

insurgency. Its confidence was enhanced in March 1999 when al-Gamaa said that it would no longer engage in violence. Two previous cease-fire offers had been spurned, but this newest offer resulted in the release of several hundred Islamists to "test its validity."

Due to the extremism of methods employed by both sides, the conflict between the regime and the fundamentalists has begun to polarize Egyptian society. As a prominent judge noted, "Islam has turned from a religion to an ideology. It has become a threat to Egypt, to civilization and to humanity."[11] In their struggle to overthrow the regime, the fundamentalists have either enlisted the support of or have declared war on scholars, journalists, teachers, and other secular intellectuals who do not openly advocate the fundamentalists' views. Censure and criticism of their works has turned to violence at times. Naguib Mahfouz, the Arab world's only Nobel laureate in literature, was seriously wounded in 1994 by a still-unidentified terrorist; and earlier, the novelist Farag Foda, a strong critic of what he called Egypt's "creeping" Islamization, was shot to death outside his Cairo home.

In 1995, the regime imposed further restrictions on Egypt's normally freewheeling press and journalistic bodies. A law would impose fines of up to $3,000 and five-yar jail sentences for articles "harmful to the state." The long arm of the law reached into the educational establishment as well. A university professor and noted Koranic scholar was charged with apostasy by clerics at Al-Azhar University, on the grounds that he had argued in his writings that the Koran should be interpreted in its historical/linguistic context alongside its identification as the Word of God. The charge came under the Islamic principle of *hisba,* "accountability." He was found guilty and ordered to divorce his wife, since a Muslim woman may not be married to an apostate. A 1996 law prohibited the use of hisba in the courts, but the damage had been done; the professor and his wife were forced into exile to preserve their marriage.

Another distinguished professor ran afoul of the government's Al-Azhar–imposed limits on free speech, as Saad Eddine Ibrahim, director of the American University at Cairo's Ibn Khaldoun Center for Democracy, was arrested in July 2000. He was charged with "defaming" Egypt in a documentary film that he had produced and distributed to encourage voter participation. The "defaming" charge came because the film mentioned fraud in earlier parliamentary elections. Ibrahim's arrest provoked a storm of international criti-

| Period of the pharaohs 2500–671 B.C. | The Persian conquest, followed by Macedonians and rule by Ptolemies 671–30 B.C. | Egypt becomes a Roman province 30 B.C. | Invading Arabs bring Islam A.D. 641 | The founding of Cairo 969 | Egypt becomes an Ottoman province 1517–1800 | Napoleon's invasion, followed by the rise to power of Muhammad Ali 1798–1831 | The Suez Canal opens to traffic 1869 | The United Kingdom establishes a protectorate 1882 |
|---|---|---|---|---|---|---|---|---|
| ● | ● | ● | ● | ● | ● | ● | ● | ● |

cism, from both governments and human-rights groups. (He holds dual Egyptian–American citizenship.) He was released, but in May 2001 he was tried and sentenced to a seven-year jail term. The case was heard by the Supreme Security Court, which bars appeals under Egyptian law. International human-rights organizations such as Amnesty International criticized the Court's decision and lack of appeals procedure as violations of international law. The head of the Group for Developing Democracy (which monitors civil rights in the country) observed, "Egypt doesn't want real democracy. The state wants us as puppets in its big show of paper democracy, and if we decide otherwise it knocks us down."[12]

Despite its huge majority in the Assembly and its ruthless pursuit of Islamic militants, the Mubarak regime thus far has failed to deal effectively with the political, economic, and social inequities and lack of freedoms that continue to hamper Egypt's development. Observers have commented on Mubarak's mindset about Islamic groups, arguing that he makes no distinction between militants and moderates. As a result, Islamists now control the trade and student unions, schools, even the judiciary, forcing the general public to choose between them and a repressive regime.

## A STRUGGLING ECONOMY

Egypt's economy rests upon a narrow and unstable base, due to rapid demographic growth and limited arable land and because political factors have adversely influenced national development. The country has a relatively high level of education and, as a result, is a net exporter of skilled labor to other Arab countries. But the overproduction of university graduates has produced a bloated and inefficient bureaucracy, as the government is required to provide a position for every graduate who cannot find other employment.

Agriculture is the most important sector of the economy, accounting for about one third of national income. The major crops are long-staple cotton and sugarcane. Egyptian agriculture since time immemorial has been based on irrigation from the Nile River. In recent years, greater control of irrigation water through the Aswan High Dam, expansion of land devoted to cotton production, and improved planting methods have begun to show positive results.

A new High Dam at Aswan, completed in 1971 upstream from the original one built in 1906, resulted from a political decision by the Nasser government to seek foreign financing for its program of expansion of cultivable land and generation of electricity for industrialization. When Western lending institutions refused to finance the dam, also for political reasons, Nasser turned to the Soviet Union for help. By 1974, just three years after its completion, revenues had exceeded construction costs. The dam made possible the electrification of all of Egypt's villages as well as a fishing industry at Lake Nasser, its reservoir. It proved valuable in providing the agricultural sector with irrigation water during the prolonged 1980–1988 drought, although at sharply reduced levels. However, the increased costs of land reclamation and loss of the sardine fishing grounds along the Mediterranean coast have made the dam a mixed blessing for Egypt.

Egypt was self-sufficient in foodstuffs as recently as the 1970s but now must import 60 percent of its food. Such factors as rapid population growth, rural-to-urban migration with consequent loss of agricultural labor, and Sadat's open-door policy for imports combined to produce this negative food balance. Subsidies for basic commodities, which cost the government nearly $2 billion a year, are an important cause of inflation, since they keep the budget continuously in deficit. Fearing a recurrence of the 1977 Bread Riots, the government kept prices in check. However, inflation, which had dropped to 8 percent in 1995 due to International Monetary Fund stabilization policies required for loans, rose to 37 percent in 1999 as the new free-market policy produced a tidal wave of imports. As a result, the foreign trade deficit increased drastically.

Egypt has important oil and natural-gas deposits, and new discoveries continue to strengthen this sector of the economy. Oil reserves increased to 3.3 billion barrels in 2001, due to new fields being brought on stream in the Western Desert. Proven natural-gas reserves are 51 trillion cubic feet, sufficient to meet domestic needs for 30 years at current rates of consumption.

A 2001 agreement with Jordan would guarantee Jordan's purchase of Egyptian natural-gas supplies, contingent on completion of the pipeline under the Red Sea from Al-Arish to Aqaba. But an earlier agreement with Israel, Egypt's closest and potentially most lucrative gas market, has been put on hold due to the renewed Palestinian–Israeli conflict. Under the agreement, Egypt would have provided $300 million a year in gas, meeting 15 percent of Israel's electric-power needs.

Egypt also derives revenues from Suez Canal tolls and user fees, from tourism, and from remittances from Egyptian workers abroad, mostly working in Saudi Arabia and other oil-producing Gulf states. The flow of remittances from the approximately 4 million expatriate workers was reduced and then all but cut off with the Iraqi invasion of Kuwait. Egyptians fled from both countries in panic, arriving home as penniless refugees. With unemployment already at 20 percent and housing in short supply, the government faced an enormous assimilation problem apart from its loss of revenue. The United States helped by agreeing to write off $4.5 billion in Egyptian military debts. By 1995, the expatriate crisis caused by returning workers had eased somewhat, with 1 million Egyptian workers employed in Saudi Arabia and smaller numbers in other Arab countries.

One encouraging sign of brighter days ahead is the expansion of local manufacturing industries, in line with government efforts to reduce dependence upon imported goods. A 10-year tax exemption plus remission of customs duties on imported machinery have encouraged a number of new business ventures, notably in the clothing industry.

In 1987, Mubarak gained some foreign help for Egypt's cash-strapped economy when agreement was reached with the International Monetary Fund for a standby credit of $325 million over 18 months to allow the country to meet its balance-of-payments deficit. The Club of Paris, a group of public and private banks from various industrialized countries, then rescheduled $12 billion in Egyptian external debts over a 10-year period.

Expanded foreign aid and changes in government agricultural policy required by the World Bank for new loans helped

| The Free Officers overthrow the monarchy and establish Egypt as a republic 1952 | Nationalization of the Suez Canal 1956 | Union with Syria into the United Arab Republic 1958–1961 | The Six-Day War with Israel ends in Israel's occupation of the Gaza Strip and the Sinai Peninsula 1967 | Gamal Abdel Nasser dies; Anwar Sadat succeeds as head of Egypt 1970 | A peace treaty is signed at Camp David between Egypt and Israel 1979 | Sadat is assassinated; he is succeeded by Hosni Mubarak; a crackdown on Islamic fundamentalists. 1980s | The government employs totalitarian tactics in its battle with fundamentalists 1990s |
| --- | --- | --- | --- | --- | --- | --- | --- |

2000s

Deep social and economic problems persist

spur economic recovery in the 1990s, especially in agriculture. Production records were set in 1996 in wheat, corn, and rice, meeting 50 percent of domestic needs. The cotton harvest for that year was 350,000 tons, with 50,000 tons exported. However, a new agricultural law passed in 1992 but not implemented until 1997 ended land rents, allowing landlords to set their own leases and in effect reclaim their properties taken over by the government during the Nasser era. The purpose is to provide an incentive for tenant farmers to grow export crops such as cotton and rice. But as a result, Egypt's 900,000 tenant farmers have faced the loss of lands held on long-term leases for several generations.

However, these economic successes must be balanced against Egypt's chronic social problems and the lack of an effective representative political system. The head of the Muslim Brotherhood made the astute observation in a 1993 speech that "the threat is not in the extremist movement. It is in the absence of democratic institutions." Until such institutions are firmly in place, with access to education, full employment, broad political participation, civil rights, and the benefits of growth spread evenly across all levels of society, unrest and efforts to Islamize the government by force are likely to continue.

By 2000, the government's harsh repression had seriously weakened the fundamentalist movement, albeit at a heavy cost. Some 1,200 police officers and militants had been killed during the 1990s, and 16,000 persons remained jailed without charges on suspicion of membership in Islamic Jihad or other organizations. However, public disaffection continues to grow and to involve inceasing numbers of nonfundamentalists. In May 2000, a demonstration by several hundred Al-Azhar students protesting the reprinting of a 1983 novel by Syrian writer Haider Haider was broken up by police. The demonstrators charged that the novel was insulting both to the Prophet Muhammad and to Islam; it had been reprinted as part of a Ministry of Culture project to promote modern Arabic literature. In 2001, the Cairo Book Fair, one of the Arab world's biggest cultural events, was boycotted by many Egyptian writers and editors, after its sponsor, the same Ministry of Culture, had banned a number of books. They were declared to be pornographic by Muslim Brotherhood members of the Legislature and criticized by Al-Azhar faculty as being offensive to Islam.

Egypt's own difficulties with fundamentalists caused some reluctance on its part when support for the U.S.–led international coalition against terrorism formed after the September 11, 2001, bombings of the World Trade Center in New York City and the Pentagon near Washington, D.C. The reluctance stemmed in part from public anger over continued American support for Israel against the Palestinians and the suffering of Iraq's fellow Arabs under the 11-year sanctions imposed on that country.

## NOTES

1. Leila Ahmed, in *A Border Passage* (New York: Farrar, Strauss & Giroux, 1999), deals at length with Egyptian vs. Arab identity from the perspective of growing up in British-controlled Egypt.

2. An English observer said, "In arms and firing they are nearly as perfect as European troops." Afaf L. Marsot, *Egypt in the Reign of Muhammad Ali* (Cambridge, England: Cambridge University Press, 1984), p. 132.

3. *Ibid.,* p. 161.

4. Quoted in P. J. Vatikiotis, *Nasser and His Generation* (New York: St. Martin's Press, 1978), p. 35.

5. Gamal Abdel Nasser, *The Philosophy of the Revolution* (Cairo: Ministry of National Guidance, 1954), p. 52.

6. Derek Hopwood, *Egypt: Politics and Society 1945–1981* (London: George Allen and Unwin, 1982), p. 77.

7. Quoted in Vatikiotis, *op. cit.,* p. 245.

8. Hopwood, *op. cit.,* p. 106.

9. David Hirst and Irene Beeson, *Sadat* (London: Faber and Faber, 1981), p. 255.

10. "Banners slung across the broad thoroughfares of central Cairo acclaimed The Hero of the Crossing (of the October 1973 War)." *Ibid.,* pp. 17–18.

11. Said Ashmawy, quoted in "In God He Trusts," *Jerusalem Post Magazine* (July 7, 1995).

12. Neged Borat, quoted in *The New York Times* (May 21, 2001).

## DEVELOPMENT

Between 1998 and 2001, Egypt's economic growth rate dropped slightly, from 5.7% to 4.9%. The tourist industry has been hard hit by the terrorist attacks in the United States and by the outbreak of renewed Palestinian–Israeli violence. However, new oil and gas discoveries and the completion of the $1.5 billion environmentally friendly Middle East Oil Refinery (MIDOR), which has a refining capacity of 100,000 b/d, have encouraged hopes for economic recovery.

## FREEDOM

The Islamic fundamentalist challenge to Egypt's secular government has caused the erosion of many rights and freedoms enshrined in the country's Constitution. A state of emergency first issued in 1981 is still in effect; it was renewed in 2001 for a 3-year period. Partly to outflank the fundamentalists, the government came down hard on the gay community. Some 52 homosexuals were arrested and charged by the Emergency State-Security Court with "habitual debauchery" and "contempt of religion"; 23 received prison sentences of 1 to 5 years with no appeal.

## HEALTH/WELFARE

Women in Egypt won a victory for their own and human rights generally in 1999 when the Supreme Administrative Court upheld a government ban on female circumcision. A new Family Law in 2001 allows women to file for divorce and to receive public assistance for nonpayment of support by their ex-husbands. However, the delays caused by overburdened courts, the huge backlog of cases, and the requirement that the husband agree to the divorce have largely negated the law. A 30-year campaign to eradicate schistosomiasis not only failed, but due to use of unsterilized needles and syringes in the necessary injections, resulted in an increase in hepatits C. It now affects 20% of Egypt's population and is rapidly reaching epidemic proportions.

## ACHIEVEMENTS

Alexandria, founded in 332 B.C. by Alexander the Great, was one of the world's great cities in antiquity, with its Library, its Pharos (Lighthouse), its palaces, and other monuments. Most of them were destroyed by fire or sank into the sea long ago, as the city fell into neglect. Then, in 1995, underwater archaelogists discovered the ruins of the Pharos; its location had not been known previously. Other discoveries followed—the palace of Cleopatra, the remains of Napoleon's fleet (sunk by the British in the Battle of the Nile), Roman and Greek trading vessels filled with amphorae, etc. The restoration of the Library was completed in 2000, with half of its 11 floors under the Mediterranean; visitors in the main reading room are surrounded by water cascading down its windows. After centuries of decay, Alexandria is again a magnet for tourists.

# Iran (Islamic Republic of Iran)

## GEOGRAPHY

*Area in Square Miles (Kilometers):* 636,294 (1,648,000) (about the size of Alaska)

*Capital (Population):* Teheran (6,836,000)

*Environmental Concerns:* air and water pollution; deforestation; overgrazing; desertification; oil pollution; insufficient potable water

*Geographical Features:* a rugged, mountainous rim; a high central basin with deserts and mountains; discontinuous plains along both coasts

*Climate:* mostly arid or semiarid; subtropical along Caspian

## PEOPLE

### Population

*Total:* 66,129,000

*Annual Growth Rate:* 0.7%

*Rural/Urban Population Ratio:* 40/60

*Major Languages:* Farsi (Persian); Azeri Turkish; Kurdish

*Ethnic Makeup:* 51% Persian; 24% Azeri; 8% Gilaki and Mazandarani; 7% Kurd; 10% others

*Religions:* 89% Shia Muslim; 10% Sunni Muslim; 1% Zoroastrian, Jewish, Christian, or Bahai

### Health

*Life Expectancy at Birth:* 69 years (male); 71 years (female)

*Infant Mortality Rate (Ratio):* 29/1,000

*Physicians Available (Ratio):* 1/1,600

### Education

*Adult Literacy Rate:* 72%

*Compulsory (Ages):* 6–10; free

## COMMUNICATION

*Telephones:* 6,600,000 main lines

*Daily Newspaper Circulation:* 20 per 1,000 people

*Televisions:* 117 per 1,000

*Internet Service Providers:* 8 (2000)

## TRANSPORTATION

*Highways in Miles (Kilometers):* 86,924 (140,200)

*Railroads in Miles (Kilometers):* 3,472 (5,600)

*Usable Airfields:* 317

*Motor Vehicles in Use:* 2,189,000

## GOVERNMENT

*Type:* theocratic republic

*Independence Date:* April 1, 1979 (Islamic Republic of Iran proclaimed)

*Head of State/Government:* Supreme Guide Ayatollah Ali Hoseini-Khamenei; President Mohammed Khatami

*Political Parties:* none legal; Islamic Iran Partnership Front unites various reform groups and holds a majority of seats in the elected Majlis

*Suffrage:* universal at 15

## MILITARY

*Military Expenditures (% of GDP):* 2.9%

*Current Disputes:* disputes with Iraq over border demarcation, prisoners of war, and the Shatt al-Arab waterway; territorial disputes with United Arab Emirates; undetermined Caspian Sea boundaries

## ECONOMY

*Currency ($ U.S. Equivalent):* 1,741 rials = $1

*Per Capita Income/GDP:* $6,300/$413 billion

*GDP Growth Rate:* 5%

*Inflation Rate:* 14%

*Unemployment Rate:* 25%

*Labor Force:* 17,300,000

*Natural Resources:* petroleum; natural gas; coal; chromium; copper; iron ore; lead; manganese; zinc; sulfur

*Agriculture:* grains; sugar beets; fruits; nuts; cotton; dairy products; wool; caviar

*Industry:* petroleum; petrochemicals; textiles; cement and other construction materials; food processing; metal fabrication; armaments

*Exports:* $25 billion (primary partners Japan, Italy, United Arab Emirates)

*Imports:* $15 billion (primary partners Germany, South Korea, Italy)

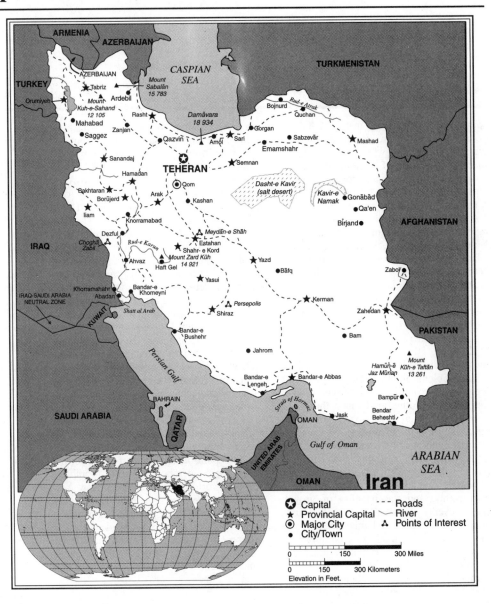

# IRAN

Iran is in many respects a subcontinent, ranging in elevation from Mount Demavend (18,386 feet) to the Caspian Sea, which is below sea level. Most of Iran consists of a high plateau ringed by mountains. Much of the plateau is covered with uninhabitable salt flats and deserts—the Dasht-i-Kavir and Dasht-i-Lut, the latter being one of the most desolate and inhospitable regions in the world. The climate is equally forbidding. The so-called Wind of 120 Days blows throughout the summer in eastern Iran, bringing dust and extremely high temperatures.

Most of the country receives little or no rainfall. Settlement and population density are directly related to the availability of water. The most densely populated region is along the Caspian Sea coast, which has an annual rainfall of 80 inches. The provinces of Azerbaijan in the northwest and Khuzestan along the Iraqi border, and the urban areas around Iran's capital, Teheran, are also heavily populated.

Water is so important to the Iranian economy that all water resources were nationalized in 1967. Lack of rainfall caused the development of a sophisticated system of underground conduits, *qanats*, to carry water across the plateau from a water source, usually at the base of a mountain. Many qanats were built thousands of years ago and are still in operation. They make existence possible for much of Iran's rural population.

Until the twentieth century, the population was overwhelmingly rural; but due to rural–urban migration, the urban population has increased steadily. Nearly all of this migration has been to Teheran, whose metropolitan area now has a population of nearly 7 million, as compared to 200,000 in 1900. Yet the rural population has also increased. This fact has had important political consequences for Iran, when it was a monarchy as well as an Islamic republic. Attachment to the land, family solidarity, and high birth rates have preserved the strong rural element in Iranian society as a force for conservatism and loyalty to religious leaders, who then are able to influence whatever regime is in power. Indeed, the rural population strongly supported the first Islamic regime and contributed much of the volunteer manpower recruited to defend the country after the invasion by Iraqi forces in 1980.

## ETHNIC AND RELIGIOUS DIVERSITY

Due to Iran's geographic diversity, the population is divided into a large number of separate and often conflicting ethnic groups. Ethnic Iranians constitute the majority. The Iranians (or *Persians,* from Parsa, the province where they first settled) are an Indo-European people whose original home was probably in Central Asia. They moved into Iran around 1100 B.C. and gradually dominated the entire region, establishing the world's first empire (in the sense of rule over various unrelated peoples in a large territory). Although its rulers failed to conquer Greece and thereby extend their empire into Europe, such achievements as their imperial system of government, the Persian language (Farsi), the monumental architecture of their capital at Persepolis, and their distinct cultural/historical heritage provide modern Iranians with pride in their ancient past and a national identity, unbroken to the present day.

The largest ethnic minority group is the Azeri (or Azerbaijani) Turks. The Azeris live in northwestern Iran. Their ethnic origin dates back to the ancient Persian Empire, when Azerbaijan was known as Atropene. The migration of Turkish peoples into this region in the eleventh and twelfth centuries A.D. encouraged the spread of the Turkish language and of Islam. These were reinforced by centuries of Ottoman rule, although Persian remained the written and literary language of the people.

Turkish dynasties originating in Azerbaijan controlled Iran for several centuries and were responsible for much of premodern Islamic Iran's political power and cultural achievements. In the late nineteenth and early twentieth centuries, Azeris were in the forefront of the constitutional movement to limit the absolute power of Iranian monarchs. They formed the core of the first Iranian Parliament. The Azeris have consistently fought for regional autonomy from the central Iranian government in the modern period and refer to their province as "Azadistan, Land of Freedom."

The Kurds are another large ethnic minority. Iran's Kurd population is concentrated in the Zagros Mountains along the Turkish and Iraqi borders. The Kurds are Sunni Muslims, as distinct from the Shia majority. The Iranian Kurds share a common language, culture, social organization, and ethnic identity with Kurds in Iraq, Turkey, and Syria. Kurds are strongly independent mountain people who lack a politically recognized homeland and who have been unable to unite to form one. The Kurds of Iran formed their own Kurdish Republic, with Soviet backing, after World War II. But the withdrawal of Soviet troops, under international pressure, caused its collapse. Since then, Iranian Kurdish leaders have devoted their efforts toward greater regional autonomy. Kurd-

ish opposition to the central Iranian government was muted during the rule of the Pahlavi dynasty (1925–1979), but it broke into the open after the establishment of the Islamic republic. The Kurds feared that they would be oppressed under the Shia Muslim government headed by Ayatollah Khomeini and boycotted the national referendum approving the republic. Central-government authority over the Kurds was restored in 1985. In 1992, Iraqi Kurdish leaders made an agreement with the Iranian government for deliveries of fuel and spare parts for their beleaguered enclave; in return, they pledged that the enclave would not be used by the People's Mujahideen or any other antigovernment group for military actions against Iran.

The Arabs are another important minority group (Iran and Turkey are the two Islamic countries in this region of the world with a non-Arab majority). The Arabs live in Khuzestan Province, along the Iraqi border. The Baluchi, also Sunni Muslims, are located in southeast Iran and are related to Baluchi groups in Afghanistan and Pakistan. They are seminomadic and have traditionally opposed any form of central-government control. The Baluchi were the first minority to oppose openly the fundamentalist Shia policies of the Khomeini government. Non-Islamic minorities include Jews, Zoroastrians, and Armenians and other Christians. Altogether they make up 1 percent of the population. They are represented in the *Majlis* (Parliament) by two Armenian deputies and one each for Zoroastrians and Jews. Zoroastrians, about 30,000 in all, follow the ancient Persian religion preached by the prophet Zoroaster 2,500 years ago. Zoroaster defined life as a constant struggle between good (*Ahura Mazda*, "light") and evil (*Ahriman*, "darkness"). Zoroastrianism was the official religion of Iran during the pre-Islamic Sassanid empire. Its priests formed a privileged class, charged with responsibility for tending the sacred fire, which was (and still is) kept burning in the fire temples that are centers of faith and worship. Zoroastrians also traditionally buried their dead atop "towers of silence" rather than pollute the ground. Their religiously based customs and traditions have carried over into modern Iranian life. Thus Nowruz ("New Year"), the beginning of spring, the most important and popular of Iranian festivals, is Zoroastrian in origin, as is the solar calendar introduced by Reza Shah to replace the Arabic lunar one.

The Armenians, another small minority, are also protected under Article 13 of the republic's Constitution. Formerly, Armenians were important middlemen and traders

Iranian society today has a considerable level of cultural conformity. Shia Islam is the dominant religion of Iran, and observance of this form of Islam permeates society, as this prayer meeting at Teheran University attests.

in Iran. Armenian hairstylists were very popular before the Revolution, but the republic's strict Islamic code on male–female contacts forced them, as men, out of business. Armenian butcher shops are also required to post signs saying "Minority Religion" because they sell pork.

The Bahais, a splinter movement from Islam founded by an Iranian mystic called the *Bab* ("Door," i.e., to wisdom) and organized by a teacher named Baha'Ullah in the nineteenth century, are the largest non-Muslim minority group. Although Baha'Ullah taught the principles of universal love, peace, harmony, and brotherhood, his proclamations of equality of the sexes, ethnic unity, the oneness of all religions, and a universal rather than a Muslim God aroused the hostility of Shia religious leaders. Bahais in Iran were protected from Shia hostility during the Qajar and Pahlavi monarchy periods. But with the overthrow of Mohammed Reza Pahlavi, the religious leaders of the Islamic Republic undertook a campaign of persecution and mistreatment described by outside observers as "the genocide of a non-combatant people."[1]

Since 1979, more than 200 Bahais have been executed, and 800 jailed for various periods. The Bahai Institute of Higher Education, opened privately since Bahais are prohibited from attending Iranian universities, was shut down in 1998 by security police. The Khatami government has been less repressive than its predecessors on the Bahais, and a number of them have been able to obtain visas to emigrate to the United States. Bahai properties and businesses have been confiscated.

Despite Iran's official hostility toward Israel, its own Jewish population is recognized as a minority under the 1979 Constitution and has lived there for centuries. Some 100,000 Jews once lived in Iran, but emigration to Israel, the United States, and elsewhere has reduced their numbers. There are about 28,000 Jews in Iran today. They have been protected as "People of the Book" for generations; they observe their dietary laws without restriction, and their divorce, burial, and other laws are accepted in the Islamic courts. They also elect one deputy to the Majlis. However, the tensions in Iranian society between those favoring more openness to the outside world and hard-liners opposed to any accommodation, particularly with the United States and its Israeli ally, brought disaster to the Jewish community in Iran in 1999. Thirteen Jews were arrested and charged with spying for Israel. They included a rabbi, a university professor, office workers, and students. The trial began in May. Despite appeals from Jewish groups abroad and international criticism of the trial itself as being politically motivated, 10 of the defendants were given prison terms of up to 13 years; three were acquitted. The relative leniency of the sentences—the death sentence for espionage is normal in the Islamic Republic—underscored the trial's political nature. It met international demands for judicial fairness as well as the need to satisfy hard-liners. However, the Iranian Supreme Court denied an appeal by defense lawyers in 2001, saying that it had no legal basis for their consideration.

## CULTURAL CONFORMITY

Despite the separatist tendencies in Iranian society caused by the existence of these various ethnic groups and religious divisions, there is considerable cultural conformity. Most Iranians, regardless of background, display distinctly Iranian values, customs, and traditions. Unifying features include the Farsi language, Islam as the overall religion, the appeal (since the sixteenth century) of Shia Islam as an Iranian nationalistic force, and a sense of nationhood derived from Iran's long history and cultural continuity.

Iranians at all levels have a strongly developed sense of class structure. It is a three-tier structure, consisting of upper, middle, and lower classes. However, some scholars distinguish two lower classes: the urban wage earner, and the landed or landless peasant. The basic socioeconomic unit in this class structure is the patriarchal family, which functions in Iranian society as a tree trunk does in relation to its branches. The patriarch of each family is not only disciplinarian and decisionmaker but also guardian of the family honor and inheritance.

The patriarchal structure, in terms of the larger society, has defined certain behavioral norms. These include the seclusion of women, ceremonial politeness *(ta'aruf)*, hierarchical authoritarianism with domination by superiors over subordinates, and the importance of face *(aberu)*—maintaining "an appropriate bearing and appearance commensurate with one's social status."[2] Under the republic, these norms have been increasingly Islamized as religious leaders have asserted the primacy of Shia Islam in all aspects of Iranian life.

## HISTORY

Modern Iran occupies a much smaller territory than that of its predecessors. The Persian Empire (sixth–fourth centuries B.C.) included Egypt, the Arab Near East, Afghanistan, and much of Central Asia, prior to its overthrow by Alexander of Macedon. The Parthian and Sassanid monarchies were major rivals of Rome. Under the latter rulers (A.D. 226–651), Zoroastrianism became the state religion. The Sassanid administrative system, which divided its territory into provinces under a single central authority, was taken over intact by invading Arab armies bringing Islam to the land.

The establishment of Islam brought significant changes into Iranian life. Arab armies defeated the Sassanid forces at the Battle of Qadisiya (A.D. 637) and the later Battle of Nihavand (A.D. 641), which resulted in the death of the last Sassanid king and the fall of his empire. The Arabs gradually established control over all the former Sassanid territories, converting the inhabitants to Islam as they went. But the well-established Iranian cultural and social system provided refinements for Islam that were lacking in its early existence as a purely Arab religion. The Iranian converts to Islam converted the religion from a particularistic Arab faith to a universal faith. Islamic culture, in the broad sense—embracing literature, art, architecture, music, certain sciences and medicine—owes a great deal to the contributions of Iranian Muslims such as the poets Hafiz and Sa'di, the poet and astronomer Omar Khayyam, and many others.

Shia Muslims, currently the vast majority of the Iranian population and represented in nearly all ethnic groups, were in the minority in Iran during the formative centuries of Islam. Only one of the Twelve Shia Imams—the eighth, Reza—actually lived in Iran. (His tomb at Meshed is now the holiest shrine in Iran.) *Taqiya* ("dissimulation" or "concealment")—the Shia practice of hiding one's beliefs to escape Sunni persecution—added to the difficulties of the Shia in forming an organized community.

In the sixteenth century, the Safavids, who claimed to be descendants of the Prophet Muhammad, established control over Iran with the help of Turkish tribes. The first Safavid ruler, Shah Ismail, proclaimed Shiism as the official religion of his state and invited all Shias to move to Iran, where they would be protected. Shia domination of the country dates from this period. Shia Muslims converged on Iran from other parts of the Islamic world and became a majority in the population.

The Safavid rulers were bitter rivals of the Sunni Ottoman sultans and fought a number of wars with them. The conflict was religious as well as territorial. The Ottoman sultan assumed the title of caliph of Islam in the sixteenth century after the conquest of Egypt, where the descendants of the last Abbasid caliph of Baghdad had taken refuge. As caliph, the sultan claimed the right to speak for, and rule, all Muslims. The Safavids rejected this claim and called on Shia Muslims to struggle against him. In more recent years, the Khomeini government issued a similar call to Iranians to carry on war against the Sunni rulers of Iraq, indicating that Shia willingness to struggle and, if necessary, incur martyrdom was still very much alive in Iran.

### King of Kings

The Qajars, a new dynasty of Turkish tribal origin, came to power after a bloody struggle at the end of the eighteenth century. They made Teheran their capital. Most of Iran's current borders were defined in the nineteenth century by treaties with foreign powers—Britain (on behalf of India), Russia, and the Ottoman Empire. Due to Iran's military weaknesses, the agreements favored the outside powers and the country lost much of its original territory.

Despite Iran's weakness in relation to foreign powers, the Qajar rulers sought to revive the ancient glories of the monarchy at home. They assumed the old Persian title *Shahinshah,* "King of Kings." At his coronation, each ruler sat on the Peacock Throne, the gilded, jewel-encrusted treasure brought to Iran by Nadir Shah, conqueror of northern India and founder of the short-lived Iranian Afshar dynasty. They assumed other grandiose titles, such as "Shadow of God on Earth" and "Asylum of the Universe." A shah once told an English visitor, "Your King, then, appears to be no more than a first magistrate. I, on the other hand, can elevate or degrade all the high nobles and officers you see around me!"[3]

Qajar pomp and grandeur were more illusion than reality, as was shown in a recent exhibit of Qajar art. Thus portraits of Fath Ali Shah, the second Qajar ruler, show him receiving the bows of European envoys, in poses meant to duplicate those of the great Sassanid rulers of the pre-Islamic Iranian past. Unfortunately, Iran's grandeur had passed. Its strategic location between British-ruled India and the Russian Empire that extended across Central Asia guaranteed that it would become a pawn in the contest for control, usually referred to as the "Great Game." Under these difficult circumstances, Qajar rulers survived mainly by manipulating tribal leaders and other groups against one another with the tacit support of the mullahs (religious leaders).

Nasr al-Din Shah, Iran's ruler for most of the nineteenth century, was responsible for a large number of concessions to European bankers, promoters, and private companies. His purpose was to demonstrate to European powers that Iran was becoming a modern state and to find new revenues without having to levy new taxes, which would have aroused more dangerous opposition. The various concessions helped to modernize Iran, but they bankrupted the treasury in the process. The shah also wanted to prove to the European powers that Iran had a modern army. A contract was signed with Russia for officers from the Cossacks, a powerful Russian group, to train an elite Iranian military unit, the Cossack Brigade.

In the mid-nineteenth century, the shah was encouraged by European envoys to turn his attention to education as a means of creating a modern society. In 1851, he opened the Polytechnic College, with European instructors, to teach military science and technical subjects. The graduates of this college, along with other Iranians who had been sent to Europe for their education and a few members of aristocratic families, became the nucleus of a small but influential intellectual elite. Along with their training in military subjects, they acquired European ideas of nationalism and progress. They were "government men" in the sense that they worked for and belonged to the shah's government.

But they also came to believe that the Iranian people needed to unite into a nation, with representative government and a European-style educational system, in order to become a part of the modern world. The views of these intellectuals put them at odds with the shah, who cared nothing for representative government or civil rights, only for tax collection. The intellectuals also found themselves at odds with the mullahs, who controlled the educational system and feared any interference with their superstitious, illiterate subjects.

The intellectuals and mullahs both felt that the shah was giving away Iran's assets and resources to foreigners. For a long time the intellectuals were the only group to complain; the illiterate Iranian masses could not be expected to protest against actions they knew nothing about. But in 1890, the shah gave a 50-year concession to a Briton named Talbot for a monopoly over the export and distribution of tobacco. Faced with higher prices for the tobacco they grew themselves, Iranians staged a general strike and boycott, and the shah was forced to cancel the concession. The pattern of local protest leading to mass rebellion, with all population groups uniting against an arbitrary ruler, was to be duplicated in the Constitutional Revolt of 1905 and again in the 1979 Revolution.

By the end of the nineteenth century, the people were roused to action, the mullahs had turned against the ruler, and the intellectuals were demanding a constitution that would limit his powers. One of the intellectuals wrote, "It is self-evident that in the future no nation—Islamic or non-Islamic—will continue to exist without constitutional law. . . . The various ethnic groups that live in Iran will not become one people until the law upholds their right to freedom of expression and the opportunity for [modern] education."[4] One century and two revolutions later, Iran is still struggling to put this formula into operation.

According to Roy Mottahedeh, "the bazaar and the mosque are the two lungs of public life in Iran."[5] The bazaar, like the Greek agora and the Roman forum, is the place where things are bought, deals are consummated, and political issues are aired for public consideration or protest. The mosque is the bastion of religious opinion; its preachers can, and do, mobilize the faithful to action through thundering denunciations of rulers and government officials. Mosque and bazaar came together in 1905 to bring about the first Iranian Revolution, a forerunner, at least in pattern, of the 1979 revolt. Two sugar merchants were bastinadoed (a punishment, still used in Iran, in which the soles of the feet are beaten with a cane) because they refused to lower their prices; they complained that high import prices set by the government gave them no choice. The bazaar then closed down in protest. With commercial activity at a standstill, the shah agreed to establish a "house of justice" and to promulgate a constitution. But six months later, he still had done nothing. Then a mullah was arrested and killed for criticizing the ruler in a Friday sermon. Further protests were met with mass arrests and then gun-

fire; "a river of blood now divided the court from the country."[6]

In 1906, nearly all of the religious leaders left Teheran for the sanctuary of Qum, Iran's principal theological-studies center. The bazaar closed down again, a general strike paralyzed the country, and thousands of Iranians took refuge in the British Embassy in Teheran. With the city paralyzed, the shah gave in. He granted a Constitution that provided for an elected Majlis, the first limitation on royal power in Iran in its history. Four more shahs would occupy the throne, two of them as absolute rulers, but the 1906 Constitution and the elected Legislature survived as brakes on absolutism until the 1979 Revolution. In this sense, the Islamic Republic is the legitimate heir to the constitutional movement.

### The Pahlavi Dynasty

Iran was in chaos at the end of World War I. British and Russian troops partitioned the country, and after the collapse of Russian power due to the Bolshevik Revolution, the British dictated a treaty with the shah that would have made Iran a British protectorate. Azeris and Kurds talked openly of independence; and a Communist group, the Jangalis, organized a "Soviet Republic" of Gilan along the Caspian coast.

The only organized force in Iran at this time was the Cossack Brigade. Its commander was Reza Khan, a villager from an obscure family who had risen through the ranks on sheer ability. In 1921, he seized power in a bloodless coup, but he did not overthrow the shah. The shah appointed him prime minister and then left the country for a comfortable exile in Europe, never to return.

Turkey, Iran's neighbor, had just become a republic, and many Iranians felt that Iran should follow the same line. But the religious leaders wanted to keep the monarchy, fearing that a republican system would weaken their authority over the illiterate masses. The religious leaders convinced Prime Minister Reza that Iran was not ready for a republic. In 1925, Reza was crowned as shah, with an amendment to the Constitution that defined the monarchy as belonging to Reza Shah and his male descendants in succession. Since he had no family background to draw upon, Reza chose a new name for his dynasty: Pahlavi. It was a symbolic name, derived from an ancient province and language of the Persian Empire.

Reza Shah was one of the most powerful and effective monarchs in Iran's long history. He brought all ethnic groups under the control of the central government

and established a well-equipped standing army to enforce his decrees. He did not tamper with the Constitution; instead, he approved all candidates for the Majlis and outlawed political parties, so that the political system was entirely responsible to him alone.

### Reza Shah's New Order

Reza Shah wanted to build a "new order" for Iranian society, and he wanted to build it in a hurry. He was a great admirer of Mustafa Kemal Ataturk, founder of the Turkish Republic. Like Ataturk, Reza Shah believed that the religious leaders were an obstacle to modernization, due to their control over the masses. He set out to break their power through a series of reforms. Lands held in religious trust were leased to the state, depriving the religious leaders of income. A new secular code of laws took away their control, since the secular code would replace Islamic law. Other decrees prohibited the wearing of veils by women and the fez, the traditional brimless Muslim hat, by men. When religious leaders objected, Reza Shah had them jailed; on one occasion, he went into a mosque, dragged the local mullah out in the street, and horsewhipped him for criticizing the ruler during a Friday sermon.

In 1935, a huge crowd went to the shrine of Imam Reza, the eighth Shia Imam, in Meshad, to hear a parade of mullahs criticize the shah's ruthless reform policies. Reza Shah ringed the shrine with troops. When the crowd refused to disperse, they opened fire, killing a hundred people. It was the first and last demonstration organized by the mullahs during Reza Shah's reign. Only one religious leader, a young scholar named Ruhollah al-Musavi al-Khomeini, consistently dared to criticize the shah, and he was dismissed as being an impractical teacher.

Iran declared its neutrality during the early years of World War II. But Reza Shah was sympathetic to Germany; he had many memories of British interference in Iran. He allowed German technicians and advisers to remain in the country, and he refused to allow war supplies to be shipped across Iran to the Soviet Union. In 1941, British and Soviet armies simultaneously occupied Iran. Reza Shah abdicated in favor of his son, Crown Prince Mohammed, and was taken into exile on a British warship. He never saw his country again.

### Mohammed Reza Pahlavi

When the new shah came to the throne, few suspected that he would rule longer than his father and hold even more power. Mohammed Reza Pahlavi was young (22) and inexperienced, and he found himself ruling a land occupied by British and Soviet troops and threatened by Soviet-sponsored separatist movements in Azerbaijan and Kurdistan. Although these movements were put down, with U.S. help, a major challenge to the shah developed in 1951–1953.

A dispute over oil royalties between the government and the Anglo-Iranian Oil Company (AIOC) aroused intense national feeling in Iran. Mohammed Mossadegh, a long-time Majlis member and ardent nationalist, was asked by the shah in 1951 to serve as prime minister and to implement the oil-nationalization laws passed by the Majlis. The AIOC responded by closing down the industry, and all foreign technicians left the country. The Iranian economy was not affected at first, and Mossadegh's success in standing up to the company, which most Iranians considered an agent of foreign imperialism, won him enormous popularity.

Mossadegh served as prime minister from 1951 to 1953, a difficult time for Iran due to loss of oil revenues and internal political wrangling. Although his policies embroiled him in controversy, Mossadegh's theatrical style—public weeping when moved, fainting fits, a preference for conducting public business from his bed while dressed in pajamas, and a propensity during speeches to emphasize a point by ripping the arm from a chair—enhanced his appeal to the Iranian people. His radio "fireside chats" soon won him a mass following; he became more popular than the shy, diffident young shah, and for all practical purposes he ruled Iran.

By 1953, Iran's economy was in bad shape. With no oil revenues coming in, there was mass unemployment and high inflation. However, political factors rather than economic ones led to Mossadegh's overthrow. By then he had suspended the Majlis, and ruled by decree. As opposition to his decrees increased, Mossadegh and his Tudeh allies responded with arrests of key opponents. Newspapers were closed if they dared to criticize the government, in an eerie mirroring of the Iran of today. Many of the prime minister's supporters had broken with him due to what they considered his unwise leadership and dictatorial policies. As a result, his main support came from the Tudeh ("Masses"), the Soviet-aligned Iranian Communist Party. The Cold War confrontation between the United States and the Soviet Union was then at its height, and the Dwight Eisenhower administration feared that Mossadegh's policies would lead to a Communist takeover of Iran.

The shah's advisers convinced him to dismiss Mossadegh and appoint General Fazlollah Zahedi, minister of interior, in his place. When the decree was announced, Mossadegh's supporters, along with Tudeh members, took to the streets to protest the dismissal. The shah then fled the country, for the first time in his life. But after a confused series of demonstrations and counter-demonstrations, a popular uprising, which started in the poor sections of Iran where the ruler had his greatest support, overthrew Mossadegh. He was arrested as he tried to climb the back fence of his house. On August 19, the shah returned to his country in triumph. He then gradually gathered all authority in his hands and developed the vast internal security network that eliminated parliamentary opposition. Mossadegh was kept in prison for three years, all the while loudly protesting his innocence. He was then tried and sentenced to house arrest at his estate at Ahmedabad, west of Teheran. He died there in March 1967.[7]

By the 1960s, the shah felt that he was ready to lead Iran to greatness. In 1962, he announced the Shah–People Revolution, also known as the White Revolution. It had these basic points: land reform, public ownership of industries, nationalization of forests, voting rights for women, workers' profit sharing, and a literacy corps to implement compulsory education in rural areas. The plan drew immediate opposition from landowners and religious leaders. But only one spoke out forcefully against the shah: Ayatollah Ruhollah Khomeini, by then the most distinguished of Iran's religious scholars. "I have repeatedly pointed out that the government has evil intentions and is opposed to the ordinances of Islam," he said in a public sermon. His message was short and definite: The shah is selling out the country; the shah must go.

Khomeini continued to criticize the shah, and in June 1963, he was arrested. Demonstrations broke out in various cities. The shah sent the army into the streets, and again a river of blood divided ruler from country. Khomeini was released, re-arrested, and finally exiled to Iraq. For the next 15 years, he continued attacking the shah in sermons, pamphlets, and broadsides smuggled into Iran through the "bazaar network" of merchants and village religious leaders. Some had more effect than others. In 1971, when the shah planned an elaborate coronation at the ancient Persian capital of Persepolis to celebrate 2,500 years of monarchy, Khomeini declared, "Islam is fundamentally opposed to the whole notion of monarchy. The title of King of Kings . . . is the most hated of all titles in the sight of God. . . . Are the people of Iran to have a festival for those whose behavior has been a scandal throughout history and who are a cause of crime and oppression . . . in the present age?"[8]

Yet until 1978, the possibility of revolution in Iran seemed to be remote. The shah controlled all the instruments of power. His secret service, SAVAK, had informers everywhere. The mere usage of a word such as "oppressive" to describe the weather was enough to get a person arrested. Whole families disappeared into the shah's jails and were never heard from again.

The public face of the regime, however, seemed to indicate that Iran was on its way to wealth, prosperity, and international importance. The shah announced a 400 percent increase in the price of Iranian oil in 1973 and declared that the country would soon become a "Great Civilization." Money poured into Iran, billions of dollars more each year. The army was modernized with the most sophisticated U.S. equipment available. A new class of people, the "petro-bourgeoisie," became rich at the expense of other classes. Instead of the concessions given to foreign business firms by penniless Qajar shahs, the twentieth-century shah became the dispenser of opportunities to businesspeople and bankers to develop Iran's great civilization with Iranian money—an army of specialists imported from abroad.

In 1976, the shah seemed at the pinnacle of his power. His major adversary, Khomeini, had been expelled from Iraq and was now far away in Paris. U.S. president Jimmy Carter visited Iran in 1977 and declared, "Under your leadership (the country) is an island of stability in one of the more troubled areas of the world." Yet just a month later, 30,000 demonstrators marched on the city of Qum, protesting an unsigned newspaper article (reputed to have been written by the shah) that had attacked Khomeini as being anti-Iranian. The police fired on the demonstration, and a massacre followed.

Gradually, a cycle of violence developed. It reflected the distinctive rhythm of Shia Islam, wherein a death in a family is followed by 40 days of mourning and every death represents a martyr for the faith. Massacre followed massacre in city after city. In spite of the shah's efforts to modernize his country, it seemed to more and more Iranians that he was trying to undermine the basic values of their society by striking at the religious leaders. Increasingly, marchers in the streets were heard to shout, "Death to the shah!"

Even though the shah held absolute power, he seemed less and less able or willing to use his power to crush the opposition. It was as if he were paralyzed. He wrote in his last book, "A sovereign may not save his throne by shedding his countrymen's blood. . . . A sovereign is not a dictator. He cannot break the alliance that exists between him and his people."[9] The shah vacillated as the opposition intensified. His regime was simply not capable of self-reform or of accepting the logical consequences of liberalization, of free elections, a return to constitutional monarchy, and the emergence of legitimate dissent.[10]

## THE ISLAMIC REPUBLIC

The shah and his family left Iran for good in January 1979. Ayatollah Ruhollah Khomeini returned from exile practically on his heels, welcomed by millions who had fought and bled for his return. The shah's Great Civilization lay in ruins. Like a transplant, it had been an attempt to impose a foreign model of life on the Iranian community, a surgical attachment that had been rejected.

In April 1979, Khomeini announced the establishment of the Islamic Republic of Iran. He called it the first true republic in Islam since the original community of believers was formed by Muhammad. Khomeini said that religious leaders would assume active leadership, serve in the Majlis, even fight Iran's battles as "warrior mullahs." A "Council of Guardians" was set up to interpret laws and ensure that they were in conformity with the sacred law of Islam. Although its rulers failed to conquer Greece and thereby extend their empire into Europe, such achievements as their imperial system of government, the Persian language (Farsi), the monumental architecture of their capital at Persepolis, and their distinct cultural/historical heritage provide modern Iranians with pride in their ancient past and a national identity, unbroken to the present day.

Khomeini, as the first Supreme Guide, embodied the values and objectives of the republic. Because he saw himself in that role, he consistently sought to remain above factional politics yet to be accessible to all groups and render impartial decisions. But the demands of the war with Iraq, the country's international isolation, conflicts between radical Islamic fundamentalists and advocates of secularization, and other divisions forced the aging Ayatollah into a day-to-day policy-making role. It was a role that he was not well prepared for, given his limited experience beyond the confines of Islamic scholarship. (Quite possibly the war with Iraq, for example, could have been settled earlier if it were not for Khomeini's vision

(UN photo)

Iran has a long Islamic tradition. This worshipper is praying at the Shah Mosque, which makes up one side of the magnificent Royal Square of Shah Abbas in Isfahan.

of a pure Shia Iran fighting a just war against the atheistic, secular regime of Saddam Hussain.)

A major responsibility of the Council of Guardians was to designate—with the Ayatollah's approval—a successor to Khomeini as Supreme Legal Guide. In 1985, the Council chose Ayatollah Hossein Ali Montazeri, a former student and close associate of the bearded patriarch. Montazeri, although politically inexperienced and lacking Khomeini's charisma, had directed the exportation of Iranian Islamic fundamentalist doctrine to other Islamic states after the Revolution, with some success. This responsibility had identified him abroad as the architect of Iranian-sponsored terrorist acts such as the taking of hostages in Lebanon. But during his brief tenure as Khomeini's designated successor, he helped make changes in prison administration, revamped court procedures to humanize the legal system and reduce prisoner mistreatment, and urged a greater role for opposition groups in political life. However, Montazeri resigned in March 1989 after publishing an open letter, which aroused Khomeini's ire, criticizing the mistakes made by Iranian leaders during the Revolution's first decade.

The Islamic Republic staggered from crisis to crisis in its initial years. Abol Hassan Bani-Sadr, a French-educated intellectual who had been Khomeini's right-hand man in Paris, was elected president in 1980 by 75 percent of the popular vote. But it was one of the few postrevolutionary actions that united a majority of Iranians. Although the United States, as the shah's supporter and rescuer in his hour of exile, was proclaimed the "Great Satan" and thus helped to maintain Iran's revolutionary fervor, the prolonged crisis over the holding of American Embassy hostages by guards who would take orders from no one but Khomeini embarrassed Iran and damaged its credibility more than any gains made from tweaking the nose of a superpower. Although the hostages were held for over a year and so damaged the credibility of President Carter as to cost him the 1980 presidential election, one group of American Embassy diplomats managed to escape and take refuge in the Canadian Embassy in Teheran. Subsequently they escaped from the country disguised as members of a Canadian film company that had supposedly produced a film on Iran, thus being the only Americans to leave Iran in the year of the hostage crisis.

Historically, revolutions often seem to end by devouring those who carry them out. A great variety of Iranian social groups had united to overthrow the shah.

They had different views of the future; an "Islamic republic" meant different things to different groups. The Revolution first devoured all those associated with the shah, in a reign of terror intended to compensate for 15 years of repression. Islamic tribunals executed thousands of people—political leaders, intellectuals, and military commanders.

The major opposition to Khomeini and his fellow religious leaders came from the radical group Mujahideen-i-Khalq. The group favored an Islamic socialist republic and was opposed to too much influence on government by religious leaders. However, the Majlis was dominated by the religious leaders, many of whom had no experience in government and knew little of politics beyond the village level. As the conflict between these groups sharpened, bombings and assassinations occurred almost daily.

The instability and apparently endless violence during 1980–1981 suggested to the outside world that the Khomeini government was on the point of collapse. Iraqi president Saddam Hussain thought so, and in September 1980, he ordered his army to invade Iran—a decision that proved to be a costly mistake. President Bani-Sadr was dismissed by Khomeini after an open split developed between him and religious leaders over the conduct of the war; he subsequently escaped to France. A series of bombings carried out by the Mujahideen in mid-1981 killed a number of Khomeini's close associates, including the newly elected president of the republic.

The Khomeini regime showed considerable resilience in dealing with its adversaries. In 1983, Mujahideen leaders were hunted down and killed or imprisoned. Their organization had been the vanguard in the Iranian Revolution, but their Marxist, atheist views caused them to be viewed by the clerical regime as an enemy. The principal Mujahideen leader, Massoud Rajavi, escaped to France, but in 1986 the French government expelled him with his followers in an effort to improve Franco–Iranian relations. Subsequently, Iraq gave them asylum.

Toward the end of the Iran–Iraq War, the Mujahideen took advantage of Iraqi successes to seize several towns inside Iran, freeing political prisoners and executing minor officials, such as prison wardens, without trial. But the organization had little internal support in the country. Its Marxist views were not shared by the majority of people, and Mujahideen claims of 90,000 executions and more than 150,000 political prisoners held by

the regime were believed to be wildly exaggerated.

However, the government of Ali Akbar Hashemi Rafsanjani, who became president in 1989, was as ruthless as the shah's in hunting down its opponents. In 1990, Rajavi's brother was killed by unknown gunmen in Geneva, Switzerland. In August 1991, Shahpour Bakhtiar, the last prime minister under the monarchy, was murdered under similar circumstances in Paris, where he had been living in exile. Although the elderly Bakhtiar had been opposed to the shah as well as to Khomeini, fellow exile and former Iranian president Bani-Sadr charged that the regime had a "hit list" of opponents, including himself and the former prime minister, slated for execution.

The other main focus of opposition was the Tudeh (Masses) Party. Although considered a Communist party, its origins lay in the Iranian constitutional movement of 1905–1907, and it had always been more nationalistic than Soviet-oriented. The shah banned the Tudeh after an assassination attempt on him in 1949, but it revived during the Mossadegh period of 1951–1953. After the shah returned from exile in 1953, the Tudeh was again banned and went underground. Many of its leaders fled to the Soviet Union. After the 1979 Revolution, the Tudeh again came out into the open and collaborated with the Khomeini regime. It was tolerated by the religious leaders for its nationalism, which made its Marxism acceptable. Being militarily weak at that time, the regime also wished to remain on good terms with its Soviet neighbor. However, the rapprochement was brief. In 1984, top Tudeh leaders were arrested in a series of surprise raids and were given long prison terms.

## PROSPECTS

The Revolution that overturned one of the most ruthless authoritarian regimes in history has been in effect long enough to provide some clues to its future direction. One clue is the continuity of internal politics. Despite wreaking savage vengeance on persons associated with the shah's regime, Khomeini and his fellow mullahs preserved most of the Pahlavi institutions of government. The Majlis, civil service, secret police, and armed forces were continued as before, with minor modifications to conform to strict Islamic practice. The main addition was a parallel structure of revolutionary courts, paramilitary Revolutionary Guards (Pasdaran), workers' and peasants' councils, plus the Council of Guardians as the watchdog over legislation.

An important change between the monarchy and the republic concerns the matter of appropriate dress. Decrees issued by Khomeini required women to wear the enveloping chador and *hijab* (headscarf) in public. Painted nails or too much hair showing would often lead to arrests or fines, sometimes jail. The decrees were enforced by Revolutionary Guards and *komitehs* ("morals squads") patrolling city streets and urban neighborhoods. Also, the robe and turban worn by Ayatollah Khomeini and his fellow clerics were decreed as correct fashion, preferred over the "Mr. Engineer" business suit and tie of the shah's time. The necktie in particular was considered a symbol of Western decadence and derided as a "donkey's tail" by the country's new leaders. In subsequent years, the dress code and other restrictions on behavior have seesawed between extremes. In Khatami's first term, most restrictions were lifted; the necktie even staged a comeback among professionals—doctors, lawyers, and others. Then, in 2001, following his reelection, the so-called hard-line conservatives who control the judiciary issued new regulations, banning neckties, wearing of heavy makeup in public places such as restaurants, and other forms of "un-Islamic" social behavior. Shopping malls were ordered not to play music or display women's underwear in their shop windows; shopkeepers and restaurateurs were warned of "heavy consequences" for violations.

The 1985 presidential election in Iran continued the secular trend. The ruling Islamic Republican Party (since dissolved) nominated President Ali Khamenei for a second term, against token opposition. However, Mehdi Bazargan, the republic's first prime minister, who subsequently went into opposition and founded the Freedom Movement, announced that he would be a candidate. The Council of Guardians vetoed his candidacy on the grounds that his opposition to the war with Iraq, although well publicized, would be damaging to national solidarity if he ran for president. Khamenei won reelection handily, but nearly 2 million votes were cast for one of the two opposition candidates, a religious leader. The relatively high number of votes for this candidate reflected increasing dissatisfaction with the Khomeini regime's no-quarter policy toward Iraq, rather than opposition to the regime itself.

In its foreign relations, the regime remained unpredictable. It played an active behind-the-scenes role in the release of Western hostages in Lebanon in 1990 and 1991, possibly reflecting a desire for improved relations with Western countries, both for economic reasons and to enable Iran to resume its important role in re-

gional affairs. However, a death sentence imposed in 1989 on Anglo-Pakistani author Salman Rushdie for his novel *The Satanic Verses,* considered by Iranian religious leaders to have defamed the Prophet Muhammad, widened the gap between Iran and the West. The sentence, issued under a *fatwa* (a religious edict), was lifted in 1998, in the sense that the Iranian government disclaimed the responsibility for carrying it out. In return, Britain restored diplomatic relations with the republic.

The regime has had difficulties in ensuring popular support and making use of its majority in the fractious Majlis to carry out necessary economic reforms. In the 1992 Majlis elections, two political groups presented candidates: the Society of Radical Clergy (*Ruhaniyat,* loosely but incorrectly translated as "moderates") and the Combatant Religious Leaders (*Ruhaniyoun,* "hard-liners"). All candidates had to be approved by the Council of Constitutional Guardians (CCG), a 12-member body of senior religious scholars, to ensure that their views were compatible with Islam.

In the 1996 Majlis elections, the distinction between Ruhaniyat and Ruhaniyoun became even more blurred, reflecting the arcane nature of Iranian politics. The former, renamed the Conservative Combatant Clergy Society, was now opposed by the Servants of Iran's Construction, a coalition of centrist supporters of then–president Rafsanjani. The Freedom Movement, now headed by former prime minister Ibrahim Yazdi, was banned by the CCG. In October 2001, 30 of its members, excluding Yazdi, were arrested and held for trial on charges of "diverting" the Islamic Revolution from its true course.

In the 2000 Majlis elections, held in three stages, new political groupings emerged, corresponding to the reformist and hard-line elements in the population. The Islamic Iran Participation Front, a coalition of disparate groups united mainly in their goal of political reform, won 200 of the seats in the Legislature, to 55 for the Executives of Construction, composed of clerical leaders and government officials opposed to reform.

## IRAN AFTER KHOMEINI
In June 1989, Ayatollah Ruhollah Khomeini died of a heart attack in a Teheran hospital. He was 86 years old and had struggled all his life against the authoritarianism of two shahs.

The Imam left behind a society entirely reshaped by his uncompromising Islamic ideals and principles. Every aspect of social life in republican Iran is governed by

these principles, from prohibition of the production and use of alcohol and drugs to a strict dress code for women outside the home, compulsory school prayers, emphasis on theological studies in education, and required fasting during Ramadan. One positive result of this Islamization program has been a renewed awareness among Iranians of their cultural identity and pride in their heritage.

Khomeini also bequeathed many problems to his country. The most immediate problem concerned the succession to him as Supreme Guide. Earlier, he had appointed an "Expediency Council" to resolve differences between the Majlis and the Council of Constitutional Guardians.

A separate body of senior religious leaders and jurists, the Assembly of Experts, resolved the succession question by electing President Khamenei as Supreme Guide. However, the choice emphasized Khomeini's unique status as both political and spiritual leader. As a *Hojatulislam* (a lower-ranking cleric), Khamenei lacked the credentials to replace the Ayatollah. But he was an appropriate choice, having served as a part of the governing team. Also, he was the most available religious leader. He had completed two terms as president and was ineligible for reelection.

## THE PRESIDENCY
The chief executive's powers in the Iranian system were greatly strengthened by a constitutional amendment abolishing the office of prime minister, approved by voters in a July 1989 referendum. But concern for a smooth transfer of power after Khomeini's death prompted the government to advance the date for electing a new president to succeed Ali Khamenei from October to July. There were only two candidates: Majlis speaker Ali Akbar Hashemi Rafsanjani, Khomeini's right-hand man almost from the start of the Revolution; and Agriculture Minister Abbas Sheibani, a political unknown. As anticipated, Rafsanjani won handily, with 95 percent of the 14.1 million votes cast.

Rafsanjani's first cabinet consisted mostly of technocrats, suggesting some relaxation of the policy of exporting the Revolution and supporting revolutionary Islamic groups outside the country. At home, there was also a slight relaxation of the strict enforcement of Islamic codes of behavior enforced by the morals squads and security police. But the easing was temporary. In 1992, the new Supreme Guide issued an edict ordering these codes enforced. A similar edict was issued for arts and culture, and the minister of culture and Islamic guidance was forced to resign after clerical leaders charged him with being "too permissive" in allowing concerts and films of a "non-Islamic" nature to be presented to the public. (His name: Mohammed Khatami.)

Rafsanjani was reelected in 1993, but by a much smaller margin of the electorate, 63 percent. The decline in his popularity was due mainly to his failure to improve the economy, but also for continuation of the strict Islamic dress and behavior codes. When his term ended, he kept his seat in the Majlis. In the February 2000 Majlis elections, he finished 29th in the contest for Teheran's 30 seats, barely avoiding a run-off. However, Ayatollah Khamenei appointed him chairman of the powerful Expediency Council, which serves as the final advisory body to the Supreme Legal Guide in political and legislative matters. In this capacity, he continued to play an important role in Iran's evolving political process.

## FOREIGN POLICY

The end of the war with Iraq left a number of issues unresolved. A prisoner exchange was agreed to in principle, but it has yet to be completed. Under the terms of an agreement negotiated by the International Red Cross, Iran released 1,999 Iraqi prisoners in April 2000, and an additional 930 in May, for a total of 2,929. Many of them had been held since the end of the war in 1988, and others since 1983.

A formal peace treaty and delimitation of navigation rights on the Shatt al-Arab have yet to be signed between the two countries. One reason for the holdup in the peace treaty is Iraq's backing of the Mujahideen. Saddam Hussain's government provides bases for its cross-border raids as well as major funding for the organization.

The unwillingness of European countries to go along with secondary sanctions on Iran, due to its economic and trade importance to them, brought an improvement in Iranian–European relations in the mid-1990s. In July 1996, Total of France was given a concession to develop newly discovered oil fields near Sirri Island in the Gulf. The concession had been granted previously to the U.S. Conoco Oil Company, but Conoco withdrew under pressure from the Clinton administration to comply with sanctions regulations.

The conviction of four Iranians in a German court in 1997 for the 1992 assassinations of Iranian Kurd opposition leaders in Berlin temporarily halted the increase in European–Iranian contacts. More than 100,000 people marched in Teheran to protest the decision, and the European Union suspended the "dialogue" with Iran on ways to sanctions. But the Iranian market remains too attractive to

Europe in terms of investment. Between 1998 and 2001, the Khatami regime negotiated $13 billion in foreign investment, most of it from European firms.

The long and often hostile relationship with Russia, dating back to the years of gradual acquisition of Iranian territory by advancing Russian armies and settlers in the 1800s, entered a new phase in the new millennium with a joint agreement for training of Iranian officers at Russian bases. Russia also agreed to complete the reparation of Iran's German-built nuclear reactor at Bushehr, badly damaged in the war with Iraq. Also, over vehement U.S. objections, Russia sold Kilo-class submarines and other weapons to Iran, including parts for a new ballistic missile.

Iran's relations with the United States remained glacially frozen, at least on the official level. For more than two decades, the only official connections had been through the Swiss Embassy in Teheran and the Pakistan Embassy in Washington, D.C. However, an indirect channel through the U.S.–Iran Claims Tribunal set up in the Hague has been quite successful. It was set up to adjudicate claims by U.S. firms for work contracted and equipment delivered to the shah's regime but not paid for due to the Revolution. The tribunal is also responsible for examining Iranian claims against U.S. companies. By 1996, it had awarded $6 billion to U.S. claimants and $4 billion to Iran for similar claims.

Although Iranians continue to view the American people favorably, the clerical regime and its hard-line supporters insist that the U.S. government is the cause of their failure to establish a sound economy, and an obstacle to improved relations with the outside world. In November 2001, the 22nd anniversary of the occupation of the U.S. Embassy in Teheran and the holding of 52 Americans as hostages for 444 days, the embassy building was reopened as a museum, with an exhibit of alleged "crimes against the Iranian people" committed by America. One exhibit showed photos of the U.S. helicopters that had crashed in the desert on a failed rescue mission.

Prior to the election of a new Iranian president in 1997, the U.S.–Iranian relationship became truly ice-bound. The Clinton administration imposed a trade embargo in 1995, calling the country a major sponsor of international terrorism. Congress then passed a bill penalizing companies that invest $40 million or more in Iran's oil and gas industry. The ban would apply equally to U.S. and foreign companies.

As might have been expected, the bill aroused a storm of protest in Europe. It was viewed as unwarranted interference in

the internal affairs of European countries, and the European Union denounced it as a violation of the principles of international free trade. It was patently unenforceable outside U.S. borders, and in May 1998, the administration approved a waiver to allow the consortium formed to exploit the former Conoco concession. In return, consortium members agreed to block sales of nuclear technology to Iran. In October 2001, Russia signed an agreement with the country to deliver $300 million annually in jet aircraft, missiles, and other weaponry. And in November, the first of two nuclear reactors was delivered to the 1,000-megawatt power station being built at Bushire. Other arms deals between the two countries have made Iran Russia's third-largest arms customer, after India and China.

President Khatami's reelection prompted a reassessment of U.S. policy toward Iran. Former secretary of state Madeleine Albright acknowledged some "mistakes of the past" shortly after the February 2000 Majlis elections. They included the overthrow of Mossadegh, U.S. support for Iraq in the war with Iran, and alignment with the shah's regime despite its brutal suppression of dissent. Tariffs on imports of Iranian caviar, carpets, pistachio nuts, and dried fruits were lifted in 2000 and remain so.

Iran's foreign policy in recent years has been essentially regional. In 2001, it signed an agreement with Saudi Arabia for joint efforts to combat terrorism and drug trafficking. Iran's relations with the newly independent Islamic republics of Central Asia expanded rapidly in the late 1990s, both in diplomatic relations and exchanges of trade. However, a dispute with Azerbaijan over oil exploration rights in the Caspian Sea—which holds an estimated 200 billion barrels of offshore oil and 600 billion cubic meters of natural gas—came to a head in July 2001, when an Iranian warship halted exploration in the offshore Alov field by Azerbaijani research vessels.

The dispute over this field reflects the larger issue of Caspian Sea boundaries. After the collapse of the Soviet Union in 1991, the five countries bordering the Caspian—Iran, Azerbaijan, Kazakhstan, Russia, and Turkmenistan—signed an agreement that gave Iran 12 percent of shoreline but left open the issue of oil and gas development. With exploration under way, Iran is demanding control of 20 percent, including the Alov field, which lies 60 miles north of its current territorial waters.

In a related dispute, Iran has objected strenuously to the U.S.-sponsored plan for a pipeline to carry Azerbaijani oil from Baku to the Turkish port of Ceyhan (Adana) on the Mediterranean, thus bypassing Iranian territory. For its part, the Azerbaijan government accused Iran of funding new mosques and paying their prayer leaders to support pro-Iranian subversive activities.

After the September 11, 2001, terrorist attacks in the United States, the government condemned the action and the killing of civilians. In a mosque sermon, Expediency Council president Rafsanjani stated that "despite all our differences we are willing to join the U.S.–international coalition against terrorism under the umbrella of the United Nations, if America does not impose its own view." Iran closed its border with Afghanistan to Afghan refugees, although it allowed private relief organizations to continue making food deliveries to that war-ravaged country.

An important element in Iran's willingness to cooperate with the United States against the Afghanistan-based al-Qaeda network and its leader, Osama bin Laden, stemmed from drug smuggling. The Taliban regime that controlled 90 percent of that country until its overthrow in late 2001 had encouraged drug cultivation as a means of income and turned a blind eye to smuggling, much of it through Iran. Since 1996, some 3,000 Iranian border guards have been killed by smugglers, and easy access to drugs has resulted in a large number of Iranian addicts.

However, President George W. Bush's expansion of the "war on terrorism" to embrace an "evil axis" that included Iran, helped to refreeze U.S.–Iranian relations. Hard-liners and reformists united to denounce the descriptive label, calling it interference in domestic affairs. In February 2002, the 23rd anniversary of the Revolution was marked by huge demonstrations, as marchers shouted "Death to America!" in an all-too-familiar refrain.

(UNHCR/A. Hollmann)

Today Iran is still in a state of internal unrest. The country's future will be in the hands of the young and how well they are educated.

## AN ELECTION SURPRISE

In May 1997, Iranian voters went to the polls to elect a new president. Four candidates had been cleared and approved by the CCG: a prominent judge; a former intelligence-agency director; Majlis speaker Ali Akbar Nalegh-Nouri; and Mohammed Khatami, the former minister of culture and Islamic guidance, a more or less last-minute candidate, since he had been out of office for five years and was not well known to the public. Speaker Nalegh-Nouri was the choice of the religious leaders and the Majlis and was expected to win easily.

In Iranian politics, though, the devil is often in the details; the unexpected may be the rule. With 25 million out of Iran's 33 million potential voters casting their ballots, Khatami emerged as the winner in a startling upset, with 69 percent of the votes as compared to 25 percent for Nalegh-Nouri. Support for the new president came mainly from women, but he was also backed by the large number of Iranians under age 25, who grew up under the republic but are deeply dissatisfied with economic hardships and Islamic restrictions on their personal freedom.

Khatami took office in August. Despite some opposition in the Majlis, all 22 of the ministers in his cabinet were approved, although his first nominee for minister of interior was later impeached by a 137–128 vote. (Khatami then assigned him to a subcabinet post.)

During the short-lived openness of Iran's 1997 version of "Prague Spring," civic and press freedom flourished, with many new newspapers and magazines appearing on the streets. *Society,* a new magazine, even dared to publish articles mildly critical of the regime and photographs of unveiled women on its front pages. Another harbinger of change was the impressive victory of Khatami supporters in the local and municipal elections, the first since the 1979 Revolution. They won the great majority of the 200,000 seats on town and city councils, including 15 seats on the influential Teheran City Council.

Greater participation of women in political life had been one of Khatami's campaign promises, and a number of women won seats on various councils.

However, Khatami's options as an agent of change are limited. Not only is he a member of the religious establishment himself, but his powers are limited constitutionally. Under the Constitution, Supreme Legal Guide Ayatollah Khamenei controls the judiciary, the Revolutionary Guards, the security and intelligence services, the Basijis (volunteers in the Iran–Iraq War who served as "guardians of public morality"), and the shadowy Ansar-e-Hezbullah, vigilantes who cruise city streets on motorcycles beating up citizens and are answerable only to Khamenei for their actions.

The president's limitations were underscored in 1998 by the murders of prominent Iranian writers and dissidents. A public outcry resulted in the uncovering of a "rogue squad" in the intelligence service responsible for these and other murders of prominent Iranians over the years—intellectual, political, and other leaders. Members of the squad were tried and convicted in 1998 by a military court, but the Iranian Supreme Court overturned the convictions on the grounds of investigative irregularities. In August 2001, a new trial of 15 "rogue agents" began in Teheran. By that time, the highest-ranking official involved, Deputy Minister Saeed Emani, had died in custody. Supporters of President Khatami had charged a cover-up in order to bring about a new trial, claiming that death squads had attempted to silence opponents of the clerical regime for more than a decade.

The contest between "hard-liners" holding fast to the Islamic structure and rules bequeathed to the republic by Ayatollah Khomeini as well as advocates of a more open society with fewer social restrictions reached flash point in 1998 and 1999. In February 1998, the popular mayor of Teheran, Gholarn Hossein Karbaschi, was arrested and charged with corruption in office. He had won popular favor with his beautification and cleanup program for the capital and had been active in Khatami's election campaign. During his trial, the embattled mayor described it as "politically motivated on the part of enemies of reform and openness." Nonetheless, he received a two-year sentence; however, in January 2000, Khamenei pardoned him in another of the unexpected twists that give Iranian politics its unique flavor.

## THE ECONOMY

Iran's bright economic prospects during the 1970s were largely dampened by the 1979 Revolution. Petroleum output was sharply reduced, and the war with Iraq crippled industry as well as oil exports. Ayatollah Khomeini warned Iranians to prepare for a decade of grim austerity before economic recovery would be sufficient to meet domestic needs. After the cease-fire with Iraq, Khomeini enlarged upon his warning, saying that the world would be watching to see if the Revolution would be destroyed by postwar economic difficulties.

Iran's remarkable turnaround since the end of the war with Iraq, despite the U.S.–imposed trade restrictions, suggests that the late Ayatollah Khomeini was a better theologian than economist. The country's foreign debts were paid off by 1990. Since then, however, loans for new development projects and purchase of equipment, including a nuclear reactor for peaceful uses set up by Russian technicians in 1998, along with reduced oil revenues, have generated foreign debts of $30 billion.

Iran was self-sufficient in food until 1970. The White Revolution redistributed a considerable amount of land, most of it from estates that Reza Shah had confiscated from their previous owners. But the new owners, most of them former tenant farmers, lacked the capital, equipment, and technical knowledge needed for productive agriculture. The revolutionary period caused another upheaval in agriculture, as farmers abandoned their lands to take part in the struggle, and fighting between government forces and ethnic groups disrupted production. Production dropped 3.5 percent in 1979–1980, the first full year of the Islamic Republic of Iran, and continued to drop at the same rate through 1982. The war with Iraq caused another upheaval. The majority of recruits came from villages, the rural population having been Khomeini's most fervent supporters. Rural youths joined the Basijis in large numbers, resulting in severe attrition in the able-bodied male farm population.[11]

These difficulties, plus large-scale rural–urban migration, have hampered development of the agricultural sector, which accounts for 20 percent of gross domestic product. Formerly self-sufficient in food, Iran is now the world's biggest wheat importer. In the non-oil sector, Iran is the world's major producer of pistachio nuts. (Former president Rafsanjani is himself a pistachio farmer in his home province of Rafsanjan, the center of production.) Other important non-oil exports are carpets, caviar from sturgeon that swim south into Iran's share of the Caspian Sea, and Persian melons. The country is also the number- one world producer of saffron; unfortunately, much of the crop is stolen by poachers and smuggled into Europe, where it sells for up to $272 per pound!

Petroleum is Iran's major resource and the key to economic development. Oil was discovered there in 1908, making the Iranian oil industry the oldest in the Middle East. Until 1951, the Anglo-Iranian Oil Company produced, refined, and distributed all Iranian oil. After the 1951–1953 nationalization period, when the industry was closed down, a consortium of foreign oil companies—British, French, and American—replaced the AIOC. In 1973, the industry was again nationalized and was operated by the state-run National Iranian Oil Company.

After the Revolution, political difficulties affected oil production, as the United States and its allies boycotted Iran due to the hostage crisis and other customers balked at the high prices ($37.50 per barrel in 1980, as compared to $17.00 per barrel a year earlier). The war with Iraq was a further blow to the industry. Japan, Iran's biggest customer, stopped purchases entirely in 1981–1982. War damage to the important Kharg Island terminal reduced Iran's export capacity by a third, and the Abadan refinery was severely crippled. Periodic Iraqi raids on other Iranian oil terminals in more distant places such as Lavan and Qeshm, reachable by longer-range aircraft, seriously decreased Iran's export output. Recovery from war damages has not only helped oil production and export but has also benefited other sectors of the oil industry. The Abadan refinery, the country's oldest, resumed full production in 1989 after a nine-year lapse and by 1996 was producing 300,000 barrels per day, half its prewar output. In 1996, a new petrochemical complex went into operation in Tabriz. It produces 400,000 tons a year of ethylene, polyethylene, and benzine.

In addition to its oil and gas reserves, Iran has important bauxite deposits, and in 1994, it reported the discovery of 400 million tons of phosphate rock to add to its mineral resources. It is now the world's sixth-largest exporter of sulfur. However, oil and gas remain the mainstays of the economy. Oil reserves are 88 billion barrels; with new gas discoveries each year, the country sits astride 70 percent of the world's reserves.

Iran's great natural resources, large population, and strong sense of its international importance have fueled its drive to become a major industrial power. The country is self-sufficient in cement, steel, petrochemicals, and hydrocarbons (as well as sugar—Iranians are heavy users). Production of electricity meets domestic

| The Persian Empire under Cyrus the Great and his successors includes most of ancient Near East and Egypt 551–331 B.C. | The Sassanid Empire establishes Zoroastrianism as the state religion A.D. 226–641 | Islamic conquest at the Battles of Qadisiya and Nihavard 637–641 | The Safavid shahs develop national unity based on Shia Islam as the state religion 1520–1730 | The constitutional movement limits the power of the shah by the Constitution and Legislature 1905–1907 | The accession of Reza Shah, establishing the Pahlavi Dynasty 1925 | The abdication of Reza Shah under Anglo–Soviet pressure; he is succeeded by Crown Prince Mohammed Reza Pahlavi 1941 |
|---|---|---|---|---|---|---|

needs, and the projected completion of nuclear plants will add to the supply. Iran now has its own small-weapons program, producing, among other items, a battle tank, the Zolfaqar. However, its efforts to develop an effective nuclear missile capability for potential use against hostile neighbors have yet to succeed. Testing of Shahab-3 missiles modeled on North Korea's No Dong, which have a 600-mile range, began in 1998 but is as yet unproven, and the civilian nuclear-power reactors being built by Russian technicians will not be operative until 2003.

Since the breakup of the Soviet Union into independent states, Iran has been active in developing trade and economic links with the mainly Islamic republics of Central Asia. A rail link from the port of Bandar Abbas to Turkmenistan was completed in 1996, giving that landlocked country access to the outside world by a watery "Silk Road" to India and the Far East.

Traditionally, Iran's economy has been controlled by the *bazaaris*, city bazaar merchants and business owners. Their support was critical to the Revolution, and they have continued to receive preferential treatment in economic transactions. This factor, among others, has caused the economy to stagnate since 1979. The nationalization of most private industries (and heavy taxes on the remaining ones) has discouraged investment. One example was Cheet-e-Ray, a government-owned textile factory that was $10 million in debt. It was privatized and sold for $2,500 to investors who promptly fired the workforce without paying salaries and then declared bankruptcy, forcing the government to issue loans to restart it.

To their credit, the reformers backing the Khatami government have set out to reform the economy. In June 2001, the Majlis approved a 26-article law to stimulate economic growth. Among other elements, it would allow imports of modern machinery to replace Iran's aging industrial equipment. But the Guardian Council, which has final authority over legislation, rejected the law, arguing that it would discriminate against domestic investment and pave the way for foreign control of the economy. It was approved and resubmitted by the Majlis, but in December 2001 the Council ruled that it was not consistent with Islamic law. With the Majlis and the

Guardian Council in total disagreement, the next step was submission to the Expediency Council, which has final mediating power in such matters. Since it is also dominated by conservatives, the chances for the law's passage seemed slim.

## WHITHER THE REPUBLIC?

Two decades after the Revolution that brought the first Islamic republic into existence, a debate is still under way to determine how "Islamic" Iranian society should be. The debate is between those Iranians who advocate strict adherence to Islamic law and those who would open up the society to diverse social behavior and norms. As noted earlier in this report, Iran's new president was the choice of women and young people, two groups who feel they have benefited little from the Revolution. As their candidate, he may expect to come under increasing pressure from this new and largely disadvantaged constituency. As one Iranologist noted, "Having united religion and politics, the regime now has to face antagonisms directed at the clerics for failing to deliver on lofty promises. Pressure from Islamic radicals to push for further purification of social and political practices has alienated important elements in society."[12]

On June 8, 2001, Mohammed Khatami was reelected handily for a second term as Iran's president, garnering 77 percent of the 28.2 million votes cast. His closest opponent, the former minister of labor, won 16.5 percent of the vote. The remainder was divided among eight other candidates. Voter turnout was 68 percent, lower than in 1997, but Khatami's victory margin was higher.

In most countries, support of such magnitude would give the winner a clear mandate for carrying out his or her programs. But politically, the Islamic Republic of Iran is a unique institution. Its population is sharply divided between "hard-liners" and "reformers," terms that do little to explain Iran's political complexities. The former, generally speaking, are those who would preserve at all costs the theocratic rule and Islamic values bequeathed to the republic by its founders. The latter, centered on Khatami as the "great white hope" in achieving their goals, seek to reshape Iran as a more open society, com-

mitted to justice and the rule of law and with personal freedom and rights guaranteed. The slogan "Iran for all Iranians" adopted by the reformers during the February 2000 Majlis elections perhaps best describes—and symbolizes—these goals.

There remains a dark side to Iranian political life. It is best illustrated by unpredictable acts of repression and violence, a country "of cultural apartheid, where people are punished for their lifestyles as well as their crimes." Khatami's first term was marred by the murders of leading writers and intellectuals, and by several violent confrontations of university students with security police, the former being at the forefront of resistance to hard-liners. A police raid on a Teheran University dormitory in 1999 resulted in a number of deaths and arrests of student leaders. Further demonstrations generated scenes reminiscent of the last days of the monarchy before the Revolution.

The election of a reformer-dominated Majlis in February 2000, and that of Khatami for a second term as president in June 2001, seemed to promise success for his reform program. Known as the Second Khordad Movement because of its date (that of his election), it would move Iranian society away from the strict Islamic interpretation of social and political behavior of the clerical regime, toward a more open society receptive to ideas and influences from the outside world, yet without compromising its Islamic nature. However, opposition from hard-liners continued to block reform in the political sphere. New newspapers were closed, often immediately after publication, and their reporters and editors were arrested for articles deemed critical of Islam or the regime. The repression was expanded to include many elderly veterans who had fought in the Revolution and had spent their lives in opposition to the shah. Their "crime," ironically, was advocacy of greater democracy and political pluralism. Even the film industry, which has benefited from the new openness, releasing a series of superb movies, is no longer exempt. In August 2001, filmmaker Tahmineh Milani was arrested after censors claimed that her film *The Hidden Half* was subversive. (It focused on participation by leftist students in the 1979 Revolution.) Milani was charged with "abusing art as

**The oil industry is nationalized under the leadership of Prime Minister Mossadegh**
**1951–1953**

**The shah introduces the White Revolution**
**1962**

**Revolution overthrows the shah; Iran becomes an Islamic republic headed by the Ayatollah Khomeini**
**1979–1980**

**The Iran-Iraq war; Khomeini dies**
**1980s**

**Iran's economy begins to recover; foreign relations improve; debate over how Islamic the Islamic Republic should be**
**1990s**

**2000s**

President Mohammed Khatami wins reelection handily

U.S. president George W. Bush calls Iran part of "evil axis" of terror, reigniting tensions with Iran

an instrument to support anti-revolutionary groups."

The hard-liners also used public floggings as a visible method of slowing the clock of political and social change. In August 2001, 13 young men were given 80 lashes each for "offenses against public order," notably use of alcohol or being seen in public with women to whom they were not related. The head of the judiciary defended the floggings as necessary to combat un-Islamic behavior and rising rates of crime and drug use.

While Khatami's reelection gave him a huge popular mandate, it did not increase his power options. Some scholars have argued that the Revolution that ended 2,000 years of off-and-on monarchy may be compared with the French Revolution, in passing through a number of phases before it settles down. The comparison is dubious because Iran's Revolution reflects the multiplicity of groups in Iranian society and the ambiguities of its political equation. The terms "reformer" and "hardliner," as well as "liberal" and "conservative," are inadequate for use in describing this diversity of thought and position. Perhaps the only constant for all groups is the argument over the proper role and structure of government; the existence of the republic as an Islamic one is not in question.

What is clear is that there is today a fundamental shift in the Iranian social structure that will ocntinue to bring about major changes in the political system. Fifty percent of Iran's population were born after the Revolution. As one observer noted, "These young people crave social

and political freedom and want their country to better integrate with the dynamic world beyond their borders. Along with a well-educated middle class, politically active women, and high unemployment, these forces form a potent combination that will ultimately make political change inevitable."

## NOTES

1. A 1991 memo from Ayatollah Khamenei ordered that Bahais should be expelled from prevented from attaining "positions of influence," and denied employment and access to education. The memo is in sharp contrast to UN General Assembly *Resolution 52/142,* which calls on Iran to "emancipate" its Bahai population.

2. Golamreza Fazel, "Persians," in Richard V. Weekes, ed., *Muslim Peoples: A World Ethnographic Survey,* 2nd ed. (Westport, CT: Greenwood Press, 1984), p. 610. "Face-saving is in fact one of the components of *Ta'aruf,* along with assertive masculinity (*gheyrat*)."

3. John Malcolm, *History of Persia* (London: John Murray, 1829), Vol. II, p. 303.

4. Behzad Yaghmaian, *Social Change in Iran* (Albany, NY: State University of New York Press, 2001), p. 127.

5. Roy Mottahedeh, *The Mantle of the Prophet* (New York: Simon & Schuster, 1985), p. 52.

6. *Ibid.,* p. 34.

7. Until recently, the CIA had always been credited with engineering Mossadegh's overthrow and had made no effort to deny this charge. Publication recently of the agency's secret history of "Operation Ajax"

clearly emphasized its limited role and lack of effectiveness. The unpublished memoirs of Ardeshir Zahedi, the general's son ("Five Decisive Days, August 14–18, 1953") indicate that U.S. involvement was incidental to a genuine popular uprising.

8. Imam Khomeini, *Islam and Revolution,* transl. by Hamid Algar, tr. (Berkeley, CA: Mizan Press, 1981), p. 175.

9. Mohammed Reza Pahlavi, Shah of Iran, *Answer to History* (New York: Stein and Day, 1980), pp. 152–153.

10. Sepehr Zabih, *Iran's Revolutionary Upheaval: An Interpretive Essay* (San Francisco, CA: Alchemy Books, 1979), pp. 46–49.

11. "They [the Basijis] usually advanced ahead of the regular Iranian troops in human wave attacks. Wearing red headbands and inspired by professional chanters before battle, their heads were filled with thoughts of death and martyrdom and going to Paradise." V. S. Naipaul, "After the Revolution," *The New Yorker* (May 26, 1997), pp. 46—69.

12. Farhad Kazemi, "The Iranian Enigma," *Current History* (January 1997), p. 40.

## DEVELOPMENT

The slow pace of economic development reflects a major difference between "reformers" and "hard-liners." The former would open Iran to foreign investment, end endemic corruption in the economic system, and reduce the control over commerce of the bazaaris (merchant class). Extensive European investment would also bypass U.S. sanctions. The Khatami government generated $10 billion in such investments in 1998–2001, mainly on a buy-back basis in hydrocarbons industries. In May 2000, the World Bank approved its first loans to the republic, $232 million for health-care projects and a sewage-treatment plant in Teheran, overriding U.S. objections.

## FREEDOM

Iran's Constitution calls its political system a "religious democracy," leaving the term ambiguous. However, the struggle between advocates of openness and justice and those who would preserve rigid orthodoxy under the clerical regime has brought periodic waves of repression, affecting the press, artists and writers, and intellectuals. The U.S. State Department's 2001 report to Congress notes that "systematic abuses" of human rights include "summary executions, widespread use of torture, disappearances and other degrading treatment."

## HEALTH/WELFARE

In recent years, Iran's efforts to interdict drug smuggling across its border with Afghanistan has earned it high marks. In 1999–2000, 253 tons of illegal drugs were seized by border guards, although 3,000 border guards have been killed in shootouts with smugglers. Ironically, during the late shah's regin, Iran was a major producer of both heroin and opium, while today it leads the world in interdiction of drug traffic. Unfortunately, ease of access and low cost has created a drug problem at home. Some 1.3 million Iranians have become addicts. In 2000, Britain donated $2.5 million to the Iranian drug enforcement program.

## ACHIEVEMENTS

Despite varying levels of strictness under Iran's interpretation of Islamic law, women have been fully integrated into society and participate actively in national life. They drive their own cars and work outside the home, albeit theoretically a husband's permission is required. Women make up 25% of the labor force and 50% of university students. They serve in the Majlis, and their literacy rate is equal to that of men. Women filmmakers such as Marzieh Meshkini and Tahmineh Milani, along with their male colleagues, are responsible for the revitalization of the Iranian film industry. In fashion, designers increasingly challenge the drab female dress code with bright topcoats and scarves.

# Iraq (Republic of Iraq)

## GEOGRAPHY
*Area in Square Miles (Kilometers):*
168,710 (437,072) (about twice
the size of Idaho)
*Capital (Population):* Baghdad
(3,842,000)
*Environmental Concerns:*
destruction of natural habitat
and wildlife due to water-
control schemes; air and water
pollution; soil degradation and
erosion; desertification
*Geographical Features:* mostly
broad plains; reedy marshes along
the Iranian border, with large
flooded areas; mountains along the
borders with Turkey and Iran
*Climate:* mostly desert; cold winters
in northern mountainous regions

## PEOPLE

### Population
*Total:* 23,332,000
*Annual Growth Rate:* 2.84%
*Rural/Urban Population Ratio:* 25/75
*Major Languages:* Arabic;
Kurdish; Assyrian; Armenian
*Ethnic Makeup:* 75%–80% Arab;
15%–20% Kurdish; 5% Turkish,
Assyrian, and others
*Religions:* 62% Shia Muslim; 35%
Sunni Muslim; 3% others

### Health
*Life Expectancy at Birth:* 66 years
(male); 68 years (female)
*Infant Mortality Rate (Ratio):*
60/1,000
*Physicians Available (Ratio):* 1/2,181

### Education
*Adult Literacy Rate:* 58%
*Compulsory (Ages):* 6–12; free

## COMMUNICATION
*Telephones:* 675,000 main lines
*Daily Newspaper Circulation:* 27 per
1,000 people
*Televisions:* 48 per 2,000 people
*Internet Service Provider:* 1 (2000)

## TRANSPORTATION
*Highways in Miles (Kilometers):* 29,435
(47,400)
*Railroads in Miles (Kilometers):* 1,262
(2,032)
*Usable Airfields:* 109
*Motor Vehicles in Use:* 1,040,000

## GOVERNMENT
*Type:* officially a republic; in reality a
single-party secular state with an
absolute ruler
*Independence Date:* October 3, 1932
(from a League of Nations mandate
under British administration)

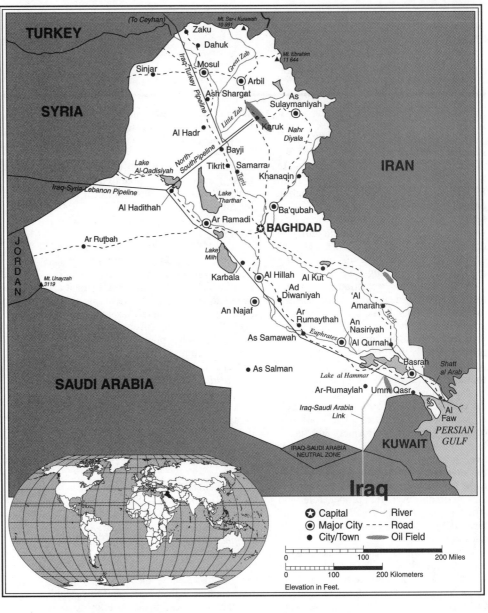

*Head of State/Government:* President
Saddam Hussein is both head of state
and head of government
*Political Parties:* Ba'th (Iraqi branch of
Arab Socialist Resurrection Party), only
legal party
*Suffrage:* universal at 18

## MILITARY
*Military Expenditures (% of GDP):* 18%
*Current Disputes:* final exchanges with
Iran resulting from 1980–1988 war not
settled; conflict with the United States
and Britain over no-fly zones in
Kurdistan and the southeast; periodic
territorial challenges to Kuwait; conflict
with Turkey over water-development
plans

## ECONOMY
*Currency ($ U.S. Equivalent):* 3,275
dinars = $1
*Per Capita Income/GDP:* $2,500/$57
billion
*GDP Growth Rate:* 15%
*Inflation Rate:* 100%
*Labor Force:* 4,400,000
*Natural Resources:* petroleum; natural gas;
phosphates; sulfur; lead; gypsum; iron ore
*Agriculture:* wheat; barley; rice;
vegetables; dates; cotton; sheep; cattle
*Industry:* petroleum; chemicals; textiles;
construction materials; food processing
*Exports:* $21.8 billion (primary partners
Russia, France, Switzerland)
*Imports:* $13.8 billion (primary partners
Egypt, Russia, France)

# IRAQ

The Republic of Iraq is a young state in a very old land. In ancient times, its central portion was called *Mesopotamia,* a word meaning "land between the rivers." Those rivers are the Tigris and the Euphrates, which originate in the highlands of Turkey and flow southward for more than a thousand miles to join in an estuary called the Shatt al-Arab, which carries their joint flow into the Persian (or, to Iraqis, the Arab) Gulf.

The fertility of the land between the rivers encouraged human settlement and agriculture from an early date. The oldest farming community yet discovered anywhere was unearthed near Nineveh, capital of the Assyrian Empire, in 1989; it dates back to 9000 B.C. Other settlements grew in time into small but important cities with local governments, their economies based on trade and crafts production in addition to agriculture. And the process of using a written alphabet with characters rather than symbols probably originated here. In 1999, President Saddam Hussain announced an international festival for the year 2000 to mark the 5,000th anniversary of this Mesopotamian invention (although recent archaeological discoveries in Egypt suggest that writing may have developed there even earlier).

Present-day Iraq (*Iraq* is an Arabic word meaning "cliff" or, less glamorously, "mud bank") occupies a much larger territory than the original Mesopotamia. Iraqi territory also includes a Neutral Zone on the border with Saudi Arabia. Iraq's other borders are with Turkey, Syria, Jordan, Kuwait, and Iran. These borders were established by the British on behalf of the newly formed Iraqi government, which they controlled after World War I. Disagreement with Kuwait over oil production and allocation from their shared Rumaila field was a factor in Iraq's 1990 invasion of Kuwait.

In 1994, Iraq accepted the border demarcated under United Nations *Resolutions 687, 773,* and *883,* formally relinquishing its claims to Kuwait and the islands of Bubiyan and Warbah. The new border, realigned northward by an international commission, removed 1,870 feet from Iraqi jurisdiction.

Iraq's other border in question, disputed with Iran, is in the Shatt al-Arab (Arab Delta), a broad, navigable estuary extending from the confluence of the Tigris and Euphrates Rivers down to the Persian Gulf. During the years of the British mandate and early independence, Iraq claimed ownership from the west to east banks. Iran's claim extended from its own (east) bank to mid-channel. Iraq recognized the Iranian claim in a 1975 agreement; in return, Iran withdrew support from Kurds in northern Iraq who were seeking autonomy within the Iraqi state. The unilateral abrogation of this agreement by Saddam Hussain was one factor in the 1980–1988 Iran–Iraq War.

# HISTORY

During its long and rich history, the "land between the rivers" has seen many empires rise and fall. Assyrians, Babylonians, Chaldeans, Persians, and others contributed layer upon layer to Mesopotamian civilization. In 1989, archaeologists digging at the site of Nimrud, a major Assyrian city, uncovered the 2,700-year-old tomb of a royal princess within the grounds of the palace of King Ashurnasirpal II, containing a vast store of her jewelry—55 pounds in all.

Despite the many varied influences, the most important influence in Iraqi social and cultural life today comes from the conquest of the region by Islamic Arabs. In A.D. 637, an Arab army defeated the Persians, who were then rulers of Iraq, near the village of Qadisiya, not far from modern Baghdad, a victory of great symbolic importance for Iraqis today. Arab peoples settled the region and intermarried with the local population, producing the contemporary Iraqi–Arab population.

During the early years of Islam, Iraq played an important role in Islamic politics. It was a center of Shia opposition to the Sunni Muslim caliphs. The tombs of Ali, Muhammad's son-in-law and the fourth and last leader of a united caliphate, and his son Husayn, martyred in a power struggle with his Damascus-based rival Yazid, are both in Iraq (at Najaf and Karbala, respectively).

In the period of the Abbasid caliphs (A.D. 750–1258), Iraq was the center of a vast Islamic empire stretching from Morocco on the west to the plains of India. Caliph al-Mansur laid out a new capital for the world of Islam, some 60 miles from the ruins of Babylon. He named his new capital Baghdad, possibly derived from a Persian word for "garden," and, according to legend, laid bricks for its foundations with his own hand. Baghdad was a round city, built in concentric circles, each one walled, with the caliph's green-domed palace and mosque at the center. It was the world's first planned city, in the sense of having been laid out in a definite urban configuration and design. Under the caliphs, Baghdad became a center of science, medicine, philosophy, law, and the arts, at a time when London and Paris were mud-and-wattle villages. The city became wealthy from the goods brought by ships from Africa, Asia, and the Far East, since it was easily reachable by shallow-draught boats from the Gulf and the Indian Ocean moving up the Tigris to its harbor.

Baghdad was destroyed by an invasion of Central Asian Mongols in A.D. 1258. The Mongols overran most of the Middle East. In addition to ravaging cities, they ruined the complex irrigation system that made agriculture possible and productive. Modern Iraq has yet to reach the level of agricultural productivity of Abbasid times, even with the use of sophisticated technology.

After the fall of Baghdad, Iraq came under the rule of various local princes and dynasties. In the sixteenth century, it was included in the expanding territory of the Safavid Empire of Iran. The Safavid shah championed the cause of Shia Islam; as a result, the Ottoman sultan, who was Sunni, sent forces to recover the area from his hated Shia foe. Possession of Iraq went back and forth between the two powers, but the Ottomans eventually established control until the twentieth century.

Iraq was administered as three separate provinces under appointed Ottoman governors. The governors paid for their appointments and were interested only in recovering their losses. The result was heavy taxation and indifference to social and economic needs. The one exception was the province of Baghdad. It was governed by a man whom today we would call an enlightened administrator. This governor, Midhat Pasha, set up a provincial newspaper, hospitals, schools, munitions factories, and a fleet of barges to carry produce downriver to ports on the Gulf. His administration also ensured public security and an equitable taxation system. Midhat Pasha later became the grand vizier (prime minister) of the Ottoman Empire and was the architect of the 1876 Constitution, which limited the powers of the sultan.

## The British Mandate

World War I found England and France at war with Germany and the Ottoman Empire. British forces occupied Iraq, which they rechristened Mesopotamia, early in the war. British leaders had worked with Arab leaders in the Ottoman Empire to launch a revolt against the sultan; in return, they promised to help the Arabs form an independent Arab state once the Ottomans had been defeated. A number of prominent Iraqi officers who were serving in the Ottoman Army then joined the British and helped them in the Iraqi campaign.

The British promise, however, was not kept. The British had made other commitments, notably to their French allies, to divide the Arab provinces of the Ottoman Empire into British and French "zones of influence." An independent Arab state in those provinces was not in the cards.

The most that the British (and the French) would do was to organize protectorates, called mandates, over the Arab provinces, promising to help the population become self-governing within a specified period of time. The arrangement was approved by the new League of Nations in 1920. Iraq then became a British mandate, with Faisal ibn Hussein as its king, but with British advisers appointed to manage its affairs. (Faisal had been ruler of the short-lived Arab kingdom of Syria set up after the war, but he was expelled when the French occupied Damascus and established their mandate.)

The British kept their promise with the mandate. They worked out a Constitution for Iraq in 1925 that established a constitutional monarchy with an elected Legislature and a system of checks and balances. Political parties were allowed, although most of them were groupings around prominent personalities and had no platform other than independence from Britain. In 1932, the mandate formally ended, and Iraq became an independent kingdom under Faisal. The British kept the use of certain air bases, and their large capital investment in the oil industry was protected through a 25-year treaty. Otherwise, the new Iraqi nation was on its own.

### The Iraqi Monarchy: 1932–1958

The new kingdom cast adrift on perilous international waters was far from being a unified nation. It was more of a patchwork of warring and competing groups. The Muslim population was divided into Sunni and Shia, as it is today, with the Sunnis forming a minority but controlling the government and business and dominating urban life. The Shias, although a majority, were mostly rural peasants and farmers, many of them migrants to the cities, where they formed a large underclass.

The country also had large Christian and Jewish communities, the latter tracing its origins back several thousand years to the exile of Jews from Palestine to Babylonia after the conquest of Jerusalem by Nebuchadnezzar. The Assyrians formed the largest Christian group. Formerly residents in Ottoman Turkey, they supported the British as "our smallest ally" in World War I and, as a result, were allowed to resettle in Iraq after the establishment of the Turkish Republic. The British protected them, recruiting Assyrians as guards for military and air bases and the British-controlled police force. As one ob-

server noted, "with their slouch hats and red and white hackles, they became a symbol for British rule in Iraq. However, when they pushed their luck to the point of demanding autonomy in 1933, the British-trained Iraqi Army moved against them, destroying villages and massacring their Assyrian inhabitants.[1] Many fled into exile, forming large communities (particularly in Detroit and San Diego). A small minority remained in Iraq, but most of them have now left, due to the country's economic difficulties. A group of 172 Assyrians took asylum in Mexico in September 2000.

The new state also included other non-Muslim communities, such as the Yazidis (called "devil-worshippers," from their religious practice) and the Sabaeans, descended from the ancient Babylonians. These social and religious divisions in the population plus great economic disparities made the new state almost impossible to govern or develop politically.[2]

King Faisal I was the single stabilizing influence in Iraqi politics, so his untimely death in 1933 was critical. His son and successor, Ghazi, was more interested in racing cars than anything else and was killed at the wheel of one in 1939. Ghazi's infant son succeeded him as King Faisal II, while Ghazi's first cousin became regent until the new ruler came of age.

After King Faisal's death and during the minority of his young son, the regent, Abd al-Ilah, governed the country along with a constantly shifting coalition of landowners, merchants, tribal leaders, and urban politicians. As a result, there was little political stability or progress toward national unity. Between 1933 and 1936, for example, 22 different cabinets held office. The late Nuri al-Said, who served as prime minister a number of times, once compared the Iraqi government to a pack of cards. You must shuffle them often, he said, because the same faces keep turning up.[3]

### THE REVOLUTION OF 1958

To their credit, the king's ministers kept the country's three broad social divisions—the Kurdish north, the Sunni Arab center, and the Shia Arab south—in relative balance and harmony. Oil revenues were channeled into large-scale development projects. Education was promoted strongly, which may explain why Iraq has a much higher literacy rate than most other Middle Eastern countries. The press was free, and, though it had a small and ingrown political elite, there was much participation in legislative elections. Despite its legitimate Arab credentials as one of the successor states fashioned by the

British after World War I, however, a new generation of pan-Arab nationalist Iraqis viewed the royal regime as a continuation of foreign rule, first Turkish and then British.

Resentment crystallized in the Iraqi Army. On July 14, 1958, a group of young officers overthrew the monarchy in a swift, predawn coup. The king, regent, and royal family were killed. Iraq's new leaders proclaimed a republic that would be reformed, free, and democratic, united with the rest of the Arab world and opposed to all foreign ideologies, "Communist, American, British or Fascist."

Iraq has been a republic since the 1958 Revolution, and July 14 remains a national holiday. But the republic has passed through many different stages, with periodic coups, changes in leadership, and political shifts, most of them violent. Continuing sectarian and ethnic hatreds, maneuvering of political factions, ideological differences, and lack of opportunities for legitimate opposition to express itself without violence have created a constant sense of insecurity among Iraqi leaders. A similar paranoia affects Iraq's relations with its neighbors. The competition for influence in the Arab world and the Persian/Arab Gulf and other factors combine to keep the leadership constantly on edge.

This pattern of political instability showed itself in the coups and attempted coups of the 1960s. The republic's first two leaders were overthrown after a few years. Several more violent shifts in the Iraqi government took place before the Ba'th Party seized control in 1968. Since that time, the party has dealt ruthlessly with internal opposition. A 1978 decree outlawed all political activity outside the Ba'th for members of the armed forces. Many Shia clergy were executed in 1978–1979 for leading antigovernment demonstrations after the Iranian Revolution; and following Saddam Hussain's rise to the presidency, he purged a number of members of the Revolutionary Command Council (RCC), on charges that they were part of a plot to overthrow the regime.

### THE BA'TH PARTY IN POWER

The Ba'th Party in Iraq began as a branch of the Syrian Ba'th founded in the 1940s by two Syrian intellectuals: Michel Aflaq, a Christian teacher, and Salah al-Din Bitar, a Sunni Muslim. Like its Syrian parent, the Iraqi Ba'th was dedicated to the goals of Arab unity, freedom, and socialism. However, infighting among Syrian Ba'th leaders in the 1960s led to the expulsion of Aflaq and Bitar. Aflaq went to Iraq, where he was accepted as the party's true leader. Eventually, he moved to Paris, where he died in 1989. His body was brought back to Iraq for burial, giving the Iraqi Ba'th a strong claim to legitimacy in its struggle with the Syrian Ba'th for hegemony in the movement for Arab unity.

The basis of government under the Ba'th is the 1970 Provisional Constitution, issued unilaterally by the Revolutionary Command Council, the party's chief decision-making body. It defines Iraq as a sovereign peoples' democratic republic. The Constitution provides for an "elected" National Assembly with responsibility for ratification of laws and RCC decisions.

An abortive coup in 1973, which pitted a civilian faction of the Ba'th against the military leadership headed by President Ahmad Hasan al-Bakr, stirred party leaders to attempt to broaden their base of popular support. They reached agreement with the Iraqi Communist Party to set up a Progressive National Patriotic Front. Other organizations and groups joined the Front later. Although the Iraqi Communist Party had cooperated with the Ba'th on several occasions, the agreement marked its first legal recognition as a party. However, distrust between the two organizations deepened as Ba'th leaders struggled to mobilize the masses. The Communists withdrew from the Front in 1979 and refused to participate in parliamentary elections. Their party was declared illegal in 1980 and has not been reinstated, largely due to its support for Iran during the Iran–Iraq War.

## SADDAM HUSSAIN

Politics in Iraq since the 1958 overthrow of the monarchy has been marked by extreme secrecy. The intrigues and maneuverings of factions within the Ba'th take place off-screen, and there is no tradition of public pressure to bring them to account. In assessing the strengths, capabilities, and prospects for survival of Iraq's Ba'th leaders, a good question beyond "Who are they?" is "Will the Iraqi ruling class please stand up?"[4] But in the late 1970s and early 1980s, one of its leaders, Saddam Hussain, emerged from the pack to become an absolute ruler.

Saddam Hussain's early history did not suggest such an achievement. He was born in 1937 in the small town of Tikrit, on the Tigris halfway between Baghdad and Mosul. Tikrit's chief claim to fame, until the twentieth century, was that it was the birthplace of Saladin, hero of the Islamic world in the Middle Ages against the Crusaders. (The Iraqi leader has at times identified himself with Saladin as another great Tikriti, although Saladin was a Kurd and Saddam Hussain's distrust of Kurds

(Homer Sykes/Katz/Woodfin)

The image of Saddam Hussain has become part of the Iraqi landscape; his portrait appears in public buildings, at the entrances to cities, in homes, even on billboards along highways.

is well known.) His family belonged to the Begat clan of the Al Bu Nasser tribe, settled around Tikrit. They lived in a nearby village and farmed some 12 acres of land. According to accounts, Saddam was a bully and street fighter from early childhood. He spent little time in school and was hired out from time to time as a shepherd. As a teenager he left home for Baghdad, lived with an uncle, and joined the Ba'th Party. He played a very minor role in the Ba'th's attempted assassination in 1959 of Abd al-Karim Qassem, leader of the 1958 Revolution, and escaped to Egypt in disguise. He returned to Iraq after Qassem's overthrow and execution and gradually worked his way up through the ranks of the Ba'th. Eventually he became vice-chairman, and then chairman, of the Revolutionary Command Council, the party's ruling body. As chairman, he automatically became president of Iraq under the 1970 Constitution. As there are no constitutional provisions limiting the terms of office for the position, the National Assembly named him president-for-life in 1990.[5]

Saddam Hussain is a somewhat unusual head of state, in that he holds supreme elective offices but has never stood as a candidate in an election, and he serves as commander of the armed forces but has never served in the military. He does have great personal courage and a gambler's instinct in decision making. Like most gamblers, though, he is often wrong, two glaring examples being the invasion of Iran and the occupation of Kuwait. Domestically, he has a surer touch. Through control of the Ba'th, the army, and the intelligence services, with their legion of informers, he has instilled a "climate of fear" in the Iraqi people, with actions that

deepen this fear. Thus, shortly after he became president he declared that a plot by other Ba'th leaders to overthrow him had been discovered. He called an emergency meeting of the RCC, read out the names of the conspirators, had them called forward to "confess," and then taken out and shot. Finally, he sent a videotape of the proceedings to other Arab heads of state "so they would understand the need for the Ba'th to destroy enemies within its ranks."[6]

The Iran–Iraq War of the 1980s was a severe test for the Ba'th and its leader. A series of Iraqi defeats with heavy casualties in the mid-1980s suggested that the Iranian demand for Saddam Hussain's ouster as a precondition for peace might ignite a popular uprising against him. But Iranian advances into Iraqi territory, and in particular the capture of the Fao Peninsula and the Majnoon oil fields, united the Iraqis behind Saddam. For one of the few times in its history, the nation coalesced around a leader and a cause.

The Iraqi leader used this support to cultivate a more popular public image. He visited the war front regularly, traveled to villages for whistle-stop appearances, helped with the harvests, and mingled with the people. Portraits of Saddam Hussain in field marshal's uniform, Bedouin robes, Ba'th Party green fatigues, and Italian designer suits, often accompanied by the peasant *keffiyeh* (headscarf) of his native region, are common everywhere in Iraq.

## RECENT DEVELOPMENTS

The end of the war with Iran and Saddam Hussain's popularity as the heroic defender of the Iraqi Arab nation against the Shia Iranian enemy prompted a certain lifting of Ba'thist repression and authoritarian rule. Emergency wartime regulations in force since 1980 were relaxed in 1989, and an amnesty was announced for all political exiles except "agents of Iran."

In July 1990, the RCC and the Arab Ba'th Regional Command, the party's governing body, approved a draft constitution to replace the 1970 provisional one. The new Constitution "legalized" the formation of political parties other than the Ba'th, as long as they conformed to Ba'thist principles. It also established freedom of the press and other civil rights, although again in conformity with Ba'thism.

The 1990 Iraqi occupation of Kuwait and the ensuing Gulf War halted even these small steps toward representative government. The draft Constitution remained in suspension; it was not issued unilaterally by the regime nor submitted to voters in a referendum. However, Saddam Hussain has taken it upon himself in recent years to open up the political process, presumably to solidify his image as the "Great Savior." He approved holding of elections for a new Majlis al-Watani in 1996, followed by local and municipal council elections. All candidates were required to be either Ba'th members or bona fide independents. These councils have the authority under a 1995 law to administer programs in health, education, and economic development in their respective localities.

Perhaps the most disturbing feature of Saddam Hussain's rule, as far as the rest of the world is concerned, is his determination to make Iraq the possessor of nuclear, chemical, and biological weapons as a major world power. According to his chief "bombmaker," in 1971 he directed a team of scientists and engineers to build a nuclear bomb equal to that exploded by the United States over Hiroshima in 1945. The first one made by Iraq would be dropped unannounced on Israel. Such a bomb was tested in 1987, but the project was halted in 1990 by the invasion of Kuwait. By that time, it had employed 12,000 engineers and scientists and cost more than $10 billion.[7]

## THE KURDS

The Kurds, the largest non-Arab minority in Iraq today, form a relatively compact society in the northern mountains. Kurdish territory was included in the British mandate after World War I. British troops were already there, and the territory was known to have important oil resources. The Kurds agitated for self-rule periodically during the monarchy; for a few months after World War II, they formed their own republic in Kurdish areas straddling the Iraq–Iran and Iraq–Turkey borders.

In the 1960s, the Kurds rebelled against the Iraqi government, which had refused to meet their three demands (self-government in Kurdistan, use of Kurdish in schools, and a greater share in oil revenues). The government sent an army to the mountains but was unable to defeat the Kurds, masters of guerrilla warfare. Conflict continued intermittently into the 1970s. Although the 1970 Constitution named Arabs and Kurds as the two nationalities in the Iraqi nation and established autonomy for Kurdistan, the Iraqi government had no real intention of honoring its pledges to the Kurds.

A major Iraqi offensive in 1974 had considerable success against the Kurdish *Pesh Merga* ("Resistance"), even capturing several mountain strongholds. At that point, the shah of Iran, who had little use for Saddam Hussain, began to supply arms to the Pesh Merga. The shah also kept the Iraq–Iran border open as sanctuary for the guerrillas.

In 1975, a number of factors caused the shah to change his mind. He signed an agreement with Saddam Hussain, redefining the Iran–Iraq border to give Iran control over half of the Shatt al-Arab. In return, the shah agreed to halt support for the Kurds. The northern border was closed and, without Iranian support, Kurdish resistance collapsed. A similar fate befell the Assyrian community. Entire villages were destroyed, and the surviving population was resettled farther south as Saddam Hussain pressed his drive to "purify" the Iraqi nation and preserve Sunni Arab minority authority.

In 1986, Iran resumed support for the Pesh Merga, to use its warriors as an auxiliary force against the Iraqis. Kurdish forces carried out a number of raids into northern Iraq.

But with the end of the war with Iran in 1988, the Iraqi Army turned on the Kurds in a savage and deliberate campaign of genocide. Operation *Anfal* ("spoils," in Arabic) involved the launching of chemical attacks on such villages as Halabja and the forced deportation of Kurdish villagers from their mountains to detention centers in the flatlands. The campaign received international exposure when 18 tons of Iraqi state documents detailing Operation Anfal were captured by Kurdish partisans during the abortive uprising that followed the Gulf War. The documents, prepared with Nazi-like thoroughness, indicated that approximately 180,000 Kurds, mostly old men, women, and children, had died or disappeared during the operation.[8]

A second exodus of Kurdish refugees took place in 1991, after uprisings of Kurdish rebels in northern Iraq were bru-

tally suppressed by the Iraqi Army, which had remained loyal to Saddam Hussain. The United States and its allies sent troops and aircraft to the Iraqi–Turkish border and barred Iraq from using its own air space north of the 36th Parallel, the main area of Kurdish settlement. Several hundred thousand refugees subsequently returned to their homes and villages.

Under this umbrella of air protection and the exclusion of Iraqi forces from the Kurdish region, the Iraqi Kurds moved toward self-rule in their region. The two main factions—the Kurdish Democratic Party (KDP), led by Massoud al-Barzani, and the Patriotic Union of Kurdistan (PUK) of Jalal al-Talabani—agreed to the formation of a joint Parliament elected by the Kurdish population. This new Parliament, which was divided equally between KDP and PUK members, approved a law defining a federal relationship with Iraq, providing for internal autonomy for the Kurdish region. Kurdish was confirmed as the official language, and a Kurdish university was established.

But the tragedy of the Kurds has always been their inability to unite unless there is an external threat. With the Iraqi regime effectively removed from Kurdistan, the traditional cleavages and inner conflicts of Kurdish society came to the surface. A new Kurdish Parliament was scheduled to be elected in September 1995. However, clashes between the two factions broke into open conflict before the elections could take place. By 1996, the PUK controlled two thirds of the region, including the major cities of Irbil and Sulaymaniyah. Barzani's KDP, although it controlled only one third, held an economic advantage over its rival because of its control over the main source of Kurdish revenues. The lion's share of these revenues came from trade (and smuggling) across the Turkish border.

The bell rang for another tragic hour in Iraqi Kurdistan in September 1996. Barzani's KDP struck a deal with Saddam Hussain to help him unseat the rival PUK; and KDP forces, backed by 30,000 to 40,000 Iraqi troops with tanks and artillery, swept down on Irbil and Sulaymaniyah to drive the PUK from its strongholds. The KDP success was brief; the PUK withdrew into the mountains to regroup and then launched a counteroffensive, which recovered all its lost territories, except Irbil, by mid-October. Saddam Hussain withdrew his forces after a blunt warning from the United States, but not before rounding up opposition dissidents who had remained there after the Gulf War and were supported by the U.S. Central Intelligence Agency to form the anti-Saddam Iraqi National Congress (INC).

Operation Provide Comfort, which was set up after the Gulf War to give the Kurds in northern Iraq a "safe haven" under U.S. and British air protection, has enabled the Kurdish population to become a self-governing state, albeit remaining part of Iraq. They have an elected Parliament and other institutions of government. In 2001, peace between the KDP and the PUK ended a decade of conflict. Currently the KDP administers the western half of the territory, the PUK the eastern half, with overall government by an elected Parliament.

Economically, Iraqi Kurdistan has prospered under the U.S.–U.K. protection. It receives income from the Iraqi oil-for-food program and a great deal more from cross-border smuggling through Turkey. Use of its own currency and language has helped the integration of thbis fractious population into a bona fide Iraqi Kurdish nation.

As one scholar has observed, the Kurds are caught in a double bind—one internal, the other international. Massoud Barzani, son of the legendary Kurdish leader Mulla Mustafa Barzani, "has always assumed that leadership of the Kurds is his birthright. [He is] unable to see the larger interest of Iraqi Kurds outside the parochial concerns of his tribal and family alliances. . . ." The "international bind" for the Kurds, both those in Iraq and in neighboring countries, is that they have always been manipulated by outside powers, always for reasons of the outsiders' self-interest.[9]

## THE OPPOSITION
Opposition to Saddam Hussain has always been fragmented. Those of his political opponents who escaped the leader's firing squads lacked a power base inside the country; they also often disagreed among themselves and preferred a comfortable exile to the ordeal of attempting the overthrow of a well-entrenched despot. But the Iraqi defeat in the Gulf War, followed by the Kurdish and Shia popular uprisings—although they were unsuccessful—suggested that there was more internal resistance to Saddam's rule than had been suspected. The success of Iraq's Kurds in establishing de facto autonomy under UN–U.S. protection also encouraged the opposition, as did the continuing UN–imposed limitations on Iraqi sovereignty. In June 1992, representatives of some 30 opposition groups met in Vienna, Austria, to form the Iraqi National Congress.

Composed of various opposition groups, the INC described its purpose as the overthrow of Saddam Hussain and the Ba'th Party and their replacement by a secular Islamic regime. The state would be governed under a constitution providing specific guarantees of human rights, protection of minorities, and a multiparty political system. The United States then began funneling funds through its Central Intelligence Agency to the INC, while other CIA operatives worked with its rival anti-Saddam organization, the Iraq National Accord (INA), based in Jordan. In 1994, a team of CIA officers went to Iraqi Kurdistan to establish a base for the INC as the starting point for a coup against the Iraqi dictator.

However, the conflict between Kurdish rival groups described above encouraged the Iraqi Army to invade their territory. The CIA/INC base was overrun. Those of its members not arrested or executed by the Iraqis were evacuated to the United States after the 1996 presidential election. A similar fate befell the INA, which was potentially more dangerous to Saddam because it was centered in units that formed the core of his support, the Republican Guards and the Security Service (the dreaded *Mukhabarat*). In June 1996, the officers involved were arrested, tortured, and executed as they prepared to stage their coup.[10]

## OTHER COMMUNITIES
The Shia community, which forms approximately two thirds of the total population of Iraq, has been ruled by the Sunni minority since independence. Shias have been consistently underrepresented in successive Ba'thist governments and are the most economically deprived component of the population. However, they remained loyal to the regime (or at least quiescent) during the war with Iran. In a belated attempt to undo decades of deprivation and assure their continued loyalty, the government invested large sums in the rehabilitation of Shia areas in southern Iraq after the war ended. Roads were built, and sacred Shia shrines were repaired.

Long-held Shia grievances against Ba'thist rule erupted in a violent uprising after Iraq's defeat in the Gulf War. The uprising was crushed, however, as Iraqi troops remained loyal to Saddam Hussain. Some 600 troops were killed in an Alamo-type siege of the sacred shrines, which were badly damaged. A few rebels escaped into the almost impenetrable marshlands of southern Iraq. But their expectations of U.S. support proved illusory. The Clinton administration feared that Iran would intervene on behalf of the Iraqi Shias. U.S. helicopters did nothing except to overfly Iraqi gunships as they strafed columns of fleeing refugees. In a half-hearted policy, the Clinton administration eventually declared a no-fly zone south of the 32nd Parallel, off limits to Iraqi aircraft. But by then, the uprising had been crushed.

The rebels' retreat into the marshlands served as an excuse for the Iraqi regime to bring another distinctive community—the Marsh Arabs—under centralized government control. This community, believed by some to be descended from the original inhabitants of southern Iraq and by others to be descended from slaves, has practiced for centuries a unique way of life based on fishing and hunting in the marshes, living in papyrus-and-mud houses and traveling in reed boats through the maze of unmarked channels of their watery region. Prior to 1990, they numbered about 750,000. Previous Iraqi governments had ignored them, but Saddam Hussain was determined to bring all Iraq under centralized government control. Using their support for Shia rebels hiding in the marshes as his excuse, he declared that their culture was "primitive, debased and non-Iraqi." Iraqi troops encircled a 3,800-square-mile area of marshlands in June 1992, rounding up the population for resettlement elsewhere and killing those who resisted, while artillery barrages leveled their villages.

At the same time, the government began a massive effort to reclaim the marshes. Aside from destroying the way of life of the Marsh Arabs, it would reclaim the area and convert millions of acres to productive farmland. A "third river," in the form of a canal between the Tigris and the Euphrates, was completed in three months early in 1993 by 6,000 workers drawn from Iraq's huge labor surplus. Some 350 miles in length, it was intended to drain salt water from approximately 330 million acres of marshland for conversion to agriculture. By June 1993, the water level in parts of the marshes had dropped by more than three feet; some 46 Arab villages were left high and dry. The no-fly exclusion zone had little effect on the campaign against the Marsh Arabs and their Shia allies, since it did not extend to artillery bombardments or infantry attacks. The canal is important to agriculture in that region since it helps drain salt from the soil. However, its impact on the 5,000-year-old way of life of the Marsh Arabs has been disastrous. The few marshlands that have not been destroyed provide a base for Shia guerrillas in their struggle against the regime. Also, the reclamation of the marshes has been detrimental not only to its inhabitants but also to the environment of the entire region. The worst dust storm in history, which blanketed Kuwait in choking dust early in 2000, was the direct result of marsh drainage.

## THE ECONOMY

Iraq's economy since independence has been based on oil production and exports. The country also has large natural-gas reserves as well as phosphate rock, sulfur, lead, gypsum, and iron ore. Ancient Mesopotamia was probably the first area in the world to develop agriculture, using the fertile soil nourished by the Tigris and Euphrates Rivers. Until recently, Iraq was the world's largest exporter of dates. However, by 1999 the UN embargo (see below) and the longest drought in a century had brought food production to a near standstill. An estimated 70 percent of wheat and barley crops, mainstays of agriculture, were lost, and government officials described the situation as a "food catastrophe" comparable to the collapse of the health-care system.

Since the Ba'th Party took control in 1968, its economic policies have emphasized state control and guidance of the economy, under the Ba'thist rubric of guided socialism. In 1987, the regime began a major economic restructuring program. More than 600 state organizations were abolished, and young technocrats replaced many senior ministers. In 1988, the government began selling off state-run industries, reserving only heavy industry and hydrocarbons for state operation. Light industries such as breweries and dairy plants would henceforth be run by the private sector.

The oil industry was developed by the British during the mandate but was nationalized in the early 1970s. Nationalization and price increases after 1973 helped to accelerate economic growth. The bulk of Iraqi oil shipments are exported via pipelines across Turkey and Syria. During the war with Iran, the Turkish pipeline proved essential to Iraq's economic survival, since the one across Syrian territory was closed and Iraq's own refineries and ports were put out of commission by Iranian attacks. Turkey closed this pipeline during the 1990–1991 Gulf crisis, a decision that proved a severe strain for the Iraqi economy (not to mention a huge sacrifice for coalition-member Turkey).

Iraq has proven oil reserves of some 100 billion barrels, the fifth largest in the world, and new discoveries continue to augment the total. Oil output was cut to 2 million barrels per day in 1986–1987, in accordance with quotas set by the Organization of Petroleum Exporting Countries, but was increased to 4.5 million b/d in 1989 as the country sought to recover economically from war damage.

The economic impact of the eight-year Iran–Iraq War was heavy, causing delays in interest payments on foreign loans, defaults to some foreign contractors, and postponement of major development projects except for dams, deemed vital to agricultural production. The war also was a heavy drain on Iraqi finances; arms purchases between 1981 and 1985 cost the government $23.9 billion. By 1986, the external debt was $12 billion. By 1988, the debt burden had gone up to nearly $60 billion, although half this total had been given by the Arab Gulf states as war aid and was unlikely ever to be repaid.

Iraq's economic recovery after the war with Iran, despite heavy external debts, suggested rapid growth in the 1990s. Gross domestic product was expected to rise by 5 percent a year due to increasing oil revenues. Even in 1988, Iraq's GDP of $50 billion was the highest in the Arab world, after Saudi Arabia's. With a well-developed infrastructure and a highly trained workforce, Iraq appeared ready to move upward into the ranks of the developed nations.

## THE UN EMBARGO

Iraq's invasion and occupation of Kuwait and the resulting Gulf War drew a red line through these optimistic prospects. Bombing raids destroyed much of Iraq's infrastructure, knocking out electricity grids, bridges, and sewage and water-purification systems. Although much of this infrastructure has been repaired, the oil industry and water and sanitation systems in particular have been operating at only about 40 percent of capacity.

The UN embargo that was imposed on Iraq after the Gulf War to force compliance with resolutions ordering the country to dismantle its weapons program has not only brought development to a halt but has also caused untold suffering for the Iraqi population. The resolutions in question were *Resolution 687,* which required the destruction of all missile, chemical, and nuclear facilities; *Resolution 713,* which established a permanent UN monitoring system for all missile test sites and nuclear installations; and *Resolution 986,* which allowed Iraq to sell 700,000 barrels of oil per day for six months, in return for its compliance with the first two resolutions. Of the $1.6 billion raised through oil sales, $300 million would be paid into a UN reparations fund for Kuwait. Another $300 million would be put aside to finance the UN monitoring system as well as providing aid for the Kurdish population. The remainder would revert to Iraq to be used for purchases of food and medical supplies.

Saddam Hussein initially refused to be bound by *Resolution 986,* calling it an infringement of Iraq's national sovereignty. But in 1996, he agreed to its terms. By then, the Iraqi people were nearly destitute, suffering from extreme shortages of food and medicines. The United Nations estimated that 750,000 Iraqi children were "severely malnourished." Half a million had died, and the monthly death toll from malnutrition-related illnesses was averaging 5,750, the majority of them children under age five, due to lack of basic medicines and hospital equipment.[11] In 1998, the Security Council increased approved Iraqi oil revenues to $5.26 billion every six months. Higher world oil prices and exemptions to make up for earlier shortfalls in its export quota due to equipment breakdowns brought total revenues to $7

(UN photo/H. Arvidsson)

UN Security Council *Resolution 687* called for the disposal of Iraq's weapons of mass destruction. Saddam Hussain had stockpiled enormous quantities of chemical munitions, and while many of these insidious weapons were indeed destroyed, large quantities remained hidden. Iraq's refusal to cooperate with international inspection teams has caused sanctions to remain in place.

billion in 1999. In all, Iraq has received $40 billion from oil sales since 1996. However, the UN Compensation Commission, which is responsible for reparations to companies and individuals for losses sustained during the occupation of Kuwait, disbursed $365 million in payment of claims in September 2001. The largest single payment, $176.3 million, went to Botas Petroleum Pipeline Corporation to cover losses caused by the shutdown in the pipeline from Iraq to the Turkish port of Iskenderun. Since its establishment, the commission has paid $35.4 billion to claimants. Agreement between the United States and Russia in the Security Council enabled it in November 2001 to extend sanctions for another six months, to May 2002, keeping the existing "oil-for-food" and its governing rules unchanged.

Where the country has profited economically in spite of the sanctions is in the numerous loopholes in the program. Due in part to the worsening Palestinian–Israeli conflict, but also to increased unwillingness on the part of many countries to honor them, the sanctions have become increasingly ineffective. By early 2001, 20 countries had resumed regular air service to Baghdad; they included Turkey, Egypt, and Syria, all part of the original Desert Storm coalition. Iraq's Arab neighbors have done their part to flout the United Nations. In January 2001, the country signed a free-trade agreement with Syria that would triple their annual trade, up to $1 billion. Much of this would come to Iraq from oil shipments through the reopened pipeline from the Kirkuk oil fields to Banias, Syria. Other Arab states have followed suit; there are sales contracts with Egypt, Jordan, Lebanon, and the United Arab Emirates, for a total of $4.7 billion.

## GLORIOUS LEADER, OR GREAT SURVIVOR?

Until very recently, army support and a ruthlessly efficient security service, with informers literally at every street corner, assured Saddam Hussain's continuation in power. In any case, internal opposition is nonexistent. Aside from a small (mostly Sunni) elite dependent upon the ruler and thus isolated from the impact of sanctions, potential opponents have been silenced or are in exile. The once prosperous and well-educated Iraqi middle class, the backbone of national development, has been reduced to near starvation, so survival has taken precedence over any form of political activity for those who have remained in the country.

Saddam Hussain's grip on total power is buttressed by his extreme visibility—not in person, but on billboards, gigantic statues, and larger-than-life posters that are omnipresent not only in cities but also in the countryside. In Baghdad, victory arches and a huge statue of the Glorious Leader trampling on scraps of U.S. missiles were erected on the first anniversary of the U.S. air strikes, which Saddam describes as a "great victory" similar to Iraq's "success" in keeping Allied forces out of its territory in the Gulf War, the "Mother of All Battles."[12]

The cult of the Glorious Leader with which Saddam surrounds himself has not kept him entirely immune from attempts to oust him from power. An army coup by officers from the Dalaimi clan, traditional rivals of his Tikriti clan, was thwarted with considerable difficulty in June 1995. A much greater threat was the defection to Jordan of two of his sons-in-law with their wives and some Sunni officers. One son-in-law, Hussein Kamel, had headed the Iraqi secret-weapons program and was a member of the inner circle around the president. Kamel was given asylum in Jordan and talked openly of leading a coup to overthrow Saddam. But in time, the Iraqi exiles became an embarrassment to their hosts. Seven months after their arrival, the party left Jordan to return to Iraq, having received an offer from Saddam to pardon them as "repentant sinners." But after they had returned and were ensconced in Tikrit, the two sons-in-law were surrounded and killed in a gun battle with members of the presidential guard belonging to another, rival tribal clan. Its leaders issued a statement that "we have cut off this treacherous branch from our noble family tree. Amnesty does not obliterate the right of our family to impose the necessary punishment."[13]

Thus far, the Glorious Leader has proven an elusive and adroit opponent for U.S. policymakers as well as the UN Security Council. He has survived sanctions, U.S. air attacks, restrictions on Iraq's territorial sovereignty, and exposure of much of his secret weapons program, and he has responded to international pressure with effective counterpressures to ensure his retention of power. Internal opposition has been muzzled; the assassination of Grand Ayatollah Sadiq al-Badr, spiritual head of the Shia coummunity, was a warning of what real or potential opponents face at the hands of Saddam and his intelligence service.

The main organized opposition group outside the country is the Iraqi National Congress. In 1999, the U.S. Congress appropriated $97 million to the INC. However, almost none of that amount was actually disbursed, and what little there was went to buy computer equipment for the organization's London office. In 2001, the George W. Bush administration continued the practice, providing $4 million for "information gathering" inside Iraq, but the expulsion of the INC from its Kurdish base and lack of observers on the ground rendered the project useless.

In August 2001, a U.S.–financed satellite-television station, Liberty TV, went into operation as an INC project. Its $1 million start-up costs and $1.3 million annual operating costs would come from congressional appropriations. The new station beams political news reports, call-in and talk shows, and other programs not only to Iraq but elsewhere in the Middle East. Being broadcast by satellite, it cannot be jammed in Iraq, although only that portion of the population with access to satellite dishes can see to it. However, INC leaders insisted that by reaching an "influential audience," many of whose members are part of the power structure around Saddam, Liberty TV should facilitate the effort to overthrow the tyrannical Iraqi leader. But in December 2001, the State Department suspended funding for INC due to its lack of proper accounting for the funds. A deadline was set for compliance, while the INC was given $500,000 to cover current expenses.

Saddam Hussain's ruthless elimination of political opponents, along with his autocratic rule, have identified him with the Iraqi nation to a greater degree than that of any of his predecessors. For more than two decades he has been the arbiter of power, the ultimate dispenser of justice, the sole formulator of national policy. As one analyst noted, "Saddam's hegemony over Iraq's policy-making, and his highly personalized, consciously mobilizational rule meant that more than in any preceding period, identity would be persistently used to serve his political needs and interests."[14]

Following the September 11, 2001, terrorist bombings in the United States, Saddam denounced the action and the killing of innocent civilians. However, there were huge public demonstrations in Baghdad, presumably government-sponsored, to protest to continued U.S. and British air raids on Iraqi territory and the U.S. military campaign in Afghanistan. Protesters carried banners that read "Down With American Terrorism Against Islam." Although U.S. officials continued to insist on a connection between Iraq and al-Qaeda and spoke loudly of a possible invasion to topple Saddam, there has been as yet no evidence of complicity. The George W. Bush administration in January 2002 included Iraq in the "evil axis" of

| Border province of the Ottoman Empire 1520–1920 | British mandate 1920–1932 | Independent kingdom under Faisal I 1932 | The monarchy is overthrown by military officers 1958 | The Ba'th Party seizes power 1968 | The Algiers Agreement between the shah of Iran and Hussain ends Kurdish insurrection 1975 | Iran–Iraq War; diplomatic relations are restored with the United States after a 17-year break 1980s | Iraq invades and occupies Kuwait, leading to the brief but intense Gulf War; Saddam Hussein retains power 1990s |
|---|---|---|---|---|---|---|---|

2000s

Despite continuing UN sanctions, Saddam remains firmly in control

countries officially sponsoring terrorism and accused it of violating the 1972 treaty banning bacteriological, chemical, and other weapons of mass destruction. (Iraq is a signatory to the treaty.)

Iraq's peculiar status as an "artificial" nation-state, a forced creation lacking the essential basis for nationhood, was described earlier in this report. It remains a nation fragmented into many groups with different, often opposed identities. By putting on these various identities at various times when it suits him, Saddam has established the basis for a modern Iraqi nation, one with a sense of nationhood. It is secularist and yet Islamic, Arabist yet firmly nationalistic, historically viable in its ancient Mesopotamian and later Islamic Abbasid roots, urban yet tribal.

What does the future hold for this battered nation? It is almost inconceivable that another power center could emerge to challenge the Ba'th. In any event, the UN sanctions have united the people around the Ba'th and its leader to a greater degree than might have been expected. The Glorious Leader of today has yet to name a prospective heir. Of his two sons, the elder, Uday, has inherited his father's bullying nature but has yet to demonstrate the latter's charisma and skillful use of power. Recently he was "elected" speaker of the National Assembly, and he serves as chair of Iraq's Olympic Committee, and he does have the protection of the Tikriti "mafia." The younger son, Qusay, formerly served as commander of the Republican Guard, and in 2001 his father appointed him head of the military committee of the RCC. Yet although rumors surface occasionally about Saddam Hussein's health, thus far he has outlasted—and befuddled—several American presidents, including one who

dealt his forces a humiliating military defeat.

## NOTES

1. K. S. Husry, "The Assyrian Affair of 1933," *International Journal of Middle East Studies* (1974), p. 166. The Assyrians are also called Chaldeans.

2. Muhammad A. Tarbush, *The Role of the Military in Politics: A Case Study of Iraq to 1941* (London: Kegan Paul, 1982), p. 50.

3. Richard F. Nyrop, *Iraq: A Country Study*. Washington D.C.: American University, Foreign Area Studies (1979), p. 38. Faisal I had noted sadly just before his death: "There is no Iraqi people but unimaginable masses of human beings, devoid of any patriotic feeling, connected by no common tie, perpetually ready to rise against any government." Quoted in Hanna Batatu, *The Old Social Classes and the Revolutionary Movements in Iraq* (Princeton, NJ: Princeton University Press, 1978), pp. 25–26.

4. Joe Stork, "State Power and Economic Structure . . ." in Tim Niblock, *Iraq: The Contemporary State* (London: Croom Helm, 1982), p. 44.

5. Milton Viorst, "Letter From Baghdad," *The New Yorker* (June 24, 1991), p. 61.

6. Ofra Bengio, *Saddam's Word: Political Discourse in Iraq* (London: Oxford University Press, 1988), p. 24.

7. Khidr Hamza, with Jeff Stein, *Saddam's Bombmaker* (New York: Scribner's, 2001). Hamza was head of the team that designed the bomb.

8. "Anafal" is the Arabic name of the 8th sura (chapter) of the Koran and appeared as a revelation to Muhammad after the battle of Badr, the first victory of the Muslims over their Meccan enemies. It was viewed by them (and by Saddam) as proof that God and right were on their

side. See Human Rights Watch, *Iraq's Crime of Genocide: The Anfal Campaign Against the Kurds* (New Haven, CT: Yale University Press, 1995), p. 4.

9. Henri J. Barkey, "Kurdish Geopolitics," *Current History* (January 1997), p. 2.

10. The INA was "managed" from Jordan by a special CIA team. After the coup had been thwarted—the regime had advance warning through penetration of the CIS's satellite-technology communications system—the team received a message: "We have arrested all your people. You might as well pack up and go home." The CIA team did just that. Andrew Cockburn and Peter Cockburn, *Out of the Ashes: The Resurrection of Saddam Hussain* (New York: HarperCollins, 1999), p. 229.

11. Stephen Kinzer, "Iraq Is a Pediatrician's Hell," *The New York Times* (December 27, 1998). The author notes that in most countries, the cure rate for leukemia is nearly 70 percent; in Iraq, it is near zero.

12. Samir al-Khalil, in *The Monument: Art, Vulgarity and Responsibility in Iraq,* notes that "many of these monuments were commissioned before the supposed victories they celebrate were even declared." Quoted in *The Economist* (March 6, 1999).

13. Cockburn and Cockburn, *op. cit.,* p. 210.

14. John Hughes, "Same Old Saddam," *The Christian Science Monitor* (February 16, 2000).

---

## DEVELOPMENT

The now 13-year sanctions on Iraq have severely crippled the economy. Although the oil-for-food program brings in needed goods and Iraq receives a substantial income from smuggling oil products to various purchasers, it is now near the bottom in indicators of national development. Despite deficiencies in equipment and shortages of technicians, oil production has held steady at 380,000 barrels per day for several years.

## FREEDOM

Although governed in theory by a provisional Consitution, with an elected legislature, in practice Iraq is an authoritarian single-party state. Civil and human rights in the international sense of the term do not exist. However, the difficulties resulting from its isolation and economic collapse have given the Iraqi people a sense of "us against the world" which helps them to overlook the Ba'th-enforced restrictions on their personal and collective freedom.

## HEALTH/WELFARE

UN sanctions have resulted in the breakdown of the national health service, once one of the best in the region. Medical supplies and food bought under the "oil-for-food" program frequently wind up in the black market. The once-prosperous, well-educated middle class has been destroyed. An entire generation has grown up under severe economic and educational deprivation, uninformed about the outside world and alienated from Western society.

## ACHIEVEMENTS

Almost the only improvement in Iraq's once-productive agriculture since the Gulf War is the Third River project, a canal dug under the Tigris and Euphrates Rivers to drain off excess salinity in the soil and thus increase freshwater irrigation.

# Israel (State of Israel)

## GEOGRAPHY

*Area in Square Miles (Kilometers):*
8,017 (20,770) (about the size of New Jersey)

*Capital (Population):* Tel Aviv (356,000) recognized by most countries; Jerusalem (591,000) claimed as the capital but not internationally recognized

*Environmental Concerns:* limited arable land and fresh water; desertification; air and groundwater pollution; fertilizers; pesticides

*Geographical Features:* desert in south; low coastal plain; central mountains; Jordan Rift Valley

*Climate:* primarily temperate

## PEOPLE

### Population

*Total:* 5,938,000
*Annual Growth Rate:* 1.58%
*Rural/Urban Population Ratio:* 9/91
*Major Languages:* Hebrew; English; Arabic
*Ethnic Makeup:* 80% Jewish; 20% non-Jewish (mostly Arab)
*Religions:* 80% Jewish; 15% Muslim; 2% Christian; 3% others

### Health

*Life Expectancy at Birth:* 77 years (male); 81 years (female)
*Infant Mortality Rate (Ratio):* 7.7/1,000
*Physicians Available (Ratio):* 1/206

### Education

*Adult Literacy Rate:* 95%
*Compulsory (Ages):* 5–16; free

## COMMUNICATION

*Telephones:* 2,656,000 main lines
*Daily Newspaper Circulation:* 271 per 1,000 people
*Televisions:* 290 per 1,000 people
*Internet Service Providers:* 21 (2000)

## TRANSPORTATION

*Highways in Miles (Kilometers):* 9,603 (15,464)
*Railroads in Miles (Kilometers):* 379 (610)
*Usable Airfields:* 54
*Motor Vehicles in Use:* 1,544,000

## GOVERNMENT

*Type:* republic
*Independence Date:* May 14, 1948 (from a League of Nations mandate under British administration)
*Head of State/Government:* President Moshe Katsav (mainly ceremonial); Prime Minister Ariel Sharon
*Political Parties:* Likud Bloc, majority party but rules in coalition with Labor Party (largest minority party); also

Shas, Meretz, Center, Yisrael Ba' Aliya, others
*Suffrage:* universal at 18

## MILITARY

*Military Expenditures (% of GDP):* 9.5%
*Current Disputes:* conflict tantamount to war with Palestinian terrorists

## ECONOMY

*Currency ($ U.S. Equivalent):* 4.91 new shekels = $1
*Per Capita Income/GDP:* $18,900/$110.2 billion
*GDP Growth Rate:* 5.9%
*Inflation Rate:* 0.1%
*Unemployment Rate:* 9%
*Labor Force:* 2,400,000

*Natural Resources:* copper; phosphates; bromide; potash; clay; sand; timber; manganese; natural gas; oil
*Agriculture:* citrus fruits; vegetables; cotton; beef; poultry; dairy products
*Industry:* food processing; diamond cutting; textiles and apparel; chemicals; high-technology projects; wood and paper; others
*Exports:* $31.5 billion (primary partners United States, United Kingdom, Benelux)
*Imports:* $35.1 billion (primary partners United States, Benelux, Germany)

 http://lcweb2.loc.gov/frd/cs/iltoc.html

---

### Map

MEDITERRANEAN SEA

LEBANON
SYRIA
UNDOF ZONE
GOLAN HEIGHTS
Mount Meron 3962
Nahariyya
'Akko
Capernaum Sinagoge
Tiberias
Sea of Galilee (Lake Tiberias)
Haifa
Mount Carmel 1789
Nazareth
Mount Tabor 1929
Caesarea
Netanya
Shechen
Mount Gilboa 1631
Herzliyya
Ramat Gan
Nablus
Petach Tikua
WEST BANK
TEL AVIV–YAFO
Ramla
Ram Allah
Jericho
Jordan River
Ashdad
JERUSALEM
Mount Scopus 2694
Ashqelon
Bethlehem
GAZA STRIP
Gaza
Eleutheropolis
Hebron
DEAD SEA 1302
Masada
Beersheba
JORDAN
Mash 'abbe Sade
Dimona
Besor
Harvat Shivta
Hazeba
Mizpe Ramon
En Yahav
Mount Ramon 3395
EGYPT
Paran
Yotvata
SAUDI ARABIA
Elat
Gulf of Aqaba
Israel

Legend:
- ⊛ Capital
- ★ District Capital
- ● City/Town
- River
- Road
- Israeli-occupied (Status to be determined)
- ⊢⊣ Canals
- △ Points of Interest

0   50   100 Miles
0   50   100 Kilometers
Elevation in Feet.

---

## ISRAEL

Israel, the Holy Land of Judeo–Christian tradition, is a very small state about the size of New Jersey. Its population is also smaller than those of most of its neighbors', with low birth and immigration rates. Population growth within these limits would be manageable. But until recently, the country's very existence was not accepted by its neighbors (even now, it is not recognized by all), and its borders remained temporary ones under the 1949 armistice agreements that ended the first Arab–Israeli War.

The country occupies a larger land area than it held at the time of its independence in 1948, due to expansion wars with its neighbors. The border with Egypt was defined by a 1979 peace treaty; subsequently, Israel retroceded the Sinai Peninsula, which had been occupied by Israeli forces in 1973. In 1994, Israel signed a peace treaty with Jordan. Among its provisions, their common border was demarcated, and areas in the Galilee were returned to Jordan. Peace treaties with Israel's other two Arab neighbors have yet to be signed. Israeli forces occupied a nine-mile-wide, self-declared "security zone" along the Lebanese border from 1982 until 2000, when they were withdrawn.

Although it is small, Israel has a complex geography, with a number of distinct regions. The northern region, Galilee, is a continuation of the Lebanese mountains, but at a lower altitude. The Galilee uplands drop steeply on three sides: to the Jordan Valley on the east; to a narrow coastal plain on the west; and southward to the Valley of Esdraelon, a broad inland valley from the Mediterranean to the Jordan River, which is fertile and well watered and has become important to Israeli agriculture.

Another upland plateau extends south from Esdraelon for about 90 miles. This area contains the ancient Jewish heartland—Judea and Samaria to Israelis, the West Bank to Palestinians—which is supposed to serve as the core of the self-governing Palestinian state as defined in the 1993 Oslo Agreement. This plateau gradually levels off into semidesert, the barren wilderness of Judea. The wilderness merges imperceptibly into the Negev, a desert region that comprises 60 percent of the land area but has only about 12 percent of the population.

## TERRITORIAL CHANGES

Israel's current territory includes three areas that were not part of the Jewish state established in the 1947 United Nations partition plan for Palestine. They are the Gaza Strip, captured from Egypt during the 1967 Six-Day War; the West Bank (of the Jordan River) and East Jerusalem, seized from Jordan at the same time; and the Golan Heights along the border with Syria, also occupied in 1967 and annexed unilaterally in 1981. Since the 1973 War, the United Nations has maintained a small observer force in the demilitarized zone between Syrian and Israeli territory on the Golan. Syria's nonrecognition of Israel and Israel's insistence that the Golan Heights are essential to its security have made resolution of the dispute all but impossible. In January 2000, Syrian and Israeli negotiators met in Shepherdstown, West Virginia, under U.S. sponsorship, but they were unable to reconcile their conflicting claims to the territory.

The 1993 Oslo Agreement and the 1998 Wye Agreement, signed by then-prime minister Benjamin Netanyahu and Yassir Arafat, leader of the nascent Palestinian state, set guidelines for the gradual transfer of these territories to Palestinian self-rule (excluding the Golan Heights, which is slated to be returned to Syria eventually). The Wye Agreement specified that 15 percent of the West Bank would be transferred by February 2000. In September 1999, Israel transferred 7 percent (160 square miles) of West Bank land to Palestinian control. An additional 5 percent was transferred in January 2000. The following summer, the new Israeli prime minister, Ehud Barak, met with Arafat at the presidential retreat in Camp David, Maryland, under U.S. sponsorship, and offered to turn over 94 percent of the West Bank for inclusion in the new Palestinian state. The Palestine National Authority (PNA) would be given administrative rule over the Dome of the Rock, excluding the Wailing Wall, as well as the non-Jewish quarters of East Jerusalem. However, the negotiations foundered, due in large measure to Arafat's insistence on the "right of return" of displaced Palestinians to their former homes and villages in Israel. Arrangements for exercise of this "right" would be determined under a complex formula set up by the United Nations. The resumption of open conflict between the PNA and Israel has not only undercut these agreements but also has left further negotiations in abeyance, with Israel in effect reestablishing the status quo of the 30-plus years of occupation.

The issue of East Jerusalem—the "Old City" sacred to three faiths but revered especially by Jews as their spiritual, emotional, and political capital—remains a difficult one to resolve. From 1949 to 1967, it was under Jordanian control, with Jews prohibited from visiting the Wailing Wall and other sites important in the history of Judaism. Almost the only contact between the divided sectors of east and west was at the Mandelbaum Gate. In the 1967 Six-Day War, Israeli forces captured the Old City in fierce fighting. Since then its holy sites, sacred to Muslims, Christians, and Jews, have been opened to denominational and religious use. The Israeli government and its people are united in regarding Jerusalem as their eternal and political capital, although it is recognized as such by very few countries. Until very recently this status was considered nonnegotiable by Israelis. In the early days of the new Christian millennium (year 5760 of the Jewish calendar), however, a number of Israeli and Arab intellectuals called for the city to be "internationalized" as a center and model for global peace with secular authority shared between Muslim Palestinians and Jews.[1]

## THE POPULATION

The great majority of the Israeli population are Jewish. Judaism is the state religion; Hebrew, the ancient liturgical language revived and modernized in the twentieth century, is the official language, although English is widely used. Language and religion, along with shared historical traditions, a rich ancient culture, and a commitment to the survival of the Jewish state, have fostered a strong sense of national unity among the Israeli people. They are extremely nationalistic, and these feelings are increased because of hostile neighbors. Most Israelis believe that their neighbors are determined to destroy their state, and this belief has helped to develop a "siege mentality" among them. This siege mentality has deep roots. Nobel Peace Prize–winner Elie Wiesel has defined it as follows: "Jewish history, flooded by suffering but anchored in defiance, describes a permanent conflict between *us* [Jews] and the others. Ever since Abraham [the father of Judaism], we have been on one side and the rest of the world on the other."[2]

Except for a small population of Jews that remained in the region (the village of Peki'in in Galilee is said to be the only one with an unbroken Jewish presence over the past 2,000 years), Jews dispersed throughout the world after Jerusalem's conquest by Roman legions in A.D. 70. Those who settled in Europe are called Ashkenazis (from Ashkenaz, Genesis 10:3). Most of them settled in France and Germany, and later in Central/Eastern Europe. Other Jewish communities found refuge in Spain, where they later prospered under Islamic rule for seven centuries (A.D. 711–1492). Such Jewish

(Israeli Government Tourism Administration)

Israelis regard Jerusalem as the political and spiritual capital of Israel. East Jerusalem was annexed from Jordan after the 1967 Six-Day War, and returning this part of the city to Jordan has never been seriously considered by Israel.

intellectual leaders as Moses Ben Maimon (Maimonides) rendered important services to Muslim rulers, and their role in trans-Mediterranean trade was so valuable that their Hispano–Moorish commercial language, Ladino, became the lingua franca of Christian–Islamic economic relations.

However, the reconquest of Spain by armies of the Christian rulers Ferdinand and Isabella imposed a tragic fate on both Jews and Muslims. They were ordered to convert to Christianity or go into exile. Even those Jews who chose conversion (the *Conversos*) often came under suspicion by the Spanish Inquisition for practicing their Jewish faith in secret. As the result of the two "Edicts of Expulsion" of 1492 and 1511, the entire Muslim population and nearly all Jews left their Spanish homeland, settling either in Ottoman lands or Morocco and other areas of Muslim North Africa.[3]

The diversity among incoming Jews, particularly the Sephardic communities, was so great during the early years of independence that the government developed a special orientation program of Hebrew language and culture, called Ulpan (which is still in use), to help with their assimilation. Some Sephardic groups have prospered and gained economic and political equality with Ashkenazis. How-

ever, the majority of Sephardim have yet to attain full equality, and this is a cause of tension. The 2000 election as president of Moshe Katsav, a Sephardic Jew originally from Yazd (Iran), has been a source of great pride to the Sephardic community.

Another difference among Israelis has to do with religious practice. The Hasidim, or Orthodox Jews, strictly observe the rules and social practices of Judaism and live in their own separate neighborhoods within cities. Reform Jews, by far the majority, are Jewish in their traditions, history, and faith, but they modify their religious practices to conform to the demands of modern life and thought. Both the Orthodox and Reform Jews have chief rabbis who sit on the Supreme Rabbinical Council, the principal interpretive body for Judaism.

A small groups of Jews of ancient origins, the Samaritans, have lived for centuries in Palestine in two locations, Holon (near Tel Aviv) and Nablus (in the West Bank). They are descended from one of the ancient Jewish tribes, one that broke away from the mainstream Jerusalem-based community over the location of Abraham's putative sacrifice of Isaac to God. (They believe that it took place on Mt. Gerizim rather than Mt. Moriah.) After the 1948 war for Israeli independence,

they were separated; the Holon community was now part of Israel, while the Nablus Samaritans came under Jordanian rule. The 1967 Six-Day War reunited them, and since then they have served as intermediaries between their Palestinian neighbors and the Israeli authorities, being acceptable to both. The Samaritan community currently numbers just over 600. Most speak Arabic as well as Hebrew and are at home in both cultures.

Relations between the majority Reform Jews in Israel and the much smaller Orthodox community were marked by occasional incidents of friction but overall coexistence until the rise to power of Menachem Begin's Likud Bloc. Begin's own political party, Herut, always emphasized the country's biblical heritage in its platform. But during Begin's period in office, the small religious parties that represent the Orthodox acquired political power because they were essential to the coalition government. The higher birth rate among haredim families, combined with exemption from military service of Orthodox youth enrolled in religious schools (*yeshivas*) and other privileges, have given them social and political influence out of proportion to their number. The ultra-Orthodox Shas Party formed a key unit in both the Netanyahu and Barak coalition governments, and Shas's defection from the coalition was an important factor in Barak's defeat in the 2000 election.

Differences in historical experiences have also divided the Ashkenazis. Most lived in Central/Eastern Europe, sometimes isolated from other Jews as well as from their Christian neighbors. At one time, "They were closed off in a gigantic ghetto called the Pale of Settlement, destitute, deprived of all political rights, living in the twilight of a slowly disintegrating medieval world."[4] However, by the nineteenth century, Jews in Western Europe had become politically tolerated and relatively well-off, and, due to the Enlightenment, found most occupations and professions open to them. These "emancipated" Jews played a crucial role in the Zionist movement, but the actual return to Palestine and settlement was largely the work of Ashkenazis from Central/Eastern Europe. The former Soviet Union, which had a Jewish population of 3.5 million, nearly all in Russia itself, had not supported the creation of the State of Israel and did not establish diplomatic relations until 1990, when a consular office was opened in Tel Aviv. However, U.S. restrictions on the entry of Soviet Jews caused the majority of them to emigrate to Israel. By 1992, some 350,000 had arrived in Israel. The majority were highly educated and professionally trained, but they were often unable to find suitable jobs and placed an added strain on housing and social services in Israel. One reason for the Israeli request to the United States for $10 billion in loan guarantees, which was held up by the George Bush administration and partially released by its successor, the Clinton administration, was to obtain funds for housing Soviet immigrants. Disillusionment with their experiences and lack of professional opportunities in Israel led the immigrants to form their own political party, Yisrael Ba'Aliya, to press for better conditions. The party joined the Benjamin Netanyahu coalition after the Knesset (Parliament) elections and shifted to support for Ehud Barak after he became prime minister. Its leader, Natan Sharansky, was named minister of interior in return for his party's support. His appointment put him in direct conflict with Shas, which had previously controlled that ministry. Yisrael Ba' Aliya was also promised $65 million for jobs and housing for Soviet emigrants.

The *Aliyah* ("going up" in Hebrew, i.e., to Israel) policy has resulted in the return of many formerly isolated Jewish communities to the new homeland. The first group to arrive were from Yemen, where they had lived in scattered villages, working as craftsmen and using Aramaic in their liturgy. Some 90 percent of them were airlifted directly to Israel. Although Yemen closed its borders in the 1960s, most of the remaining Jews were allowed to emigrate, leaving about 300 members of this oldest of diaspora communities. However, the Yemeni Jews have often felt like second-class citizens in Israel. In recent years, about 100 families have left Israel for New York City, under the aegis of Satmar, an anti-Zionist Hasidic organization based in Williamsburg, Virginia.

Israel has two important non-Jewish minorities, totaling about 1 million—about 20 percent of the population. The larger group consists of Muslim and some Christian Arabs who stayed after Israel achieved statehood. This Arab population was ruled under military administration from 1948 until 1966, when restrictions were lifted and the Arabs ostensibly became full citizens. However, they were not allowed to serve in the armed forces; and until recently they did not have parity with Israelis in job training and opportunities, and access to higher education, housing, and political representation. When the Israeli state was formed in 1948, they were primarily farmers living in small villages; by the 1980s, however, some 60 percent were employed in construction and other industries and in public service. Higher

educational access for Arabs has greatly improved.

For Arabs, the ability to attain economic and social parity with Israeli Jews is primarily a matter of greater political representation. The first Arab political party was formed in 1988 and won one seat in the Knesset. In 1996, the party won four seats. In 1999, 95 percent of the Arab electorate voted for Barak; they were a major factor in his victory over Netanyahu.

Thus far, political representation in the Knesset has not been accompanied by social and economic equality for Israel's Arabs. The Barak government took several small steps in that direction in the new century. El Al, the Israeli airline, hired its first Arab flight attendant. Lands confiscated from the Arab village of Kafr Kassem, scene of a 1956 massacre, were returned to their former owners. Unfortunately, the renewal of the Palestinian intifada in 2000 after Ariel Sharon's visit to the Islamic holy places in Jerusalem has had a spin-off effect on Israeli Arabs. Demonstrations in October in sympathy with the Palestinians turned violent, with 13 Arabs killed and dozens injured in clashes with the police.

A second non-Jewish minority, the Druze, live not only in Israel but also in mountain enclaves in Lebanon and Syria. They form a majority of the population in the Golan Heights, occupied by Israeli forces in the 1967 Six-Day War and annexed in 1981. They practice a form of Islam that split off from the main body of the religion in the tenth century. Most Druze have remained loyal to the Israeli state. In return, they have been given full citizenship, are guaranteed freedom to practice their faith under their religious leaders, and may serve in the armed forces. Some 233 Druze have died in Israel's wars.

At present about 70,000 Druze live in Israel in 16 large villages in the Galilee and near Haifa. Another 16,000 Druze live in the Israeli-annexed Golan Heights, where they are physically separated from their families on the Syrian side by the UN demilitarized zone. These Druze have rejected Israeli citizenship. When Israel annexed the Golan Heights unilaterally in 1981, they reacted with a six-month-long general strike; it ended only when the government agreed not to force citizenship on the Druze. In 1997, on the 15th anniversary of the strike, the villagers showed their continued defiance of Israeli rule by flying the Syrian flag over their schools.

Despite their relative freedom, the Druze in Israel, like the Israeli Arabs, experience some discrimination in educa-

tional and work opportunities. The discrepancy is particularly noticeable for Druze women. In 1988, the first national movement for the advancement of Druze women was formed. Named the Council of Druze Women, it works to help them to reach the educational and social levels of Israeli women and to protect them from the abuses of what is still a patriarchal society, one in which there is even a religious ban on women driving.

There are two other small minority groups in Israel, both Sunni Muslims. The Circassians, descendants of warriors from the Caucasus brought in centuries ago to help Muslim armies drive the Christian Crusaders from Palestine, have been completely integrated into Israeli society. The second minority group, the Bedouins, formerly roamed the barren uplands of Judea and the Negev Desert. Those in Judea have been completely urbanized. But the Negev Bedouins, some 100,000 in number, maintained their traditional nomadic way of life until very recently. This way of life has come under attack from many quarters. A major one stems from the government policy of settling them in permanent homes in new towns. Thus far, seven such towns have been established. The largest, Rahat (population 30,000), was given city status in 1994. However, fewer than half of the Bedouins have accepted the government's offer of money to build homes (called *Bneh Beitcha,* "Build your own home") and a *dunam* (one-quarter acre) of land. The remaining Bedouins continue to live in tents or illegally constructed block dwellings that are subject to demolition and eviction of residents under the 1992 building code. Like the Druze, Bedouins have limited education and job opportunities; and restrictions on their traditional right to roam and pasture their herds on rented, leased, or open land have driven many to become day laborers.

## HISTORY
The land occupied by the modern State of Israel has been a crossroads for conquering armies and repository for many civilizations during its long history. As such, it is part of biblical history and an important component of the Judeo-Christian heritage. The ruins of Megiddo, near Haifa, are believed by scholars to be the site of Armageddon, described in *Revelations* as the final clash between good and evil resulting in the end of the world.

Jews believe that Israel is the modern fulfillment of the biblical covenant between God and a wanderer named Abraham (Abram) that granted him a homeland in a particular place. Jews have held fast to this covenant during the centuries of

(UN photo/John Isaac)

The Wailing Wall, a focal point of Jewish worship, is all that remains of the ancient temple destroyed by the Roman legions led by Titus in A.D. 70. The Wailing Wall stands as a place of pilgrimage for devout Jews throughout the world.

their exile and captivity in foreign lands. Each of these periods of exile is called a *diaspora* ("dispersion"). The most important one, in terms of modern Israel, took place in the first century A.D. Abraham's descendants through Isaac had called the land given to them in covenant Judea and Samaria; and when it became part of the expanding Roman Empire, it was known as the province of Judea. Due to the unruly nature of the Jews, the Romans preferred to rule them indirectly through appointed governors such as Herod the Great who ruled in the time of Jesus Christ.[5] After his death, the Romans imposed direct rule under appointed governors called procurators. In A.D. 69–70, the Jews rebelled. The forces of Roman general (later emperor) Titus then besieged Jerusalem. The city fell in A.D. 70, and Roman legions sacked and destroyed much of it, leaving only a portion of the Wailing Wall (so called because it is the center of prayer and pilgrimage for Jews in Jerusalem).

From then until the twentieth century, most Jews were dispersed, living among alien peoples and subject to foreign rulers. Periodically persecuted and often mistrusted, they coexisted with the populations around them, in part by preserving

their ancient rituals and customs but also due to the restrictions imposed on them by their non-Jewish rulers. Thus, in the Islamic world Jews were required to wear distinctive dress with armbands and pay a separate poll tax in order to observe their religious ceremonies. Their places of worship as well as their homes could not be built higher than Islamic ones, and in other ways they were made to feel inferior to their Muslim neighbors.

## Zionism

The organized movement to reestablish a national home for dispersed Jews in biblical Judea and Samaria in accordance with God's promise is known as Zionism. It became, however, more of a political movement formed for a particular purpose: to establish by Jewish settlement a homeland where dispersed Jews may gather, escape persecution, and knit together the strands of traditional Jewish faith and culture. As a political movement, it differs sharply from spiritual Zionism, the age-old dream of "the return." Most Orthodox Jews and traditionalists opposed *any* movement to reclaim Palestine; they believed that it is blasphemy to do so, for only God can perform the miracle of restoring the Promised Land. The reality of

the establishment of the Jewish state by force of arms, with a secular political system backed by strong Jewish nationalism, has created what one author calls "an unprecedented Jewish dialogue with power, an attempt to historicize the Jewish experience as a narrative of liberation by armed Jews."[6]

Zionism as a political movement began in the late nineteenth century. Its founder was Theodore Herzl, a Jewish journalist from Vienna, Austria. Herzl had grown up in the Jewish Enlightenment period. Like other Western European Jews, he came to believe that a new age of full acceptance of the Jewish community into European life had begun. He was bitterly disillusioned by the wave of Jewish persecution that swept over Central/Eastern Europe after the murder of the liberal Russian czar, Alexander II, in 1881. He was even more disillusioned by the trial of a French Army officer, Alfred Dreyfus, for treason. Dreyfus, who was Jewish, was convicted after a trumped-up trial brought public protests that he was part of an antigovernment Jewish conspiracy.

Herzl concluded from these events that the only hope for the long-suffering Jews, especially those from Central/Eastern Europe, was to live together, separate from non-Jews. In his book *The Jewish State,* he wrote: "We have sincerely tried everywhere to merge with the national communities in which we live, seeking only to preserve the faith of our fathers. It is not permitted to us."[7]

Herzl had attended the Dreyfus trial as a journalist. Concerned about growing anti-Semitism in Western Europe, he organized a conference of European Jewish leaders in 1897 in Basel, Switzerland. The conference ended with the ringing declaration that "the aim of Zionism is to create a Jewish homeland in Palestine secured by public law." Herzl wrote in an appendage: "In Basel I have founded the Jewish state."[8]

The Zionists hoped to be allowed to buy land in Palestine for Jewish settlements. But the Ottoman government in Palestine would not allow them to do so. Small groups of Eastern European Jews escaping persecution made their way to Palestine and established communal agricultural settlements called *kibbutzim.* Those immigrants believed that hard work was essential to the Jewish return to the homeland. Work was sacred, and the only thing that gave the Jews the right to the soil of Palestine was the "betrothal of toil." This belief became a founding principle of the Jewish state.

## The Balfour Declaration

Although the Zionist movement attracted many Jewish supporters, it had no influence with European governments, nor with the Ottoman government. The Zionists had difficulty raising money to finance land purchases in Palestine and to pay for travel of emigrants.

It appeared in the early 1900s that the Zionists would never reach their goal. But World War I gave them a new opportunity. The Ottoman Empire was defeated, and British troops occupied Palestine. During the war, a British Zionist named Chaim Weizmann, a chemist, had developed a new type of explosive that was valuable in the British war effort against Germany. Weizmann and his associates pressed the British government for a commitment to support a home for Jews in Palestine after the war. Many British officials favored the Zionist cause, among them Winston Churchill. During his term as colonial secretary after World War I, he organized the 1921 Cairo Conference, which among other issues confirmed the League of Nations' assignment of Palestine to Britain as a mandate. Churchill then planted a tree on Mt. Scopus next to the new Hebrew University as a symbol of the British commitment to "some sort of national home there" for the Zionists.[9]

## The British Mandate

The peace settlement arranged after World War I by the new League of Nations gave Palestine to Britain as a mandate. As a result, the name Palestine came into common usage for the territory. It is probably derived from Philistine, from the original tribal inhabitants (who are also called Canaanites), but this covenanted land had been ruled by many other peoples and their rulers for centuries, due to its location as a strategic corridor between Asia and Africa. After it became part of the Ottoman Empire, along with Lebanon it was divided into *vilayets* (provinces), those of Beirut and Acre respectively; Jerusalem was administered separately as a *sanjak* (subprovince). The majority of the population were small farmers living in compact villages and rarely traveling elsewhere. Most were Muslims, but there was a substantial minority of Christians. Leadership, such as it was, was held by a small urban elite, the principal families being the Husseinis and Nashashibis of Jerusalem.

After World War I and the peace settlement, the Zionists assumed that the Balfour Declaration authorized them to begin building a national home for dispersed Jews in Palestine. Weizmann and his colleagues established the Jewish Agency to organize the return. Great Britain's obligation under the mandate was to prepare Palestine's inhabitants for eventual self-government. British officials assigned to Palestine tended to favor Jewish interests over those of the native population. This was due in part to their Judeo–Christian heritage, but also to the active support of Jews to Britain during the war. In addition to Weizmann's contribution, the Jewish Legion, a volunteer group, had fought with British forces against the Turks.

Britain's "view with favor" toward Zionism weighed heavily in the application of mandate requirements to Palestine. Jews were allowed to emigrate, buy land, develop agriculture, and establish banks, schools, and small industries. The Jewish Agency established a school system, while former members of the dispersed Jewish Legion regrouped into what became Haganah, the defense force for the Jewish community.

Compounding the difficulties of adjustment of two different peoples to the same land was the fact that most Zionist leaders had never been to Palestine. They envisaged it as an empty land waiting for development by industrious Jews. David Ben-Gurion, for example, once claimed that one could walk for days there without meeting a soul; Palestine, he told his compatriots, was a land without a people for

a people without a land. Palestine was indeed underpopulated, but it did have a substantial population, many of its members living in villages settled by their ancestors centuries earlier. Referring to the Balfour Declaration, Tom Segev observed that "the Promised Land had, by the stroke of a pen, become twice-promised."[9]

Palestinian Arabs were opposed to the mandate, to the Balfour Declaration, and to Jewish immigration. They turned to violence on several occasions, against the British and the growing Jewish population. In 1936, Arab leaders called a general strike to protest Jewish immigration, which led to a full-scale Arab rebellion. The British tried to steer a middle ground between the two communities. But they were unwilling (or unable) either to accept Arab demands for restrictions on Jewish immigration and land purchases or Zionist demands for a Jewish majority in Palestine. British policy reports and White Papers during the mandate wavered back and forth. In 1937, the Peel Commission, set up after the Arab revolt, recommended a halt to further Jewish immigration, and subsequently the 1939 "White Paper" stated that the mandate should be replaced by a self-governing Arab state with rights assured for the Jewish minority.

One important difference between the Palestinian Arab and Jewish communities was in their organization. The Jews were organized under the Jewish Agency, which operated as a "state within a state" in Palestine. Jews in Europe and the United States also contributed substantially to the agency's finances and made arrangements for immigration. The Palestinian Arabs, in contrast, were led by heads of urban families who often quarreled with one another. The Palestinian Arab cause also did not have outside Arab support; leaders of neighboring Arab states were weak and were still under British or French control.

A unique feature of Zionism that helped strengthen the Jewish pioneers in Palestine in their struggle to establish their claim to the land were the kibbutzim. Originally, there were two types, *moshavim* and *kibbutzim.* The moshavim, cooperative landholders' associations whose members worked the land under cooperative management and lived in nearby villages, have largely disappeared with urbanization. The kibbutzim, in contrast, were collective-ownership communities with self-contained, communal-living arrangements; members shared labor, income, and expenses. Over the years, kibbutzim have played a role that is disproportionate to their size and numbers, not only in building an integrated Jewish community in Palestine but also in the formation of the Israeli state.

David Ben-Gurion, Israel's first prime minister, lived in and retired to Kibbutz Sde Boker, in the Negev. Shimon Peres, twice prime minister and longtime public official, wrote of his youth on a kibbutz in these moving terms: "We saw it as the solution to the evils of urban industrialized society. I dreamed of my future as a brawny, sunburned kibbutz farmer, plowing the fields by day, guarding the perimeter by night on a fleet-footed horse. The kibbutz would break new ground, literally; it would make the parched earth bloom and beat back the attacks of marauders who sought to destroy our pioneering lives."[10]

Adolf Hitler's policy of genocide (total extermination) of Jews in Europe, developed during World War II, gave a special urgency to Jewish settlement in Palestine. American Zionist leaders condemned the 1939 British White Paper and called for unrestricted Jewish immigration into Palestine and the establishment of an independent, democratic Jewish state. After World War II, the British, still committed to the White Paper, blocked Palestine harbors and turned back the crowded, leaking ships carrying desperate Jewish refugees from Europe. World opinion turned against the British. Supplies of smuggled weapons enabled Haganah to fend off attacks by Palestinian Arabs, while Jewish terrorist groups such as the Stern Gang and Irgun Zvai Leumi carried out acts of murder and sabotage against British troops and installations.

## PARTITION AND INDEPENDENCE
In 1947, the British decided that the Palestine mandate was unworkable. They asked the United Nations to come up with a solution to the problem of "one land, two peoples." A UN Special Commission on Palestine recommended partition of Palestine into two states—one Arab, one Jewish—with an economic union between them. A minority of UNSCOP members recommended a federated Arab–Jewish state, with an elected legislature and minority rights for Jews. The majority report was approved by the UN General Assembly on November 29, 1947, by a 33–13 vote, after intensive lobbying by the Zionists. The partition would establish a Jewish state, with 56 percent of the land, and a Palestinian Arab state, with 44 percent. The population at that time was 60 percent Arab and 40 percent Jewish. Due to its special associations for Jews, Muslims, and Christians, Jerusalem would become an international city administered by the United Nations.

Abba Eban, who had been "present at the creation" and served the Israeli state with distinction in many capacities, noted in his memoirs, "President Truman told me: 'Quite simply, you got your state because you made feasible proposals and your adversaries did not. If Israel had asked for a Jewish state in the whole of the land of Israel it would have come away with nothing. An Arab and a Jewish state side by side with integrated economies was something that American ethics and logic could absorb.' "[11]

The Jewish delegation, led by Eban and David Ben-Gurion, accepted the partition plan approved by the UN General Assembly. But Palestinian Arab leaders, backed strongly by the newly independent Arab states, rejected the plan outright. On May 14, 1948, in keeping with Britain's commitment to end its mandate, the last British soldiers left Palestine. Ben-Gurion promptly announced the "birth of the new Jewish State of Israel." On May 15, the United States and the Soviet Union recognized the new state, even as the armies of five Arab states converged on it to "push the Jews into the sea."

## INDEPENDENT ISRAEL
Long before the establishment of Israel, the nation's first prime minister, David Ben-Gurion, had come to Palestine as a youth. After a clash between Arab nomads and Jews from the kibbutz where he lived had injured several people, Ben-Gurion wrote prophetically, "It was then I realized . . . that sooner or later Jews and Arabs would fight over this land, a tragedy since intelligence and good will could have avoided all bloodshed."[12] In the five decades of independence, Ben-Gurion's prophecy has been borne out in five Arab–Israeli wars. In between those wars, conflict between Israel and the Palestinians has gone on more or less constantly, like a running sore.

Some 700,000 to 800,000 Palestinians fled Israel during the War for Independence. After the 1967 Six-Day War, an additional 380,000 Palestinians became refugees in Jordan. Israeli occupation of the West Bank brought a million Palestinians under military control.

The unifying factor among all Palestinians is the same as that which had united the dispersed Jews for 20 centuries: the recovery of the sacred homeland. Abu Iyad, a top Palestine Liberation Organization leader, once said, " . . . our dream. . . [is] the reunification of Palestine in a secular and democratic state shared by Jews, Christians and Muslims rooted in this common land. . . . There is no doubting the irrepressible will of the Palestinian people to pursue their struggle . . . and one day, we will have a country."[13] The land

vacated by the Palestinians has been transformed in the decades of Israeli development. Those Israelis actually born in Palestine—now in their third generation—call themselves *Sabras,* after the prickly pear cactus of the Negev. The work of Sabras and of a generation of immigrants has created a highly urbanized society, sophisticated industries, and a productive agriculture. Much of the success of Israel's development has resulted from large contributions from Jews abroad, from U.S. aid, from reparations from West Germany for Nazi war crimes against Jews, and from bond issues. Yet the efforts of Israelis themselves should not be understated. Ben-Gurion once wrote, "Pioneering is the lifeblood of our people....We had to create a new life consonant with our oldest traditions as a people. This was our struggle."[14]

## ISRAELI POLITICS: DEMOCRACY BY COALITION
Israel is unique among Middle Eastern states in having been a multiparty democracy from its establishment as a state. It does not have a written constitution, mainly because secular and Orthodox communities cannot agree on its provisions. The Orthodox community, for example, argues that it already has its consitution, in the Bible and Torah. For the Orthodox, a constitution would be something imported from a foreign country such as a Canada or Sweden, not a document that truly belonged to Israel.

In place of a constitution, the Israeli state is governed by a series of Basic Laws. They include the Law of Return, by which diaspora Jews may return and are automatically granted Israeli citizenship. In addition, a series of seven Basic Laws established the Knesset, the national army (Israel Defense Forces), the office of president, the legal system, and so on. Two new Basic Laws issued in 1992 provide for direct election of the prime minister and for recognition of human dignity and rights before the power of the state. The Law for Direct Election of the prime minister was invoked in the last elections but has been criticized, and will probably be revoked in the near future.

Power in the Israeli political system rests in the unicameral Knesset. It has 120 members who are elected for four-year terms under a system of proportional representation from party lists. The prime minister and cabinet are responsible to the Knesset, which must approve all policy actions. The new Direct Elections law also has a provision for the removal from office of a prime minister, either through a 61-member no-confidence vote or through impeachment for "crimes of moral turpitude." The possibility of this type of removal loomed large for a time in 1997 during the Bar-On affair, "Israel's Watergate."[15]

Ben-Gurion's Labor Party controlled the government for the first three decades of independence. However, the party seldom had a clear majority in the Knesset. As a result, it was forced to join in coalitions with various small parties. Israeli political parties are numerous. Many of them have merged with other parties over the years or have broken away to form separate parties. The Labor Party itself is a merger of three Socialist labor organizations. The two oldest parties are Agudath Israel World Organization (founded in 1912), which is concerned with issues facing Jews outside of Israel as well as within, and the Israeli Communist Party (Rakah, founded in 1919).

The Labor Party's control of Israeli politics began to weaken seriously after the October 1973 War. Public confidence was shaken by the initial Israeli defeat, heavy casualties, and evidence of Israel's unpreparedness. Austerity measures imposed to deal with inflation increased Labor's unpopularity. In the 1977 elections, the opposition, the Likud bloc, won more seats than Labor but fell short of a majority in the Knesset. The new prime minister, Menachem Begin, was forced to make concessions to smaller parties in order to form a governing coalition.

However, the Israeli invasion of Lebanon in 1982 weakened the coalition. It seemed to many Israelis that for the first time in its existence, the state had violated its own precept that wars should be defensive and waged only to protect Israeli land. The ethical and moral implications of Israel's occupation, and in particular the massacre by Lebanese Christian militiamen of Palestinians in refugee camps in Beirut who were supposedly under Israeli military protection, led to the formation in 1982 of Peace Now, an organization of Israelis who mounted large-scale demonstrations against the war and are committed to peace between Israel and its Arab neighbors.

Begin resigned in 1983, giving no reason but clearly distressed not only by the difficulties in Lebanon but also by the death of his wife. He remained in seclusion for the rest of his life. He died in 1992.

## RECENT INTERNAL POLITICS
The Labor Party won the majority of seats in the Knesset in the 1984 elections—but not a clear majority. As a result, the two major blocs reached agreement on a "government of national unity," the first in Israel's history. The arrangement established alternating two-year terms for each party's leader as prime minister. Shimon Peres (Labor) held the office from 1984 to 1986 and Yitzhak Shamir (Likud) from 1986 to 1988.

In the 1988 elections, certain fundamental differences between Labor and Likud emerged. By this time the first Palestinian *intifada* ("uprising") was in full swing. It would not only change the relationship between Israelis and Palestinians forever but would also alter the norms of Israeli politics. Labor and Likud differed over methods of handling the uprising, but they differed even more strongly in their views of long-term settlement policies toward the Palestinians. Labor's policy was to "trade land for peace," with some sort of self-governing status for the occupied territories and peace treaties with its Arab neighbors guaranteeing Israel's "right to exist." Likud would give away none of the sacred land; it could not be bartered for peace.

The election results underscored equally deep divisions in the population. Neither party won a clear majority of seats in the Knesset; Likud took 40 seats, Labor 39. Four minority ultra-religious parties gained the balance of power, with 15 percent of the popular vote and 18 seats. Their new-found political power encouraged the religious parties to press for greater control on the part of Orthodox Jewry over Israeli life. However, a proposed bill to amend the Law of Return to allow only Orthodox rabbis to determine "who is a Jew" for citizenship purposes aroused a storm of protest among diaspora Jews, who are mostly Reform or Conservative and would be barred from citizenship. In February 2002, the Israeli Supreme Court ruled that both movements would be listed as Jews in the official census registry. For Reform and Conservative Jews living in Israel, it was a major step toward official recognition.

The 1992 Knesset election ended 15 years of Likud dominance. Labor returned to power, winning a majority of seats. However, the splintered, multiparty Israeli electoral system denied it an absolute majority. Concessions to minority parties enabled Labor to establish a functioning government, and party leader Yitzhak Rabin was named prime minister. With the support of these minority parties, notably Shas, an ultra-religious, non-Zionist party of mostly Sephardic Jews, and the left-wing Meretz Party, the Rabin government could count on 63 votes in the Knesset. This majority ensured support for the government's policies, including the 1993 Oslo agreements with the Palestinians.

## JEWISH EXTREMISTS, ARAB EXTREMISTS
The deep divisions in Israeli society regarding future relations with the Palestinian population in the occupied territories (for many Israelis, these lands are Judea and Samaria, part of the ancestral Jewish homeland) were underscored by the uncovering in the 1980s of a Jewish underground organization that had attacked Palestinian leaders in violent attempts to keep the territories forever Jewish. The group had plotted secretly to blow up the sacred Islamic shrines atop the Dome of the Rock. A number of the plotters were given life sentences by a military court. But such was the outcry of support from right-wing groups in the population that their sentences were later commuted by then-president Chaim Herzog.

A more virulent form of anti-Arab, anti-Palestinian violence emerged in 1984 with the founding of Kach, a political party that advocated expulsion of all Arabs from Israel. Its founder, Brooklyn, New York–born Rabbi Meir Kahane, was elected to the Knesset in 1984, giving him parliamentary immunity, and he began organizing anti-Arab demonstrations. The Knesset subsequently passed a law prohibiting any political party advocating racism in any form from participation in national elections. On that basis, the Israeli Supreme Court barred Kach and its founder from participating in the 1988 elections. Kahane was murdered by an Egyptian-American while in New York for a speaking engagement. His son Binyamin formed a successor party, *Kahane Chai* ("Kahane Lives"), based in the West Bank Jewish settlement of Tapuah. Both Kach and Kahane Chai were labeled terrorist groups by the U.S. Department of State. They were also outlawed in Israel after a member, Baruch Goldstein, murdered 29 Muslims in a mosque in Hebron. In September 2000, Binyamin Kahane and his wife were killed in an ambush while driving their children to school, in another blow to the struggling Palestinian–Israeli peace negotiations.

Arab extremism, or, more accurately, Palestinian extremism, evolved in the 1990s largely as a result of Palestinian anger and disillusionment over the peace agreements with Israel, which were seen as accommodation on the part of Palestinian leaders, notably Yassir Arafat, to Israel rather than negotiations to establish a Palestinian state. The main Palestinian extremist group is *Hamas* (the Arabic acronym for the Islamic Resistance Movement, or IRM). Hamas developed originally as a Palestinian chapter of the Muslim Brotherhood, which has chapters in various Islamic Arab countries where it seeks to replace their secular regimes by a government ruled under Islamic law. However, Hamas broke with its parent organization over the use of violence, due largely to the lack of success of the intifada in achieving Palestinian self-rule.

A number of violent attacks on Israelis, including the murder of a border policeman in 1992, led Israel to deport 415 Hamas activists to southern Lebanon. However, the Lebanese government refused to admit them. Lebanon and other Arab countries filed a complaint with the UN Security Council. The Council passed *Resolution 799,* calling for the return of the deportees. Although Israel seldom responds to UN resolutions, in this case the 1993 Oslo Agreement provided additional motivation, and eventually the deportees were allowed to return to their homes.

## DIASPORA RELATIONS

Israel's relationship with the United States has been close since the establishment of the Jewish state, in large part due to the large American Jewish population and its unstinting support. This friendship has been severely tested on two occasions. During the 1967 Six-Day War, the *Liberty,* a slow-moving, lightly armed U.S. Navy ship working with the U.S. National Security Agency to monitor the conflict, was attacked by Israeli aircraft and torpedo boats off the Mediterranean coast. Thirty-four American sailors were killed, and 171 wounded. Israeli statements that the attack was a "mistake" were accepted at face value by the Lyndon Johnson administration, which was concerned with maintaining good relations with Israel at that time of wartime crisis. However, more recent information from the National Security Agency and other archives suggest that it was deliberate.

A second major strain on U.S.–Israeli relations was the Pollard affair. It involved an American Jew, Jonathan Jay Pollard, who was convicted of spying on his own country for Israel. Pollard's reports on U.S. National Security Agency intelligence-collecting methods and his duplication of military satellite photographs seriously compromised U.S. security. They also damaged Israel's image in the American Jewish community. One U.S. Jewish leader asked, "Is Israel becoming an ugly little Spartan state instead of the light of the world?"[16]

The puzzling question of "Who is a Jew?" became a major issue separating Orthodox and Reform and Conservative Jewry in 1998 and 1999. A bill introduced in the Knesset in 1997 by the three religious parties would ban Reform and Conservative Jews from serving on religious councils. The action was rejected by the Israeli Supreme Court, and in January 1998, the first non-Orthodox representatives took their seats on the Haifa Council.

In December 1998, the Court ruled that the system of exemptions from military service for yeshiva students (those enrolled in religious-study programs) was illegal because it was not anchored in law. The court ordered the Knesset to pass legislation dealing with the issue. Ehud Barak had pledged the end of the draft-deferral system during his campaign for the prime ministership. But after his election, he approved changing the system rather than eliminating it. Under the changes, yeshiva students would be exempt from service from ages 18 to 23. They would be allowed a "year of deliberation" thereafter; they could go to trade school or get jobs. At age 24, if they decided to leave the yeshiva, they would be required to do four months' service, either national or military, in a special unit.

Despite Barak's backtracking on the draft-deferral issue, other issues continued to divide Orthodox from secular Jews. Shas, flexing its political muscle after joining Barak's coalition, gained control of the Labor Ministry and promptly enforced a 1953 law that banned employment of Jewish teenagers on the Sabbath. As a result, a McDonald's franchise in Jerusalem was hit with $20,000 in fines.

Other issues separating the two communities include closing of roads near haredim neighborhoods on the Sabbath, and the government's refusal to recognize non-Orthodox Conservative, Reform, and Reconstruction Judaism as legitimately Jewish, for fear of offending the Orthodox community. Until recently, for example, only Orthodox rabbis could perform marriage ceremonies and grant divorces. In 2001, however, new Interior Minister Sharansky, appointed by Barak to replace the Shas incumbent, ruled that the ministry would recognize and register civil marriages performed at foreign consulates in Israel. The new ruling provided a solution for Russian immigrants, who are prohibited from marrying Israelis because under Orthodox rules they are not Jewish!

One of the contentious issues dividing Orthodox and secular Jews is that of a written constitution. As noted earlier in this chapter, Israel has been governed by a series of Basic Laws since independence. These laws do not address the range of civil and human rights covered in most Western constitutions. Nor are they "the law of the land," since they can be overturned by a simple majority in the Knesset.

In recent years, a group of academic scholars and political leaders in the Israel Democracy Institute have worked to lay the groundwork for the country's first written constitution, 50-odd years after one was supposed to be adopted under the terms of the declaration of independence of the state. In September 2000, the effort snowballed when Ehud Barak proposed its adoption as part of his "civil-social agenda." Three new Basic Laws were presented to the Knesset. They concerned due process of law, freedom of expression, and the right to education and housing for all citizens. If adopted, they would add important rights planks to the constitutional structure. However, political developments halted the process in midstream—the collapse of Barak's coalition; the election of a right-wing government under Ariel Sharon, dependent on Orthodox support; and the renewal of the Palestinian intifada. As a result, prospects for a constitution that would reflect the popular will, recognize human rights, separate religion from the state, and establish basic equality for Jews and non-Jews remained remote and divorced from reality.

## THE INTIFADA

The Palestinian intifada in the West Bank and Gaza Strip, which began in December 1987, came as a rude shock to Israel. Coming as it did barely $2\frac{1}{2}$ years after the trauma of the Lebanon War, the uprising found the Israeli public as well as its citizen army unprepared. The military recall of middle-aged reservists and dispatch of new draftees to face stone-throwing Palestinian children created severe moral and psychological problems for many soldiers. John Freymann, an eyewitness to the first Palestinian–Israeli conflict, wrote sadly: "Forty years later the grandsons of the refugees I saw huddled in these camps clash daily with the grandsons of the Israelis with whom I endured the siege of Jerusalem."[17]

Military authorities devised a number of methods to deal with the uprising. They included deportation of suspected terrorists, demolition of houses, wholesale arrests, and detention of Palestinians without charges for indefinite periods. However, growing international criticism of the policy of "breaking the bones" of demonstrators (particularly children) developed by then–defense minister Yitzhak Rabin brought a change in tactics, with the use of rubber or plastic dum-dum bullets, whose effect is less lethal except at close range.

The government also tried to break the Palestinian resistance through arbitrary higher taxes, arguing that this was necessary to compensate for revenues lost due to refusal of Palestinians to pay taxes, a slowdown in business, and lowered exports to the territories. A value added tax (VAT) imposed on olive presses just prior to the processing of the West Bank's major crop was a particular hardship. Along with the brutality of its troops, the tax-collection methods drove Palestinians and Israelis further apart, making the prospect of any amicable relationship questionable.

The opening of emigration to Israel for Soviet Jews added an economic dimension to the intifada. Increased expropriation of land on the West Bank for new immigrant families, along with the expansion of Jewish settlements there, added to Palestinian resentment. Many Palestinians felt that because the new immigrants were unable to find professional employment, they were taking menial jobs ordinarily reserved for Palestinian workers in Israel.

In October 1990, the most serious incident since the start of the intifada occurred in Jerusalem. Palestinians stoned a Jewish group, the Temple Mount Faithful, who had come to lay a symbolic cornerstone for a new Jewish Temple near the Dome of the Rock. Israeli security forces then opened fire, killing some 20 Palestinians and injuring more than 100. The UN Security Council approved a resolution condemning Israel for excessive response (one of many that the Israeli state has ignored over the years). Israel appointed an official commission to investigate the killings. The commission exonerated the security forces, saying that they had acted in self-defense.

**Shamir's Election Plan**
In May 1989, responding to threats by Labor to withdraw from the coalition and precipitate new elections, the government approved a plan drafted by Defense Minister Rabin for elections in the West Bank and Gaza as a prelude to "self-government." Under the plan, the Palestinians would elect one representative from each of 10 electoral districts to an Interim Council. The Council would then negotiate with Israeli representatives for autonomy for the West Bank and Gaza, as defined in the 1979 Camp David treaty. Negotiations on the final status of the territories would begin within three years of the signing of the autonomy agreement.

The implementation of the Rabin plan would have forced Israelis to decide between the Zionist ideal of "Eretz Israel" (the entire West Bank, along with the coast from Lebanon to Egypt, as the Jewish homeland) and the trading of "land for peace" with another nation struggling for its independence. The success of the intifada lay in demonstrating for Israelis the limits to the use of force against a population under occupation. It also served as a pointed reminder to Israelis that "incorporating the occupied territories would commit Israel to the perpetual use of its military to control and repress, not 'Arab refugees' but the whole Palestinian population living in these lands."[18]

**THE PEACE AGREEMENT**
Prior to September 1993, there were few indications that a momentous breakthrough in Palestinian–Israeli relations was about to take place. The new Labor government had cracked down on the Palestinians in the occupied territories harder than had its predecessor in six years of the intifada. In addition to mass arrests and deportations of persons allegedly associated with Hamas, the government sealed off the territories, not only from Israel itself but also from one another. With 120,000 Palestinians barred from their jobs in Israel, poverty, hunger, and unemployment became visible facts of life in the West Bank and the Gaza Strip.

However, what 11 rounds of peace talks, five wars, and 40 years of friction had failed to achieve was accomplished swiftly that September, with the signing of a peace and mutual-recognition accord between Israel and its long-time enemy. The accord was worked out in secret by Israeli and PLO negotiators in Norway and under Norwegian Foreign Ministry sponsorship. It provided for mutual recognition, transfer of authority over the Gaza Strip and the West Bank city of Jericho (but not the entire West Bank) to an elected Palestinian council that would supervise the establishment of Palestinian rule, withdrawal of Israeli forces and their replacement by a Palestinian police force, and a Palestinian state to be formed after a transitional period.

Opposition to the accord from within both societies was to be expected, given the intractable nature of Palestinian–Israeli differences—two peoples claiming the same land. Implementation of the Oslo agreements has been hampered from the start by groups opposed to any form of Palestinian–Israeli accommodation. On the Israeli side, some settler groups formed vigilante posses for defense, even setting up a "tent city" in Jerusalem to protest any giveaway of sacred Jewish land. Palestinian gunmen and suicide bombers responded with attacks on Jews, sometimes in alleyways or on lonely stretches of road outside the cities, but also in public places. One of the bloodiest incidents in this tragic vendetta was the killing of 29 Muslim worshippers in a mosque in Hebron by an American emigrant, an Orthodox Jew, during their Friday service.

Labor's return to power in 1992 suggested that, despite this virulent opposition, the peace process would go forward under its own momentum. The new government, headed by Rabin as prime minister and Peres as foreign minister, began to implement the disengagement of Israeli forces and the transfer of power over the territories to Yassir Arafat's Palestine National Authority (PNA). The Gaza Strip, Jericho, and several West Bank towns were turned over to PNA control. Israel's seeming commitment to the peace process at that time helped to improve relations with its Arab neighbors. The Arab boycott of Israeli goods and companies was lifted. In 1994, the country signed a formal peace treaty with Jordan and opened trade offices in several Gulf states.

**RABIN'S DEATH**
**AND ITS CONSEQUENCES**
The second stage in transfer of authority over the West Bank had barely begun when Rabin was assassinated by an Orthodox Jew while speaking at a Peace Now rally in Jerusalem on November 4, 1995. The assassination climaxed months of increasingly ugly anti-Rabin rhetoric orchestrated by Orthodox rabbis, settlers, and right-wing groups who charged the prime minister with giving away sacred Jewish land while gaining little in return. The assassin, Yigal Amir, stated in court that God had made him act, since the agreement with the Palestinians contradicted sacred Jewish religious principles. He stated: "According to *halacha* [Judaic tradition] a Jew who like Rabin gives over his people and his land to the enemy must be killed. My whole life I have been studying the *halacha* and I have all the data."[19]

Rabin's assassination marked a watershed in Israeli political life; for the first time an Israeli leader had been struck down by one of his own people. Amir's action was condemned abroad. Most secular Israelis regard it as a terrible and useless tragedy, and Israeli society as a whole has yet to come to terms with the murder of its most respected statesman. Unfortunately, many Orthodox Jews subscribed to Amir's stated belief that he had acted rightly to preserve the sacred homeland. Rabin's widow, Leah, continued to call Amir a traitor to his country until her own death in 2001, and she traveled throughout the world to promote the cause of Israeli–Palestinian coexistence. In August 2001, however, President Katsav pardoned Amir's co-conspirator Margalit Has-Sheft, who had been serving a nine-month jail term for complicity in the assassination. Amir's brother and others associated with his plot remain in prison, but the pardon re-exposed the deep fault lines in Israeli society that had emerged with Rabin's death.

After Rabin's death, Peres was confirmed as his successor by a 111–9 Knesset vote. However, he was defeated in the 1996 elections by the new Likud leader, Benjamin Netanyahu. It was Israel's first direct election for prime minister. Peres had hurt his cause by undertaking the ill-advised "Operation Grapes of Wrath" into Lebanon, which resulted in the deaths of many Lebanese civilians. The vote was close, a razor-thin margin of 50.3 percent for Netanyahu to 49.6 percent for Peres. However, Likud failed to win a majority of seats in the Knesset and was forced into another coalition with the religious parties. Labor actually won more seats than Likud (34 to 32), but support from Shas and the National Religious Party (20 seats) and the Russian-immigrant Yisrael Ba'Aliya party gave Netanyahu a narrow majority in the Knesset.

Netanyahu's victory, by a scant 16,000 votes, foreshadowed what would prove to be a near-total deadlock in the peace process. The deadlock was also marked by a deep and angry division within the Isareli population. Israeli social observer Amos Elon wrote that "Zionism, as originally conceived, seemed to have successfully achieved most of its purposes. Yet in its current interpretation by hardliners and religious fundamentalists [it] has been a stumbling block to peace."[20] Israel's 50th birthday in May 1998 underscored the divisions. Even the reelection of Ezer Weizman to the largely ceremonial office of president in March for a second five-year term generated controversy. The Likud, angered at Weizman's public criticism of its policies, nominated an unknown to run against the popular president. However, Weizman was easily reelected by a 63–49 vote in the Knesset.

In contrast to the vision of Israel's founders of Jewish immigrants from many countries and cultures unified into a model democracy, Israeli society as it exists today would be better described as a land of contentious tribes, traceable back to Abraham's expulsion of Hagar and her son Ishmael (ancestor of the Arabs) in favor of Isaac and his descendants. In addition to not honoring the Oslo agreements, Netanyahu encouraged increased Jewish

settlements in the West Bank and Gaza. He used his office to cultivate various groups and parties at the expense of other groups, changing sides when it suited him. A Labor Party official observed before the 1999 election that Israeli elections are more anthropology than politics; the nation does not have a democratic "pendulum" that swings voters away from a leader en masse when his policies seem to be failing.

Elections for the office of prime minister had been scheduled for 2000, but Netanyahu advanced them by a year to preempt increasing opposition to his policies. However, his principal rival, retired general Ehud Barak, defeated him handily in the election, and Netanyahu gave up his seat in the Knesset and retired to private life. Unfortunately for Israel, Barak's large popular majority was negated by the country's multiparty system, which makes a majority difficult to establish in the Knesset. One Israel (formerly Labor), which was now the majority party, held 27 seats to 17 for Shas, 10 for the left-of-center Mereta Party, six each for Center (a new party) and Yisrael Ba' Aliya, and five each for the ultra-Orthodox United Torah Judaism and National Religious Party. Barak was forced to form a coalition of several parties in order to retain support for his peace initiatives with the Palestinians.

Effective coalition government requires concessions to minority parties in Israel's fractious political system. In return for Shas's support, the party was granted four ministerial portfolios, including that of the powerful Interior Ministry. Shas leaders then demanded more concessions; they included $36 million to bail out its bankrupt religious-schools system, as well as debt relief and tax exemptions for the party's social services. When these demands were rejected, Shas pulled out of the coalition. (Earlier, its leader, Rabbi Aryeh Deri, had been convicted of fraud, bribery, and misuse of public power while he was a cabinet minister. He was given a three-year jail sentence.) A similar misuse of public power blocked a bid by supporters of President Ezer Weizman to have him serve a third term. The office, although it is largely ceremonial, requires Knesset confirmation. Weizman had been charged with receiving cash gifts from business people and keeping them rather than turning them over to the state. The court found insufficient evidence for more than a reprimand, but Weizman resigned rather than continue in office under a cloud.

Ariel Sharon's well-publicized visit on September 28, 2000, to the Dome of the

Rock not only set off a new Palestinian intifada; it also had a direct impact on the muddled Israeli political system. The collapse of Barak's coalition left him in the awkward position of negotiating a settlement with the Palestinians without the support of the Knesset or of his own people, particularly the latter, since the negotiations involved territorial concessions. As former Likud leader, Netanyahu seemed poised to take back the office of prime minister. However, Israel's election laws require that a candidate must be a Knesset member. With Netanyahu unable to run, the election narrowed to a choice for the voters between Barak and Sharon, with the latter winning by another huge margin. One major difference from the previous election was that voter turnout was 60 percent. Of those who voted, 62 percent either voted for Barak or turned in blank ballots in protest. Also, only 18 percent of Israeli Arabs cast their ballots; they had been a significant factor in Barak's 1999 election victory, supporting him by 95 percent.

The new prime minister took office amid foreboding on the part of many Israelis, as well as by the country's Arab neighbors and the world at large. Noting Sharon's record, which includes masterminding the 1982 invasion of Lebanon and ultimate responsibility for the slaughter of Palestinians by Israel's Christian allies in Lebanese refugee camps, one author suggests that his election "looked like appointing the village pyromaniac to head its fire brigade." In 2001, survivors of the families killed at the camps filed suit against him in a Belgian court, under the new international statute allowing for prosecution of national leaders for war crimes such as genocide.

Sharon's first year in office coincided with the renewal of the Palestinian intifada, which has brought Israel and the Palestinians into a head-on conflict verging on total war. The accelerated cycle of violence has been marked by new tactics on both sides—relentless suicide bombings by Palestinians, mostly against Israeli civilians; and use of massive retaliation by Israeli tanks, missiles, and helicopter gunships. The first Israeli government official was killed in November, and since then Israel has embarked on a policy of targeting Palestinians suspected of leading the violence. The death toll is modest compared with that in other areas of conflict, in Africa and elsewhere. But the impact of the conflict on the two societies has been traumatic.

By early 2002, the conflict was taking on more and more of a civil-war aspect. On the Palestinian side, despite Israel's interception of a ship laden with heavy weapons allegedly funded by Iran, the Palestinians have significantly improved their weaponry and tactics and have seriously eroded Israeli social morale. Although Palestinian casualties are triple those of Israelis, that country increasingly feels itself under siege. The result is an increased polarization of its society. Thus in February 2002, some 100 reservists refused to serve in the West Bank and Gaza. Although the Israeli left has been splintered by the violence and no longer argues uniformly for "trading land for peace," such tactics as mass destruction of Palestinian homes and reoccupation of towns scheduled for inclusion in the new Palestinian state have generated not only widespread international criticism but also domestic concern. (Such action is banned under the Fourth Geneva Convention governing military occupation of foreign territory.)

To some extent, the Palestinian–Israeli conflict has become one of a personal vendetta between Ariel Sharon and Yassir Arafat. Bolstered by the hawks in his government and party, Sharon declared Arafat "irrelevant" to the peace process in December 2001, and Israeli tanks blockaded the Palestinian leader in his Ramallah headquarters. The blockade was lifted in May 2002 under heavy U.S. pressure. But given the supercharged atmosphere of Palestinian–Israeli hatred and the Sharon–Arafat personal vendetta, only strong and unremitting external mediation could create the conditions for a truce and peace negotiations.[21]

## THE ECONOMY

In terms of national income and economic and industrial development, Israel is ahead of a number of Middle Eastern states that have greater natural resources. Agriculture is highly developed; Israeli engineers and hydrologists have been very successful in developing new irrigation and planting methods that not only "make the desert bloom" but also are exported to other nations under the country's technical-aid program. Agriculture contributes 7.5 percent of gross domestic product annually. However, the prolonged drought that began in 1998 has seriously affected agriculture. Israel also faces a serious water shortage, due to depletion of aquifers. In 2001, there was a 30 percent shortfall in water supplies.

The cutting and export of diamonds and other gemstones is a small but important industry. Since 1996, exports of rough diamonds from the Ramat Gan diamond exchange have increased 80 percent, from $5.2 billion to $9.8 billion. However, in June 2001, the DeBeers Consolidated Mines of South Africa, colossus of the diamond world, announced that it would privatize and sell its own diamond jewelry rather than go through Israeli merchants in the exchange. The action poses a serious threat to the Israeli share of the industry. The aircraft industry is the largest single industrial enterprise, but it has fallen on hard times. The national airline, El Al, which began its existence with the founding of the state, was restructured as a public enterprise in 1982 by the Begin government. It continued to lose money, in part due to high operating costs and unique security arrangements. A $600 million upgrade in equipment enabled the company to expand its flights, and in 1998, it showed a modest $25 million profit. In 2001, the high-speed wireless companies BreezeCom and Floware merged to form a single company capitalized at $330 million.

In January 2001, under the rubric "business is business" and despite strained diplomatic relations, Israel signed an agreement with Egypt to import $3 billion in natural gas annually until 2012. The arrangement would quadruple Egyptian–Israeli trade volume. Unfortunately, the renewal of Palestinian–Israeli conflict on a major scale has put the project on hold for the time being.

An added boost for the Israeli economy was the discovery recently of large natural-gas deposits offshore near the Gaza Strip, by the British energy company BP. Development of these resources will help meet Israel's chronic freshwater shortages by providing energy for the new desalinization plants under construction near Tel Aviv. Using energy-efficient filtration devices pioneered by Israeli scientists, the price for desalted water internationally has dropped from $6 per 1,000 gallons in 1990 to $2 per 1,000. With Israeli aquifers and its main reservoir at the Sea of Galilee down to their lowest levels on record, the country faces a critical water shortage until the new plants are in production.

Providing further evidence of the high level of Israeli technology, the Israel-based Solel Solar Systems currently produces 50 kilowatts annually of solar power, meeting 80 percent of the country's power needs in hotels, hospitals, and other public buildings. Thus far, it is the only solar power system in the world that generates electricity from conventional turbines.

Israel's military superiority over that of its Arab neighbors was reemphasized in 2001 by successful tests of its Arrow II ABM missile. The Arrow II intercepted and destroyed a simulated missile similar to the Scuds fired by Iraq during the 1991 Gulf War.

The Israeli economy has been strengthened through the success of its high-technology companies, many of which are subsidiaries of U.S. firms like Net Manage and Geotek Communications. Its cadre of army-trained computer experts and skilled Russian emigrés made the country second to the United States in the number of start-up companies in the 1990s.

Israel has 34 producing oil wells. After the 1967 War and the occupation of the Sinai Peninsula, Israel was able to exploit Sinai petroleum resources as well as the Alma oil fields in the Gulf of Suez. Twenty-five percent of domestic oil needs came from the Alma fields. In accordance with the Egyptian–Israeli peace treaty, these fields were returned to Egypt, with the stipulation that Israel be able to purchase Sinai oil at less than prices set by the Organization of Petroleum Exporting Countries (OPEC) for Egyptian oil on the world market.

Prior to 1977, when the Likud Bloc came to power, the economy was managed largely by the state in tandem with Histadrut, the Israeli labor confederation. Histadrut functions partly as a union but also as an employer, and it is the controlling factor in many industries. It negotiates for most labor contracts through bargaining with the government. The cost-of-living increases built into these contracts and the country's high level of defense expenditures sent the inflation rate out of sight in the 1980s.

Inflation was also fueled by Likud's fiscal policies. Foreign-exchange controls were abolished, along with the travel tax and import licenses. The currency was allowed to float, and Israelis could open bank accounts in foreign currency. The results were balance-of-payments deficits and a drop in foreign-exchange reserves due to luxury imports paid for in foreign currencies. By 1985, the inflation rate had reached 800 percent.

The Labor government took office amid warnings from U.S. and other economists, plus its own advisers, that the economy was on the point of collapse. Peres introduced a package of draconian reforms. Wages and prices were frozen, and imports of all but essential goods were banned. The package included devaluation of the shekel, replacing it with the Israeli new shekel, pegged to the dollar. Cost-of-living increases were eliminated from labor contracts, and 10,000 jobs were cut from the government bureaucracy.

These drastic measures, plus an annual $3 billion in U.S. aid, enabled the economy to rebound. By 2001, the inflation rate had dropped to 1.3 percent, although unemployment had risen to 9.1 percent. Israel's per capita income of $18,900 makes it for all practical pur-

**Timeline:**

The Zionist movement is organized by Theodor Herzel
**1897**

The Balfour Declaration
**1917**

British mandate over Palestine
**1922–1948**

A UN partition plan is accepted by the Jewish community; following British withdrawal, the State of Israel is proclaimed
**1947–1948**

Armistices are signed with certain Arab states, through U.S. mediation
**1949**

The Six-Day War; Israeli occupation of East Jerusalem, the Gaza Strip, and the Sinai Peninsula
**1967**

Yom Kippur War
**1973**

Peace treaty with Egypt
**1979**

The Israeli invasion of Lebanon
**1980s**

Israeli–Palestinian efforts toward peace; violence escalates on both sides in response; Prime Minister Yitzhak Rabin is assassinated
**1990s**

**2000s**

Ariel Sharon becomes prime minister

The Palestinian–Israeli conflict reaches new extremes of violence

poses a "developed" country in consort with the U.S. and other European and Asian countries.

An added "peace dividend" for Israeli business and industry from a settlement not only with the Palestinians but also with the country's Arab neighbors would be greatly increased foreign investment. It reached $24 billion after the 1993 Oslo Agreement, but dropped 40 percent to $2 billion by 1998, owing to concerns among international investors about the stability and peace commitments of the Netanyahu government.

## NOTES

1. Menachem Froman, "A Modest Proposal," *Jerusalem Report* (October 25, 1999).

2. John Noble Wilford, "A New Armageddon Erupts Over Ancient Battlefields," *The New York Times* (January 6, 2000).

3. Ashkenazi, derived from Ashkenaz (Genesis 10:3), is the name given to Jews who lived in Europe, particularly Germany, and followed particular traditions of Judaism handed down from biblical days. Sephardim (from Sepharah, Obadiah 1:20) refers to Jews originally from Spain who were expelled and emigrated to the Middle East–North Africa. R. J. Zwi Werblowsky and Geoffrey Wigoder, eds., *The Encyclopedia of the Jewish Religion* (New York: Holt, Rinehart & Winston, 1965).

4. Dan V. Segre, *A Crisis of Identity: Israel and Zionism* (Oxford, England: Oxford University Press, 1980), p. 25.

5. Recent excavations of Herod's summer palace at Herodium near Bethlehem reveal an 18- by 30-foot indoor swimming pool, saunas, and baths adorned with mosaics and frescoes, confirming the king's achievements as the "Great Builder" of Judea in early Christian times.

6. Yaron Ezrahi, *Rubber Bullets: Power and Conscience in Modern Israel* (New York: Farrar, Straus & Giroux, 1997), p. 269.

7. Abraham Shulman, *Coming Home to Zion* (Garden City, NY: Doubleday, 1979), p. 14.

8. The text is in "Documents on Palestine," *The Middle East and North Africa* (London: Europa Publications, 1984), p. 58.

9. See Roy Jenkins, *Churchill: A Biography* (London: Macmillan, 2001) p. 360. The author also notes that Churchill had spoken out favorably about the Arabs at the Cairo Conference: "The British government is well-disposed to them and cherishes Arab friendship." A more specific commitment came in the form of a letter from Arthur James Balfour to Lord Rothschild, prominent statesman and a Zionist sympathizer, in 1917. Although the latter's qualified endorsement favoring a Jewish national home in Palestine included a commitment to guarantee the rights of the indigenous population, its approval by the cabinet was taken by the Zionists as official British support for their cause. In this way the letter became "The Balfour Declaration."

10. Shimon Peres, *Battling for Peace: A Memoir,* David Landau, ed. (New York: Random House, 1995), pp. 20–21.

11. Abba Eban, "Rebirth of a Nation," *Jerusalem Post* Supplement 5757 (May 1997), p. 2.

12. David Ben-Gurion, *Memoirs* (Cleveland: World Publishing, 1970), p. 58.

13. Abu Iyad with Eric Rouleau, *My Home, My Land: A Narrative of the Palestinian Struggle,* Linda Butler Koseoglu, tr. (New York: New York Times Books, 1981), pp. 225–226.

14. Ben-Gurion, *op. cit.,* p. 57.

15. The Bar-On affair involved Netanyahu's appointment of a "mediocre lawyer," Roni Bar-On, as attorney-general, supposedly as a favor to the leader of Shas, in return for his party's support for the coalition government. The Israeli Supreme Court ruled in June 1997 that there was insufficient evidence to prosecute Netanyahu, but the near-scandal led to a no-confidence resolution in the Knesset that the prime minister survived by a 55–50 vote. See *The New York Times* (June 24, 1997).

16. Robert Schreiber, in *New Outlook* (May/June 1987), p. 42.

17. John Freymann, in *Foreign Service Journal* (May 1988), p. 30.

18. Ezrahi, *op. cit.,* pp. 274–275.

19. Quoted in Amos Elon, *A Blood-Dimmed Tale: Despatches from the Middle East* (New York: Columbia University Press, 1997) (originally appeared in *The New York Review of Books,* December 21, 1995).

20. *Ibid.,* p. 2.

21. See "Arafat and Sharon Endgame," *World Press Review* (April 2002), a series of articles by Israeli and foreign journalists.

## DEVELOPMENT

Israel is now labeled a "developed" country, in contrast to its Arab neighbors, under international standards and norms. As such, its energy needs are greater than the current sources of supply. The discovery of large natural-gas deposits offshore near Gaza will increase expenditures in the energy sector but will be compensated for by increased energy supplies at below-global costs.

## FREEDOM

Israel is a multiparty democracy with a Parliament (Knesset) and representative political and judicial institutions. Its Basic Laws guarantee free speech, among other human rights. However, these laws and basic rights have not been applied equally to the Arab population in such areas as housing, access to education, and political representation. In February 2002, an Arab lawmaker went on trial for speeches praising the Lebanese Hizbullah and recommending that the Palestinians adopt its terrorist tactics in the West Bank and Gaza Strip.

## HEALTH/WELFARE

Intifada II and the steady escalation of conflict have seriously damaged the mental and psychological health of both Israeli and Palestinian societies and have had an especially negative effect on youth. Thus the Zionist religious youth movement Bnei Akiva, which has traditionally emphasized youth activities such as summer camp, has become a front-line organization in the figting, its efforts concentrated on bereavement therapy, family losses, and orphanhood. And to young Palestinians, the suicide bomber has become a familiar tragic figure, often a youth who has lost all hope for the future.

## ACHIEVEMENTS

The Inter-Religious Coordinating Council serves as an umbrella organization for some 70 groups and seeks through joint projects, workshops, school programs, and informal social gatherings to build understanding between Israeli Jews and Israeli Arabs, with their different cultures and long history of conflict. One such project resulted in a book, *Common Values, Different Sources,* which is used in both school systems. Another project, the Center for Social Concern, brings school principals and community leaders together to discuss environmental issues of common concern, such as water usage.

# Jordan (Hashimite Kingdom of Jordan)

## GEOGRAPHY

*Area in Square Miles (Kilometers):*
(92,300) (about the size of
Indiana)

*Capital (Population):* Amman
(483,000)

*Environmental Concerns:* limited
natural freshwater reserves;
deforestation; overgrazing; soil
erosion; desertification

*Geographical Features:* mostly
desert plateau in the east; a
highland area in the west; the
Great Rift Valley separates the
east and west banks of the
Jordan River

*Climate:* mostly arid desert; a
rainy season in the west

## PEOPLE

### Population

*Total:* 5,154,000
*Annual Growth Rate:* 3%
*Rural/Urban Population Ratio:*
28/72
*Major Language:* Arabic
*Ethnic Makeup:* 98% Arab; 1%
Circassian; 1% Armenian
*Religions:* 92% Sunni Muslim;
6% Christian and others

### Health

*Life Expectancy at Birth:* 75 years
(male); 80 years (female)
*Infant Mortality Rate (Ratio):*
20.3/1,000
*Physicians Available (Ratio):* 1/616

### Education

*Adult Literacy Rate:* 86.6%
*Compulsory (Ages):* 6–16; free

## COMMUNICATION

*Telephones:* 403,000 main lines
*Daily Newspaper Circulation:* 62
per 1,000 people
*Televisions:* 176 per 1,000
*Internet Service Providers:* 5 (2000)

## TRANSPORTATION

*Highways in Miles (Kilometers):* 4,968
(8,000)
*Railroads in Miles (Kilometers):* 420 (677)
*Usable Airfields:* 18
*Motor Vehicles in Use:* 265,000

## GOVERNMENT

*Type:* constitutional monarchy
*Independence Date:* May 25, 1946 (from
League of Nations mandate)
*Head of State/Government:* King Abdullah
II; Prime Minister Ali Abul Ragheb
*Political Parties:* Al-Umma (Nation)
Party; Jordanian Democratic Popular

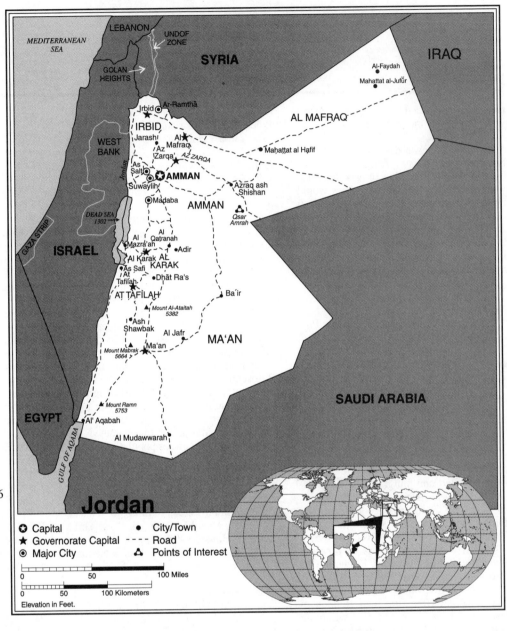

Jordan

| | |
|---|---|
| ⊕ Capital | ● City/Town |
| ★ Governorate Capital | - - - Road |
| ◉ Major City | ▲ Points of Interest |

Elevation in Feet.

Unity Party; Islamic Action Front;
National Constitutional Party;
many others
*Suffrage:* universal at 20

## MILITARY

*Military Expenditures (% of GDP):* 7.8%
*Current Disputes:* none

## ECONOMY

*Currency ($ U.S. Equivalent):* 0.712 dinar
= $1
*Per Capita Income/GDP:* $3,500/$17.3 billion
*GDP Growth Rate:* 2%
*Inflation Rate:* 0.7%
*Unemployment Rate:* officially 15%; more
likely 25%–30%

*Labor Force:* 1,150,000
*Natural Resources:* phosphates; potash;
shale oil
*Agriculture:* wheat; barley; fruits;
tomatoes; olives; livestock
*Industry:* phosphate mining; petroleum
refining; cement; potash; light
manufacturing
*Exports:* $2 billion (primary partners
Iraq, India, Saudi Arabia)
*Imports:* $4 billion (primary partners
Iraq, Germany, United States)

http://lcweb2.loc.gov/frd/cs/jotoc.html
http://www.odci.gov/cia/publications/
factbook/index.html

Jordan Tourism Authority

Amman is a city built on seven hills. Against the slope of one hill is this large Roman amphitheater. The amphitheater, restored to its original seating capacity of 6,000, is now being used once again for grand performances, as it was almost 2,000 years ago.

# JORDAN

The Hashimite Kingdom of Jordan (previously called Transjordan; usually abbreviated to Jordan) is one of the smaller Middle Eastern nations. The country formerly consisted of two regions: the East Bank (lying east of the Jordan River) and the West Bank of the Jordan. Israel occupied the West Bank in June 1967, although the region continued to be legally and administratively attached to Jordan and salaries of civil servants and others were paid by the Jordanian government. In 1988, King Hussein formally severed the relationship, leaving the West Bank under Israeli occupation de facto as well as de jure. Between 1948 and 1967, Jordanian-occupied territory also included the old city of Jerusalem (East Jerusalem), which was annexed during the 1948 Arab–Israeli War.

Modern Jordan is an "artificial" nation, the result of historical forces and events that shaped the Middle East in the twentieth century. It had no prior history as a nation and was known simply as the land east of the Jordan River, a region of diverse peoples, some nomadic, others sedentary farmers and herders. Jordan's current neighbors are Iraq, Syria, Saudi Arabia, and Israel. Their joint borders were all established by the British after World War I, when Britain and France divided the territories of the defeated Ottoman Empire between them.

Jordan's borders with Iraq, Syria, and Saudi Arabia do not follow natural geographical features. They were established mainly to keep nomadic peoples from raiding; over time, these borders have been accepted by the countries concerned. The boundary with Israel, which formerly divided the city of Jerusalem between Jordanian and Israeli control, became an artificial barrier after the 1967 Six-Day War and Israel's occupation of Jerusalem and the West Bank (of the Jordan River). The Jordan–Israel Peace Treaty of 1994 has resulted in a redrafting of borders. Israel returned 340 square miles captured in 1967 in the Arava Valley and south of the Galilee to Jordanian control. However, Israeli *kibbutzim* (communal farm settlements) will be allowed to continue cultivating some 750 acres in the territory under a 25-year lease.

## HISTORY

The territory of modern Jordan was ruled by outside powers until it became an independent nation in the twentieth century. Under the Ottoman Empire, it was part of the province of Syria. The Ottoman authorities in Syria occasionally sent military patrols across the Jordan River to "show the flag" and collect taxes, but otherwise they left the people of the area to manage their own affairs.[1]

This tranquil existence ended with World War I. The Ottomans were defeated and their provinces were divided into protectorates, called mandates, set up by the League of Nations and assigned to Britain and/or France to administer and prepare for eventual self-government. The British received a mandate over Palestine and extended its territory to include Transjordan east of the River Jordan. Due to their commitment to help Jews dispersed throughout the world to establish a national home in Palestine, the British decided to govern Transjordan as a separate mandate.

The terms of the mandate system required the protecting power (in this case, Britain) to appoint a native ruler. During the war, the British had worked with Sharif Husayn to organize an Arab revolt against the Ottomans. Husayn was a prominent Arab leader in Mecca who held the honorary position of "Protector of the Holy Shrines of Islam." Two of the sharif's sons, Faisal and Abdullah, had led the revolt, and the British felt that they owed them something. When Iraq was set up as a mandate, the British made Faisal its king. Abdullah was offered the Transjordan territory. Because the population was primarily pastoral, he chose the traditional title of emir, rather than king, considering it more appropriate.

## EMIR ABDULLAH

Through his father, Abdullah traced his lineage back to the Hashim family of Mecca, the clan to which the Prophet Muhammad belonged. This ancestry gave him a great deal of prestige in the Arab world, particularly among the nomads of Transjordan, who had much respect for a person's genealogy. Abdullah used the connection assiduously to build a solid base of support among his kinspeople. When the country became fully independent in 1946, Abdullah named the new state the Hashimite Kingdom of Jordan.

Abdullah's new country had little to recommend it to outsiders except some fine Roman ruins and a great deal of empty land. It was a peaceful, quiet place, consisting entirely of what is today the East Bank of the Jordan River, with vaguely defined borders across the desert. The population was about 400,000, mostly rural peasants and nomads; the capital, Amman, was little more than a large village spread over some of those Roman ruins.

During the period of the mandate (1921–1946), Abdullah was advised by resident British officials. The British helped him draft a constitution in 1928, and Transjordan became independent in everything except financial policy and foreign relations. But Emir Abdullah and his advisers ran the country like a private club. In traditional Arab desert fashion, Abdullah held a public meeting outside his palace every Friday; anyone who wished could come and present a complaint or petition to the emir.

Abdullah did not trust political parties or institutions such as a parliament, but he

agreed to issue the 1928 Constitution as a step toward eventual self-government. He also laid the basis for a regular army. A British Army officer, John Bagot Glubb, was appointed in 1930 to train the Transjordanian Frontier Force to curb Bedouin raiding across the country's borders. Under Glubb's command, this frontier force eventually became the Arab Legion; during Emir Abdullah's last years, it played a vital role not only in defending the kingdom against the forces of the new State of Israel but also in enlarging Jordanian territory by the capture of the West Bank and East Jerusalem.[2]

When Britain gave Jordan its independence in 1946, the country was not vastly different from the tranquil emirate of the 1920s. But events beyond its borders soon overwhelmed it, like the dust-storm rolling in from the desert that sweeps everything before it. The conflict between the Arab and Jewish communities in neighboring Palestine had become so intense and unmanageable that the British decided to terminate their mandate. They turned the problem over to the United Nations. In November 1947, the UN General Assembly voted to partition Palestine into separate Arab and Jewish states, with Jerusalem to be an international city under UN administration.

The partition plan was not accepted by the Palestine Arabs, and as British forces evacuated Palestine in 1947–1948, they prepared to fight the Jews for possession of all Palestine. The State of Israel was proclaimed in 1948. Armies of the neighboring Arab states, including Jordan, immediately invaded Palestine. But they were poorly armed and untrained. Only the Jordanian Arab Legion gave a good account of itself. The Legion's forces seized the West Bank, originally part of the territory allotted to a projected Palestinian Arab state by the United Nations. The Legion also occupied the Old City of Jerusalem (East Jerusalem). Subsequently, Abdullah annexed both territories, despite howls of protest from other Arab leaders, who accused him of landgrabbing from his "Palestine brothers" and harboring ambitions to rule the entire Arab world.

Jordan now became a vastly different state. Its population tripled with the addition of half a million West Bank Arabs and half a million Arab refugees from Israel. Abdullah still did not trust the democratic process, but he realized that he would have to take firm action to strengthen Jordan and to help the dispossessed Palestinians who now found themselves reluctantly included in his kingdom. He approved a new Constitution, one that provided for a bicameral

Legislature (similar to the U.S. Congress), with an appointed Senate and an elected House of Representatives. He appointed prominent Palestinians to his cabinet. A number of Palestinians were appointed to the Senate; others were elected to the House of Representatives.

On July 20, 1951, King Abdullah was assassinated as he entered the Al Aqsa Mosque in East Jerusalem for Friday prayers. His grandson Hussein was at his side and narrowly escaped death. Abdullah's murderer, who was killed immediately by royal guards, was a Palestinian. Many Palestinians felt that Abdullah had betrayed them by annexing the West Bank and because he was thought to have carried on secret peace negotiations with the Israelis (recent evidence suggests that he did so). In his *Memoirs,* King Abdullah wrote, "The paralysis of the Arabs lies in their present moral character. They are obsessed with tradition and concerned only with profit and the display of oratorical patriotism."[3]

Abdullah dealt with the Israelis because he despaired of Arab leadership. Ironically, Abdullah's proposal to Britain in 1938 for a unified Arab–Jewish Palestine linked with Jordan, if it had been accepted, would have avoided five wars and hundreds of thousands of casualties. Yet this same proposal forms the basis for discussion of the Palestinian–Israeli settlement in recent years.[4]

## KING HUSSEIN

Abdullah's son Crown Prince Talal succeeded to the throne. He suffered from mental illness (probably schizophrenia) and had spent most of his life in mental hospitals. When his condition worsened, advisers convinced him to abdicate in favor of his eldest son, Hussein.

At the time of his death from cancer in February 1999, Hussein had ruled Jordan for 46 years, since 1953—the longest reign to date of any Middle Eastern monarch and one of the longest in the world in the twentieth century. To a great extent he *was* Jordan, developing a small desert territory with no previous national identity into a modern state. A popular Jordanian saying was, "Hussein is Jordan and Jordan is Hussein," underlining the fusion of ruler and nation.

Yet during his long reign, Hussein faced and overcame many crises and challenges to his rule. These crises stemmed mainly from Jordan's involvement in the larger Arab–Israeli conflict. Elections for the Jordanian Parliament in 1956 resulted in a majority of West Bank Palestinian candidates. Controversy developed as these representatives pressed the king to declare his all-out support for the Palestinian cause. At one point, the rumor spread that he had been killed. Hussein immediately jumped into a jeep and rode out to the main Arab Legion base at Zerqa, near Amman. He then presented himself to the troops to prove that he was still alive and in command.[5]

The "Zerqa incident" illustrated Hussein's fine sense of timing, undertaking bold actions designed to throw real or potential enemies off balance. It also emphasized the importance of army support for the monarchy. The majority of the Arab Legion's soldiers came from Bedouin tribes, and for them, loyalty to the crown has always been automatic and unfailing.

Other challenges followed. Syrian fighters tried to shoot down King Hussein's plane in 1958, and Communists and Palestinian leaders plotted his overthrow.

The June 1967 Six-Day War produced another crisis in Jordan, this one not entirely of its own making. Israeli forces occupied 10 percent of Jordanian territory, including half of its best agricultural lands. The Jordanian Army suffered 6,000 casualties, most of them in a desperate struggle to hold the Old City of Jerusalem against Israeli attack. Nearly 300,000 more Palestinian refugees from the West Bank fled into Jordan. To complicate things further, guerrillas from the Palestine Liberation Organization, formerly based in the West Bank, made Jordan their new headquarters. The PLO considered Jordan its base for the continued struggle against Israel. Its leaders talked openly of removing the monarchy and making Jordan an armed Palestinian state.

By 1970, Hussein and the PLO were headed toward open confrontation. The guerrillas had the sympathy of the population, and successes in one or two minor clashes with Israeli troops had made them arrogant. They swaggered through the streets of Amman, directing traffic at intersections and stopping pedestrians to examine their identity papers. Army officers complained to King Hussein that the PLO was really running the country. The king became convinced that unless he moved against the guerrillas, his throne would be in danger. He declared martial law and ordered the army to move against them.

The ensuing Civil War lasted until July 1971, but in the PLO annals, it is usually referred to as "Black September," because of its starting date and because it ended in disaster for the guerrillas. Their bases were dismantled, and most of the guerrillas were driven from Jordan. The majority went to Lebanon, where they reorganized. In time they became as powerful there as they had been in Jordan.

For the remainder of his reign, there were no serious internal threats to King Hussein's rule. Jordan shared in the general economic boom in the Arab world that developed as a result of the enormous price increases in oil after the 1973 Arab–Israeli War. As a consequence, Hussein was able to turn his attention to the development of a more democratic political system. Like his grandfather, he did not entirely trust political parties or elected legislatures, and he was leery of the Palestinians' intentions toward him. He was also convinced that Jordan rather than the PLO should be the natural representative of the Palestinians. But he realized that in order to represent them effectively and to build the kind of Jordanian state that he could safely hand over to his successors, he would need to develop popular support in addition to that of the army. Accordingly, Hussein set up a National Consultative Council in 1978, as what he called an interim step toward democracy. The Council had a majority of Palestinians (those living on the East Bank) as members.

Hussein's arbitrary separation of Jordan from the West Bank has had important implications for internal politics in the kingdom. It enabled the king to proceed with political reforms without the need to involve the Palestinian population there. The timetable was accelerated by nationwide protests in 1989 over price increases for basic commodities. The protests turned swiftly to violence, resulting in the most serious riots in national history. Prime Minister Zaid Rifai was dismissed; he was held personally responsible for the increases and for the country's severe financial problems, although these were due equally to external factors. King Hussein appointed a caretaker government, headed by his cousin, to oversee the transitional period before national elections for the long-promised lower chamber of the Legislature.

In 1990, the king and leaders of the major opposition organization, the Jordanian National Democratic Alliance (JANDA), signed a historic National Charter, which provides for a multiparty political system. Elections were set under the Charter for an 80-member House of Representatives. Nine seats would be reserved for Christians and three for Circassians, an ethnic Muslim minority originally from the Caucasus.

In 1992, Hussein abolished martial law, which had been in effect since 1970. Henceforth, security crimes such as espionage would be dealt with by state civilian-security courts. New laws also undergirded constitutional rights such as a free press, free speech, and the right of public assembly.

With political parties now legalized, 20 were licensed by the Interior Ministry to take part in Jordan's first national parliamentary election since 1956. The election was scheduled for November 1993. However, the September 13 accord between Israel and the PLO raised questions about the process. Many people in Jordan committed to democratization feared that the election would become a battle between supporters and opponents of the accord, since half the Jordanian population are of Palestinian descent. As a result, the government placed strict limits on campaigning. Political rallies were banned; the ban was rescinded by the courts several weeks before the election. Hussein also suspended the Parliament elected in 1990; and an amendment was added to the election law stipulating that voting would be "one person, one vote" rather than by party lists.

Despite these forebodings, the election went off on schedule, with few hitches. The results were an affirmation of Hussein's policy of gradual democratization. Pro-monarchy candidates won 54 of the 80 seats in the House of Representatives to 16 for the Islamic Action Front, the political arm of the Muslim Brotherhood. The remaining seats were spread among minor parties and independents. Voter turnout was 68 percent, far higher than in the 1990 election. The electorate also surprised by choosing the first woman member, Toujan Faisal, a feminist and television personality who, in the earlier campaign had been charged with apostasy by the Muslim Brotherhood.

The 1997 parliamentary elections, which took place in November, continued the trend toward Hussein's version of representative government under firm monarchical rule. Government supporters won 62 of 80 seats in the lower house; the remainder went to independent candidates and Islamic Action Front candidates. However, a restrictive press law imposed in May led to the suspension of 13 weekly newspapers. Opposition groups then called for a boycott of the election. The law was thrown out by the Higher Court of Justice (Jordan's Supreme Court) after the election. But the damage to Jordan's fledgling democracy had been done. Barely 50 percent of the country's 800,000 registered voters cast their ballots. The poor turnout was not a criticism of the king as much as it was due to public disappointment with the lack of visible benefits from the peace treaty with Israel and the widening gap between rich and poor in Jordan.

## FOREIGN POLICY

During the 40-year cycle of hostilities between Israel and its Arab neighbors, there were periodic secret negotiations involving Jordanian and Israeli negotiators, including at times King Hussein himself, as Jordan sought to mend fences with its next-door neighbor. But in 1991 and 1992, Jordan became actively involved in the "peace process" initiated by the United States to resolve the vital issue of Palestinian self-government. As these negotiations proceeded, opponents of the process in Jordan did their best to derail them. Islamic Action Front members of the lower house of Parliament called for a vote of no-confidence in the government (but not in Hussein's leadership) for "treachery to Jordan and the Arab nation." However, the motion failed; most Jordanians supported the peace talks, and a majority of members of the House disagreed with the motion and voted against it.

Peace with Israel became a reality in October 1994, with Jordan the second Arab nation to sign a formal treaty with the Israeli state. Subsequently, the normalization of relations moved ahead with lightning speed. In July 1995, the Senate voted to annul the last anti-Israel laws still on the books. Embassies opened in Amman and Tel Aviv under duly accredited ambassadors. As Israel's first ambassador to Jordan observed, "I don't think there have ever been two countries at war for such a long time that have moved so quickly into peaceful cooperation."[6]

The treaty produced some positive results. Direct mail service between the two countries went into effect in February 1995. The maritime boundary in the Gulf of Aqaba was formally demarcated at mid-channel, and Israeli tourists flocked to visit Petra and other historic Jordanian sites.

However, the benefits anticipated from the peace agreement and its spin-off in terms of U.S. aid and renewed close relations have been negated largely by the breakdown of the Oslo and subsequent agreements for Palestinian statehood. The late king Hussein worked tirelessly to mediate the conflict. King Abdullah II has been less involved. Other than closing down the Amman office of Hamas—the militant Islamic anti-Israeli organization in the West Bank and Gaza Strip—Abdullah's government observes the letter but not the spirit of the peace treaty. Early in 2001, Abdullah and Egyptian president Hosni Mubarak submitted a joint proposal to end the violence and to reinstate the peace talks on the basis of equality. Israel would halt settlement building in the West Bank in return for an end to the Palestinian intifada. but thus far, the proposal has achieved no results.

The Jordanian people have yet to follow up the peace treaty with cultural and social interchanges. Journalists who attended a workshop with their Israeli counterparts in Haifa in September 1999 were even expelled from the Jordan Press Association. They were reinstated only after issuing a public statement that "we still view Israel to be a conquest state and hold that it is impossible to conduct policies of normalization with her."[7]

The peace agreement has to some extent isolated Jordan from other Arab countries. Iraq, its major trading partner, broke relations after the Jordanian government allowed the Iraq National Accord, an umbrella opposition group working to overthrow Saddam Hussain, to set up an office in Amman. Inter-Arab solidarity was restored after the breakdown of the Palestinian–Israeli peace negotiations in 2000–2001. Saudi Arabia resumed oil shipments to Jordan after an eight-year break, caused by Jordan's alignment with Iraq, its principal supplier and trade partner. Kuwait also agreed to provide Jordan with 30 million barrels per day of oil; and in 2001, with the border open, regular deliveries of Iraqi oil were resumed.

The positive relationship established with successive U.S. administrations by the late king Hussein has been seriously weakened by the renewed cycle of Israeli–Palestinian conflict. In October 2001, the U.S. Senate approved the free-trade agreement with Jordan negotiated by the Bill Clinton administration and supported by that of George W. Bush. As a result, Jordan became the fourth country (after Canada, Mexico, and Israel) to enjoy a tariff-free association with the United States. Although it had been in the works long before the September 11, 2001, terrorist attacks on the United States, it offered an added incentive for Jordan to join the international coalition against terrorism. In November, King Abdullah offered troops in support of the offensive against Osama bin Laden and his Al Qaeda network. But he insisted that, in return, the United States would work for a "speedy solution" to the Israeli–Palestinian conflict. Early in 2002, the king strongly criticized Israel's blockade of palestinian leader Yassir Arafat in his Ramallah headquarters. In a February 26 editorial, *The Jordan Times,* which reflects official government policy, accused Israeli prime minister Ariel Sharon of seeking to overthrow the legitimate recognized leader of the nascent Palestinian state.

In any case, the country has had more than its share of Islamic extremism to deal with. At the end of the century, Jordanian intelligence agents uncovered a plot to bomb Amman hotels filled with American and Israeli tourists who had come to celebrate the millennium, and another scheme that would blow up Christian holy sites in Jordan. The plotters included a number of Jordanians who had fought the Soviets in Afghanistan and returned home after the Soviet withdrawl from that country.

## THE ECONOMY

Jordan is rich in phosphates. Reserves are estimated at 2 billion tons, and new deposits are constantly being reported. Phosphate rock is one of the country's main exports, along with potash, which is mined on the Jordanian side of the Dead Sea.

The mainstay of the economy is agriculture. The most productive agricultural area is the Jordan Valley. A series of dams and canals from the Jordan and Yarmuk Rivers has increased arable land in the valley by 264,000 acres and made possible production of high-value vegetable crops for export to nearby countries.

During the years of Israeli occupation of the West Bank, Jordan was estimated to have been deprived of 80 percent of its citrus crops and 45 percent of its vegetable croplands. It also lost access to an area that had provided 30 percent of its export market, as Israeli goods replaced Jordanian ones and the shekel became the medium of exchange there. The peace treaty guaranteed Jordan 7.5 billion cubic feet of water annually from the Jordan and Yarmuk Rivers, but to date the country has received less than half the agreed-on amount.

Jordan's economy traditionally has depended on outside aid and remittances from its large expatriate skilled labor force to make ends meet. A consequence of the Gulf War was the mass departure from Kuwait of some 350,000 Jordanian and Palestinian workers. Despite the loss in remittances and the added burden on its economy, Jordan welcomed them. But their return to Jordan complicated the nation's efforts to meet the requirements of a 1989 agreement with the International Monetary Fund for austerity measures as a prerequisite for further aid. The government reduced subsidies, but the resulting increase in bread prices led to riots throughout the country. The subsidies were restored; but they were again reduced in 1991, this time with basic commodities (including bread) sold at fixed low prices under a rationing system. Later price increases that were required to meet budgetary deficits in 1996 and 1998 met

| Establishment of the British mandate of Transjordan **1921** | The first Constitution is approved by the British-sponsored Legislative Council **1928** | Treaty of London; the British give Jordan independence and Abdullah assumes the title of emir **1946** | The Arab Legion occupies the Old City of Jerusalem and the West Bank during the first Arab–Israeli War **1948** | Jordanian forces are defeated by Israel in the Six-Day War; Israelis occupy the West Bank and Old Jerusalem **1967** | "Black September"; war between army and PLO guerrillas ends with expulsion of the PLO from Jordan **1970–1971** | Politically, economically, and socially, Jordan is one of the primary losers in the Gulf crisis; Jordan signs a peace treaty with Israel; King Hussein dies and is succeeded by his son Abdullah **1990s** |

**2000s**

The Aqaba Special Economic Zone opens

Jordan supports the antiterrorism coalition

with little public protest, as the population settled down stoically to face a stagnating economy. One opposition leader remarked, "I don't want us to end up as an economic colony of the United States and Israel, enslaved as cheap labor."[8]

Jordan has backed strongly the development of a Palestinian state governed by the Palestine National Authority. Initially, the Jordanian government set up a preferential tax and customs exemption system for 25 Palestinian export products. A transit agreement reached in 1996 allows Palestinian exporters direct access to Aqaba port.

King Hussein's death and the accession to the throne of Abdullah rather than Crown Prince Hassan, the late king's brother, has caused concern over Jordan's political future. But a greater concern is that of the country's economic progress. As the result of the high birth rate—75 percent of the population are under age 29, with those age 15 to 29 accounting for 34.4 percent—there are not enough jobs. Unemployment for this age group is about 30 percent. A UN–financed Jordan Human Development Report 2000 found that Jordan's youth "are not well-equipped to meet the challenges of a globalizing world."

In addition to the free-trade pact, the United States has helped Jordan to set up a number of free-trade zones. A $300 million supplemental aid package for Jordan was approved by the U.S. Congress in 1999, and the country currently ranks fourth in the Middle East in U.S. aid appropriations (after Israel, Egypt, and Turkey).

Despite his youth and political inexperience, Abdullah's early actions indicated a much greater awareness of and concern for Jordan's economic problems than his late father, at least during Hussein's last years on the throne. Like the caliphs of old, King Abdullah went out in public in

disguise, accompanied only by his driver, to learn about these problems first-hand. "There are sightings all over the place," he told an interviewer. "The bureaucrats are terrified. It's great"—as he changes into a wig, plastic glasses, false beard, and cane, before visiting the Finance Ministry.[9] He has inspected the free-trade zones incognito to hear complaints about fiscal mismanagement. Abdullah envisions Jordan as a "Middle Eastern Singapore," a model for development. "We can be symbols," he says, "for someone in Yemen who might say 'I don't want my country to be like it is today. I want it to be like the Jordanian or the Bahraini model, modern and progressive.'"[10]

There are many obstacles to both Jordan's political development and economic progress. On the political side, continued limits on press freedom and public assembly, the prevalence of nepotism, an entrenched bureaucracy, and the king's role as final arbiter hamper the growth of representative government. In July 2001, a new election law raised the number of deputies in Parliament from 80 to 120. Election boundaries were redistricted to allow for the expanded membership. However, the parliamentary elections scheduled for mid-summer were postponed indefinitely after the Muslim Brotherhood, which is strong in Jordan although not represented as a political party, threatened a boycott.

A new cabinet was appointed in early 2002, and parliamentary elections originally scheduled for 2001 were postponed again, to September 2002, to allow the new government to strengthen the economy through the free-trade pact with the United States.

**NOTES**

1. The Ottomans paid subsidies to nomadic tribes to guard the route of pilgrims headed south for Mecca. Peter Gubser, *Jordan: Crossroads of Middle Eastern Events* (Boulder, CO: Westview Press, 1983).

2. Years later, Glubb wrote, "In its twenty-eight years of life it had never been contemplated that the Arab Legion would fight an independent war." Quoted in Harold D. Nelson, ed., *Jordan, A Country Study* (Washington, D.C.: American University, Foreign Area Studies, 1979), p. 201.

3. King Abdullah of Jordan, *My Memoirs Completed,* Harold W. Glidden, trans. (London: Longman, 1951, 1978), preface, xxvi.

4. The text of the proposal is in Abdullah's *Memoirs, Ibid.,* pp. 89–90.

5. Naseer Aruri, *Jordan: A Study in Political Development (1925–1965)* (The Hague, Netherlands: Martinus Nijhoff, 1967), p. 159.

6. Quoted in *Middle East Economic Digest* (June 16, 1995).

7. Helen Schary Motro, "Israel the Invisible," *The Christian Science Monitor,* (January 12, 2000).

8. Laith Shbeilat, quoted in William A. Orme, "Neighbors Rally to Jordan," *The New York Times* (February 18, 1999).

9. Jeffrey Goldberg, "Learning to Be a King," *The New Times Magazine* (February 8, 2000).

10. *Ibid.*

---

**DEVELOPMENT**

Jordan's treaty with Israel brought the cancellation of $683 million in debts to the United States and $210 million to European countries. But continued budgetary deficits and expanded imports have increased foreign indebtedness. The United States helped to set up a number of free-trade zones in 2000 and 2001. These have already generated 13,000 new jobs. The free-trade agreement with the United States resulted in a 25% increase in Jordanian exports in 2001 over 1999 totals.

**FREEDOM**

The National Charter guarantees full civil and other rights to all Jordanians. In practice, however, press freedom, political activity, and other rights are often circumscribed. The free-trade agreement with the United States commits Jordan to recognize the right of labor unions to organize and bargain.

**HEALTH/WELFARE**

Article 340 of the Jordan Penal Code, which imposes light sentences, or in some cases complete acquittal, for men who carry out "honor killings"—the murder of wives or female relatives who are deemed to have defamed family honor by their actions—has recently come under attack not only by human-rights groups in Jordan but also by international organizations such as Amnesty International. Legislation is now pending in Jordan to provide stiff penalties.

**ACHIEVEMENTS**

In January 2001, the new Aqaba Special Economic Zone was opened for business. It offers low taxes, duty-free privileges, and streamlined investment procedures for foreign companies considering a Jordan location. The intent of Jordanian officials is to transform Aqaba from an underdeveloped region to "an engine for Jordanian economic growth." By 2020, the zone is expected to bring $6 billion in investment and generate 70,000 jobs.

# Kuwait (State of Kuwait)

## GEOGRAPHY

*Area in Square Miles (Kilometers):*
6,880 (17,818) (about the size
of New Jersey)

*Capital (Population):* Kuwait
(277,000)

*Environmental Concerns:* limited
natural freshwater reserves; air
and water pollution; desertification

*Geographical Features:* flat to
slightly undulating desert plain

*Climate:* intensely hot and dry
summers; short, cool winters

## PEOPLE

### Population

*Total:* 2,200,000
*Annual Growth Rate:* 3.3%
*Rural/Urban Population Ratio:* 3/97
*Major Languages:* Arabic;
English
*Ethnic Makeup:* 45% Kuwaiti; 35%
other Arab; 9% South Asian; 4%
Iranian; 7% others
*Religions:* 85% Muslim; 15%
Christian, Hindu, Parsi, and
others

### Health

*Life Expectancy at Birth:* 75 years
(male); 77 years (female)
*Infant Mortality Rate (Ratio):*
11.1/1,000
*Physicians Available (Ratio):* 1/533

### Education

*Adult Literacy Rate:* 78.6%
*Compulsory (Ages):* 6–14; free

## COMMUNICATION

*Telephones:* 412,000 main lines
*Daily Newspaper Circulation:* 401
per 1,000 people
*Televisions:* 390 per 1,000 people
*Internet Service Providers:* 2 (2000)

## TRANSPORTATION

*Highways in Miles (Kilometers):* 2,763
(4,450)
*Railroads in Miles (Kilometers):* none
*Usable Airfields:* 8
*Motor Vehicles in Use:* 700,000

## GOVERNMENT

*Type:* nominal constitutional monarchy
*Independence Date:* June 19, 1961 (from
the United Kingdom)
*Head of State/Government:* Emir Jabir
al-Ahmad al-Jabir al-Sabah; Prime Minister (Crown Prince) Saad al-Abdullah
al-Salim al-Sabah
*Political Parties:* none legal

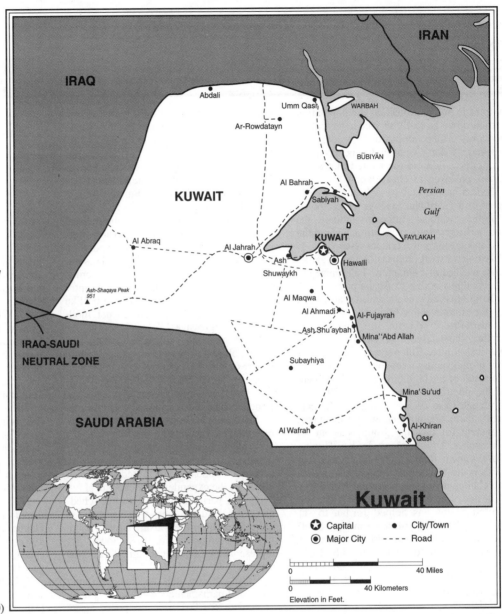

*Suffrage:* limited to male citizens over 21,
including those naturalized; women and
members of the armed services excluded

## MILITARY

*Military Expenditures (% of GDP):* 8.7%
*Current Disputes:* none

## ECONOMY

*Currency ($ U.S. Equivalent):* 0.305
dinars = $1
*Per Capita Income/GDP:* $15,000/$29.3
billion
*GDP Growth Rate:* 6%
*Inflation Rate:* 3%
*Unemployment Rate:* 1.8% (official rate)
*Labor Force:* 1,300,000

*Natural Resources:* petroleum; fish;
shrimp; natural gas
*Agriculture:* fish
*Industry:* petroleum; petrochemicals;
desalination; food processing;
construction materials; salt; construction
*Exports:* $23.2 billion (primary partners
Japan, United States, Singapore)
*Imports:* $7.6 billion (primary partners
United States, Japan, United Kingdom)

http://lcweb2.loc.gov/frd/cs/kwtoc.html
http://kuwait-info.org

# KUWAIT
The State of Kuwait consists of a wedge-shaped, largely desert territory located near the head of the Persian Gulf and just southwest of the Shatt al-Arab. Kuwaiti territory includes the islands of Bubiyan and Failaka in the Gulf, both of them periodically claimed by Iraq. Kuwait also shares a Neutral Zone, consisting mainly of oil fields, which it administers jointly with Iraq and Saudi Arabia; oil production is supposedly divided equally among them. The Iraqi accusation that Kuwait was taking more than its share was one of the points of contention that led to Iraq's invasion of Kuwait in 1990.

Kuwait's location has given the country great strategic importance in the modern rivalries of regional powers and their outside supporters. The country played a major role in the Iran–Iraq War, supporting Iraq financially and serving as a conduit for U.S. naval intervention through the reflagging of Kuwaiti tankers. The Iraqi invasion reversed roles, with Iraq the aggressor and Kuwait both the victim and the target of UN/U.S.–led military action during the brief Gulf War in 1991.

## HISTORY
Kuwait was inhabited entirely by nomadic peoples until the early 1700s. Then a number of clans of the large Anaiza tribal confederation settled along the Gulf in the current area of Kuwait. They built a fort for protection from raids—*Kuwait* means "little fort" in Arabic—and elected a chief to represent them in dealings with the Ottoman Empire, the major power in the Middle East at that time. The ruling family of modern Kuwait, the al-Sabahs, traces its power back to this period.

Kuwait prospered under the al-Sabahs. Its well-protected natural harbor became headquarters for a pearl-fishing fleet of 800 dhows (boats). The town (also called Kuwait) became a port of call for British ships bound for India.

In the late 1700s and early 1800s, Kuwait was threatened by the Wahhabis, fundamentalist Muslims from central Arabia. Arab piracy also adversely affected Kuwait's prosperity. Kuwait's ruling shaykhs paid tribute to the Ottoman sultan in return for protection against the Wahhabis. However, the shaykhs began to fear that the Turks would occupy Kuwait, so they turned to the British. In 1899, Shaykh Mubarak, who reigned from 1896 to 1915, signed an agreement with Britain for protection. In return, he agreed to accept British political advisers and not to have dealings with other foreign governments. In this way, Kuwait became a self-governing state under British protection.

During the 1890s, Kuwait had given refuge to Ibn Saud, a leader from central Arabia whose family had been defeated by its rivals. Ibn Saud left Kuwait in 1902, traveled in secret to Riyadh, the rivals' headquarters, and seized the city in a surprise raid. Kuwait thus indirectly had a hand in the founding of its neighbor state, Saudi Arabia.

## INDEPENDENCE
Kuwait continued its peaceful ways under the paternalistic rule of the al-Sabahs until the 1950s. Then oil production increased rapidly. The small pearl-fishing port became a booming modern city. In 1961, Britain and Kuwait jointly terminated the 1899 agreement, and Kuwait became fully independent under the al-Sabahs.

A threat to the country's independence developed almost immediately, as Iraq refused to recognize Kuwait's new status and claimed the territory on the grounds that it had once been part of the Iraqi Ottoman province of Basra. Iraq was also interested in controlling Kuwaiti oil resources. The ruling shaykh, now called emir, asked Britain for help, and British troops rushed back to Kuwait. Eventually, the Arab League agreed that several of its members would send troops to defend Kuwait—and, incidentally, to ensure that the country would not revert to its previous protectorate status. The Arab contingents were withdrawn in 1963. A revolution had overthrown the Iraqi government earlier in the year, and the new government recognized Kuwait's independence. However, the Ba'thist Party's concentration of power in Saddam Hussain's hands in the 1970s led to periodic Iraqi pressure on Kuwait, culminating in the 1990 invasion and occupation. After the expulsion of Iraqi forces, Kuwait requested a realignment of its northern border; and in 1992, the United Nations Boundary Commission approved the request, moving the border approximately 1,880 feet northward. The change gave Kuwait full possession of the Rumaila oil fields and a portion of the Iraqi Umm Qasr naval base. Kuwait had argued that the existing border deprived it of its own resources and access to its territorial waters as specified in the 1963 agreement. Some 3,600 UN observers were assigned to patrol the new border; and Kuwaiti workers dug a 130-mile trench, paid for by private donations, as a further protection for the emirate.

## REPRESENTATIVE GOVERNMENT
Kuwait differs from other patriarchally ruled Arabian Peninsula states in having a Constitution that provides for an elected National Assembly. Its 50 members are elected for four-year terms.

Friction developed between the Assembly and the ruling family soon after independence. Assembly members criticized Shaykh Abdullah and his relatives, as well as the cabinet, for corruption, press censorship, refusal to allow political parties, and insufficient attention to public services. Since all members of the ruling family were on the government payroll, there was some justification for the criticism.

Abdullah died in 1965, but his successor, Shaykh al-Sabah, accepted the criticism as valid. Elections were held in 1971 for a new Assembly.

Unfortunately for democracy in Kuwait, the new Assembly paid more attention to criticism of the government than to law making. In 1976, it was suspended by Shaykh al-Sabah. He died the following year, but his successor, Shaykh Jabir, reaffirmed the ruling family's commitment to the democratic process. A new Assembly was formed in 1981, with different members. The majority were traditional patriarchs loyal to the rulers, along with technical experts in various fields, such as industry, agriculture, and engineering. But the new Assembly fared little better than its predecessor in balancing freedom of expression with responsible leadership. The ruler suspended it, along with the Constitution, in 1986.

Pressures to reinstate the Assembly have increased in recent years. Just prior to the Iraqi invasion, the ruler had convened a 75-member National Council "to appraise our parliamentary experiment." The process was halted during the Iraqi occupation; but, after the Iraqi withdrawal and the return to Kuwait of the ruling family, the emir pledged to hold elections for a new Assembly in October 1992. The vote was limited to males over age 21 who could trace their residence in Kuwait back to 1920 or earlier. Under these rules, some 82,000 voters would elect two candidates from each of 25 constituencies to the 50-member Assembly.

The emir kept his pledge, and on October 5, 1992, the election took place as scheduled. More than half of the seats were won by critics of the government. They had campaigned on a platform of demands for government accountability and broadening of the franchise to include women. In the next Assembly election, in 1996, progovernment candidates won the majority of seats. But to appease his critics, the emir appointed a new cabinet with nine non-Sabah family members as ministers.

The most important election to date in Kuwait's brief and somewhat troubled his-

(UN photo/B. Cirone)

Before the advent of tremendous oil revenues, most Kuwaitis relied on livelihoods that revolved around a nomadic life. The nomadic population has now dwindled to a small segment of the population. The need to cope with new surroundings is typified by this Bedouin family confronting modern city life.

tory of democratization was held in July 1999. The emir had suspended the Assembly in May, after opposition deputies had paralyzed government action in clashes with cabinet ministers presenting their budgetary programs.

While the Assembly was suspended, the emir issued a decree giving women the right to vote and run for public office, to take effect in the 2003 parliamentary elections. (Currently only male Kuwaiti citizens over age 21 may vote or hold cabinet offices; women are excluded, along with the police and members of the armed forces.) But in November 1999, the newly elected Assembly, in one of its first actions, rejected the decree in a close vote. A bill that included similar provisions for women's suffrage was also defeated in December by a 32–30 vote. Women have taken the issue to the courts, but as yet without success.

## VULNERABILITY

Kuwait's location and its relatively open society make the country vulnerable to external subversion. In the early 1970s, the rulers were the target of criticism and threats from other Arab states because they did not publicly support the Palestinian cause. For years afterward, Kuwait provided large-scale financial aid not only to the Palestine Liberation Organization but also to Arab states such as Syria and Jordan that were directly involved in the struggle with Israel because of their common borders.

A new vulnerability surfaced with the Iranian Revolution of 1979, which overthrew the shah. Kuwait has a large Shia Muslim population, while its rulers are Sunni. Kuwait's support for Iraq and the development of closer links with Saudi Arabia (and indirectly the United States) angered Iran's new fundamentalist rulers. Kuwaiti oil installations were bombed by Iranian jets in 1981, and in 1983 truck bombs severely damaged the U.S. and French Embassies in Kuwait City. The underground organization Islamic Jihad claimed responsibility for the attacks and threatened more if Kuwait did not stop its support of Iraq. Kuwaiti police arrested 17 persons; they were later jailed for complicity in the bombings. Since Islamic Jihad claimed links to Iran, the Kuwaiti government suspected an Iranian hand behind the violence and deported 600 Iranian workers.

Tensions with Iran intensified in the mid-1980s, as Iranian jets and missile-powered patrol boats attacked Kuwaiti tankers in the Gulf and pro-Iranian terrorists carried out a series of hijackings. A 1988 hijacking caused international concern when a Kuwaiti Airways 747 jet with several members of the royal family aboard was seized and its passengers held for 16 days while being shuttled from airport to airport. The hijackers demanded the release of the 17 truck bombers as the price for the hostages' freedom. The Kuwaiti government refused to negotiate; after the hostages were released through

mediation by other Arab states, it passed a law making hijacking punishable by death.

Fear of Iran led Kuwait to join the newly formed Gulf Cooperation Council in 1981. The country also began making large purchases of weapons for defense, balancing U.S. with Soviet equipment. Its arms buildup made it the world's third-highest defense spender, at $3.1 billion, an average of $2,901 per capita.

During the Iran–Iraq War, Kuwait loaned 13 tankers to the United States. They were reflagged and given U.S. naval escort protection to transit the Gulf. After the United States assumed a major role in the region due to the Iraqi invasion and the resulting Gulf War, Kuwait signed a 10-year mutual-defense pact, the first formal agreement of its kind for the Gulf states.

## THE IRAQI OCCUPATION AND AFTERMATH

The seven months of Iraqi occupation (August 1990–February 1991) had a devastating effect on Kuwait. Some 5,000 Kuwaitis were killed, and the entire population was held hostage to Iraqi demands. Oil production stopped entirely. Iraqi forces opened hundreds of oil storage tanks as a defense measure, pouring millions of gallons of oil into the sea, thus creating a serious environmental hazard. (As they retreated, the Iraqis also set 800 oil wells afire, destroying production capabilities and posing enormous technical and environmental problems. These conflagrations were not extinguished for nearly a year.) In Kuwait City, basic water, electricity, and other services were cut off; public buildings were damaged; shops and homes were vandalized; and more than 3,000 gold bars, the backing for the Kuwaiti currency, were taken to Iraq.

Some 605 Kuwaitis out of thousands taken to Iraq are still unaccounted for. Most of them are civilians, including 120 students, whose "crime" was noncooperation with the Iraqi occupation forces. In November 2001, two Iraqi defectors from Saddam Hussein's intelligence services told interviewers in London that 80 of the Kuwaitis were held in a secret prison outside Baghdad, refuting the Iraqi government's insistence that all Kuwaitis jailed during the occupation had been released.

In 2001, the UN Repatriations Commission, set up to recompense Kuwaitis and others for losses sustained during the occupation, approved payment of more than $360 million for this purpose. As a result, 230 Kuwait-based companies are to share $174 million in payment for their claims against Iraq.

| Establishment of the al-Sabah family as the rulers of Kuwait 1756 | Agreement with Great Britain making Kuwait a protectorate 1899 | Independence, followed by Iraqi claim and British/Arab League intervention 1961–1963 | Elections for a new National Assembly 1971 | The ruler suspends the Assembly on the grounds that it is a handicap to effective government 1976 | Bombings by Islamic Jihad; massive deportation of Iranians after public buildings and oil installations are sabotaged; the government places the tanker fleet under U.S. protection by reflagging ships and providing naval escorts in the Gulf 1980s | Iraqi forces occupy Kuwait: Kuwait is liberated in the Gulf War; tension between the government and the Assembly; tensions rise between Kuwaitis and foreign workers 1990s |

2000s

Kuwait joins the international coalition against terrorism

Iraqi maneuvers near the Kuwait border and the incursion of Iraqi forces into UN–protected Kurdistan led the United States in 1996 to invoke the mutual-defense pact by sending an additional 5,000 ground troops to Kuwait to take part in a new attack on Iraq. The Kuwaiti government, which had not been consulted, agreed to accept only 3,500. But the contest of wills between the Clinton administration and Saddam Hussein over Iraq's secret weapons program and the resulting fears of Kuwaitis of an Iraqi missile attack on the emirate led it to allow the stationing of 10,000 U.S. troops on its territory, along with Patriot missiles and fighter aircraft. After the September 11, 2001, terrorist bombings in the United States, Kuwait joined with other Gulf Cooperation Council member states in supporting the international coalition against terrorism. Its banking community donated $1 million toward New York City's recovery effort, and the presence of American troops and weaponry on its soil made it in effect a front-line state in the campaign against the Taliban and Osama bin Laden in Afghanistan. However, both the leadership and the Kuwaiti public qualified their support with condemnation of Israel's "terror tactics" against the Palestinians.

### THE PEOPLE

Until the economic recession in the region, the country had a high rate of immigration. As a result, there are more non-Kuwaitis than Kuwaitis in the population, though dislocation resulting from the Iraqi occupation has changed the balance. Today, approximately 45 percent of the population are native Kuwaitis.

About one third of the total population, both citizens and noncitizens, are Shia Muslims. After the 1979 Revolution in Iran, they were blamed for much of the unrest in the country; Shia terrorists were charged with the 1983 truck bombings of embassies in Kuwait City. The improvement in Kuwait–Iran relations that followed the end of the Iran–Iraq War lessened this Shia antigovernment activity, and Shia and Sunni residents suffered equally under the Iraqi occupation.

Before the Gulf War, the largest non-native population group was Palestinian. Although denied citizenship, the Palestinians were generally better educated and more industrious than the native Kuwaitis. Palestinians formed the nucleus of opposition to the ruling family, and a number of them collaborated with the Iraqi occupation forces. After the war, more than 600 Palestinians were tried and sentenced to prison terms for collaboration. Some 300,000 Palestinians abruptly left for Jordan. However, their management skills were not entirely missed, as their places were filled by Lebanese or Western expatriates. Low-level jobs also filled rapidly with the arrival of workers from less-developed countries. But their low pay and lack of fringe benefits triggered riots in April 2000 over a government plan to levy annual payments, up to $155, on foreign workers in return for their inclusion in the national health service. A Filipino doughnut-shop employee commented: "It's not a steep price, but it hurts when there's been no increase in my $300 a month salary."[1]

### THE ECONOMY

Kuwait's only abundant resource is petroleum. Less than 1 percent of the land can be cultivated, and there is almost no fresh water. Drinking water comes from sea water converted to fresh water by huge desalination plants.

Kuwait's oil reserves of 94 billion barrels are the world's third largest, comprising 10 percent of global reserves. According to a 1996 study by the International Monetary Fund, the oil industry—and, with it, the economy—has recovered "impressively" from the effects of the Iraqi occupation. Oil production in 1997 reached 2 million barrels per day. The 1995–2000 Five-Year Plan approved by the Assembly projects a balanced budget by the end of the plan, largely through privatization of state enterprises, increased oil and non-oil revenues, and expansion of petrochemical industries.

Kuwait's economic recovery following the Iraqi occupation was hampered not only by the damage to its oil industry but also by an overstaffed public sector, huge welfare subsidies, and other factors. Despite some opposition in the Assembly, mainly on procedural grounds, the government went ahead with the reforms.

As a result, the Kuwaiti economy has rebounded to such an extent that, in 1996, Kuwait became the first Gulf state to receive an "A" rating from the International Banking Credit Association, an organization that evaluates countries on the basis of short- and long-term risks.

In addition to restoring its oil fields to full production, by 2001 nearly all the land mines left by the retreating Iraqis had been cleared from Kuwait's vast stretches of desert. An enormous oil slick from oil-well destruction that had threatened to pollute the water supply (which comes from desalinization) had also been cleared up.

### NOTES

1. Cameron Barr, in *The Christian Science Monitor* (March 2001).

**DEVELOPMENT**

Declining oil revenues resulted in budgetary deficits, which reached $6 billion in 1998 and 1999. With the Assembly dissolved, the emir issued some 60 decrees, intended to begin to privatize the economy and reduce expenditures by 20%. In 2001, 35% of ownership in the Kuwait Cement Company was turned over to private management.

**FREEDOM**

Although women have not yet succeeded in gaining voting rights, the government submitted a decree for Assembly approval in May 2001 that would allow them to join the police force. It was subsequently approved.

**HEALTH/WELFARE**

The 1.4 million foreign workers in Kuwait have had little protection under law until very recently. In November 2000, a large number of unemployed or underemployed Egyptians, the largest component of the expatriate labor force, rioted over bad working conditions and exploitation by sponsors who charge up to $3,000 for residency and work permits. The government agreed to review labor laws to limit payments to sponsors by mutual agreement.

**ACHIEVEMENTS**

Despite their exclusion from the franchise, Kuwaiti women have done well in other areas of national life. They may now serve in the police force. And in April 2000, the first all-female soccer tournament was held for teams from Kuwait University, institutes, and foreign schools, despite criticism from Islamic fundamentalists that such a public activity was "forbidden and a disobedience to God."

# Lebanon (Lebanese Republic)

Lebanon

- ⊛ Capital
- ★ Provincial Capital
- ◉ Major City
- • City/Town
- ～ River
- --- Road
- ▲ Points of Interest

Elevation in Feet.

0   15   30 Miles
0   15   30 Kilometers

## GEOGRAPHY

*Area in Square Miles (Kilometers):*
4,015 (10,452) (smaller than Connecticut)

*Capital (Population):* Beirut (1,826,000)

*Environmental Concerns:* deforestation; soil erosion; air and water pollution

*Geographical Features:* a narrow coastal plain; the Biqa' Valley separates Lebanon and the Anti-Lebanon Mountains

*Climate:* Mediterranean (hot, humid summers; cool, damp winters); heavy winter snows in mountains

## PEOPLE

### Population

*Total:* 3,628,000
*Annual Growth Rate:* 1.38%
*Rural/Urban Population Ratio:* 12/88
*Major Languages:* Arabic; French; English
*Ethnic Makeup:* 95% Arab; 4% Armenian; 1% others
*Religions:* 70% Muslim; 30% Christian (Maronite, Greek Orthodox, Melkite, Armenian, and Protestant)

### Health

*Life Expectancy at Birth:* 69 years (male); 74 years (female)
*Infant Mortality Rate (Ratio):* 28.3/1,000
*Physicians Available (Ratio):* 1/529

### Education

*Adult Literacy Rate:* 90.8%

## COMMUNICATION

*Telephones:* 620,000 main lines
*Daily Newspaper Circulation:* 172 per 1,000 people
*Televisions:* 291 per 1,000 people
*Internet Service Providers:* 22 (2000)

## TRANSPORTATION

*Highways in Miles (Kilometers):* 4,380 (7,300)
*Railroads in Miles (Kilometers):* 138 (222)
*Usable Airfields:* 8
*Motor Vehicles in Use:* 1,183,000

## GOVERNMENT

*Type:* republic
*Independence Date:* November 22, 1943 (from League of Nations mandate under French administration)
*Head of State/Government:* President Emile Lahoud; Prime Minister Rafiq Hariri
*Political Parties:* various parties are identified with religious or denominational groups; each group nominates candidates for the Chamber of Deputies (Parliament)
*Suffrage:* compulsory for males at 21; authorized for women at 21 with elementary-school education

## MILITARY

*Military Expenditures (% of GDP):* 4.8%
*Current Disputes:* conflicts between the Shia Hizbullah militia and Israeli troops in southern Lebanon; Syrian troops in northern, central, and eastern Lebanon

## ECONOMY

*Currency ($ U.S. Equivalent):* 1,569 pounds = $1
*Per Capita Income/GDP:* $5,100/$18.2 billion
*GDP Growth Rate:* 1%
*Inflation Rate:* 0%
*Unemployment Rate:* 18%
*Labor Force:* 1,300,000 (plus as many as 1,000,000 foreign workers)
*Natural Resources:* limestone; iron ore; salt; water; arable land
*Agriculture:* fruits; vegetables; olives; tobacco; hemp (hashish); sheep; goats
*Industry:* banking; food processing; jewelry; cement; textiles; mineral and chemical products; wood and furniture products; oil refining; metal fabricating
*Exports:* $700 million (primary partners United Arab Emirates, Saudi Arabia, Syria)
*Imports:* $6.2 billion (primary partners Italy, France, Germany)

# LEBANON

The Lebanese Republic is located at the eastern end of the Mediterranean Sea. The coastal plain, which contains the capital, Beirut, and all the other important cities, is narrow, rising just a few miles east of Beirut to a rugged mountain range, Mount Lebanon. Beyond Mount Lebanon is the Biqa', a broad, fertile valley that is the country's main wheat-growing region. At the eastern edge of the Biqa', the land rises again abruptly to the snow-capped Anti-Lebanon Range, which separates Lebanon from Syria.

Lebanon's geography has always been important strategically. Many invaders passed through it over the centuries on their conquests—Egyptians, Assyrians, Persians, Crusaders, Arabs, and Turks. However, they were seldom able to gain control of Mount Lebanon. For this reason, the mountain served as a refuge for ethnic and religious minorities, and it became in time the nucleus of the modern Lebanese state.

Lebanon's Mediterranean ports have traditionally served as an outlet for goods from the region's interior, notably Syria. Lebanese merchants have profited for centuries by being middlemen for this trade. However, its strategic location and its role as a commercial entrepôt have hampered Lebanon's unification as a nation in the twentieth century. Unification and the establishment of a national identity have also been blocked by religious divisions and territorial rivalries by various clans. A Lebanese scholar described the country's political system as "a feudal hierarchy with fluctuating political influence, as powerful families asserted themselves to acquire power and prominence."[1]

# HISTORY

In ancient times, Lebanon was known as Phoenicia. The Phoenicians were great traders who traveled throughout the Mediterranean and probably out into the Atlantic Ocean as far north as Cornwall in England, in search of tin, copper, and iron ore, which were valued in the ancient world for their many uses. Phoenician merchants established trading posts, some of which eventually grew into great cities.

No central government was ever established in Phoenicia itself. Phoenician towns like Byblos, Tyre, Sidon, and Tripoli were independent states, often in conflict or rivalry over trade with one another. This city–state rivalry has always been a feature of Lebanese life and is another reason for today's lack of a national Lebanese sense of unity.

Lebanon began to develop a definite identity much later, in the seventh century A.D. when a Christian group, the Maronites, took refuge in Mount Lebanon after they were threatened with persecution by the government of the East Roman or Byzantine Empire because of theological disagreements over the nature of Christ. The Muslim Arabs brought Islam to coastal Lebanon at about the same time, but they were unable to dislodge or convert the Maronites. Mount Lebanon's sanctuary tradition attracted other minority groups, Muslim as well as Christian. Shia Muslim communities moved there in the ninth and tenth centuries to escape persecution from Sunni Muslims, the Islamic majority. In the eleventh century, the Druze, adherents of an offshoot of Islam who followed the teachings of an Egyptian mystic and also faced persecution from Sunni Muslims, established themselves in the southern part of Mount Lebanon. These communities were originally quite separate. In the modern period of Lebanese history, however, they have tended to overlap, a fact, David Gordon says, "that makes both for unity and in troubled times for a dangerous struggle for turf."[2]

Lebanon acquired a distinct political identity under certain powerful families in the sixteenth and seventeenth centuries. The Ottoman Turks conquered it along with the rest of the Middle East, but they were content to leave local governance in the hands of these families in return for tribute. The most prominent was the Ma'an family, who were Druze. Their greatest leader, Fakhr al-Din (1586–1635), established an independent principality that included all of present-day Lebanon, Israel, and part of Syria. It was during al-Din's rule that French religious orders were allowed to establish missions in the country, which facilitated later European intervention in Lebanon.

The Ma'ans were succeeded by the Shihabs, who were Maronites. Their descendants continue to hold important positions in the country, underscoring the durability of the extended-family system, which still dominates Lebanese politics. They also allied the Maronite Church with the Roman Catholic Church, an action that had great consequences in the twentieth century, when the Maronites came to view Lebanon as a "Christian island in a Muslim sea," preserving its unique Lebanese identity only through Western support.

European countries began to intervene directly in Lebanon in the nineteenth century, due to conflict between the Maronite and Druze communities. Mount Lebanon was occupied by Egyptian armies of the Ottoman khedive (viceroy) of Egypt, Mu-

hammad Ali, in the 1830s. Egyptian development of Beirut and other coastal ports for trade purposes, particularly exports of Lebanese silk (still an important cash crop) at the expense of Mount Lebanon, and heavy taxes imposed by the khedive's overseers led to peasant uprisings in 1840 and 1857. By then the Ottomans had reestablished their authority, with European help. However, the European powers refused to allow the sultan to change Mount Lebanon's special status as an autonomous province. Ottoman governors resorted to intrigues with Maronite and Druze leaders, playing one against the other. The result was a Maronite–Druze civil war, which broke out in 1860. The cause was insignificant—"an affray between two boys, the shooting of a partridge or the collision of two pack animals," asserts one author; but whatever the spark, the two communities were ready to go for each other's throats.[3]

Although the Maronite fighters greatly outnumbered the Druze, the latter had better leadership. The Druze massacred 12,000 Christians and drove 100,000 from their homes during a four-week period. At that point, the European powers intervened to protect their coreligionists. French troops landed in Beirut and moved on to occupy Damascus. France and England forced the Ottoman sultan to establish Mount Lebanon as a self-governing province headed by a Christian governor. The province did not include Beirut. Although many Lebanese emigrated during this period because Mount Lebanon was small, rather poor, and provided few job opportunities, those who stayed (particularly the Maronites) prospered. Self-government under their own leader enabled them to develop a system of small, individually owned farms and to break their former dependence on absentee landowners. A popular saying among Lebanese at the time was, "Happy is he who has a shed for one goat in Mount Lebanon."[4]

### The French Mandate

After the defeat of Ottoman Turkey in World War I, Lebanon became a French mandate. The French had originally intended the country to be included in their mandate over Syria; but in 1920, due to pressure from Maronite leaders, they separated the two mandates. "New" Lebanon was much larger than the old Maronite–Druze territory up on Mount Lebanon. The new "Greater Lebanon" included the coast—in short, the area of the current Lebanese state. The Maronites found themselves linked not only with the Druze but also with both Sunni and Shia Muslims. The Maronites already distrusted the

Druze, out of bitter experience. Their distrust was caused by fear of a Muslim majority and fear that Muslims, being mostly Arabs, would work to incorporate Lebanon into Syria after independence.

France gave Lebanon its independence in 1943, but French troops stayed on until 1946, when they were withdrawn due to British and American pressure on France. The French made some contributions to Lebanese development during the mandate, such as the nucleus of a modern army, development of ports, roads, and airports, and an excellent educational system dominated by the Université de St. Joseph, training ground for many Lebanese leaders. The French language and culture served until recently as one of the few things unifying the various sects and providing them with a sense of national identity.

## THE LEBANESE REPUBLIC

The major shortcoming of the mandate was the French failure to develop a broad-based political system with representatives from the major religious groups. The French very pointedly favored the Maronites. The Constitution, originally issued in 1926, established a republican system under an elected president and a Legislature. Members would be elected on the basis of six Christians to five Muslims. The president would be elected for a six-year term and could not serve concurrently. (The one exception was Bishara al-Khuri [1943–1952], who served during and after the transition period to independence. The Constitution was amended to allow him to do so.) By private French–Maronite agreement, the custom was established whereby the Lebanese president would always be chosen from the Maronite community.

In the long term, perhaps more important to Lebanese politics than the Constitution is the National Pact, an oral agreement made in 1943 between Bishara al-Khuri, as head of the Maronite community, and Riad al-Sulh, his Sunni counterpart. The two leaders agreed that, first, Lebanese Christians would not enter into alliances with foreign (i.e., Christian) nations and Muslims would not attempt to merge Lebanon with the Muslim Arab world; and second, that the six-to-five formula for representation in the Assembly would apply to all public offices. The pact has never been put in writing, but in view of the delicate balance of sects in Lebanon, it has been considered by Lebanese leaders, particularly the Maronites, as the only alternative to anarchy.

Despite periodic political crises and frequent changes of government due to shifting alliances of leaders, Lebanon functioned quite well during its first two decades of independence. The large extended family, although an obstacle to broad nation building, served as an essential support base for its members, providing services that would otherwise have to have been drawn from government sources. These services included education, employment, bank loans, investment capital, and old-age security. Powerful families of different religious groups competed for power and influence but also coexisted, having had "the long experience with each other and with the rules and practices that make coexistence possible."[5] The freewheeling Lebanese economy was another important factor in Lebanon's relative stability. Per capita annual income rose from $235 in 1950 to $1,070 in 1974, putting Lebanon on a level with some of the oil-producing Arab states, although the country does not have oil.

The private sector was largely responsible for national prosperity. A real-estate boom developed, and many fortunes were made in land speculation and construction. Tourism was another important source of revenues. Many banks and foreign business firms established their headquarters in Beirut because of its excellent communications with the outside world, its educated, multilingual labor force, and the absence of government restrictions.

## THE 1975–1976 CIVIL WAR

The titles of books on Lebanon in recent years have often contained adjectives such as "fractured," "fragmented," and "precarious." These provide a generally accurate description of the country's situation as a result of the Civil War of 1975–1976. The main destabilizing element, and the one that precipitated the conflict, was the presence and activities of Palestinians.

In some ways, Palestinians have contributed significantly to Lebanese national life. The first group, who fled there after the 1948 Arab–Israeli War, consisted mostly of cultured, educated, highly urbanized people who gravitated to Beirut and were absorbed quickly into the population. Many of them became extremely successful in banking, commerce, journalism, or as faculty members at the American University of Beirut. A second Palestinian group arrived as destitute refugees after the 1967 Six-Day War. They have been housed ever since in refugee camps run by the United Nations Relief and Works Agency. The Lebanese government provides them with identity cards but no passports. For all practical purposes, they are stateless persons.

Neither group was a threat to Lebanese internal stability until 1970, although Lebanon backed the Palestine Liberation Organization cause and did not interfere with guerrilla raids from its territory into Israel. After the PLO was expelled from Jordan, the organization made its headquarters in Beirut. This new militant Palestinian presence in Lebanon created a double set of problems for the Lebanese. Palestinian raids into Israel brought Israeli retaliation, which caused more Lebanese than Palestinian casualties. Yet the Lebanese government could not control the Palestinians. To many Lebanese, especially the Maronites, their government seemed to be a prisoner in its own land.

In April 1975, a bus carrying Palestinians returning from a political rally was ambushed near Beirut by the Kata'ib, members of the Maronite Phalange Party. The incident triggered the Lebanese Civil War of 1975–1976. The war officially ended with a peace agreement arranged by the Arab League.[6] But the bus incident also brought to a head conflicts derived from the opposing goals of various Lebanese power groups. The Palestinians' goal was to use Lebanon as a springboard for the liberation of Palestine. The Maronites' goal was to drive the Palestinians out of Lebanon and preserve their privileged status. Sunni Muslim leaders sought to reshape the National Pact to allow for equal political participation with the Christians. Shia leaders were determined to get a better break for the Shia community, generally the poorest and least represented in the Lebanese government.[7] The Druze, also interested in greater representation in the system and traditionally hostile to the Maronites, disliked and distrusted all of the other groups.

Like most civil wars, the Lebanese Civil War was fought by Lebanon's own people. It was a war that made no sense, where sides changed frequently and battles raged from street to street in Beirut, while in the hinterland, neighboring towns and villages became the front line for ethnic and particularly religious conflict. The uncertainty of the period is clearly illustrated in remarks by a hostess to her guests at a Beirut dinner party: "Would you like to eat now, or wait for the next cease-fire?"

Eventually Lebanon's importance as a regional trade, banking, and transit center ensured that outside powers would intervene. Syrian troops were ordered by the Arab League to occupy the country. Their purpose was not only to end the conflict but also to block Palestinian aspirations to use Lebanon as a launching pad for the recovery of their lands in Israel. The Israelis encouraged a renegade Lebanese officer to set up an "independent free Lebanon" adjoining the Israeli border. The complexity of the situation was described in graphic terms by a Christian religious leader:

> The battle is between the Palestinians and the Lebanese. No! It is between the Palestinians and the Christians. No! It is between Christians and Muslims. No! It is between Leftists and Rightists. No! It is between Israel and the Palestinians on Lebanese soil. No! It is between international imperialism and Zionism on the one hand, and Lebanon and neighboring states on the other.[8]

## THE ISRAELI INVASION

The immediate result of the Civil War was to divide Lebanon into separate territories, each controlled by a different faction. The Lebanese government, for all practical purposes, could not control its own territory. Israeli forces, in an effort to protect northern Israeli settlements from constant shelling by the Palestinians, established control over southern Lebanon. The Lebanese–Israeli border, ironically, became a sort of "good fence" open to Lebanese civilians for medical treatment in Israeli hospitals.

In March 1978, PLO guerrillas landed on the Israeli coast near Haifa, hijacked a bus, and drove it toward Tel Aviv. The hijackers were overpowered in a shootout with Israeli troops, but 35 passengers were killed along with the guerrillas. Israeli forces invaded southern Lebanon in retaliation and occupied the region for two months, eventually withdrawing after the United Nations, in an effort to separate Palestinians from Israelis, set up a 6,000-member "Interim Force" in Lebanon, made up of units from various countries, in the south. But the Interim Force was not able to do much to control the Palestinians; most Lebanese and Israelis referred sarcastically to the Force as the "United Nothings."

The Lebanese factions themselves continued to tear the nation apart. Political assassinations of rival leaders were frequent. Many Lebanese settlements became ghost towns; they were fought over so much that their residents abandoned them. Some 300,000 Lebanese from the Israeli-occupied south fled to northern cities as refugees. In addition to the thousands of casualties, a psychological trauma settled over Lebanese youth, the "Kalashnikov generation" that knew little more than violence, crime, and the blind hatred of religious feuds. (The Kalashnikov, a Soviet-made submachine gun, became the standard toy of Lebanese children.)[9]

The Israeli invasion of Lebanon in June 1982 was intended as a final solution to the Palestinian problem. It didn't quite work out that way. The Israeli Army surrounded Beirut and succeeded with U.S. intervention in forcing the evacuation of PLO guerrillas from Lebanon. Some of the Lebanese factions were happy to see them go, particularly the Maronites and the Shia community in the south. But they soon discovered that they had exchanged one foreign domination for another. The burden of war, as always, fell heaviest on the civilian population. A Beirut newspaper estimated almost 50,000 civilian casualties in the first two months of the invasion. Also, the Lebanese discovered that they were not entirely free of the Palestinian presence. The largest number of PLO guerrillas either went to Syria and then returned secretly to Lebanon or retreated into the Biqa' Valley to take up new positions under Syrian Army protection.

Israeli control over Beirut enabled the Christians to take savage revenge against the remaining Palestinians. In September 1983, Christian Phalange militiamen entered the refugee camps of Sabra and Shatila in West Beirut and massacred hundreds of people, mostly women and children. The massacre led to an official Israeli inquiry and censure of Israeli government and military leaders for indirect responsibility. But the Christian-dominated Lebanese government's own inquiry failed to fix responsibility on the Phalange.

The Lebanese Civil War supposedly ended in 1976, but it was not until 1990 that the central government began to show results in disarming militias and establishing its authority over the fragmented nation. Until then, hostage taking and clan rivalries underlined the absence in Lebanon of a viable national identity.

The 1982 Israeli invasion brought a change in government; the Phalange leader, Bashir Gemayel, was elected to head a "government of national salvation." Unfortunately for Bashir, his ruthlessness in his career had enabled him to compile an impressive list of enemies. He was killed by a bomb explosion at Phalange headquarters before he could take office. Gemayel was succeeded by his older brother, Amin. The new president was persuaded by U.S. negotiators to sign a troop-withdrawal agreement with Israel. However, the agreement was not supported by leaders of the other Lebanese communities, and in March 1984, Gemayel unilaterally repudiated it. The Israelis then began working their way out of the "Lebanese quagmire" on their own, and in June 1985, the last Israeli units left Lebanon. (However, the Israelis did reserve a "security zone" along the border for necessary reprisals for attacks by PLO or Shia guerrillas.)

The Israelis left behind a country that had become almost ungovernable. Gemayel's effort to restructure the national army along nonsectarian lines came to nothing, since the army was not strong enough to disband the various militias. The growing power of the Shia Muslims, particularly the Shia organization Amal, presented a new challenge to the Christian leadership, while the return of the Palestinians brought bloody battles between Shia and PLO guerrillas. As the battles raged, cease-fire followed cease-fire and conference followed conference, but without noticeable success.

The Israeli withdrawal left the Syrians as the major power brokers in Lebanon. In 1985, Syrian president Hafez al-Assad masterminded a comprehensive peace and reform agreement with Elie Hobeika, the commander of the Christian Falange militia that carried out the 1983 massacres of Palestinians at Sabra and Shatila refugee camps. The agreement would expand the National Pact to provide equal Christian–Muslim representation in the Chamber of Deputies. Hobeika was later ousted by one of his rivals and went into exile in Syria; his departure made the agreement worthless. He returned to Lebanon at the end of the Civil War and held several ministerial portfolios. In January 2002, however, he was killed in a car-bomb blast.

## SYRIA INTERVENES

The collapse of peace efforts led Syria to send 7,000 heavily armed commandos into west Beirut in 1987 to restore law and order. They did restore a semblance of order to that part of the capital and opened checkpoints into east Beirut. But the Syrians were unable, or perhaps unwilling, to challenge the powerful Hizbullah faction (reputed to have held most Western hostages), which controlled the rabbit warren of narrow streets and tenements in the city's southern suburbs.

Aside from Hizbullah, Syria's major problem in knitting Lebanon together under its tutelage was with the Maronite community. With President Gemayel's six-year term scheduled to end in September 1988, the Syrians lobbied hard for a candidate of their choice. (Under the Lebanese parliamentary system, the president is elected by the Chamber of Deputies.) Unfortunately, due to the Civil War, only 72 of the 99 deputies elected in 1972, when the last elections had been held, were still in office. They rejected Syria's candidate, former president Suleiman Franjieh (1970–1976), because of his identification with the conflict and his ties with the Assad regime. When the Chamber failed to agree on an acceptable candidate, the office became vacant. Gemayel's last act before leaving office was to appoint General Michel Aoun, the commander of Christian troops in the Lebanese Army, to head an interim government. But the Muslim-dominated civilian government of Prime Minister Salim al-Hoss contested the appointment, declaring that it remained the legitimate government of the country.

## BREAKDOWN OF A SOCIETY

The assassination in 1987 of Prime Minister Rachid Karami (a bomb hidden in the army helicopter in which he was traveling blew up) graphically underlined the mindless rejection of law and order of the various Lebanese factions. The only show of Lebanese unity in many years occurred at the funeral of former president Camille Chamoun, dead of a heart attack at age 87. Chamoun's last public statement, made the day before his death, was particularly fitting to this fractured land. "The nation is headed toward total bankruptcy and famine," he warned. The statement brought to mind the prophetic observations of a historian, written in 1966: "Lebanon is too conspicuous and successful an example of political democracy and economic liberalism to be tolerated in a region that has turned its back on both systems."[10]

The death of the Mufti (the chief religious leader of the Sunni Muslim community) in a car-bomb attack in 1989 confirmed Chamoun's gloomy prediction. The Mufti had consistently called for reconciliation and nonviolent coexistence between Christian and Muslim communities. The political situation remained equally chaotic. Rene Moawwad, a respected Christian lawyer, was elected by the Chamber to fill the presidential vacancy. However, he was murdered after barely 17 days in office. The Chamber then elected Elias Hrawi, a Christian politician from the Maronite stronghold of Zahle, as president. General Aoun contested the election, declaring himself the legitimate president of Lebanon, and holed up in the presidential palace in east Beirut, defended strongly by his Maronite militiamen.

But the Maronite community was as fragmented as the larger Lebanese community. Aoun's chief Christian rival, Samir Geagea, rejected his authority, and early in 1990, a renewed outbreak of fighting between their militias left east Beirut in shambles, with more than 3,000 casualties. After another shaky cease-fire had been reached, Syrian Army units supporting the regular Lebanese Army surrounded the Christian section. Aoun's palace became an embattled enclave, with supplies available only by running the Syrian blockade or from humanitarian relief organizations.

Aoun's support base eroded significantly in the spring, when his rival recognized the Hrawi government as legitimate and endorsed the Taif Accord.[11] In October, Hrawi formally requested Syrian military aid for the Lebanese Army. After an all-out assault on the presidential palace by joint Syrian–Lebanese forces, the general surrendered, taking refuge in the French Embassy and then going into exile.

Aoun's departure enabled the Hrawi government to begin taking the next step toward rebuilding a united Lebanon. This involved disarming the militias. The continued presence of Syrian forces was a major asset to the reconstituted Lebanese Army as it undertook this delicate process. A newspaper publisher observed that "the Syrian presence is a very natural fact for the Lebanese," echoing the Syrian president's statement to an interviewer: "Lebanon and Syria are one nation and one people, but they are two distinct states."[12] It was the first clear statement from any Syrian leader that Lebanon had a legitimate existence as a state.

Following the reestablishment of central-government authority, a new transitional Council of Ministers (cabinet) was appointed by President Hrawi in 1992. Its responsibilities were to stabilize the economy and prepare for elections for a new Chamber of Deputies. The election law was amended by decree in June to enlarge the Chamber from 108 to 128 seats, in order to establish a better confessional balance.

The first national elections since the start of the Civil War were held in 1992. Due in part to a boycott by Christian parties, which had demanded Syrian withdrawal as their price for participation, Shia candidates won 30 seats. Shia Amal leader Nibih Berri was elected speaker; Rafiq Hariri, a Sunni Muslim and millionaire (who had made his fortune as a contractor in Saudi Arabia) was named prime minister.

In any case, the growing demographic imbalance of Muslims and Christians indicated that, in the not too distant future, Lebanon would no longer be "a Christian island in a Muslim sea." By 1997, Christians numbered at most 30 percent of the population (composed of 800,000 Maronites, 400,000 Greek Orthodox, 300,000 Greek Catholics or Melkites, and 75,000 Armenians). Half a million Christians had left the country during the Civil War, along with top leaders such as Michel Aoun, Amin Gemayel, and Raymond Edde, in exile in Paris.

A 1999 election law set up 14 constituencies in place of the former governorates. Some of the latter were combined in a single constituency; others were spread among several constituencies. The number of seats per constituency in the Chamber of Deputies would vary, from six to 16. Essentially, the law was designed to punish opposition leaders and reward loyal ones. Overall, the seats remained equally divided between Christians and Muslims, despite their differences in population size.

An earlier (1996) amendment to the election law allowed government officials to run for office. The amendment enabled General Emile Lahoud, the Lebanese Army chief of staff, to run for president at the end of President Hrawi's term. Lahoud was elected in 1999 in the first peaceful transfer of power in the country in more than two decades.

As army chief of staff, Lahoud, a Maronite, had been responsible for disarming the country's numerous militias. By 1993, the one remaining armed organization was Hizbullah. Its members were allowed to keep their weapons in order to deal with Israeli forces in the "security zone" along the border and with their allies, the South Lebanon Army (SLA). With weapons and training supplied by Iran and Syria, Hizbullah developed into a formidable fighting force. In 1998, its fighters succeeded in overrunning the main SLA base at Jezzin. The impending defeat of its Lebanese ally and the endless "war of attrition" with Hizbullah led to a complete withdrawal of Israeli forces from the self-proclaimed "security zone," but inside the Lebanese border, in May 2000. Israeli prime minister Ehud Barak had originally set July 2000 for the withdrawal, but he accelerated the process for policy reasons. On May 24, the last Israeli soldiers pulled out of the zone, ending a 22-year occupation. Commenting on the precipitate departure, an Israeli tank officer observed: "You can't win a guerrilla war. We withdrew with dignity. I don't think we ran away."[13] Hizbullah leaders held a different view: To them, it was proof that the invincible Israeli Army had its weaknesses and could be defeated by unorthodox tactics.

The Israeli withdrawal resulted in jubilant celebrations throughout Lebanon. The government declared May 24 a national holiday, National Resistance Day, as crowds danced in the streets. Some 6,000 SLA militiamen fled into Israel with their families, fearing retribution by Hizbullah. Although the Israeli government provided housing and other benefits for them, the exiles felt uncomfortable in a "foreign" setting. They also faced unremitting hostility from Israeli Arabs. In 2000, they began returning to their homes in south Lebanon; by the end of 2001, some 2,344 had returned. The anticipated sectarian bloodbath did not materialize, and as a result the area remained at peace, ending 30 years of conflict.

Under the terms of UN *Resolution 425,* which had called for Israel's withdrawal as long ago as 1978, units of the United Nations Interim Force in Lebanon (UNFIL) moved to the border as peacekeepers. The border has been quiet since then—with one exception: Shebaa Farms. This mountain region of 15.6 square miles was originally Lebanese territory but had been awarded to Syria by the League of Nations in 1920, after the establishment of the Syrian and Lebanese mandates. For that reason, the United Nations had excluded it from Israel's "security zone." In May 2001, Hizbullah guerrillas abducted several Israeli soldiers stationed there, on the grounds that they were actually on Lebanese territory. Israel's response was an air attack on a nearby Syrian radar installation. It was Israel's first attack on Syria in 22 years.

Along with guerrilla warfare, Hizbullah engaged in a "propaganda war" with Israel through its satellite-television station, *Al-Manar* ("The Beacon"). Its programs were greatly expanded after the Israeli withdrawal from Lebanon and the revived Palestinian intifada. Its broadcasts in Hebrew to Israelis and in Arabic to the Palestinians, with video images of clashes and casualties, helped to strengthen the resolve of the Palestinians against the Israelis.

## LEBANON AND THE WORLD
Aside from its vulnerability to international and inter-Arab rivalries because of internal conflicts, Lebanon drew world attention in the 1980s for its involvement in hostage taking. Lebanese militias such as Hizbullah, a Shia group backed by Iran as a means of exporting the Islamic Revolution, and shadowy organizations like the Islamic Jihad, Revolutionary Justice, and Islamic Jihad for the Liberation of Palestine kidnapped foreigners in Beirut. The conditions set for their release were rarely specific, and the refusal of the U.S. and other Western governments to "deal with terrorists" left them languishing in unknown prisons for years, seemingly forgotten by the outside world.

The changing Middle East situation and Lebanon's slow return to normalcy in the 1990s began to move the hostage-release process forward. Release negotiations were pursued by then–UN general-secretary Javier Pérez de Cuéllar. The UN team worked on two levels: Pérez de Cuéllar ran a high-profile diplomatic campaign by

repeatedly visiting Iran, Syria, and Israel, while his long-time associate Giandomenico Picco conducted behind-the-scenes talks with Shia operatives in the Biqa' Valley located in the eastern part of Lebanon. Their efforts began to bear fruit: within a few months. The hostages, mostly British and American, were freed individually or in small groups. They included Terry Waite, an envoy of the archbishop of Canterbury originally sent to negotiate the hostages' release (he was charged mistakenly with espionage). Several had been professors at the American University of Beirut or Beirut College for Women, and the last to be released was Terry Anderson, a well-known *New York Times* correspondent.

Since then, Lebanese–American relations have remained stable. However, the September 11 terrorist bombings in the United States and President George W. Bush's effort to form an international antiterrorism coalition that would include Muslim states placed the Lebanese government in an awkward position. The U.S. ambassador to Lebanon commented in October 2001 that the country continued to shelter "terrorist organizations," including Hizbullah, since it had been responsible for the 1983 destruction of the American Embassy in Beirut and a truck-bomb onslaught on a U.S. Marine barracks that killed 241 Americans. Despite Hizbullah's newfound respectability as a social-service organization and political party represented in the Chamber of Deputies, the government feared that its past actions might motivate the United States to seek retribution, including Lebanon in its antiterrorism campaign. A Bush administration request to the Lebanese government to freeze Hizbullah assets as a "terrorist organization" was rejected.

Syria, with 30,000 troops stationed in Lebanon, remains the dominant factor in Lebanon's relations with the larger world. In addition to its military presence, some 250,000 Syrian workers are employed in Lebanon, most of them in low-level jobs. In other complaints about Syrian overlordship, Lebanese farmers argue that their market is being ruined by imports of cheap, duty-free Syrian produce. As the Lebanese economy has sagged in recent years, criticism of the Syrian presence has become more vocal. In September 2000, Druze leader Walid Jumblatt and the Maronite patriarch separately called for a Syrian withdrawal. In a partial response, Syrian troops withdrew from Beirut in June 2001. They were redeployed in bases in the Biqa' and eastern Lebanon, where their presence was not as visible as in the Lebanese capital. However, in the fall of

2001, the government's Central Security Council banned supporters of Aoun and Samir Gaegea from political activity. Both of these Christian groups had campaigned actively since 1990 for the removal of all Syrian troops from Lebanon.

## THE ECONOMY
In the mid-1970s, the Lebanese economy began going steadily downhill. The Civil War and resulting instability caused most banks and financial institutions to move out of Beirut to more secure locations, notably Jordan, Bahrain, and Kuwait. Aside from the cost in human lives, Israeli raids and the 1982 invasion severely damaged the economy. The cost of the invasion in terms of damages was estimated at $1.9 billion. Remittances from Lebanese emigrants abroad dropped significantly. The Lebanese pound, valued at 4.74 to U.S. $1 in 1982, reached a record low of 3,000 to $1 in 1992.

Yet by a strange irony of fate, some elements of the economy continued to display robust health. Most middle-class Lebanese had funds invested abroad, largely in U.S. dollar accounts, and thus were protected from economic disaster.

The expansion of the Civil War in 1989–1990 and the intervention of Syrian troops tested the survival techniques of the Lebanese people as never before. But they adjusted to the new "Battle of Beirut" with great inventiveness. A newspaper advertisement announced: "Civilian fortifications, 24-hour delivery service. Sandbags and barrels, full or empty." With the Syrian–Christian artillery exchanges concentrated at night, most residents fled the city then, returning after the muezzin's first call for morning prayers had in effect silenced the guns, to shop, to stock up on fuel smuggled ashore from small tankers, or to sample the luxury goods that in some mysterious way had appeared on store shelves.

The long, drawn-out civil conflict badly affected Lebanese agriculture, the mainstay of the economy. Both the coastal strip and the Biqa' Valley are extremely fertile, and in normal times produce crop surpluses for export. Lebanese fruit, particularly apples (the most important cash crop) and grapes, is in great demand throughout the Arab world. But these crops are no longer exported in quantity. Israeli destruction of crops, the flight of most of the farm labor force, and the blockade by Israeli troops of truck traffic from rural areas into Beirut had a devastating effect on production.

Lebanon produces no oil of its own, but before the Civil War and the Israeli inva-

**Timeline:**

Establishment of Mount Lebanon as a sanctuary for religious communities
**9th–11th centuries**

The first Civil War, between Maronites and Druze, ending in foreign military intervention
**1860–1864**

French mandate
**1920–1946**

Internal crisis and the first U.S. military intervention
**1958**

Civil war, ended (temporarily) by an Arab League–sponsored cease-fire and peacekeeping force of Syrian troops
**1975–1976**

Israeli occupation of Beirut; Syrian troops reoccupy Beirut; foreigners are seized in a new outbreak of hostage taking; the economy nears collapse
**1980s**

The withdrawal of Israeli forces from Lebanon; all foreign hostages are released; Lebanon begins rebuilding
**1990s**

**2000s**

Hizbullah's presence in Lebanon causes tension with the United States

sion, the country derived important revenues from transit fees for oil shipments through pipelines across its territory. The periodic closing of these pipelines and damage to the country's two refineries sharply reduced revenues. The well-developed manufacturing industry, particularly textiles, was equally hard hit.

In August 1998, Hariri resigned as prime minister. He had been charged with spending the country into debt with huge construction schemes, notably the rebuilding of Beirut. His successor, Salam al-Hoss, also failed to turn the economy around. In the fall 2000 elections for the Chamber of Deputies, the voters returned a majority of Hariri supporters to the Chamber of Deputies, and Hariri was returned to office.

Armed with $458 million in aid from the World Bank, the European Union, and the Paris-based Mediterranean Development Agency, Hariri launched a major economic reform drive in February 2001. He laid off 500 employees from the bloated public sector, and privatized the state-owned electricity company as a start toward further privatization. The cabinet also agreed to shut down the state-owned TeleLiban, saving $33 million a year. Elimination of the sugar subsidy will save another $40 million annually.

Hariri's reform program faced significant obstacles. Lebanon's current public debt is $28 billion, 165 percent of gross domestic product and the fourth-highest debt-to-GDP ratio in the world (after Nicaragua, Zambia, and Malawi). Another obstacle is the time-honored practice of *wasta* (bribes), needed for all public services. In 2001, Syria stopped supplying Lebanon with electricty, due to an unpaid $120 million bill. In February 2001, the government intorduced a value added tax (VAT) of 10 percent on most goods; it should generate $500 million in income. Increased tourism and a rise in purchases of real estate by wealthy Gulf Arabs offered some hope that the economy would rebound.

## NOTES

1. Abdo Baaklini, *Legislative and Political Development: Lebanon 1842–1972* (Durham, NC: Duke University Press, 1976), pp. 32–34.

2. David C. Gordon, *The Republic of Lebanon: Nation in Jeopardy* (Boulder, CO: Westview Press, 1983), p. 4.

3. Samir Khlaf, *Lebanon's Predicament* (New York: Columbia University Press, 1987), p. 69.

4. Gordon, *op. cit.,* p. 19.

5. *Ibid.,* p. 25. See also Baaklini, *op. cit.,* pp. 200–202, for a description of the coexistence process as used by Sabri Hamadeh, for many years head of the assembly.

6. Whether the Civil War ever really ended is open to question. A cartoon in a U.S. newspaper in August 1982 shows a hooded skeleton on a television screen captioned "Lebanon" saying, "And now we return to our regularly scheduled civil war." Gordon, *op. cit.,* p. 113.

7. Shia religious leader Imam Musa al-Sadr's political organization was named Harakat al-Mahrumin ("Movement of the Disinherited") when it was founded in 1969–1970. See Marius Deeb, *The Lebanese Civil War* (New York: Praeger, 1980), pp. 69–70.

8. Gordon, *op. cit.,* p. 110.

9. *Ibid.,* p. 125.

10. Charles Issawi, "Economic Development and Political Liberalism in Lebanon," in Leonard Binder, ed., *Politics in Lebanon* (New York: John Wiley, 1966), pp. 80–81.

11. The Taif Accord, signed under Arab League auspices in Taif, Saudi Arabia, changes the power-sharing arrangement in the Lebanese government from a 6:5 Christian–Muslim ratio to one of equal representation in the government. The powers of the president are also reduced.

12. *Middle East Economic Digest* (October 10, 1990).

13. Joel Greenberg, in *The New York Times* (May 24, 2000).

## DEVELOPMENT

Considerable progress has been made since 1994 in rebuilding Lebanon's infrastructure. In 1995, GDP was $11.4 billion, almost double the 1994 level. The growth rate has remained steady at 3% since then, but due to Hariri's reforms, was expected to reach 5% in 2001. Lebanon's $28 billion foreign debt and limited resources indicate that external aid for its development will need to be continued for the foreseeable future. In September 2001, the cabinet approved a draft budget with revenues of $36 billion. However, expenditures will exceed this figure.

## FREEDOM

Under an unwritten agreement made by Christian and Muslim leaders at independence, Lebanon is a "confessional democracy," with political representation based on religious affiliation. By tradition, the president is a Maronite Christian, the prime minister a Sunni Muslim, and the speaker of the Chamber of Deputies a Shia Muslim. Other government posts are similarly apportioned among the various religious denominations. However, demographic changes resulting in a non-Christian majority have yet to be reflected in the political structure.

## HEALTH/WELFARE

The withdrawal of Israeli forces from southern Lebanon left Hizbullah as the sole on-site agency for reconstruction of that war-torn region. In late 2000, teams of fighters-turned-humanitarian-workers cleaned village streets, set up potable water dispensers, sent mosquito-spraying trucks into the villages, and established and equipped mobile health clinics. Schools were reopened, and the former Israeli hospital at Bint Jbail, the regional capital, is now managed completely by Hizbullah doctors and nurses.

## ACHIEVEMENTS

Since 1996, with U.S. Department of Agriculture help, the Lebanese government has been encouraging farmers in the Biqa region to switch from opium-poppy production to alternative crops, dairy cows in particular. But the U.S. cows did not take well to Lebanese grass and fodder. In March 2001, Iran provided $50 million for the same purpose. Its components include not only dairy cows but also farm credits, training in beekeeping and hives for bees, fish farming, and a food-processing factory.

# Libya (Socialist People's Libyan Arab Jamahiriya)

## GEOGRAPHY

*Area in Square Miles (Kilometers):*
679,147 (1,759,450) (about
the size of Alaska)

*Capital (Population):* Tripoli
(1,681,000)

*Environmental Concerns:*
desertification; very limited
freshwater resources

*Geographical Features:* mostly
barren, flat to undulating
plains, plateaus, depressions

*Climate:* Mediterranean along
the coast; dry, extreme desert
in the interior

## PEOPLE

### Population
*Total:* 5,241,000
*Annual Growth Rate:* 2.4%
*Rural/Urban Population Ratio:*
14/86
*Major Languages:* Arabic;
English; Italian
*Ethnic Makeup:* 97% Berber and
Arab; 3% others
*Religions:* 97% Sunni Muslim;
3% others

### Health
*Life Expectancy at Birth:* 74
years (male); 78 years (female)
*Infant Mortality Rate (Ratio):*
28.9/1,000
*Physicians Available (Ratio):*
1/948

### Education
*Adult Literacy Rate:* 76.2%
*Compulsory (Ages):* 6–15

## COMMUNICATION
*Telephones:* 380,000 main lines
*Daily Newspaper Circulation:*
15 per 1,000 people
*Televisions:* 105 per 1,000 people
*Internet Service Provider:* 1
(2000)

## TRANSPORTATION
*Highways in Miles (Kilometers):* 15,180
(24,484)
*Railroads in Miles (Kilometers):* none
*Usable Airfields:* 136
*Motor Vehicles in Use:* 904,000

## GOVERNMENT
*Type:* officially an "Arab" republic
(*Jamahiriya*), with authority vested
in the General People's Congress, with
members elected by popular vote
*Independence Date:* December 24, 1951
(from Italy)
*Head of State/Government:* Revolutionary
Leader Colonel Muammar al-Qadhafi;
Premier Mubarak al-Shamekh
*Political Parties:* none

*Suffrage:* universal and compulsory at 18

## MILITARY
*Military Expenditures (% of GDP):* 3.9%
*Current Disputes:* territorial claims in
Niger and Algeria

## ECONOMY
*Currency ($ U.S. Equivalent):* 1.34 dinars
= $1
*Per Capita Income/GDP:* $8,900/$45.4 bil-
lion
*GDP Growth Rate:* 6.5%
*Inflation Rate:* 18.5%
*Unemployment Rate:* 30%
*Labor Force:* 1,500,000
*Natural Resources:* petroleum; natural gas;
gypsum

*Agriculture:* wheat; barley; olives; dates;
citrus fruits; vegetables; peanuts; beef;
eggs
*Industry:* petroleum; food processing;
textiles; handicrafts; cement
*Exports:* $13.9 billion (primary partners
Italy, Germany, Spain)
*Imports:* $7.6 billion (primary partners
Italy, Germany, Tunisia)

http://lcweb2.loc.gov/frd/cs/lytoc.html
http://home.earthlink.net/~dribrahim/

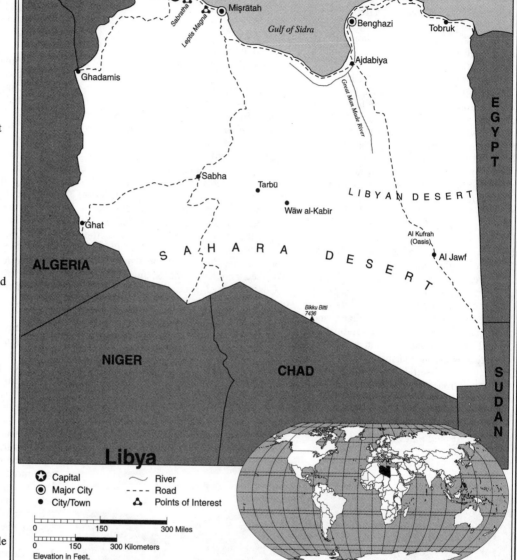

## LIBYA

The Socialist People's Libyan Arab Jamahiriya (Republic), commonly known as Libya, is the fourth largest of the Arab countries. Since it became a republic in 1969, it has played a role in regional and international affairs more appropriate to the size of its huge territory than to its small population.

Libya consists of three geographical regions: Tripolitania, Cyrenaica, and the Fezzan. Most of the population live in Tripolitania, the northwestern part of the country, where Tripoli, the capital and major port, is located. Cyrenaica, in the east along the Egyptian border, has a narrow coastline backed by a high plateau (2,400-feet elevation) called the Jabal al-Akhdar ("Green Mountain"). It contains Libya's other principal city, Benghazi. The two regions are separated by the Sirte, an extension of the Sahara Desert that reaches almost to the Mediterranean Sea. Most of Libya's oil fields are in the Sirte.

The Fezzan occupies the central part of the country. It is entirely desert, except for a string of widely scattered oases. Its borders are with Chad, Algeria, Niger, and Sudan. The border with Chad, established during French colonial rule in sub-Saharan Africa, was once disputed by Libya. The matter was settled through international mediation, with the border formally demarcated in 1994. Libya also claims areas in northern Niger and southeastern Algeria left over from the colonial period, when they formed part of the French West

African empire. In the Libyan view, these areas should have been transferred to its control under the peace treaty that established the Libyan state and relinquishment of French control.

## HISTORY

Until modern times, Libya did not have a separate identity, either national or territorial. It always formed a part of some other territorial unit and in most cases was controlled by outsiders. However, control was usually limited to the coastal areas. The Berbers of the interior were little affected by the passing of conquerors and the rise and fall of civilizations.

Libya's culture and social structure have been influenced more by the Islamic Arabs than by any other invaders. The Arabs brought Islam to Libya in the early seventh century. Arab groups settled in the region and intermarried with the Berber population to such an extent that the Libyans became one of the most thoroughly Arabized peoples in the Islamic world.

Coastal Libya, around Tripoli, was an outlying province of the Ottoman Empire for several centuries. Like its urban neighbors Tunis and Algiers, Tripoli had a fleet of corsairs who made life dangerous for European merchant ships in the Mediterranean. When the United States became a Mediterranean trading nation, the corsairs of Tripoli included American ships among their targets. The USS *Philadelphia* was sent to Tripoli to "teach the corsairs a lesson" in 1804, but it got stuck on a sandbar

and was captured. Navy Lieutenant Stephen Decatur led a commando raid into Tripoli harbor and blew up the ship, inspiring the words to what would become the official U.S. Marine hymn: "From the halls of Montezuma to the shores of Tripoli. . . ."

### The Sanusiya Movement

At various stages in Islam's long history, new groups or movements have appeared committed to purifying or reforming Islamic society and taking it back to its original form of a simple community of believers led by just rulers. Several of these movements, such as the Wahhabis of Saudi Arabia, were important in the founding of modern Islamic states. The movement called the Sanusiya was formed in the nineteenth century. In later years, it became an important factor in the formation of modern Libya.

The founder, the Grand Sanusi, was a religious teacher from Algeria. He left Algeria after the French conquest and settled in northern Cyrenaica. The Grand Sanusi's teachings attracted many followers. He also attracted the attention of the Ottoman authorities, who distrusted his advocacy of a strong united Islamic world in which Ottomans and Arabs would be partners. In 1895, to escape from the Ottomans, the Grand Sanusi's son and successor moved Sanusiya headquarters to Kufra, a remote oasis in the Sahara.

The Sanusiya began as a peaceful movement interested only in bringing new converts to Islam and founding a network of *zawiyas* ("lodges") for contemplation and monastic life throughout the desert. But when European countries began to seize territories in North and West Africa, the Sanusi became warrior-monks and fought the invaders.

### Italy Conquers Libya

The Italian conquest of Libya began in 1911. The Italians needed colonies, not only for prestige but also for the resettlement of poor and landless peasants from Italy's crowded southern provinces. The Italians expected an easy victory against a weak Ottoman garrison; Libya would become the "Fourth Shore" of a new Roman Empire from shore to shore along the Mediterranean. But the Italians found Libya a tougher land to subdue than they had expected. Italian forces were pinned to Tripoli and a few other points on the coast by the Ottoman garrison and the fierce Sanusi warrior-monks.

The Italians were given a second chance after World War I. The Ottoman Empire had been defeated, and Libya was ripe for the plucking. The new Italian government

(UN photo/pcd)

The Fezzan occupies the central part of Libya and is entirely desert, except for some widely scattered oases. This oasis is called Bu Gheilan.

(UN photo/Rice)

After the 1969 Revolution, the government strove to develop many aspects of the country. These local chiefs are meeting to plan community development.

of swaggering dictator Benito Mussolini sent an army to occupy Tripolitania. When the Italians moved on Cyrenaica, the Grand Sanusi crossed the Egyptian border into exile under British protection. The Italians found Cyrenaica much more difficult to control than Tripolitania. It is ideal guerrilla country, from the caves of Jabal al-Akhdar to the stony plains and dry, hidden *wadis* (river beds) of the south. It took nine years (1923–1932) for Italy to overcome all of Libya, despite Italy's vast superiority in troops and weapons. Sanusi guerrilla bands harried the Italians, cutting supply lines, ambushing patrols, and attacking convoys. Their leader, Shaykh Omar Mukhtar, became Libya's first national hero.

The Italians finally overcame the Sanusi by the use of methods that do not shock us today but seemed unbelievably brutal at the time. Cyrenaica was made into a huge concentration camp, with a barbed-wire fence along the Egyptian border. Nomadic peoples were herded into these camps, guarded by soldiers to prevent them from aiding the Sanusi. Sanusi prisoners were pushed out of airplanes, wells were plugged to deny water to the people, and flocks were slaughtered. In 1931, Omar Mukhtar was captured, court-martialed, and hanged in public. The resistance ended with his death.

The Italians did not have long to cultivate their Fourth Shore. During the 1930s, they poured millions of lire into the colony. A paved highway from the Egyptian to the Tunisian border along the coast was completed in 1937; in World War II, it became a handy invasion route for the British. A system of state-subsidized farms was set up for immigrant Italian peasants. Each was given

free transportation, a house, seed, fertilizers, a mule, and a pair of shoes as inducements to come to Libya. By 1940, the Italian population had reached 110,000, and about 495,000 acres of land had been converted into productive farms, vineyards, and olive groves.[1]

**Independent Libya**

Libya was a major battleground during World War II, as British, German, and Italian armies rolled back and forth across the desert. The British defeated the Germans and occupied northern Libya, while a French army occupied the Fezzan. The United States later built an important air base, Wheelus Field, near Tripoli. Thus the three major Allied powers all had an interest in Libya's future. But they could not agree on what to do with occupied Libya.

Italy wanted Libya back. France wished to keep the Fezzan as a buffer for its African colonies, while Britain preferred self-government for Cyrenaica under the Grand Sanusi, who had become staunchly pro-British during his exile in Egypt. The Soviet Union favored a Soviet trusteeship over Libya, which would provide the Soviet Union with a convenient outlet in the Mediterranean. The United States waffled but finally settled on independence, which would at least keep the Soviet tentacles from enveloping Libya.

Due to lack of agreement, the Libyan "problem" was referred to the United Nations General Assembly. Popular demonstrations of support for independence in Libya impressed a number of the newer UN members; in 1951, the General Assembly approved a resolution for an independent Libyan state, a kingdom under the Grand Sanusi, Idris.

## THE KINGDOM OF LIBYA

Libya has been governed under two political systems since independence: a constitutional monarchy (1951–1969); and a Socialist republic (1969– ), which has no constitution because all power "belongs" to the people. Monarchy and republic have had almost equal time in power. But Libya's sensational economic growth and aggressive foreign policy under the republic need to be understood in relation to the solid, if unspectacular, accomplishments of the regime that preceded it.

At independence, Libya was an artificial union of the three provinces. The Libyan people had little sense of national identity or unity. Loyalty was to one's family, clan, village, and, in a general sense, to the higher authority represented by a tribal confederation. The only other loyalty linking Libyans was the Islamic religion. The tides of war and conquest that had washed over them for centuries had had little effect on their strong, traditional attachment to Islam.[2]

Political differences also divided the three provinces. Tripolitanians talked openly of abolishing the monarchy. Cyrenaica was the home and power base of King Idris; the king's principal supporters were the Sanusiya and certain important families. The distances and poor communication links between the provinces contributed to the impression that they should be separate countries. Leaders could not even agree on the choice between Tripoli and Benghazi for the capital. For his part, the king distrusted both cities as being corrupt and overly influenced by foreigners. He had his administrative capital at Baida, in the Jabal al-Akhdar.

The greatest problem facing Libya at independence was economics. Per capita income in 1951 was about $30 per year; in 1960, it was about $100 per year. Approximately 5 percent of the land was marginally usable for agriculture, and only 1 percent could be cultivated on a permanent basis. Most economists considered Libya to be a hopeless case, almost totally dependent on foreign aid for survival. (It is interesting to note that the Italians were seemingly able to force more out of the soil, but one must remember that the Italian government poured a great deal of money into the country to develop the plantations, and credit must also be given to the extremely hard-working Italian farmer.)

Despite its meager resources and lack of political experience, Libya was valuable to the United States and Britain in the 1950s and 1960s because of its strategic location. The United States negotiated a long-term lease on Wheelus Field in 1954, as a vital link in the chain of U.S. bases built around the southern perimeter of the Soviet Union due to the Cold War. In return, U.S. aid of $42 million sweetened the pot, and Wheelus became the single largest employer of Libyan labor. The British had two air bases and maintained a garrison in Tobruk.

Political development in the kingdom was minimal. King Idris knew little about parliamentary democracy, and he distrusted political parties. The 1951 Constitution provided for an elected Legislature, but a dispute between the king and the Tripolitanian National Congress, one of several Tripolitanian parties, led to the outlawing of all political parties. Elections were held every four years, but only property-owning adult males could vote (women were granted the vote in 1963). The same legislators were reelected regularly. In the absence of political activity, the king was the glue that held Libya together.

### THE 1969 REVOLUTION

At dawn on September 1, 1969, a group of young, unknown army officers abruptly carried out a military coup in Libya. King Idris, who had gone to Turkey for medical treatment, was deposed, and a "Libyan Arab Republic" was proclaimed by the officers. These men, whose names were not known to the outside world until weeks after the coup, were led by Captain Muammar Muhammad al-Qadhafi. He went on Benghazi radio to announce to a startled Libyan population: "People of Libya . . . your armed forces have undertaken the overthrow of the reactionary and corrupt regime. . . . From now on Libya is a free, sovereign republic, ascending with God's help to exalted heights."[3]

Qadhafi's new regime made a sharp change in policy from that of its predecessor. Wheelus Field and the British air bases were evacuated and returned to Libyan control. Libya took an active part in Arab affairs and supported Arab unity, to the extent of working to undermine other Arab leaders whom Qadhafi considered undemocratic or unfriendly to his regime.[4]

### REGIONAL POLICY

To date, Qadhafi's efforts to unite Libya with other Arab states have not been successful. A 1984 agreement for a federal union with Morocco, which provided for separate sovereignty but a federated Assembly and unified foreign policies, was abrogated unilaterally by the late King Hassan II, after Qadhafi had charged him with "Arab treason" for meeting with Israeli leader Shimon Peres. Undeterred,

(Gamma-Liaison/Christian Vioujard)

Muammar al-Qadhafi led a group of army officers in the military coup of 1969 that deposed King Idris. In later years, Qadhafi gained worldwide notoriety for his apparent sanction of terrorism.

Qadhafi tried again in 1987 with neighboring Algeria, receiving a medal from President Chadli Bendjedid but no other encouragement.

Although distrustful of the mercurial Libyan leader, other North African heads of state have continued to work with him on the basis that it is safer to have Qadhafi inside the circle than isolated outside. Tunisia restored diplomatic relations in 1987, and Qadhafi agreed to compensate the Tunisian government for lost wages of Tunisian workers expelled from Libya during the 1985 economic recession. Qadhafi also accepted International Court of Justice arbitration over Libya's dispute with Tunisia over oil rights in the Gulf of Gabes. In 1989, Libya joined with other North African states in the Arab Maghrib Union, which was formed to coordinate their respective economies. However, the AMU has yet to become a viable organization due to political differences among its members, in particular the Western Sahara dispute between Algeria and Morocco.

With little to show for his efforts to unite the Arab countries, Qadhafi turned his attention to sub-Saharan Africa. He had abolished the Secretariat for Arab Unity as a government ministry in 1997, and subsequently black African workers were invited to come and work in Libya. By 2000, nearly a million had arrived, most of them from Nigeria, Chad, and Ghana. Economic problems in sub-Saha-

ran Africa caused thousands more to use Libya as an escape route for Europe, many of them also fleeing from civil war in Côte d' Ivoire and Sierra Leone. The flood of migrants generated tension between them and Libyan natives; the latter viewed the migrants as agents of social misbehavior ranging from prostitution to drug usage and AIDS. In August 2000, the Libyan government deported several thousand African workers. They were hauled to the Niger border in trucks and dumped across the border there. Qadhafi had announced earlier that a "United States of Africa" would come into existence in March 2001 under Libyan sponsorship. But for once the Libyan people did not agree with him; "We are native Arabs, not Africans," they told their leader.

### SOCIAL REVOLUTION

Qadhafi's desert upbringing and Islamic education gave him a strong, puritanical moral code. In addition to closing foreign bases and expropriating properties of Italians and Jews, he moved forcefully against symbols of foreign influence. The Italian cathedral in Tripoli became a mosque, street signs were converted to Arabic, nightclubs were closed, and the production and sale of alcohol were prohibited.

But Qadhafi's revolution went far beyond changing names. In a three-volume work entitled *The Green Book,* he described his vision of the appropriate political system for Libya. Political parties would not be allowed, nor would constitutions, legislatures, even an organized court system. All of these institutions, according to Qadhafi, eventually become corrupt and unrepresentative. Instead, "people's committees" would run the government, business, industry, and even the universities. Libyan embassies abroad were renamed "people's bureaus" and were run by junior officers. (The takeover of the London bureau in 1984 led to counterdemonstrations by Libyan students and the killing of a British police officer by gunfire from inside the bureau. The Libyan bureau in Washington, D.C., was closed by the U.S. Federal Bureau of Investigation and the staff deported on charges of espionage and terrorism against Libyans in the United States.) The country was renamed the Socialist People's Libyan Arab Jamahiriya, and titles of government officials were eliminated. Qadhafi became "Leader of the Revolution," and each government department was headed by the secretary of a particular people's committee.

Qadhafi then developed a so-called Third International Theory, based on the belief that neither capitalism nor communism could solve the world's problems. What was needed, he said, was a "middle way" that would harness the driving forces of human history—religion and nationalism—to interact with each other to revitalize humankind. Islam would be the source of that middle way, because "it provides for the realization of justice and equity, it does not allow the rich to exploit the poor."[5]

## THE ECONOMY

Modern Libya's economy is based almost entirely on oil exports. Concessions were granted to various foreign companies to explore for oil in 1955, and the first oil strikes were made in 1957. Within a decade, Libya had become the world's fourth-largest exporter of crude oil. During the 1960s, pipelines were built from the oil fields to new export terminals on the Mediterranean coast. The lightness and low sulfur content of Libyan crude oil make it highly desirable to industrialized countries, and, with the exception of the United States, differences in political viewpoint have had little effect on Libyan oil sales abroad.

After the 1969 Revolution, Libya became a leader in the drive by oil-producing countries to gain control over their petroleum industries. The process began in 1971, when the new Libyan government took over the interests of British Petroleum in Libya. The Libyan method of nationalization was to proceed against individual companies rather than to take on the "oil giants" all at once. It took more than a decade before the last company, Exxon, capitulated. However, the companies' $2 billion in assets were left in limbo in 1986, when the administration of U.S. president Ronald Reagan imposed a ban on all trade with Libya to protest Libya's involvement in international terrorism. President George Bush extended the ban for an additional year in 1990, although he expressed satisfaction with reduced Libyan support for terroristic activities, one example being the expulsion from Tripoli of the Palestine Liberation Front, a radical opponent of Yassir Arafat's Palestine Liberation Organization.

Recent discoveries have increased Libya's oil reserves 30 percent, to 29.5 billion barrels, and recoverable natural-gas reserves to 1.6 billion cubic meters. With oil production reaching a record 1.4 million barrels per day, Libya has been able to build a strong petrochemical industry. The Marsa Brega petrochemical complex is one of the world's largest producers of urea, although a major contract with India

was canceled in 1996 due to UN sanctions on trade with Libya.

Until recently, industrial-development successes based on oil revenues enabled Libyans to enjoy an ever-improving standard of living, and funding priorities were shifted from industry to agricultural development in the budget. But a combination of factors—mismanagement, lack of a cadre of skilled Libyan workers, absenteeism, low motivation of the workforce, and a significant drop in revenues (from $22 billion in 1980 to $7 billion in 1988)—cast doubts on the effectiveness of Qadhafi's *Green Book* socialistic economic policies.

In 1988, the leader began closing the book. As production incentives, controls on both imports and exports were eliminated, and profit sharing for employees of small businesses was encouraged. In 1990, the General People's Congress (GPC), Libya's equivalent of a parliament, began a restructuring of government, adding new secretariats (ministries) to help expand economic development and diversity the economy.

In January 2000, Qadhafi marched into a GPC meeting waving a copy of the annual budget. He tore up the copy and ordered most of the secretariats abolished. Their powers would be transferred to "provincial cells" outside of Tripoli. Only five government functions—finance, defense, foreign affairs, information, and African unity—would remain under central-government control. In October of that year, Qadhafi ordered further cuts, continuing his direct management of national affairs. For the first time he named a prime minister, Mubarak al-Shamekh, to head the stripped-down government. The secretariat for information was abolished, and the heads of the justice and finance secretariats summarily dismissed. The head of the National Oil Company (NOC), Libya's longest-serving government official, was transferred to a new post; Qadhafi had criticized the NOC for mismanagement of the oil industry and lack of vision.

Libya also started developing its considerable uranium resources. A 1985 agreement with the Soviet Union provided the components for an 880-megawatt nuclear-power station in the Sirte region. Libya has enough uranium to meet its foreseeable domestic needs. The German-built chemical-weapons plant at Rabta, described by Libyans as a pharmaceutical complex but confirmed as to its real function by visiting scientists, was destroyed in a mysterious fire in the 1980s. A Russian-built nuclear reactor at Tajoora, 30 miles from Tripoli, suffered a similar fate, not from fire but due to faulty ventilation

and high levels of radiation. But the Libyans have pressed on. An underground complex at Mount Tarhuna, south of Tripoli, was completed in 1998 and closed subsequently to international inspection. Libya claims that it is part of the Great Man-Made River (GMR) project and thus not subject to such inspections. The country also refuses to sign the 1993 UN convention outlawing chemical weapons.

In addition to its heavy dependence on oil revenues, another obstacle to economic development in Libya is derived from an unbalanced labor force. One author observed, "Foreigners do all the work. Moroccans clean houses, Sudanese grow vegetables, Egyptians fix cars and drive trucks. Iraqis run the power stations and American and European technicians keep the equipment and systems humming. All the Libyans do is show up for makework government jobs."[6] But thanks to all this help, Libya is self-sufficient in cement; in iron and steel; and in the agricultural sector in poultry, vegetables, and cereals.

## AN UNCERTAIN FUTURE

The revolutionary regime has been more successful than the monarchy was in making the wealth from oil revenues available to ordinary Libyans. Per capita income, which was $2,170 the year after the revolution, had risen to $10,900 by 1980. (With the drop in world oil prices and the residual effect of sanctions, it fell to $8,900 by 2001.)

This influx of wealth changed the lives of the people in a very short period of time. Seminomadic tribes such as the Qadadfas of the Sirte (Qadhafi's kin) have been provided with permanent homes, for example. Extensive social-welfare programs, such as free medical care, free education, and low-cost housing, have greatly enhanced the lives of many Libyans. However, this wealth has yet to be spread evenly across society. The economic downturn of the 1990s produced a thriving black market, along with price gouging and corruption in the public sector. In 1996, Libya organized "purification committees," mostly staffed by young army officers, to monitor and report instances of black-market and other illegal activities.

Until recently, opposition to Qadhafi was confined almost entirely to exiles abroad, centered on former associates living in Cairo, Egypt, who had broken with the Libyan leader for reasons either personal or related to economic mismanagement. But economic downturns and dissatisfaction with the leader's wildly unsuccessful foreign-policy ventures increased popular discontent at home. In

1983, Qadhafi had introduced two domestic policies that also generated widespread resentment: He called for the drafting of women into the armed services, and he recommended that all children be educated at home until age 10. The 200 basic "people's congresses," set up in 1977 to recommend policy to the national General People's Congress (which in theory is responsible for national policy), objected strongly to both proposals. Qadhafi then created 2,000 more people's congresses, presumably to dilute the opposition, but withdrew the proposals. In effect, suggested one observer, *The Green Book* theory had begun to work, and Qadhafi didn't like it.

Qadhafi's principal support base rests on the armed forces and the "revolutionary committees," formed of youths whose responsibility is to guard against infractions of *The Green Book* rules. "Brother Colonel" also relies upon a small group of collaborators from the early days of the Revolution, and his own relatives and members of the Qadadfa form part of the inner power structure. This structure is highly informal, and it may explain why Qadhafi is able to disappear from public view from time to time, as he did after the United States conducted an air raid on Tripoli in 1986, and emerge having lost none of his popularity and charismatic appeal.

In recent years, disaffection within the army has led to a number of attempts to overthrow Qadhafi. The most serious coup attempt took place in 1984, when army units allied with the opposition Islamic Front for the Salvation of Libya, based in Cairo and headed by several of Qadhafi's former associates, attacked the central barracks in Tripoli where he usually resides. The attackers were defeated in a bloody gun battle. A previously unknown opposition group based in Geneva, Switzerland, claimed in 1996 that its agents had poisoned the camel's milk that Qadhafi drinks while eating dates on his desert journeys, but proof of this claim is lacking.

However, the Libyan leader's elusiveness and penchant for secrecy make assessments of his continued leadership risky. According to the Tripoli rumor mill, someone attempts to assassinate Qadhafi every couple of months. But as yet no organized internal opposition has emerged, and the mercurial Libyan leader remains not only highly visible but also popular with his people.

## INTERNAL CHANGES

Qadhafi has a talent for the unexpected that has made him an effective survivor. In 1988, he ordered the release of all political prisoners and personally drove a bulldozer through the main gate of Tripoli's prison to inaugurate "Freedom Day." Exiled opponents of the regime were invited to return under a promise of amnesty, and a number did so.

In June of that year, the GPC approved a "Charter of Human Rights" as an addendum to *The Green Book*. The charter outlaws the death penalty, bans mistreatment of prisoners, and guarantees every accused person the right to a fair trial. It also permits formation of labor unions, confirms the right to education and suitable employment for all Libyan citizens, and places Libya on record as prohibiting production of nuclear and chemical weapons. In March 1995, the country's last prison was destroyed and its inmates freed in application of the charter's guarantees of civil liberty.

## THE WAR WITH CHAD

Libyan forces occupied the Aouzou Strip in northern Chad in 1973, claiming it as an integral part of the Libyan state. Occupation gave Libya access also to the reportedly rich uranium resources of the region. In subsequent years, Qadhafi played upon political rivalries in Chad to extend the occupation into a de facto one of annexation of most of its poverty-stricken neighbor.

But in late 1986 and early 1987, Chadian leaders patched up their differences and turned on the Libyans. In a series of spectacular raids on entrenched Libyan forces, the highly mobile Chadians, traveling mostly in Toyota trucks, routed the Libyans and drove them out of northern Chad. Chadian forces then moved into the Aouzou Strip and even attacked nearby air bases inside Libya. The defeats, with casualties of some 3,000 Libyans and loss of huge quantities of Soviet-supplied military equipment, exposed the weaknesses of the overequipped, undertrained, and poorly motivated Libyan Army.

In 1989, after admitting his mistake, Qadhafi signed a cease-fire with then–Chadian leader Hissène Habré and agreed to submit the dispute over ownership of Aouzou to the International Court of Justice (ICJ). The ICJ affirmed Chadian sovereignty in 1994 on the basis of a 1955 agreement arranged by France as the occupying power there. Libyan forces withdrew from Aouzou in May, and since then the two countries have enjoyed a peaceful relationship. In 1998, the border was opened completely, in line with Qadhafi's policy of "strengthening neighborly relations."

## FOREIGN POLICY

Libya's relations with the United States have remained hostile since the 1969 Revolution, which not only overthrew King Idris but also resulted in the closing of the important Wheelus Field air base. Despite Qadhafi's efforts in more recent years to portray himself and Libya as respectable members of the world of nations, the country remains on the U.S. Department of State's list as one of the main sponsors of international terrorism. In 1986, U.S. war planes bombed Tripoli and Benghazi in retaliation for the bombing of a disco in Berlin, Germany, which killed two U.S. servicemen and injured 238 others. The retaliatory U.S. air attack on Libya killed 55 Libyan civilians, including Qadhafi's adopted daughter. After numerous delays and conflicting evidence about Libya's role in the Berlin bombing, a trial began in 1998 for four persons implicated in the attack. Only one, a diplomat in the embassy in East Berlin (now closed), was a Libyan national. The trial ended in 2001 with the conviction of the four; they were given 12- to 14-year sentences.

Libya resumed its old role of "pariah state" in 1992 by refusing to extradite two officers of its intelligence service suspected of complicity in the 1988 bombing of a Pan American jumbo jet over Lockerbie, Scotland. The United States, France, and Britain had demanded the officers' extradition and introduced a resolution to that effect in the UN Security Council; in the event of noncompliance on Libya's part, sanctions would be imposed on the country. *Resolution 748* passed by a 10-to-zero vote, with five abstentions. A concurrent ruling by the ICJ ordered Libya to turn over the suspects or explain in writing why it was not obligated to do so.

Qadhafi, however, refused to comply with *Resolution 748*. He argued that the suspects should be tried (if at all) in a neutral country, since they could not be given a fair trial either in Britain or the United States.

The Security Council responded by imposing partial sanctions on Libya. Despite the partial embargo, Libya's leader continued to reject compliance with the resolution. As a result, the Security Council in 1993 passed *Resolution 883,* imposing much stiffer sanctions on the country. The new sanctions banned all shipments of spare parts and equipment sales and froze Libyan foreign bank deposits. International flights to Libya were prohibited. The only area of the economy not affected was that of oil exports, since Britain and other Western European countries are dependent on low-sulfur Libyan crude for their economies.

Despite the sanctions and Libya's isolation, Qadhafi continued to refuse to sur-

| | | | | | | |
|---|---|---|---|---|---|---|
| Tripoli becomes an Ottoman province with the Sanusiya controlling the interior **1835** | Libya becomes an Italian colony, Italy's "Fourth Shore" **1932** | An independent kingdom is set up by the UN under King Idris **1951** | The Revolution overthrows Idris; the Libyan Arab Republic is established **1969** | Qadhafi decrees a cultural and social revolution with government by people's committees **1973–1976** | A campaign to eliminate Libyan opponents abroad; the United States imposes economic sanctions in response to suspected Libya-terrorist ties; U.S. planes attack targets in Tripoli and Benghazi; Libyan troops are driven from Chad, including the Aouzou Strip **1980s** | Libya's relations with its neighbors improve; the UN votes to impose sanctions on Libya for terrorist acts; Qadhafi comes to an agreement with the UN regarding the trial of the PanAm/Lockerbie bombing suspects **1990s** |

**2000s**

Qadhafi makes changes to governmental structure

render the two Lockerbie suspects. He maintained that they were innocent and could not receive a fair trial except in a neutral country under international law.

The tug-of-war between the United Nations and its recalcitrant member went on for six years. In March 1998, the United Nations, set a 60-day deadline for compliance. Subsequently Qadhafi reversed his stance on the Lockerbie suspects. While he insisted that the Libyan government was not involved, he agreed to turn over the suspects to be tried in a neutral court under Scottish law. The two were then flown to the Netherlands, where they were tried in a court set up in an abandoned Dutch air base, Camp Zeist. The trial was marked by intricate legal maneuverings and some questionable evidence. In 2000, one of the suspects was acquitted. The other, former Libyan intelligence agent Abdel Basset al-Megrahi, was found guilty and sentenced to life imprisonment. Late in 2001, his attorneys appealed the conviction, promising that hitherto undisclosed evidence would prove that there had been a miscarriage of justice.

## PROSPECTS
The tide of fundamentalism sweeping across the Islamic world and challenging secular regimes has largely spared Libya thus far, although there were occasional clashes between fundamentalists and police in the 1980s, and in 1992, some 500 fundamentalists were jailed briefly. However, the bloody civil uprisings against the regimes in neighboring Algeria and Egypt caused Qadhafi in 1994 to reemphasize Libya's Islamic nature. New laws passed by the General People's Congress would apply Islamic law (Shari'a) and punishments in such areas as marriage and divorce, wills and inheritance, crimes of theft and violence (where the Islamic pun-

ishment is cutting off a hand), and for apostasy. Libya's tribal-based society and Qadhafi's own interpretation of Islamic law to support women's rights and to deal with other social issues continue to serve as obstacles to Islamic fundamentalism.

On September 7, 1999, the Libyan leader celebrated his 30th year in power with a parade of thousands of footsoldiers, along with long-range missiles and tanks, through the streets of Tripoli. Libyan jets, many of them piloted by women, flew overhead.

At 60-plus the charismatic Libyan leader shows no sign of relinquishing power and seems in excellent health. In the absence of a formal succession process (Qadhafi has no official title), speculation centers on his oldest son, Muhammad Sayf al-Islam. However, a younger son, El-Saadi, represented Libya on an official visit to Japan in 2001.

The lifting of UN sanctions on the country resulted from Qadhafi's acceptance of international jurisdiction in the Lockerbie case. As a result, relations with Europe have been normalized. However, the United States continues to insist that the country is a sponsor of global terrorism. In July 2001, the U.S. Senate approved a five-year extension of the Iran–Libya Sanctions Act (ILSA). The act bars U.S. companies from doing business in Libya, imposing fines for those investing more than $20 million in Libyan development projects. With U.S. firms effectively barred, European companies rushed to take advantage of the end of sanctions and Libya's need to revitalize and repair its oil industry.

Although he is certainly no friend of the United States and bitterly opposes Israel, Qadhafi spoke out strongly after the terrorist bombings of the World Trade Center and the Pentagon. He condemned the attacks as "horrifying and destructive" and

said that U.S. retaliation would be an act of self-defense. He urged Libyans to donate blood for the victims and denounced the use of anthrax as "demonic."

## NOTES
1. "[I]rrigation, colonization and hard work have wrought marvels. Everywhere you see plantations forced out of the sandy, wretched soil." A. H. Broderick, *North Africa* (London: Oxford University Press, 1943), p. 27.

2. Religious leaders issued a *fatwa* ("binding legal decision") stating that a vote against independence would be a vote against religion. Omar el Fathaly, et al., *Political Development and Bureaucracy in Libya* (Lexington, KY: Lexington Books, 1977).

3. See *Middle East Journal,* vol. 24, no. 2 (Spring 1970), Documents Section.

4. John Wright, *Libya: A Modern History* (Baltimore, MD: Johns Hopkins University Press, 1982), pp. 124–126. Qadhafi's idol was former Egyptian president Nasser, a leader in the movement for unity and freedom among the Arabs. While he was at school in Sebha, in the Fezzan, he listened to Radio Cairo's Voice of the Arabs and was later expelled from school as a militant organizer of demonstrations.

5. *The London Times* (June 6, 1973).

6. Khidr Hamza, with Jeff Stein, *Saddam's Bombmaker* (New York: Scribner's, 2000), p. 289. The author was head of the Iraqi nuclear-weapons program before defecting to Libya and eventually the United States.

7. Donald G. McNeil Jr., in *The New York Times* (February 1, 2001).

---

## DEVELOPMENT

Although continued U.S. sanctions prohibit American firms from operating in Libya, improved relations with other countries have begun to generate diversification of the Libyan economy. An agreement with Ireland to import 50,000 live Irish cattle was concluded in March 2001, and Italy's export credit agency wrote off $230 million in Libyan debts to encourage investment by Italian firms. New oil discoveries in the Murzuq field.

## FREEDOM

The General People's Congress has the responsibility for passing laws and appointing a government. In 1994, the GPC approved legislation making Islamic law applicable in the country. They concerned retribution and blood money; rules governing wills, crimes of theft and violence, protection of society from things banned in the Koran, marriage, and divorce; and a ban on alcohol use.

## HEALTH/WELFARE

In addition to 1 million sub-Saharan African workers, Libya has made use of skilled workers as well as unskilled ones from many other Arab countries. Palestinian workers were expelled after the 1993 Oslo Agreement with Israel, which Qadhafi opposed vehemently. A GPC regulation issued in 2001 fixed the total number of skilled foreign workers at 40,000.

## ACHIEVEMENTS

The latest phase of the Great Man-Made River (GMR) project—Libya's self-financed plan to bring potable and irrigation water from Saharan aquifers to coastal cities and farmlands—began in 2001. It consists of a 120-mile pipeline, three pumping stations, and a 300,000-cubic-meter concrete reservoir at Abu Zayan. But construction problems continue to delay project completion.

# Morocco (Kingdom of Morocco)

## GEOGRAPHY
*Area in Square Miles (Kilometers):*
(446,550) this figure does not
include Western Sahara (about
the size of California)
*Capital (Population):* Rabat
(1,293,000)
*Environmental Concerns:* land
degradation; desertification; soil
erosion; overgrazing; contamination of water supplies; oil pollution of coastal waters
*Geographical Features:* the northern
coast and interior are
mountainous, with large areas of
bordering plateaux, intermontane
valleys, and rich coastal plains
*Climate:* varies from Mediterranean
to desert

## PEOPLE

### Population
*Total:* 30,646,000
*Annual Growth Rate:* 1.71%
*Rural/Urban Population Ratio:* 47/53
*Major Languages:* Arabic; Tama-
zight; various Berber dialects;
French
*Ethnic Makeup:* 64% Arab; 35%
Berber; 1% non-Morroccan and
Jewish
*Religions:* 99% Sunni Muslim; 1%
Christian and Jewish

### Health
*Life Expectancy at Birth:* 67 years
(male); 72 years (female)
*Infant Mortality Rate (Ratio):*
48/1,000
*Physicians Available (Ratio):* 1/2,923

### Education
*Adult Literacy Rate:* 43.7%
*Compulsory (Ages):* 7–13

## COMMUNICATION
*Telephones:* 1,515,000 main lines
*Daily Newspaper Circulation:* 13
per 1,000 people
*Televisions:* 93 per 1,000 people
*Internet Service Providers:* 8 (2000)

## TRANSPORTATION
*Highways in Miles (Kilometers):* 37,649
(60,626)
*Railroads in Miles (Kilometers):* 1,184
(1,907)
*Usable Airfields:* 69
*Motor Vehicles in Use:* 1,278,000

## GOVERNMENT
*Type:* constitutional monarchy
*Independence Date:* March 2, 1956 (from
France)
*Head of State/Government:* King
Muhammad VI; Prime Minister
Abderrahmane Youssoufi

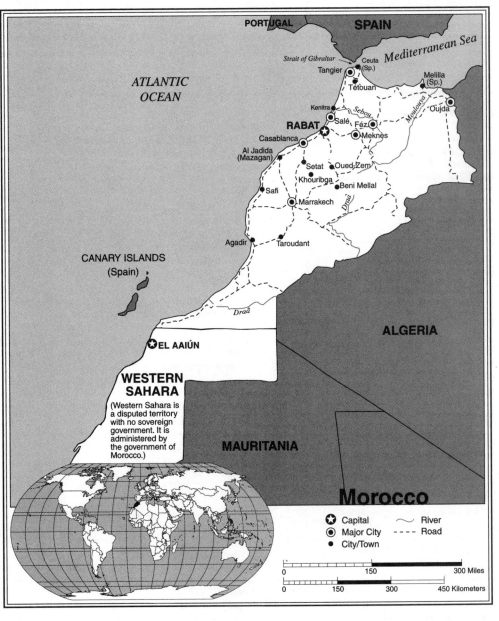

*Political Parties:* National Rally of Inde-
pendents; Popular Movement; National
Democratic Party; Constitutional Union;
Socialist Union of Popular Forces;
Istiqlal; Kutla Bloc; Party of Progress
and Socialism; others
*Suffrage:* universal at 21

## MILITARY
*Military Expenditures (% of GDP):* 4%
*Current Disputes:* final resolution on the
status of Western Sahara remains to be
worked out; disputes with Spain over
Ceuta and Melilla as well as several
small islands

## ECONOMY
*Currency ($ U.S. Equivalent):* 11.25
dirhams = $1

*Per Capita Income/GDP:* $3,500/$105
billion
*GDP Growth Rate:* 8%
*Inflation Rate:* 2%
*Unemployment Rate:* 23%
*Labor Force:* 11,000,000
*Natural Resources:* phosphates, iron ore;
manganese; lead; zinc; fish; salt
*Agriculture:* barley; wheat; citrus fruits;
wine; vegetables; olives; livestock
*Industry:* phosphate mining and process-
ing; food processing; leather goods;
textiles; construction; tourism
*Exports:* $7.6 billion (primary partners
France, Spain, United Kingdom)
*Imports:* $12.2 billion (primary partners
France, Spain, Italy)

# MOROCCO

The Kingdom of Morocco is the western-most country in North Africa. Morocco's population is the second largest (after Egypt) of the Arab states. The country's territory includes the Western Sahara (a claim made under dispute), formerly two Spanish colonies, Rio de Oro and Saguia al-Hamra. Morocco annexed part in 1976 and the balance in 1978, after Mauritania's withdrawal from its share, as decided in an agreement with Spain. Since then, Morocco has incorporated the Western Sahara into the kingdom as its newest province.

Two other territories physically within Morocco remain outside Moroccan control. They are the cities of Ceuta and Melilla, both located on rocky peninsulas that jut out into the Mediterranean Sea. They have been held by Spain since the fifteenth century. (Spain also owns several small islands off the coast in Moroccan territorial waters.) The economic advantages to Morocco of the free-port status of Ceuta and Melilla, plus the fact that they employ a large expatriate Moroccan labor force, have thus far outweighed the desire among Moroccan leaders to press hard for their return. A 1986 Spanish law excluding Moroccan Muslim residents of the two cities from Spanish citizenship led to riots among the mostly Berber population. The Moroccan government took no action in their support, and in 1988, the question of ownership became moot, when the Spanish Parliament passed a law formally incorporating Ceuta and Melilla into Spain as Spanish cities with locally elected legislatures. Spain also backed Morocco's application to the European Union for admission as an associate member. The injection of EU funds into the economies of the two enclaves has improved living standards for both the Christian and the Muslim populations.

Morocco is a rugged land, dominated by several massive mountain ranges. The Rif Range, averaging 7,000 feet in elevation, runs parallel to the Mediterranean, isolating the northern region from the rest of the country. The Atlas Mountains dominate the interior of Morocco. The Middle Atlas begins south of the Rif, separated by the Taza Gap (the traditional gateway for invaders from the east), and extends from northeast to southwest to join the High Atlas, a snowcapped range containing North Africa's highest peak. A third range, the Anti-Atlas, walls off the desert from the rest of Morocco. These ranges and the general inaccessibility of the country have isolated Morocco throughout most of its history, not only from outside invaders but internally as well, because of the geographical separation of peoples.

Moroccan geography explains the country's dual population structure. About 35 percent of the population are Berbers, descendants of the original North Africans. The Berbers were, until recently, grouped into tribes, often taking the name of a common ancestor, such as the Ait ("Sons of") 'Atta of southern Morocco.[1] Invading Arabs converted them to Islam in the eighth century but made few other changes in Berber life. Unlike the Berbers, the majority of the Arabs who settled in Morocco were, and are, town-dwellers. To a much greater degree than the Arab, the Berber was conditioned by traditional family structure and values; "a web of kinship bound the rural individual to his tribal territory, to his immediate family, and to his more distant kin."[2]

The fact that the Arabs were invaders caused the majority of the Berbers to withdraw into mountain areas. They accepted Islam but held stubbornly to their basic independence. Much of Morocco's past history consisted of efforts by various rulers, both Berber and Arab, to control Berber territory. The result was a kind of balance-of-power political system. The rulers had their power bases in the cities, while the rural groups operated as independent units. Moroccan rulers made periodic military expeditions into Berber territory to collect tribute and if possible to secure full obedience from the Berbers. When the ruler was strong, the Berbers paid up and submitted; when he was weak, they ignored him. At times Berber leaders might invade "government territory," capturing cities and replacing one ruler with another more to their liking. When they were not fighting with urban rulers, different Berber groups fought among themselves, so the system did little to foster Moroccan national unity.

## HISTORY

Morocco has a rich cultural history, with many of its ancient monuments more or less intact. It has been governed by some form of monarchy for over a thousand years, although royal authority was frequently limited or contested by rivals. The current ruling dynasty, the Alawis, assumed power in the 1600s. One reason for their long rule is the fact that they descend from the Prophet Muhammad. Thus, Moroccans have had a real sense of Islamic traditions and history through their rulers.

The first identifiable Moroccan "state" was established by a descendant of Muhammad named Idris, in the late eighth century. Idris had taken refuge in the far west of the Islamic world to escape civil war in the east. Because of his piety, learning, and descent from Muhammad, he was accepted by a number of Berber groups as their spiritual and political leader. His son and successor, Idris II, founded the first Moroccan capital, Fez. Father and son established the principle whereby descent from the Prophet was an important qualification for political power as well as social status in Morocco.

The Idrisids ruled over only a small portion of the current Moroccan territory, and, after the death of Idris II, their "nation" lapsed into decentralized family rule. In any case, the Berbers had no real idea of nationhood; each separate Berber group thought of itself as a nation. But in the eleventh and twelfth centuries, two Berber confederations developed that brought imperial grandeur to Morocco. These were the Almoravids and the Almohads. Under their rule, North Africa developed a political structure separate from that of the eastern Islamic world, one strongly influenced by Berber values.

The Almoravids began as camel-riding nomads from the Western Sahara who were inspired by a religious teacher to carry out a reform movement to revive the true faith of Islam. (The word *Almoravid* comes from the Arabic *al-Murabitun,* "men of the ribat," rather like the crusading religious orders of Christianity in the Middle Ages.) Fired by religious zeal, the Almoravids conquered all of Morocco and parts of western Algeria.

A second "imperial" dynasty, the Almohads, succeeded the Almoravids but improved on their performance. They were the first, and probably the last, to unite all of North Africa and Islamic Spain under one government. Almohad monuments, such as the Qutubiya tower, the best-known landmark of Marrakesh, and the Tower of Hassan in Rabat, still stand as reminders of their power and the high level of the Almohads' architectural achievements.

The same fragmentation, conflicts, and Berber/Arab rivalries that had undermined their predecessors brought down the Almohads in the late thirteenth century. From then on, dynasty succeeded dynasty in power. An interesting point about this cyclical pattern is that despite the lack of political unity, a distinctive Moroccan style and culture developed. Each dynasty contributed something to this culture, in architecture, crafts, literature, and music. The interchange between Morocco and Islamic Spain was constant and fruitful. Poets, musicians, artisans, architects, and others traveled regularly between Spanish and Moroccan cities. One can visit the city of Fez today and be instantly transported back into the Hispano-Moorish way of life of the Middle Ages.

## Mulay Ismail

The Alawis came to power and established their rule partly by force, but also as a result of their descent from the Prophet Muhammad. This link enabled them to win the support of both Arab and Berber populations. The real founder of the dynasty was Mulay Ismail, one of the longest-reigning and most powerful monarchs in Morocco's history.

Mulay Ismail unified the Moroccan nation. The great majority of the Berber groups accepted him as their sovereign. The sultan built watchtowers and posted permanent garrisons in Berber territories to make sure they continued to do so. He brought public security to Morocco also; it was said that in his time, a Jew or an unveiled woman could travel safely anywhere in the land, which was not the case in most parts of North Africa, the Middle East, and Europe.

Mulay Ismail was a contemporary of Louis XIV, and the reports of his envoys to the French court at Versailles convinced him that he should build a capital like it. He chose Meknes, not far from Fez. The work was half finished when he died of old age. The slaves and prisoners working on this "Moroccan Versailles" threw down their shovels and ran away. The enormous unfinished walls and arched Bab al-Mansur ("Gate of the Victorious") still stand today as reminders of Mulay Ismail's dream.

Mulay Ismail had many wives and left behind 500 sons but no instructions as to which should succeed him. After years of conflict, one of his grandsons took the throne as Muhammad II. He is important for giving European merchants a monopoly on trade from Moroccan ports (in wool, wax, hides, carpets, and leather) and for being the first non-European monarch to recognize the United States as an independent nation, in 1787.[3]

## The French Protectorate

In the 1800s and early 1900s, Morocco became increasingly vulnerable to outside pressures. The French, who were established in neighboring Algeria and Tunisia, wanted to complete their conquests. The nineteenth-century sultans were less and less able to control the mountain Berbers and were forced to make constant expeditions into the "land of dissidence," at great expense to the treasury. They began borrowing money from European bankers, not only to pay their bills but also to finance arms purchases and the development of ports, railroads, and industries to create a modern economy and prove to the European powers that Morocco could manage its own affairs. Nothing worked;

(Hamilton Wright/Government of Morocco)

Morocco has a rich history. The Karawiyyin Mosque at Fez was founded in the ninth century A.D. and is the largest mosque in North Africa. It is also the seat of one of Africa's oldest universities.

by 1900, Morocco was so far in debt that the French took over the management of its finances. (One sultan, Abd al-Aziz, had bought one of everything he was told about by European salesmen, including a gold-plated toy train that carried food from the kitchen to the dining room of his palace.) Meanwhile, the European powers plotted the country's downfall.

In 1904, France, Britain, Spain, and Germany signed secret agreements partitioning the country. The French would be given the largest part of the country, while Spain would receive the northern third as a protectorate plus some territory in the Western Sahara. In return, the French and Spanish agreed to respect Britain's claim to Egypt and Germany's claim to East African territory.

The ax fell on Morocco in 1912. French workers building the new port of Casablanca were killed by Berbers. Mobs attacked foreigners in Fez, and the sultan's troops could not control them. French troops marched to Fez from Algeria to restore order. The sultan, Mulay Hafidh (Hafiz), was forced to sign the Treaty of Fez, establishing a French protectorate over southern Morocco. The sultan believed that he had betrayed his country and died shortly thereafter, supposedly of a broken heart. Spain then occupied the

northern third of the country, and Tangier, the traditional residence of foreign consuls, became an international city ruled by several European powers.

The French protectorate over Morocco covered barely 45 years (1912–1956). But in that brief period, the French introduced significant changes into Moroccan life. For the first time, southern Morocco was brought entirely under central government control, although the "pacification" of the Berbers was not complete until 1934. French troops also intervened in the Spanish Zone to help put down a rebellion in the Rif led by Abd al-Krim, a *Qadi* ("religious judge") and leader of the powerful Ait Waryaghar tribe.[4]

The organization of the protectorate was largely the work of the first French resident-general, Marshal Louis Lyautey. Lyautey had great respect for Morocco's past and its dignified people. His goal was to develop the country and modernize the sultan's government while preserving Moroccan traditions and culture. He preferred the Berbers to the Arabs and set up a separate administration under Berber-speaking French officers for Berber areas.[5]

Lyautey's successors were less respectful of Moroccan traditions. The sultan, supposedly an independent ruler, became a figurehead. French *colons* (settlers) flocked to Morocco to buy land at rock-bottom prices and develop vineyards, citrus groves, and orchards. Modern cities sprang up around the perimeters of Rabat, Fez, Marrakesh, and other cities. In rural areas, particularly in the Atlas Mountains, the French worked with powerful local chiefs (qaids). Certain qaids used the arrangement to become enormously wealthy. One qaid, al-Glawi, as he was called, strutted about like a rooster in his territory and often said that he was the real sultan of Morocco.[6]

### Morocco's Independence Struggle

The movement for independence in Morocco developed slowly. The only symbol of national unity was the sultan, Muhammad ibn Yusuf. But he seemed ineffectual to most young Moroccans, particularly those educated in French schools, who began to question the right of France to rule a people against their will.

The hopes of these young Moroccans got a boost during World War II. The Western Allies, Great Britain and the United States, had gone on record in favor of the right of subject peoples to self-determination after the war. When U.S. president Franklin D. Roosevelt and British prime minister Winston Churchill came to Casablanca for an important wartime conference, the sultan was convinced to meet them privately and get a commitment for Morocco's independence. The leaders promised their support.

However, Roosevelt died before the end of the war, and Churchill was defeated for reelection. The French were not under any pressure after the war to end the protectorate. When a group of Moroccan nationalists formed the Istiqlal ("Independence") Party and demanded the end of French rule, most of them were arrested. A few leaders escaped to the Spanish Zone or to Tangier, where they could operate freely. For several years, Istiqlal headquarters was the home of the principal of the American School at Tangier, an ardent supporter of Moroccan nationalism.

With the Istiqlal dispersed, the sultan represented the last hope for national unity and resistance. Until then, he had gone along with the French; but in the early 1950s, he began to oppose them openly. The French began to look for a way to remove him from office and install a more cooperative ruler.

In 1953, the Glawi and his fellow qaids decided, along with the French, that the time was right to depose the sultan. The qaids demanded that he abdicate; they said that his presence was contributing to Moroccan instability. When he refused, he was bundled into a French plane and sent into exile. An elderly uncle was named to replace him.

The sultan's departure had the opposite effect from what was intended. In exile, he became a symbol for Moroccan resistance to the protectorate. Violence broke out, French settlers were murdered, and a Moroccan Army of Liberation began battling French troops in rural regions. Although the French could probably have contained the rebellion in Morocco, they were under great pressure in neighboring Algeria and Tunisia, where resistance movements were also under way. In 1955, the French abruptly capitulated. Sultan Muhammad ibn Yusuf returned to his palace in Rabat in triumph, and the elderly uncle retired to potter about his garden in Tangier.

### INDEPENDENCE

Morocco became independent on March 2, 1956. (The Spanish protectorate ended in April, and Tangier came under Moroccan control in October, although it kept its free-port status and special banking and currency privileges for several more years.) It began its existence as a sovereign state with a number of assets—a popular ruler, an established government, and a well-developed system of roads, schools, hospitals, and industries inherited from the protectorate. Against these assets were the liabilities of age-old Arab–Berber and inter-Berber conflicts, little experience with political parties or democratic institutions, and an economy dominated by Europeans.

The sultan's goal was to establish a constitutional monarchy. His first action was to give himself a new title, King Muhammad V, symbolizing the end of the old autocratic rule of his predecessors. He also pardoned the Glawi, who crawled into his presence to kiss his feet and crawled out backwards as proof of penitence. (He died soon thereafter.) However, the power of the qaids and pashas ended; "they were compromised by their association with the French, and returned to the land to make way for nationalist cadres, many . . . not from the regions they were assigned to administer."[7]

Muhammad V did not live long enough to reach his goal. He died unexpectedly in 1961 and was succeeded by his eldest son, Crown Prince Hassan. Hassan II ruled until his death in 1999. While he fulfilled his father's promise immediately with a Constitution, in most other ways Hassan II set his own stamp on Morocco.

The Constitution provided for an elected Legislature and a multiparty political system. In addition to the Istiqlal, a number of other parties were organized, including one representing the monarchy. But the results of the French failure to develop a satisfactory party system soon became apparent. Berber–Arab friction, urban–rural distrust, city rivalries, and inter-Berber hostility all intensified. Elections failed to produce a clear majority for any party, not even the king's.

In 1965, riots broke out in Casablanca. The immediate cause was labor unrest, but the real reason lay in the lack of effective leadership by the parties. The king declared a state of emergency, dismissed the Legislature, and assumed full powers under the Constitution.

For the next dozen years, Hassan II ruled as an absolute monarch. He continued to insist that his goal was a parliamentary system, a "government of national union." But he depended on a small group of cronies, members of prominent merchant families, the large Alawi family, or powerful Berber leaders as a more reliable group than the fractious political parties. The dominance of "the king's men" led to growing dissatisfaction and the perception that the king had sold out to special interests. Gradually, unrest spread to the army, previously loyal to its commander-in-chief. In 1971, during a diplomatic reception, cadets from the main military academy invaded the royal palace near Rabat. A number of foreign diplomats were killed and the king held prisoner briefly before loyal troops could crush the rebellion. The next year, a plot by air-force pilots to shoot down the king's plane was narrowly averted. The two escapes helped confirm in Hassan's mind his invincibility under the protection of Allah.

But they also prompted him to reinstate the parliamentary system. A new Constitution issued in 1972 defined Morocco "as a democratic and social constitutional monarchy in which Islam is the established religion."[8] However, the king retained the constitutional powers that, along with those derived from his spiritual role as "Commander of the Faithful" and lineal descendant of Muhammad, undergirded his authority.

### INTERNAL POLITICS

Morocco's de facto annexation of the Western Sahara has important implications for future national development due to the territory's size, underpopulation, and mineral resources, particularly shale oil and phosphates. But the annexation has been equally important to national pride and political unity. The "Green March" of 350,000 unarmed Moroccans into Spanish territory in 1975 to dramatize Morocco's claim was organized by the king and sup-

(Hamilton Wright/Government of Morocco)

Tangier was once a free city and port. Just across the Strait of Gibraltar from Spain, it now is Morocco's northern metropolis. Modernization and expansion of port facilities to accommodate large cruise ships and tankers got under way in 1999.

ported by all segments of the population and the opposition parties. In 1977, opposition leaders agreed to serve under the king in a "government of national union." The first elections in 12 years were held for a new Legislature; several new parties took part.

· The 1984 elections continued the national unity process. The promonarchist Constitutional Union (UC) party won a majority of seats in the Chamber of Representatives (Parliament). A new party, the National Rally of Independents (RNI), formed by members with no party affiliations, emerged as the chief rival to the UC.

New elections were scheduled for 1989 but were postponed three times; the king said that extra time was needed for the economic-stabilization program to show results and generate public confidence. The elections finally took place in two stages in 1993: the first for election of party candidates, and the second for trade-union and professional-association candidates. The final tally showed 195 seats for center-right (royalist) candidates, to 120 for the Democratic-bloc opposition. As a result, coalition government became necessary. The two leading opposition parties, however—the Socialist Union of Popular Forces (USFP) and the Istiqlal—refused to participate, claiming election irregularities. Opposition from members of these parties plus the Kutla Bloc, a new party

formed from the merger of several minor parties, blocked legislative action until 1994. At that point, the entire opposition bloc walked out of the Legislature and announced a boycott of the government.

King Hassan resolved the crisis by appointing then–USFP leader Abdellatif Filali as the new prime minister, thus bringing the opposition into the government. The king continued with this method of political reconciliation by appointing the new head of the USFP, Abderrahmane Youssoufi, to the position after the latter's return from political exile in 1998.

Previously, in 1992, voters had approved a new Constitution in a referendum. Its main provisions are a stated commitment to human rights, transfer of responsibility for cabinet appointments from the king to the prime minister, and the establishment of a Constitutional Council with the power to arbitrate parliamentary disputes. Also, 20 was set as the minimum voting age.

A national referendum in 1996 endorsed several constitutional amendments. One of them established a bicameral national legislature, the assembly, to replace the existing unicameral one. Members of the lower house would be elected directly; the upper chamber (Senate) would be two-thirds elected and one-third appointed by the king.

## FOREIGN RELATIONS

During his long reign, King Hassan II served effectively in mediating the long-running Arab–Israeli conflict. He took an active part in the negotiations for the 1979 Egyptian–Israeli peace treaty and for the treaty between Israel and Jordan in 1994. For these services he came to be viewed by the United States and by European powers as an impartial mediator. However, his absolute rule and suppression of human rights at home caused difficulties with Europe. The European Union suspended $145 million in aid in 1992; it was restored only after Hassan had released long-time political prisoners and pardoned 150 alleged Islamic militants. In 1995, Morocco became the second African country, after Tunisia, to be granted associate status in the EU.

Thus far, Morocco's only venture in "imperial politics" has been in the Western Sahara. This California-size desert territory, formerly a Spanish protectorate and then a colony after 1912, was never a part of the modern Moroccan state. Its only connection is historical—it was the headquarters and starting point for the Almoravid dynasty, camel-riding nomads who ruled western North Africa and southern Spain in the eleventh century. But the presence of so much empty land, along with millions of tons of phosphate rock and potential oil fields, encouraged the king to "play international politics" in order to secure the territory. The 1975 Green March described in the "Theater of Conflict" essay of this book has been followed up by large-scale settlement of Moroccans there in the past two decades. Like the American West in the nineteenth century, it was Morocco's "last frontier." Moroccans were encouraged to move there, with government pledges of free land, tools, seeds, and equipment for farmers, as well as housing.

Since the 1976 partition, ownership of the Western Sahara has been challenged by the Polisario, an independence movement backed by Algeria. Acting under the aegis of its responsibility for decolonization and self-government of colonized peoples, the United Nations established a peacekeeping force for the Western Sahara (MINURSO) in 1991. A UN resolution thereafter called for a referendum that would give the population a choice between independence and full integration with Morocco. Voter registration would precede the referendum, in order to determine eligibility of voters.

A decade later, the referendum seems less and less likely to be held. King Hassan II unilaterally named the territory Morocco's newest province, and by 2001 Moroccan settlers formed a majority in the population of 244,593. In December 2001, French president Jacques Chirac made an official visit to Morocco and saluted the country for the development of its "southern provinces." Earlier, the United Nations had appointed former U.S. secretary of state James Baker as mediator between Morocco and the Polisario. After several failed attempts at mediation, Baker submitted a plan for postponement of the referendum until 2006. In the interim, the Sahrawis would elect an autonomous governing body, with its powers limited to local and provincial affairs. The voting list would include all residents. The Security Council approved the Baker plan. But in view of the extensive Moroccanization of the territory, its self-government under Sahrawi leadership remained highly unlikely. King Muhammad made his first visit there in 2002, receiving a thunderous welcome from the Moroccan settler population. Emphasizing its integration into the kingdom as its newest province, he approved offshore oil-exploration concessions and released 56 Sahrawi political prisoners as a "sign of affection for the sons of the Sahara."

## THE ECONOMY

Morocco has many of certain resources but too little of other, critical ones. It has two thirds of the world's known reserves of phosphate rock and is the top exporter of phosphates. The major thrust in industrial development is in phosphate-related industries. Access to deposits was one reason for Morocco's annexation of the Western Sahara, although to date there has been little extraction there due to the political conflict. The downturn in demand and falling prices in the global phosphates market brought on a debt crisis in the late 1980s. Increased phosphate demand globally and improved crop production following the end of several drought years have strengthened the economy. Gross domestic product grew by 6 percent in 2000 and was projected to increase to 8 percent in 2001.

The country also has important but undeveloped iron-ore deposits and a small but significant production of rare metals such as mercury, antimony, nickel, and lead. In the past, a major obstacle to development was the lack of oil resources. Prospects for oil improved in 2000 when the U.S. oil company Skidmore Energy was thought to have struck oil near Talsinnt, in the eastern Sahara. But the find, which the king had declared to be God's gift to Morocco, turned out to be mud. In 2001, the French oil company TotalFinaElf and Kerr-McGee of Texas were granted parallel concessions of 44,000 square miles offshore in Western Saharan waters near Dakhla.

Although recurring droughts have hampered improvement of the agricultural sector, it still accounts for 20 percent of gross domestic product and employs 50 percent of the labor force. Production varies widely from year to year, due to fluctuating rainfall. The cereals harvest of 2000–2001 was sufficient to boost GDP to the 8 percent figure. Better weather conditions and abundant rainfall in 2001 resulted in a 25 percent increase in agricultural output over the previous year.

The fisheries sector is equally important to the economy, with 2,175 miles of coastline and half a million square miles of territorial waters to draw from. Fisheries account for 16 percent of exports; annual production is approximately 1 million tons. The agreement with the European Union for associate status has been very beneficial to the industry. Morocco received $500 million in 1999–2001 from European countries in return for fishing rights for their vessels in Moroccan territorial waters.

But the economic outlook and social prospects remain bleak for most people. Although the birth rate has been sharply reduced, job prospects are limited for the large number of young Moroccans entering the labor force each year. They are emigrating to Europe in ever-increasing numbers, most of them to Spain (as the nearest European country). Many do not succeed, paying large sums to smugglers who ferry them across the Strait of Gibraltar in leaky, overcrowded, and unseaworthy boats, only to drown when the boats capsize. Many more are arrested and deported by Spanish authorities, usually to the Spanish port of Melilla on the African mainland, from whence they are marched across the border into Morocco.

## PROSPECTS

King Hassan II died in July 1999. The monarch had ruled his country for 38 years—the second-longest reign in the Middle East. Like King Hussein of Jordan, Hassan became identified with his country to such a degree that "Hassan was Morocco, and Morocco was Hassan." But unlike Jordan's ruler, Hassan combined religious with secular authority. Among his many titles was that of "Commander of the Faithful," and the affection felt for him by most Moroccans, particularly women and youth, was amply visible during his state funeral. His frequent reminders to the nation in speeches and broadcasts that "I am the person entrusted by God to lead you" clearly identified him in the public mind not only as their religious leader but also as head of the family.

The king's eldest son, Crown Prince Muhammad, succeeded him without incident as Muhammad VI. Morocco's new ruler began his reign with public commitments to reform human-rights protections and an effort to atone for some aspects of Hassan's autocratic rule. The king's declared commitment to human rights and political reform have been undercut to a large extent by the repressive structure inherited from his father. This structure, comprising the security services, army leaders, and a coterie of senior ministers, is a major obstacle to civil change. One of his first acts was the dismissal of longtime Interior Minister Driss Basri, considered the power behind the throne during Hassan II's reign. He was felt by most Moroccans to be in charge of everything from garbage collection to the torture of political prisoners, and even important foreign-policy decisions. But Basri's elaborate security apparatus was left largely intact.

Muhammad VI also publicly admitted the existence of the Tazmamat "death camp" and other camps in the Sahara, where rebel army officers and political prisoners were held, often for years and without trial or access to their families. (The family of General Oufkir, leader of the 1972 attempted coup who was later

| | | | | | | | | Bread riots; agreement with Libya for a federal union; the king unilaterally abrogates the 1984 treaty of union with Libya | Elections establish parliamentary government; King Hassan dies and is succeeded by King Muhammad VI |
|---|---|---|---|---|---|---|---|---|---|---|

The foundations of Moroccan nation are established by Idris I and II, with the capital at Fez
**788–790**

The Almoravid and Almohad dynasties, Morocco's "imperial period"
**1062–1147**

The current ruling dynasty, the Alawi, establishes its authority under Mulay Ismail
**1672**

Morocco is occupied and placed under French and Spanish protectorates
**1912**

Independence under King Muhammad V
**1956**

The accession of King Hassan II
**1961**

The Green March into the Western Sahara dramatizes Morocco's claim to the area
**1975**

Bread riots; agreement with Libya for a federal union; the king unilaterally abrogates the 1984 treaty of union with Libya
**1980s**

Elections establish parliamentary government; King Hassan dies and is succeeded by King Muhammad VI
**1990s**

**2000s**

King Muhammad VI works to improve human rights

The economic picture brightens

executed, were among those held, but they managed to escape.)[9] The new king also committed $3.8 million in compensation to the families of those who had been imprisoned.

The rise of Islamic fundamentalism as a political force is an obstacle to Muhammad VI's vision of Morocco. Hassan II kept fundamentalists on a tight rein. He suppressed the main Islamist movement, Adil wa Ihsan ("Justice and Charity"), and sent its leader to a mental institution. Hassan also used his religious credentials to pose as a fundamentalist leader of his people. Muhammad VI seems more willing to integrate the fundamentalists into the political structure. Recently he issued a "National Action Plan" guaranteeing rights for women, approving a free press, and promising other civil rights long absent from Moroccan society.

In March 2000, half a million people took to the streets to declare their support for the action plan. Independent, nongovernment newspapers appeared on the newsstands. The king's popularity soared as he traveled about the country to learn about problems at first hand, and he was hailed as the "king of the poor" by the people.

Early in 2001, the public mood changed sharply. The "Islamist" label provoked a violent counter-demonstration by hard-liners. The new independent newspapers were closed; they included *Le Journal*, Morocco's most popular French-language magazine. Adil wa Ihsan was denied a license to register as a political party. The head of the Moroccan Association for Human Rights was arrested and beaten, and riot police broke up demonstrations protesting the restrictions, arresting 800 persons. A police officer noted that "we don't

want the chaos of a second intifada," a reference to the current Palestinian uprising against Israel. But Muhammad VI struggled on. In December 2000, he announced an annual prize for services to human rights. The label "cool king on a hot throne" seemed a fitting one for Morocco's new ruler.[10]

Partly to ward off the fundamentalist threat, but also to placate Berber leaders (who have long felt excluded from the political process and marginalized as a culture group), the king in his July 2001 Speech from the Throne announced the formation of a Royal Institute for the Preservation of Berber Culture. He also directed the Ministry of Education to incorporate Tamazight, the principal Berber language, into the national educational curriculum.

**NOTES**

1. See David M. Hart, *Dadda 'Atta and His Forty Grandsons* (Cambridge, England: Menas Press, 1981), pp. 8–11. Dadda 'Atta was a historical figure, a minor saint or marabout.

2. Harold D. Nelson, ed., *Morocco, A Country Study* (Washington, D.C.: American University, Foreign Area Studies, 1978), p. 112.

3. The oldest property owned by the U.S. government abroad is the American Consulate in Tangier; a consul was assigned there in 1791. *Ibid.*, p. 40.

4. See David Woolman, *Rebels in the Rif: Abd 'al Krim and the Rif Rebellion* (Palo Alto, CA: Stanford University Press, 1968). On the Ait Waryaghar, see David M. Hart, *The Ait Waryaghar of the Moroccan Rif: An Ethnography and a History* (Tucson, AZ: University of Arizona Press,

1976). Abd 'al Krim had annihilated a Spanish army and set up a Republic of the Rif (1921–1926).

5. For a detailed description of protectorate tribal administration, see Robin Bidwell, *Morocco Under Colonial Rule* (London: Frank Cass, 1973).

6. He once said: "Morocco is a cow, the Qaids milk her while France holds the horns." Nelson, *op. cit.,* p. 53.

7. Mark Tessler, "Morocco: Institutional Pluralism and Monarchical Dominance," in W. I. Zartman, ed., *Political Elites in North Africa* (New York: Longman, 1982), p. 44.

8. Nelson, *op. cit.,* p. 205.

9. See Malika Oufkir, with Michele Fitoussi, *Stolen Lives: Twenty Years in a Desert Jail* (New York: Hyperion Books, 1999). Another prisoner, Ahmed Marzouki, recently published his memoir of life there. Entitled *Cell 10*, it has sold widely in Morocco.

10. Nicholas Pelham, in *The Christian Science Monitor* (December 14, 2000).

**DEVELOPMENT**

Other than certain rare metals, fisheries, and citrus exports to Europe at favorable terms under its associate membership, Morocco has few resources on which to base economic development. Oil discoveries in the Moroccan Sahara in 2000 proved abortive, and the large phosphate deposits in the Western Sahara have yet to be fully developed.

**FREEDOM**

The absence of respect for constitutional and human rights was standard practice during Hassan II's reign. Muhammad VI has closed the Saharan "death camps" that had held political prisoners for years without trial. The king's "national action plan" is particularly beneficial to women. It allocates 200 of the Assembly's 600 seats to women, restricts polygamy, raises the legal marriage age to 18, and gives women equal rights in inheritance. It is scheduled to become law when approved by the Assembly in its next session.

**HEALTH/WELFARE**

In October 2000, the International Labor Organization (ILO) ranked Morocco as the 3rd-highest country in the world, after China and India, in the exploitation of child labor. Moroccan children as young as 5, all girls, are employed in the carpet industry, working up to 10 hours per day weaving the carpets that are at present Morocco's major source of foreign currency. Weaving and other crafts employ children at the expense of their education. Over a million children are sent into the streets by their families every day, to earn what they can as shoeshine boys, windshield washers, and prostitutes.

**ACHIEVEMENTS**

Moroccans take pride in the fact that a Moroccan, Abdelkader Mouaziz, was the victor in 2000 in the 31st New York City Marathon. His 2-minute, 20-second finish ahead of his nearest competitor was one of the biggest margins in the race's history.

# Oman (Sultanate of Oman)

## GEOGRAPHY

*Area in Square Miles (Kilometers):* 82,009 (212,460) (about the size of Kansas)

*Capital (Population):* Muscat (400,000)

*Environmental Concerns:* rising soil salinity; beach pollution from oil spills; very limited freshwater

*Geographical Features:* central desert plain; rugged mountains in the north and south

*Climate:* coast, hot and humid; interior, hot and dry

## PEOPLE

### Population

*Total:* 2,623,000

*Annual Growth Rate:* 3.45%

*Rural/Urban Population Ratio:* 22/78

*Major Languages:* Arabic; English; Sheba

*Ethnic Makeup:* almost entirely Arab; small Baluchi, South Asian, and African groups

*Religions:* 75% Ibadi Muslim; remainder Sunni Muslim, Shia Muslim, some Hindu

### Health

*Life Expectancy at Birth:* 70 years (male); 74 years (female)

*Infant Mortality Rate (Ratio):* 22.5/1,000

*Physicians Available (Ratio):* 1/852

### Education

*Adult Literacy Rate:* nearly 80%

## COMMUNICATION

*Telephones:* 220,000 main lines

*Daily Newspaper Circulation:* 31 per 1,000 people

*Televisions:* 711 per 1,000 people

*Internet Service Provider:* 1 (2000)

## TRANSPORTATION

*Highways in Miles (Kilometers):* 20,369 (32,800)

*Railroads in Miles (Kilometers):* none

*Usable Airfields:* 143

*Motor Vehicles in Use:* 347,000

## GOVERNMENT

*Type:* monarchy; the monarch's absolute power is limited by the 1996 Basic Law

*Independence Date:* 1650 (expulsion of the Portuguese)

*Head of State/Government:* Sultan and Prime Minister Qabus ibn Said Al Said is both head of state and head of government

*Political Parties:* none

*Suffrage:* extended in 2001 to 175,000 male and female Omanis for elected Majlis al-Shura (Consultative Council)

## MILITARY

*Military Expenditures (% of GDP):* 13%

*Current Disputes:* the boundary with the United Arab Emirates has not been bilaterally defined; section in the Musandam Peninsula is an administrative boundary

## ECONOMY

*Currency ($ U.S. Equivalent):* 0.385 rial = $1

*Per Capita Income/GDP:* $7,700/$19.6 billion

*GDP Growth Rate:* 4.6%

*Inflation Rate:* -0.8%

*Labor Force:* 850,000

*Natural Resources:* petroleum; copper; asbestos; marble; limestone; chromium; gypsum; natural gas

*Agriculture:* dates; limes; bananas; alfalfa; vegetables; camels; cattle; fish

*Industry:* crude-oil production and refining; natural-gas production; construction; cement; copper

*Exports:* $11.1 billion (primary partners Japan, China, Thailand)

*Imports:* $4.5 billion (primary partners United Arab Emirates, Japan, United Kingdom)

 http://lcweb2.loc.gov/frd/cs/omtoc.htm
http://www.oman.org/

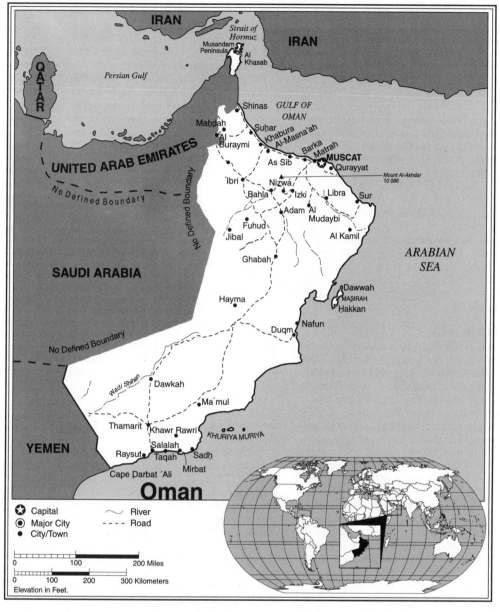

Oman

- ★ Capital
- ◉ Major City
- ● City/Town
- ～ River
- ---- Road

0  100  200 Miles
0  100  200  300 Kilometers
Elevation in Feet.

## OMAN

The Sultanate of Oman was, at least until about 1970, one of the least-known countries in the world. Yet it is a very old country with a long history of contact with the outside world. Merchants from Oman had a near monopoly on the trade in frankincense and myrrh. Oman-built, shallow-draught, broad-beamed ships called dhows crisscrossed the Indian Ocean, trading with India and the Far East.

In the twentieth century, Oman became important to the outside world for two primary reasons: it began producing oil in the 1960s; and it has a strategic location on the Strait of Hormuz, the passageway for supertankers carrying Middle Eastern oil to the industrialized nations. Eighty percent of Japan's oil needs passes through Hormuz, as does 60 percent of Western Europe's. A Swiss journalist called the Omanis "sentinels of the Gulf" because they watch over this vital traffic.

### GEOGRAPHY

Oman is the third-largest country in the Arabian Peninsula, after Yemen and Saudi Arabia. However, the population is small, and large areas of land are uninhabited or sparsely populated. The geographic diversity—rugged mountains, vast gravelly plains, and deserts—limits large-scale settlement. The bulk of the population is centered in the Batinah coastal plain, which stretches from the United Arab Emirates border south to the capital, Muscat. Formerly this area was devoted to fishing and agriculture; but with the rapid development of Oman under the current sultan, it has become heavily industrialized, with extensive commerce. The ancient system of *falaj*—underground irrigation channels that run for miles, bringing water downhill by gravity flow—has made farming possible, although the agricultural sector has been adversely affected in recent years by prolonged drought. Oman's southern Dhofar Province is more fertile and productive than the rest of the country, due to monsoon rains. In addition to citrus and other tropical fruits, Oman is the major world source of frankincense, gum from a small tree that grows wild and has been prized since ancient times.

Behind Oman's coast is the Jabal al-Akhdar ("Green Mountain"), a spine of rugged mountains with peaks over 10,000 feet. The mountains form several disconnected chains, interspersed with deep, narrow valleys where village houses hang like eagles' nests from the mountaintops, above terraced gardens and palm groves.

Most of Oman's oil wells are located in the interior of the country. The interior is a broad, hilly plain dotted with oasis vil-lages, each one a fortress with thick walls to keep out desert raiders. The stony plain eventually becomes the Rub al-Khali ("Empty Quarter"), the great uninhabited desert of southeastern Arabia.

Omani territory includes the Musandam Peninsula, at the northeastern tip of Arabia projecting into the Strait of Hormuz. The peninsula and the neighboring Midha oasis are physically separated from the rest of Oman by U.A.E. territory. In 1995, the Omani border with Yemen was formally demarcated in accordance with a UN–sponsored 1992 agreement. The oasis of Buraimi, on the Oman/Saudi Arabia/U.A.E. border, is currently under U.A.E. control, although it is claimed by both Saudi Arabia and Yemen. The surrounding desert hinterland is shared by the three states and remains undefined.

### HISTORY

As was the case elsewhere in Arabia, the early social structure of Oman consisted of a number of tribal groups. Many of them were and still are nomadic (Bedouin), while others became settled farmers and herders centuries ago. The groups spent much of their time feuding with one another. Occasionally, several would join in an alliance against others, but none of them recognized any higher authority than their leaders.

In the seventh century A.D., the Omanis were converted to Islam. They developed their own form of Islam, however, called Ibadism, meaning "Community of the Just," a branch of Shia Islam. The Ibadi peoples elect their own leader, called an Imam. The Ibadi Imams do not have to be descendants of the prophet Muhammad, as do the Imams in the main body of Shia Muslims. The Ibadi community believes that anyone, regardless of background, can be elected Imam, as long as the individual is pious, just, and capable. If no one is available who meets those requirements, the office may remain vacant.

Ibadi Imams ruled interior Oman with the support of family shaykhs until the eighteenth century. Well before then, however, coastal Oman was being opened up to foreign powers. The Portuguese captured Muscat in the 1500s for use as a stopping place for their ships on the trade route to India. (An Omani served as navigator to Portuguese admiral Vasco da Gama in his voyage across the Indian Ocean to India.) They built two great forts guarding the entrance to Muscat harbor, forts that still stand, giving the town its picturesque appearance. The Portuguese were finally driven out in 1650. Since that time, Oman has not been ruled directly by any foreign power.

The current ruling dynasty in Oman is the Al Bu Said Dynasty. It has been in power since 1749, when a chief named Ahmad ibn Said defeated an Iranian invasion and established his authority over most of Oman. But, for most of the period, Oman actually had two rulers—a sultan ruling in Muscat and an Imam ruling in the interior at the same time.

The most successful Omani sultan before the twentieth century was Said ibn Sultan (1804–1856). He added Dhofar Province and Zanzibar, on the East African coast, to Omani territory. Sultan Said had good relations with Britain. He signed a treaty with the British that stated, "the friendship between our two states shall remain unshook to the end of time." The sultan also signed a friendship treaty with the United States in 1833; and in 1836, to the surprise of the New York Port authorities, an Omani ship docked in New York harbor. Its captain said that the sultan had sent him to get to know the Americans whom he had heard so much about and to arrange trade contacts. Friendship between the United States and Oman operates on a different basis today. Now it is the Omanis who allow the Americans the use of the British-built Masirah Island base and share responsibility for patrolling the Strait of Hormuz, the strategic entrance point for the strife-ridden Persian Gulf. But this friendship has its roots in Sultan Said's mission.

After Said's death, a number of ethnic, tribal, and religious differences re-asserted themselves, and Oman lost its importance in regional affairs. Its territory was again restricted to its small corner of southeastern Arabia. The opening of the Suez Canal in 1869 diverted shipping to new Red Sea routes, and ships no longer called at Muscat harbor. Piracy and the slave trade, both of which had provided revenues for the sultan, were prohibited by international law. For the rest of the 1800s and most of the 1900s, Oman sank back into isolation, forgotten by the world. Only Britain paid the Omanis any attention, giving the sultan a small subsidy in the event that Oman might be of some future use to it.

In the early twentieth century, the Imams of inner Oman and the sultans ruling in Muscat came to a complete parting of the ways. In 1920, a treaty between the two leaders provided that the sultan would not interfere in the internal affairs of inner Oman. Relations were reasonably smooth until 1951, when Britain recognized the independence of the Sultanate of Muscat-Oman, as it was then called, and withdrew its advisers. Subsequently, the Imam declared inner Oman to be a separate state from the sultanate. A number of Arab states supported the Imam, on the grounds that the sultan was a British puppet. Conflict between the Imam and the sultan dragged on until 1960, when the sultan finally reestablished his authority.

Oman's ruler for nearly four decades in the twentieth century was Sultan Said ibn Taimur (1932–1970). The most interesting aspect of his reign was the way in which he stopped the clock of modernization. Oil was discovered in 1964 in inland Oman; within a few years, wealth from oil royalties began pouring in. But the sultan was afraid that the new wealth would corrupt his people. He refused to spend money except for the purchase of arms and a few personal luxuries such as an automobile, which he liked to drive on the only paved road in Salalah. He would not allow the building of schools, houses, roads, or hospitals for his people. Before 1970, there were only 16 schools in all of Oman. The sole hospital was the American mission in Muscat, established in the 1800s by Baptist missionaries; and all 10 of Oman's qualified doctors worked abroad, because the sultan did not trust modern medicine. The few roads were rough caravan tracks; many areas of the country, such as the Musandam Peninsula, were inaccessible.

The sultan required the city gates of Muscat to be closed and locked three hours after sunset; no one could enter or leave the city after that. Flashlights were prohibited, since they were a modern invention; so were sunglasses and European shoes. Anyone found on the streets at night without a lighted kerosene lantern could be imprisoned. In the entire country, there were only about 1,000 automobiles; to import a car, one had to have the sultan's personal permission. On the darker side, slavery was still a common practice. Women were almost never seen in public and had to be veiled from head to foot if they so much as walked to a neighbor's house to visit. And on the slightest pretext, prisoners could be locked up in the old Portuguese fort at Muscat and left to rot.

As the 1960s came to an end, there was more and more unrest in Oman. The opposition centered around Qabus ibn Said, the sultan's son. Qabus had been educated in England. When he came home, his father shut him up in a house in Salalah, a town far from Muscat, and refused to give him any responsibilities. He was afraid of his son's "Western ideas."

On July 23, 1970, supporters of Crown Prince Qabus overthrew the sultan, and Qabus succeeded him. Sultan Qabus ibn Said brought Oman into the twentieth century in a hurry. The old policy of isolation was reversed.

(UN photo/A221)

Boys study the Koran at a village in Oman. When Qabus ibn Said came to power in 1970, replacing his father, he targeted education, health care, and transportation as prime development areas.

Qabus also ended a long-running rebellion in Dhofar. The rebellion had developed originally from the social and economic neglect of the province by the Taimur government. The Dhofar rebels were supported and armed by the then–People's Democratic Republic of Yemen, Oman's neighbor. Relations between the two countries remained poor even after the sultan had crushed the rebellion in 1975, with the help of troops from Britain and Iran. The unification of the two Yemens in 1990 improved prospects for an Omani–Yemeni reconciliation, which was confirmed by the 1992 border agreement and the 1995 demarcation.

## OMANI SOCIETY

Oman today is a land in flux, its society poised between the traditional past and a future governed increasingly by technology. An Omani business executive or industrial chief may wear a Western suit and tie to an appointment, but more than likely he will arrive for his meeting in a *dishdasha* (the traditional full-length robe worn by Gulf Arabs), with either a turban or an embroidered skullcap to complete the outfit. A ceremonial dagger called *kanjar* will certainly hang from his belt or

sash. He will have a cellular phone pressed to his right ear and a digital watch on his wrist, courtesy of Oman's extensive trade with Japan. Older Omani women are also traditional in costume, covered head to toe with the enveloping *chador* and their faces (except for the eyes) hidden behind the black *batula,* the eagle-like mask common in the region. But increasingly their daughters and younger sisters opt for Western clothing, with only headscarves to distinguish them as Muslims.

In social, economic, and even political areas of Omani life, Qabus has brought about changes that have proceeded at a dizzying pace during his three-decade rule. Education, health care, and roads were his three top priorities when he took office. By the 2001–2002 school year, 542,063 students were enrolled in the country's 1,000 state schools. The enrollment is 48.7 percent female. Sultan Qabus University, which opened in 1986 with a student body of 3,000, now has 6,000 students. These efforts, along with numerous adult-education programs, have increased Oman's literacy rate to 80 percent.

The sultan has also begun the process of replacing authoritarian rule by representative government. In 1996, his silver-

The Portuguese seize Muscat and build massive fortresses to guard the harbor
**1587–1588**

The Al Bu Said Dynasty is established; extends Omani territory
**1749**

The British establish a de facto protectorate; the slave trade is supposedly ended
**late 1800s**

Independence
**1951**

Sultan Said ibn Taimur is deposed by his son, Prince Qabus
**1970**

With British and Iranian help, Sultan Qabus ends the Dhofar rebellion
**1975**

Oman joins the Gulf Cooperation Council

Sultan Qabus sets up a Consultative Assembly as the first step toward democratization
**1980s**

The sultan focuses on expanding Oman's industrial base
**1990s**

**2000s**

Democratization continues with the extension of suffrage

WHO rates Oman's health-care system 8th best in the world

Oman supports the coalition against terrorism

anniversary year, he issued a Basic Law setting up a Majlis al-Shura (Council of State). Its 82 members are appointed by the ruler to represent Oman's provinces (*wilayats*) and cities. The Majlis has neither veto nor legislative powers, but it acts as an advisory body in the drafting of laws and the national budget. In 1998, an amendment to the Basic Law established local and municipal councils, in order to exercise internal authority in these areas.

## THE ECONOMY

Oman began producing and exporting oil in limited quantities in 1967. The industry was greatly expanded after the accession of Sultan Qabus. It is managed by a national corporation, Petroleum Development Oman (PDO). Oil production in the 1990s reached 900,000 barrels per day but was reduced to 860,000 bpd in 2000–2001, in accordance with OPEC production cuts. Oman's oil reserves are 5.7 billion barrels. Natural-gas reserves are 29.3 trillion cubic feet. The new liquefied natural gas (LNG) plant at Qalhat produced 6.6 million tons of LNG in 2001. Some 4 million tons were exported to South Korea in 2000; it was the largest single gas-export contract arranged with two state companies.

In its search for ways to supplement its oil income, Oman in 1996 formed a Caspian Sea Consortium with Russia, Kazakhstan, and several U.S. oil companies to link its refinery with Kazakh oil fields via new pipelines. Consortium ownership is divided between Russia (24 percent), Kazakhstan (19 percent), and Oman (7 percent), with the balance being held by the U.S. companies Chevron, Lukoil, and Arco. In 2000, PDO signed a supplemental agreement with Arco and Exxon for oil exploration in Kazakhstan's part of the Caspian Sea.

Barely 2 percent of Oman's land is arable. Rainfall averages two to four inches annually except in monsoon-drenched Dhofar, and recent drought has largely dried up the long-established falaj system. The interior oases and Dhofar provide for intensive cultivation of dates. They also grow coconuts and various other fruits. Agriculture provides 35 percent of non-oil exports and employs 12 percent of the labor force.

The fishing industry employs 10 percent of the working population, but obsolete equipment and lack of canning and freezing plants have severely limited the catch in the past. Another problem is the unwillingness of Omani fishermen to move into commercial production; most of them catch just enough fish for their own use. The Oman Fish Company was formed in 1987 to develop fishery resources, financing the purchase by fishermen of aluminum boats powered by outboard motors to replace the seaworthy but slow traditional wooden dhows. Completion of the enlarged fishing harbor at Raysut, along with a $34 million fish-processing plant at Rusayl, will enable the current Five-Year Plan to achieve a 5.6 percent increase in the fishing sector by 2003.

## FOREIGN RELATIONS

Oman joined with other Arab countries in opening links with Israel after its Oslo agreements with the Palestine Liberation Organization for Palestinian autonomy and the 1994 Jordan–Israel peace treaty. However, the freeze in Arab–Israeli relations ordered by the Arab League caused Oman to cancel the proposed Israeli trade mission in Muscat.

As a member of the Gulf Cooperation Council, Oman has become active in regional affairs, a role emphasized by its strategic location. Its long history of deal-

ings with the United States—a relationship dating back to Andrew Jackson's presidency—has made Oman a natural partner in U.S. efforts to promote stability in the Gulf region. In 1980, Oman granted American military and naval personnel use of its Masirah Island and other military bases and the right to station troops and equipment there. In turn, the United States has provided new equipment to the Omani armed forces and built base housing for American personnel. During the Iran–Iraq War of 1980–1988, the country provided logistical support for U.S. warships escorting oil tankers in the Gulf to protect them from Iranian attacks, and U.S. jet fighters were based in Oman during the 1991 Gulf War.

After the September 11, 2001, terrorist attacks on the World Trade Center and the Pentagon, Sultan Qabus took the lead among the Gulf states in supporting the U.S.–led international coalition against terrorism. In October, 20,000 British troops arrived in Muscat to supplement the U.S. forces already there. The United States also reached agreement for a $1.1 billion arms sale to Oman. It included 12 F-16 fighter aircraft, Sidewinder air-to-air missiles, and Harpoon antiship missiles.

---

## DEVELOPMENT

Vision Oman 2020, the sultan's blueprint for long-term growth, sets among its objectives increasing economic diversity to reduce dependence on oil, developing a competitive private sector producing manufactured goods for export, and Omanization of the labor force. With one-half million youths entering the job market by 2005, reducing dependence on foreign workers is critical.

## FREEDOM

Although Qabus is, both in theory and practice, an absolute ruler and governs by royal decree, in 1996 he issued a Basic Law that provides for an appointed Council of State (including a few women members) and a Majlis al-Shura, also appointed, which may draft legislation on social issues for his approval. If approved, the draft then becomes law. Unlike in other Gulf states, most Omani women are educated, and many play an active part in national life.

## HEALTH/WELFARE

Mobile health units that travel to remote areas have helped bring about a steep decline in infant mortality rates, from 34.3 per 1,000 in 1995 to the current 22.5 per 1,000. In addition, vigorous family-planning programs have lowered the birth rate from an astronomical 3.36% (in 1998) to 2.5%. Oman's health-care system was rated 8th best in the world by the World Health Organization in 2000.

## ACHIEVEMENTS

A new Iranian-built power plant began operations in 1999 in Oman, meeting domestic needs for electricity. Oman is also self-sufficient in cement and textiles, most of the latter made in factories located in the Rusayl free-trade zone near Muscat. The zone now has more than 60 industries and produces $60 million in finished goods, generating $24 million in exports.

# Qatar (State of Qatar)

## GEOGRAPHY

*Area in Square Miles (Kilometers):*
4,400 (11,400) (about the
size of Connecticut)
*Capital (Population):* Doha
(340,000)
*Environmental Concerns:* limited
natural freshwater supplies;
increasing dependence on
large-scale desalination facilities
*Geographical Features:* mostly
flat and barren desert covered
with loose sand and gravel
*Climate:* desert; hot and dry;
humid and sultry summers

## PEOPLE

### Population
*Total:* 769,000
*Annual Growth Rate:* 3.18%
*Rural/Urban Population Ratio:* 8/92
*Major Languages:* Arabic;
English widely used
*Ethnic Makeup:* 40% Arab;
18% Pakistani; 18% Indian;
10% Iranian; 14% others
*Religions:* 95% Muslim; 5%
others

### Health
*Life Expectancy at Birth:* 72
years (male); 77 years (female)
*Infant Mortality Rate (Ratio):*
21.4/1,000
*Physicians Available (Ratio):* 1/793

### Education
*Adult Literacy Rate:* 79.4%

## COMMUNICATION

*Telephones:* 150,500 main lines
*Daily Newspaper Circulation:* 143
per 1,000 people
*Televisions:* 451 per 1,000 people
*Internet Service Provider:* 1 (2000)

## TRANSPORTATION

*Highways in Miles (Kilometers):*
764 (1,230)
*Railroads in Miles (Kilometers):* none
*Usable Airfields:* 4
*Motor Vehicles in Use:* 183,000

## GOVERNMENT

*Type:* traditional monarchy
*Independence Date:* September 3, 1971
(from the United Kingdom)
*Head of State/Government:* Emir Hamad
bin Khalifa al-Thani; Prime Minister
Abdallah bin Khalifa al-Thani
*Political Parties:* none
*Suffrage:* limited to municipal elections

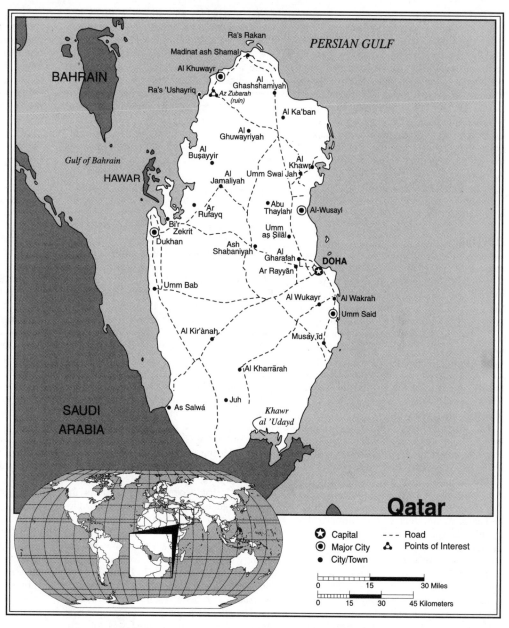

Qatar

## MILITARY

*Military Expenditures (% of GDP):* 10%
*Current Disputes:* none; territorial dispute
with Bahrain settled in 2001 by the
International Court of Justice

## ECONOMY

*Currency ($ U.S. Equivalent):* 3.64 rials =
$1 (fixed rate)
*Per Capita Income/GDP:* $20,300/$15.1
billion
*GDP Growth Rate:* 4%
*Inflation Rate:* 2.5%
*Labor Force:* 233,000

*Natural Resources:* petroleum; natural gas;
fish
*Agriculture:* fruits; vegetables; poultry;
dairy products; beef; fish
*Industry:* crude-oil production and
refining; fertilizers; petrochemicals;
steel reinforcing bars; cement
*Exports:* $9.8 billion (primary partners
Japan, Singapore, South Korea)
*Imports:* $3.8 billion (primary partners
United Kingdom, Japan, Germany)

 http://lcweb2.loc.gov/frd/cs/
qatoc.html
http://www.qatar-info.com/

# QATAR

Qatar is a shaykhdom on the eastern (Gulf) coast of Arabia. It is the second-smallest Middle Eastern state, after Bahrain; but due to its oil wealth, it has an extremely high per capita annual income. Before 1949, when its oil exports began, there were about 20,000 Qataris, all descendants of peoples who had migrated to the coast centuries ago in search of a dependable water supply. Since then, rapid economic growth has attracted workers and residents from other Arab countries and distant Muslim states such as Pakistan. As a result, Qatar has a high number of immigrants and expatriates, which makes for some tension.

## HISTORY

Although the peninsula has been inhabited since 4000 B.C., little is known of its history before the nineteenth century. At one time, it was ruled by the al-Khalifa family, the current rulers of Bahrain. It became part of the Ottoman Empire formally in 1872, but the Turkish garrison was evacuated during World War I. The Ottomans earlier had recognized Shaykh Qassim al-Thani, head of the important al-Thani family, as emir of Qatar, and the British followed suit when they established a protectorate after the war.

The British treaty with the al-Thanis was similar to ones made with other shaykhs in Arabia and the Persian Gulf in order to keep other European powers out of the area and to protect their trade and communications links with India. In 1916, the British recognized Shaykh Abdullah al-Thani, grandfather of the current ruler, as ruler of Qatar and promised to protect the territory from outside attack either by the Ottomans or overland by hostile Arabian groups. In return, Shaykh al-Thani agreed not to enter into any relationship with any other foreign government and to accept British political advisers.

Qatar remained a tranquil British protectorate until the 1950s, when oil exports began. Since then, the country has developed rapidly, though not to the extent of producing the dizzying change visible in other oil-producing Arab states.

## INDEPENDENCE

Qatar became independent in 1971, and the ruler, Shaykh Ahmad al-Thani, took the title of emir. Disagreements within the ruling family led the emir's cousin, Shaykh Khalifa, to seize power in 1972. Khalifa made himself prime minister as well as ruler and initiated a major program of social and economic development, which his cousin had opposed.

Shaykh Khalifa limited the privileges of the ruling family. There were more than 2,000 al-Thanis, and most of them had been paid several thousand dollars a month whether or not they worked. Khalifa reduced their allowances and appointed some nonmembers of the royal family to the Council of Ministers, the state's chief executive body. In 1992, he set up a Consultative Council of 30 members to advise the cabinet on proposed legislation and budgetary matters. Subsequently, the cabinet itself was enlarged, with new ministries of Islamic affairs, finance, economy, and industry and trade. While the majority of cabinet and Consultative Council members belonged to the royal family, the appointment of a number of nonfamily members to both these organizations heralded the "quiet revolution" toward power sharing to which Shaykh Khalifa was committed.

## FOREIGN RELATIONS

Because of its small size, great wealth, and proximity to regional conflicts, Qatar is vulnerable to outside intervention. The government fears especially that the example of the Iranian Shia Revolution may bring unrest to its own Shia Muslim population. After the discovery of a Shia plot to overthrow the government of neighboring Bahrain in 1981, Qatari authorities deported several hundred Shia Qataris of Iranian origin. But thus far, the government has avoided singling out the Shia community for heavy-handed repression, preferring to concentrate its efforts on economic and social progress. On the 10th anniversary of Qatar's independence, the emir said that "economic strength is the strongest guarantee that safeguards the independence of nations, their sovereignty, rights and dignity."[1]

Fears of a possible attack by Iran led the country to sign a bilateral defense agreement with Saudi Arabia in 1982. The Iraqi invasion of Kuwait exposed Saudi military weakness, and, as a result, Qatar turned to the United States for its defense. A Qatar official noted, "Saudi Arabia was the protector, but the war showed that the emperor had no clothes."[2] However, the close alliance has not brought full acceptance of U.S. Middle East policy. The emir joined other Arab leaders in criticizing Israel and its principal ally for repression of the renewed Palestinian intifada (uprising) after the collapse of the 1993 Oslo agreements for Palestinian self-determination. In 2000, the Israeli trade mission in Qatar, the last one active for the Gulf states, was ordered closed.

The continued U.S./UN sanctions imposed on Iraq after the Gulf War drew increased opposition among Qataris, as the extent of harm to the Iraqi civilian population became more evident. Qatar was the first Gulf state to criticize openly U.S. and British air attacks on Iraq.

However, the expanded U.S. military presence in the Gulf, and the Qatari government's fears of a threat to its territory by a remilitarized Iraq, resulted in 2000 in the establishment in the country of the largest American military base outside the continental United States. The base was placed on full military alert in July 2000, after the attack on the U.S. destroyer *Cole* in Aden (Yemen) harbor. The emir also completed the $1 billion air base at Al-Ubeid, which holds up to 100 fighter aircraft (Qatar's total air force consists of 10 aircraft). An attack in November 2001 by a lone gunman on guards at the base was a reminder of the unpopularity of the U.S. military presence in the Gulf region despite its low profile. But when he was criticized by Islamic opposition leaders with "Christianizing" the country by making the base available to the United States, the emir responded: "We intend to be essential to the American presence in the Gulf. What do we get in exchange? We don't need to spend a lot of money on defense, we'll be attractive to U.S. businessmen, and we'll get international status and prestige."[3]

Inasmuch as Iraq was apparently not involved or charged with complicity in the September 11, 2001, terrorist attacks on the United States, the Qatari government felt less constrained about actively participating in the international coalition being formed to combat global terrorism than it had before the attacks. The American military and air bases in Qatar went on full alert for the invasion of Afghanistan, and the troops were reinforced by U.S. special forces and fighter aircraft.

Qatar's main foreign-policy concern has involved the islands of Hawar and Fishat al-Duble, which lie off of its northwest coast. Ownership was disputed with Bahrain, which controlled them under arrangements made in the 1930s, when both countries were British protectorates. In 1992, Qatar unilaterally extended its territorial waters to 12 nautical miles to bring the islands and adjacent seabed under Qatari sovereignty. Bahrain filed a complaint with the International Court of Justice (the ICJ, or World Court). In 2001, the World Court confirmed Bahraini ownership of the islands and adjacent territorial waters. The Qatari emir had said previously that he would not accept World Court arbitration, but following the issuance of the Court's decision, he agreed to accept Bahraini sovereignty. Under the terms of the Court's ruling, Qatar was awarded sovereignty over Zabarah and Janan Islands, and the elevation at low tide of Fasht and Dubal. Qatari ships were also guaranteed the right of unobstructed passage through the Bahrain territorial sea.

| Britain recognizes Shaykh Abdullah al-Thani as emir **1916** | The start of oil production in Qatar **1949** | An abortive federation with Bahrain and the Trucial States (U.A.E.), followed by independence **1971** | The ruler is deposed by Shaykh Khalifa **1972** | Qatar condemns the Iraqi invasion of Kuwait and expels resident Palestinians; Crown Prince Hamad al-Thani deposes his father and takes over as emir **1990s** |

**2000s**

The World Court decides a territorial dispute in favor of Bahrain

Qatari-funded Al Jazeerah news station achieves global prominence

## THE ECONOMY

The Qatari economy is currently based on oil, but in the very near future, oil will be replaced by natural gas as its major mineral resource. Until recently, the Qatari oil industry was considered to be in a state of terminal decline, with dwindling reserves and low production. New discoveries and production-sharing agreements have revived the industry. Proven oil reserves are sufficient for 23 years at current rates of production.

Depletion of water supplies due to heavy demand and dependence on outdated desalination plants for its fresh water has prompted the country to undertake some innovative food-production projects. One such project, begun in 1988, uses solar energy and seawater to cultivate food crops on sand. As a result of such projects, Qatar produces sufficient food both to meet domestic needs and to export vegetables to neighboring states.

## SOCIETAL CHANGES

Qatar was originally settled by nomadic peoples, and their influence is still strong. Traditional Bedouin values, such as honesty, hospitality, pride, and courage, have carried over into modern times.

Most Qataris belong to the strict puritanical Wahhabi sect of Islam, which is also dominant in Saudi Arabia. They are similar to Saudis in their conservative outlook, and Qatar generally defers to its larger neighbor in foreign policy. There are, however, significant social differences between Qataris and Saudis. Western movies may be shown in Qatar, for example, but not in Saudi Arabia. Furthermore, Qatar does not have religious police or "morals squads" to enforce Islamic conventions, and foreigners may purchase alcoholic beverages legally.

Qatar also differs from its Arab peninsular neighbors and the Arab world generally in permitting free discussion in the media of issues generally suppressed by Arab rulers. Following his accession to the throne, the new emir abolished press censorship and eliminated the Information Ministry from his cabinet. In 1997, the government licensed the satellite news channel Al Jazeerah ("Peninsula" in Arabic). As the only uncensored news station in the Arab world, it not only provides freewheeling coverage, CNN-fashion, of ongoing conflicts such as the Palestinian intifada, but also of repressive measures taken by Arab rulers. As one writer noted, "Its reporters have no qualms about challenging today's Arab rulers . . . they openly challenge the sycophantic tone of the state-run Arab media and the quiescence of the mainstream Arab press, both of which play down controversy and dissent."[4] Its main themes, however, are anti-Americanism and anti-Zionism.

The most significant societal change in Qatar involves the position of women. The first school for girls opened there in 1956. But change in women's rights and roles has accelerated in recent years. In 1998, the new emir, who had deposed his father in 1995 while the latter was vacationing in Switzerland, granted women the right to vote and to run for and hold public office.

Roughly 30 percent of Qatari women are employed in the labor force, and many are not only educated but also well-qualified professionally. Unlike their sisters in some other Gulf states, they drive cars, work in offices, juggle careers and family responsibilities. As a Qatari female journalist told an interviewer: "It is not easy for a man to permit his wife to work, to appear on TV, to drive a car. We have special clubs for women, separate cinema areas, even women's banks, to reinforce each other."[5]

## INTERNAL POLITICS

Crown Prince Shaykh Hamad bin Khalifa's "palace coup" was bloodless, although several attempts by supporters of the deposed ruler to overthrow his son have been thwarted. In July 1999, Shaykh Hamid al-Thani, the ruling emir's cousin and former chief of police, was arrested and brought back from his hiding place "somewhere abroad" for trial. He was charged with being the leader and organizer of the attempted coups. The ex-emir also agreed to return $2 billion in government funds that he had deposited abroad over the years in personal accounts.

The "quiet revolution" initiated by the new emir entered a new stage in March 1999, with elections for a Doha Central Municipal Council, the country's first public elections. The Council does not have executive powers, but it is intended as a transitional body between patriarchal rule and the establishment of an elected parliament. All Qataris over age 18 were allowed to vote, including women (who make up 44 percent of registered voters). Six women ran with 221 men for the Council's 29 seats.

## NOTES

1. Qatar News Agency (November 23, 1981).

2. Douglas Jehl, *The New York Times International* (July 20, 1997).

3. Mary Anne Weaver, "Democracy by Decree," *The New Yorker* (November 20, 2000), p. 57.

4. Fouad Ajami, "What the Muslim World Is Watching," *The New York Times Magazine* (November 18, 2001).

5. Weaver, *op cit.*

## DEVELOPMENT

Qatar's huge gas reserves are among the largest in the world, but are concentrated in a single field. They form the basis for ongoing economic development. New petrochemical and related fertilizer industries are beginning to diversify sources of revenue.

## FREEDOM

Since he deposed his father, the ruling emir has abolished press censorship, established Al Jazeerah as a service of uncensored news to the Arab world, and appointed younger members of the ruling family to replace his father's advisers and ministers.

## HEALTH/WELFARE

Qatar's first private hospital opened in 1996 and is now fully staffed by Qatari doctors and nurses, who have replaced expatriate medical personnel. Among the Arab states, Qatar has an unusually high ratio of physicians to population.

## ACHIEVEMENTS

Qatar played host to the World Trade Conference annual meeting in November 2001. Despite threats of disruption by activists opposed to WTO policies, the meeting opened on schedule, albeit under tight security. It produced a compromise agreement among the 144 member states on global-market reforms that will expedite free trade while protecting the interests of the poorer nations.

# Saudi Arabia (Kingdom of Saudi Arabia)

## GEOGRAPHY

*Area in Square Miles (Kilometers):*
756,785 (1,960,582) (about ⅕ the size of the United States)

*Capital (Population):* Riyadh (2,625,000)

*Environmental Concerns:* desertification; depletion of underground water resources; coastal pollution from oil spills

*Geographical Features:* mostly uninhabited sandy desert

*Climate:* harsh, dry desert, with great extremes of temperature

## PEOPLE

### Population

*Total:* 22,758,000

*Annual Growth Rate:* 3.2%

*Rural/Urban Population Ratio:* 16/84

*Major Languages:* Arabic; English widely used

*Ethnic Makeup:* 90% Arab; 10% Afro-Asian

*Religion:* 100% Muslim

### Health

*Life Expectancy at Birth:* 66 years (male); 70 years (female)

*Infant Mortality Rate (Ratio):* 51.2/1,000

*Physicians Available (Ratio):* 1/590

### Education

*Adult Literacy Rate:* 62.8%

## COMMUNICATION

*Telephones:* 2,900,000 main lines

*Daily Newspaper Circulation:* 54 per 1,000 people

*Televisions:* 257 per 1,000 people

*Internet Service Providers:* 42 (2001)

## TRANSPORTATION

*Highways in Miles (Kilometers):* 87,914 (146,524)

*Railroads in Miles (Kilometers):* 863 (1,390)

*Usable Airfields:* 205

*Motor Vehicles in Use:* 2,800,000

## GOVERNMENT

*Type:* hereditary monarchy

*Independence Date:* September 23, 1932 (unification)

*Head of State/Government:* King Fahd bin Abdal-Aziz al-Saud is titular head of state and head of government; de facto leader is Crown Prince Abdallah

*Political Parties:* none; prohibited

*Suffrage:* none

## MILITARY

*Military Expenditures (% of GDP):* 13%

*Current Disputes:* boundary with Yemen not fully defined; boundary with United Arab Emirates not final

## ECONOMY

*Currency ($ U.S. Equivalent):* 3.75 riyals = $1

*Per Capita Income/GDP:* $10,500/$232 billion

*GDP Growth Rate:* 4%

*Inflation Rate:* 0.5%

*Labor Force:* 7,000,000

*Unemployment Rate:* 14% for male Saudis

*Natural Resources:* petroleum; natural gas; iron ore; gold; copper

*Agriculture:* wheat; barley; tomatoes; melons; dates; citrus fruits; mutton; chickens; eggs; milk

*Industry:* crude-oil production; petroleum refining; basic petrochemicals; cement; construction; fertilizer; plastics

*Exports:* $81.2 billion (primary partners Japan, United States, South Korea)

*Imports:* $30.1 billion (primary partners United States, Japan, Germany)

 http://lcweb2.loc.gov/frd/cs/satoc.html
http://www.saudinf.com/main/start.htm

## SAUDI ARABIA

The Kingdom of Saudi Arabia is the geographical giant of the Arabian Peninsula. It is also a giant in the world economy, because of its oil. To many people, the name Saudi Arabia is a synonym for oil wealth. Indeed, its huge oil reserves, large financial surpluses from oil production, and ability to use oil as a political weapon (as in the 1973 embargo) enable the country to play an important part in international as well as regional affairs.

Saudi Arabia's population is small in relation to the country's size and is heavily urbanized. Urban growth has been very rapid, considering that only 1 percent of the land can be used for agriculture and all employment opportunities are in the cities or in the oil-producing regions. The kingdom has relied strongly on expatriate workers, skilled as well as unskilled, in its development. The economic dislocation of the Gulf War, along with the support given Iraq by Palestinians and the government of Yemen, led to the expulsion of nearly 1 million foreign workers, most of them Palestinians and Yemenis. But due to the unwillingness of most Saudis to take on low-paying work that seems to be below them professionally, the government has had to continue its dependence on expatriates. Some 67 percent of government jobs and 95 percent of those in private industry are still held by foreigners.

The country contains three main geographical regions: the Hejaz, along the Red Sea; the Nejd, a vast interior plateau that comprises the bulk of Saudi territory; and the Eastern Province. The kingdom's largest oases, al-Hasa and Safwa, are located in this third region, along with the major oil fields and industrial centers. The Empty Quarter (al-Rub' al-Khali), an uninhabited desert where rain may not fall for a decade or more, occupies the entire southeastern quadrant of the country.

## THE WAHHABI MOVEMENT

In the eighteenth century, most of the area included in present-day Saudi Arabia was the home of nomads, as it had been for centuries. These peoples had no central government and owed allegiance to no one except their chiefs. They spent much of their time raiding one another's territories in the struggle for survival. Inland Arabia was a great blank area on the map—a vast, empty desert.

The only part of modern Saudi Arabia under any government control in the eighteenth century was the Hejaz, which includes the Islamic holy cities of Mecca and Medina. It was a province of the Ottoman Empire, the major power in the Middle East at that time.

Saudi Arabia became a nation, in the modern sense of the word, in 1932. But the origins of the Saudi nation go back to the eighteenth century. One of the tribes that roamed the desert beyond Ottoman control was the tribe of Saud. Its leader, Muhammad ibn Saud, wanted to gain an advantage over his rivals in the constant search for water and good grazing land for animals. He approached a famous religious scholar named Abd al-Wahhab, who lived in an oasis near the current Saudi capital, Riyadh (then a mud-walled village). Abd al-Wahhab promised Allah's blessing to ibn Saud in his contests with his rivals. In return, the Saudi leader agreed to protect al-Wahhab from threats to his life by opponents of the strict doctrines he taught and preached, and he swore an oath of obedience to these doctrines. The partnership between these two men gave rise to a crusading religious movement called Wahhabism.

Wahhabism is basically a strict and puritanical form of Sunni Islam. The Wahhabi code of law, behavior, and conduct is modeled on that of the original Islamic community established in Mecca and Medina by the Prophet Muhammad. Although there has been some relaxation of the code due to the country's modernization, it remains the law of Saudi Arabia today. Interpretation of Islamic law is the responsibility of the *ulema* (a body of religious scholars and jurists, in Sunni Islam). As a result, Saudi society is more conservative and puritanical than many other Islamic societies, including those of its Persian Gulf neighbors. The Taliban, the Islamic fundamentalist movement that held power in Afghanistan from 1996 to 2001, is thus far the only movement in Islam to have embraced Wahhabism.

Wahhabi-based social and cultural restrictions and strict observance of Islamic law are still the norm in Saudi Arabia. The government maintains separate schools for boys and girls at the precollege level. Women are not allowed to drive cars, although this may change with the continued economic downturn, as more women are forced to enter the workforce. And Islamic law continues to be applied with severity. Alcohol consumption is prohibited, and its use may bring jail sentences or expulsion of foreigners. Public floggings, amputations, and even executions are mandatory for crimes ranging from harassment of women to robbery, homosexual behavior in public, adultery, or occasionally murder.

The ulema includes a number of Wahhab's descendants—he had a very large family—and the Saudi–Wahhabi partnership has enabled them to play an important role in decision making. The late grand mufti, Shaykh Abd al-Aziz Bin Baz (who was famous for declaring that Earth was not round but flat), played such a role in the crisis that followed the Iraqi invasion of Kuwait.

The September 11, 2001, terrorist attacks in the United States and the resulting war on terrorism proclaimed by President George W. Bush against Osama bin Laden and his al-Qaeda network placed the Saudi government in an awkward position. As a valued ally, it was expected to provide active support for the international antiterrorism coalition. But a large section of the Saudi population is opposed to U.S. policy in the Middle East because of its support for Israel. A number of Wahhabi religious leaders ranged themselves in opposition to the monarchy due to its alliance with the "infidel West," some of them even urging its overthrow. In October 2001, a senior Wahhabi cleric, Shaykh Hamoud Ben Oqla, issued a *fatwa* (religious edict) to the effect that "it is a duty to wage jihad on anyone who supports the [American] attack on Afghanistan by hand, tongue or money; whoever helps the infidel against Muslims is to be considered an infidel." Although the Saudi government in October ended its recognition of the Taliban as the legitimate government of Afghanistan, the presence of 5,000 U.S. troops on "sacred Saudi Islamic soil" and bin Laden's popularity as a symbol of Muslim defiance against American "arrogance" in stationing them there forced the monarchy to walk a tightrope in balancing its international obligations with the views of its own people.

Fears that Saudi Arabia would be next on Saddam Hussein's invasion list after Kuwait led to the formation of the coalition of United Nations–sponsored forces that carried out Operation Desert Storm. This action involved stationing of American and other non-Muslim troops in the kingdom. The Saudi leadership was divided on the issue. But at this critical juncture, Bin Baz issued a fatwa. His edict said that in an extreme emergency, it was permissible for an Islamic state to seek help from non-Islamic ones. A later edict ruled that the campaign against Iraq was a jihad, further justifying the coalition and buildup of non-Muslim troops on Saudi soil.

In the late 1700s, the puritanical zeal of the Wahhabis led them to declare a "holy war" against the Ottoman Turks, who were then in control of Mecca and Medina, in order to restore these holy cities to the Arabs. In the 1800s, Wahhabis captured the cities. Soon the Wahhabis threatened to undermine Ottoman authority

(Aramco photo)

The Great Mosque at Mecca, in Saudi Arabia, is the holiest of shrines to Muslims. Historically, Mecca was the site at which Islam was founded, in the seventh century A.D., by the Prophet Muhammad. Pilgrims today flock to the Great Mosque to fulfill their Muslim duties as set down by the Five Pillars of Islam.

elsewhere. Wahhabi raiders seized Najaf and Karbala in Iraq, centers of Shia pilgrimage, and desecrated Shia shrines. In Mecca, they removed the headstones from the graves of members of the Prophet's family, because in their belief system, all Muslims are supposed to be buried unmarked.

The Ottoman sultan did not have sufficient forces at hand to deal with the Wahhabi threat, so he called upon his vassal, Muhammad Ali, the khedive (viceroy) of Egypt. Muhammad Ali organized an army equipped with European weapons and trained by European advisers. In a series of hard-fought campaigns, the Egyptian Army defeated the Wahhabis and drove them back into the desert.

Inland Arabia reverted to its old patterns of conflict. The Saudis and other rival tribes were Wahhabi in belief and practice, but this religious bond was countered by age-old disputes over water rights, territory, and control over trade routes. In the 1890s, the Saudis' major rivals, the Rashidis, seized Riyadh. The Saudi chief escaped across the desert to Kuwait, a town on the Persian Gulf that was under

British protection. He took along his young son, Abd al-Aziz ibn Saud.

## IBN SAUD

Abd al-Aziz al-Rahman Al Sa'ud, usually referred to simply as Ibn Saud (son of Sa'ud), was the father of his country, in both a political and a literal sense.[1] He grew up in exile in Kuwait, where he brooded and schemed about how to regain the lands of the Saudis. When he reached age 21, in 1902, he decided on a bold stroke to reach his goal. On 5 Shawwal 1319 (January 1902), he led a force of 48 warriors across the desert from Kuwait to Riyadh. They scaled the city walls at night and seized the Rashidi governor's house, and then the fort in a daring dawn raid. The population seems to have accepted the change of masters without incident, while Bedouin tribes roaming in the vicinity came to town to pledge allegiance to Ibn Saud and applaud his exploit.

Over the next three decades, Ibn Saud steadily expanded his territory. He said that his goal was "to recover all the lands of our forefathers."[2] In World War I, he became an ally of the British, fighting the Ottoman Turks in Arabia. In return, the

British provided arms for his followers and gave him a monthly allowance. The British continued to back Ibn Saud after the war, and in 1924, he entered Mecca in triumph. His major rival, Sharif Husayn, who had been appointed by the Ottoman government as the "Protector of the Holy Places," fled into exile. (Sharif Husayn was the great-grandfather of King Hussein I of Jordan.)

Ibn Saud's second goal, after recovering his ancestral lands, was to build a modern nation under a central government. He used as his motto the Koranic verse, "God changes not what is in a people until they change what is in themselves" (Sura XIII, 2). The first step was to gain recognition of Saudi Arabia as an independent state. Britain recognized the country in 1927, and other countries soon followed suit. In 1932, the country took its current name of Saudi Arabia, a union of the three provinces of Hejaz, Nejd, and al-Hasa.

## INDEPENDENCE

Ibn Saud's second step in his "grand design" for the new country was to establish order under a central government. To do this, he began to build settlements and to encourage the nomads to settle down, live in permanent homes, and learn how to grow their own food rather than relying on the desert. Those who settled on the land were given seeds and tools, were enrolled in a sort of national guard, and were paid regular allowances. These former Bedouin warriors became in time the core of the Saudi armed forces.

Ibn Saud also established the country's basic political system. The basis for the system was the Wahhabi interpretation of Islamic law. Ibn Saud insisted that "the laws of the state shall always be in accordance with the Book of Allah and the Sunna (Conduct) of His Messenger and the ways of the Companions."[3] He saw no need for a written constitution, and as yet Saudi Arabia has none. Ibn Saud decreed that the country would be governed as an absolute monarchy, with rulers always chosen from the Saud family. He was unfamiliar with political parties and distrusted them in principle; political organizations were therefore prohibited in the kingdom. Yet Ibn Saud was himself democratic, humble in manner, and spartan in his living habits. He remained all his life a man of the people and held every day a public assembly (*majlis*) in Riyadh at which any citizen had the right to ask favors or present petitions. (The custom of holding a daily majlis has been observed by Saudi rulers ever since.) More often than not, petitioners would address Ibn Saud not as Your Majesty but simply as Abd al-Aziz (his given name), a dramatic example of Saudi democracy in action.

Ibn Saud died in 1953. He had witnessed the beginning of rapid social and economic change in his country due to oil revenues. Yet his successors have presided over a transformation beyond the wildest imaginations of the warriors who had scaled the walls of Riyadh half a century earlier. Riyadh then had a population of 8,000. Today, it has 2.6 million inhabitants. It is one of the fastest-growing cities in the world.[4]

Ibn Saud was succeeded by his eldest surviving son, Crown Prince Saud. A number of royal princes felt that the second son, Faisal, should have become the new king because of his greater experience in foreign affairs and economic management. Saud's only experience was as governor of Nejd.

Although he was large and corpulent and lacked Ibn Saud's forceful personality, the new king was like his father in a number of ways. He was more comfortable in a desert tent than running a bureaucracy or meeting foreign dignitaries. Also, like his father, he had no idea

(UPI/Corbis-Bettman)

King Faisal was instrumental in bringing Saudi Arabia into the world's international community and in establishing domestic plans that brought his country into the twentieth century.

of the value of money. Ibn Saud would carry a sackful of riyals (the Saudi currency) to the daily majlis and give them away to petitioners. His son, Saud, not only doled out money to petitioners but also gave millions to other members of the royal family. One of his greatest extravagances was a palace surrounded by a bright pink wall.[5]

By 1958, the country was almost bankrupt. The royal family was understandably nervous about a possible coup supported by other Arab states, such as Egypt and Syria, which were openly critical of Saudi Arabia because of its lack of political institutions. The senior princes issued an ultimatum to Saud: First he would put Faisal in charge of straightening out the kingdom's finances, and, when that had been done, he would abdicate. When the financial overhaul was complete, with the kingdom again on a sound footing, Saud abdicated in favor of Faisal.

The transfer of authority from Saud to Faisal illustrates the collective principle of government of the Saudi family monarchy. The sovereign rules in theory; but in practice, the inner circle of Saudi senior princes, along with ulema leaders, make all decisions concerning succession, foreign policy, the economy, and other issues. The reasons for a decision must always be guessed at; the Saudis never explain them. It is a system very different from the open, freewheeling one of Western democracies,

yet it has given Saudi Arabia stability and leadership on occasions when crises have threatened the kingdom.

## FAISAL AND HIS SUCCESSORS
In terms of state-building, the reign of King Faisal (1964–1975) is second in importance only to that of Ibn Saud. One author wrote of King Faisal during his reign, "He is leading the country with gentle insistence from medievalism into the jet age."[6] Faisal's gentle insistence showed itself in many different ways. Encouraged by his wife, Queen Iffat, he introduced education for girls into the kingdom. Before Faisal, the kingdom had had no systematic development plans. In introducing the first five-year development plan, the king said that "our religion requires us to progress and to bear the burden of the highest tradition and best manners."[7]

In foreign affairs, Faisal ended the Yemen Civil War on an honorable basis for both sides; took an active part in the Islamic world in keeping with his role as Protector of the Holy Places; and, in 1970, founded the Organization of the Islamic Conference, which has given the Islamic nations of the world a voice in international affairs. Faisal laid down the basic strategy that his successors have followed, namely, avoidance of direct conflict, mediation of disputes behind the scenes, and use of oil wealth as a political weapon when necessary. The king never understood the American commitment to Israel, any more than his father had. (Ibn Saud had met U.S. president Franklin D. Roosevelt in Egypt during World War II. Roosevelt, motivated by American Jewish leaders to help in the establishment of a Jewish homeland in Palestine, sought to convince Ibn Saud, as head of the only independent Arab state at that time, to moderate Arab opposition to the project.) But Faisal's distrust of communism was equally strong. This distrust led him to continue the ambivalent yet close Saudi alliance with the United States that has continued up to the present.

King Faisal was assassinated in 1975 by a deranged nephew while he was holding the daily majlis. The assassination was another test of the system of rule by consensus in the royal family, and the system held firm. Khalid, Faisal's eldest half-brother, his junior by six years, succeeded him without incident. He ruled until his death in 1982. The next-oldest half-brother, Fahd, succeeded him.

## THE MECCA MOSQUE SIEGE
One of the most shocking events in Saudi Arabia since the founding of the kingdom

was the seizure of the Great Mosque in Mecca, Islam's holiest shrine, by a group of fundamentalist Sunni Muslims in November 1979. The leader of the group declared that one of its members was the *Mahdi* (in Sunni Islam, the "Awaited One") who had come to announce the Day of Judgment. The group occupied the mosque for two weeks. The siege was finally overcome by army and national guard units, but with considerable loss of life on both sides. No one knows exactly what the group's purpose was, nor did it lead to any general expressions of dissatisfaction with the regime. But the incident reflects the very real fear of the Saudi rulers of a coup attempted by the ultra-religious right.

Although the Saudi government remains staunchly conservative, it has before it the example of Iran, where a similar Islamic fundamentalist movement overthrew a well-established monarchy. Furthermore, the Shia Muslim population of the country is concentrated in al-Hasa Province, where the oil fields are located. The government's immediate fear after the Great Mosque seizure was of an outside plot inspired by Iran. When this plot did not materialize, the Saudis feared Shia involvement. Outside of increased security measures, the principal result of the incident has been a large increase in funding for the Shia community to ease socioeconomic tensions.

## THE ECONOMY

Oil was discovered in Saudi Arabia in 1938, but exports did not begin until after World War II. Reserves in 1997 were 261 billion barrels, 26 percent of the world's oil supply. The oil industry was controlled by Aramco (Arabian–American Oil Company), a consortium of four U.S. oil companies. In 1980, it came under Saudi government control, but Aramco continued to manage marketing and distribution services. The last American president of Aramco retired in 1989 and was succeeded by a Saudi. The company was renamed Saudi Aramco. But after a quarter-century of exclusion of foreign firms from the oil and gas industry, Saudi Arabia opened the gates in June 2001. A consortium of foreign oil companies was granted exploration rights in a desert area the size of Ireland. As a spin-off from the concession, the consortium will develop the existing South Ghawar gas field, and related power, desalination, and petrochemical plants.

The pressures of unemployment (14 percent for male Saudis), a population growth rate of 3.2 percent annually, and a stagnating economy, have motivated the government to seek foreign capital investment. The new investment law passed in 2000 permits 100 percent foreign ownership of projects. Import duties were reduced from 12 to 5 percent in 2001. As a result, foreign investment doubled to $9 billion. Some 60 percent of this amount comes from two projects: a Japanese-built desalination plant, and a U.S. contract to build 3,000 schools with connections to the Internet.

King Faisal's reorganization of finances and development plans in the 1960s set the kingdom on an upward course of rapid development. The economy took off after 1973, when the Saudis, along with other Arab oil-producing states, reduced production and imposed an export embargo on Western countries as a gesture of support to Egypt in its war with Israel. After 1973, the price per barrel of Saudi oil continued to increase, to a peak of $34.00 per barrel in 1981. (Prior to the embargo, it was $3.00 per barrel; in 1979, it was $13.30 per barrel.) The outbreak of the Iran–Iraq War in 1980 caused a huge drop in world production. The Saudis took up the slack.

The huge revenues from oil made possible economic development on a scale undreamed of by Ibn Saud and his Bedouin warriors. The old fishing ports of Yanbu, on the Red Sea, and Jubail, on the Persian Gulf, were transformed into new industrial cities, with oil refineries, cement and petrochemical plants, steel mills, and dozens of related industries. Riyadh experienced a building boom; Cadillacs bumped into camels on the streets, and the shops filled up with imported luxury goods. Every Saudi, it seemed, profited from the boom through free education and health care, low-interest housing loans, and guaranteed jobs.

The economic boom also lured many workers from poor countries, attracted by the high wages and benefits available in Saudi Arabia. Most came from such countries as Pakistan, Korea, and the Philippines, but the largest single contingent was from Yemen, next door. However, the bottom dropped out of the Saudi economy in the late 1980s. Oil prices fell, and the kingdom was forced to draw heavily on its cash reserves. Yemen's support for Iraq during the Gulf War was the last straw; the Saudi government deported 850,000 Yemeni workers, seriously disrupting the Yemeni economy with the shutdown in remittances.

Continued low world oil prices in the 1990s had a very bad effect on what was formerly a freewheeling economy. As one reporter noted, "the days of oil and roses are over for ordinary Saudis."[8] In 1998, the country's oil income dropped 40 percent, to $20 billion; after a two-year surplus, the budget showed a $13 billion deficit. Lowered oil prices accounted only in part for the deficit. Monthly stipends ranging from $4,000 to $130,000 given to the 20,000-plus descendants of Ibn Saud continued to drain the treasury, while free education, health care, and other benefits guaranteed for all Saudis under the Basic Law of Government generated some $170 billion in internal debts. The general downturn in the economy, particularly in the private sector, which is described as "quite anemic" by Saudi economists, has continued into the new millennium, despite significantly higher oil prices and Saudi insistence as the largest oil producer in the Organization of Petroleum Exporting Countries (OPEC), in maintaining current levels of production.

A major concern of the Saudi monarchy is the health of its current ruler. King Fahd has had lasting health effects from a stroke in 1995, but he remains the titular ruler of the kingdom. Crown Prince Abdallah serves de facto in his stead, at an age when most men are ready for retirement. Other prominent royal princes are at or beyond the same age. To his credit, Abdallah initiated various reforms in 2000–2001 to keep the country solvent. The state telephone service and several other public enterprises were privatized. Visa document fees for foreign workers were doubled, and subsidies for gasoline and electricity were discontinued. For the first time in 18 years, national income equaled public debt.

What will this aloof and rigidly Islamic nation be like in future years? One Saudi prince observed: "We wake up each morning complaining about management, not legitimacy. We never debate direction. We debate its focus, speed, style, emphasis, colors."[9]

## THE FUTURE

Its size, distance from major Middle Eastern urban centers, and oil wealth historically have insulated Saudi Arabia from the winds of political change. Domestic and foreign policy alike evolve from within the ruling family. Officials who undertake independent policy actions are quickly brought into line (an example being the freewheeling former oil minister Shaykh Zamani). The ruling family is also closely aligned with the ulema; Saudi rulers since Ibn Saud's time have held the title "Guardians of the Holy Mosques" (of Mecca and Medina), giving them a preeminent position in the Islamic world. The modern version of the Saudi–Wahhab partnership permits the ruler to appoint the Council of Senior Theologians, whose job it is to ensure Islamic cultural and social "rules" (such as women driving). In return, their presence and prescripts on Islamic behavior serve as an endorsement of the monarchy. But as one Saudi scholar told an interviewer, "the clerics can issue edicts to their hearts' content, answering weighty questions like whether or not a wife can wear jeans in front of her husband. Our clerics' religion has little to do with ethics, only lifestyle. They never do what they should do—denounce tyranny, injustice, corruption."[10]

Pressure to broaden participation in political decision making outside of the royals has increased markedly in recent years. This is due not only to greater contact by educated Saudis with more democratic political systems, but also to the vastly increased use of satellite dishes and the Internet. While agreeing in principle to changes, the House of Saud, strongly supported by the religious leaders, has held fast to its patriarchal system.

Given these strictures, it was somewhat surprising in 1991 when the ulema submitted a list of 11 "demands" to King Fahd. The most important one was the formation of a *Majlis al-Shura* (Consultative Council), which would have the power to initiate legislation and advise the government on foreign policy. The king's response, developed in deliberate stages with extensive behind-the-scenes consultation, in typical Saudi style, was to issue in February 1992 an 83-article "Organic Law," comparable in a number of respects to a Western constitution. The law sets out the basic rules for Saudi government; it went into effect by royal decree in August 1993. It defines the Saudi governing system as comprising the Majlis al-Shura; the Council of Ministers (cabinet); and regional, provincial, and local councils. The first Majlis was appointed in 1993 for a four-year term. At the time of expiration of its term, the speaker stated that the new Shura would be appointed rather than elected as requested by groups interested in broadening the political process.

Saudi Arabia is defined in the Organic Law as an Arab Islamic sovereign state (Article 5), with Islam the state religion (Article 1), and as a monarchy under the rule of Ibn Saud's descendants. Other articles establish an independent judiciary under Islamic law (*shari'a*) and define the powers and responsibilities of the ruler.

Aside from some internal pressures, mainly from intellectuals, the main reason for Fahd's decision to broaden the political process was the Gulf War, which exposed the Saudi system to international scrutiny and pointed up the risks of patriarchal government. A major difference between the Saudi Organic Law and Western-style constitutions is the absence of references to political, civil, and social rights. Political parties as such remain illegal; but, in 1993, the first human-rights organization in the country, the Committee for the Defense of Legitimate Rights, was formed by a group of academics, tribal leaders, and government officials. Its members included the second-ranking religious scholar, Shaykh Abdullah al-Jubrien, and the former head of Diwan al-Mazalem, the Saudi equivalent of ombudsman. The Committee's goal was the elimination of oppression and injustice, which is considered an important part of its members' religious duty. But its emergence was perceived as a threat to the ulema. An edict condemned it, stating that there was no need for such an organization in a country ruled by Islamic law.

Satellite television, instant worldwide communications, the Internet, and other features of the contemporary interlinked world certainly threaten the self-imposed isolation of regimes such as Saudi Arabia's. In 2001, 42 Internet service providers were operational in the country. Although Internet usage is controlled through a single central-government authority that may block out Web sites considered pornographic or politically objectionable, Saudi Arabia's huge youth population (nearly 50 percent are under age 15) has easy access to satellite television or foreign Web sites, enabling viewers to circumvent such control. The opening of the U.S.–style Faisalah Mall in Riyadh in 2000 has at least provided Saudi young people with a public meeting-place and entertainment venue in the absence of movie theaters and other mass media centers.

Since the Gulf War, the country's purchases of large amounts of weaponry and the stationing of 5,000 American air and ground forces on Saudi soil have been strongly criticized by the Saudi public as well as by other Arab countries. Other Arab leaders have even accused Saudi Arabia (and Kuwait) of becoming U.S. satellites! In the past, the monarchy ignored such criticism; alignment with United States as its major ally and protector have been cornerstones of Saudi foreign policy since World War II. However, perceptions of U.S. bias in the Palestinian–Israeli conflict has weakened this long-time alliance. In June 1996, a truck-bomb explosion at Khobar, an American air base built with Saudi money, killed 24 American service personnel. The authorities arrested a number of Saudis in connection with the bombing. However, in 2001, it was announced that they would be tried in Saudi courts. The government rejected U.S. extradition requests for those arrested along with an indictment issued in the United States that called for their trial in American courts.

Despite the American presence and its own vigilance, the country continues to be threatened by Islamic fundamentalists. After the seizure of the Great Mosque in Mecca by Sunni fundamentalists in 1979, several hundred of them were deported to Afghanistan, where they joined the resistance to the Soviet occupation. After the Soviet withdrawal in 1989, many of these "Arab Afghans" returned to Saudi Arabia and other Middle Eastern Islamic countries. Some even migrated to Europe or Canada, ultimately entering the United States. Most of them were Saudi nationals; they included Osama bin Laden. Although bin Laden was deprived of his Saudi citizenship and deported (to Sudan) in 1994, the nucleus of his terrorist organization remained in Saudi Arabia. It presents a serious underground threat to the monarchy. One scholar noted: "The jihad effort [in Afghanistan] may have brought the Saudi royal family an extra 25 years. . . but it faces an extended period of even greater vulnerability. Here is a group of young Saudis, a couple hundred, maybe a couple thousand. They have become anti-Western and anti-American, but first and foremost they are anti-Saudi."[11]

Saudi vulnerability stems from internal weaknesses rather than external threats, as was the case a decade age when Iraqi forces had seized Kuwait and stood on the borders of the kingdom. King Fahd marked his 20th anniversary on the throne in 2001 in poor health, confined to a wheelchair, and reportedly suffering from Alzheimer's disease. Crown Prince Abdullah has become for all practical purposes the country's leader and, despite a lack of governmental and foreign experience, has governed effectively. In 2000, he formed a family council to manage royal-family affairs for the 7,000 or so princes; in 2001, he directed members to pay their own electricity and phone bills and placed a five-year moratorium on military contracts, another source of graft and kickbacks.

## FOREIGN POLICY

The Iraqi invasion and occupation of Kuwait caused a major shift in Saudi policy, away from mediation in regional conflicts and bankrolling of popular causes (such as the Palestinian) to one of direct confrontation. For the first time in its history, the Saudi nation felt directly threatened by the actions of an aggressive neighbor. Diplomatic relations were broken with Iraq

Wahhabis seize
Mecca and
Medina
**1800**

Ibn Saud
captures Riyadh
in a daring
commando raid
**1902**

Ibn Saud is
recognized by
the British as the
king of Saudi
Arabia
**1927**

Oil exports get
under way
**1946**

King Saud, the
eldest son and
successor of Ibn
Saud, is deposed
in favor of his
brother Faisal
**1963**

Faisal is
assassinated;
succession
passes by
agreement to
Khalid
**1975**

The Great
Mosque in
Mecca is
seized by a
fundamentalist
Muslim group
**1979**

King Khalid dies;
succession
passes to Crown
Prince Fahd;
Saudi jets shoot
down an Iranian
jet for violation of
Saudi air space
**1980s**

Saudi Arabia
hosts foreign
troops and
shares command
in the Gulf War
**1990s**

2000s

The Saudi
economy stabilizes

The Saudi–U.S.
relationship is scrutinized
in the wake of the
September 11
terrorist attacks

and subsequently with Jordan and Yemen, due to their support of the Iraqi occupation. Yemeni workers were rounded up and expelled, and harsh restrictions were imposed on Yemeni business owners in the kingdom. Establishment of the UN/U.S.–led coalition against Iraq led to the stationing of foreign non-Muslim troops on Saudi soil, also a historic first.

The continued survival of Saddam Hussain's regime in Iraq resulted in huge Saudi purchases of U.S. military equipment, although a $1.7 billion arms deal was cancelled in 1999 due to the economic recession. In the last few years, the purchase of U.S. arms and the stationing of 5,000 American troops on Saudi soil has drawn criticism from other Arab countries. They have even accused the kingdom of becoming a U.S. satellite. In the past, Saudi rulers have ignored such criticism. Alignment with the United States as its major ally and arms supplier has been the cornerstone of Saudi policy since World War II. However, all-out U.S. support for Israel in its conflict with the Palestinians began to erode the alliance in 2000–2001. The government authorized public anti-American demonstrations in several Saudi cities, while the crown prince and other officials angrily criticized both the Clinton and George W. Bush administrations for their lack of even-handedness in the conflict. One observer noted: " The Islamists think the Saudis have sold out to the Americans, and the Americans think they have sold out to the terrorists. Eventually this translates into an erosion of legitimacy—that if you are not satisfying the Arabs and Washington, you're on your own."[12]

The country's often difficult relationship with Iran underwent another change

in 1991. The fall of the Iranian monarchy and establishment of the Islamic Republic had initially been welcomed by Saudi rulers because of the new regime's fidelity to Islamic principles. But, in 1987, Iranian pilgrims attending the pilgrimage to Mecca undertook anti-Saudi demonstrations that led to a violent confrontation with police, resulting in more than 400 casualties. The two countries broke diplomatic relations; and, in 1988, Saudi Arabia established a quota system for pilgrims on the basis of one pilgrim per 1,000 population. The quota system was described as necessary to reduce congestion on the annual pilgrimages, but in fact it would limit Iran to 50,000 pilgrims and limit Iranian-inspired political activism. Iran boycotted the pilgrimage in 1988 and 1989 as a result.

Relations with neighboring Gulf states have also improved. Long-time border disputes with Qatar and Yemen have been resolved amicably, with demarcation through largely featureless desert territory. In the Yemeni case, the border was demarcated by a joint arbitration commission to extend from Jebel Thar to the Omani border, on the basis of the 1934 Treaty of Taif.

After a less violent incident in 1992, the Saudi government banned all parades and demonstrations for the foreseeable future. Subsequent pilgrimages passed without incident. In 1997, the government increased the Iranian pilgrim quota to 100,000.

## NOTES

1. He had 24 sons by 16 different women during his lifetime (1880–1953). See William Quandt, *Saudi Arabia in the 1980's* (Washington, D.C.: Brookings Institution, 1981), Appendix E, for a genealogy.

2. George Rentz, "The Saudi Monarchy," in Willard A. Beling, ed., *King Faisal and*

*the Modernization of Saudi Arabia* (Boulder, CO: Westview Press, 1980), pp. 26–27.

3. *Ibid.,* p. 29.

4. "Saudi Arabia's Centennial," *Aramco World,* Vol. 50, No. 1 (January–February 1999), pp. 21–22. The walls and gates were demolished in 1953 under the "relentless pressure" of modernization, but the Masmak and other structures dating from Ibn Saud's time have been preserved as museums to celebrate the nation's past.

5. The wall was torn down by his successor, King Faisal. Justin Coe, in *The Christian Science Monitor* (February 13, 1985).

6. Gordon Gaskill, "Saudi Arabia's Modern Monarch," *Reader's Digest* (January 1967), p. 118.

7. Ministry of Information, Kingdom of Saudi Arabia, *Faisal Speaks* (n.d.), p. 88.

8. Douglas Jehl, in *The New York Times* (March 20, 1999).

9. Susan Sachs, in *The New York Times* (December 4, 2000).

10. David Hirst, "Corruption, Hard Times Fuel Desert Discontent," *The Washington Times* (September 29, 1999), p. 150.

11. Joseph Kechichan, in *The Christian Science Monitor* (October 4, 2001).

12. Mamoun Fandy, interviewed in *The New York Times* (November 4, 2001).

## DEVELOPMENT

The new Saudi 5-Year Plan sets a growth rate of 3.16% annually, with increased diversification of the economy to reduce dependence on oil. With revenues dropping to half of the 1980 totals, an abnormally high birth rate and high unemployment, there are simply not enough jobs being created for the 100,000 Saudis entering the workforce each year.

## FREEDOM

Saudi Arabia's strict adherence to Islamic law not only imposes harsh punishments for many crimes but also restricts human rights. The country ranks second in the world in executions per million population: 123 in 2000. Sharia law applies equally to Saudis and non-Saudis; in 2001, 4 Britons were flogged publicly for dealing in alcohol. A new Code of Criminal Procedure took effect in July 2001. It allows defendants to be represented in court by a lawyer. Also special courts have been set up by the government to bypass Sharia in such matters as labor disputes and the progressive income tax, for which there are no precedents, as well as traffic offenses.

## HEALTH/WELFARE

Overcrowded schools and universities and an overabundance of graduates in Islamic studies or liberal arts who are untrained in modern technology continue to affect both economic and social development. In addition to large-scale school construction to meet the demands of a growing school-age population, a new curriculum emphasizes English educaiton and global studies.

## ACHIEVEMENTS

Aside from the pilgrimage to Mecca, with its influx of 2 million pilgrims a year, tourism in the kingdom has been nonexistent. In 2000, a special commission was set up to encourage nonpilgrimage visits; it is headed by Prince Sultan, the country's first astronaut. Asir Province, with its lofty mountains and uncrowded Red Sea beaches, is the main focus of tourist development, with a network of resorts built in record time to accommodate an estimated 700,000 visitors.

# Sudan (Republic of the Sudan)

## GEOGRAPHY

*Area in Square Miles (Kilometers):*
892,068 (2,505,810) (about ¼ the size of the United States)

*Capital (Population):* Khartoum (948,000)

*Environmental Concerns:* little potable water; threatened wildlife populations; soil erosion; desertification

*Geographical Features:* generally flat, featureless plain; mountains in the east and west

*Climate:* varies from arid desert in the north to tropical in the south

## PEOPLE

### Population
*Total:* 36,081,000
*Annual Growth Rate:* 2.79%
*Rural/Urban Population Ratio:* 68/32
*Major Languages:* Arabic; Dinka; Nubian; Nuer; others
*Ethnic Makeup:* 52% black; 39% Arab; 6% Beja; 3% others
*Religions:* 70% Sunni Muslim in north; 25% indigenous beliefs; 5% Christian, mostly in the south and Khartoum

### Health
*Life Expectancy at Birth:* 58 years (male); 56 years (female)
*Infant Mortality Rate (Ratio):* 68.7/1,000
*Physicians Available (Ratio):* 1/11,300

### Education
*Adult Literacy Rate:* 46%

## COMMUNICATION
*Telephones:* 162,000 main lines
*Daily Newspaper Circulation:* 21 per 1,000 people
*Televisions:* 8.2 per 1,000 people
*Internet Service Provider:* 1 (2000)

## TRANSPORTATION
*Highways in Miles (Kilometers):* 7,390 (11,900)
*Railroads in Miles (Kilometers):* 3,425 (5,516)
*Usable Airfields:* 61
*Motor Vehicles in Use:* 75,000

## GOVERNMENT
*Type:* transitional
*Independence Date:* January 1, 1956 (from Egypt and the United Kingdom)
*Head of State/Government:* President Omar Hassan al-Bashir is both head of state and head of government
*Political Parties:* political "associations" now allowed: include the National Congress Party; Popular National Congress; Umma; Democratic Unionist Party; National Democratic Alliance; Sudan People's Liberation Army
*Suffrage:* universal at 17

## MILITARY
*Military Expenditures (% of GDP):* 7.3% (est.)
*Current Disputes:* civil war; disputed boundary with Kenya; territorial dispute with Egypt

## ECONOMY
*Currency ($ U.S. Equivalent):* 2,582 pounds = $1
*Per Capita Income/GDP:* $1,000/$35.7 billion
*GDP Growth Rate:* 7%
*Inflation Rate:* 10%
*Unemployment Rate:* 4%
*Labor Force:* 11,000,000
*Natural Resources:* petroleum; small reserves of iron ore, copper, chromium ore, zinc, tungsten, mica, silver, and gold
*Agriculture:* cotton; groundnuts; sorghum; millet; wheat; gum arabic; sesame; sheep
*Industry:* cotton ginning; textiles; cement; edible oils; sugar; soap distilling; shoes; petroleum refining; armaments
*Exports:* $1.7 billion (primary partners Saudi Arabia, Italy, Germany)
*Imports:* $1.2 billion (primary partners China, Libya, Saudi Arabia)

 http://lcweb2.loc.gov/frd/cs/sdtoc.html

## SUDAN

Sudan is the largest nation on the African continent. It extends from its northern border with Egypt and the Libyan and Nubian Deserts southward deep into tropical Africa. Its territory includes the Blue and White Nile Rivers, which join at Khartoum to form the Nile, Egypt's lifeline.

The name of the country underscores its distinctive social structure. Centuries ago, Arab geographers named it Bilad al-Sudan, "Land of the Blacks." The northern half, including Khartoum, is Arabic in language, culture, and traditions, and Islamic in religion. However, the admixture of Arab and African peoples over 2,000 years has produced a largely black Arab population.

Southern Sudan is the home of a large number of black African tribes and groups—Dinka, Nuer, Lopit, and others. The British administration and the presence of Christian missionaries who established schools has resulted in a large Christian population. About 25 percent of southerners are Christian; the remainder are animists, who believe in natural forces and presences.

The two halves of Sudan have little or nothing in common. The country's basic political problem is how to achieve unity between these two different societies, which were brought together under British rule to form an artificial nation.

## HISTORY

The ancient history of Sudan, at least of the northern region, was always linked with that of Egypt. The pharaohs and later conquerors of Egypt—Persians, Greeks, Romans, and eventually the Arabs, Turks, and British—periodically attempted to extend their power farther south. The connection with Egypt became very close when the Egyptians were converted to Islam by invading armies from Arabia, in the seventh century A.D. As the invaders spread southward, they converted the northern Sudanese people to Islam, developing in time an Islamic Arab society in northern Sudan. Southern Sudan remained comparatively untouched, because it was isolated by the geographical barriers of mountain ranges and the great impassable swamps of the Nile.

The two regions were forcibly brought together by conquering Egyptian armies in the nineteenth century. The conquest became possible after the exploration of sub-Saharan Africa by Europeans. After the explorers and armies came slave traders and then European fortune hunters, interested in developing the gold, ivory, diamonds, timber, and other resources of sub-Saharan Africa.

The soldiers and slave traders were the most brutal of all these invaders, particularly in southern Sudan. In fact, many of the slave traders were Muslim Sudanese from the north. The Civil War between the Islamic north and the Christian/animist south, which began in 1955 and is still going on, had its roots in the nineteenth-century experiences of the southerners, as "memories of plunder, slave raiding and suffering" at the hands of slavers and their military allies were passed down from generation to generation.[1]

## THE ORIGINS OF
## THE SUDANESE STATE

The first effort to establish a nation in Sudan began in the 1880s, when the country was ruled by the British as part of their protectorate over Egypt. The British were despised as foreign, non-Muslim rulers. The Egyptians, who made up the bulk of the security forces assigned to Sudan, were hated for their arrogance and mistreatment of the Sudanese.

In 1881, a religious leader in northern Sudan announced that he was the *Mahdi,* the "Awaited One," who, according to Sunni Islamic belief, would appear on Earth, sent by God to rid Sudan of its foreign rulers. The Mahdi called for a *jihad* (struggle or holy war) against the British and the Egyptians.

Sudanese by the thousands flocked to join the Mahdi. His warriors, fired by revolutionary zeal, defeated several British-led Egyptian armies. In 1885, they captured Khartoum, and, soon thereafter, the Mahdi's rule extended over the whole of present-day Sudan. For this reason, the Mahdi is remembered, at least in northern Sudan, as Abu al-Istiqlal, the "Father of Independence."[2]

The Mahdi's rule did not last long; he died in 1886. His chief lieutenant and successor, the Khalifa Abdallahi, continued in power until 1898, when a British force armed with guns mowed down his spear-carrying, club-wielding army. Sudan was ruled jointly by Britain and Egypt from then until 1955. Since the British already ruled Egypt as a protectorate, for all practical purposes joint rule meant British rule.

Under the British, Sudan was divided into a number of provinces, and British university graduates staffed the country's first civil service.[3] But the British followed two policies that have created problems for Sudan ever since it became independent. One was "indirect rule" in the north. Rather than developing a group of trained Sudanese administrators who could take over when they left, the British governed indirectly through local chiefs and religious leaders. The second policy was to separate southern from northern Sudan through "Closed Door" laws, which prohibited northerners from working in, or even visiting, the south.

Sudan became independent on New Year's Day 1956, as a republic headed by a civilian government. The first civilian government lasted until 1958, when a military group seized power "to save the country from the chaotic regime of the politicians."[4] But the military regime soon became as "chaotic" as its predecessor's. In 1964, it handed over power to another civilian group. The second civilian group was no more successful than the first had been, as the politicians continued to feud, and intermittent conflict between government forces and rebels in the southern region turned into all-out civil war.

In 1969, the Sudanese Army carried out another military coup, headed by Colonel Ja'far (or Gaafar) Nimeiri. Successive Sudanese governments since independence, including Nimeiri's, have faced the same basic problems: the unification of north and south, an economy hampered by inadequate transportation and few resources, and the building of a workable political system. Nimeiri's record in dealing with these difficult problems is one explanation for his longevity in power. A written Constitution was approved in 1973. Although political parties were outlawed, an umbrella political organization, the Sudan Socialist Union (SSU), provided an alternative to the fractious political jockeying that had divided the nation before Nimeiri.[5]

Nimeiri's firm control through the military and his effectiveness in carrying out political reforms were soon reflected at the ballot box. He was elected president in 1971 for a six-year term and was re-elected in 1977. Yet broad popular support did not generate political stability. There were a number of attempts to overthrow him, the most serious in 1971 and 1976, when he was actually captured and held for a time by rebels.

One reason for his survival may be his resourcefulness. After the 1976 coup attempt, for example, instead of having his opponents executed, he invited them and other opposition leaders to form a government of national unity. One of Nimeiri's major opponents, Sadiq al-Mahdi, a great-grandson of the Mahdi and himself an important religious leader, accepted the offer and returned from exile.

Nimeiri's major achievement was to end temporarily the Civil War between north and south. An agreement was signed in 1972 in Addis Ababa, Ethiopia, mediated by Ethiopian authorities, between his gov-

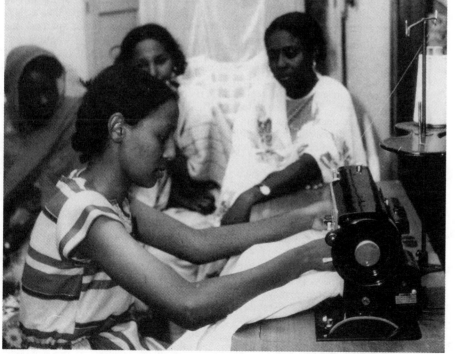

ernment and the southern Anya Anya resistance movement. The agreement provided for regional autonomy for the south's three provinces, greater representation of southerners in the National People's Assembly, and integration of Anya Anya units into the armed forces without restrictions.

### THE COUP OF 1985

Nimeiri was reelected in 1983 for a third presidential term. Most of his political opponents had apparently been reconciled with him, and the army and state security forces were firmly under his control. It seemed that Sudan's most durable leader would round out another full term in office without too much difficulty. But storm clouds were brewing on the horizon. Nimeiri had survived for 16 years in power largely through his ability to keep opponents divided and off balance by his unpredictable moves. From 1983 on, however, his policies seemed designed to unite rather than divide them.

The first step in Nimeiri's undoing was his decision to impose Islamic law (*Shari'a*) over the entire country. The impact fell heaviest on the non-Muslim southern region. In a 1983 interview, Nimeiri explained his reasons for the action. His goal from the start of his regime, he said, was "to raise government by the

book [i.e., the Koran] from the level of the individual to that of government." If the Sudanese, with their numerous ethnic and cultural differences and the country's vast size, were governed properly by God's Book, they would provide an example of peace and security to neighboring countries.[6]

In Nimeiri's view, the application of Islamic restrictions on alcohol, tobacco, and other prohibited forms of behavior was appropriate to Sudanese Muslims and non-Muslims alike, since "Islam was revealed to serve man and all its legislation has the goal of regulating family, social, and individual life and raising the level of the individual."[7]

The new draconian measures were widely resented, but particularly in the south, where cigarettes and home-brewed beer were popular palliatives for a harsh existence. When Nimeiri continued his "Islamic purification" process with a reorganization of Sudanese administration into several large regions in order to streamline the cumbersome bureaucracy inherited from the British, the southerners reacted strongly. Consolidation of three autonomous provinces into one directly under central-government control was seen by them as a violation of the commitment made to regional autonomy that had ended the Civil War. An organized

guerrilla army, the Sudan People's Liberation Army (SPLA), resumed civil war under the expert leadership of U.S.–trained colonel John Garang. The rebels' new strategy was not only to oppose government troops but also to strike at development projects essential to the economy. Foreign workers in the newly developed oil fields in southwestern Sudan were kidnapped or killed; as a result, Chevron Oil Company halted all work on the project.

A crackdown on Islamic fundamentalist groups, particularly the Muslim Brotherhood, added to Nimeiri's growing list of opponents. Members of the Brotherhood had been active in implementing Islamic law as the law of the land, but Nimeiri felt that they had gone too far. By late 1984, it appeared that the president had angered or alienated everybody in the country, all for different reasons.

In the end, it was the failure of his economic policies rather than anything else that brought about Nimeiri's fall. The International Monetary Fund imposed strict austerity requirements on Sudan in 1984 as a prerequisite to a $90 million standby loan to enable the country to pay its mounting food and fuel bills. The food bills were aggravated by famine, the fuel bills by the necessity to import almost all fuel requirements. The IMF insisted on drastic budget cuts, devaluation of currency, and an end to subsidies on basic commodities. If Nimeiri had been able to carry out these reforms, he would have stood a chance of restoring the country to solvency and his own rule to respectability. Protests turned to riots, mainly over the end of price subsidies and a consequent 33 percent increase in the prices of such necessities as bread, sugar, and cooking oil. Other protests erupted over the application of Islamic law, especially the ban on alcohol, which brought thousands of Sudanese into the streets shouting "We want beer! We want beer!"

Nimeiri's departure for the United States to seek further economic help triggered a general strike in 1985. A genuine national movement arose, uniting students and professionals with the urban poor, all demanding that Nimeiri resign. Fearing anarchy or an uprising by young army officers, the senior military leaders moved quickly, took over the government, and ordered Nimeiri deposed. Crowds in Khartoum shouted, "Nimeiri the butcher is finished; the country belongs to the people." "He's nothing, let him sell lemons," cried one demonstrator, and others tore Nimeiri's picture from their devalued banknotes.[8]

The new military government, headed by General Abd al-Rahman Swareddahab,

(UN photo/Louise Gubb)

The attainment of political stability is important to Sudanese development, but it will be a strong economy that makes for lasting peace. Job training is extremely important. This woman in a sewing class in Khartoum represents the need to create a skilled-labor pool.

a highly respected senior officer, promised to hold elections within a year to restore civilian rule and to revive political parties. That promise was kept: In 1986, elections were held for a new People's Assembly. Two revived pre-Nimeiri parties, the Umma and the Democratic Unionist Party (DUP), won the majority of seats, with the fundamentalist National Islamic Front emerging as a strong third party. Sadiq al-Mahdi, head of the Umma, automatically became prime minister; his principal rival, DUP leader Ahmed Ali al-Mirghani, was chosen as president. The new prime minister chose a coalition cabinet to begin the arduous process of restoring the democratic process to Sudan after 15 years of Nimeiri.

But the euphoria over the departure of "Nimeiri the Butcher" soon gave way to the realization that the problems that had daunted him remained unresolved. They included heavy foreign indebtedness, a weak economy, inefficient agricultural production, an inadequate transportation system, party and personal rivalries, and extreme distrust between north and south in the divided Sudanese nation.

**INTERNAL PROBLEMS**
The al-Mahdi government had no more success than its predecessors in resolving Sudan's endemic political disunity. Efforts to limit the application of Islamic law throughout the country were blocked by the National Islamic Front (NIF) in 1988. The Civil War then heated up. SPLA success in capturing the principal towns in the south led the DUP to sign a separate agreement with the rebels for a cease-fire. The People's Assembly rejected the agreement, and the DUP then withdrew from the government.

Faced with the imminent collapse of civilian authority, the armed forces again seized power, in Sudan's fourth military coup since independence. The army moved after food shortages and soaring inflation, fed by war costs of $1 million a day, led to riots in Khartoum and other cities. A Revolutionary Council, headed by Lieutenant General Omar Hassan al-Bashir, suspended the Constitution and arrested government leaders.

In 1992, Bashir appointed a 300-member National Transitional Assembly to lay the groundwork—at least in theory—for a return to civilian rule. Its members included military leaders (those who sat on the ruling Revolutionary Council), provincial (state) governors, and some former government leaders. Its primary function was to implement Council decrees; during the transitional period, however, it could develop legislation.

The regime also sought to broaden its popular base through the establishment of local elections. The elections were held in two stages, the first stage being the election of people's congresses (at the village and town level); in the second stage of the process, the congresses then elected provincial legislatures. Due to the Civil War, the southern region remained unrepresented.

The regime's international isolation as a "rogue" state committed to the support of global terrorism has blocked needed foreign aid for the nearly bankrupt Sudanese economy. As a result, it has begun slowly to restore representative government. Elections were held in 1996 for a 400-member National People's Assembly and to choose a president. Not surprisingly, Bashir was elected president; he received 75.5 percent of the 5.5 million votes cast. (The south was excluded from the election process.) Subsequently, Hassan al-Turabi, leader of the NIF and the architect of Sudanese Islam, was elected Speaker of the new Assembly.

In June 1998, the regime enacted a number of constitutional reforms. They allow political parties to form, although they are to be registered officially as "associations." Freedoms of speech, assembly, and the press are guaranteed under the reforms, although political parties that receive foreign funding or "go beyond the bounds of religion" can be proscribed.

In 1998 and 1999, the regime called on political opponents to return and help build a "new democratic Sudan." Several did so. They included Nimeiri and Sadeq al-Mahdi. However, rivalry between Bashir and Turabi, which came to a head in 1999, halted the restoration of representative government. Turabi presented constitutional amendments to the Assembly in December. If approved, they would abolish the position of prime minister (held under the 1998 reorganization of his government) as well as his control over provincial governorships. The president could also be impeached by a two-thirds vote in the Assembly. Inasmuch as Turabi's party controlled the great majority of its 400 seats, approval of the amendments seemed inevitable.

On December 12, however, the embattled president struck back. He declared a three-month state of emergency, suspended the Constitution and the Assembly, and dismissed his entire cabinet. In January 2000, he removed all state governors from office and appointed a new cabinet, with most of the ministries now held by his own supporters. "God willing with this team we will guide Sudan toward peace," he told the nation in a public address.

In March 2001, the conflict between the two leaders intensified when Turabi was arrested. He was charged with complicity with the southern rebels, because he had signed a "memorandum of understanding" with SPLA leaders. The memorandum called for an end to the two-year-old state of emergency and recognition of Sudan's religious and cultural pluralism.

Prior to his arrest, Turabi had formed a political "association" (so called because political parties remain banned) to replace the NIF. The new association, the Popular National Congress (PNC), had boycotted the December 2000 presidential election on grounds that the election had been "cooked and prearranged" by Bashir and his supporters. Bashir was then reelected by an 86 percent majority of voters, although only 66 percent of those eligible to vote cast their ballots. Former Sudanese dictator Jaafar Nimeiri, invited to return after years of exile in Egypt, ran against the president as an independent, receiving 9 percent of the popular vote.

Military rule eased in 2001. Bashir announced an amnesty for opponents of his regime, and two important civilian leaders accepted the offer. Former prime minister Sadeq al-Mahdi returned from voluntary exile in December 2000. In December 2001, Ahmed al-Mirghani, deputy head of the Democratic Unionist opposition party, returned to a welcome by tens of thousands after a 12-year exile in Egypt. He was greeted by Bashir in person as a "unifying symbol of the state," part of the president's newest effort at political reconciliation as a prelude to restoration of civilian government.

**THE CIVIL WAR**
The government gained some ground against rebels in the Civil War in late 1991, when the SPLA split into contending factions. One faction, led by Lieutenant Rick Machar, accused SPLA commander John Garang of a dictatorial reign of terror within the organization. The split became tribal when Nuer troops of Machar's faction invaded Dinka territory; the Dinkas are Garang's main supporters. Some 100,000 Dinkas fled their homeland during the fighting. Sudan government forces took advantage of internal SPLA rivalry to capture several important southern towns during an offensive in March 1992.

The ethnic killings of Nuers and Dinkas, along with famine (which has been intensified by the SPLA infighting), led other African states and, in late 1993, the United States to attempt to mediate and bring the two factions together as a prelude to ending the Civil War. But even the presence of former U.S. president

Jimmy Carter as mediator failed to bridge the differences separating the two SPLA leaders. And the major differences between southerners and northerners—imposition of Islamic law on non-Muslims, revenue sharing among regions, states' rights and powers versus those of the national government—seemed insurmountable.

In the late 1990s, the National Islamic Front, renamed the National Congress Party in an effort to soften its fundamentalist image, won almost complete control over the Revolutionary Council. The security forces, the judiciary, and the universities were purged of moderate or liberal staff members and replaced by NIF fundamentalists. In 1991, the regime had bowed to NIF pressure and issued an edict making Islamic law the "law of the land" in both north and south Sudan. As a result, the Civil War intensified.

In 1997, the government signed peace agreements with several SPLA factions after rebel successes threatened to win the entire southern region. The agreements specified a four-year autonomy period for the south. At the end of the period, the population could choose between independence and integration on a basis of equality with the Muslim north.

The appointment in October 2001 by the George W. Bush administration of former senator John Danforth as its special envoy to mediate the Civil War underscored expanded U.S. concern about Sudan's involvement as a state sponsor of terrorism. But of equal concern was the Sudanese regime's record of repression and denial of human rights to its southern non-Muslim population.

Earlier, the Garang and Machar factions of the SPLA had patched up their differences to present a united front against government forces. Although he had arrived with no detailed peace program, Danforth urged an end to attacks on civilians, abudctions, and forced slavery of southerners; and asked for a permanent cease-fire in the Nuba Mountains, whose inhabitants have been caught between government and SPLA forces and deprived of food. Danforth negotiated a cease-fire in that region in January 2002. In February, however, a series of helicopter attacks by the Sudanese military on UN food-distribution centers, which killed a number of civilians, caused the envoy to suspend his efforts to end Africa's longest-running civil war.

In February 2002, the government accepted a Libyan–Egyptian peace proposal. It would pave the way for an interim government of all political groups. If the proposal held, it would be a major step toward ending the war.

## THE ECONOMY

Although the attainment of political stability is important to Sudanese development, much depends on building the economy. The Sudanese economy is largely dependent on agriculture. The most important crop is cotton. Until recently, the only other Sudanese export crop of importance was gum arabic.

Because Sudan has great agricultural potential, due to its rivers, alluvial soils, and vast areas of unused arable land, Nimeiri had set out in the 1970s to develop the country into what experts told him could be the "breadbasket" of the Middle East. To reach this ambitious goal, some cotton plantations were converted to production of grain crops. The huge Kenana sugar-refinery complex was started with joint foreign and Sudanese management; the long-established Gezira cotton scheme was expanded; and work began on the Jonglei Canal, intended to drain a vast marshy area called the Sudd ("swamp") in the south, in order to bring hundreds of thousands of acres of marshlands under cultivation. But the breadbasket was never filled. Mismanagement and lack of skilled labor delayed some projects, while others languished because the roads and communications systems needed to implement them did not exist.

It may be that oil, rather than agriculture, holds the key to Sudan's economic growth and indirectly its internal peace. Oil was discovered by Chevron in the southwestern region in the 1970s. The two oil fields there were being developed when the north–south war resumed. In 1984, three foreign oil workers were killed by rebels in an attack on the Bentiu facility, and Chevron withdrew and closed down its entire installation.

In the late 1990s, a temporary halt to the Civil War made resumption of oil exploration feasible. A consortium of three foreign oil companies (Talisman of Canada and the state oil companies of China and Malaysia), along with the Sudan National Oil Company, built a 936-mile, $1.2 billion pipeline from the former Chevron fields near Haglig northeast to Port Sudan. The pipeline was completed in less than a year. Initial exports of 120,000 barrels per day from the Port Sudan refinery had risen to 220,000 b/d by 2002, with an anticipated output of 500,000 b/d by 2005.

Although it was criticized for supporting a repressive government with oil revenues, enabling it to purchase new weaponry, Talisman officials insisted that they were helping the Sudanese people to meet urgent social needs.

But the message reached only deaf ears in the United States. In June 2001, Congress passed a series of measures that would prohibit foreign oil companies working in Sudan from raising capital in the United States, or trading their securities in American financial markets in order to finance their oil operations. The actions would force them to give up their seats on the New York Stock Exchange or Nasdaq.

## FAMINE

The Sudanese people traditionally have lived in a barter economy, with little need for money. Huge budget deficits and high prices for basic commodities hardly affect the mass of the population. But the Civil War and a 12-year drought cycle in the sub-Saharan Sahel region, which includes Sudan, have changed their subsistence way of life into one of destitution.

The drought became critical in 1983, and millions of refugees from Ethiopia and Chad, the countries most affected, moved into temporary camps in Sudan. Then it was Sudan's turn to suffer. Desperate families fled from their villages as wells dried up, cattle died, and crops wilted. By 1985, an estimated 9 million people, half of them native Sudanese, were dying of starvation. Emergency food supplies from many countries poured into Sudan; but due to inadequate transportation, port delays, and diversion of shipments by incompetent or dishonest officials, much of this relief could not be delivered to those who most needed it. Bags of grain lay on the docks, waiting for trucks that did not come because they were immobilized somewhere else, stuck in the sand or mired in the mud of one of Sudan's few passable roads.

Heavy rains in the rainy season regularly washed out sections of track of Sudan's one railroad, the only link with remote provinces other than intermittent air drops. By 1987, it was estimated that 2,000 children a day were dying from malnutrition-related diseases.

Prodded into action in 1989, after a drought-related famine had caused 250,000 deaths, the United Nations organized "Operation Lifeline Sudan," a consortium of two of its agencies (Unicef and the World Food Program) and 40 humanitarian nongovernmental organizations (NGOs). Humanitarian aid averaging $1 million a day reduced the number of Sudanese reguiring emergency relief in the 1990s. However, prolonged drought and the ongoing Civil War increased their numbers significantly in 2000. As of January 2001, the World Food Program (WFP) was feeding 1.7 million people in Sudan, most of them in the provinces of Darfur, Kordofan, Equatoria, and Jonglei. A ban

An Egyptian province under Muhammad Ali
**1820**

Mahdi rebellion against the British and Egyptians
**1881**

The British recapture Khartoum; establishment of joint Anglo-Egyptian control
**1898**

The Civil War begins
**1955**

Sudan becomes an independent republic
**1956**

Nimeiri seizes power
**1969**

Nimeiri is overthrown in a bloodless coup; millions of people die of starvation; the Civil War resumes in the south
**1980s**

The regime institutes systematic slavery
**1990s**

**2000s**

Sudan remains ravaged by the Civil War

Sudan cooperates in the international effort against terrorism

on cattle imports due to outbreaks of foot-and-mouth disease elsewhere added to the misery of southerners, many of whom have only their cattle herds as their assets.

These difficulties have been compounded by the periodic ban on relief flights imposed by the government and requisitioning of food stocks, sometimes by the military, but also by the SPLA or local militias. The Sudanese military's policy forcibly removing villagers from oil-field areas and using food as a weapon, along with rape, forced labor, and abduction of southern youths to be taken to Khartoum as slaves or household servants for Muslim families, has turned a civil war into one of extermination of people.

## FOREIGN POLICY

Aside from the internal devastation of the Civil War, Sudan's somewhat unwitting involvement in events outside its borders has affected its economic survival as well as its political stability. The country sided with Iraq during the Gulf War, and consequently 300,000 Sudanese expatriate workers were expelled from the Arab states in that area. Their return put in further strain on the weak economy and eliminated $445 million annually in worker remittances, which had been an important source of revenue. The regime's reinstatement of Parliament and gradual steps toward representative government helped to improve Sudan's relations with its neighbors. Diplomatic relations were restored with Egypt and Eritrea in 2000. A treaty with Uganda withdrew Sudanese support for the Lord's Resistance Army, an opposition force to the Ugandan government.

Sudan's identification with international terrorism led the UN Security Council to approve *Resolution 1044* in 1996. It imposed economic sanctions on the country. The United States put into

place its own sanctions after Sudanese nationals were implicated in the 1993 bombing of the World Trade Center building in New York.

In August 1998, the Clinton administration's firm belief that Sudan was a major sponsor of international terrorism led to the bombing of the Al-Shifa pharmaceutical plant near Khartoum. The plant, one of six in the country, produced drugs, medicines, and veterinary medications. In January it had been granted a $199,000 contract to ship 100,000 cartons of Shifa-zole (an antibiotic used to treat parasites in animals) to Iraq. The shipment was to be made for humanitarian purposes; hence, it would be exempt from UN–imposed sanctions on that country. But the United States claimed that the shipment would include a chemical that could be used to manufacture the nerve gas UFX. Subsequent investigation proved that the Al-Shifa plant was involved exclusively in production of pharmaceuticals and that the United States had erred in bombing it.

Ironically, the American missile attack united the Sudanese people behind their often-reviled regime. Mobs destroyed the unmanned U.S. embassy in Khartoum as angry demonstrators shouted "the tomb will await our enemies whatever the cost." A Sudanese scholar-professor and former member of the government, ousted for his arguments in favor of secular Islamic reform, noted that "The U.S. has shot itself in the foot. . . . This is not terrorism. You don't deal with a resurgent Muslim world through cruise missiles."

U.S. sanctions on Sudan for its support of international terrorism and harboring of terrorist mastermind Osama bin Laden led to his expulsion from Sudan in 1996. In its continuing effort to regain international respectability, the regime also offered the use of its military facilities to

the United States after the September 11, 2001, terrorist bombings. It signed UN Security Council *Resolutions 1044, 1054, and 1066*, which require the suspension of support for terrorist groups, and began rounding up the remaining members of bin Laden's network. As one observer noted, "Sudan is now effectively eliminated as one of the biggest bases of operation for bin Laden."[9]

## NOTES

1. Dunstan Wai, *The African-Arab Conflict in the Sudan* (New York: Africana Publishing, 1981), p. 32.

2. Southerners are not so favorable; in the south, the Mahdi's government was as cruel as the Egyptian. *Ibid.,* p. 31.

3. Peter M. Holt, in *The History of the Sudan,* 3rd ed. (London: Weidenfeld and Nicolson, 1979), p. 123, quotes the British governor as saying that they were recruited on the basis of "good health, high character and fair abilities."

4. *Ibid.,* p. 171.

5. The SSU is defined as "a grand alliance of workers, farmers, intellectuals, business people and soldiers." Harold D. Nelson, ed., *Sudan, A Country Study* (Washington, D.C.: American University, Foreign Area Studies, 1982), p. 199.

6. Quoted in Tareq Y. Ismael and Jacqueline S. Ismael, *Government and Politics in Islam* (New York: St. Martin's Press, 1985), Appendix, pp. 148–149.

7. *Ibid.,* p. 150.

8. *The Christian Science Monitor* (April 16, 1985).

9. Robin Wright, in *The Los Angeles Times* (October 2001).

## DEVELOPMENT

The Middle East's poorest country made a 180° turn economically in 2000 with the reactivation of its dormant oil fields. Production in 2000 generated revenues of $550 million. Annual revenues are estimated to average $300–$400 million, given the size and reserves of the fields. However, large-scale arms purchases, mostly from China, and other costs of the Civil War, have cut deeply into development projects.

## FREEDOM

Sudan's 1998 Constitution guarantees civil rights for all citizens and establishes separation of powers in government and a multiparty political system. Although the National Assembly has been reinstated and a presidential election was held in 2000, civil rights are limited by the state of emergency and the exclusion from the political process of the southern region.

## HEALTH/WELFARE

Development of the oil industry by an international consortium of oil companies has been widely criticized abroad because it excludes the non-Muslim population from the benefits of production and export. In March 2000, the Clinton administration barred U.S. companies from doing business with the consortium for this reason.

## ACHIEVEMENTS

Although Sudan failed to win a seat on the UN Security Council in 2000, the country gained one on the Human Rights Council when the U.S. seat became vacant.

# Syria (Syrian Arab Republic)

## GEOGRAPHY
*Area in Square Miles (Kilometers):*
71,500 (185,170) (about the size
of North Dakota)
*Capital (Population):* Damascus
(1,549,000)
*Environmental Concerns:*
deforestation; overgrazing; soil
erosion; desertification; water
pollution; insufficient potable
water
*Geographical Features:* primarily
semiarid and desert plateau;
narrow coastal plain; mountains
in the west
*Climate:* predominantly desert;
considerable variation between
the interior and coastal regions

## PEOPLE

### Population
*Total:* 16,730,000
*Annual Growth Rate:* 2.54%
*Rural/Urban Population Ratio:*
47/53
*Major Languages:* Arabic, Kurdish;
Armenian
*Ethnic Makeup:* 90% Arab; 10%
Kurd, Armenian, and others
*Religions:* 74% Sunni Muslim; 16%
Alawite, Druze, and other
Muslim sects; 10% Christian
and Jewish

### Health
*Life Expectancy at Birth:* 68 years
(male); 70 years (female)
*Infant Mortality Rate (Ratio):*
33.8/1,000
*Physicians Available (Ratio):* 1/953

### Education
*Adult Literacy Rate:* 70.8%
*Compulsory (Ages):* 6–12

## COMMUNICATION
*Telephones:* 1,313,000 main lines
*Daily Newspaper Circulation:* 19 per
1,000 people
*Televisions:* 49 per 1,000 people
*Internet Service Provider:* 1 (2000)

## TRANSPORTATION
*Highways in Miles (Kilometers):* 25,741
(41,451)
*Railroads in Miles (Kilometers):* 1,650
(2,750)
*Usable Airfields:* 100
*Motor Vehicles in Use:* 353,000

## GOVERNMENT
*Type:* republic under a military regime
since March 1963
*Independence Date:* April 17, 1946 (from
a League of Nations mandate under
French administration)

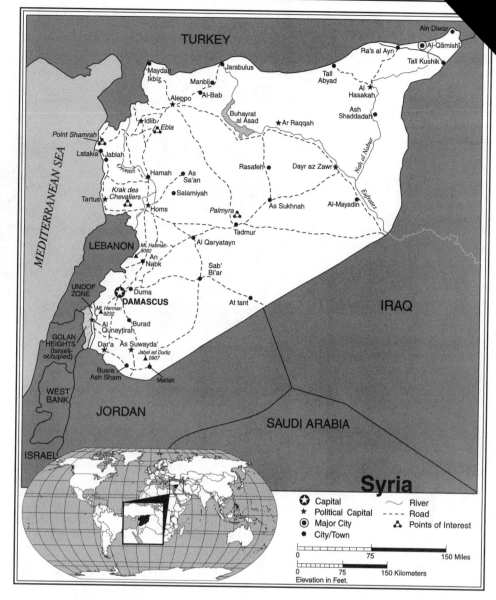

*Head of State/Government:* President
Bashar al-Assad; Prime Minister
Muhammed Miru
*Political Party:* Ba'th (Arab Socialist
Resurrection Party) only legal party
*Suffrage:* universal at 18

## MILITARY
*Military Expenditures (% of GDP):* 5.9%
*Current Disputes:* Golan Heights is Israeli-
occupied; dispute with Turkey over
Turkish water-development plans;
Syrian troops in Lebanon

## ECONOMY
*Currency ($ U.S. Equivalent):* 50.52
pounds = $1
*Per Capita Income/GDP:* $3,100/$50.9 billion
*GDP Growth Rate:* 3.5%
*Inflation Rate:* 1.5%

*Unemployment Rate:* 30%
*Labor Force:* 4,700,000
*Natural Resources:* petroleum; phosphates;
chrome and manganese ores; asphalt;
iron ore; rock salt; marble; gypsum;
hydropower
*Agriculture:* wheat; barley; cotton; lentils;
chickpeas; olives; sugar beets; beef;
mutton; eggs; poultry; milk
*Industry:* petroleum; textiles; food
processing; beverages; tobacco;
phosphate-rock mining
*Exports:* $4.8 billion (primary partners
Germany, Italy, France)
*Imports:* $3.5 billion (primary partners
France, Italy, Germany)

 http://lcweb2.loc.gov/frd/cs/
sytoc.html

is a pale shadow
t various times in
ingdom, incorpo-
ent-day Lebanon,
a part of Turkey
ncient Syria was
also a part of the great civilization centered
in Mesopotamia. Recent discovery by archaeologists of a 6,000-year-old city at
Hamonkar, in northeastern Syria near the
Iraqi and Turkish borders, has pushed back
the start of urban design centuries earlier
than that of the Sumerians.

Syrian kings figure prominently in the
Old Testament as rivals to those of Israel
and Judah. One of these kings, Antiochus,
divided the empire of Alexander the Great,
after the death of that world conqueror,
with his other generals. Antiochus's kingdom dominated the Near East prior to the
establishment of the Roman empire, with
Syria as its center.

Syria also figured prominently in the
expansion of Islam. After the death of the
Prophet Muhammad, his successors,
called *caliphs*, expanded Islamic rule over
a territory greater than Rome. They moved
their capital from Mecca to Damascus.
The Umayyad Caliphate, so called because of its family origins in Muhammad's clan, spread the Arabic language
and Islamic culture from North Africa to
the western border of India. Due to its
centrality, Arab geographers and cartogra-
phers termed Syria *Bilad ash-Sham,* literally "east," whence the sun rose over the
lands of Islam.

Modern Syria is a nation of artificial
boundaries. Its borders were determined
by agreement between France and Britain
after World War I. The country's current
boundaries are with Turkey, Iraq, Jordan,
Israel, and Lebanon. (The only one of
these boundaries in dispute is the Golan
Heights, which was seized and annexed by
Israel in the 1970s.) The border with Turkey is defined by a single-track railroad,
perhaps the only case in the world of a
railroad put to that use. Syria's other borders are artificial lines established by outside powers for convenience.

Syria is artificial in another sense: Its political system was established by outside
powers. Since becoming independent in
1946, the Syrians have struggled to find a
political system that works for them. The
large number of coups and frequent changes
in government are evidence of this struggle.
The most stable government in Syria's independent history is the current one, which
has been in power since 1970.

Syrian political instability stems from
the division of the population into separate
ethnic and religious groups. The Syrians

(The Bettmann Archive)

A view of Damascus, probably the oldest city in the world.

are an amalgamation of many different
ethnoreligious groups that have settled the
region over the centuries. The majority of
the population are Sunni Muslim Arabs.
The Alawis form the largest minority
group. Although the Alawis are nominally
Shia Muslims, the Sunni Muslims distrust
them—not primarily because of religion,
but because of the secret nature of their
rituals and because as a minority they are
very clannish. The next-largest minority,
the Druze, live in Israel and Lebanon as
well as Syria. They are nominally Muslims, but their (secret) rituals include
Christian liturgical elements such as the
Eucharist, when they drink the blood and
eat the body not of Christ but of Ali, Muhammad's closest relative.

Non-Arab minorities in Syria include a
small, long-established community of
Jews; and the Kurds, Sunni Muslims also
found in much larger numbers in Iraq,
Turkey, and Iran. Fewer than 10 percent
of Syria's people are Christian. Hafez al-
Assad's regime, no doubt due to its own
minority status (Alawi), was the most religiously tolerant in the Middle East.
Christian communities have been and presumably still are allowed to hold drum parades and carry effigies of the crucified
Christ through city streets at Easter, and
Muslims and Christians visit each other's
houses of worship and participate jointly
in such festivals as Christmas and Mouloud, the Prophet Muhammad's birthday.

Although Syrian cities are slowly becoming more homogeneous in population,

the different communities still constitute a
majority in certain areas. Thus, Alawis
make up 60 percent of the population of
the northern coast, and Druze predominate
in Jabal Druze, near the Lebanese border,
and in that part of the Golan Heights still
under Syrian control. Kurds are found
mostly north of Aleppo and eastward toward the Turkish border.

## HISTORY

Syria's greatest period was probably that
of the Umayyad caliphs (A.D. 661–750).
These caliphs were rulers of a vast Islamic
empire. The first Umayyad caliph, Mua-
wiya, is considered one of the political
geniuses of Islam. He described his political philosophy to a visitor as follows:

> I apply not my lash where my tongue
> suffices, nor my sword where my
> whip is enough. If there be one hair
> binding me to my fellow men I let it
> not break. If they pull I loosen; if they
> loosen I pull.[1]

During this period of Umayyad rule,
Damascus became a great center of learning and culture. But later Umayyad caliphs were no more successful than their
modern Syrian counterparts in developing
effective government. They ruled by fear,
repression, and heavy taxation. They also
made new non-Arab converts to Islam pay
a special tax from which Arab Muslims
were exempted. They were finally overthrown by non-Arab Muslim invaders

from Iraq. From that time until Syria became an independent republic, its destiny was determined by outsiders.

Syria was ruled by the Ottoman Turks for four centuries as a part of their empire. It was divided into provinces, each governed by a pasha whose job it was to collect taxes and keep order (with the help of an Ottoman garrison). In mountain areas such as Lebanon, then part of Syria, the Ottomans delegated authority to the heads of powerful families or leaders of religious communities. The Ottomans recognized each of these communities as a *millet,* a Turkish word meaning "nation." The religious head of each millet represented the millet in dealings with Ottoman officials. The Ottomans, in turn, allowed each millet leader to manage the community's internal affairs. The result was that Syrian society became a series of sealed compartments. The millet system has disappeared, but its effects have lingered to the present, making national unity difficult.

### The French Mandate
In the nineteenth century, as Ottoman rule weakened and conflict developed among Muslim, Christian, and Druze communities in Syria, the French began to intervene directly in Syria to help the Maronite Christians. French Jesuits founded schools for Christian children. In 1860, French troops landed in Lebanon to protect the Christian Maronites from massacres by the Druze. French forces were withdrawn after the Ottoman government agreed to establish a separate Maronite region in the Lebanese mountains. This arrangement brought about the development of Lebanon as a nation separate from Syria. The Christians in Syria were less fortunate. About 6,000 of them were slaughtered in Damascus before Ottoman troops restored order.[2]

In the years immediately preceding World War I, numbers of young Syrian Christians and some Muslims were exposed through mission schools to ideas of nationalism and human rights. A movement for Arab independence from Turkish rule gradually developed, centered in Damascus and Beirut. After the start of World War I, the British, with French backing, convinced Arab leaders to revolt against the Ottoman government. The Arab army recruited for the revolt was led by Emir Faisal, the second son of Sharif Husayn of Mecca, leader of the powerful Arab Hashimite family, and the Arab official appointed by the Ottomans as "Protector of the Holy Shrines of Islam." Faisal's forces, along with a British army, drove the Ottomans out of Syria. In 1918,

(UPI/Bettmann)

In 1920, following the successful expulsion of the Ottoman government from Syria in 1918, Emir Faisal (pictured above) was named king of Syria.

the emir entered Damascus as a conquering hero, and in 1920 he was proclaimed king of Syria.

Faisal's kingdom did not last long. The British had promised the Arabs independence in a state of their own, in return for their revolt. However, they had also made secret agreements with France to divide the Arab regions of the defeated Ottoman Empire into French and British protectorates. The French would govern Syria and Lebanon; the British would administer Palestine and Iraq. The French now moved to collect their pound of flesh. They sent an ultimatum to Faisal to accept French rule. When he refused, a French army marched to Damascus, bombarded the city, and forced him into exile. (Faisal was brought back by the British and later was installed as the king of Iraq under a British protectorate.)

What one author calls the "false dawn" of Arab independence was followed by the establishment of direct French control over Syria.[3] The Syrians reacted angrily to what they considered betrayal by their former allies. Resistance to French rule continued throughout the mandate period (1920–1946), and the legacy of bitterness over their betrayal affects Syrian attitudes toward outside powers, particularly Western powers, to this day.

The French did some positive things for Syria. They built schools, roads, and hospitals, developed a productive cotton industry, and established order and peaceful relations among the various communities. But the Syrians remained strongly attached to the goals of Arab unity and Arab independence, first in Syria, then in a future Arab nation.[4]

### INDEPENDENT SYRIA
Syria became independent in 1946. The French had promised the Syrians independence during World War II but delayed their departure after the war, hoping to keep their privileged trade position and military bases. Eventually, pressure from the United States, the Soviet Union, and Britain forced the French to leave both Syria and Lebanon.

The new republic began under adverse circumstances. Syrian leaders had little experience in government; the French had not given them much responsibility and had encouraged personal rivalries in their divide-and-rule policy. The Druze and Alawi communities feared that they would be under the thumb of the Sunni majority. In addition, the establishment in 1948 of the State of Israel next door caused great instability in Syria. The failure of Syrian armies to defeat the Israelis was blamed on weak and incompetent leaders.

For two decades after independence, Syria had the reputation of being the most unstable country in the Middle East. There were four military coups between 1949 and 1954 and several more between 1961 and 1966. There was also a brief union with Egypt (1958–1961), which ended in an army revolt.

One reason for Syria's chronic instability was that political parties, were simply groups formed around individuals. At independence, the country had many such parties. Other parties were formed on the basis of ideology, such as the Syrian Communist Party. In 1963, one party, the Ba'th, acquired control of all political activities. Since then, Syria has been a single-party state.

### THE BA'TH
The Ba'th Party (the Arabic word *ba'th* means "resurrection") began in the 1940s as a political party dedicated to Arab unity. It was founded by two Damascus schoolteachers, both French-educated: Michel Aflaq, a Greek Orthodox Christian, and Salah Bitar, a Sunni Muslim. In 1953, the Ba'th merged with another political party, the Arab Socialist Party. Since then, the formal name of the Ba'th has been the Arab Socialist Resurrection Party.

The Ba'th was the first Syrian political party to establish a mass popular base and to draw members from all social classes. Its program called for freedom, Arab unity, and socialism. The movement for Arab unity led to the establishment of the branches of the party in other Arab countries, notably Iraq and Lebanon. The party appealed particularly to young officers in the armed forces; and it attracted strong support from the Alawi community, because it called for social justice and the equality of all Syrians.

The Ba'th was instrumental in 1958 in arranging a merger between Syria and Egypt as the United Arab Republic (U.A.R.). The Ba'thists had hoped to undercut their chief rival, the Syrian Communist Party, by the merger. But they soon decided that they had made a mistake. The Egyptians did not treat the Syrians as equals but as junior partners. Syrian officers seized control and expelled the Egyptian advisers. It was the end of the U.A.R.

For the next decade, power shifted back and forth among military and civilian factions of the Ba'th Party. The process had little effect on the average Syrian, who liked to talk about politics but was wary, with good reason, of any involvement. Gradually, the military faction got the upper hand; and, in 1970, Lieutenant General Hafez al-Assad, the defense minister of one of the country's innumerable previous governments, seized power in a bloodless coup.[5]

## THE HAFEZ AL-ASSAD REGIME

Syria can be called a presidential republic, in the sense that the head of state has extensive powers, which are confirmed in the Constitution approved in 1973. He decides and executes policies, appoints all government officials, and commands the armed forces. He is also head of the Ba'th Party. Under the Constitution, he has unlimited emergency powers "in case of grave danger threatening national unity or the security . . . of the national territory" (Article 113), which only the president can determine.

Hafez al-Assad ruled Syria for nearly three decades, becoming in the process the longest-serving elected leader of any Arab state. He was first elected in 1971 (as the only candidate), and thereafter for five consecutive seven-year terms, the last in 1999. Over the years he broadened the political process to some extent, establishing a People's Assembly with several small socialist parties as a token opposition body in the Legislature. In 1990, elections were held for an enlarged, 250-member Assembly. Ba'th members won 134 seats to 32 for the opposition; the remainder were won by independents. Assad then approved the formation of a National Progressive Front, which included the independents. But mindful of Syria's long history of political instability in the years before he took office, he decreed that its only function would be approval of laws issued by the Ba'th Central Committee.

## Syria's Role in Lebanon

Assad's position was strengthened domestically in the 1970s due to his success (or perceived success) in certain foreign-policy actions. The Syrian Army fought well against Israel in the October 1973 War, and Syria subsequently received both military and financial aid from the Soviet Union as well as its Arab brothers. The invitation by the Arab League for Syria to intervene in Lebanon, beginning with the 1975–1976 Lebanese Civil War, was widely popular among Syrians. They never fully accepted the French action of separating Lebanon from Syria during the mandate period, and they continue to maintain a proprietary attitude toward Lebanon. Assad's determination to avoid conflict with Israel led him in past years to keep a tight rein on Syrian-based Palestine Liberation Organization (PLO) operations. The al-Saiqa Palestinian Brigade was integrated into the Syrian Army, for example. However, Assad's agreement to join a Middle East conference with other Arab states and Israel in 1991 resulted in the release of all PLO activists held in detention in Syria.

When the Lebanese Civil War broke out, Assad pledged that he would control the Palestinians in Lebanon. He sent about 2,000 al-Saiqa guerrillas to Beirut in early 1976. The peacekeeping force approved by the Arab League for Lebanon included 30,000 regular Syrian troops. For all practical purposes, this force maintained a balance of power among Lebanese factions until the Israeli invasion of June 1982. It then withdrew to the eastern Biqa' Valley, avoiding conflict with Israeli forces and providing sanctuary to Palestinian guerrillas escaping from Beirut.

From this vantage point, Syria made a number of attempts to broker a peace agreement among the various Lebanese factions. However, all of them failed, owing in large measure to the intractable hostility separating Muslim from Christian communities and intercommunal rivalries among the militias. In 1987, faced with a near-total breakdown in public security, Assad ordered 7,000 elite Syrian commandos into West Beirut. Syrian forces maintained an uneasy peace in the Lebanese capital until 1989, when they were challenged directly by the Christian militia of General Michel Aoun, who refused to accept Syrian authority and declared himself president. Syrian forces surrounded the Christian enclave and, early in 1990, mounted a massive assault, backed by heavy artillery, that finally broke the Christian resistance. Aoun took refuge in the French Embassy and then went into exile.

Syria reduced its forces in Lebanon to 30,000–35,000 after the end of the Lebanese Civil War. In June 2001, the Syrian garrison in Beirut, which included tanks and armor, was moved to bases in eastern Lebanon. The surprise move came after Israel had withdrawn its troops from southern Lebanon, resulting also from months of complaints by Lebanese Christians of Syrian interference in their internal affairs.

## Internal Opposition

Opposition to the Hafez al-Assad regime was almost nonexistent in the 1990s. A major cause for resentment among rank-and-file Syrians, however, is the dominance of the Alawi minority over the government, armed forces, police, and intelligence services. The main opposition group was the Syrian branch of the Muslim Brotherhood (a Sunni organization spread throughout the Arab world). The Brotherhood opposed Assad because of his practice of advancing Alawi interests over those of the Sunni majority. Its main stronghold was the ancient city of Hama, famed for its Roman waterwheels. In 1982, Assad's regular army moved against Hama after an ambush of government officials there. The city was almost obliterated by tanks and artillery fire, with an estimated 120,000 casualties. Large areas were bulldozed as a warning to other potentially disloyal elements in the population.[6]

The "lessons of Hama" have not been forgotten. The calculated savagery of the attack was meant not only to inflict punishment but to provide a warning for future generations of Syrians. It did have a positive result. In ensuring the survival of his regime, Assad guaranteed political stability, along with prosperity for the largely Sunni merchant class. Thus other Arab states look toward the "Hama solution" with nostalgia.

Assad's control over the various levers of power, notably the intelligence services (mukhabarat), the security police, and the military, ensured his rule during his lifetime, despite his narrow support base as head of a minority group. After Hama, no organized opposition group remained to challenge his authority. As a result, he was able to give Syria the political stability that his predecessors had never provided.

Syrian popular support for the aging president grew in the 1990s, as he continued to resist accommodation with Israel, while other Arab states were establishing relations or even recognizing the State of Israel. This broader support enabled Assad to loosen the reins of government. At the start of his fourth term he included several Sunni ministers in his cabinet. Political prisoners were released, most of them Muslim Brotherhood members. In 1999, he ordered a general amnesty for 150,000 prisoners to "clean out the jails"; most of them had been jailed for smuggling, desertion from the armed forces, or various economic crimes.

## THE ECONOMY

At independence, Syria was primarily an agricultural country, although it had a large merchant class and a free-enterprise system with considerable small-scale industrial development. When it came to power, the Ba'th Party was committed to state control of the economy. Agriculture was collectivized, with land expropriated from large landowners and converted into state-managed farms. Most industries were nationalized in the 1960s. The free-enterprise system all but disappeared.

Cotton was Syria's principal export crop and money earner until the mid-1970s. But with the development of oil fields, petroleum became the main export. Syria produced enough oil for its own needs until 1980. However, the changing global oil market and the reluctance of foreign companies to invest in Syrian oil exploration under the unfavorable concession terms set by the government have hampered development. Oil production, formerly 580,000 barrels per day, fell to 340,000 b/d in the mid-1990s. It increased to 450,000 b/d in 2000 and 550,000 b/d in 2001, due largely to imports of Iraqi oil for further export through the Kirkuk-Banias pipeline. Syria's position is that the arrangement does not violate the United Nation's oil-for-food program anymore than that of Iraqi exports of crude oil to Jordan.

Agriculture, which accounts for 30 percent of gross domestic product annually at present and employs 33 percent of the labor force, benefited in the early 1990s from expanded irrigation, which brought additional acreage under cultivation. Production of cotton, the major agricultural crop, reached a record 1.1 million tons in 2000, with 270,000 tons exported.

The end of Syria's special relationship with the Soviet Union due to the breakup of that country in 1991 encouraged a modest liberalization of the Ba'thist economic system. A prominent exiled businessman who had been one of Assad's bitterest critics returned in 1993 to set up a retail store chain similar to London's Marks & Spencer, taking advantage of new tax exemptions and other incentives. Syria's large number of educated and skilled managers, along with a dependable and productive labor force, has encouraged foreign investment. Foreign companies

such as Benetton, Adidas, and Kentucky Fried Chicken have established franchises in the country to take advantage of its substantial consumer market.

Hafez al-Assad's death in June 2000 and the accession of his son Bashar to the presidency have been felt most strongly in the economic sector. In December 2000, the Ba'th Regional Command, the party's central committee, approved the establishment of private banks, ending 40 years of state monopoly over banking and foreign-exchange transactions. For the first time in the lives of most of them, Syrians no longer had to go across the Lebanese border to stash their illegal dollars in Lebanese banks or to use them to buy imported goods unavailable in their own country.

## FOREIGN RELATIONS

Syria's often prickly relations with its neighbors and its rigid opposition to Israel have made the country the "odd man out" in the region at various times. Syria's hostility to the rival Ba'thist regime in Iraq resulted in periodic border closings and a shutdown in shipments of Iraqi oil through Syrian pipelines to refineries on the Mediterranean coast in the 1980s. The border was closed definitively after Syria sided with Iran during its war with Iraq and remained so in the Gulf War, as Syrian troops formed part of the coalition that drove Iraqi forces out of Kuwait. The UN sanctions on Iraq brought the two Arab neighbors closer together. The border was reopened in 1997, and the new regime removed all restrictions on travel to Iraq in 2001. In February, the two Ba'th regimes signed a free-trade agreement; and in August, Syrian prime minister Muhammed Moru made the first official visit to Baghdad of any Syrian government leader since 1979. Current trade volume between the countries is $500 million.

Assad expelled Abdullah Ocalan, leader of insurgent Kurdish forces fighting for independence from Turkey, in February 1999. The Kurdish leader had been useful to Syria as a bargaining chip with Turkey, particularly for increased allocation of water from the Euphrates River.

Syria's role as an alleged major sponsor of international terrorism has adversely affected its relations with Western countries for years. In 1986, a number of these countries broke diplomatic relations after the British discovered a Syrian-funded plot to blow up an Israeli airliner at Heathrow Airport in London, England. Relations were restored after the Assad regime disassociated itself from terrorist actions, and the image of Syria as a terrorist sponsor largely disappeared after the country sent troops to aid in the expulsion

of Iraq from Kuwait. The U.S. Department of State recently removed Syria from its list of countries supporting international terrorism, providing a further incentive for foreign investment in the Syrian economy.

Syria's inclusion in the Department of State list as a state supporter of terrorism had been based on the harboring of groups engaged in violence, usually against Israel but also against Yassir Arafat's Palestinian organization. The groups included Hamas, the Popular Front for the Liberation of Palestine (PFLP), and Islamic Jihad. However, the Assad government was careful not to allow them to launch anti-Israeli operations from Syrian territory. The September 11, 2001, terrorist attacks on the United States brought a change in the equation. President Bashar denounced the terrorist attacks and criticized Osama bin Laden and his al-Qaeda network for giving Islam a bad name. However, he declared that the Palestinian–Israeli conflict ultimately bore responsibility for the terrorism. In March 2002, Bashar announced strong support for the Saudi proposal for recognition of Israel by the Arab states in return for Israel's withdrawal to its pre-1967 borders.

The 1993 Oslo agreements between Israel and the Palestinians and the 1994 Jordan–Israel peace treaty encouraged Assad to begin serious discussions with the Israelis for a settlement of the Golan Heights issue. Talks began with the Rabin government, but they were broken off after the election of Benjamin Netanyahu as Israel's prime minister. His defeat in the 1999 elections made possible the revival of negotiations, inasmuch as incoming prime minister Ehud Barak had stressed settlement of the Golan as part of his 15-month plan for regional peace.

Syrian and Israeli representatives met in January 2000 in the resort town of Shepherdstown, West Virginia, with then-president Bill Clinton serving as moderator. Their talks ended inconclusively, as the Syrian and Israeli positions remained far apart on such issues as the Golan Heights. However, the death of Hafez al-Assad makes the pursuit of a peace treaty with Israel less urgent for the new Syrian regime. Its priorities of necessity have concentrated on internal reform and revitalization of the economy. As one scholar observed, [Israel] took 90 percent of Assad's energy. Israel was a legitimizing factor for the regime—Syria must always have an enemy to help create political cohesion."[7]

## PROSPECTS

Hafez al-Assad died on June 10, 2000, the last of a group of autocratic rulers who

| The capital of Umayyads is removed to Damascus; Syria becomes the center of the Islamic world **661–750** | Ottoman province **1517–1917** | An independent Arab Kingdom of Syria is proclaimed under Faisal; shot down by French **1920** | French mandate, followed by independence **1920–1946** | Union with Egypt into the United Arab Republic **1958–1961** | Syrian troops are sent to Lebanon as a peacekeeping force **1976** | Syria's association with international terrorism leads some European countries to break relations and some to impose economic sanctions **1980s** | Assad's efforts to gain the release of hostages in Lebanon leads the United States and other countries to resume aid and diplomatic relations **1990s** | **2000s** |

Hafez al-Assad dies; his son Bashar is elected to succeed him

Syria denounces the September 11, 2001, terrorist attacks

had dominated the Middle East for more than a generation. His younger son, Bashar, was elected to succeed him on June 25 by the People's Assembly, confirmed by 97.5 percent of voters in a nationwide referendum. The Syrian Constitution, which precludes anyone under age 40 from serving as president, was conveniently set aside by the Ba'th Party Regional Command, since Bashar will not attain that exalted status until 2005.

Syria's new leader was trained as an opthalmologist in Britain and had little experience in national politics before being summoned back to replace his elder brother Basil (killed in an auto accident in 1994) as the heir-apparent. His only public post was that of commander of the Republican Guard. After his election to the presidency (he was the only candidate, like his father), Bashar became head of the armed forces and of the Ba'th Regional Command.

While cynical observers joked that Syria had exchanged a dictator for an eye doctor, Bashar brought fresh air into a moribund political system and a stagnant economy. He began by enforcing the rule requiring retirement at age 60, which is mandatory for the military but had never been adhered to. As a result, many senior commanders were forced to retire. They included Hafez al-Assad's long-serving chief of staff and the head of the mukhabarat. In March 2002, the entire cabinet resigned, as the president continued to turn to new faces to strengthen political support and help liberalize the economy.

Bashar also shook up the Ba'th Regional Command. It now includes 10 women and several younger army commanders. In other reforms, private universities are allowed to organize, ending half a century of Ba'thist monopoly over

higher education. The first privately owned newspaper hit the stands in 2001; entitled *Al-Doumari* ("The Lamplighter") it is a 16-page weekly devoted to satirical pieces on the "mistakes" of the government and the Arab world in general. And as president also of the Syrian Computer Society, Bashar was instrumental in linking his people into the Internet and other features of today's technological world.

Bashar's release of political prisoners, one of his pre-election pledges, has reduced the prison population to less than 1,000. His promised economic reforms have been less successful. Nightmarish Soviet-style bureaucratic controls remain in force, with an outmoded technology and lack of privatization of national industries being a serious hindrance to economic development. The main prop for the economy is the 200,000 barrels per day of oil from Iraq, under a barter arrangement allowing the country to increase its own oil exports.

Bashar's tentative steps toward a more open Syrian society and representative government generated a negative reaction in 2001, largely on the part of old-guard conservative elements, with their vested interest in the status quo. In addition to other reforms, the young president encouraged the formation of some 300 "salons," private forums where Syrians could freely discuss political and economic issues and recommend changes. But beginning in February, the salons were gradually shut down and new ones denied permission to organize. A series of arrests of leading intellectuals, opposition leaders in Parliament, and human-rights activists followed. They were charged with attempting to change the Constitution illegally and encourage sectarian conflict.

**NOTES**

1. The statement is found in many chronicles of the Umayyads. See Richard Nyrop, ed., *Syria, A Country Study* (Washington, D.C.: American University, Foreign Area Studies, 1978), p. 13.

2. Philip Khoury, *Urban Notables and Arab Nationalism: The Politics of Damascus 1860–1920* (Cambridge, England: Cambridge University Press, 1983), pp. 8–9.

3. Umar F. Abd-Allah, *The Islamic Struggle in Syria* (Berkeley, CA: Mizan Press, 1983), p. 39.

4. "Syrians had long seen themselves as Arabs... who considered the Arab world as rightly a single entity." John F. Devlin, *Syria: Modern State in an Ancient Land* (Boulder, CO: Westview Press, 1983), p. 44.

5. He was barred from attending a cabinet meeting and then surrounded the meeting site with army units, dismissed the government, and formed his own. *Ibid.,* p. 56.

6. Thomas L. Friedman, in *From Beirut to Jerusalem*, coined the phrase "Hama rules" to describe Assad's domestic political methods. "Hama rules" means no rules at all.

7. Quoted in Scott Peterson, in *The Christian Science Monitor* (July 12, 2000).

---

**DEVELOPMENT**

New currency and banking and investment laws were issued in March 2000 as the country moved slowly toward a free-market economy. Private banks are authorized, but they must have at least $33 million available for capital investments. The 2001 budget increased expenditures by 17% due to a 25% increase in salaries for public employees. A $19.3 million grant from the European Union covered most of the increase.

**FREEDOM**

The 1973 Constitution defines Syria as a socialist, populist democracy. The Hafez al-Assad regime limited press freedom along with human rights. President Bashar has restored some of these rights. Also, the new budget was presented to the People's Assembly for approval before being issued. But the country still has a long way to go to become truly free, populist, and democratic.

**HEALTH/WELFARE**

Syria's high birth rate has generated a young population. With insufficient jobs available, the unemployment rate is around 30%. A mandatory family-planning program will eventually lower the birth rate, and a grant from the European Union is being used to expand the public sector and provide salary increases for those already employed there.

**ACHIEVEMENTS**

Ghada Shonaa brought honor and glory to Syria when she became the first Syrian to win an Olympic gold medal. She won the women's heptathlon at the 1996 Olympic Games in Atlanta, Georgia. And although the United States and Syria remain estranged politically, the Host House Trio, an American jazz group, joined with Syrian musicians in 1999 in a concert in Damascus.

# Tunisia (Republic of Tunisia)

## GEOGRAPHY

*Area in Square Miles (Kilometers):*
63,153 (163,610) (about the size of Georgia)

*Capital (Population):* Tunis (675,000)

*Environmental Concerns:* hazardous-waste disposal; water pollution; limited fresh water resources; deforestation; overgrazing; soil erosion; desertification

*Geographical Features:* mountains in north; hot, dry central plain; semiarid south merges into Sahara

*Climate:* hot, dry summers; mild, rainy winters; desert in the south, temperate in the north

## PEOPLE

### Population

*Total:* 9,705,000

*Annual Growth Rate:* 1.15%

*Rural/Urban Population Ratio:* 37/63

*Major Languages:* Arabic; French

*Ethnic Makeup:* 98% Arab–Berber; 1% European; 1% others

*Religions:* 98% Muslim; 1% Christian; less than 1% Jewish

### Health

*Life Expectancy at Birth:* 72 years (male); 76 years (female)

*Infant Mortality Rate (Ratio):* 2.9/1,000

*Physicians Available (Ratio):* 1/1,640

### Education

*Adult Literacy Rate:* 66.7%

*Compulsory (Ages):* 6–16

## COMMUNICATION

*Telephones:* 655,000 main lines

*Daily Newspaper Circulation:* 45 per 1,000 people

*Televisions:* 156 per 1,000 people

*Internet Service Provider:* 1 (2000)

## TRANSPORTATION

*Highways in Miles (Kilometers):* 14,345 (23,100)

*Railroads in Miles (Kilometers):* 1,403 (2,260)

*Usable Airfields:* 32

*Motor Vehicles in Use:* 531,000

## GOVERNMENT

*Type:* republic

*Independence Date:* March 20, 1956 (from France)

*Head of State/Government:* President Zine El Abidine Ben Ali; Prime Minister Mohammed Ghannouchi

*Political Parties:* Democratic Constitutional Rally (RCD), majority party; others are Movement for Democratic Socialism (MDS), Ettajdid, Unionist Democratic Rally, and Socialist Liberal Party. Ennahda ("Resistance") and other Islamic fundamentalist parties are currently outlawed

*Suffrage:* universal at 20

## MILITARY

*Military Expenditures (% of GDP):* 1.5%

*Current Disputes:* none

## ECONOMY

*Currency ($ U.S. Equivalent):* 1.46 dinars = $1

*Per Capita Income/GDP:* $6,500/$62.8 billion

*GDP Growth Rate:* 5%

*Inflation Rate:* 3%

*Unemployment Rate:* 15.6%

*Labor Force:* 2,650,000

*Natural Resources:* petroleum; phosphates; iron ore; lead; zinc; salt

*Agriculture:* olives; dates; oranges; almonds; grain; sugar beets; grapes; poultry; beef; dairy products

*Industry:* petroleum; mining; tourism; textiles; footwear; food; beverages

*Exports:* $6.1 billion (primary partners Germany, France, Italy)

*Imports:* $8.4 billion (primary partners France, Germany, Italy)

 http://www.cia.gov/cia/publications/factbook/index.html

http://www.tunisiaonline.com

## TUNISIA

Tunisia, the smallest of the four North African countries, is less than one tenth the size of Libya, its neighbor to the east. However, its population is nearly twice the size of Libya's.

Tunisia's long coastline has exposed it over the centuries to a succession of invaders from the sea. The southern third of the country is part of the Sahara Desert; the central third consists of high, arid plains. Only the northern region has sufficient rainfall for agriculture. This region contains Tunisia's single permanent river, the Madjerda.

The country is predominantly urban. There is almost no nomadic population, and there are no high mountains to provide refuge for independent mountain peoples opposed to central government. The Tunis region and the Sahel, a coastal plain important in olive production, are the most densely populated areas. Tunis, the capital, is not only the dominant city but also the hub of government, economic, and political activity.

## HISTORY

Tunisia has an ancient history that is urban rather than territorial. Phoenician merchants from what is today Lebanon founded a number of trading posts several thousand years ago. The most important one was Carthage, founded in 814 B.C. It grew wealthy through trade and developed a maritime empire. Its great rival was Rome; after several wars, the Romans defeated the Carthaginians and destroyed Carthage. Later, the Romans rebuilt the city, and it became great once again as the capital of the Roman province of Africa. Rome's African province was one of the most prosperous in the empire. The wheat and other commodities shipped to Rome from North African farms were vitally needed to feed the Roman population. When the ships from Carthage were late due to storms, lost at sea, or seized by pirates, the Romans suffered hardship. Modern Tunisia has yet to reach the level of prosperity it had under Roman rule.

The collapse of the Roman Empire in the fifth century A.D. affected Roman Africa as well. Cities were abandoned; the irrigation system that had made the farms prosperous fell into ruin. A number of these Roman cities, such as Dougga, Utica, and Carthage itself, which is now a suburb of Tunis, have been preserved as historical monuments of this period.

Arab armies from the east brought Islam to North Africa in the late seventh century. After some resistance, the population accepted the new religion, and from that time on the area was ruled as the Arab–Islamic province of *Ifriqiya*. The Anglicized form of this Arabic word, "Africa," was eventually applied to the entire continent.

The Arab governors did not want to have anything to do with Carthage, since they associated it with Christian Roman rule. They built a new capital on the site of a village on the outskirts of Carthage, named Tunis. The fact that Tunis has been the capital and major city in the country for 14 centuries has contributed to the sense of unity and nationhood among most Tunisians.[1]

The original Tunisian population consisted of Berbers, a people of unknown origin. During the centuries of Islamic rule, many Arabs settled in the country. Other waves of immigration brought Muslims from Spain, Greeks, Italians, Maltese, and many other nationalities. Until recently, Tunisia also had a large community of Jews, most of whom emigrated to the State of Israel when it was founded in 1948. The blending of ethnic groups and nationalities over the years has created a relatively homogeneous and tolerant society, with few of the conflicts that marked other societies in the Islamic world.

From the late 1500s to the 1880s, Tunisia was a self-governing province of the Ottoman Empire. It was called a regency because its governors ruled as "regents" on behalf of the Ottoman sultan. Tunis was already a well-established, cosmopolitan city when it became the regency capital. Its rulers, called beys, were supported by an Ottoman garrison and a corsair fleet of fast ships that served as auxiliaries to the regular Ottoman navy. The corsairs, many of them Christian renegades, ruled the Mediterranean Sea for four centuries, raiding the coasts of nearby European countries and preying on merchant vessels, seizing cargoes and holding crews for ransom. The newly independent United States was also affected, with American merchant ships seized and cargoes taken by the corsairs. In 1799, the United States signed a treaty with the bey, agreeing to pay an annual tribute in return for his protection of American ships.

In the nineteenth century, European powers, particularly France and Britain, began to interfere directly in the Ottoman Empire and to seize some of its outlying provinces. France and Britain had a "gentleman's agreement" about Ottoman territories in Africa—the French were given a free hand in North Africa and the British in Egypt. In 1830, the French seized Algiers, capital of the Algiers Regency, and began to intervene in neighboring Tunisia in order to protect their Algerian investment.

The beys of Tunis worked very hard to forestall a French occupation. In order to do this, they had to satisfy the European powers that they were developing modern political institutions and rights for their people. Ahmad Bey (1837–1855) abolished slavery and piracy, organized a modern army (trained by French officers), and established a national system of tax collection. Muhammad al-Sadiq Bey (1859–1882) approved in 1861 the first written Constitution in the Islamic world. This Constitution had a declaration of rights and provided for a hereditary (but not an absolute) monarchy under the beys. The Constitution worked better in theory than in practice. Provincial landowners and local chiefs opposed the Constitution because it undermined their authority. The peasants, whom it supposedly was designed to protect, opposed the Constitution because it brought them heavy new taxes, collected by government troops sent from Tunis. In 1864, a popular rebellion broke out against the bey, and he was forced to suspend the Constitution.

In 1881, a French army invaded and occupied all of Tunisia, almost without firing a shot. The French said that they had intervened because the bey's government could not meet its debts to French bankers and capitalists, who had been lending money for years to keep the country afloat. There was concern also about the European population. Europeans from many countries had been pouring into Tunisia, ever since the bey had given foreigners the right to own land and set up businesses.

The bey's government continued under the French protectorate, but it was supplemented by a French administration, which held actual power. The French collected taxes, imposed French law, and developed roads, railroads, ports, hospitals, and schools. French landowners bought large areas and converted them into vineyards, olive groves, and wheat farms. For the first time in 2,000 years, Tunisia exported wheat, corn, and olive oil to the lands on the other side of the Mediterranean.

Because Tunisia was small, manageable, and primarily urban, its society, particularly in certain regions, was influenced strongly by French culture. An elite developed whose members preferred the French language to their native Arabic. They were encouraged to enroll their sons in Sadiki College, a European-type high school set up in Tunis by the French to train young Tunisians and expose them to Western subjects. After completing their studies at Sadiki, most were sent to France to complete their education in such institutions as the Sorbonne (University of Paris). The experience helped shape their political thinking, and on their return to Tunisia a number of them formed a movement for self-government that they called Destour (*Dustur* in Arabic), meaning "Constitution." The name was logical, since these young men had observed that independent countries such as France based their sovereignty on such a document. They were convinced that nationalism, "in order to be effective against the French, had to break loose from its traditional power base in the urban elite and mobilize mass support."[2] In 1934, a group of young nationalists quit the Destour and formed a new party, the Neo-Destour. The goal of the Neo-Destour Party was Tunisia's independence from France. From the beginning, its leader was Habib Bourguiba.

## HABIB BOURGUIBA

Habib Ben Ali Bourguiba, born in 1903, once said he had "invented" Tunisia, not historically but in the sense of shaping its existence as a modern sovereign nation. The Neo-Destour Party, under Bourguiba's leadership, became the country's first mass political party. It drew its membership from shopkeepers, craftspeople, blue-collar workers, and peasants, along with French-educated lawyers and doctors. The party became the vanguard of the nation, mobilizing the population in a campaign of strikes, demonstrations, and violence in order to gain independence. It was a long struggle. Bourguiba spent many years in prison. But eventually the Neo-Destour tactics succeeded. On March 20, 1956, France ended its protectorate and Tunisia became an independent republic, led by Habib Bourguiba.

One of the problems facing Tunisia today is that its political organization has changed very little since independence. A Constitution was approved in 1959 that established a "presidential republic"—that is, a republic in which the elected president has great power. Bourguiba was elected president in 1957.

Bourguiba was also the head of the Neo-Destour Party, the country's only legal political party. The Constitution provided for a National Assembly, which is responsible for enacting laws. But to be elected to the Assembly, a candidate had to be a member of the Neo-Destour Party. Bourguiba's philosophy and programs for national development in his country were often called Bourguibism. It was tailored to the particular historical experience of the Tunisian people. Since ancient Carthage, Tunisian life has been characterized by the presence of a strong central government able to impose order and bring relative stability to the people. The

predominance of cities and villages over nomadism reinforced this sense of order. The experience of Carthage, and even more so that of Rome, set the pattern. "The Beys continued the pattern of strong order while the French developed a strongly bourgeois, trade-oriented society, adding humanitarian and some authoritarian values contained in French political philosophy."[3] Bourguiba considered himself the tutor of the Tunisian people, guiding them toward moral, economic, and political maturity.

In 1961, Bourguiba introduced a new program for Tunisian development that he termed "Destourian Socialism." It combined Bourguibism with government planning for economic and social development. The name of the Neo-Destour Party was changed to the Destour Socialist Party (PSD) to indicate its new direction. Destourian Socialism worked for the general good, but it was not Marxist; Bourguiba stressed national unanimity rather than class struggle and opposed communism as the "ideology of a godless state." Bourguiba took the view that Destourian Socialism was directly related to Islam. He said once that the original members of the Islamic community (in Muhammad's time in Mecca) "were socialists . . . and worked for the common good."[4] For many years after independence, Tunisia appeared to be a model among new nations because of its stability, order, and economic progress. Particularly notable were Bourguiba's reforms in social and political life. Islamic law was replaced by a Western-style legal system, with various levels of courts. Women were encouraged to attend school and enter occupations previously closed to them, and they were given equal rights with men in matters of divorce and inheritance.

Bourguiba strongly criticized those aspects of Islam that seemed to him to be obstacles to national development. He was against women wearing the veil; polygyny; and ownership of lands by religious leaders, which kept land out of production. He even encouraged people not to fast during the holy month of Ramadan, because their hunger made them less effective in their work.

There were few challenges to Bourguiba's leadership. His method of alternately dismissing and reinstating party leaders who disagreed with him effectively maintained Destourian unity. But in later years Bourguiba's periodic health problems, the growth of Islamic fundamentalism, and the disenchantment of Tunisian youth with the single-party system raised doubts about Tunisia's future under the PSD.

The system was provided with a certain continuity by the election of Bourguiba as president-for-life in 1974, when a constitutional amendment was approved specifying that at the time of his death or in the event of his disability, the prime minister would succeed him and hold office pending a general election. One author observed: "Nobody is big enough to replace Bourguiba. He created a national liberation movement, fashioned the country and its institutions."[5] Yet he failed to recognize or deal with changing political and social realities in his later years.

The new generation coming of age in Tunisia is deeply alienated from the old. Young Tunisians (half the population are under age 15) increasingly protest their inability to find jobs, their exclusion from the political decision-making process, the unfair distribution of wealth, and the lack of political organizations. It seems as if there are two Tunisias: the old Tunisia of genteel politicians and freedom fighters; and the new one of alienated youths, angry peasants, and frustrated intellectuals. Somehow the two have gotten out of touch with each other.

The division between these groups has been magnified by the growth of Islamic fundamentalism, which in Bourguiba's view was equated with rejection of the secular, modern Islamic society that he created. The Islamic Tendency Movement (MTI) emerged in the 1980s as the major fundamentalist group. MTI applied for recognition as a political party after Bourguiba had agreed to allow political activity outside of the Destour Party and had licensed two opposition parties. But MTI's application was rejected.

## THE END OF AN ERA

In 1984, riots over an increase in the price of bread in 1984 signaled a turning point for the regime. For the first time in the republic's history, an organized Islamic opposition challenged Bourguiba, on the grounds that he had deformed Islam to create a secular society. Former Bourguiba associates urged a broadening of the political process and formed political movements to challenge the Destour monopoly on power. Although they were frequently jailed and their movements proscribed or declared illegal, they continued to press for political reform.

However, Bourguiba turned a deaf ear to all proposals for political change. Having survived several heart attacks and other illnesses to regain reasonably good health, he seemed to feel that he was indestructible. His personal life underwent significant change as he became more authoritarian. He had divorced his French wife, apparently in response to criticism that a true Tunisian patriot would not have a French spouse. His second wife, Wassila, a member of the prominent Ben Ammar family, soon became the power behind the throne. As Bourguiba's mental state deteriorated, he divorced her arbitrarily in 1986. At that time the president-for-life assemed direct control over party and government. As he did so, his actions became increasingly irrational. He would appoint a cabinet minister one day and forget the next that he had done so. Opposition became an obsession with him. The two legal opposition parties were forced out of local and national elections by arrests of leaders and a shutdown of opposition newspapers. The Tunisian Labor Confederation (UGTT) was disbanded, and the government launched a massive purge of fundamentalists.

The purge was directed by General Zine el-Abidine Ben Ali, the minister of the interior, regarded by Bourguiba as one of the few people he could trust. There were mass arrests of Islamic militants, most of them belonging to the outlawed Islamic Tendency Movement, a fundamentalist organization that Bourguiba outlawed as subversive. (It was later reorganized as a political party, Ennahda—"Renaissance"—but was again banned by Ben Ali after he became president.)

Increasingly, it seemed to responsible leaders that Bourguiba was becoming senile as well as paranoid. "The government lacks all sense of vision," said a long-time observer. "The strategy is to get through the day, to play palace parlor games." A student leader was more cynical: "There is no logic to [Bourguiba's] decisions; sometimes he does the opposite of what he did the day before."[6]

A decision that would prove crucial to the needed change in leadership was made by Bourguiba in September 1987, when he named Ben Ali as prime minister. Six weeks later, Ben Ali carried out a bloodless coup, removing the aging president under the 1974 constitutional provision that allows the prime minister to take over in the event of a president's "manifest incapacity" to govern. A council of medical doctors affirmed that this was the case. Bourguiba was placed under temporary house arrest in his Monastir villa, but he was allowed visitors and some freedom of movement within the city (after 1990).

Habib Bourguiba died in April 2001, at the age of 96. He was buried next door to this villa, in a mausoleum of white marble. The words inscribed on its door— "Liberator of women, builder of modern Tunisia"—seem an appropriate inscription for the "inventor" of his country.

## NEW DIRECTIONS

President Ben Ali (elected to a full five-year term in April 1989) initiated a series of bold reforms designed to wean the country away from the one-party system. Political prisoners were released under a general amnesty. Prodded by Ben Ali, the Destour-dominated National Assembly passed laws ensuring press freedom and the right of political parties to form as long as their platforms are not based exclusively on language, race, or religion. The Assembly also abolished the constitutional provision establishing the position of president-for-life, which had been created expressly for Bourguiba. Henceforth Tunisian presidents would be limited to three consecutive terms in office.

Ben Ali also undertook the major job of restructuring and revitalizing the Destour Party. In 1988, it was renamed the Constitutional Democratic Assembly (RCD). Ben Ali told delegates to the first RCD Congress that no single party could represent all Tunisians. There can be no democracy without pluralism, fair elections, and freedom of expression, he said.

Elections in 1988 underscored Tunisia's fixation on the single-party system. RCD candidates won all 141 seats in the Chamber of Deputies, taking 80 percent of the popular vote. Two new opposition parties, the Progressive Socialist Party and the Progressive Socialist Rally, participated but failed to win more than 5 percent of the popular vote, the minimum needed for representation in the Chamber. MTI candidates, although required to run as independents because of the ban on "Islamic" parties under the revised election law, dominated urban voting, taking 30 percent of the popular vote in the cities. However, the winner-take-all system of electing candidates shut them out as well.

Local and municipal elections have confirmed the RCD stranglehold on Tunisian political life; its performance was the exact opposite of that of the National Liberation Front in neighboring Algeria, where the dominant party was discredited over time and finally defeated in open national elections by a fundamentalist party. In the 1995 local and municipal council elections, RCD candidates won 4,084 out of 4,090 contested seats, with 92.5 percent of Tunisia's 1,865,401 registered voters casting their ballots.

Efforts to mobilize an effective opposition movement earlier were hampered when Ahmed Mestiri, the long-time head of the Movement of Socialist Democrats (MDS), the major legal opposition party, resigned in 1992. In the 1994 elections, the only opposition party to increase its support was the former Tunisian Commu-

nist Party, renamed the Movement for Renewal. It won four seats in the Chamber as Tunisia continued its slow progress toward multiparty democracy.

Developments since the 1994 election have emphasized the regime's commitment to political pluralism. The Chamber of Deputies was enlarged from 144 to 160 members, with 20 seats reserved for opposition deputies. Ben Ali was reelected for a third five-year presidential term, and again in 1999 for his fourth term. However, he faced opposition in this latter election, for the first time in his (and Tunisia's) republican history. Perhaps as a result, his victory margin was "only" 99.44 percent. Opposition-party leaders denouced the election as window-dressing and an insult to their intelligence. One observer noted: "It will become more difficult for an Arab president to win a presidency without a contest. [He] can no longer take his public for granted."[7]

## THE ECONOMY

The challenge to Ben Ali lies not only in broadening political participation but also in improving the economy. After a period of impressive expansion in the 1960s and 1970s, the growth rate began dropping steadily, largely due to decreased demand and lowered prices for the country's three main exports (phosphates, petroleum, and olive oil). Tunisia is the world's fourth-ranking producer of phosphates, and its most important industries are those related to production of superphosphates and fertilizers.

Problems have dogged the phosphate industry. The quality of the rock mined is poor in comparison with that of other phosphate producers, such as Morocco. The Tunisian industry experienced hard times in the late 1980s with the drop in global phosphate prices; a quarter of its 12,000-member workforce were laid off in 1987. However, improved production methods and higher world demand led to a 29 percent increase in exports in 1990.

Tunisia's oil reserves are estimated at 1.65 billion barrels. The main producing fields are at El Borma and offshore in the Gulf of Gabes. New offshore discoveries and a 1996 agreement with Libya for 50/50 sharing of production from the disputed Gulf of Gabes oil field have improved oil output, currently about 4.3 million barrels annually.

Tunisia's associate-member status in the European Union has brought the country some economic benefits. In addition, the economic stabilization program begun in 1986 as a consequence of International Monetary Fund insistence on reforms as a prerequisite for further loans, has provided

| Wars between Rome and Carthage, ending in the destruction of Carthage and its rebuilding as a Roman city 264–146 B.C. | The establishment of Islam in Ifriqiya, with its new capital at Tunis A.D. 800–900 | The Hafsid dynasty develops Tunisia as a highly centralized urban state 1200–1400 | Ottoman Turks establish Tunis as a corsair state to control Mediterranean sea lanes 1500–1800 | French protectorate 1881–1956 | Tunisia gains independence, led by Habib Bourguiba 1956 | An abortive merger with Libya 1974 | Bourguiba is removed from office in a "palace coup;" he is succeeded by Ben Ali 1980s | Tunisia's economic picture brightens; Ben Ali seeks some social modernization; women's rights are expanded 1990s |

2000s

Human-rights abuses continue

a strong stimulus to the economy. The growth rate reached a record 6.9 percent in 1996 but has averaged 5 percent annually since then.

The country's political stability and effective use of its limited resources for development have made it a favored country for foreign aid. Since the 1970s it has received more World Bank loans than any other Arab or African country. The funding has been equitably distributed, so that 60 percent of the population are middle class, and 80 percent own their own homes.

## THE FUTURE

Tunisia's progress as an economic beacon of stability in an unstable region has been somewhat offset by a decline in its long-established status as a successful example of a secular, progressive Islamic state. Following President Ben Ali's ouster of his predecessor in 1987, he proclaimed a new era for Tunisians, based on respect for law, human rights, and democracy. Tunisia's "Islamic nature" was reaffirmed by such actions as the reopening of the venerable Zitouna University in Tunis, a center for Islamic scholarship. But the rise of Islamic fundamentalism, in Tunisia as elsewhere in the Islamic world, has seriously damaged the country's reputation as an "oasis of openness." An attack on RCD party headquarters in February 1991 by members of An-Nahda, a fundamentalist group that advocates a Tunisian government based on Islamic law, was a turning point. Since then, the government has pursued a policy of extreme repression of Ennahda and related groups.

In subsequent years, Tunisia has become an increasingly closed society. The press is heavily censored. Bourguiba's death was not even reported in Tunisia, and the obligatory seven days of mourning were countered by instructions to banks and government offices to keep regular hours. Telephones are routinely tapped. More than 1,000 Ennahda members have been arrested and jailed without trial. In December 2000, a dozen members of another Islamic fundamentalist group were given 17-year jail sentences for forming an illegal organization; their lawyers walked out of the trial to protest the court's bias and procedural abuses.

The regime's repression of Islamic groups, even moderate nonviolent ones, has changed its former image as a tolerant, progressive Islamic country. The Tunisian League for Human Rights, oldest in the Arab world, was closed in 1992. Arrest and harassment of intellectuals, journalists, and others for alleged criticism of the regime are routine. Foreign publications are banned, and opposition leaders are pilloried in the state-controlled press as fundamentalists. Almost the only positive step in the human-rights area was a press code amendment in 2001 that precluded use of torture or physical punishment of journalists.

Following his "tainted" election victory in 1999, Ben Ali announced a new program designed to provide full employment by 2004. Called the 21–21 program, it would supplement an earlier 26–26 one that had brought the public and private sectors together to end poverty and increase home ownership, notably among the poor. In his address announcing the new program, Ben Ali stated: "Change comes from anchoring the democratic process in a steady and incremental progress aimed at avoiding setbacks or losing momentum."[8] However, his own lack of charisma (when compared with his illustrious predecessor), and his regime's continued repression of human rights, suggested otherwise. One analyst wondered if Bourguiba's funeral had marked a watershed after all, "galvanizing a generation too frightened to speak."[9]

## NOTES

1. Harold D. Nelson, ed., *Tunisia: A Country Study* (Washington, D.C.: American University, Foreign Area Studies, 1979), p. 68.

2. *Ibid.*, p. 42.

3. *Ibid.*, p. 194. What Nelson means, in this case, by "authoritarianism" is that the French brought to Tunisia the elaborate bureaucracy of metropolitan France, with levels of administration from the center down to local towns and villages.

4. *Ibid.*, p. 196.

5. Jim Rupert, in *The Christian Science Monitor* (November 23, 1984).

6. Louise Lief, in *The Christian Science Monitor* (April 10, 1987).

7. Mamoun Fandy, in *The Christian Science Monitor* (October 25, 1999).

8. Georgie Ann Geyer, in *The Washington Post* (October 23, 1999).

9. Noted in *The Economist* (April 15, 2000).

## DEVELOPMENT

Tunisia's average annual GDP growth rate has held steady at 5% in recent years. However, a 16.5% rise in imports in 2000 generated a significant negative trade balance. Imports were up 8.7%, offsetting a 94% increase in oil exports. Associate status with the European Union has helped the economy, mainly in agricultural exports.

## FREEDOM

The curtailment of civil rights, imposed by the Ben Ali government in its campaign against Islamic fundamentalists, has resulted in the jailing of nearly 2,000 political prisoners. Although most were given short sentences and then released, the government often bans foreign travel, confiscates passports, or harasses their families as a means of control. In June 1999, Tunisia was expelled from the World Press Association for its restrictions on press freedom. An amendment to the press law in 2001 removes some of these restrictions. In particular, it makes a distinction between "critical" articles and those that "defame" the state.

## HEALTH/WELFARE

Tunisia has overhauled its school and university curricula to emphasize respect for other monotheistic religions. They require courses on the Universal Declaration of Human Rights, democracy, and the value of the individual. The new curricula are at variance with government repressive policies, but they do stress Islamic ideals of tolerance for the school-age population.

## ACHIEVEMENTS

The tourism sector of the economy has grown dramatically in recent years to become the country's second-largest industry after textiles. Revenues in 1999 were $1.3 billion. Filming of episodes of *Star Wars* in the cave dwellings of Matmata, in the far south, brought unexpected wealth to a region where the monthly income averages $137.

# Turkey (Republic of Turkey)

## GEOGRAPHY

*Area in Square Miles (Kilometers):*
301,303 (780,580) (about the size of Texas)

*Capital (Population):* Ankara (2,940,000)

*Environmental Concerns:* water and air pollution; deforestation; threat of oil spills from Bosporus ship traffic

*Geographical Features:* mostly mountains; a narrow coastal plain; a high central plateau (Anatolia)

*Climate:* varied temperate

## PEOPLE

### Population

*Total:* 66,494,000
*Annual Growth Rate:* 1.24%
*Rural/Urban Population Ratio:* 29/71
*Major Languages:* Turkish; Kurdish; Arabic
*Ethnic Makeup:* 80% Turk; 17% Kurd; 3% others
*Religions:* 99% Muslim (about 79% Sunni, 20% Shia); 1% others

### Health

*Life Expectancy at Birth:* 69 years (male); 74 years (female)
*Infant Mortality Rate (Ratio):* 47.3/1,000
*Physicians Available (Ratio):* 1/1,200

### Education

*Adult Literacy Rate:* 85%
*Compulsory (Ages):* 6–16

## COMMUNICATION

*Telephones:* 17,000 main lines
*Daily Newspaper Circulation:* 44 · per 1,000 people
*Televisions:* 171 per 1,000 people
*Internet Service Providers:* 22 (2000)

## TRANSPORTATION

*Highways in Miles (Kilometers):* 237,747 (382,397)
*Railroads in Miles (Kilometers):* 5,336 (8,607)
*Usable Airfields:* 121
*Motor Vehicles in Use:* 4,320,000

## GOVERNMENT

*Type:* republican parliamentary democracy
*Independence Date:* October 29, 1923 (successor state to the Ottoman Empire)
*Head of State/Government:* President Ahmed Necdet Sezer; Prime Minister Bulent Ecevit

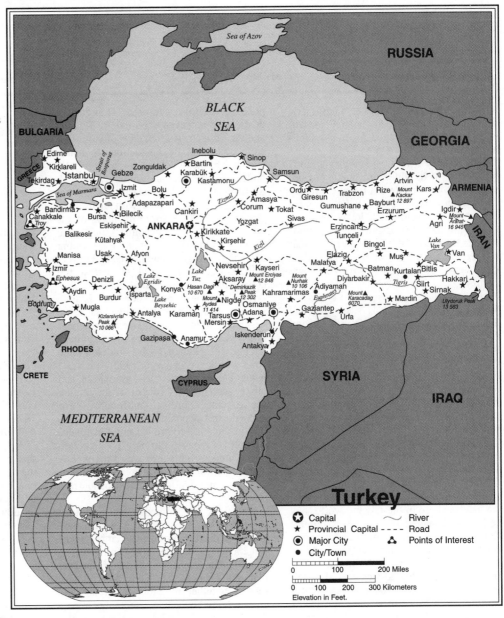

*Political Parties:* Democratic Left; Justice and Development; Nationalist Action Party; True Path; others
*Suffrage:* universal at 18

## MILITARY

*Military Expenditures (% of GDP):* 5.6%
*Current Disputes:* complex disputes with Greece; Cyprus question; periodic friction with Syria and Iraq over Euphrates River's water resources

## ECONOMY

*Currency ($ U.S. Equivalent):* 1,489,652 lira = $1
*Per Capita Income/GDP:* $6,800/$444 billion
*GDP Growth Rate:* 6%
*Inflation Rate:* 39%

*Unemployment Rate:* 5.6% (plus underemployment)
*Labor Force:* 23,000
*Natural Resources:* antimony; coal; chromium ore; mercury; copper; borate; sulfur; iron ore; meerschaum; arable land; hydropower
*Agriculture:* tobacco; cotton; grains; olives; sugar beets; pulse; citrus; livestock
*Industry:* textiles; food processing; automobiles; mining; steel; petroleum; construction; lumber; paper
*Exports:* $26.9 billion (primary partners Germany, United States, United Kingdom)
*Imports:* $55.7 billion (primary partners Germany, Italy, United States)

# TURKEY

Except for a small area in extreme South-eastern Europe called Thrace, the Republic of Turkey comprises the large peninsula of Asia Minor (Anatolia), which forms a land bridge between Europe and Asia. Asiatic Turkey is separated from European Turkey by the Bosporus, a narrow strait connecting the Black Sea with the Aegean Sea and the Mediterranean Sea via the Sea of Marmara. Throughout history, the Bosporus and the Dardanelles, at the Mediterranean end, have been important strategic waterways, fought over by many nations.

Except for the Syrian border, Asiatic Turkey's borders are defined by natural limits, with seas on three sides and rugged mountains on the fourth. European Turkey's frontiers with Greece and Bulgaria are artificial; they fluctuated considerably in the nineteenth and twentieth centuries before the Republic of Turkey was established.

Modern Turkey occupies a much smaller area than did its predecessor, the Ottoman Empire. The Ottoman Turks were the dominant power in the Middle East for more than five centuries. After the defeat of the empire in World War I, Turkey's new leader, Mustafa Kemal Ataturk, turned away from the imperial past, limiting the new republic to territory with a predominantly Turkish population. Since then, Turkey has not attempted to annex land beyond its natural Anatolian borders—with two exceptions. One was the Hatay, formerly a province of Syria that was ceded to Turkey by the French (who then controlled Syria under mandate from the League of Nations). The annexation was considered justified since the majority of the population was Turkish. The second exception was Cyprus. This island republic has a Greek majority in the population, but a significant minority (20 percent) are Turkish Cypriots, descended from Turkish families that settled there when Cyprus was Ottoman territory. Although it is a sovereign state, fears of violence against the Cypriot Turks led Turkish forces to occupy the northern third of the island in 1974. They have been there since then, with no agreement as yet on reunification of Cyprus. Some years ago, the Turkish government officially recognized the area under its control as the Republic of Northern Cyprus, but no other country has done so.

Asia Minor has an ancient history of settlement. Most of the peninsula is a plateau ringed by mountains. The mountains are close to the coast; over the centuries, due to volcanic action, the coastline became cracked, with deep indentations and islands just offshore. The inland plateau has an area of arid steppe with dried-up salt lakes at the center, but most of it is rolling land, well suited to agriculture. Consequently, people settled in small, self-contained villages at an early period and began to cultivate the land. Over the centuries, nomadic peoples migrated into Asia Minor, but the geographical pattern there did not encourage them to remain nomadic.

In terms of national unity, the modern Turkish state has not had the thorny problem of ethnic conflicts—with two important exceptions. One is the Armenians, an ancient Christian people who ruled over a large part of what is now eastern Turkey many centuries ago. The great majority were forced to leave their homeland during World War I, because the Turkish government suspected them of aiding the invading Russian armies. Hundreds of thousands of Armenians died or were killed outright during this series of forced emigrations. Although the republican government has consistently disclaimed responsibility for all wartime actions of its Ottoman predecessor, including the massacres of Armenians, Armenian terrorist groups carried out a number of attacks on Turkish diplomats abroad in the 1970s and 1980s. The Secret Army for the Liberation of Armenia (ASALA) killed some 30 diplomats and embassy staff in various countries.

When violence proved unproductive, Armenian community leaders undertook a lobbying campaign with the U.S. government and European governments to encourage them to put pressure on Turkey for an admission of its indirect responsibility for the deportations, since they had been carried out by its predecessor. This persistent lobbying finally brought results. In March 2001, the U.S. House of Representatives approved a resolution calling on Turkey to "recognize publicly the Armenian genocide." A similar resolution was approved in April by the European Parliament, the deliberative body of the European Union. The latter resolution went a step further, in calling on Turkey to withdraw its forces from northern Cyprus.

Subsequently, in perhaps the most damaging blow to Turkish pride, the French National Assembly approved a resolution to the effect that the Armenian deportations were in fact *genocide*, the intentional elimination of a people. Turkey reacted by recalling its ambassador to France. Turkish trade with the country was suspended, and the government cancelled $350 million in military contracts with French firms. But as yet the government of the republic has not changed its official position, that the deportations were justified at the time and that it cannot be held responsible, nearly a century later, for the policies and actions of its Ottoman predecessor.[1]

The other exception to Turkish homogeneity is the Kurds, who make up 17 percent of the population officially but may be closer to 20 percent. There are also Kurdish populations in Iraq, Syria, and Iran, but Turkey's Kurds form the largest component of this "people without a nation," one of the last ethnic peoples in the world who do not have their own indigenous government. Their clannish social structure and fierce spirit of independence have led to periodic Kurdish uprisings against the governments that rule them. In Turkey, the Ataturk regime crushed Kurdish rebellions in the 1920s, and from then on, Kurds were officially referred to as "Mountain Turks." Until the 1980s, Turkey's Kurds were considered an unimportant, albeit economically deprived, population group. Many emigrated to the cities or abroad, mainly to Germany and the Netherlands. Turkey's Kurdish population is concentrated in its southeastern region and its provincial capital, Diyarbakir. A large number of them have moved to Istanbul, Ankara, and other cities and have been assimilated into the surrounding Turkish culture. Those who remain are grouped in compact villages and are mostly farmers or herders.

In addition to those in Cyprus, there are two other important populations of ethnic Turks outside of Turkey. They are in Bulgaria and western (Greek) Thrace. Those in Bulgaria make up about 10 percent of the population. In the 1980s, they were suppressed by the Communist Bulgarian regime as foreigners and as Muslims, although they had lived in peace with their neighbors for centuries. About one third fled to Turkey as refugees. This forced assimilation policy was reversed after the fall of the Communist regime, and most of them have now returned to their Bulgarian homes.

There are also about 120,000 ethnic Turks in Greek Thrace, left over from the forced exchange of Greek and Turkish populations in 1922. However, they have never been granted Greek citizenship and are discriminated against in various ways. In 1990, the Greek government unilaterally abrogated the 1923 Treaty of Lausanne, which, among other things, guaranteed the Turkish minority the right to choose its own religious leaders. They are not interfered with in their religious practices and have their own elected prayer leaders (Imams). The great majority are small farmers or petty traders. In all other respects they remain a disadvantaged minority in Christian Greece.

An estimated 20 percent of Turkey's population are *Alevis,* a blanket term for various Muslim communities whose Islamic rituals and beliefs differ from those of the Sunni majority. Some are Shias; others are ethnic and religious compatriots of the Alawis, who currently rule Syria, and live close by in the Hatay and other areas near the Syrian border. Other Alevis form compact communities in such small Anatolian towns as Sivas, Corum, and Kahramanras, and Istanbul has a substantial Alevi population. Alevi rituals differ from those of both Sunnis and Shias in that they incorporate music and dancing into their services. They have no religious leaders, but each Alevi community has a *dede* ("old man") who directs community affairs. One observer said of them, "They claim to live according to the inner meaning of religion (*batin*) rather than by external (*zahir*) demands . . . , prayer, the fast in Ramadan, *zakat* and *hajj* are alien."[2]

In the years of the Ottoman Empire, a large Jewish population settled in Turkey's lands, invited there from Spain after their expulsion from that country by its Christian rulers. Nearly every Ottoman city had its Jewish quarter and synagogue. But with the establishment of Israel and the rise of Turkish nationalism, the great majority of Jews left Turkey. Small Jewish communities still survive in Ankara, Istanbul, and Antakya. Most of the country's synagogues have become architectural museums, beautifully designed monuments to the multiethnic, multireligious Ottoman past.

## HISTORY:
## A PARADE OF PEOPLES

The earliest political unit to develop in the peninsula was the Empire of the Hittites (1600–1200 B.C.), inventors of the two-wheeled chariot and one of the great powers of the ancient Near East. Other Asia Minor peoples made important contributions to our modern world through their discoveries and inventions. We are indebted to the Lydians for our currency system. They were great warriors but also great traders, developing a coinage based on gold and silver to simplify trade exchanges. The gold was panned from the Pactolus River near their capital of Sardis. It was then separated from other metals by melting through capellation—mixing the particles with salt, heating in an earthenware container, and finally smelting until ready to mint. The Lydian king, Croesus (561–547 B.C.), who ruled when Lydian trade was at its peak, has become a familiar figure, "rich as Croesus" as a result of this process.[3]

Following the collapse of the Roman Empire in the fifth century A.D., Asia Minor became the largest part of the East Roman or Byzantine Empire, named for its capital, Byzantium. The city was later renamed Constantinople, in honor of the Roman emperor Constantine, after he had become Christian. For a thousand years, this empire was a center and fortress of Christianity against hostile neighbors and later against the forces of Islam.

### The Ottoman Centuries[4]

Various nomadic peoples from Central Asia began migrating into Islamic lands from the ninth century onward. Among them were the ancestors of the Turks of today. They settled mostly along the borders between Christian and Islamic powers in Asia Minor and northwest Iran. Although divided into families and clans and often in conflict, the Turks had a rare sense of unity as a nation. They were also early converts to Islam. Its simple faith and requirements appealed to them more than did Christian ritual, and they readily

(UN photo/Rice)

Turkey has been populated for thousands of years by a myriad of peoples, including Hittites, Greeks, and Romans. This ancient Turkish artifact is mute evidence of one of these many bygone civilizations.

joined in Islam's battles as *Ghazis,* "warriors for the faith." Asia Minor, having been wrested from the Greeks by the Turks, also gave the Turks a strong sense of identification with that particular place. To them it was Anadolu (Anatolia), "land of the setting sun," a "sacred homeland" giving the Turks a strong sense of national identity and unity.

The Ottomans were one of many Turkish clans in Anatolia. They took their name from Osman, a clan leader elected because of certain qualifications considered ideal for a Ghazi chieftain—wisdom, prudence, courage, skill in battle, and justice, along with a strong belief in Islam.[5] Osman's clan members identified with their leader to such an extent that they called themselves *Osmanlis,* "sons of Osman," rather than *Turks,* a term they equated with boorish, unwashed peasants.

Although the Ottomans started out with a small territory, they were fortunate in that Osman and his successors were extremely able rulers. Osman's son, Orkhan, captured the important Greek city of Bursa, across the Sea of Marmara from Constantinople (modern-day Istanbul). It became the first Ottoman capital. Later Ottoman rulers took the title of sultan to signify their temporal authority over expanding territories. A series of capable sultans led the Ottoman armies deep into Europe. Constantinople was surrounded, and on May 29, A.D. 1453, Mehmed II, the seventh sultan, captured the great city amid portents of disaster for Christian Europe.[6]

The North African corsair city-states of Algiers, Tripoli, and Tunis, which owed nominal allegiance to the sultan but were in practice self-governing, aligned their swift fleets with his from time to time in the contest with European states for control of the Mediterranean. On two occasions his armies besieged Vienna, and during the rule of Sultan Sulayman I, a contemporary of Queen Elizabeth I of England, the Ottoman Empire was the largest and most powerful in the world.

One reason for the success of Ottoman armies was the Janissaries, an elite corps recruited mostly from Christian villages and converted to Islam by force. Janissary units were assigned to captured cities as garrisons. Those in Constantinople enjoyed special privileges. They had their own barracks and served on campaigns as the sultan's personal guard. Invading Ottoman armies were preceded by marching bands of drummers and cymbal players, like the bagpipers who marched ahead of Scottish armies. These Janissary bands made such terrifying noises that villagers fled in terror at their arrival, while enemy forces surrendered after hearing their "fearsomely loud sounds, like an alarm."[7]

Another factor that made the Ottoman system work was the religious organization of non-Muslim minority groups as self-governing units termed *millets,* a Turkish word meaning "nations." Each millet was headed by its own religious leader, who was responsible to the sultan for the leadership and good behavior of his people. The three principal millets in Turkey were the Armenians, Greek Orthodox Christians, and Jews. Although Christians and Jews were not considered equal to freeborn Muslims, they were under the sultan's protection. Armenian, Greek, and Jewish merchants rendered valuable services to the empire due to their linguistic skills and trade experience, particularly after the wars with Europe were replaced by peaceful commerce.

### The "Sick Man of Europe"

In the eighteenth and nineteenth centuries, the Ottoman Empire gradually weakened, while European Christian powers grew stronger. European countries improved their military equipment and tactics and began to defeat the Ottomans regularly. The sultans were forced to sign treaties and lost territories, causing great humiliation, since they had never treated Christian rulers as equals before. To make matters worse, the European powers helped the Greeks and other Balkan peoples to win their independence from the Ottomans.

The European powers also took advantage of the millet system to intervene directly in the Ottoman Empire's internal affairs. French troops invaded Lebanon in 1860 to restore order after civil war broke out there between the Christian and Druze communities. The European powers claimed the right to protect the Christian minorities from mistreatment by the Muslim majority, saying that the sultan's troops could not provide for their safety.

One or two sultans in the nineteenth century tried to make reforms in the Ottoman system. They suppressed the Janissaries, who by then had become an unruly mob, and organized a modern army equipped with European weapons, uniforms, and advisers. Sultan Mahmud II issued an imperial decree called *Tanzimat* (literally, "reordering"). It gave equal rights under the law to all subjects, Muslims and non-Muslims alike, in matters such as taxation, education, and property ownership. Provincial governors were directed to implement its provisions. In one province, Baghdad, the governor, Miidhat Pasha, established free schools and hospitals, invited foreign missionaries to develop a Western-style curriculum for these schools, reduced taxes, and restored public security in this traditionally unruly border province.

Subsequently Midhat Pasha was appointed grand vizier (e.g., prime minister) by the new sultan, Abdul Hamid II. In 1876, prodded by Russian and British threats of a takeover, the sultan agreed to Midhat Pasha's urgings and issued a Constitution, the first such document in the empire's history. It would limit the sultan's absolute power by establishing an elected Grand National Assembly (GNA), which would represent all the classes, races, creeds, and ethnic, and linguistic groups within the empire. (The GNA survived the fall of the empire and was reborn as the Legislature of the Turkish Republic.)

However, the forces of reaction, represented by the religious leaders, the sultan's courtiers, and the sultan himself, were stronger than the forces for reform. Abdul-Hamid had no real intention of giving up the absolute powers that Ottoman sultans had always had. Thus, when the first Grand National Assembly met in 1877 and the members ventured to criticize the sultan's ministers, he dissolved the Assembly.

The European powers became convinced that the Ottomans were incapable of reform. European rulers compared the healthy state of their economies and the growth of representative government in their countries to the grinding poverty and lack of rights for Ottoman subjects, as a healthy person looks at an ill one in a hospital bed. The European rulers referred to the sultan as the "Sick Man of Europe" and plotted his death.

But the Sick Man's death was easier to talk about than to carry out, primarily because the European rulers distrusted one another almost as much as they disliked the sultan. If one European ruler seemed to be getting too much territory, trade privileges, or control over the sultan's policies, the others would band together to block that ruler.

### World War I:
### Exit Empire, Enter Republic

During World War I, the Ottoman Empire was allied with Germany against Britain, France, and Russia. Ottoman armies fought bravely against heavy odds but were eventually defeated. A peace treaty signed in 1920 divided up the empire into British and French protectorates, except for a small part of Anatolia that was left to the sultan. The most devastating blow of all was the occupation by the Greeks of western Anatolia, under the provisions of a secret agreement that brought Greece into the war. It seemed to the Turks that their former subjects had become their rulers.

At this point in the Turkish nation's fortunes, however, a new leader appeared. He would take it in a very different direction. This new leader, Mustafa Kemal, had risen through the ranks of the Ottoman Army to become one of its few successful commanders. He was largely responsible for the defeat of British and Australian forces at the Battle of Gallipoli, when they attempted to seize control of the strategic Dardanelles (Straits) in 1915.

Mustafa Kemal took advantage of Turkish anger over the occupation of Anatolia by foreign armies, particularly the Greeks, to launch a movement for independence. It would be a movement not only to recover the sacred Anatolian homeland but also for independence from the sultan.

The Turkish independence movement began in the interior, far from Constantinople. Mustafa Kemal and his associates chose Ankara, a village on a plateau, as their new capital. They issued a so-called National Pact stating that the "New Turkey" would be an independent republic. Its territory would be limited to areas where Turks were the majority of the population. The nationalists resolutely turned their backs on Turkey's imperial past.

The Turkish War of Independence lasted until 1922. It was fought mainly against the Greeks. The nationalists were able to convince other occupation forces to withdraw from Anatolia by proving that they controlled the territory and represented the real interests of the Turkish people. The Greeks were defeated in a series of fierce battles; and eventually France and Britain signed a treaty recognizing Turkey as a sovereign state headed by Mustafa Kemal.

### THE TURKISH REPUBLIC
The Turkish republic has passed through several stages of political development since it was founded. The first stage, dominated by Mustafa Kemal, established its basic form. "Turkey for the Turks" meant that the republic would be predominantly Turkish in population; this was accomplished by rough surgery, with the expulsion of the Armenians and most of the Greeks. Mustafa Kemal also rejected imperialism and interference in the internal affairs of other nations. He once said, "Turkey has a firm policy of ensuring [its] independence within set national boundaries."[8] Peace with Turkey's neighbors and the abandonment of imperialism enabled Mustafa Kemal to concentrate on internal changes. By design, these changes would be far-reaching, in order to break what he viewed as the dead hand of Islam on Turk-

ish life. Turkey would become a secular democratic state on the European model. A Constitution was approved in 1924, the sultanate and the caliphate were both abolished, and the last Ottoman sultan went into exile. Religious courts were also abolished, and new European law codes were introduced to replace Islamic law. An elected Grand National Assembly was given the responsibility for legislation, with executive power held by the president of the republic.

The most striking changes were made in social life, most bearing the personal stamp of Mustafa Kemal. The traditional Turkish clothing and polygyny were outlawed. Women were encouraged to work, were allowed to vote (in 1930), and were given equal rights with men in divorce and inheritance. Turks were now required to have surnames; Mustafa Kemal took the name *Ataturk,* meaning "Father of the Turks."

Mustafa Kemal Ataturk died on November 10, 1938. His hold on his country had been so strong, his influence so pervasive, that a whole nation broke down and wept when the news came. The anniversary of his death is still observed in Turkey by a moment of silence. He died aboard his private yacht, *Savarona,* the largest of its kind in the world at the time.

Ismet Inonu, Ataturk's right-hand man, succeeded Ataturk and served as president until 1950. Ataturk had distrusted political parties; his brief experiment with a two-party system was abruptly cancelled when members of the officially sponsored "loyal opposition" criticized the Father of the Turks for his free lifestyle. The only political party he allowed was the Republican People's Party (RPP). It was not dedicated to its own survival or to repression, as are political parties in many single-party states. The RPP based its program on six principles, the most important, in terms of politics, being *devrim-cilik* ("revolutionism" or "reformism"). It meant that the party was committed to work for a multiparty system and free elections. One author noted, "The Turkish single party system was never based on the doctrine of a single party. It was always embarrassed and almost ashamed of the monopoly [over power]. The Turkish single party had a bad conscience."[9]

Agitation for political reforms began during World War II. Later, when Turkey applied for admission to the United Nations, a number of National Assembly deputies pointed out that the UN Charter specified certain rights that the government was not providing. Reacting to popular demands and pressure from Turkey's allies, Inonu announced that political parties could be established. The first new

party in the republic's history was the Democratic Party, organized in 1946. In 1950, the party won 408 seats in the National Assembly, to 69 for the Republican People's Party. The Democrats had campaigned vigorously in rural areas, winning massive support from farmers and peasants. Having presided over the transition from a one-party system with a bad conscience to a two-party one, President Inonu stepped down to become head of the opposition.

### MILITARY INTERVENTIONS
Modern Turkey has struggled for decades to develop a workable multiparty political system. An interesting point about this struggle is that the armed forces have seized power three times, and three times they have returned the nation to civilian rule. This fact makes Turkey very different from other Middle Eastern nations, whose army leaders, once they have seized power, have been unwilling to give it up.

Ataturk deliberately kept the Turkish armed forces out of domestic politics. He believed that the military had only two responsibilities: to defend the nation in case of invasion and to serve as "the guardian of the reforming ideals of his regime."[10] Since Ataturk's death, military leaders have seized power only when they have been convinced that the civilian government had betrayed the ideals of the founder of the republic.

The first military coup took place in 1960, after a decade of rule by the Democrats. Army leaders charged them with corruption, economic mismanagement, and repression of the opposition. After a public trial, the three top civilian leaders were executed. Thus far, they have been the only high-ranking Turkish politicians to receive the death sentence. (After the 1980 coup, a number of civilian leaders were arrested, but the most serious sentence imposed was a ban on political activity for the next 10 years for certain party chiefs.)

The military leaders reinstated civilian rule in 1961. The Democratic Party was declared illegal, but other parties were allowed to compete in national elections. The new Justice Party, successor to the Democrats, won the elections but did not win a clear majority. As a result, the Turkish government could not function effectively. More and more Turks, especially university students and trade union leaders, turned to violence as they became disillusioned with the multiparty system. As the violence increased, the military again intervened, but it stopped short of taking complete control.

In 1980, the armed forces intervened for the third time, citing three reasons: failure of the government to deal with political violence; the economic crisis; and the revival of Islamic fundamentalism, which they viewed as a total surrender of the secular principles established by Ataturk. (The National Salvation Party openly advocated a return to Islamic law and organized huge rallies in several Turkish cities in 1979–1981.) The National Assembly was dissolved, the Constitution was suspended, and martial law was imposed throughout the country. The generals said that they would restore parliamentary rule—but not before terrorism had been eliminated.

## RETURN TO CIVILIAN RULE

The military regime approved a new Constitution in 1982. It provided for a multiparty political system, although pre-1980 political parties were specifically excluded. (Several were later reinstated, notably the Republican People's Party, or RPP). Three new parties were allowed to present candidates for a new Grand National Assembly (GNA), and elections were scheduled for 1983. However, the party least favored by the generals, the Motherland Party (ANAP), ran an American-style political campaign, using the media to present its candidates to the country. It won handily. Its leader, Turgut Ozal, became the first prime minister in this phase of Turkey's long, slow progress toward effective multiparty democracy.

Ozal, an economist by profession, had served as minister of finance under the military government in 1980–1982. In that capacity, he developed a strict austerity program that stabilized the economy. But the prime ministership was another matter, especially with five generals looking over his shoulder. The Motherland Party's popularity declined somewhat in 1986–1987, a decline that owed more to a broadening of the political process than to voter disenchantment.

On September 6, 1987, the nation took a significant step forward—although some analysts viewed it as sideways—toward full restoration of the democratic process. Voters narrowly approved the restoration of political rights to about 100 politicians who had been banned from party activity for 10 years after the 1980 coup: The vote was 50.23 percent "yes" to 49.77 percent "no" in a nationwide referendum, a difference of fewer than 100,000 votes. The results surprised many observers, particularly the most prominent political exiles, former prime ministers Suleyman Demirel of the Justice Party and Bulent Ecevit, leader of the banned Republican People's Party. They had expected a heavy vote in their favor. Prime Minister Ozal's

argument that the nation should not return to the "bad old days" before the 1980 coup, when a personal vendetta between these two leaders had polarized politics and paralyzed the economy and there were several dozen murders a day, had clearly carried weight with the electorate.[11]

Thus encouraged, Ozal scheduled new elections for November 1, 1987, a year ahead of schedule. But in October, the Constitutional Court ruled that a December 1986 electoral law was invalid because it had eliminated the primary system, thereby undermining the multiparty system. The elections were held on November 29 under new electoral guidelines. The Motherland Party won easily, taking 292 of 450 seats in the GNA. The Social Democratic Populist Party (SHP), a newcomer to Turkish politics, ran second, with 99 seats; while True Path (DYP), founded by Demirel to succeed the Justice Party, ran a distant third, with 59.

The Motherland Party's large parliamentary majority enabled Ozal to have himself elected president to succeed General Evren in 1989, at the end of the latter's term in office. Although the Turkish presidency is largely a ceremonial office, Ozal continued to run the nation as if it were not, with less successful results than those he had attained during his prime ministership. As a result, popular support for his party continued to erode. In the October 1991 elections for a new National Assembly, candidates of the opposition True Path Party won 180 seats to 113 for the Motherland Party, taking 27 percent of the popular vote, as compared to 24 percent for the majority party. The Social Democratic Populist Party garnered 20 percent of the vote, followed by the Islamic Welfare Party (Refah), whose growing strength was reflected in its 16 percent support from voters.

Lacking a majority in the Assembly, the DYP formed a coalition government with the SHP in November 1991. Party leader Suleyman Demirel became prime minister. The DYP–SHP coalition improved its political position in local elections early in 1992, when its candidates won a majority of urban mayorships. In July of that year, the ban on political parties existing before the 1980 military coup was lifted; most of them had been incorporated into new parties, but the Republican People's Party, founded by Ataturk, reentered the political arena. It drew a number of defections from Assembly members, due in large part to the charismatic appeal of its leader, Deniz Baykal; as a result, the coalition was left with a shaky six-vote majority in the Legislature.

President Ozal died in April 1993, abruptly ending the long political feud be-

tween him and Demirel that had weakened government effectiveness. Demirel succeeded him as president. The DYP elected Tansu Ciller, a U.S.–trained economist and university professor, as Turkey's first woman prime minister, one of two in the Muslim world (the other was Benazir Bhutto of Pakistan).

Ciller's first two years in office were marked by economic difficulties; growing tendencies toward Islamic fundamentalism, spearheaded by Refah; and intensified violence by Kurdish separatists of the Workers' Party of Kurdistan (PKK), in the southeastern region. Nevertheless, her government, a coalition of the DYP and the Republican People's Party, representing the center left and the center right, seemed to be governing effectively in at least some respects. By early 1995, the army had regained control of much of the southeast from PKK forces, and in March, agreement was reached for a customs union with the European Union. Municipal elections in June also favored the ruling coalition. It won 61.7 percent of Council seats against 17.4 percent for Refah candidates and 13.4 percent for those of ANAP.

Thus, the collapse of the coalition government in September came as a surprise to most observers. Republican People's party head Deniz Baykal had set certain terms for continuation of his party's alliance with DYP. These included repeal of a strict antiterrorism law, which had drawn international condemnation for its lack of rights for detained dissidents; tighter controls over Islamic fundamentalists; and pay raises of 70 percent for public workers to offset inflation. When these terms were rejected, he withdrew his party from the coalition.

Elections in December 1995 brought another shock, with Refah winning 158 seats to 135 for True Path and 132 for ANAP. For the first time in modern Turkish history, an Islamic-oriented party had won more seats in the Grand National Assembly than its rivals. Refah leader Necmettin Erbakan was named Turkey's first "Islamist" prime minister, taking office in April 1996. However, his party lacked a clear majority in the Assembly. As a result, coalition government became necessary. Erbakan's cabinet included ministers from the three major parties, and Ciller became foreign minister.

The septuagenarian Erbakan initially brought a breath of fresh air into the country's stale political system. With his round face and Italian designer ties, he seemed more like a Turkish uncle than an Islamic fundamentalist. And during his year in office, his government reaffirmed traditional secularism, state social-ism, and other elements of the legacy of Ataturk. The government also stressed NATO membership in its foreign policy and continued the drive for an economic and customs union with the European Community begun by its predecessors.

With Refah's victory at the polls, Tur-key's military leaders believed that the party was determined to dismantle the secular state founded by Ataturk and re-place it with an Islamized one. In 1997, they demanded Erbakan's resignation. In-asmuch as they have final authority over political life under the 1980 Constitution, Erbakan had no choice. After his resigna-tion, the state prosecutor filed suit to out-law Refah on the grounds that its programs were intended to impose Islamic law on Turkish society. The court agreed, and Erbakan was barred from politics for five years.

President Demirel then named ANAP leader Mesut Yilmaz to head a caretaker government. But he also resigned follow-ing a no-confidence resolution in the Grand National Assembly (GNA).

In the April 1999 GNA elections, how-ever, a relatively new party, Democratic Left, surprised observers by winning a clear majority of seats. A strong pro-nationalistic party, Nationalist Action (MHP), ran second, with 18 percent of the popular vote, winning 130 seats. The Vir-tue Party, re-formed from the ruins of Re-fah, finished with 102 seats and 15 percent of the popular vote.

Virtue then set out to distance itself from Islamic fundamentalism. Its mem-bers opposed the ban on wearing headscarves in university classes and gov-ernment offices. Its governing board even approved the celebration of St. Valentine's Day (!) as an appropriate secular holiday.

Unfortunately, the "new image" of Vir-tue did not convince the country's military and civilian leaders, who are adamant in their defense of Ataturk's legacy. In July 2000, an appeals court upheld the one-year jail sentence imposed on Erbakan, and the following year the Constitutional Court, the country's highest court, banned Virtue as a political party. The action came over the objections of many political lead-ers, including Ecevit. Despite the ban, Vir-tue deputies in the GNA would be allowed to keep their seats, as independents.

In August 2001, yet another Islamic-re-lated political party was formed, the 281st since the 1876 Constitution allowed their formation. Named Justice and Develop-ment, its founders were mostly reformist former members of Virtue, led by the popular former mayor of Istanbul. He had been banned from politics for five years

in 1998 for criticizing the country's nonadherence to traditional Islam, but he was released under the 2000 amnesty law for political prisoners.

The debate between Islamists and secu-larists over Turkey's Islamic identity is far from being resolved. In May 2001, the de-bate shifted to the presidency. Ecevit had proposed a change in the constitution to allow Suleyman Demirel, the incumbent, to run for a second term but to reduce his term to five years rather than seven. Demirel's election was seen as a sure thing, once the GNA had accepted the pro-posed changes. But the GNA rejected the proposal. The deputies then elected Ah-med Necdet Sezer, chief judge of the Con-stitutional Court, as the country's 10th president. (The position is largely ceremo-nial, but all laws passed by the GNA must be signed by him before they can go into effect.)

Sezer's election was a bitter blow to Ecevit, and when the president refused to sign a controversial measure that would cause thousands of government employees to lose their jobs if they were suspected of separatist or Islamic fundamentalist ac-tivities, there was open warfare between the two leaders. Sezer's support for the re-peal of the restrictive press laws, an end to the ban on use of the Kurdish language in schools and on official documents, and civilian control over the military leader-ship has put him at odds with military leaders as well, although Turkey's accep-tance as a member of the European Union depends on the implementation of such re-forms.

One EU requirement is that of a reduction in the powers of the National Security Coun-cil. The 10-member body, composed of the president, four cabinet ministers, and the five top military commanders, sets the agenda for all important issues, even laws, before they may be debated by the GNA. The order for dismissal of government em-ployees for their "Islamist" beliefs was originally issued as a directive to the GNA by the council. It did not go into effect be-cause Sezer refused to sign it, not as a coun-cil member but in his capacity as president.

### THE "KURDISH PROBLEM"

Ataturk's suppression of Kurdish political aspirations and a separate Kurdish identity within the nation effectively removed all traces of a "Kurdish problem" from na-tional consciousness during the first dec-ades of the republic. From the 1930s to the 1970s, the Kurdish areas were covered by a blanket of silence. Posters in Diyar-bakir, the regional capital, proclaimed Ataturk's message: "Happy is he who says he is a Turk."

However, the general breakdown in law and order in Turkey in the late 1970s led to a revival of Kurdish nationalism. The Workers' Party of Kurdistan (PKK), founded as a Marxist-Leninist organiza-tion, was the first left-wing Kurdish group to advocate a separate Kurdish state. It was outlawed after the 1980 military coup; some 1,500 of its members were given jail sentences, and several leaders were executed for treason.

The PKK then went underground. In 1984, it began a campaign of guerrilla warfare. Its leader, Abdullah ("Apo") Oca-lan, had won a scholarship in political sci-ence at Ankara University. While there, he became influenced by Marxist ideology and went into exile in Syria. From his Syr-ian base, and with Syrian support and fi-nancing, he called for a "war of national liberation" for the Kurds. Prior to the 1991 Gulf War, PKK guerrillas mounted mostly cross-border attacks into Turkey from bases in northern Lebanon, where they came under Syrian protection. But with Iraq's defeat and the establishment of an autonomous Kurdish region in northern Iraq, the PKK set up bases there to sup-plement their Lebanese bases.

Use of these bases posed a problem for Iraq's Kurdish leaders. On the one hand, they were committed to the cause of Kurd-ish sovereignty. But the cross-border raids brought Turkish retaliation, endangering their hard-won freedom from the long arm of Saddam Hussein's government. In 1992, after the raids had brought on mas-sive Turkish counterattacks, they an-nounced that they no longer supported the PKK and would not allow their territory to be used for its attacks on Turkish vil-lages and police and army posts.

However, the momentum of the conflict left little maneuvering room for the groups involved. Turkey imposed martial law on its eastern provinces, and Turkish forces carried out large-scale raids on PKK bases in north-ern Iraq, seriously hampering PKK effec-tiveness. Ocalan called a unilateral cease-fire in 1993, but the Turkish government said that it would not deal with terrorists. The PKK then resumed the conflict, which by 2000 had claimed 40,000 lives, the majority of them villagers caught between security forces and the guerrillas. Some 3,000 vil-lages had been destroyed and 2 million Kurds made refugees.

Yet despite Turkey's huge military su-periority, its struggle with the PKK re-mained a stalemate until 1999. Syria meanwhile had expelled Ocalan after the Turks had threatened to invade its territory under the international "right to self-de-fense." The PKK leader went first to Italy. The Ecevit government demanded his extradition, but the Italians refused, on grounds that their Constitution forbids extradition to countries that observe the death penalty. However, by this time Ocalan had become a huge embarrassment to his hosts. He left Italy for Greece and was finally given sanctuary in the Greek Embassy in Nairobi, Kenya.

Acting on a tip from Greek intelligence, Turkish commandos abducted Ocalan from the embassy and placed him in solitary confinement on an island in the Sea of Marmara. He was then tried for treason. Although the Turkish government insisted that the trial was an internal matter, UN and European Union observers were permitted to attend it.

Testifying in his own defense, Ocalan said that he had learned his lesson. He renounced violence as a "mistaken policy" and asserted that he would work as a loyal citizen toward the goal of peace and brotherhood. "We want to give up the armed struggle and have full democracy, so the PKK can enter the political arena," he said. "I will serve the state because now I see that it is necessary."[12] The court was unconvinced, and on June 29, Ocalan was sentenced to death. The criminal appeals court, the only one in the Turkish legal system, upheld his conviction on appeal.

Ocalan's execution has yet to be carried out. In 2001, his lawyers took his case before the European Court of Human Rights. The court began hearing the case in the spring of 2002. Should it rule in his favor, Turkey's rejection of the verdict would impose a major obstacle to Turkish acceptance as a member of the European Union.

For its part, the PKK said that it would obey its imprisoned leader's direction and end the armed struggle. Its leader stated: "The Kurdish and Turkish people are as inseparable as flesh and blood."[13]

As the result of the tentative steps toward a Turkish–Kurdish rapprochement, violence in the southeastern region lessened in 2000–2001. The Kurdish areas were opened to tourists, although they were still under martial law. In March, the Kurdish population was permitted to celebrate publicly its traditional Newroz (spring) festival, albeit under strict military security.

## FOREIGN POLICY

Despite its bitter disagreements with the United States and European countries over the Armenian genocide, Turkey has retained a strong Western alignment in its foreign policy. The country has also played a positive role in regional affairs. Thus "Operation Provide Comfort," set up after the 1991 Gulf War to protect Iraq's Kurd and Shia populations from "Saddam Hussain's revenge" after their failed uprisings, enables U.S. and British planes to patrol "no-fly zones" in northern and southern Iraq. The planes are based at Turkey's Inciirlik Air Base, by agreement with the Turkish government. The agreement has been renewed by the GNA every six months since it was negotiated, most recently in June 2001.

Turkey's relations with Iraq are complex. The decade of UN sanctions on that country have cost Turkey $40 billion in lost trade, much of it from Iraqi oil exports. These were suspended entirely and then limited to 75,000 barrels per day, insufficient to meet Turkish home needs. Turkey's need for Iraqi oil generated a huge illegal cross-border trade in 2000 and 2001, much of it in low-grade fuel and diesel oil. The supplies are trucked to the Habur border point through Iraqi Kurdistan and then smuggled into Turkey. Despite Turkey's support for the sanctions on Iraq, its government allows this illegal trade to continue because it brings in revenues for the impoverished southeastern region and compensates to some degree for the limit on its oil imports from Iraq. And despite the sanctions, relations with Saddam Hussain's regime continue to improve. Turkey was the ninth country to send relief flights of humanitarian supplies to Iraq, disregarding the UN embargo. In 2001, the first Turkish ambassador in a decade arrived at his post in Baghdad.

Turkey's relatively independent posture in foreign policy has been marked by agreements with Iran and Israel for training of its air-force pilots. The country reached agreement with Israel in April 2001 for water deliveries, as a part of its "water for peace" program for the Middle East. Under the terms of the agreement, Israel would receive 50 million cubic meters annually of water from the Tigris and Euphrates Rivers. Both of them rise in Turkey.

The country has also improved its links with the newly independent Turkish-speaking nations of Central Asia. Turkey was the first country to recognize the independence of Kazakhstan and Azerbaijan. In 2000, the government signed a 15-year agreement with Azerbaijan for imports of natural gas from the Shaykh Deniz field, offshore in the Caspian Sea. Another important agreement, among Turkey, Georgia, Azerbaijan, and Kazakhstan, has initiated construction of the thousand-mile oil pipeline from Baku, Azerbaijan, to Ceyhan (Adana) on Turkey's Mediterranean coast. When completed in 2003, the pipeline will deliver a million barrels per day to the Turkish port.

## THE ECONOMY

Turkey has a relatively diversified economy, with a productive agriculture and considerable mineral resources. Cotton is the major export crop, but the country is the world's largest producer of sultana raisins and hazelnuts. Other important crops are tobacco, wheat, sunflower seeds, sesame and linseed oils, and cotton-oil seeds. Opium was once an important crop, but, due to illegal exportation, poppy growing was banned by the government in 1972. The ban was lifted in 1974 after poppy farmers were unable to adapt their lands to other crops; production and sale are now government-controlled.

Mineral resources include bauxite, chromium, copper, and iron ore, and there are large deposits of lignite. Turkey is one of the world's largest producers of chromite (chromium ore). Another important mineral resource is meerschaum, used for pipes and cigarette holders. Turkey supplies 80 percent of the world market for emery, and there are rich deposits of tungsten, perlite, boron, and cinnabar, all important rare metals.

Turkey signed a customs agreement with the European Union in 1996. The agreement eliminated import quotas on Turkish textiles and slashed customs duties and excise taxes on Turkish imports of manufactured iron and steel products from the European Union.

The agreement was intended as a first step toward full membership in the EU. However, the country's poor human-rights record, its political instability, and more recently its financial crisis of 2000–2001 have delayed the process.

The "liquidity crisis" that nearly overwhelmed the Turkish economy in 2001 resulted from a combination of factors. Ironically, one of them was the economic-reform program introduced by the Ecevit government to meet EU requirements. Corruption in economic and fiscal management was another factor, while a third grew from the public dispute between Sezer and Ecevit over privatization of state-owned enterprises. The feud between the two leaders, plus the slow pace of privatization, led to a fiscal crisis in November 2000. The liquidity crisis followed, with a run on foreign-currency reserves in the Central Bank as worried Turks and foreign investors rushed to retrieve their funds. The bank lost $7.5 billion in reserves in a two-day period. The government's stopgap decision to end currency controls and allow the Turkish lira to float caused it to lose nearly 50 percent of its value. In December, 10 banks collapsed; they included Ihlas Finans, the country's largest Islamic bank. (Under Turkish

| The founding of Constantinople as the Roman Christian capital, on the site of ancient Byzantium **330** | The capture of Constantinople by Sultan Mehmed II; the city becomes the capital of the Islamic Ottoman Empire **1453** | The Ottoman Empire expands deep into Europe; the high-water mark is the siege of Vienna **1683** | The defeat of Ottomans and division of territories into foreign protectorates **1918–1920** | Turkey proclaims its independence **1923** | The first military coup **1960** | Military coup; civilian rule later returns; the government imposes emergency rule **1980s** | The Kurdish problem intensifies; Alawi and Kurdish social unrest; thousands die as earthquakes devastate Turkey **1990s** | **2000s** |

Serious financial crises threaten the nation

Turkey continues to try to meet requirements for EU membership

banking laws, deposits in such banks, which are interest-free under Islamic prohibitions against usury, are not covered by federal deposit guarantees. Consequently, 200,000 depositors lost their life savings.)

The crisis was averted temporarily when the International Monetary Fund agreed "in principle" to provide $5 billion in emergency aid. However, the IMF's insistence on fiscal reform as a precondition brought on another crisis in March–April 2001. The government then appointed Kermal Dervis, a Turkish-born World Bank economist, as minister of the economy. He was charged with bringing economic order out of fiscal chaos. Dervis presented his reform package in April. It included a 9 percent limit on government expenditures and a hiring freeze in the bloated public sector. But despite $16 billion in loans from the IMF and the World Bank, the economy continued to slide downward, with gross domestic product down 11.8 percent for 2001. Inflation rose, and the lira continued to lose ground to the U.S. dollar. The Ecevit government's failure to turn the economy around or inspire confidence among foreign investors further eroded its popularity. A September 2001 poll indicated that it would have received 2.8 percent of the popular vote if elections were held then.

The country does have a fairly large skilled labor force, and Turkish contractors have been able to negotiate contracts for development projects in oil-producing countries, such as Libya, with partial payment for services in oil shipments at reduced rates. The large Turkish expatriate labor force, much of it in Germany, provided an important source of revenue through worker remittances. (Prospects for the 1.8 million Turks living and working in Germany, however, deteriorated sharply in 1993 as neo-Nazi "skinheads" carried out a series of violent attacks on them as part of the campaign of the German far right to force foreigners to leave the country.) New World Bank loans of $12 billion in 2002 brought total aid to Turkey since 1999 to $31 billion.

## NOTES

1. The New York Life Insurance Company agreed recently to pay $10 million to the heirs or relatives of Armenians killed during the deportations in claims on policies issued before 1915. The agreement resulted from a bill passed by the California state legislature that extends the statute of limitations on such claims. California has a large Armenian community, and the company chose to pay the claims rather than incur numerous lawsuits.

2. Martin van Bruinessen, "Kurds, Turks and the Alevi Revival in Turkey," *Middle East Report* (July–Sept 1996), p. 7.

3. John Noble Wilford, "The Secrets of Croesus' Gold," *The New York Times* (August 15, 2000) Another Asia Minor ruler, King Midas of Phrygia, was said to have the "golden touch," because everything he touched (including his daughter) turned to gold; he had angered the gods, it seemed.

4. Cf. Lord Kinross, *The Ottoman Centuries: The Rise and Fall of the Turkish Empire* (New York: William Morrow, 1977).

5. *Ibid.,* p. 25.

6. An American astronomer, Kevin Pang, advanced the proposal that the fall of the Byzantine capital was preceded by a "darkening of the skies" and other portents of doom related to the eruption of the volcano Kuwae, in the New Hebrides, in 1453. See Lynn Teo Simarski, "Constantinople's Volcanic Twilight," *Aramco World* (November/December 1996), pp. 8–13.

7. The marching bands at football games and parades in our society apparently derive from Janissary bands of drummers and cymbal players who marched ahead of invading Ottoman armies, striking terror in their enemies with their loud sounds.

8. V. A. Danilov, "Kemalism and World Peace," in A. Kazancigil and E. Ozbudun, eds., *Ataturk, Founder of a Modern State* (Hamden, CT: Archon Books, 1981), p. 110.

9. Maurice Duverger, *Political Parties* (New York: John Wiley, 1959), p. 277.

10. C. H. Dodd, *Democracy and Development in Turkey* (North Humberside, England: Eothen Press, 1979), p. 135.

11. *The Economist* (August 22, 1987) noted that ballots would be colored orange (for "yes") and blue (for "no") to simplify the process for rural voters, who made up half of the electorate and were mostly illiterate.

12. Stephen Kinzer, in *The New York Times,* (June 1, 1999).

13. *Ibid.*

---

## DEVELOPMENT

The loans pledged by the IMF and World Bank to resolve Turkey's economic crisis require the country to maintain a 4% budget surplus, excluding interest on foreign debts. Inflation and the loss of purchasing power have made that objective almost impossible to reach. A new tracking system that requires an official personal identification number (PIN) for transactions over $3,000 or to hold a bank or stock account should reduce cheating and create a financial database. It will also provide for more equitable tax collection.

## FREEDOM

In October 2001, the Grand National Assembly approved 34 amendments to the Constitution as part of Turkey's drive to join the European Union. The amendments include elimination of the death penalty except for acts of terrorism or treason. Public demonstrations may be held without legal barriers, and a court order is required for searches of private property. Some 30,000 prisoners were released in 2000 under a new amnesty law; however, the amnesty did not apply to political prisoners or rapists.

## HEALTH/WELFARE

Appalling prison conditions are an obstacle to the country's acceptance into the European Union. A prison-reform law issued in 2000 transfers prisoners from their dormitory-style wards to isolated cells. Prisoners in various jails then went on a 9-month hunger strike. They protested that the new maximum-security system left them isolated and vulnerable to torture or beatings by prison guards. By September 2001, 31 prisoners had starved to death.

## ACHIEVEMENTS

Changes to update the 1926 civil code have given women full equality with men for the first time in matters of divorce and in the workplace. The 1926 code guaranteed them equal rights in other areas, but they were required to obtain their husbands' permission to work outside the home and entitled only to that property held in their names in the event of divorce. The new code grants women half of all property acquired by the couple during their marriage.

# United Arab Emirates

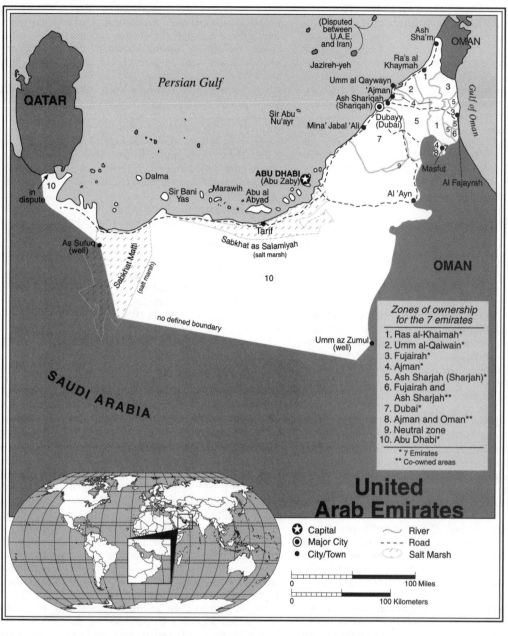

## GEOGRAPHY

*Area in Square Miles (Kilometers):* 31,992 (82,880) (about the size of Maine)

*Capital (Population):* Abu Dhabi (799,000)

*Environmental Concerns:* lack of natural freshwater; desertification; oil pollution of beaches and coastal waters

*Geographical Features:* flat, barren coastal plain merging into rolling sand dunes of vast desert; mountains in the east

*Climate:* hot, dry desert; cooler in the eastern mountains

## PEOPLE

### Population

*Total:* 2,408,000

*Annual Growth Rate:* 1.6%

*Rural/Urban Population Ratio:* 16/84

*Major Languages:* Arabic; Persian (Farsi); English; Hindi

*Ethnic Makeup:* 19% Emirati; 23% other Arab and Iranian; 50% South Asian; 8% East Asian and Westerner

*Religions:* 96% Muslim (80% Sunni, 16% Shia); 4% Hindu, Christian, and others

### Health

*Life Expectancy at Birth:* 72 years (male); 77 years (female)

*Infant Mortality Rate (Ratio):* 16.6/1,000

*Physicians Available (Ratio):* 1/545

### Education

*Adult Literacy Rate:* 79.2%

*Compulsory (Ages):* 6–12

## COMMUNICATION

*Telephones:* 916,000 main lines

*Daily Newspaper Circulation:* 135 per 1,000 people

*Televisions:* 18 per 1,000 people

*Internet Service Provider:* 1 (2000)

## TRANSPORTATION

*Highways in Miles (Kilometers):* 3,002 (4,835)

*Railroads in Miles (Kilometers):* none

*Usable Airfields:* 40

*Motor Vehicles in Use:* 400,000

## GOVERNMENT

*Type:* federation of emirates

*Independence Date:* December 2, 1971 (from the United Kingdom)

*Head of State/Government:* Supreme Council of Rulers of the 7 emirates: President Zayed bin Sultan al-Nuhayyan; Prime Minister Maktum bin Rashid al-Maktoum

*Political Parties:* none

*Suffrage:* none

## MILITARY

*Military Expenditures (% of GDP):* 3.1%

*Current Disputes:* boundary issues with Saudi Arabia and Oman; other territorial disputes

## ECONOMY

*Currency ($ U.S. Equivalent):* 3.673 dirhams = $1

*Per Capita Income/GDP:* $22,800/$54 billion

*GDP Growth Rate:* 4%

*Inflation Rate:* 4.5%

*Labor Force:* 1,400,000

*Natural Resources:* petroleum; natural gas

*Agriculture:* dates; vegetables; watermelons; poultry; dairy products; fish

*Industry:* petroleum; fishing; petrochemicals; construction materials; boat building; handicrafts; pearling

*Exports:* $46 billion (primary partners Japan, India, Singapore)

*Imports:* $34 billion (primary partners Japan, United States, United Kingdom)

 http://lcweb2.loc.gov/frd/cs/aetoc.html

## THE UNITED ARAB EMIRATES

The United Arab Emirates (U.A.E.) is a federation of seven independent states with a central governing Council located on the northeast coast of the Arabian Peninsula. The states—called emirates, from the title of their rulers—are Abu Dhabi, Ajman, Dubai, Fujairah, Ras al-Khaimah, Sharjah, and Umm al-Qaiwain. They came under British "protection" in the 1800s and were given their independence of Great Britain by treaty in 1971. At that time, they joined in the federal union. From its modest beginnings, the U.A.E. has come to play an important role in Middle East Arab affairs, because of its oil wealth.

Abu Dhabi, the largest emirate, contains 87 percent of the U.A.E. in area. Its capital, also called Abu Dhabi, is the largest city in the federation. Dubai, the second-largest emirate, has the federation's only natural harbor, which has been enlarged to handle supertankers. Abu Dhabi, Dubai, and Sharjah produce oil; Sharjah also has important natural-gas reserves and cement. Fujairah port is a major entrepôt for shipping. The other emirates have little in the way of resources and have yet to find oil in commercial quantities.

The early inhabitants of the area were fishermen and nomads. They were converted to Islam in the seventh century A.D., but little is known of their history before the sixteenth century. By that time, European nations, notably Portugal, had taken an active interest in trade with India and the Far East. Gradually, other European countries, particularly the Netherlands, France, and Britain, challenged Portuguese supremacy. As more and more European ships appeared in Arabian coastal waters or fought over trade, the coastal Arabs felt threatened with loss of their territory. Meanwhile, the Wahhabis, militant Islamic missionaries, spread over Arabia in the eighteenth century. Wahhabi agents incited the most powerful coastal group, the Qawasim, to interfere with European shipping. European ships were seized along with their cargoes, their crews held for ransom. To the European countries, this was piracy; to the Qawasim, however, it was defense of Islamic territory against the infidels. Ras al-Khaimah was their chief port, but soon the whole coast of the present-day U.A.E. became known as the Pirate Coast.

Piracy lasted until 1820, when the British, who now controlled India and thus dominated Eastern trade, convinced the principal chiefs of the coast to sign a treaty ending pirate activities. A British naval squadron was stationed in Ras al-Khaimah to enforce the treaty. In 1853,

the arrangement was changed into a "Perpetual Maritime Truce." Because it specified a *truce* between the British and the chiefs, the region became known as the Trucial Coast, and the territory of each chief was termed a "trucial state." A British garrison was provided for each ruler, and a British political agent was assigned to take charge of foreign affairs. Britain paid the rulers annual subsidies; in most cases, it was all the money they could acquire. There were originally five Trucial States (also called emirates); Sharjah and Ras al-Khaimah were reorganized as separate emirates in 1966.

The arrangement between Great Britain and the Trucial States worked smoothly for more than a century, through both world wars. Then, in the 1960s, the British decided—for economic and political reasons—to give up most of their overseas colonies, including those in the Arabian Peninsula, which were technically protectorates rather than colonies. In 1968, they proposed to the Trucial Coast emirs that they join in a federation with Bahrain and Qatar, neighboring oil-producing protectorates. But Bahrain and Qatar, being larger and richer, decided to go it alone. Thus, the United Arab Emirates, when it became independent in 1971, included only six emirates. Ras al-Khaimah joined in 1972.

## PROBLEMS OF INTEGRATION

Differences in size, wealth, resources, and population have hampered U.A.E. integration since it was formed. Another problem is poor communications. Until recently, one could travel from emirate to emirate only by boat, and telephone service was nonexistent. These limitations are disappearing rapidly, however, as the U.A.E. develops.

There are some internal disagreements among the emirates. Ras al-Khaimah and Umm al-Qaiwain have yet to reach agreement on demarcation of their common border, and Sharjah's border with neighboring Oman, on the Musandam Peninsula, is also in dispute. Differences in resources and allocation of revenues are another point of disagreement, separating the oil-rich emirates from the oil-poor ones.

The U.A.E. federal system is defined in the 1971 Constitution. The government consists of a Supreme Council of Rulers of the seven emirates; a Council of Ministers (cabinet), appointed by the president of the Council; and a unicameral Federal National Assembly of 40 members appointed by the ruling emirs on a proportional basis, according to size and population.

One of the strengths of the system is that Shaykh Zayed, the ruler of Abu Dhabi, has served as president of the Council of Rulers since its inception. The

federal capital is located in Abu Dhabi, the largest and richest emirate. The ruler of Dubai, the second largest of the emirates, serves as vice-president. Other unifying features of the U.A.E. are a common commercial-law code, currency, and defense structure. The sharing of revenues by the wealthy emirates with the less prosperous ones has also helped to foster U.A.E. unity.

The 1979 Iranian Revolution, which seemed to threaten the U.A.E.'s security, accelerated the move toward centralization of authority over defense forces, abolition of borders, and merging of revenues. In 1981, the U.A.E. joined with other states in the Gulf Cooperation Council (GCC) to establish a common-defense policy toward their large and powerful neighbor. The U.A.E. also turned to the United States for help; the two countries signed a Defense Cooperation Agreement in 1994. Under the agreement, a force of several hundred U.S. military personnel is stationed in the emirates to supervise port facilities and air refueling for American planes patrolling the no-fly zone in southern Iraq.

Early in 2001, the U.A.E. joined with other GCC members in a mutual-defense pact, the first in the region. With support from the United States, the pact would increase the current rapid-deployment force from 5,000 to 22,000. Each GCC member would contribute to the force in proportion to its size and population.

The September 11, 2001, terrorist attacks on the United States intensified the importance of increased security for oil operations on the part of Abu Dhabi and Dubai, the chief oil-producing U.A.E. states. The Federal Council supported the newly formed international coalition against terrorism in a public statement, and the U.A.E. withdrew its recognition of the Taliban as the legitimate government of Afghanistan. The apparent involvement of U.A.E. nationals in funding bank transfers to Osama bin Laden's al-Qaeda network led the emirates collectively to tighten their banking practices. A revised banking law was approved by the Council in November.

The governments of the emirates themselves are best described as patriarchal. Each emir is head of his own large "family" as well as head of his emirate. The ruling emirs gained their power a long time ago from various sources—through foreign trade, pearl fishing, or ownership of lands—and in recent years, they have profited from oil royalties to confirm their positions as heads of state.

Disagreements within the ruling families have sometimes led to violence or "palace coups," there being no rule or law of pri-

| Peace treaties between Great Britain and Arab shaykhs establishing the Trucial States **1853, 1866** | Establishment of the Trucial Council under British advisers, the forerunner of federation **1952** | Independence **1971** | The U.A.E. becomes the first Arab oil producer to ban exports to the U.S. after the Yom Kippur War **1973** | Balanced federal Assembly and cabinet are established **1979** | The U.A.E. reduces its dependence on oil revenues; the free-trade zone proves a success **1990s** |

The U.A.E. joins with other GCC members in a mutual-defense pact

The U.A.E. supports the international coalition against terrorism

mogeniture. The ruler of Umm al-Qaiwain came to power when his father was murdered in 1929. Shaykh Zayed deposed his brother, Shaykh Shakbut, in 1966, when the latter refused to approve a British-sponsored development plan for the protectorate. In 1987, Shaykh Abd al-Aziz, the elder brother of the ruler of Sharjah, attempted to overthrow his brother, on the grounds that economic development was being mishandled. The U.A.E. Supreme Council mediated a settlement, and Abd al-Aziz retired to Abu Dhabi. However, he continued to demand authority over Sharjah's economic policies in his capacity as minister for National Development. In 1990, the ruler dismissed him by abolishing the position.

Ajman and Umm al-Qaiwain are coastal ports with agricultural hinterlands. Ras al-Khaimah has continually disappointed oil seekers; its only natural resource is aggregate, which is used in making cement. Fujairah, although lacking in energy resources, has become a major oil-bunkering and -refining center. In 1996, the new bunkering terminal in its port went into operation. Built by the Dutch-owned Van Ommeren Tank Company, the world's largest independent operator, the facilities will eventually double the millions of tons of cargo now being handled by the port.

## AN OIL-DRIVEN ECONOMY
In the past, the people of the Trucial Coast made a meager living from breeding racing camels, some farming, and pearl fishing. Pearls were the main cash crop. But twentieth-century competition from Japanese cultured pearls ruined the Arabian pearl-fishing industry.

In 1958, Shaykh Zayed, then in his teens, led a party of geologists into the remote desert near the oasis of al-Ain, following up the first oil-exploration agreement signed by Abu Dhabi with foreign oil companies. Oil exports began in 1962, and from then on the fortunes of the Gulf Arabs improved dramatically. Production was 14,200 barrels per day in 1962; by 1982, it was 1.1 million b/d, indicating how far the country's oil-driven economy had moved in just two decades. Oil reserves are approximately 98 billion barrels, while gas reserves are 205 trillion cubic feet—10 percent of global reserves. They are expected to last well into the twenty-first century at current rates of extraction.

The bulk of hydrocarbon production and reserves is in Abu Dhabi. Dubai, not content with second place in U.A.E. development, launched a Strategic Development Plan in 1998, intended to increase its non-oil income to $20,000 per capita by 2010. Its government earlier had established a free-trade zone in the port of Jebel Ali. It provides 100 percent foreign ownership, full repatriation of capital and profits, and a 15-year exemption from corporate and other taxes. By 1996, more than 1,000 companies had located in the zone. In October 2000, the Dubai City Internet free-trade zone opened for business. The zone is in the process of creating a "wired economy" for the emirates, to link them with global markets and the media. Companies such as Microsoft, Compaq and IBM are helping to establish Dubai as the marketing hub of the region.[1]

Although they are not blessed with the vast petroleum-based wealth of Abu Dhabi and Dubai, the other emirates do have some important economic assets. Liquefied natural gas (LNG) was discovered in Sharjah in 1992, and by 2001 its onshore Kahaif and Sajaa fields were producing 40 million cubic feet per day, sufficient to meet domestic needs. The oil refinery at Fujairah, closed from 1997 to 1999, resumed production in 2001; current output is 105,000 barrels per day of refined petroleum products. Fujairah's port was enlarged in 2000 to accommodate tankers up to 90,000 deadweight tons; it is now the largest bunkering port in the Middle East. In addition to its gas reserves, Sharjah has become the emirate of choice for small and medium-size industries; they generate 48 percent of the U.A.E.'s non-oil, industrial share of gross domestic product.

The U.A.E.'s dependence on expatriate workers, who comprise approximately 80 percent of the labor force, has been an obstacle to self-sufficiency and diversification. In October 1996, a strict new residency law governing expatriate labor was approved by the Supreme Council. The law limits both immigration numbers and length of stay; it is aimed particularly at low-level Asian workers. As a result, some 400,000 "guest workers"—approximately 15 percent of the total expatriate population—left the federation.

The U.A.E. celebrated its silver anniversary in December 1996 with a 69-ton birthday cake. An even larger one, 50 feet long by 6 feet across, was unveiled in 1998 for the country's children. A $200 million Internet City, free-trade zones, international tennis and golf tournaments, and a new three-mile offshore resort island are among other attractions promoted by Dubai and to a lesser extent by Abu Dhabi, the "Washington, D.C." of the Gulf. Sinbad the Sailor, the legendary traveler, would be amazed at the changes if he returned to his old harbor, the creek at Dubai.

## NOTE
1. Steve Krettman, "Oil Realm Embraces a Wired Economy," *The New York Times* (June 10, 2001).

## DEVELOPMENT

Abu Dhabi and Dubai have taken the lead in the past couple of years in diversifying the economy. New non-oil projects include Aluminium Dubai, petro-chemical plants, and the world's largest drydock, also in Dubai. With oil reserves slated for exhaustion by 2010, the clock is ticking for diversification.

## FREEDOM

The Supreme Council of the U.A.E. exercises overall federal authority, but rulers of the emirates have full control over their territories. Although the patriarchal system of government and Arab tradition preclude the introduction of a Western-model democratic system with checks and balances, the custom of weekly *majlises* (public assemblies) provides an outlet for citizen concerns.

## HEALTH/WELFARE

The first all-female taxi service in the Gulf went into operation in the U.A.E. June 2000, as participation by women in the labor force increased. Also in 2000, U.A.E. banks set a quota system for employment of nationals to replace departed foreign workers. The quota is to be increased by 4% a year until the banks are fully staffed by U.A.E. nationals.

## ACHIEVEMENTS

Nearly 2 million acres of desert have been reclaimed for cultivation. In 1997, Shaykh Zayed, the moving spirit behind the U.A.E. drive for self-sufficiency in food and the "greening" of the desert, received the Gold Panda award from the Worldwide Fund for Nature for his services to global conservation— the first head of state to be so honored. In 2000, the U.A.E.'s first satellite went into orbit, another first for the Gulf region.

# Yemen (Republic of Yemen)

## GEOGRAPHY

*Area in Square Miles (Kilometers):*
203,796 (527,970) (about twice
the size of Wyoming)

*Capital (Population):* San'a
(political capital) (972,000);
Aden (economic capital)
(562,000)

*Environmental Concerns:* limited
freshwater supplies; inadequate
potable water; overgrazing; soil
erosion; desertification

*Geographical Features:* a narrow
coastal plain backed by hills
and mountains; dissected
upland desert plains in the
center slope into desert

*Climate:* mostly desert; hot,
with minimal rainfall except in
mountain zones

## PEOPLE

### Population
*Total:* 18,079,000
*Annual Growth Rate:* 3.38%
*Rural/Urban Population Ratio:*
66/34
*Major Language:* Arabic
*Ethnic Makeup:* predominantly
Arab; small Afro-Arab, South
Asian, and European communi-
ties
*Religions:* nearly 100% Muslim;
small numbers of Christians,
Jews, and Hindus

### Health
*Life Expectancy at Birth:* 58 years
(male); 62 years (female)
*Infant Mortality Rate (Ratio):*
68.5/1,000
*Physicians Available (Ratio):*
1/4,530

### Education
*Adult Literacy Rate:* 38%
*Compulsory (Ages):* 6–15

## COMMUNICATION
*Telephones:* 221,000 main lines
*Televisions:* 6.5 per 1,000 people
*Internet Service Provider:* 1 (2000)

## TRANSPORTATION
*Highways in Miles (Kilometers):* 37,557
(69,263)
*Railroads in Miles (Kilometers):* none
*Usable Airfields:* 50
*Motor Vehicles in Use:* 510,000

## GOVERNMENT
*Type:* republic, formed by merger of former
Yemen Arab Republic and People's
Democratic Republic of Yemen

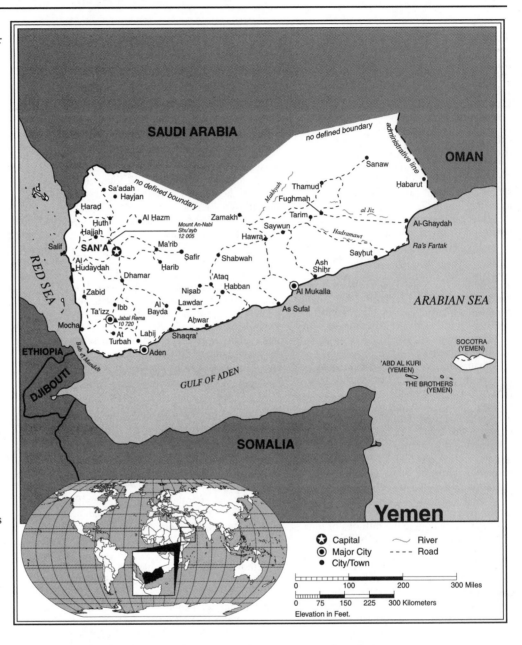

*Independence Date:* formally united May
22, 1990 (date of merger)
*Head of State/Government:* President
(Field Marshall) Ali Abdullah Saleh;
Prime Minister Abdul-Kader Bajammal
*Political Parties:* General People's Con-
gress; Islamic Reform Party; Yemen
Socialist Party
*Suffrage:* universal at 18

## MILITARY
*Military Expenditures (% of GDP):* 7.6%
*Current Disputes:* final boundary with
Saudi Arabia remains to be resolved

## ECONOMY
*Currency ($ U.S. Equivalent):* 174.59
rials = $1
*Per Capita Income/GDP:* $820/$14.4 billion

*GDP Growth Rate:* 6%
*Inflation Rate:* 10%
*Unemployment Rate:* 30%
*Natural Resources:* petroleum; fish; rock
salt; marble; small deposits of coal,
gold, lead, nickel, and copper; fertile
soil in west
*Agriculture:* grain, fruits; vegetables; qat;
coffee; cotton; livestock; fish
*Industry:* petroleum; cotton textiles and
leather goods; food processing; handi-
crafts; aluminum products; cement
*Exports:* $4.2 billion (primary partners
Thailand, China, South Korea)
*Imports:* $2.7 billion (primary partners
Saudi Arabia, United Arab Emirates;
United States)

# YEMEN

The Republic of Yemen occupies the extreme southwest corner of the Arabian Peninsula. It consists of three distinct regions, which until 1990 had been separated geographically for centuries and divided politically into two states: the Yemen Arab Republic (North Yemen, or Y.A.R.) and the People's Democratic Republic of Yemen (South Yemen, or P.D.R.Y.). Until the twentieth century, the entire area was known simply as Yemen; and with the merger of the two states, it has resumed its former geographic identity. The former Y.A.R.'s territory consists of two distinct regions: a hot, humid coastal strip, the Tihama, along the Red Sea; and an interior region of mountains and high plains that shade off gradually into the bleak, waterless South Arabian Desert.

Yemeni territory also includes Socotra, a remote island 550 miles from Aden, and two other small islands, Abd al-Khuri and the Brothers, which lie off the African coast of Somalia. Socotra is the only world habitat for Dragon's Blood trees, which produce cinnabar resin, and of some 850 other plants that exist nowhere else.

The Yemeni interior is very different not only from the Tihama but also from other parts of the Arabian Peninsula. It consists of highlands and rugged mountains ranging up to 12,000 feet. At the higher elevations, the mountain ridges are separated by deep, narrow valleys, usually with swift-flowing streams at the bottom. The ample rainfall allows extensive use of terracing for agriculture. The main crops are coffee, cereals, vegetables, and qat (a shrub whose leaves are chewed as a mildly intoxicating narcotic).

This part of Yemen has been for centuries the home of warlike but sedentary peoples who have formed a stable, stratified society living in villages or small cities. These groups have been the principal support for the Shia Zaidi Imams, whose rule was the political nucleus of Yemen from the ninth century A.D. to the establishment of the republic in 1962. The Yemeni political capital, San'a, is located in these northern highlands.

The former P.D.R.Y., almost twice the size of its neighbor but less favored geographically, consists of the port and hinterland of Aden (today Yemen's economic capital); the Hadhramaut, a broad valley edged by desert and extending eastward along the Arabian Sea coast; the Perim and Kamaran Islands, at the south end of the Red Sea; and Socotra Island.

Until the recent discoveries of oil, South Yemen was believed to have no natural resources. The dominant physical feature is the Wadi Hadhramaut. It is one of the few regions of the country with enough water for irrigation. Except for Aden, the area has little rainfall; in some sections, rain may fall only once every 10 years. Less than 2 percent of the land is cultivable.

In ancient times, the whole of Yemen was known to the Greeks, Romans, and other peoples as Arabia Felix ("Happy Arabia"), a remote land that they believed to be fabulously wealthy. They knew it as the source of frankincense, myrrh, and other spices as well as other exotic products brought to Mediterranean and Middle Eastern markets from the East. In Yemen itself, several powerful kingdoms grew up from profits earned in this trade. One kingdom in particular, the Sabaeans, also had a productive agriculture based on irrigation. The water for irrigation came from the great Marib Dam, built around 500 B.C. Marib was a marvel of engineering, built across a deep river valley. The Sabaean economy supported a population estimated at 300,000 in a region that today supports only a few thousand herders.

The Sabaeans were followed by the Himyarites. Himyarite rulers were converted to Christianity by wandering monks in the second century A.D. The Himyarites had contacts with Christian Ethiopia across the Red Sea and for a time were vassals of Ethiopian kings. An Ethiopian army invaded South Arabia but was defeated by the Himyarites in A.D. 570, the "Year of the Elephant" in Arab tradition, so called because the Ethiopian invaders were mounted on elephants. (The year was also notable for the birth of Muhammad, the founder of Islam.)

Sabaeans and Himyarites ruled long ago, but they are still important to Yemenis as symbols of their long and rich historical past. The Imams of Yemen, who ruled until 1962, used a red dye to sign their official documents in token of their relationship to Himyarite kings. (The word *Himyar* comes from the same root as *hamra,* "red.")

The domestication of the camel and development of an underground irrigation system of channels (*falaj*) made this civilization possible. Ships and camel caravans brought the frankincense, myrrh, and musk from Socotra and silks and spices from India and the Far East to northern cities in Egypt, Persia, and Mesopotamia. Aden was an important port for this trade, due to its natural harbor and its location at the south end of the Red Sea.

Yemenis were among the first converts to Islam. The separation of the Yemenis into mutually hostile Sunni and Shia Muslims took place relatively early in Islamic history. Those living in the Tihama, which was easily accessible to missionaries and warriors expanding the borders of the new Islamic state, became Sunnis, obedient to the caliphs (the elected "successors" of Muhammad). The Yemeni mountaineers were more difficult to reach; and when they were converted to the new religion, it was through the teachings of a follower of the Shi'at Ali, "Party of Ali," those who felt that Muhammad's son-in-law Ali and his descendants should have been chosen as the rightful leaders of the Islamic community. Yemenis in Aden and the Hadhramaut, as well as those in the Tihama, became Sunni, creating the basis for an intra-Yemeni conflict, which still exists.

Yemen was the home of a small Jewish community for at least 2,500 years, dating from the time of the Babylonian captivity. Although its members were excluded from all professions, except silversmithing, and were required to wear identifying clothing and sidecurls, the community lived side by side with Muslims without incident. After the establishment of Israel in 1948, 48,000 Jews were airlifted to the new Jewish state. Some 24,000 others left Yemen for Israel in later years. Today only 300 Jews remain in Yemen.

## THE ZAIDI IMAMATE

In the late ninth century A.D., a feud among certain nominally Muslim groups in inland Yemen led to the invitation to a religious scholar living in Mecca to come and mediate in their dispute. (Use of an outside mediator was common in Arabia at that time.) This scholar brought with him a number of families of Ali's descendants who sought to escape persecution from the Sunnis. He himself was a disciple of Zaid, Ali's great-grandson. He settled the feud, and, in return for his services, he was accepted by both sides of the conflict as their religious leader, or Imam. His followers received lands and were given a protected status, so that in time they became a sort of theocratic aristocracy. This was the beginning of the Zaidi Imamate, a theocratic state that lasted for a thousand years (until 1962).

The first Zaidi Imam had some personal qualities that enabled him to control the unruly mountain people and bend them to his will. He was a shrewd judge of character, using his knowledge and his prestige as a member of the family of Ali to give personal favors or to give his power of *baraka* (special powers from God) to one group or withhold it from another. He had great physical strength. It was said of him that he could grind corn with his fingers and pull a camel apart barehanded. He wrote 49 books on Islamic jurisprudence and theology, some of which are still studied by modern Yemeni scholars. He was also said to bring good (or bad) fortune to a subject merely by a touch or a glance from his piercing black eyes.[1]

In a reversal of the ancient process whereby South Arabian merchants carried goods to the far-flung cities of the north, from the late 1400s on, the towns of the bleak Arabian coast attracted the interest of European seafaring powers as way stations or potential bases for control of their expanding trade with the East Indies, India, and China. Aden was a potentially important base, and expeditions by Portuguese and other Europeans tried without success to capture it at the time. In 1839, a British expedition finally succeeded. It found a town of "800 miserable souls, huddled in huts of reed matting, surrounded by guns that would not fire," or so the American traveler Joseph Osgood described the scene.

Under British rule, Aden became an important naval base and refueling port for ships passing through the Suez Canal and down the Red Sea en route to India. For many British families bound for India, Aden was the last land, with the last friendly faces, that they would see before arriving many days later in the strange wonderland of India. The route through the Suez Canal and down the Red Sea past Aden was the lifeline of the British Empire. In order to protect Aden from possible attack by hostile peoples in the interior, the British signed a series of treaties with their chiefs, called shaykhs or sometimes sultans. These treaties laid the basis for the South Arabian Protectorates. British political agents advised the rulers on policy matters and gave them annual subsidies to keep them happy. One particular agent, Harold Ingrams, was so successful in eliminating feuds and rivalries that "Ingrams's Peace" became a symbol of the right way to deal with proud, independent local leaders.

The Zaidi Imams continued to rule inland Yemen until the nineteenth century, when the Ottoman Turks, who controlled the Tihama, sent an army to conquer all of Yemen (except for Aden, which remained under British protection). The Turks installed an Ottoman governor in San'a and made Yemen a province (*vilayet*) of the empire. But this action did not sit well with the mountain peoples. A Yemeni official told a British visitor: "We have fought the Turks, the tribes . . . and we are always fighting each other. We Yemenis submit to no one permanently. We love freedom and we will fight for it."[2]

The Turkish occupation sparked a revolt. Turkish forces were unable to defeat the mountain peoples, and in 1911, they signed a treaty that recognized Imam Yahya as ruler in the highlands. In return, the

Imam recognized Turkish rule in the Tihama. At the end of World War I, the Turks left Yemen for good. The British, who now controlled most of the Middle East, signed a treaty with Imam Yahya, recognizing his rule in all Yemen.

The two Yemens followed divergent paths in the twentieth century, accounting in large measure for the difficulties that they faced in incorporating into a single state. North Yemen remained largely uninvolved in the political turmoil that engulfed the Middle East after World War II. Imam Yahya ruled his feudal country as an absolute monarch with a handful of advisers, mostly tribal leaders, religious scholars, and members of his family. John Peterson notes that the Imamate "was completely dependent on the abilities of a single individual who was expected to be a competent combination of religious scholar, administrator, negotiator, and military commander."[3] Yahya was all of these, and his forceful personality and ruthless methods of dealing with potential opposition (with just a touch of magic) ensured his control over the population.

Yahya's method of government was simplicity itself. He held a daily public meeting (*jama'a*) seated under an umbrella outside his palace, receiving petitions from anyone who wished to present them and signing approval or disapproval in Himyarite red ink. He personally supervised tax collections and kept the national treasury in a box under his bed. The Imam distrusted the Ottomans, against whom he had fought for Yemeni independence, and refused to accept their coinage. He also rejected the British currency because it represented a potential foreign influence.

Yahya was determined to keep foreign influences out of Yemen and to resist change in any form. Although Yemen was poor by the industrial world's standards, it was self-sufficient, free, and fully recognized as an independent state. Yahya hoped to keep it that way. He even refused foreign aid because he felt that it would lead to foreign occupation. But he was unable to stop the clock entirely and to keep out all foreign ideas and influences.

Certain actions that seemed to be to his advantage worked against him. One was the organization of a standing army. In order to equip and train an army that would be stronger than tribal armies, Yahya had to purchase arms from abroad and to hire foreign advisers to train his troops. Promising officers were also sent for training in Egypt, and upon their return, they formed the nucleus of opposition to the Imam.

In 1948, Imam Yahya was murdered in an attempted coup. He had alienated not only army officers who resented his re-

pressive rule but also leaders from outside the ruling family who were angered by the privileges given to the Imam's sons and relatives. But the coup was disorganized, the conspirators unsure of their goals. Crown Prince Ahmad, the Imam's eldest son and heir, was as tough and resourceful as his 80-year-old father had been.[4] He gathered support from leaders of other clans and nipped the rebellion in the bud.

Imam Ahmad (1948–1962) ruled as despotically as his father had ruled. But the walls of Yemeni isolation inevitably began to crack. Unlike Yahya, Ahmad was willing to modernize a little. Foreign experts came to design and help build the roads, factories, hospitals, and schools that the Imam felt were needed. Several hundred young Yemenis were sent abroad for study. Those who had left the country during Imam Yahya's reign returned. Many Yemenis emigrated to Aden to work for the British and formed the nucleus of a "Free Yemen" movement.

In 1955, the Imam foiled an attempted coup. Other attempts, in 1958 and 1961, were also unsuccessful. The old Imam finally died of emphysema in 1962, leaving his son, Crown Prince Muhammad al-Badr, to succeed him.

### THE MARCH TO INDEPENDENCE

The British wanted to hold on to Aden as long as possible because of its naval base and refinery. It seemed to them that the best way to protect British interests was to set up a union of Aden and the South Arabian Protectorates. This was done in 1963, with independence promised for 1968. However, the British plan proved unworkable. In Aden, a strong anti-British nationalist movement developed in the trade unions among dock workers and refinery employees. This movement organized a political party, the People's Socialist Party, strongly influenced by the socialist, anti-Western, Arab nationalist programs of President Gamal Abdel Nasser in Egypt.

The party had two branches: the moderate Front for the Liberation of Occupied South Yemen (FLOSY) and the leftist Marxist National Liberation Front (NLF). About all they had in common was their opposition to the British and the South Arabian sultans, whom they called "lackeys of imperialism." FLOSY and the NLF joined forces in 1965–1967 to force the British to leave Aden. British troops were murdered; bombs damaged the refinery. By 1967, Britain had had enough. British forces were evacuated, and Britain signed a treaty granting independence to South Yemen under a coalition government made up of members of both FLOSY and the NLF.

Muhammad al-Badr held office for a week and then was overthrown by a military coup. Yemen's new military leaders formed a Revolution Command Council and announced that the Imam was dead. Henceforth, they said, Yemen would be a republic. It would give up its self-imposed isolation and would become part of the Arab world. But the Revolution proved to be more difficult to carry out than the military officers had expected. The Imam was not dead, as it turned out, but had escaped to the mountains. The mountain peoples rallied to his support, helping him to launch a counterrevolution. About 85,000 Egyptian troops arrived in Yemen to help the republican army. The coup leaders had been trained in Egypt, and the Egyptian government had not only financed the Revolution but also had encouraged it against the "reactionary" Imam.

For the next eight years, Yemen was a battleground. The Egyptians bombed villages and even used poison gas against civilians in trying to defeat the Imam's forces. But they were unable to crush the people hidden in the mountains of the interior. Saudi Arabia also backed the Imam with arms and kept the border open. The Saudi rulers did not particularly like the Imam, but he seemed preferable to an Egyptian-backed republican regime next door.

After Egypt's defeat by Israel in the 1967 Six-Day War, the Egyptian position in Yemen became untenable, and Egyptian troops were withdrawn. It appeared that the royalists would have a clear field. But they were even more disunited than the republicans. A royalist force surrounded San'a in 1968 but failed to capture the city. The Saudis then decided that the Imam had no future. They worked out a reconciliation of royalists and republicans that would reunite the country. The only restriction was that neither the Imam nor any of his relatives would be allowed to return to Yemen.

Thus, as of 1970, two "republics" had come into existence side by side. The Yemen Arab Republic was more of a tribal state than a republic in the modern political sense of the term. Prior to 1978, its first three presidents either went into exile or were murdered, victims of rivalry within the army. Colonel Ali Abdullah Saleh, a career army officer, seized power in that year and was subsequently chosen as the republic's first elected president. He was reelected in 1983 and again in 1988 for consecutive five-year terms. (With unification, he became the first head of state of all Yemen.)

Saleh provided internal stability and allowed some broadening of the political process in North Yemen. A General People's Congress (GPC) was established in 1982. A Consultative Council, elected by popular vote, was established in 1988 to provide some citizen input into legislation. Saleh displayed great skill in balancing tribal and army factions and used foreign aid to develop economic projects such as dams for irrigation to benefit highland and Tihama Yemenis alike.

## SOUTH YEMEN: A MARXIST STATE

With the British departure, the South Arabian Federation collapsed. Aden and the Hadhramaut were united under Aden political leadership in 1970 as the People's Democratic Republic of Yemen. It began its existence under adverse circumstances: Britain ended its subsidy for the Aden refinery, and the withdrawal of British forces cut off the revenues generated by the military payroll.

But the main problem was political. A power struggle developed between FLOSY and the NLF. The former favored moderate policies, good relations with other Arab states, and continued ties with Britain. The NLF were leftist Marxists. By 1970, the Marxists had won. FLOSY leaders were killed or went into exile. The new government set its objectives as state ownership of lands, state management of all business and industry, a single political organization with all other political parties prohibited, and support for antigovernment revolutionary movements in other Arab states, particularly Oman and Saudi Arabia.

During its two decades of existence, the P.D.R.Y. modeled its governing structure on that of the Soviet Union, with a Presidium, a Council of Ministers, a Supreme People's Legislative Council, and provincial and district councils, in descending order of importance. In 1978, the ruling (and only legal) political party took the name Yemen Socialist Party, to emphasize its Yemeni makeup.

Although the P.D.R.Y. government's ruthless suppression of opposition enabled it to establish political stability, rivalries and vendettas among party leaders led to much instability within the ruling party. The first president, Qahtan al-Sha'bi, was overthrown by pro-Soviet radicals within the party. His successor, Salim Rubayyi Ali, was executed after he had tried and failed to oust his rivals on the party Central Committee. Abd al-Fattah Ismail, the country's third president, resigned in 1980 and went into exile due to a dispute over economic policies. Ali Nasir Muhammad, the fourth president, seemed to have consolidated power and to have won broad party support, until 1986, when he tried to purge the Central Committee of potential opponents. The peoples of the interior, who formed Muhammad's original support base, stayed out of the fighting. After 10 days of bloody battles with heavy casualties, the president's forces were defeated. He then went into exile and was convicted of treason in absentia. He returned to Yemen in 1996 after the end of the Civil War and the reunification of the "two Yemens."

## UNIFICATION

Despite their natural urge to unite in a single Yemeni nation, the two Yemens were more often at odds with each other than united in pursuing common goals. This was due in part to the age-old highland–lowland, Sunni–Shia conflict that cut across Yemeni society. But it was also due to their very different systems of government. There were border clashes in 1972, 1975, and 1978–1979, when the P.D.R.Y. was accused of plotting the overthrow of its neighbor. (A P.D.R.Y. envoy brought a bomb hidden in a suitcase to a meeting with the Y.A.R. president, and the latter was killed when the bomb exploded.)

Improved economic circumstances and internal political stability in both Yemens revived interest in unity in the 1980s, especially after oil and natural-gas discoveries in border areas promised advantages to both governments through joint exploitation. In May 1988, President Saleh and Prime Minister al-Attas of the P.D.R.Y. signed the May Unity Pact, which ended travel restrictions and set up a Supreme Yemeni Council of national leaders to prepare a constitution for the proposed unitary state.

From then on, the unity process snowballed. In 1989, the P.D.R.Y. regime freed supporters of former President Ali Nasir Muhammad. Early in 1990, the banks, postal services, ports administration, and customs of the two republics were merged, followed by the merger under joint command of their armed forces.

Formal unification took place on May 22, 1990, with approval by both governments and ratification of instruments by their legislative bodies. Ali Abdullah Saleh was unanimously chosen as the republic's first president, with a four-member Presidential Council formed to oversee the transition. A draft constitution of the new republic established a 39-member Council of Ministers headed by P.D.R.Y. prime minister al-Attas, with ministries divided equally between North and South. In a national referendum in May 1991, voters approved the new all-Yemen Constitution. (The Constitution was opposed by the newly formed Islah Party, representing the tribes and Islamic fundamentalists, on the grounds that it did not conform fully to Islamic law.)

The Constitution provides for elections to a 301-member Parliament. Elections were scheduled for November 1992 but were postponed until April 1993 after the elections committee protested that insufficient time had been allocated for voter registration, preparation of candidate lists, drawing of constituency borders, and campaigning.

The campaign itself was marred by violence, much of it directed at officials of the Yemen Socialist Party by tribal opponents of unification or others who feared that the election would result in greater influence for the more liberal, ex-Marxist Southerners in the government. In 1992, an economic crisis also hit the country; in December people took to the streets protesting price increases and a 100 percent inflation rate.

Despite the disruption, the elections were held on schedule. President Saleh's General People's Congress won 147 seats in Parliament, just shy of a majority. The elections were carried out in open democratic fashion, with women and the small Yemenite Jewish community allowed to vote, in sharp contrast to election practice in other parts of the Middle East.

A coalition government was formed in May 1993 between the General People's Congress, the Yemen Socialist Party, and Islah, which ran third in the balloting. But rivalry between the former political elites of North and South, plus differences in outlook, continued to impede progress toward full unification. Early in 1994, Ali al-Beidh, Yemen Socialist Party (YSP) leader and vice president of the ruling coalition, presented a set of 18 demands whose acceptance was a prerequisite for his return to the government. They were rejected by President Saleh, and civil war broke out in May 1994. Initially, the South Yemeni forces had the better of it, but the larger and better-equipped army of the North, moving slowly southward, surrounded Aden and captured the city after a brief siege. Vice-President al-Beidh fled into exile, effectively depriving the rebellion of its chief leader, and his Yemen Socialist Party was excluded from the governing coalition, although it was allowed to continue as a political party.

The end of the Civil War, more or less on North Yemen's terms, offered Saleh another opportunity to unify the nation. The first step would be the restoration of representative government. A 1992 law was reinstated to require political parties to have 5,000 or more members, plus offices in each governorate, in order to present candidates in the forthcoming national elections.

The election was held on April 27, 1993. Some 2,300 candidates vied for the 301 seats in the unicameral Yemeni national Legislature. As expected, the GPC won a large majority, 239 seats, to 62 for Islah, the main opposition party. The Yemen Socialist Party, which boycotted the elections, was shut out of legislative participation entirely.

What struck outside observers about the election was its faithful adherence to political democracy. The entire process was supervised by the Supreme Election Commission, established by law as an independent body with balanced political representation. Despite having one of the lowest literacy rates in the world, Yemenis participated with enthusiasm and in great numbers, illiterate voters being assisted by literate volunteers to mark their ballots inside the curtained polling booths. Ballots were tabulated by hand by representatives of the Supreme Election Council, prompting an American observer to ask why "they didn't use voting machines and computers; they said they would not trust such a system because it would not be transparent."[5]

In September 1999, Yemen's first direct presidential election marked a milestone in the slow progress of the state—and Arab states in general—toward Western-style representative government. Prior to the election, the Constitution was amended to allow an incumbent to serve for two consecutive five-year terms. Although he was nominated by both his own party and the opposition Islah Party, President Ali Abdullah Saleh faced opposition for the first time in a presidential election. Admittedly the opposition consisted of token, unknown candidates, and Saleh won reelection with ease. However, despite its flawed nature, the election underlined not only the president's popularity among his people but also his serious commitment to representative government.

Although on the surface Yemen seems to offer fertile ground for Islamic fundamentalism due to its poverty, its high unemployment rate, and its divisions between a tribal north and a Marxist south, until recently no homegrown Islamic fundamentalist movement existed there. Following the withdrawal of Soviet troops from Afghanistan in 1989, a large number of Afghan resistance fighters (*mujahideen*) and Muslim volunteers from other countries who had gone to Afghanistan to defend Islam against atheistic Communists fled to Yemen. At the end of the 1994, one mujahideen group, Aden-Abyan Islamic Jihad, carried out a number of bombings and kidnappings of foreign tourists and oil company employees. Its objectives were unclear, but it was said that the group was seeking to enforce the strict observance of Islamic law in Yemen. The group was subdued by government forces in 1999, and in January 2000, the Yemen high court convicted 10 of its members of terrorism. Three were sentenced to death, and the leader was immediately executed.

### THE ECONOMY

Discoveries of significant oil deposits in the 1980s should have augured well for Yemen's economic future. Reserves are estimated at 1 billion barrels in the Marib basin and 3.3 billion in the Shabwa field northeast of Aden, with an additional 5.5 billion in the former neutral zone shared by the two Yemens and now administered by the central government. Yemen also has large deposits of natural gas, with reserves estimated at 5.5 trillion cubic feet.

Unfortunately, the political conflicts of the 1990s had a negative effect on these rosy prospects. The Gulf War, in which Yemen supported Iraq against the UN–U.S.–Saudi coalition, caused Saudi Arabia to deport some 850,000 Yemeni workers. And the Civil War in 1994 seriously damaged the infrastructure, requiring some $200 million in repairs to schools, hospitals, roads, and power stations.

Until very recently, both Yemens were among the poorest and least-developed countries in the Middle East. This description is somewhat misleading in North Yemen's case, however, since the highland regions have traditionally supported a sizable population, due to fertile soil, de-

| | | | | | | |
|---|---|---|---|---|---|---|
| Yemen is recognized as an independent nation under Imam Yahya **1934** | A revolution overthrows Imam al-Badr; a military group proclaims a republic in North Yemen **1962** | Civil war between supporters of Badr and Egyptian-backed republicans; protectorates merge with Aden Crown Colony **1962–1969** | British forces withdraw from Aden; the National Liberation Front proclaims South Yemen an independent republic **1967** | Major oil and natural-gas discoveries **1980s** | The two Yemens unite on May 22, 1990; free elections are held on April 27, 1993; civil war in 1994 **1990s** | **2000s** |

The U.S. destroyer *Cole* is attacked in Aden harbor

Yemen states willingness to join international coalition against terrorism

pendable and adequate rainfall, and effective use of limited arable land. South Yemen's resources were mostly unexploited during the 130 years of British rule, except for a small local fishing industry and the Aden port and refinery. During its brief period of independence, the P.D.R.Y.'s budget came mostly (70 percent) from the Soviet Union and other Communist countries. The reduction in Soviet aid from $400 million in 1988 to $50 million in 1989 was one of the economic factors that encouraged reunification from the South Yemen side.

In ancient times, Yemen, particularly in the South, had a flourishing agriculture based on monsoon rains, supplemented by a sophisticated system of small dams and canals and centered in the Wadi Hadhramaut. But long neglect and two decades of disastrous Soviet-style state-farm management adversely affected agricultural production.

Since reunification, most state-owned lands in the Hadhramaut have been privatized. And oil drilling in the region has resulted in discovery of important underground water resources. As a result, and with aid from the World Bank, the region has recovered much of its former agricultural productivity. Today, date-palm groves, fields of corn, orchards, and beehives flourish.

## FOREIGN RELATIONS
Prior to unification with South Yemen, North Yemen's geographical isolation and tribal social structure limited its contact with other Arab states. South Yemen's Marxist regime, in contrast, actively attempted to subvert the governments of its neighbors. Reunification has brought better and closer relations with these states. In 1995, the flags of Yemen and Oman

flew side by side on their newly demarcated common border, based on a 1992 agreement to accept UN mediation.

Yemen's relations with Saudi Arabia have followed an uneven course. Yemeni workers in the kingdom were deported en masse after the Gulf War, due to Yemeni support for Iraq. The action was a severe blow to the Yemeni economy, as 20 to 25 percent of the national budget had come from expatriate-worker remittances. The relationship improved after 1995, when Syrian mediators arranged for a reconfirmation of the 1934 Treaty of Taif, which had demarcated their common border. The resulting "Memorandum of Understanding of Taif" recognizes Saudi sovereignty over Asir, Najran, and Jizan Provinces in return for Yemeni sovereignty over the Marib oil fields.

Yemen's nongovernmental associations with anti–U.S. terrorism were emphasized by the bombing of the U.S. Navy destroyer *Cole* in October 2000 while it was in Aden harbor for refueling. Seventeen American naval personnel were killed in the attack, which was carried out by men in a small boat filled with explosives. The attack was unexpected, given the extent of the Yemeni government's cooperation with the United States. American warships had been given permission to use Aden as a port of call, American specialists had arrived to train Yemenis in removal of land mines from the interior, and Peace Corps volunteers were providing English-language and agricultural training in villages throughout the country.

The *Cole* attackers were believed to be part of Osama bin Laden's al-Qaeda terrorist network, and American FBI agents were initially invited to take part in the investigation. However, as the search proceeded, Yemeni authorities imposed severe

restrictions on these agents. Their access to senior military and religious leaders was prohibited, and subsequently they withdrew from the country.

Following the September 11, 2001, terrorist attacks in the United States, the Yemeni government declared its willingness to join the international antiterror coalition. It arrested 20 Yemenis suspected of having been trained in al-Qaeda camps in Afghanistan before returning to their own country. To underscore Yemen's cooperation, Prime Minister Abdul-Kader Bajammal indicated that 4,000 Yemenis trained in such camps had been expelled.

## NOTES
1. Robin Bidwell, *The Two Yemens* (Boulder, CO: Westview Press, 1983), p. 10.
2. Quoted in Robert Stookey, *Yemen: The Politics of the Yemen Arab Republic* (Boulder, CO: Westview Press, 1978), p. 168.
3. John Peterson, "Nation-building and Political Development in the Two Yemens," in B. R. Pridham, ed., *Contemporary Yemen: Politics and Historical Background* (New York: St. Martin's Press, 1985), p. 86.
4. Yemenis believed that he slept with a rope around his neck to terrify visitors, that he could turn twigs into snakes, and that he once outwrestled the devil. Bidwell, *op. cit.,* p. 121.
5. William A. Rugh, "A (Successful) Test of Democracy in Yemen," *The Christian Science Monitor* (May 28, 1997), p. 19.

---

### DEVELOPMENT

Yemen's modest growth, averaging 2% in the 1990s, is due in part to political instability but also to a lack of aggressive development of its oil and gas resources. Unemployment holds steady at 35%, and although some of the 850,000 Yemeni workers expelled from Saudi Arabia have been allowed to return, expatriate remittances are far below what they were before 1991.

### FREEDOM

The 1991 Constitution established a parliamentary republic in unified Yemen. Elections in 1997 for the national Legislature resulted in a two-party division of power, with majority (GPC) and minority (Islah) parties represented. The press is free, and women enjoy full civil rights and may run for public office. Yemen's legal code, based on Islamic law and approved by referendum in 1994, is also unusual in outlawing the death penalty for juvenile offenders under age 18. However, tribal law makes the ban difficult to enforce in the country's rural areas.

### HEALTH/WELFARE

Yemenis spend many hours chewing qat, the leaves of a shrub that are mildly narcotic. Arguing that qat-chewing was an obstacle to development, President Saleh launched a nationwide campaign to "kick the habit" in 1999. But because qat provides 30% of GDP, farmers have been reluctant to plant other crops such as coffee and sorghum, which bring them less than 1/5 of the return from their qat crop.

### ACHIEVEMENTS

In April 2000, the government approved a master plan developed by the Socotra Diversity Project, a $5 million offshoot of the 1992 Rio de Janeiro (Brazil) environmental summit conference. The plan calls for the UN to designate Socotra Island as a "human and biosphere preserve." Socotra will be managed and its status protected by the Yemeni government's Environmental Protection Council.

# Annotated Table of Contents for Articles

## Articles from the World Press

*Article 1*

*The World & I,* September 1997

TAKING THE MYSTERY OUT OF ISLAM

# WHAT IS ISLAM?

*Islam, a great monotheistic religion, provides spiritual and moral life,
and cultural and sometimes national identity, to more than a billion people.*

## ABDULAZIZ SACHEDINA

In the mass media, Islam and Muslims are frequently depicted as the "other" in global politics and cultural warfare. The Iranian revolution under Ayatollah Khomeini in 1978–79, the tragic death of 241 marines near Beirut airport in 1983, and the bombing of the World Trade Center in New York in 1993 are among the violent images associated with Muslims. But those images resonate poorly with the majority of Muslims. Most Muslims, like other

human beings, are engaged in their day-to-day life in this world, struggling to provide for their usually large extended families, working for peaceful resolution to the conflicts that face them, and committed to honor universal human values of freedom and peace with justice.

Muslims in general take their religion seriously. For many it is the central focus of their spiritual and moral life. For others, less religiously inclined, it remains a source of their cultural and sometimes national identity. So the word *Islam* carries broader ramifications than is usually recognized in the media. As the name of the religion, *Islam* means "submission to God's will." It is also applied to cultures and civilizations that developed under its religious impulse.

Historically as well as psychologically, Islam shares the monotheistic religious genome with Judaism and Christianity. Islamic civilization has acted as the repository of the Hebrew, Persian, Indian, and Hellenistic intellectual traditions and cultures.

### Historical Development

Islam was proclaimed by Muhammad (570–632), the Prophet of Islam and the founder of Islamic polity, in Arabia. Seventh-century Arabia was socially and politically ripe for the emergence of new leadership. When Muhammad was growing up in Mecca, by then an important center of flourishing trade between Byzantium and the Indian Ocean, he was aware of the social inequities and injustices that existed in the tribal society dominated by a political oligarchy.

Before Islam, religious practices and attitudes were determined by the tribal aristocracy, who also upheld tribal values—bravery in battle, patience in misfortune, persistence in revenge, protection of the weak, defiance of the strong, generosity, and hospitality—as part of their moral code. The growth of Mecca as a commercial center had weakened this tribal moral code and

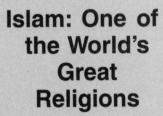

## Islam: One of the World's Great Religions

*Islam was proclaimed by Muhammad (570–632), the Prophet of Islam and the founder of Islamic polity.*

*After Muhammad's death, the Islamic community divided into the Sunni ("people of tradition") and the Shiites ("partisans").*

*The Sunni have mostly a quietist and authoritarian stance, while the Shiites tend to be more activist and radical.*

*The Muslim faith is built on Five Pillars.*

*Islam today continues to inspire more than a billion people to go beyond a self-centered existence to establish a just society.*

concern for the less fortunate in society, leaving them without any security. It was in the midst of a serious socioeconomic imbalance between the rich and the poor, between extreme forms of individualism and tyrannical tribal solidarity, that Islam came to proclaim an ethical order based on interpersonal justice.

## The founder and his community

Muhammad's father died before he was born, and his mother died when he was only six years old. In accordance with Arab tribal norms, he was brought up first by his grandfather and then, following his grandfather's death, by his uncle. As a young man he was employed by a wealthy Meccan woman, Khadija, as her trade agent. He was twenty-five when he accepted a marriage offer from Khadija, who was fifteen years his senior. When Muhammad received his prophetic call at the age of forty, Khadija was the first person to become "Muslim" ("believer in Islam").

Meccan leadership resisted Muhammad and persecuted him and his followers, who were drawn mainly from among the poor and disenfranchised. Muhammad decided to emigrate to Medina, an oasis town in the north. This emigration in 622 marks the beginning of the Muslim calendar, as well as the genesis of the first Islamic polity. (Muslims marked their new year, 1418, on May 8, 1997.)

Muhammad as a statesman instituted a series of reforms to create his community, the Umma, on the basis of religious affiliation. This also established a distinctive feature of Islamic faith, which does not admit any separation between the religious and temporal spheres of human activity and has insisted on the ideal unity of civil and moral authority under the divinely ordained legal system, the Shari'ah.

At Muhammad's death, he had brought the whole of Arabia under the Medina government, but he apparently left no explicit instruction regarding succession to his religious-political authority. The early Muslim leaders who succeeded him as caliph (meaning political and spiritual "successor") exercised Muhammad's political authority,

making political and military decisions that led to the expansion of their domain beyond Arabia. Within a century Muslim armies had conquered the region from the Nile in North Africa to the Amu Darya in Central Asia east to India.

This phenomenal growth into a vast empire required an Islamic legal system for the administration of the highly developed political systems of the conquered Persian and Byzantine regions. Muslim jurists therefore formulated a comprehensive legal code, using the ethical and legal principles set forth in the Qur'an.

Differences of opinion on certain critical issues emerged as soon as Muhammad died. The question of succession was one of the major issues that divided the community into the Sunni and the Shiites. Those supporting the candidacy of Abu Bakr (ca. 573–634), an elderly associate of the Prophet, as caliph formed the majority of the community and gradually came to be known as the Sunni ("people of tradition"); those who acclaimed 'Ali (ca. 600–661), Muhammad's cousin and son-in-law, as the "imam" (religious and political leader) designated by the Prophet formed the minority group, known as the Shiites ("partisans").

The civil strife in Muslim polity gave rise to two distinct, and in some ways contradictory, attitudes among Muslims that can be observed even today: quietist and activist. Those upholding a quietist posture supported an authoritarian stance, to the point of feigning unquestioning and immediate obedience to almost any nominally Muslim political authority. Exponents of an activist posture supported radical politics and taught that under certain circumstances people had the right to revolt against evil Muslim rulers.

Gradually the quietist and authoritarian stance became associated with the majority Sunni Muslims, although every now and then they had their share of radicalism, as seen in the assassination of Egyptian President Anwar Sadat in 1981. The activist-radical stance came to be associated with Shiite Islam, represented by Iran today.

The Muslim community has continued to live in the shadow of the idealized history of early Islam, when religious and secular authority was

united under pious caliphs. Efforts to actualize this ideal today give rise to radical politics among a number of religious-minded Muslim groups, usually designated pejoratively as "fundamentalists," who regard *jihad* (war) against their corrupt rulers as a legitimate tool for change.

## What do Muslims believe?

Muslims derive their religious beliefs and practices from two sources: the Qur'an, which they regard as the "Book of God," and the Sunna, or the exemplary conduct of the Prophet. The Qur'an consists of the revelations Muhammad received intermittently over the twenty-two years from the time of his calling in 610 until his death. Muslims believe that the Qur'an was directly communicated by God through the archangel Gabriel, and accordingly, it is regarded as inerrant and immutably preserved. It has served as the normative source for deriving principal theological, ethical, and legal doctrines. The Sunna (meaning "trodden path") has functioned as the elaboration of the Qur'anic revelation. It provides details about each and every precept and deed attributed to Muhammad. The narratives that carried such information are known as *hadith*. In the ninth century, Muslim scholars developed an elaborate system for the theological and legal classification of these hadith to derive certain beliefs and practices.

In this connection it is relevant to remember the Rushdie affair of the 1980s. Salman Rushdie's novel *The Satanic Verses* was directed toward discrediting both the Qur'an and the Prophet as the normative sources for Muslim religiosity, which, understandably, enraged more than a billion Muslims around the world. And while many Muslims may not have endorsed the death sentence passed on Rushdie by the Ayatollah Khomeini, they unanimously condemned the novel for its profanity in connection with the founder of Islam and Muslim scriptures.

## The Five Pillars of Islam

The Muslim faith is built upon Five Pillars, as follow:

**The First Pillar** is the *shahada,* the profession of faith: "There is no deity but God, and Muhammad is the messenger of God." This is the formula through which a person converts to Islam. Belief in God constitutes the integrity of human existence, individually and as a member of society. The Qur'an speaks about God as the being whose presence is felt in everything that exists; everything that happens is an indicator of the divine. God is the "knower of the Unseen and the Visible; . . . the All-merciful, the All-compassionate, . . . the Sovereign Lord, the All-holy, the Giver of peace, the Keeper of faith, the All-preserver, the All-mighty, the All-powerful, the Most High" (Qur'an, 59:23). Faith in God results in being safe, well integrated, sound, and at peace.

Human beings are not born in sin, but they are forgetful. To help them realize their potential God sends prophets to "remind" humanity of their covenant with God (7:172). Noah, Abraham, Moses, Jesus, and Muhammad are regarded as "messengers" sent to organize their people on the basis of the guidance revealed by God.

**The Second Pillar** is daily worship (*salat*), required five times a day: at dawn, midday, afternoon, evening, and night. These prayers are short and require bowing and prostrations. Muslims may worship anywhere, preferably in congregation, facing Mecca. They are required to worship as a community on Fridays at midday and on two major religious holidays.

**The Third Pillar** is the mandatory "alms-levy" (*zakat*). The obligation to share what one possesses with those less fortunate is stressed throughout the Qur'an. The Muslim definition of the virtuous life includes charitable support of widows, wayfarers, orphans, and the needy. Although zakat has for the most part been left to the conscience of Muslims, the obligation to be charitable and contribute to the general welfare of the community continues to be emphasized. In a number of poor Muslim countries this benevolence provided by wealthy individuals has underwritten badly needed social services for those who cannot afford them.

**The Fourth Pillar** is the fast during the month of Ramadan, observed according to the Muslim lunar calendar, which has been in use since the seventh century. Since the lunar year is some ten days shorter than the solar year, the fasting and all Muslim festivals occur in different seasons. During the fast, which lasts from dawn to dusk, Muslims are required not only to refrain from eating, smoking, and drinking; they are also to refrain from sexual intercourse and acts leading to sensual behavior. The end of the month is marked by a festival, Eid al-Fitr, after which life returns to normal.

**The Fifth Pillar** is the *hajj,* or pilgrimage to Mecca, which all Muslims are required to undertake once in their lives, provided they have the financial means. The pilgrimage brings together Muslims of diverse cultures and nationalities to achieve a purity of existence and a communion with God that will exalt the pilgrims for the rest of their lives.

The Islamic ethical-legal system, known as the Shari'ah, was developed to determine normative Islamic conduct.

## Muslim moral and legal guidance

The Islamic ethical-legal system, known as the Shari'ah, was developed to determine normative Islamic conduct. The Shari'ah is the divinely ordained blueprint for human conduct, which is inherently and essentially religious. The juridical inquiry in discovering the Shari'ah code was comprehensive because it necessarily dealt with every case of conscience covering God-human relations, as well as the ethical content of interpersonal relations in every possible sphere of human activity. Most of the legal activity, however, went into settling more formal interpersonal activities that affected the morals of the community. These activities dealt with the obligation to do good to Muslims and guard the interests of the community.

Islamic legal theory recognized four sources on the basis of which judicial decisions could be deduced: the Qur'an, the Sunna, consensus of the early community of Muslims, and analogical reasoning, which attempts to discover the unknown from the known precedent. Ash-Shafi'i (767–820), a rigorous legal thinker, systematically and comprehensively linked the four sources to derive the entire legal system covering all possible contingencies. The legal precedents and principles provided by the Qur'an and Sunna were used to develop an elaborate system of rules of jurisprudence. Human conduct was to be determined in terms of how much legal weight was borne by a particular rule that rendered a given practice obligatory or merely recommended.

As Islamic law became a highly technical process, disputes about method and judicial opinions crystallized into legal schools designated by the names of prominent jurists. The legal school that followed the Iraqi tradition was called "Hanafi," after Abu Hanafi (669–767), the great imam in Iraq. Those who adhered to the rulings of Malik ibn Anas (ca. 715–795), in Arabia and elsewhere, were known as "Malikis." Ash-Shafi'i founded a legal school in Egypt whose influence spread widely to other regions of the Muslim world. His followers were known as Shafi'is. Another school was associated with Ahmad ibn Hanbal (780–855), who compiled a work on traditions that became the source for juridical decisions for Hanbalis.

The Shiites developed their own legal school, whose leading authority was Imam Ja'far ibn Muhammad (ca. 702–765). Normally, Muslims accept one of the legal schools prevalent in their region. Most of the Sunni follow Hanifi or Shafi'i, whereas the Shiites follow the Ja'fari school. In the absence of an organized "church" and ordained "clergy" in Islam, determination of valid religious practice is left to the qualified scholar of religious law known as a *mufti* (the one who issues a *fatwa,* or decree).

## Muslim family law

In Islamic family law, the rights of women, children, and other dependents are protected against the male head of the family, who, on the average, is stronger than a woman and more independent, since he is free of pregnancy

# Islam and the Arabic Language

By Tamara Sonn

*Those are the verses of the glorious book. We have revealed it as an Arabic recitation, so that you will understand.* (Qur'an, 12:2)

These words from Islamic scripture, and others like them, reveal the integral relationship between the Arabic language and Islam. Muslims believe that all revelation comes from the same divine source, so there is no need to be concerned that the Jews have their Torah and the Christians have their Gospels, for example. The Qur'an is simply divine revelation sent to speakers of Arabic, according to this sacred book. "Yet before it was the Book of Moses for a model and a mercy; and this is a book confirming in Arabic, to warn the evil-doers and bring good tidings to the good-doers" (46:11–12). The Qur'an, therefore, is essentially Arabic. But that does not mean Islam is only for Arabs.

According to the Qur'an, no one can be forced to convert. "In matters of religion there is no compulsion" (2:256). But those who choose to become Muslim must pray five times a day, reciting from the Qur'an in Arabic. The role of the Arabic language in Islam, therefore, remains central, despite the fact that the vast majority of Muslims are neither Arab nor Arabic speaking.

The majority of Muslims worldwide today "read" Arabic for prayer the way Roman Catholics used to "read" Latin at mass. They can make out the words but know the general ideas represented primarily through vernacular interpretations. Yet there is no movement to substitute the vernacular for the original language, as there was in Catholicism before the Second Vatican Council. On the contrary, emphasis on the importance of studying Arabic is increasing.

Only one country has ever authorized a translation of the Qur'an. Turkey, created after the breakup of the Ottoman Empire in World War I, stressed the Turkish language in an effort to distinguish itself from the rest of the Muslim world. Even in Turkey, however, prayer continued to be in Arabic, and today there is a strong movement to return to Arabic as the universal language of Islam.

Part of the contemporary stress on Arabic results from the worldwide movement of rebirth (*al-nahda*) in Islam. After centuries of eclipse and Euro-Christian domination, the Muslim world entered the twentieth century with a renewed commitment to its roots as a means of reviving both cultural strength and political independence. Formal independence from colonial control, however, left most of the Muslim world afflicted with severe economic and political underdevelopment. Experiments with European-style social and political models have been judged failures, benefiting only a few. The result has been a populist call for "the Islamic solution," religiously based cultural and political identity. Renewed emphasis on the Qur'an—and with it, Arabic—is an integral part of this "Islamist" movement. As a result, the Arabic language is being studied more widely than ever.

The Islamist stress on Islamic and therefore Arabic studies, however, should not be confused with another modern movement known as Arabism (*'urubah*). Arabism stresses not only the centrality of the Arabic language to Islamic identity but the dominance of Arab culture. Early proponents described Islam as "the highest moment of consciousness" of Arab culture. Therefore, as people become Muslim, they actually become Arab as well, at least to a certain degree. Some see Arabism as simply a religiously oriented version of the Arab nationalist movement.

A controversial movement from the outset, Arabism has declined in popularity with the rise of Islamism, although its echoes can still be heard. In a recent speech, Sadek Jawad Sulaiman, former ambassador of Oman to the United States, stressed the centrality of Arabism to Islam: "Outside its repository of Arabic culture, Islam is left with little form or substance."

The majority of those who stress the importance of Arabic believe they are simply following the Qur'an's own teaching. The Qur'an repeatedly refers to the power and beauty of its language. It tells of Prophet Muhammad being an illiterate (or unlettered) orphan and yet producing a work of such splendor that it challenges his detractors to match it (10:38–9, 11:13–16, 28:49). Even today, non-Muslim Arabic speakers are awed by its beauty. Undoubtedly, the book's inherent beauty and power would suffer in translation. Beyond aesthetic concerns, however, is recognition of the insidious effect of translation on understanding.

Even so, Muslims agree that fluency in Arabic is no guarantee that one will be moved by the Qur'an or be a good Muslim. As the Qur'an teaches, "God summons to the abode of peace and guides whomsoever he will to a straight path" (3:27). Islam enters "through the heart," according to Qur'anic metaphor. It is primarily a turning of the will toward God, an inner transformation. This transformation may or may not be prompted by the power of the Qur'an. The Qur'an counts among the believers anyone—including Jews and Christians—who believes in God and does good deeds. For at its core, Islam is a matter of behavior rather than words: "Woe betide those who pray, yet are neglectful of their prayers—those who pray for show and yet refuse charity" (107:1–7).

*Tamara Sonn is a professor in the Department of Religious Studies at the University of South Florida, Tampa.*

and immediate care of children. Islamic marital rules encourage individual responsibility by strengthening the nuclear family. The Shari'ah protects male prerogative as the one who is required to support the household, whereas a woman is protected primarily by her family. All schools give a husband one-sided divorce privileges, because for a woman to divorce a man would mean to unsettle her husband's economic investment. Under these rules a husband could divorce a wife almost at will, but a wife who wished to leave her husband had to show good reason. The main legal check upon the man in divorce is essentially financial and a matter of contract between equal parties that includes a provision about the bridal gift. The man pays part of the gift, which might be substantial, at the time of marriage; if he divorces her without special reason, he has to pay her the rest.

The Muslim woman can own property, and it cannot be touched by any male relative, including her husband, who is required to support her from his own funds. Moreover, she has a personal status that might allow her to go into business on her own. However, this potential feminine independence was curbed primarily by cultural means, keeping marriages within the extended family, so that family property would not leave the family through women marrying out.

All schools of Islam, although tending to give men an extensive prerogative, presupposed a considerable social role for women. The Qur'anic injunction to propriety was stretched by means of the Sunna to impose seclusion. The veil for women was presented simply in terms of personal modesty, the female

Muslims, like Christians, have raised critical questions about human responsibility in view of God's overpowering will.

apartments in terms of family privacy.

In the patriarchal family structures, and not necessarily in the Shari'ah, women were assigned a subordinate role in the household and community. Here, the term *Islam* is being used in the sense of culture or local tradition. And it is precisely in the confusion between normative Islam and cultural practices that we find tension in ethical and legal formulations among Muslims.

In some parts of the Muslim world women are victims of traditional practices that are often harmful to them and to their children's well-being. One controversial and persistent practice is female circumcision (*khafd or khifad*), without which it is believed that girls could not attain the status of womanhood. Islamic views of female circumcision are ambiguous. The operation was performed long before the rise of Islam, and it is not a practice in many Muslim countries, including Saudi Arabia, Tunisia, Iran, and Turkey. There is nothing in the Qur'an that sanctions female circumcision, especially its most severe form, infibulation. The Prophet opposed the custom, found among pre-Islamic Arabs, since he considered it harmful to women's sexual well-being. Yet the official position adopted by a

majority of Sunni jurists is that female circumcision is sanctioned by the tradition. They concede, however, that the Shari'ah does not regard it as an obligatory requirement.

## Are humans free agents of God?

Muslims, like Christians, have raised critical questions about human responsibility in view of God's overpowering will. In the first half of the eighth century, the rudiments of the earliest systematic theology were developed by a group called the Mu'tazilites. Before them, some Muslim thinkers had developed theological arguments, including a doctrine of God and human responsibility. The Mu'tazilites undertook to show that there was nothing repugnant to reason in the Islamic revelation. Their theological system was worked out under five headings: (1) belief in God's unity, which rejected anything that smacked of anthropomorphism; (2) the justice of God, which denied any ascriptions of injustice to God's judgment of human beings, with the consequence that humans alone were responsible for all their acts and thus punishable for evil actions; (3) the impending judgment, which underscored the importance of daily righteousness and rejected laxity in matters of faith; (4) the middle position of the Muslim sinner, who, because of disobeying God's commandments was neither condemned to hell nor rewarded with paradise; and (5) the duty to command the good and forbid evil to ensure an ethical social order.

The traditionalist Ash'arites, reacting to Mu'tazilite rationalism, limited speculative theology to a defense of the doctrines given in the hadith, which were regarded as more reliable than abstract reason in deriving individual doctrines. The Ash'arites emphasized the absolute will and power of God and denied nature and humankind any decisive role. In their effort to maintain the effectiveness of a God who could and did intervene in human affairs, they maintained that good and evil are what God decrees them to be. Accordingly, good and evil cannot be known from nature but must be discovered in the Qur'an and the tradition. Ash'arite theological views have remained dominant

throughout Islamic history, well into modern times, and had a profound effect upon scientific theory and practice among the Sunni.

The attitude of resignation, a by-product of belief in predestination, is summed up in the Sunni creedal confession: "What reaches you could not possibly have missed you; and what misses you could not possibly have reached you" (*Fiqh akbar*, Article 3).

The Shiite Muslims, on the other hand, have developed a rational theology and ethical doctrines resembling those of the Mu'tazilites. Hence, they believe that humans are free agents of God who are responsible for their own actions. Moreover, the justice of God requires that God provide a constant source of guidance through reason and exemplary leaders, known as imams, for human advancement toward perfection. This belief is the source of the emergence of Khomeini-like leadership in Shitte Iran today.

## Mystical dimension of Islam

From the early days of the Islamic empire (eighth century) the ascetic reaction to growing worldliness in the Muslim community took the form of mysticism of personality in Islam, whose goal was spiritual and moral perfection of an individual. Sufism, as Islamic mysticism came to be known, aimed to internalize the ritual acts by emphasizing rigorous self-assessment and self-discipline. In its early form Sufism was mainly a form of ascetic piety that involved ridding oneself of any dependence on satisfying one's desire, in order to devote oneself entirely to God. Mystical practices developed by the Sufi masters comprised a moral process to gain the relative personal clarity that comes at moments of retreat and reflection.

From daily moments of reflection the mystic experienced more intense levels of awareness, which could take ecstatic forms, including ecstatic love of God. This aspect of Sufism brought the mystics into direct conflict with the traditionalist Muslims, who emphasized active obedience to God as the highest goal of religious meaning and purpose.

By the eleventh century, the Sufi masters had developed a new form of religious orientation that brought about the acceptance of Sufism by the ordinary people in many places. Near the end of the twelfth century, the Sufi organized several formal brotherhoods or orders (*tariqa*) in which women also participated. Each order taught a pattern of invocation and meditation that used devotional practices to organize a group of novices under a master. Through special control of breath and bodily posture accompanied by invocative words or syllables, they developed more intense concentration.

These brotherhoods, however, degenerated into antisocial groups that caused much damage to the teachings of Islam about societal and familial obligations. Moreover, because of their unquestioning devotion to the Sufi masters, both living and dead, a shrine culture leading to almost saint worship took deep roots among ordinary peoples attracted to this folk Islam. This condition elicited a strong reaction against Sufism in the Muslim world in modern times. Both the traditionalist reformers, like the Wahhabis of Saudi Arabia, and the

champions of secularist modernism, like the founder of modern Turkey, Kemal Atatürk (1881–1938), disbanded Sufism as being totally un-Islamic.

Nevertheless, the formal approval of Sufism as a genuine form of Islamic piety by the great scholar Abu Hamid al-Ghazal (1058–1111), who taught Islamic law and theology in Baghdad, has been revived in many countries. There sufism continues to thrive as a bastion of religious tolerance and free-spirited religiosity.

### Islam today

Islam as a religion, culture, and civilization continues to inspire a billion people worldwide to take up the challenge to go beyond one's self-centered existence to establish a just society that will reflect "submission to God's will." As an Abrahamic faith, Islam has accepted the pluralism of human responses to spiritual guidance as a divine mystery. And although its interaction with history is not free of tension, and even contradictions, on the whole Islam has devel-

oped an enviable system of coexistence among religious communities. Its vision of a global community working toward the common good of humanity has been overshadowed by political upheavals in the postcolonial Muslim world. Unless the violated justice of the ordinary people is restored, like its other Abrahamic forebears Islam will continue to inspire activist response to social and political injustices in the Muslim world.

*Abdulaziz Sachedina is professor of religious studies at the University of Virginia.*

---

*Article 2*

*The American Prospect*, November 19, 2001

# Why Don't They Like Us?

How America Has Become the Object of Much of the Planet's Genuine Grievances—and Displaced Dicontents

Stanley Hoffmann

IT WASN'T ITS INNOCENCE THAT THE UNITED STATES LOST ON SEPtember 11, 2001. It was its naiveté. Americans have tended to believe that in the eyes of others the United States has lived up to the boastful clichs propagated during the Cold War (especially under Ronald Reagan) and during the Clinton administration. We were seen, we thought, as the champions of

freedom against fascism and communism, as the advocates of decolonization, economic development, and social progress, as the technical innovators whose mastery of technology, science, and advanced education was going to unify the world.

Some officials and academics explained that U.S. hegemony was the best thing for a troubled world and unlike past hegemonies would last—not only because there were no challengers strong enough to steal the crown but, above all, because we were benign rulers who threatened no one.

But we have avoided looking at the hegemon's clay feet, at what might neutralize our vaunted soft power and undermine our hard power. Like swarming insects exposed when a fallen tree is lifted, millions who dislike or distrust the hegemon have suddenly appeared after September 11, much to our horror and disbelief. America became a great power after World War II, when we faced a rival that seemed to stand for everything we had been fighting against—tyranny, terror, brainwashing—and we thought that our international reputation would benefit from our standing for liberty and stability (as it still does in much of Eastern Europe). We were not sufficiently marinated in history to know that, through the ages, nobody—or almost nobody—has ever loved a hegemon.

Past hegemons, from Rome to Great Britain, tended to be quite realistic about this. They wanted to be obeyed or, as in the case of France, admired. They rarely wanted to be loved. But as a combination of high-noon sheriff and proselytizing missionary, the United States expects gratitude and affection. It was bound to be disappointed; gratitude is not an emotion that one associates with the behavior of states.

## The New World Disorder

This is an old story. Two sets of factors make the current twist a new one. First, the so-called Westphalian world has collapsed. The world of sovereign states, the universe of Hans Morgenthau's and Henry Kissinger's Realism, is no longer. The unpopularity of the hegemonic power has been heightened to incandescence by two aspects of this collapse. One is the irruption of the public, the masses, in international affairs. Foreign policy is no longer, as Raymond Aron had written in *Peace and War*, the closed domain of the soldier and the diplomat. Domestic publics—along with their interest groups, religious organizations, and ideological chapels—either dictate or constrain the imperatives and preferences that the governments fight for. This puts the hegemon in a difficult position: It often must work with governments that represent but a small percentage of a country's people—but if it fishes for public support abroad, it risks alienating leaders whose cooperation it needs. The United States paid heavily for not having had enough contacts with the opposition to the shah of Iran in the 1970s. It discovers today that there is an abyss in Pakistan, Saudi Arabia, Egypt, and Indonesia between our official allies and the populace in these countries. Diplomacy in a world where the masses, so to speak, stayed indoors, was a much easier game.

The collapse of the barrier between domestic and foreign affairs in the state system is now accompanied by a disease that attacks the state system itself. Many of the "states" that are members of the United Nations are pseudo-states with shaky or shabby institutions, no basic consensus on values or on procedures among their heterogeneous components, and no sense of national identity. Thus the hegemon—in addition to suffering the hostility of the government in certain countries (like Cuba, Iraq, and North Korea) and of the public in others (like, in varying degrees, Pakistan, Egypt, and even France)—

can now easily become both the target of factions fighting one another in disintegrating countries and the pawn in their quarrels (which range over such increasingly borderless issues as drug trafficking, arms trading, money laundering, and other criminal enterprises). In addition, today's hegemon suffers from the volatility and turbulence of a global system in which ethnic, religious, and ideological sympathies have become transnational and in which groups and individuals uncontrolled by states can act on their own. The world of the nineteenth century, when hegemons could impose their order, their institutions, has been supplanted by the world of the twenty-first century: Where once there was order, there is now often a vacuum.

What makes the American Empire especially vulnerable is its historically unique combination of assets and liabilities. One has to go back to the Roman Empire to find a comparable set of resources. Britain, France, and Spain had to operate in multipolar systems; the United States is the only superpower.

But if America's means are vast, the limits of its power are also considerable. The United States, unlike Rome, cannot simply impose its will by force or through satellite states. Small "rogue" states can defy the hegemon (remember Vietnam?). And chaos can easily result from the large new role of nonstate actors. Meanwhile, the reluctance of Americans to take on the Herculean tasks of policing, "nation building," democratizing autocracies, and providing environmental protection and economic growth for billions of human beings stokes both resentment and hostility, especially among those who discover that one can count on American presence and leadership only when America's material interests are gravely threatened. (It is not surprising that the "defense of the national interest" approach of Realism was developed for a multipolar world. In an empire, as well as in a bipolar system, almost anything can be described as a vital interest, since even peripheral disorder can unravel the superpower's eminence.) Moreover, the complexities of America's process for making foreign-policy decisions can produce disappointments abroad when policies that the international community counted on—such as the Kyoto Protocol and the International Criminal Court—are thwarted. Also, the fickleness of U.S. foreign-policy making in arenas like the Balkans has convinced many American enemies that this country is basically incapable of pursuing long-term policies consistently.

NONE OF THIS MEANS, OF COURSE, THAT THE UNITED STATES HAS no friends in the world. Europeans have not forgotten the liberating role played by Americans in the war against Hitler and in the Cold War. Israel remembers how President Harry Truman sided with the founders of the Zionist state; nor has it forgotten all the help the United States has given it since then. The democratizations of postwar Germany and Japan were huge successes. The Marshall Plan and the Point Four Program were revolutionary initiatives. The decisions to resist aggression in Korea and in Kuwait demonstrated a commendable farsightedness.

But Americans have a tendency to overlook the dark sides of their course (except on the protesting left, which is thus constantly accused of being un-American), perhaps because they perceive international affairs in terms of crusades between good and evil, endeavors that entail formidable pressures for unanimity. It is not surprising that the decade following the Gulf War was marked both by nostalgia for the clear days of the Cold War and by a lot of floundering and hesitating in a world without an overwhelming foe.

## Strains of Anti-Americanism

The main criticisms of American behavior have mostly been around for a long time. When we look at anti-Americanism today, we must first distinguish between those who attack the United States for what it does, or fails to do, and those who attack it for what it is. (Some, like the Islamic fundamentalists and terrorists, attack it for both reasons.) Perhaps the principal criticism is of the contrast between our ideology of universal liberalism and policies that have all too often consisted of supporting and sometimes installing singularly authoritarian and repressive regimes. (One reason why these policies often elicited more reproaches than Soviet control over satellites was that, as time went by, Stalinism became more and more cynical and thus the gap between words and deeds became far less wide than in the United States. One no longer expected much from Moscow.) The list of places where America failed at times to live up to its proclaimed ideals is long: Guatemala, Panama, El Salvador, Chile, Santo Domingo in 1965, the Greece of the colonels, Pakistan, the Philippines of Ferdinand Marcos, Indonesia after 1965, the shah's Iran, Saudi Arabia, Zaire, and, of course, South Vietnam. Enemies of these regimes were shocked by U.S. support for them—and even those whom we supported were disappointed, or worse, when America's cost-benefit analysis changed and we dropped our erstwhile allies. This Machiavellian scheming behind a Wilsonian facade has alienated many clients, as well as potential friends, and bred strains of anti-Americanism around the world.

A second grievance concerns America's frequent unilateralism and the difficult relationship between the United States and the United Nations. For many countries, the United Nations is, for all its flaws, the essential agency of cooperation and the protector of its members' sovereignty. The way U.S. diplomacy has "insulted" the UN system—sometimes by ignoring it and sometimes by rudely imposing its views and policies on it—has been costly in terms of foreign support.

Third, the United States' sorry record in international development has recently become a source of dissatisfaction abroad. Not only have America's financial contributions for narrowing the gap between the rich and the poor declined since the end of the Cold War, but American-dominated institutions such as the International Monetary Fund and the World Bank have often dictated financial policies that turned out to be disastrous for developing countries—most notably, before and during the Asian economic crisis of the mid-1990s.

Finally, there is the issue of American support of Israel. Much of the world—and not only the Arab world—considers America's Israel policy to be biased. Despite occasional American attempts at evenhandedness, the world sees that the Palestinians remain under occupation, Israeli settlements continue to expand, and individual acts of Arab terrorism—acts

that Yasir Arafat can't completely control—are condemned more harshly than the killings of Palestinians by the Israeli army or by Israeli-sanctioned assassination squads. It is interesting to note that Israel, the smaller and dependent power, has been more successful in circumscribing the United States' freedom to maneuver diplomatically in the region than the United States has been at getting Israel to enforce the UN resolutions adopted after the 1967 war (which called for the withdrawal of Israeli forces from then-occupied territories, solving the refugee crisis, and establishing inviolate territorial zones for all states in the region). Many in the Arab world, and some outside, use this state of affairs to stoke paranoia of the "Jewish lobby" in the United States.

## Antiglobalism and Anti-Americanism

Those who attack specific American policies are often more ambivalent than hostile. They often envy the qualities and institutions that have helped the United States grow rich, powerful, and influential.

The real United States haters are those whose anti-Americanism is provoked by dislike of America's values, institutions, and society—and their enormous impact abroad. Many who despise America see us as representing the vanguard of globalization—even as they themselves use globalization to promote their hatred. The Islamic fundamentalists of al-Qaeda—like Iran's Ayatollah Khomeini 20 years ago—make excellent use of the communication technologies that are so essential to the spread of global trade and economic influence.

We must be careful here, for there are distinctions among the antiglobalist strains that fuel anti-Americanism. To some of our detractors, the most eloquent spokesman is bin Laden, for whom America and the globalization it promotes relentlessly through free trade and institutions under its control represent evil. To them, American-fueled globalism symbolizes the domination of the Christian-Jewish infidels or the triumph of pure secularism: They look at the United States and see a society of materialism, moral laxity, corruption in all its forms, fierce selfishness, and so on. (The charges are familiar to us because we know them as an exacerbated form of right-wing anti-Americanism in nineteenth- and twentieth-century Europe.) But there are also those who, while accepting the inevitability of globalization and seem eager to benefit from it, are incensed by the contrast between America's promises and the realities of American life. Looking at the United States and the countries we support, they see insufficient social protection, vast pockets of poverty amidst plenty, racial discrimination, the large role of money in politics, the domination of the elites—and they call us hypocrites. (And these charges, too, are familiar, because they are an exacerbated version of the left-wing anti-Americanism still powerful in Western Europe.)

On the one hand, those who see themselves as underdogs of the world condemn the United States for being an evil force because its dynamism makes it naturally and endlessly imperialistic—a behemoth that imposes its culture (often seen as debased), its democracy (often seen as flawed), and its conception of individual human rights (often seen as a threat to more communitarian and more socially concerned approaches) on other societies. The United States is perceived as a bully ready to use all means, including overwhelming force, against those who resist it: Hence, Hiroshima, the horrors of Vietnam, the rage against Iraq, the war on Afghanistan.

On the other hand, the underdogs draw hope from their conviction that the giant has a heel like Achilles'. They view America as a society that cannot tolerate high casualties and prolonged sacrifices and discomforts, one whose impatience with protracted and undecisive conflicts should encourage its victims to be patient and relentless in their challenges and assaults. They look at American foreign policy as one that is often incapable of overcoming obstacles and of sticking to a course that is fraught with high risks—as with the conflict with Iraq's Saddam Hussein at the end of the Gulf War; as in the flight from Lebanon after the terrorist attacks of 1982; as in Somalia in 1993; as in the attempts to strike back at bin Laden in the Clinton years.

Thus America stands condemned not because our enemies necessarily hate our freedoms but because they resent what they fear are our Darwinian aspects, and often because they deplore what they see as the softness at our core. Those who, on our side, note and celebrate America's power of attraction, its openness to immigrants and refugees, the uniqueness of a society based on common principles rather than on ethnicity or on an old culture, are not wrong. But many of the foreign students, for instance, who fall in love with the gifts of American education return home, where the attraction often fades. Those who stay sometimes feel that the price they have to pay in order to assimilate and be accepted is too high.

## What Bred bin Laden

This long catalog of grievances obviously needs to be picked apart. The complaints vary in intensity; different cultures, countries, and parties emphasize different flaws, and the criticism is often wildly excessive and unfair. But we are not dealing here with purely rational arguments; we are dealing with emotional responses to the omnipresence of a hegemon, to the sense that many people outside this country have that the United States dominates their lives.

Complaints are often contradictory: Consider "America has neglected us, or dropped us" versus "America's attentions corrupt our culture." The result can be a gestalt of resentment that strikes Americans as absurd: We are damned, for instance, both for failing to intervene to protect Muslims in the Balkans and for using force to do so.

But the extraordinary array of roles that America plays in the world—along with its boastful attitude and, especially recently, its cavalier unilateralism—ensures that many wrongs caused by local regimes and societies will be blamed on the United States. We even end up being seen as responsible not only for anything bad that our "protectorates" do—it is no coincidence that many of the September 11 terrorists came from America's protégés, Saudi Arabia and Egypt—but for what our allies do, as when Arabs incensed by racism and joblessness in France take up bin Laden's cause, or when Muslims talk about American violence against the Palestinians. Bin Laden's extraordinary appeal and prestige in the Muslim world do not mean that his apocalyptic nihilism (to use Michael Ig-

natieff's term) is fully endorsed by all those who chant his name. Yet to many, he plays the role of a bloody Robin Hood, inflicting pain and humiliation on the superpower that they believe torments them.

Bin Laden fills the need for people who, rightly or not, feel collectively humiliated and individually in despair to attach themselves to a savior. They may in fact avert their eyes from the most unsavory of his deeds. This need on the part of the poor and dispossessed to connect their own feeble lot to a charismatic and single-minded leader was at the core of fascism and of communism. After the failure of pan-Arabism, the fiasco of nationalism, the dashed hopes of democratization, and the fall of Soviet communism, many young people in the Muslim world who might have once turned to these visions for succor turned instead to Islamic fundamentalism and terrorism.

One almost always finds the same psychological dynamics at work in such behavior: the search for simple explanations—and what is simpler and more inflammatory than the machinations of the Jews and the evils of America—and a highly selective approach to history. Islamic fundamentalists remember the promises made by the British to the Arabs in World War I and the imposition of British and French imperialism after 1918 rather than the support the United States gave to anticolonialists in French North Africa in the late 1940s and in the 1950s. They remember British opposition to and American reluctance toward intervention in Bosnia before Srebrenica, but they forget about NATO's actions to save Bosnian Muslims in 1995, to help Albanians in Kosovo in 1999, and to preserve and improve Albanians' rights in Macedonia in 2001. Such distortions are manufactured and maintained by the controlled media and schools of totalitarian regimes, and through the religious schools, conspiracy mills, and propaganda of fundamentalism.

## What Can Be Done?

Americans can do very little about the most extreme and violent forms of anti-American hatred—but they can try to limit its spread by addressing grievances that are justified. There are a number of ways to do this:

- First—and most difficult—drastically reorient U.S. policy in the Palestinian-Israeli conflict.
- Second, replace the ideologically market-based trickle-down economics that permeate American-led development institutions today with a kind of social safety net. (Even *New York Times* columnist Thomas Friedman, that ur-celebrator of the global market, believes that such a safety net is indispensable.)
- Third, prod our allies and protégés to democratize their regimes, and stop condoning violations of essential rights (an approach that can only, in the long run, breed more terrorists and anti-Americans).
- Fourth, return to internationalist policies, pay greater attention to the representatives of the developing world, and make fairness prevail over arrogance.
- Finally, focus more sharply on the needs and frustrations of the people suffering in undemocratic societies than on the authoritarian regimes that govern them.

America's self-image today is derived more from what Reinhold Niebuhr would have called pride than from reality, and this exacerbates the clash between how we see ourselves and foreign perceptions and misperceptions of the United States. If we want to affect those external perceptions (and that will be very difficult to do in extreme cases), we need to readjust our self-image. This means reinvigorating our curiosity about the outside world, even though our media have tended to downgrade foreign coverage since the Cold War. And it means listening carefully to views that we may find outrageous, both for the kernel of truth that may be present in them and for the stark realities (of fear, poverty, hunger, and social hopelessness) that may account for the excesses of these views.

Terrorism aimed at the innocent is, of course, intolerable. Safety precautions and the difficult task of eradicating the threat are not enough. If we want to limit terrorism's appeal, we must keep our eyes and ears open to conditions abroad, revise our perceptions of ourselves, and alter our world image through our actions. There is nothing un-American about this. We should not meet the Manichaeanism of our foes with a Manichaeanism of self-righteousness. Indeed, self-examination and self-criticism have been the not-so-secret weapons of America's historical success. Those who demand that we close ranks not only against murderers but also against shocking opinions and emotions, against dissenters at home and critics abroad, do a disservice to America.

*Stanley Hoffmann is the Paul and Catherine Buttenwieser University Professor at Harvard University.*

---

*Article 3*

*Middle East Journal*, Autumn 2001

# The nature of succession in the Gulf

The unfolding crisis of succession in the Middle East has received considerable attention in recent years. This is particularly true in the Gulf where four of the six states of the Gulf Cooperation Council (GCC) are led by aging rulers and the other two rulers, younger and recently enthroned, have chosen to take their small states on unprecedented and somewhat radical courses. It is disturbing that the mechanisms for the transferral of power remain disconcertingly vague and ambiguous. Effective leadership depends on having the right personalities in charge, and this is never an easy task in a hereditary system. As the Gulf regimes complete their transformation from shaykhly systems to monarchies, the question of succession will become an increasingly difficult problem.

## J. E. Peterson

The unfolding crisis of succession in the Middle East has received considerable attention in recent years. Succession is a problem faced by nearly all Arab states, regardless of type of political system. Hereditary succession is of course a defining characteristic of monarchies but the Arab republics, as autocratic regimes weak in institutionalization, also face serious dilemmas as the current generation of leaders reach the end of their careers.

While recent instances of succession in the region—King Husayn to his son 'Abdullah in Jordan, King Hasan to his son Muhammad in Morocco, and President Hafiz al-Asad to his son Bashar [Bashshar] in Syria—appear to have progressed smoothly, a plethora of question marks remain for other countries.

This is particularly true in the Gulf where four of the six states of the Gulf Cooperation Council (GCC) are led by aging rulers and the other two rulers, younger and recently enthroned, have chosen to take their small states on unprecedented and somewhat radical courses. Despite widespread awareness of the problem confronting the GCC states, there is little detailed written consideration regarding succession scenarios and problems in the GCC, with the partial exception of Saudi Arabia.[1] The following pages provide brief sketches of the situation existing in each of the six countries.

# SAUDI ARABIA

Much concern has been expressed by outsiders over King Fahd's poor health in recent years because of the attendant question mark for them over succession. In fact, the peril of suitable succession has troubled the Saudi state since its initial emergence in the 18th century. This has been true as well of the Third Saudi State, i.e. the renewed regime founded by King 'Abd al-'Aziz (commonly known in the West as Ibn Sa'ud) after he recaptured the ancestral home of Riyadh in 1902. Despite paying lip service to the "traditional Arab" principle that a ruler had no right to name his heir but that succession should go to the strongest claimant who simply seized power, from the early 1930s at least King 'Abd al-'Aziz in fact prepared his eldest surviving son Sa'ud to succeed him, naming him as Heir Apparent and securing family allegiance to Sa'ud's succession.[2] This set in train two related phenomena. First, the principle was established of succession through the sons of King 'Abd al-'Aziz in chronological order, albeit with some exceptions. Second, because these sons display varying qualities as rulers, a pattern of rivalries between sons has been a feature over the last sixty years.[3]

The introduction of a Basic Law in 1992 laid down some principles regarding succession but did not answer all outstanding questions. The Basic Law stipulated that succession must go to the next oldest and most fit candidate (emphasis added). By requiring that succession remain in the line of the descendants of King 'Abd al-'Aziz, the way is paved for the grandsons to assume the throne in due course. But the Basic Law, probably deliberately, does not explain what methods should be chosen when succession reaches that point.

It is clear that the accession of Sa'ud on the death of King 'Abd al-'Aziz in 1953, instead of his far more capable brother Faysal, came close to destroying the kingdom. Sa'ud's recklessness in spending nearly bankrupted the state and his on/off flirtation with Egypt's President Jamal 'Abd al-Nasir [Nasser] at a time when Egyptian troops were threatening Saudi Arabia from across the Yemen border finally provoked the ruling family to persuade Faysal to replace him in 1964. But Faysal's successful reign, marked by stability in external affairs and a measure of liberalization and development at home, was brought to a premature close by an assassin's bullet in 1975. Another son, and Faysal's half-brother, Khalid succeeded—but in tandem with yet another son, Fahd: at first, Khalid reigned while in effect Fahd ruled, as had been agreed, although Khalid soon acquired a taste for rule.[4] Khalid's apparent success owed much to Fahd's competent handling of affairs and the prosperity brought about by the first oil price revolution. But Fahd, after he succeeded Khalid in 1982, was hit by the double blow of collapsing oil prices and eventually his own failing health.

Thus the present succession situation in Saudi Arabia bears resemblance to preceding ones, at least in Western eyes. There is no question that the next king—if not the next two or three—will be drawn from the numerous remaining sons of King 'Abd al-'Aziz. But the sons are growing old and their capabilities diminish as one nears the end of the line. As of mid-2001, 'Abdullah was not only Heir Apparent but the kingdom's effective ruler. King Fahd's six full brothers, the Al Fahd (or, as they—plus the king—are sometimes called in the West, the Sudayri Seven, after the family of their mother) undoubtedly wish Fahd to hang on as long as possible, in part because every additional year of Fahd is likely to mean one less year for 'Abdullah, who is about 77 years old and only a year younger than King Fahd. But this is a double-edged sword because the next-in-line is Sultan, presently Minister of Defense and Aviation and the next oldest of the Al Fahd at about 76, who is not likely to long out-live 'Abdullah.

Much has been made of 'Abdullah's Shammari mother, as well as his Syrian and other Arab connections. Factors with probably more relevance to most Saudis are his conservatism and image of moral rectitude, especially when compared to Fahd's lingering playboy reputation, and the fact that Fahd has become indelibly associated with bad times economically. It is sometimes assumed that Nayif (about 67, presently the Minister of the Interior) and then Salman (about 64, presently the Governor of Riyadh Province) will follow after Sultan. But of course the longer 'Abdullah waits to become king, and the longer 'Abdullah then rules, the less time will be left to these individuals, if indeed they do succeed. More importantly, the longer 'Abdullah is king, the more opportunity he will have to put his stamp on the kingdom. This undoubtedly will include replacing Fahd's men with his own— at least in the Royal Diwan if not the Council of Ministers (which requires maintenance of a delicate balance)—and possibly even altering the progress of succession away from the Al Fahd. It seems safe to say that succession will move beyond the sons of 'Abd al-'Aziz to another generation within this decade. Furthermore, although Salman is noted for his competence and dedication, it seems unlikely that Nayif will prove to be a capable king, should he unexpectedly succeed. Conceivably, another spell with an unsuitable king (as with Sa'ud, Khalid, and latterly Fahd) will speed up the change and deny Salman his turn.[5]

A principal factor in persisting with the present line is the dilemma of agreeing where any change in the procedure will lead. With the number of males from the Al Sa'ud running into the thousands, there is no shortage of potential candidates. King Fahd may well prefer for one of his own sons to succeed him. The most politically prominent of his sons has been Muhammad (born 1950), Governor of the Eastern Province (which contains the great majority of the country's oil production) since 1985. But Muhammad's slim chances of succession are seriously handicapped by his reputation as a high-powered businessman grown wealthy on commissions and his playboy lifestyle. The King's favorite, however, has always been his youngest, 'Abd al-'Aziz (born about 1974). Even as a teenager, 'Abd al-'Aziz accompanied his father on state visits and GCC summits. In 1998, the King appointed this son a Minister of State and sent him on a high-profile visit to the United States.[6] But 'Abd al-'Aziz is regarded as a lightweight with no place in the succession. Given a scenario of King Fahd's early death and a longish reign by 'Abdullah, it is not impossible, although unlikely, that 'Abdullah's sons might also move into contention.[7]

Stronger candidates, however, have been the talented sons of the late King Faysal. Best-known among them is Sa'ud al-Faysal (born 1940), Minister of Foreign Affairs since 1975 and Deputy Minister of Petroleum before that. Highly qualified and dedicated, Sa'ud has suffered from certain intrusions of his cousin Bandar bin Sultan into his realm of foreign affairs, although he is well-regarded by both 'Abdullah and Sultan. His brother Turki al-Faysal (born 1945) served as the Director-General of Intelligence from 1978 to 2001, but is not generally considered a candidate. A third capable brother is Khalid al-Faysal (born 1941), Governor of the southern province of 'Asir since 1971 and heavily involved in promoting the King Faysal Foundation. Khalid's advantages are that he is close to his uncle Sultan and is better known to the people on the personal level than his brother Sa'ud.[8] Conventional wisdom has held that the fortunes of this group have been kept on hold because of the threat they pose to the Al Fahd.[9] Their natural alliance has been with Crown Prince 'Abdullah and it will be interesting to speculate if they prosper under 'Abdullah as King.

Any discussion of potential successors should include two dark-horse candidates, both grandsons of King 'Abd al-'Aziz. Bandar bin Sultan (born 1949) is the son of Sultan bin 'Abd al-'Aziz (Minister of Defense and Aviation) and the son-in-law of the late King Faysal. An air force pilot by background, Bandar rose to prominence in the diplomatic world when he was named ambassador to the United States in the 1980s. The granting of ministerial rank in 1995 in some ways was simply a recognition of his unofficial role as a roving ambassador and personal emissary of King Fahd—leading some to regard him as Foreign Minister in all but name. Still, the circumstances of his birth and mother probably rule him out. Al-Walid bin Talal has shot to world-wide prominence in recent years for his business acquisitions and by some accounts is reckoned one of the world's richest men. Although occasionally mentioned as a contender, al-Walid's interests have centered on business and not politics (he has never held an official position). Furthermore, he is undoubtedly burdened by his father's reputation. Talal bin 'Abd al-'Aziz was one of the "liberal princes," Minister of Communications and then Finance under King Sa'ud but his advocacy of democratic practices in Saudi Arabia pushed him into several years of exile in the early 1960s. Although he has lived in the kingdom since then, he never held government office again and his influential but controversial pronouncements from time to time on political and social matters keep him at the edge of Al Sa'ud society.

# KUWAIT

Succession in Kuwait is constitutionally limited to the descendants of Shaykh Mubarak, who reigned from 1896 to 1915 and secured Kuwait's independence from the Ottoman Empire by tying the country to the British. But rivalries within the family produced an ad hoc system of alternation between two branches of Shaykh Mubarak's descendants. These derive from the two sons who followed Mubarak: Jabir (ruled 1915–1917) and Salim (ruled 1917–1921). When the succession moved to the next generation, the penultimate ruler's son Ahmad al-Jabir was chosen instead of Salim's son 'Abdullah. For three decades, the family was split between the Al Jabir, the family of the late Amir Jabir and headed by Amir Ahmad, and the Al Salim, the family of the late Amir Salim and headed by 'Abdullah. The Al Salim regained ascendancy when 'Abdullah finally succeeded in 1950 and they kept the office when Sabah al-Salim replaced his brother as Amir in 1965. But the accession of the present Amir, Jabir al-Ahmad al-Jabir, in 1977, restored the alternation back to the Al Jabir.[10]

Kuwait's constitution also requires that the Amir name his Heir Apparent and that this choice be approved by the elected National Assembly. The Assembly was in suspension at the time of Amir 'Abdullah's death and the selection of an Heir Apparent by the family was never formally approved. It stood to reason that the new Heir Apparent to Amir Jabir should be chosen from the Al Salim according to the principle of alternation. The most prominent candidate was the former Deputy Prime Minister and Minister of Information, Jabir al-'Ali. But he was regarded as too abrasive and uncontrolled and his cousin, Sa'd al-'Abdullah, was picked as a compromise. Of mean origin, inarticulate, and plagued by poor health, Sa'd has not been a popular Heir Apparent and his standing has been diminished even further by constant attacks in the National Assembly against the government which he heads as Prime Minister. It is widely believed that the Al Jabir have encouraged dissent within the National Assembly as a way of weakening the Heir Apparent, and there is speculation that the Al Jabir seek to eliminate the alternation altogether. Certainly, the Al Salim have grown far weaker than their rivals and even though Jabir al-'Ali was still reckoned to have a chance to succeed should Sa'd die before becoming Amir, Jabir died in 1994.

The sole remaining candidate from the same generation of this branch was until recently Salim al-Sabah al-Salim, the son of Amir Sabah and long-time Deputy Prime Minister and Minister of Defense (and previously Minister of the Interior). But Salim was considered weak and not much of a match for his Al Jabir rival, Sabah al-Ahmad al-Jabir, the brother of Amir Jabir and long-time Deputy Prime Minister and Foreign Minister. He also suffers from Parkinson's disease and withdrew from politics in early 2001.

According to logical protocol, should Sa'd succeed Amir Jabir, Sabah should be appointed Heir Apparent as the Al Jabir candidate. But this is by no means certain. Sabah is not well-liked, lacks basic political skills, is resented for his extensive business interests, and bears part of the taint of "losing" Kuwait to the Iraqis in 1990.

The experience of invasion and occupation, so traumatic for most Kuwaitis, in fact has changed the country's political climate and has worked both to discredit the present generation of Al Sabah leaders and to bolster popular opposition to the ruling family's political dominance. Amir Jabir is said to be a shadow of his former self and suffered a stroke in September 2001; Shaykh Sa'd is at the helm only fitfully; Shaykh Sabah is discredited and in feud with Shaykh Sa'd; and Shaykh Salim is out of the picture.[11] For the future of the family, it may well be necessary to select the next Amir—or, more precisely, the next Heir

Apparent after Sa'd—from a new generation. But the present generation took up public positions when in their 20s and 30s and have spent the last 40 to 50 years proving themselves and running the country. The following generation has never had the opportunity to prove themselves even though they are now into their 50s.

None of the ruling triumvirate's sons hold senior government positions. Although Amir Jabir is said to have fathered between 30 and 100 offspring, none are in prominent government positions nor is there a sign of any being groomed for succession. The most capable appears to be Salim al-Jabir (born 1947), who earned a doctorate from the Sorbonne during his career in the Foreign Ministry and served as ambassador to the United Nations in Geneva at the time of the Iraqi invasion. But he has spent most of his career abroad and is not well known in Kuwait.[12]

The older children of Shaykh Sa'd were all daughters and his only son Fahd was born in 1960, who shows no aptitude for politics. Shaykh Sabah's sons Nasir and Hamad are active partners with their father in running one of Kuwait's biggest commercial concerns but there is no indication that Hamad is interested in politics. Nasir apparently is quite interested in becoming Amir and recently acquired a position as adviser to Shaykh Sa'd, thus strengthening his ties to the al-Salim branch.[13] Still, many feel that Nasir is more interested in spending his time outside the country and is not willing to do the work necessary to succeed. Sons of Shaykh Salim, such as Basil (born 1959), have not shown interest in politics either.

When Shaykh Salim retired from politics, he suggested that one of his brothers take his place. The most qualified was Dr. Muhammad (born 1955), who had received his Ph.D. in economics from Harvard University, taught at Kuwait University, and been appointed Ambassador to the United States in 1993. Muhammad apparently had long resisted his brother's efforts to bring him back to Kuwait to groom him for succession but was appointed Minister of State for Foreign Affairs in the new cabinet of February 2001.[14]

The new Council of Ministers contains five Al Sabah outside the ruling tri-umvirate, none of whom is closely related to the present Amir. The most capable of these appears to be Shaykh Muhammad al-Khalid al-Hamad, from another branch of the ruling family but a great-grandson of Shaykh Mubarak (ruled 1896–1915), probably the most renowned of the Al Sabah Amirs. Muhammad has held the key post of Minister of the Interior since 1996 and also received the title of Deputy Prime Minister in 2001. Another Deputy Prime Minister and the replacement for Shaykh Salim as Minister of Defense is Shaykh Jabir al-Mubarak al-Hamad who had been out of politics since resigning as Minister of Information shortly after the Iraqi invasion in 1990.

The other two Al Sabah (aside from Dr. Shaykh Muhammad) are Ahmad al-'Abdullah al-Ahmad, a banker and former Minister of Finance who was named Minister of Communications, and Ahmad al-Fahd al-Ahmad. The latter, named Minister of Information, had succeeded his father Fahd as head of the Kuwaiti Olympic Committee and soccer federation after Fahd was killed resisting the Iraqi invasion. Shaykh Ahmad was also active in the resistance and made headlines in 1996 when he declared his intention to be the first Al Sabah to be elected to Kuwait's National Assembly. In short, there are no obvious candidates as the next Heir Apparent, even amongst the younger generation of Al Sabah, despite the advancing ages of the family's inner circle.[15]

## BAHRAIN

The death on March 6, 1999, of the Amir of Bahrain, Shaykh 'Isa bin Salman Al Khalifa, removed one of the question marks regarding succession in the Gulf for the foreseeable future. The unchallenged accession of his son and Heir Apparent Hamad bin 'Isa (born 1950, Heir Apparent since 1964) marks the fourth consecutive occasion in this century that primogeniture has governed succession in Bahrain. Yet the emergence of Amir Hamad still leaves a considerable number of questions unanswered.[16]

Amir 'Isa was a "hands-off" ruler, largely content to enjoy life and to serve as a respected and beloved head of state. The day-to-day business of running the government was left in the hands of his brother and Prime Minister, Khalifa bin Salman, and it had long been thought that 'Isa would have abdicated years ago if he could have been certain that Khalifa would step aside and allow Hamad to rule as well as reign. But Khalifa seemed to have no intention of retiring from the center of power, especially since his activities as Prime Minister dovetailed closely with his business interests and this combination has made him one of the wealthiest men in Bahrain.

The first few months of Amir Hamad's reign seemed to indicate, however, that the two men are able to work together. The new cabinet announced on May 31, 1999, was largely unchanged from the previous one—and thus full of Shaykh Khalifa's men. In addition, there was some indication that the new Amir was prepared to make some conciliatory responses to defuse the tensions and unrest that plagued Bahrain during the 1990s. But far more substantial steps were required to address Bahrain's serious underlying problems. The Al Khalifa ruling family of Bahrain is one of the largest in the Gulf. More significantly, they are the only family that has come to power by invasion and conquest. The consequence has been an often arrogant Al Khalifa attitude toward the state and its population and the polarization of Bahraini society to a degree unmatched elsewhere in the Gulf.

There are four main categories of social stratification in Bahrain. The Al Khalifa enjoy a monopoly of political power at the top, supported by their tribal allies, originally from the Najd region of what is today Saudi Arabia, who either accompanied the Al Khalifa during the initial invasion in the 18th century or were subsequently invited to Bahrain. The Hawla families constitute the second stratum and are still the principal economic elite. These families migrated to Bahrain from the Iranian coast over the last several centuries but claim to be Arab, Sunni, and originally from the Arabian Peninsula. The largest stratum by far, however, is formed by the Baharina (singular, Bahrani), presumed to be the original farming inhabitants of the islands. Concentrated in Bahrain's villages and increasingly in poorer urban neighborhoods, the Baharina are Arab but entirely Shi'i.[17] The Persian population forms the fourth and bottom stratum. Although Iran—previously called Persia—controlled Bahrain at times prior to the 18th century, nearly all Persians in Bahrain today were immigrants during the 20th century, first as small merchants and then especially as workers in the oil fields during the 1930s and 1940s.

There have always been rich and poor in the Gulf states, powerful and powerless, those with correct genealogies and others without clear origin. But the divisions in Bahrain are sharper than elsewhere and, in part because of Bahrain's paucity of oil and economic opportunities, more persistent. Unrest has been recurrent with periods of sustained and often organized dissidence occurring in 1921–1923, 1934–1935, 1938, 1947–1948, 1953–1956, 1965, 1975, and 1994–1999. The grievances remain remarkably constant: more equitable economic distribution and a measure of political participation. In the earlier years of this century, Sunnis and Shi'is pursued their goals independently and the two communities often clashed. But by the 1950s, an alliance was formed and an underground organization formed to press demands on the ruling family. Although this movement failed, it led to the creation of similarly nonsectarian groups on the secular left during the 1960s and 1970s.

The Iranian Revolution of 1979, with its appeal for Islamic revolution everywhere, and especially the Iran-Iraq War of 1980–1988 served to break the sectarian alliance. The discovery of Iran-sponsored subversive cells in the 1980s deepened suspicions of local Shi'a. The cycle of opposition, dormant since the mid-1970s, re-emerged in 1994 under the leadership of a younger class of Iran-trained, rural mullahs (religious leaders). This new wave of opposition, while serious and prolonged, failed to threaten fundamentally the regime. Although much of the population shared many of the goals, including greater economic opportunities, an end to discrimination, and restoration of the elected National Assembly (suspended in 1975), the concentration of activists in Baharina villages under the apparent direction of polemical mullahs prevented any wider participation.

By 1999, the unrest had dissipated, but this was due more to the temporary success of the government's policy of repression and the movement's exhaustion, rather than the achievement of any permanent solution of the underlying problems. The regime's response to the demand for participation was the creation of an appointed Majlis al-Shura, which satisfied virtually no one. Soon after his accession, Amir Hamad pardoned the most prominent mullah, Shaykh 'Abd al-'Amir al-Jahri, in what seemed to be a conciliatory measure (although the opposition charged that he was being kept under house arrest). In September 2000, he expanded the Majlis al-Shura. But many Bahrainis remained unconvinced that this marked any significant change in policy. Amir Hamad had lost much credibility during his years as Heir Apparent and was believed by many to be under Saudi influence.

But expectations were raised in late 2000 and early 2001 by a series of developments set in chain by the new amir. A National Charter for the country was announced in December 2000, with the most significant provisions promising the independence of the judiciary, the creation by 2004 of a bicameral legislative body, including an elected house, and the provision that Bahrain would become a monarchy (*mamlaka*) and the amir a king. The National Charter was put to a national referendum in February 2001 and was approved by over 98% of the eligible population. During the same period, the amir took other positive steps. Political prisoners were released, the hated State Security Court was abolished, the British head of security much-reviled by the opposition apparently left for good, and an amnesty was announced for all exiles. The mood in Bahrain was suddenly brighter than it had been for decades and anticipation of real political change was widespread.

With his popularity thus soaring, Amir Hamad seems set to remain in power for many years to come. His first decree was to appoint his son Salman (born about 1969) as Heir Apparent in a continuation of the policy of primogeniture in conformity with the 1973 Constitution, which stipulates that succession should pass through the eldest son unless the Amir should choose to appoint another son. However, he must

carry through on his promises and he has yet to relieve Shaykh Khalifa of his position. Although it is unlikely that Shaykh Khalifa would ever accede, it is not entirely impossible that he will be able to maneuver the line of succession to one of his sons, particularly 'Ali bin Khalifa (born around the late 1950s) who has served as Minister of Transportation since 1993. A recrudescence of popular unrest, combined with a failure to provide employment for a rapidly growing population, may yet place succession and even the Al Khalifa in jeopardy. On the other hand, the closeness of the Bahraini state and the Al Khalifa to Saudi Arabia provides a certain assurance against such a scenario. In Bahrain's case, the generational change in leadership has resulted in considerable promise of change—a welcome situation given the underlying requirements for change and adaptation.

## QATAR

Qatar is the other Gulf state experiencing a recent change of rulers,[18] Although its experience is clearly unique, there are aspects that may well apply in the near future for some of its neighbors. In 1972, Khalifa bin Hamad became Amir by deposing his cousin Ahmad bin 'Ali. Although the Al Thani ruling family had agreed that Khalifa should succeed Amir 'Ali bin 'Abdullah, Amir 'Ali instead ensured that succession went to his son Ahmad on 'Ali's death in 1960. The result was a situation similar to others mentioned above: for 12 years, Ahmad reigned while Khalifa essentially ran the country. Finally, six months after independence in 1971, Khalifa ousted his cousin Ahmad during one of the latter's frequent absences from Qatar and added the title of Amir to the duties he had been carrying out already.

Shaykh Khalifa's personality and workload were essential to the operation of the small state, as the Amiri Diwan (i.e. the palace) was responsible for nearly every operation of any import. Having already formed the country's first proper government on the eve of independence, Shaykh Khalifa spent the following years engineering the country's development plans, putting the long-declared Advisory Council into action and later expanding it, and wresting ministerial portfolios away from collateral branches of the fractious Al Thani family. But his refusal to delegate hampered institutionalization and, as his health failed and ennui set in, he handed over more and more responsibilities to his son and Heir Apparent Hamad bin Khalifa (born 1950).

In June 1995, Hamad seized power while his father was abroad. It was the first successful palace coup in the Gulf since that of Khalifa himself 23 years earlier. The Gulf states recognized the new ruler, albeit with some hesitation, and thereby re-legitimized the principle of extra-constitutional succession.[19] It is alleged that Shaykh Hamad acted to prevent his father from regaining powers he had delegated to Hamad. Not surprisingly, given Khalifa's personality, he did not give up easily. He had retained control of finances with the consequence that most of the state's financial reserves—said to be as much as $3 billion—remained under his power. But when the new regime persuaded the Swiss and French governments in 1996 to block the accounts under Shaykh Khalifa's control, the former Amir was forced to acquiesce in a token reconciliation with his son and successor in Rome at the end of that year.

Basking in his success, the new Amir swiftly moved to put his unique stamp on Qatari and regional politics. In his first months of *de jure* rule, Shaykh Hamad seemed to enjoy deliberately provoking his GCC allies. As Prime Minister, he had already permitted Israel to open a trade office in Doha and drawn closer to Iran. He pointedly accused his neighbors of supporting his father's alleged counter-coup in February 1996. Relations with Bahrain had been troubled for decades over territorial disputes, so it was not surprising that Hamad would accuse Bahrain. Although Qatar traditionally has been close to Saudi Arabia, relations with Riyadh had worsened in the past decade, in part due to a 1992 border skirmish. Finally, Qatar and Abu Dhabi had been traditional rivals and the reaction of Shaykh Zayid of Abu Dhabi may well have been to support a legitimate ruler of his own generation against a coupmaker—a development in reaction to possible repercussions up and down the Gulf.[20]

Furthermore, faced with criticism over his new policies, Shaykh Hamad deliberately strengthened his relations with the United States as a counter. Some of Shaykh Hamad's domestic policies may have unnerved his neighboring monarchs as well— among them the abolition of Qatar's Ministry of Information and press censorship, municipal elections in 1999 (in a promised preview of parliamentary elections) and granting permission for a provocative satellite television channel ("al-Jazira" or, as the network spells it, Al-Jazeera) which gathered controversy for its airing of subjects generally kept hidden in the Gulf.

In appointing his third son Jasim (born 1978) as Heir Apparent in 1996, Shaykh Hamad broke with the principle of primogeniture but confirmed descent through the Amir's offspring.[21] Once again, the action raised questions for the future. Does this mean that succession by primogeniture in Qatari politics was just a momentary aberration? And, although the new Amir chose a son to succeed him, will that be accepted by the other sons? Will the next succession be constitutional or not?

The possibility still exists of a struggle between competing sons of ex-Amir Khalifa. Khalifa's second son, 'Abd al-'Aziz, had been sacked from the cabinet reshuffle put together by Hamad as Prime Minister in 1992 and subsequently lived abroad.[22] On the other hand, an alliance exists between Amir Hamad and his brother (Khalifa's third son) 'Abdullah, who was appointed Prime Minister by his brother to go along with his existing position of Minister of the Interior. Khalifa's fourth son Muhammad, Minister of Finance at the time of the coup, initially appeared to join his father in exile but soon returned to Doha to take up a position as Deputy Prime Minister.[23] Al Thani waters have been further muddied by the failed February 1996 counter-coup and the new regime's decision to place those accused of involvement on trial—33 defendants were sentenced to life imprisonment in early 2000.[24]

## UNITED ARAB EMIRATES

In the late 1960s, Britain, knowing that withdrawal from the Gulf was just ahead, began urging the nine small states of the lower Gulf to unify in protection against the challenges ahead. But it was a difficult task. Bahrain felt its longer period of development entitled it to special status; Qatar was reluctant to share its oil income; Abu Dhabi held the same attitude until its ruler was ousted in 1966; and the six smaller states simply were unable to agree amongst themselves. The accession of Shaykh Zayid bin Sultan as Amir of Abu Dhabi in 1966 was a key turning point as he threw his weight and his increasing income behind the project.[25] Although Bahrain and Qatar both chose to go it alone in 1971, the remaining seven shaykhdoms banded together in the United Arab Emirates. The early years of the UAE, however, were full of questions about what union really meant and how the responsibilities and obligations were to be sorted out. Constitutionally, the UAE remains a union of monarchies with legislative and executive authority vested in the Council of Ministers.[26]

The fundamental question during the UAE's nearly 30 years of existence has been whether the union constituted a federation or a confederation. On the one hand, the UAE unquestionably is a single state, with a capital, flag, bureaucracy, currency, and international recognition. On the other, the writ of the federal government, although increasing, has been limited. Individual emirates have been able to resist some federal dictates and regulations and to retain local control over perceived core areas of domestic administration.

Integration has not been helped by the diffusion of the constituent states into three ranks because of wealth, size, and personality of individual rulers. The two largest states, Abu Dhabi and Dubai, compete over opposing conceptions of the federal role. Abu Dhabi pushes for greater integration since, as the largest and richest member, a stronger federal unity will increase its control. Dubai opposes Abu Dhabi for the very same reason, seeking to maintain as much control of its domestic affairs as possible while accepting only what it perceives as beneficial aspects of federal membership. The middle two—Sharja and Ra's al-Khayma—seek to steer a middle course and maintain a measure of independence as far as is financially possible. The only choice of the small trio—al-Fujayra, Umm al-Qaywayn, and 'Ajman—is to follow along. In practice, this tends to mean keeping on Abu Dhabi's good side because of that emirate's control of the federal government and the largesse it bestows.[27]

If Shaykh Zayid's accession was necessary for the formation of the UAE, it follows that his continued leadership may be essential for the future health of the union. In part, his election and subsequent re-elections as President of the UAE were due to his personal capabilities and qualities of leadership.[28] But even more, Shaykh Zayid has served as President since 1971 because he heads the richest and most powerful constituent state. Herein lies the difficulty, as future UAE leadership is dependent on succession in Abu Dhabi. The next set of UAE rulers is likely to pit Shaykh Muhammad of Dubai, as the strongest and most capable personality of the lot, against a weaker successor to Shaykh Zayid in Abu Dhabi. Under the present system, it is inconceivable that the office of UAE President should be held by anyone but the ruler of Abu Dhabi, serving as a sort of quasi-king of the country. It would require a radical change in the mix of rulers' personalities and considerably more political participation for the most capable of the seven rulers to be selected as President. And the substitution of a system of rotation, as in Malaysia, with the *de facto* executive authority selected from outside the Council of Rulers, is only a distant prospect.

## Abu Dhabi

With Shaykh Zayid advancing in years and facing increasing health problems, the time for a successor cannot be far off. A few years ago, Abu Dhabi confronted the possibility of a schism within the ruling Al Nahyan family through the posting of a challenge by the Bani Muhammad, a group of brothers from another line of the family. In the 1980s, three brothers were prominent: Hamdan (UAE Deputy Prime Minister), Surur (President of the [Abu Dhabi] Amiri Diwan and married to one of Shaykh Zayid's daughters), and Tahnun (Chairman of the Abu Dhabi

National Oil Company [ADNOC], [Abu Dhabi] ruler's Representative in the Eastern Region [i.e. al-'Ayn], and also married to a daughter of Shaykh Zayid). Of these, Surur stood perhaps the best chance of succeeding: although his formal role was limited to Abu Dhabi, he acted much like a *de facto* Prime Minister for the UAE (especially after the *de jure* Prime Minister and ruler of Dubai, Shaykh Rashid, slipped into a long coma that only ended with his death in 1990). But the threat of the Bani Muhammad faded in the 1990s. Hamdan died in 1989, Surur lost influence (and his position) to the growing numbers of adult sons of Shaykh Zayid, and Tahnun—though regarded by Shaykh Zayid almost as a son—was probably never a viable candidate for succession anyway.

Shaykh Zayid's health has deteriorated markedly in the last few years. He spent several months in 1996 recovering from surgery at the Mayo Clinic in Minnesota and another four months at the Cleveland Clinic in 2000. His eldest son Khalifa has been Heir Apparent since 1969 and there is no question that he will succeed his father. Although dull and lacking in charisma, and plagued by his own history of health problems, Khalifa has filled in more than adequately for his father. A few years ago, it was speculated that Khalifa might well choose to abdicate after an acceptable period of rule, say one or two years, but this scenario clearly depended on his Heir Apparent. More recently, however, Khalifa has strengthened his control over much of Abu Dhabi's affairs and shows every sign of ruling capably if and when he succeeds.[29]

Khalifa's appointment as Heir Apparent was a departure from Abu Dhabi norms—the four rulers between 1909 and 1928 were all sons of Zayid bin Khalifa, the father of the modern Abu Dhabi state, and three became rulers following murders by brothers. Shaykh Zayid himself overthrew his brother Shakhbut to become ruler in 1966, although this act was accomplished without violence but with British complicity and was widely welcomed in the emirate due to Shakhbut's inability to lead Abu Dhabi into the oil age. Thus the Al Nahyan face the dilemma after Khalifa of whether to accept his brothers as rulers

in turn, as the emirate did in the past and as Saudi Arabia still does, or to stick to the short-lived principle of primogeniture.

There is no dearth of sons of Shaykh Zayid to choose from— he has at least 19. The next oldest after Khalifa is Sultan (born ca. 1955) who was appointed Commander-in-Chief of the Armed Forces by his father in 1978 but allegedly scandalous behavior drove him to the sidelines. Over the last 10 years, though, Sultan has clearly captured his father's eye again and has worked himself back into positions of responsibility as Deputy Prime Minister of the UAE (1990), Deputy Chairman of the Abu Dhabi Executive Council (i.e the cabinet for the emirate) and Chairman of Abu Dhabi's Public Works Department (1991). Sultan faces formidable competition if he should seek succession himself and most likely will support Khalifa against Muhammad bin Zayid. Muhammad bin Zayid is next in age (born ca. 1960) and he is well-known for his ambition. Muhammad has parlayed an early career as an air force pilot into Commander of the UAE Air Force (about 1987), Deputy Chief of Staff of the UAE Armed Forces (about 1991), and Chief of Staff (about 1993). His supporters have grown increasingly uneasy, however, over his over-reaching actions and behavior.

Muhammad undoubtedly will benefit as well from his support network of full-brothers, sons of Zayid's most beloved wife, Shaykha Fatima. This is an advantage neither Khalifa nor Sultan, their respective mothers' only sons, can claim despite their apparent greater general popularity. The brothers include Hamdan (UAE Minister of State for Foreign Affairs), Hazza' (Director-General of Intelligence), 'Abdullah (UAE Minister of Information and Culture), Mansur (Director-General of the President's Office), and Tahnun (Chairman of the President's Private Department).[30] The alternative to the path of brotherly succession is continuation of primogeniture. Khalifa bin Zayid has been grooming his son but Sultan bin Khalifa is still young, inexperienced, more interested in being a playboy, and, most importantly, faces the combined opposition of his many uncles.

## Dubai

So much of the modern history of Dubai was embodied in the person of Shaykh Rashid bin Sa'id. Although his father Sa'id laid the foundations of the merchant state that Dubai has become, Rashid undoubtedly was responsible for the present success and prosperity of the emirate. Taking over the day-to-day reins from his father in the 1940s, Shaykh Rashid crafted a strategy that made the most of Dubai's modest oil revenues and central location to create a laissez-faire entrepôt that remains without equal in the Gulf. His reign was marred only by the serious illness that struck him in the early 1980s and left him comatose in his final years until his death in 1990. Since then, his son Muhammad has thoroughly and competently taken up the *de facto* reins in Dubai.

But Rashid's decision to rely on primogeniture and his wife's injunction to her sons not to fight each other has left the process of succession in Dubai in a muddle. Rashid's eldest son Maktum succeeded in 1990 but it was clear well before Rashid's death that the third son Muhammad held the real power in the emirate. The situation was formally normalized by Maktum's decree in 1995 to appoint the second of Rashid's four sons, Hamdan, Deputy Ruler but to make Muhammad the Heir Apparent.[31] While Muhammad was likely to succeed in any case, the question now is whether succession will revert to primogeniture in the future, i.e. to Muhammad's eldest son Rashid.

## Sharja

The problem of succession in the two middle-rank UAE members should be mentioned as well. Until the 1960s, Sharja was perhaps the leading settlement and the seat of British representation on what was known as the Trucial Coast. Its ruling family is from the al-Qawasim, or al-Qasimi in the singular, who had constituted the leading power of the southern Gulf until vanquished by the British in the early 19th century. This memory of past glory probably contributed to the independent attitude of Shaykh Saqr bin Sultan, the ruler with Arab nationalist leanings from 1951 until his deposition with British assistance in 1965. The troubled political history of the emirate continued when Saqr's failed attempt to regain control in 1972 ended with the death of his cousin and successor, Khalid bin Muhammad. Since then, the emirate has been ruled by Khalid's brother, Sultan bin Muhammad, the only ruler in the Gulf to have earned a Ph.D.

But his ambitious brother 'Abd al-'Aziz, one of Sharja's leading businessmen and commander of Sharja's Emiri Guards, took advantage of one of Shaykh Sultan's trips abroad to seize power in 1987, justifying his action by pointing out that the emirate was approximately $1 billion in debt and alleging that Sultan was avoiding his responsibilities by his preoccupation with academic pursuits.[32] The matter would have ended there had not the Al Maktum of Dubai welcomed Sultan to come back to Dubai and then persuaded King Fahd of Saudi Arabia to mediate and convince Shaykh Zayid of Abu Dhabi to use his considerable influence to annul the coup days later.[33] Ten days after the coup, Shaykh Sultan returned to Sharja in his capacity as ruler.

Although 'Abd al-'Aziz was formally named Heir Apparent, this appeared to be little more than a face-saving device and he left for exile in Abu Dhabi two years later.[34] Since then, Shaykh Sultan named Ahmad bin Sultan, younger brother of former ruler Saqr bin Sultan, as Deputy Ruler in 1990 in an apparent attempt to heal the breach between the two branches of the family. But speculation that this solution might evolve into a formula of alternating power between the two al-Qasimi branches on the Kuwaiti line faded when Shaykh Sultan named Sultan bin Muhammad bin Sultan, his cousin and the brother of his beloved wife Juwahir, as Heir Apparent in May 1999.[35] The rivalries and violence within the family makes charting the path of succession in Sharja particularly unpredictable. It is not inconceivable that the position of Heir Apparent might be switched to one of Shaykh Sultan's younger sons when they grow older.

## Ra's al-Khayma

The situation in Ra's al-Khayma is not so complicated but perhaps more urgent. If the al-Qawasim of Sharja resented their decline in political position, this was even more true of Shaykh Saqr bin Muhammad, ruler of Ra's al-Khayma since 1948. The al-Qasimi branch in Ra's al-Khayma long ago fell out with the other branch in Sharja and the political subservience of Ra's al-Khayma to Sharja until 1952 has not been forgotten. Like his namesake, Shaykh Saqr of Sharja, Saqr bin Muhammad flirted with Arab nationalism in the 1960s as a way of escaping British influence and then held aloof from the founding of the UAE in late 1971 when it became clear that Ra's al-Khayma would not be regarded as the equal of Abu Dhabi and Dubai within the union. But he was forced to swallow his pride and join the UAE a few months later when his hopes of a major oil discovery were dashed. Ra's al-Khayma's relative lack of resources leaves it poorer than the three larger states and thus more dependent on federal assistance, to Shaykh Saqr's fury. Primogeniture applies in Ra's al-Khayma as Saqr's eldest son Khalid (born 1940) has been Heir Apparent for many years. Educated in Cairo, Britain, and the US, first commander of the Ra's al-Khayma army, and formerly active on the federal scene, Khalid has been patient and his turn must come soon with Shaykh Saqr entering his 80s.

## OMAN

Unlike the ruling families of the other Gulf states, the Al Bu Sa'id in Oman constitute a small and relatively weak ruling family.[36] There is no strong son for the ruler to rely on or brother to take the day-to-day reins of state (and conversely of course the Sultan is free from threats from close relations). The family is small and, for historical reasons, without influence on the ruler. There is no inner circle of family members who must be consulted on every significant decision and their consensus obtained. Because the father of Sultan Qabus bin Sa'id married in the country's southern region of Dhufar and Qabus remains single,[37] there are no pressures from nonsanguineous relations.

Indeed, the Sultan rules with few constraints from any direction. Naturally, he must appear just and rule according to Islamic norms but otherwise he is free from domestic challenge.

There are no key national families occupying the next rungs of power. All senior members of the government, as well as all other important political figures such as tribal leaders, are fully dependent on the Sultan's blessing for the retention of their positions. Traditional religious leadership remains in the background and there is little evidence of any popular Islamic dissent.

But Sultan Qabus is unique among Gulf rulers in another way. The lack of a direct heir and a paucity of reliable close family members mean that succession to Qabus is dramatically problematic. This situation is unique in modern Omani history as well. From the latter part of the 19th century until now, a pattern of primogeniture (specifically succession through the eldest son by a suitable Arab mother) governed the Sultanate. That this is no longer being possible has raised decades-long concern in Oman, the Gulf, and elsewhere over who shall succeed the Sultan and whether it will be a peaceful process.

For years, Sultan Qabus seemed oblivious to these concerns. Not only did he fail to groom an heir, he refused to give up the formal post of Prime Minister and seemed to deny would-be contenders any opportunity to prove their suitability. The only indication he had even considered the matter remains the Basic Law, promulgated in 1996.[38]

There is no viable candidate outside the ruling family. Many of the prominent ministers and merchants come from Muscat families, especially ethnic and/or sectarian minorities, and have no power base outside the capital. The Dhufari ministers owe their positions to this Sultan and most likely will lose their jobs on his disappearance from the scene. No tribal leader seems to possess sufficient standing to make a run for power and in any case any ambitious tribal leader would be opposed by competing tribes. The primacy of the religious establishment died with the demise of the Imamate in the 1950s. There is no sign of politicization in the security forces.

Thus it seems rather definite that succession will remain within the Al Bu Sa'id by default. The highest-ranking member in terms of protocol, Thuwayni bin Shihab, who holds the title of the Sultan's Personal Representative (which ranks as the equivalent of a deputy

prime minister), is excluded by personality. Next in line is Fahd bin Mahmud, another cousin to the Sultan and Deputy Prime Minister for Council of Ministers Affairs. His chances of succession are rated as minimal because of his aloofness from the family and public alike, the alleged animosity of the Sultan (who seems to have downgraded Fahd in 1994 from his previous position as Deputy Prime Minister for Legal Affairs), the fact that his children are of a French mother and thus not suitable for succession in turn, and the apprehension generated by a history of mental illness in his branch of the family. The most likely candidates for succession are three of the sons of the late Tariq bin Taymur, the formidable uncle of the Sultan who served briefly as the Sultan's only Prime Minister (in the early 1970s) and died in 1980: Shihab, Haytham, and As'ad. Shihab bin Tariq has served as the Commander of the Royal Navy of Oman since 1990 and generally rates high marks for his seriousness and his successful command. Haytham bin Tariq was appointed Under-Secretary in the Ministry of Foreign Affairs in 1986, at the same time that Hamdan bin Zayid received a similar appointment in the UAE. But whereas Hamdan has since become Minister of State for Foreign Affairs, Haytham remains in the same position (albeit with an upgraded title to Secretary-General), presumably because of his lack of dedication to public service. His continuing reputation as a playboy has left him out of the running in the eyes of many Omanis. The strongest alternative to Shihab thus remains his brother As'ad bin Tariq, who some would say is the stronger of the two candidates. Although As'ad displays the same serious demeanor, his position vis-à-vis the Sultan is not clear. In 1993, As'ad was removed from his powerful—and popular—position commanding the Sultan of Oman's Armor (which has built up to nearly a separate service in Oman), and given the less prestigious job of Secretary-General for Conferences.

## FUTURE PATTERNS OF SUCCESSION

The success of ruling families in the Gulf in the 20th century in large part depended upon exceptional leaders who

appeared at a propitious point when tribal societies began to coalesce into quasi nation-states. Thus the roles of King 'Abd al-'Aziz bin 'Abd al-Rahman (ruled 1902–1953) in forging the modern Kingdom of Saudi Arabia, that of Shaykh Mubarak al-Sabah (r. 1896–1915) in creating an independent Kuwait, Shaykh 'Abdullah bin Jasim (r. 1913–1949) in sharpening Qatar's separate identity, and Shaykh Zayid bin Khalifa (r. 1855–1909) in melding the tribes into the discernible state of Abu Dhabi.

By the close of the century, all of the Gulf states had undergone tremendous socio-economic change. In addition to the roads, industrial complexes, and welfare systems, all had built modern governments with professional bureaucracies. Their populations had changed, become much larger in size, dramatically better educated, and more socially diverse, yet the fundamental basis of politics remained much the same. The effectiveness of leadership varied markedly from one ruler to the next and the quality of vision, as possessed by the prominent forebears named above, more often than not was lacking at a time when challenges to the regimes seemed more profound than ever.

Thus it is disturbing that the mechanisms for the transferral of power remain disconcertingly vague and ambiguous. Succession no longer occurs through patricide or fratricide, although palace coups apparently are still not entirely ruled out. The procedure for the immediate hand over of power on the death of an incumbent is no longer in doubt either since the practice of naming and respecting an Heir Apparent has been adopted in all six countries. Generally, there seems to be a trend towards primogeniture, with its advantages in defusing family rivalries and assuring an orderly succession. Of course this method is not accepted in either Saudi Arabia or Kuwait and cannot be the means for the next succession in Oman. But in the end, of course, effective leadership depends on having the right personalities in charge. This is never an easy task in a hereditary system. As the Gulf regimes complete their transformation from shaykhly systems to monarchies, the question of succession will become an increasingly difficult problem.

TABLE 1

Rulers and Succession in the Gulf States

| Country | Ruling Family | Present Ruler (year of birth) (with date of accession and formal positions held) | Heir Apparent (year of birth) (with date of appointment and formal positions held) | Relationship of Heir Apparent to Ruler | Constitutional Rules of Succession | Putative Line of Succession |
|---|---|---|---|---|---|---|
| Saudi Arabia | Al Sa'ud | Fahd bin 'Abd al-'Aziz (1921) *King (1982), Prime Minister* | 'Abdullah bin 'Abd al-'Aziz (1923 *Heir Apparent (1982), First Deputy Prime Minister, Head of National Guard* | half-brother | yes | sons of the late King 'Abd al-'Aziz in chronological succession, although Basic Law of 1992 stipulates that sons and grandsons should be consulted |
| Kuwait | Al Sabah | Jabir al-Ahmad (1926) *Amir (1977)* | Sa'd al-'Abdullah (1930) *Heir Apparent (1978), Prime Minister* | cousin | yes | alternation between al-Jabir and al-Salim branches of family |
| Bahrain | Al Khalifa | Hamad bin 'Isa (1950) Amir (1999) | Salman bin Hamad (1969) *Heir Apparent (1999), Under-Secretary in the Ministry of Defense* | eldest son | yes | Primogeniture |
| Qatar | Al Thani | Hamad bin Khalifa (1950) *Amir (1995)* | Jasim bin Hamad (1978) *Deputy Ruler Heir Apparent (1996)* | 3rd son | no | Primogeniture or father-to-son |
| Oman | Al Bu Sa'id | Qabus bin Sa'id (1940) *Sultan (1970), Prime Minister, Minister of Defense, Minister of Foreign Affairs* | None | n.a. | yes | previously primogeniture but now to be governed by stipulations of Basic Law |
| United Arab Emirates | n.a. | Zayid bin Sultan Al Nahyan (late 80s?) | Maktum bin Rashid Al Maktum (1941) *Vice-President (1971), Prime Minister* | n.a. | yes | election by Supreme Council of Rulers but in effect Ruler of Abu Dhabi |
| Abu Dhabi | Al Nahyan | Zayid bin Sultan (ca. 1912?) *Amir (1966)* | Khalifa bin Zayid (1949) *Heir Apparent (late 1960s?), Deputy Supreme Commander of UAE Armed Forces* | eldest son | no | previously mixed, now primogeniture (?) |

| Country | Ruling Family | Present Ruler (year of birth) (with date of accession and formal positions held) | Heir Apparent (year of birth) (with date of appointment and formal positions held) | Relationship of Heir Apparent to Ruler | Constitutional Rules of Succession | Putative Line of Succession |
|---|---|---|---|---|---|---|
| Dubai | Al Maktum | Maktum bin Rashid (1941) *Amir 1990* | Muhammad bin Rashid (1948) *Heir Apparent (1995), UAE Minister of Defense* | full brother | no | previously primogeniture, now mixed (?) |
| Sharja | al-Qasimi (al-Qawasim) | Sultan bin Muhammad (1942) *Amir (1972)* | Sultan bin Muhammad (1990) *Heir Apparent (1987)* | cousin | no | previously mixed, now mixed |
| Ra's al-Khayma | al-Qasimi (al-Qawasim) | Saqr bin Muhammad (1920) *Amir (1948)* | Khalid bin Saqr (1943) *Heir Apparent (?), Deputy Ruler* | eldest son | no | previously mixed, now primogeniture (?) |
| Al-Fujayra | al-Sharqiyin | Hamad bin Muhammad (1948) *Amir (1974)* | Hamad bin Sayf (?) *Heir Apparent (?), Deputy Ruler* | uncle | no | primogeniture |
| Umm al-Qaywayn | Al 'Ali (Al Mu'alla) | Rashid bin Ahmad (1930) *Amir (1981)* | Sa'ud bin Rashid (1952) *Heir Apparent (?)* | eldest son | no | primogentiture |
| 'Ajman | al-Nu'aymi | Humayd bin Rashid (1930) *Amir (1981)* | 'Ammar bin Humayd (?) *Heir Apparent (1993)* | eldest son | no | |

Note: dates of birth for older generations are often approximate.

TABLE 2

*Rulers and Heirs Apparent: Years in Office, Ages, Generations*

| | GCC Rulers (6) | GCC + UAE Rulers (12) | GCC Heirs Apparent (5) | GCC + UAE Heirs Apparent (11) |
|---|---|---|---|---|
| Average years in office | 19½ | 21½ | 12 (4 without Abu Dhabi) | 18 (8 of 11 total) |
| Average age | 68 | 67 | 51½ | 52 (8 of 11 total) |
| Oldest | Ca. 92 | Ca. 92 | 76 | 76 |
| Youngest | 51 | 51 | 23 | 23 |
| Change of generation from predecessor | 4 | 9 | 3 | 8 (?) |

# NOTES

1. Recent works touching on succession and related political dilemmas in the Gulf states include F. Gregory Gause, III, *Oil Monarchies: Domestic and Security Challenges in the Arab Gulf States* (New York: Council on Foreign Relations Press, 1994); Muhammad al-Rumaihi, "The Gulf Monarchies: Testing Time," *Middle East Quarterly*, Vol. 3, No. 4 (December 1996), pp. 45–51; Rosemarie Said Zahlan, *The Making of the Modern Gulf States: Kuwait, Bahrain, Qatar, the United Arab Emirates and Oman* (London: Unwin Hyman, 1989; rev. ed.; Reading: Ithaca Press, 1998); and Michael Herb, *All in the Family: Absolutism, Revolution, and Democratic Prospects in the Middle Eastern Monarchies* (Albany: State University of New York Press, 1999).

2. L/P&S/12/2085: HEJAZ-NEJD ANNUAL REPORTS (1930–1937); Sir A. Ryan, Jedda, to Sir John Simon, FO, 26 Feb. 1933, Annual Report for Hejaz-Nejd, 1932; FO/905/57; R.W. Bullard, Jidda, to Viscount Halifax, 25 Apr. 1938.

3. The perceived importance of succession in the kingdom is illustrated by the number of works on the subject, including: A.R. Kelidar, "The Problem of Succession in Saudi Arabia," *Asian Affairs* (London), Vol. 65 (N.S. 9), Pt. 1 (February 1978), pp. 23–30; Mashaal Abdullah Turki Al Saud, "Permanence and Change: An Analysis of the Islamic Political Culture of Saudi Arabia As It Faces the Challenges of Development with Special Reference to the Royal Family" (Ph.D. dissertation, Claremont Graduate School, 1982); Gary Samuel Samore, "Royal Family Politics in Saudi Arabia (1953–1982)" (Ph.D. dissertation, Harvard University, 1983); Alexander Bligh, *From Prince to King: Royal Succession in the House of Saud in the Twentieth Century* (New York: New York University Press, 1984); and Joseph Nevo, "The Saudi Royal Family: The Third Generation," *Jerusalem Quarterly*, No. 31 (Spring 1984), pp. 79–90. Three more recent works focusing on the subject are Simon Henderson, *After King Fahd: Succession in Saudi Arabia* (Washington: Washington Institute for Near East Policy, 1994; Washington Institute Policy Papers, No. 37); Sarah Yizraeli, *The Remaking of Saudi Arabia: The Struggle Between King Sa'ud and Crown Prince Faysal, 1953–1962* (Tel Aviv: Tel Aviv University Moshe Dayan Center for Middle Eastern and African Studies, 1997); and Joseph A. Kechichian, *Succession in Saudi Arabia* (New York: Palgrave, 2001).

4. Muhammad bin 'Abd al-'Aziz was next in age to Faysal but had already surrendered his right to succession and so was passed over without resistance, presumably because of his dissolute reputation and since his full-brother Khalid was next in line.

5. Some observers caution against counting Nayif out, however, and it should be remembered that, as Minister of the Interior, he controls the most important security agency in the kingdom. Mention should also be made of Ahmad, the youngest of the Al Fahd whose strengths include his neutrality between his brothers and his role as member of numerous important councils.

6. Of Fahd's other sons, his eldest, Faysal (born 1946) served as Director-General of Youth Welfare until his death in August 1999; Sa'ud (born 1950) is Deputy Director-General of Intelligence; and Sultan (born 1951) was the Deputy Director-General of Youth Welfare until the death of his brother Faysal.

7. One of his approximately one dozen sons, Mut'ib, presently is a full general in the National Guard, which is controlled by his father, where he serves as Assistant Deputy Commander for Military Affairs.

8. Another son of note is Muhammad (born 1937), who served as Deputy Minister of Agriculture and Water for Desalination Affairs—which sparked his well-publicized idea of towing an iceberg from Antarctica to Saudi Arabia to provide water—but he left government service following the death of his father and is not a player.

9. At the very least, they aroused the ire of Fahd when they tried to push through their late father's reforms during King Khalid's reign.

10. Sources on the recent political situation in Kuwait include Abdul-Reda Assiri and Kamal Al-Monoufi, "Kuwait's Political Elite: The Cabinet," *Middle East Journal*, Vol. 42, No. 1 (Winter 1988), pp. 48–58; Jill Crystal, *Oil and Politics in the Gulf: Rulers and Merchants in Kuwait and Qatar* (Cambridge: Cambridge University Press, 1990); Abdullah K. Al-shayeji, "Kuwait at the Crossroads: The Quest for Democratization," *Middle East Insight*, Vol. 8 (May-June 1992), pp. 41–46; Mary Ann Tetreault, "Designer Democracy in Kuwait," *Current History*, Vol. 96, No. 606 (January 1997), pp. 36–39; and Shafeeq Ghabra, "Kuwait and the Dynamics of Socio-Economic Change," *Middle East Journal*, Vol. 51, No. 3 (Summer 1997), pp. 359–372.

11. The fifth member of the Al Sabah pentarchy running the government at the time of the invasion was the Amir's brother Nawwaf al-Ahmad. Appointed Minister of the Interior in 1978, he was shifted to Minister of Defense in 1988. Widely regarded as a non-entity holding high position only to keep the senior ranks within the hands of the Al Jabir, Nawwaf was widely condemned for Kuwait's lack of preparation in 1990. He was shifted to Social Affairs and Labor in the first post-liberation government and then dropped entirely in 1992.

12. In fact, there is some speculation that this has been a deliberate strategy by his opponents. After Geneva, he was named ambassador to Malaysia and then Oman.

13. Nasir and his wife Husa (the daughter of former Amir Sabah al-Salim) have been prominent collectors of Islamic art and their loans have formed the core of the Kuwait National Museum, most of which miraculously survived the Iraqi invasion in 1990.

14. The other brother suggested, Badr (born about 1958), is a businessman with no government experience.

15. Another prominent member of the family is Shaykh Sa'ud al-Nasir al-Sa'ud. A career in the Foreign Ministry culminated with ambassadorial posts in London and Washington. As a result of his favorable performance in Washington during the period of occupation, he was given the portfolio of Minister of Information

in 1992. However, opposition by Islamists within the National Assembly led to his transfer to Minister of Oil in 1998 where he remained until dropped from the cabinet in 2001. But Shaykh Sa'ud has not been very popular and he belongs to a distant branch of the Al Sabah which resided in Iraq.

16. Recent treatments of Bahraini politics include: Munira Fakhro, "The Uprising in Bahrain: An Assessment," in Gary G. Sick and Lawrence G. Potter, eds., *The Persian Gulf at the Millennium: Essays in Politics, Economy, Security, and Religion* (New York: St. Martin's Press, 1997), pp. 167–188, Louay Bahry, "The Opposition in Bahrain: A Bellwether for the Gulf?" *Middle East Policy*, Vol. 5, No. 2 (May 1997), pp. 42–57; and Abdul Hadi Khalaf, "The New Amir of Bahrain: Marching Side-Ways," *Civil Society*, Vol. 9, No. 100 (April 2000), pp. 6–13.

17. The Shi'a are the largest sect to break away from mainstream or Sunni Islam. The Baharina of Bahrain belong to the Ja'fari or Twelver subsect of Shi'a, the largest Shi'a subdivision to which most Iranians also belong. The word Shi'ah, derived from an Arabic word meaning "party" is a collective; an individual member is a Shi'i. Recent media usage has corrupted the term to Shiite.

18. Qatari developments have been covered in Crystal, *Oil and Politics in the Gulf*; Louay Bahry, "Elections in Qatar: A Window of Democracy Opens in the Gulf," *Middle East Policy*, Vol. 4, No. 4 (June 1999), pp. 118–127; Andrew Rathmell and Kirsten Schulze, "Political Reform in the Gulf: The Case of Qatar," *Middle Eastern Studies*, Vol. 36, No. 4 (October 2000), pp. 47–62.

19. This was in seeming contradiction to the stance taken in Sharja in 1987 when the ruler was briefly ousted by his brother (see below). It should be noted, though, that Sharja is a constituent member of the UAE and not an independent state and that the UAE federal government officially acted to restore the legal ruler.

20. When Shaykh Khalifa made his first post-coup trip to the Gulf in December 1995, his first stop was Abu Dhabi (followed by Bahrain, Kuwait, and Saudi Arabia) and Shaykh Zayid permitted the deposed ruler to remain in Abu Dhabi. It appears that Saudi Arabia also offered asylum to Khalifa on condition that he refrain from political activity.

21. There had been some speculation that Shaykh Hamad's eldest son Mish'al, an official in the Foreign Ministry, would become Heir Apparent, but the role went to Jasim apparently because of his better education and perceived leadership qualities—he passed out of Sandhurst two months before the announcement. The second son Muhammad allegedly was passed over because of his religious conservatism and lack of interest in government. Constitutional changes after the coup limited succession to the Amir's son and provided for the removal of the Heir Apparent should he prove unsatisfactory.

22. Although 'Abd al-'Aziz had taken over the finance portfolio from his father in 1972, he was reputed to be primarily interested in his playboy pursuits. Consequently, another reason for Hamad's action in 1995 was said to be his fa-

ther's attempt to bring 'Abd al-'Aziz back to Qatar.

23. 'Abdullah and Muhammad are full-brothers whose mother also raised Hamad after the death of his mother. Shaykh Khalifa's three other sons were not involved in politics in 1995 because of their youth.

24. According to the Qatari government, the "coup" involved an attempt to capture a tank at a border post by bedouin retainers of the former Amir, backed by former Minister of Economy and Trade (and police chief) Shaykh Hamad bin Jasim bin Hamad. More than 100 people were arrested and Shaykh Hamad was captured by subterfuge in 1999; he was one of those sentenced to life imprisonment the following year.

25. Another important factor was the strong relationship between two key advisers, Ahmad al-Suwaydi in Abu Dhabi and Mahdi al-Tajir in Dubai, who did much to bring their pivotal rulers together.

26. Relevant politics in the UAE has been the subject of Christian Huxley, "A Central American Situation in the Gulf," *MERIP Reports*, Vol. 17, No. 5 (September-October 1987), pp. 33–34; J.E. Peterson, "The Future of Federalism in the United Arab Emirates," in H. Richard Sindelar, III, and J.E. Peterson, eds., *Cross-Currents in the Gulf: Arab, Regional, and Global Interests* (London: Routledge, 1988), pp. 198–230; William A. Rugh, "The United Arab Emirates: What are the Sources of Its Stability?" *Middle East Policy*, Vol. 5, No. 3 (September 1997), pp. 14–24; ibid., "Leadership in the UAE: Past, Present and Future," in Joseph A. Kechichian, ed., *A Century in Thirty Years: Shaykh Zayed and the United Arab Emirates* (Washington, DC: Middle East Policy Council, 2000), pp. 235–271; and Joseph A. Kechichian, "From Trucial Shaykhdoms to a Federation: Sociopolitical Origins of Emirati Leaders," in Kechichian, ed., *A Century in Thirty Years*, pp. 49–72 {St. John Armitage e-mail 6 Feb. 2000.}.

27. This situation is evolving, however. The prospect that Dubai's oil reserves will be depleted by 2010 has led the emirate to integrate its local armed forces into the federal structure, with local control over internal security, police, and health administration to follow. A similar prospect of an imminent end to oil income affects Sharja's attitude as well. As a consequence, the federation will likely be strengthened as the authority of individual emirates gradually fades.

28. The term of the UAE President is fixed constitutionally at five years and is renewable.

29. Shaykh Khalifa is Chairman of the Abu Dhabi Executive Council (which serves as the cabinet for the emirate) and heads both the Abu Dhabi Petroleum Company and the Abu Dhabi Investment Authority. In fact, he seems to be in control of almost everything except defense (although in fact he also holds the title of Deputy Commander of the UAE Armed Forces and it has been reported that he has formed his own Amiri Guard, to serve a similar function as the Saudi Arabian National Guard).

30. Other sons of Shaykh Zayid with prominent positions are Ahmad (Under-Secretary at the UAE Ministry of Finance and Industry), Diyab (Director of the Presidential Court), 'Isa (Under-Secretary in the Abu Dhabi Public Works Department), Sa'id (Chairman of the Abu Dhabi Seaports Authority), and Sayf (Under-Secretary in the UAE Ministry of Interior).

31. Hamdan continues to hold the federal appointment of Minister of Finance and Industry while Muhammad serves as the UAE Minister of Defense; the fourth—and far younger—son is Ahmad.

32. Although 'Abd al-'Aziz was older than Sultan, he had not succeeded in 1972 because he was believed to have been responsible for plotting an assassination of his brother Khalid bin Muhammad in 1970.

33. It was widely believed in the UAE that 'Abd al-'Aziz had been encouraged in his actions by either Shaykh Zayid directly or the Bani Muhammad of Abu Dhabi, acting during a time when Shaykh Zayid was in de facto semi-retirement outside the country. The role of Dubai in restoring Shaykh Sultan, the ruler of Dubai's traditional rival, to power was remarkable and would have been inconceivable if (a) Shaykh Rashid had still been on the scene, (b) Sultan had not already recommended himself to the Al Maktum by his willingness to compromise over the Dubai-Sharja boundary, and (c) Abu Dhabi had not been implicated in the coup attempt.

34. This put Shaykh Zayid in the unusual position of playing host to two failed Sharja putschists: Saqr bin Sultan, whom Shaykh Zayid had brought back from exile in Egypt, and 'Abd al-'Aziz.

35. The decree was issued barely a month after British media reported that Shaykh Sultan's eldest son Muhammad died in England from a drug overdose.

36. The situation in Oman has been discussed by J.E. Peterson, "Legitimacy and Political Change in Yemen and Oman," *Orbis*, Vol. 27, No. 4 (Winter 1984), pp. 971–998; Calvin H. Allen, Jr., "The Sultanate of Oman and American Security Interests in the Arabian Gulf," in Robert W. Stookey, ed., *The Arabian Peninsula: Zone of Ferment* (Stanford, CA: Hoover Institution Press, 1984), pp. 1–16; Ian Skeet, *Oman: Politics and Development* (London: Macmillan, 1992); and Calvin H. Allen and W. Lynn Rigsbee, II, *Oman Under Qaboos: From Coup to Constitution, 1970–1996* (London: Frank Cass, 2000).

37. Qabus married his first cousin Nawwal (later known as Kamilah), daughter of Tariq bin Taymur, in 1976 but he divorced her soon after.

38. On succession, the Basic Law stipulates that the council of the Ruling Family has three days in which to choose a successor. If it is unable to do so, the Defense Council, made up of the Minister of Palace Office Affairs (now the Royal Office) and the heads of the security services, is to appoint the individual whose name has been left in a sealed letter from the deceased Sultan.

J. E. Peterson's most recent positions have been in the Office of the Deputy Prime Minister for Security and Defence of the Sultanate of Oman and at the International Institute for Strategic Studies, London (www.JEPeterson.net). The analysis in this article relies principally on observations and interviews during several decades of travel to and residence in the Gulf. Because these do not lend themselves easily to citation, references to relevant published sources have been provided for each country. An opportunity to update information in the Gulf during January-February 2001 was provided by the International Institute for Strategic Studies and a grant from the MacArthur Foundation. The author is also grateful for the comments on an earlier draft provided by Dr. Rosemarie Said Zahlan, H. St. John B. Armitage, and Dr. Hassan al-Alkim.

*Article 4*            *Current History,* January 2000

# The Middle East's Information Revolution

"It may be some time before the Internet becomes firmly entrenched in much of the Middle East. The obstacles to adoption, especially with the current technology, appear significant. But the information revolution has already arrived in the Middle East, and it poses significant challenges for the status quo."

JON B. ALTERMAN

The visionaries of the information age see a future in which mankind and machines are fused. Computers, telephones, and pagers will morph into a single appliance, while everything from refrigerators to washing machines will be connected to the Internet. We will become ever more enveloped in information, and we will be able to devote progressively more of our energies to purposive activities instead of the minutiae that crowd our present lives.

In painting such a picture, futurologists tend not to give much thought to whom the word "we" represents. They assume that "we" is shorthand for the world, or perhaps more narrowly the developed world, or even more narrowly still, the very rich in the developed world. They pointedly do not concentrate on the technologies available to the vast portion of the world's population, or those technologies most likely to be adopted.

In the Middle East, it would be a mistake to predict that the bulk of the region's people will be "wired"—connected to the Internet and other interactive communications, constantly sending and receiving signals through the electronic ether—anytime soon. But it would also be a mistake to assert that the Middle East is beyond the reach of the information revolution enveloping the developed world. Fax machines, videocassette recorders, and photocopiers are found throughout the region, and are even reaching into the villages. Indeed, the Middle East is undergoing its own information technology revolution—it is simply different than that occurring in the West.

## "NET" GAINS?

The United States has been a pioneer both in developing the Internet and in adopting it for popular use. In the 1990s the "net" went from being a mode of communication for a small number of hobbyists, scientists, and educators to being something akin to a national craze. A large number of advertisements now sport website addresses for commercial sponsors, although the entire concept of the world wide web is little more than a half decade old.

A robust Middle Eastern presence can already be felt on the Internet. Middle East–oriented news-groups have existed for more than a decade, encouraging discussions on subjects as broad as Middle Eastern politics and as narrow as Algerian rai music. Middle Eastern chat rooms can also be found. Newspapers from throughout the region have begun maintaining a presence on the web, often posting the contents of their newspapers free of charge. *Ha'aretz,* an Israeli newspaper that publishes in Hebrew, posts an English-language version of its newspaper on its website daily. Even radio and television stations have taken to the web, and in the last few years an increasing number have begun webcasting their programming.

> Satellite television and the Internet in the Middle East allow expatriates living in the West to play an intimate role in their homelands' cultures.

Governments and organizations also host websites, and many sites run by expatriates link to many sites involving their home countries. The Muslim Students Association, an American collegiate organization, maintains an impressive news website that has links to sites throughout the Muslim world (msanews.mynet.net/Launchpad/index.html). Explicitly religious organizations have taken to the web as well. One recently launched site, Islam Online (www.islam-online.net), offers netsurfers the ability to solicit a custom-tailored religious decree, or *fatwa,* in Arabic or English. Political opposition groups have also taken to the web; Lebanon's Hezbollah maintains an active web page (www.hizbollah.org), as does the Saudi opposition group, the Movement for Islamic Reform in Arabia (www.miraserve.com).

Most of the Internet activity involving the Middle East is carried out by Middle Easterners residing overseas rather than in the region itself. In fact, the Internet has been embraced much more tentatively in the Middle East than in the United States and Western Europe. One barrier has been expense. Computers alone cost about $1,000, and on-line access in most Middle Eastern countries is approximately $30 a month, and in some cases much higher. While these costs may seem relatively affordable to many Americans, they remain out of reach to most Middle Easterners. Saudi Arabia, once one of the richest countries in the region, has seen its annual per capita income decline from a high of about $24,000 in 1982 to a relatively paltry $6,500 today. In the most populous Arab country, Egypt, per capita income is even lower, at about $1,290 per year. Israel, with a per capita income of $15,940, bucks this trend, and accordingly has a higher level of Internet penetration.

Money is not the only barrier to the Internet in the Middle East. Using the Internet remains baffling for many, especially those who are not proficient in English. Technology is improving to represent foreign languages on the web (especially languages that are difficult to represent, such as Arabic, Hebrew, and Farsi), and a few Arabic search engines exist. But upward of 80 percent of the world wide web is in English, and in a medium whose utility is a function of its size and comprehensiveness, lack of a facility with English is a major drawback.

Language aside, personal computers in general and the Internet in particular remain difficult for novices to use. Typing is a slow process for many, and efforts to simplify interfaces collide with rapidly expanding operating systems that automate increasingly more tasks. Computers still crash, browsers cause internal conflicts, viruses proliferate, and hard drives decay over time. While these problems may be manageable in an environment where help is a phone call away, it can turn a computer in a developing country into a paperweight. In many developing countries, clusters of unused computers sit under dust covers, protected from users who might introduce some insoluble problem to the systems.

E-mail, which appears to be the primary use of the Internet in the United States, is typing-intensive and also offers somewhat less robust support for non-Western languages than the web. In some chat rooms, participants transliterate non-Western languages into the Latin alphabet, using commonly agreed on numbers for sound that do not exist in English. Such an approach underscores both the lack of support for less common languages, as well as the need to be at least moderately Western-language literate to participate.

## THE INTERNET'S FRIENDS AND FOES

Governments in the Middle East have taken strikingly different approaches to the Internet. Some, like Egypt and Jordan, have been quiet boosters, building global Internet connections while promoting the establishment of local Internet service providers. The Egyptian government has promised not to monitor Internet activity, and the Jordanian government has encouraged universities to provide Internet services to students. In what may be a sign of tolerance (or a sign that Internet use remains the province of a small group of elites), Egyptian and Jordanian authorities have not intervened when newspaper articles banned by local censors have been made available on the web.

Other governments, such as Saudi Arabia, have been slow to adapt. For most Saudis, domestic Internet connections did not arrive until January 1999, almost two years after the decision to allow access and four years after the issue was first considered. Until last January, many Saudis dialed into neighboring Bahrain for their Internet connections. The Internet available in Saudi Arabia is still subject to many restrictions, filters, and "firewalls" to prevent access to what the government holds is undesirable information. According to at least one account, any effort by a Saudi to reach a banned site results in an instantaneous message alerting the user that his or her effort to reach the site has been noted and logged. The Saudi Internet infrastructure is also swamped with users, prompting recent complaints that it is hard to get on-line.

The Syrian government has evinced interest in the Internet, and President Hafez al-Asad's son (and some assume, successor) Bashar al-Asad heads the Syrian Computing Society. Still, Internet access remains limited to a small group of perhaps several hundred, with an unknown number dialing up through Lebanon. Libya and Iraq prohibit access outright. Iran allows access, especially for e-mail, but the extent of monitoring remains unclear.

The remaining governments tend to regard the Internet somewhat warily. Bahrain and Tunisia openly monitor Internet traffic, and the United Arab Emirates and Yemen use proxy services that can prevent access to undesirable sites.

User figures are difficult to establish and tend to change rapidly. Questions such as how many users operate from a single account remain as baffling as exactly who is accessing the Internet in the Middle East. In general, data is much better regarding Israeli Internet use, which also includes in its figures many users in areas administered by the Palestinian National Authority. Estimates put Israeli Internet use at more than 600,000 users, which may be as much as double the number in the entire Arab world. Countries like the United Arab Emirates (UAE) have relatively high levels of Internet use, although estimates placing it as high as 9 percent of the population are significantly exaggerated (at least in part because of the large number of expatriates in the UAE, who are more likely than the local population to have Internet connections, and less likely to share those connections widely). Other countries are more like Oman, with an estimated 1.6 percent of the population using the Internet, or Egypt, with an estimated 3 percent (although expatriates may be inflating that number as well). Iranian Internet use is also difficult to estimate, but it is certainly low. The lack of many high-speed international connections means that use of the world wide web is frustratingly slow, and most people are restricted to e-mail use.

In recent years the Western philanthropic community has worked to expand Internet connectivity to nongovernmental organizations in the Middle East. Human rights organizations, think tanks, and charitable organizations increasingly have web pages and communicate through e-mail with their Western donors. The long-term effects of these efforts are unclear. Such efforts certainly facilitate contacts among regional organizations, and create access to resources that may be hard to come by in many developing countries. They can also be monitored with relative ease by government authorities, should they choose to do so. The major question is how effectively the organizations will use the Internet both to gain influence in their own countries and draw strength from the international community. A subsidiary question is whether nongovernmental organizations' Internet use will spur wider Internet use among a broader segment of the Middle Eastern societies. At this point, these answers appear murky.

## POISED NOT TO GROW?

How quickly will the Internet spread in the Middle East? Will the region's Internet adoption be characterized by the exponential growth that has marked its use in the United States and Western Europe, or will it follow a flatter trajectory?

It is not easy to answer these questions when looking regionwide, because of large disparities in income, education, literacy, and language ability. From a broader perspective, however, it appears that for some (mainly wealthy, Western-educated elites) adoption of the Internet is a rather easy process, while for others (most graduates of the region's public education systems) the process is more difficult. Although numbers are extremely difficult to obtain, it appears that the elites do not comprise more than about 5 percent of the population of most Middle Eastern countries, with few indications that the number is likely to expand soon. This small percentage means that Internet growth will plateau in most countries in the next five years, with the main question being whether at 1 percent, 5 percent, or 10 percent of the population.

Assessing the impact of the information technology revolution solely in terms of Internet use would be a huge mistake, however. A number of technological innovations have had a far-reaching effect on life in the Middle East, and are poised to have an even greater impact in the years to come.

## THE NEWS . . . AND HAYFA TOO

The explosion of satellite television in the Middle East is often overlooked. Whereas television broadcasting once was the sole province of government within its borders, the shrinking size of satellite dishes, their plummeting cost (now about $200 for a fixed dish), and the rapid expansion of programming choices have created regional audiences where none existed even five years ago. The change is most marked in the Arab world, where 22 nations are united by language but divided by political borders. Satellite television stations, programming in Arabic, reach an audience that may be as large as between 20 and 30 percent of the region's population.

A Saudi-owned channel called the Middle East Broadcasting Center (MBC) pioneered regional programming. Owned by Shaikh Walid al-Ibrahim, whose sister is married to King Fahd, the station has used its London base to broadcast a mix of news and entertainment since 1991. MBC has been pioneering in some respects: it was the first Arab television station to open a Jerusalem bureau, for example, and it has broadcast documentaries on wars with Israel and Iraq that included interviews with former adversaries. But MBC is thought to have gone stale in recent years, perhaps hobbled by Saudi sensitivities not to push the envelope too much on issues such as regional political reform or relations between the sexes.

Into the gap has leaped upstart al-Jazeera, which broadcasts from Qatar. Al-Jazeera was formed, ironically, when the Saudi owners of another Arab station, Orbit, shut down a joint news operation with the British Broadcasting Corporation's Arabic service because the British-based reporters had violated Saudi sensibilities. The Qataris took much of the BBC operation and exported it to their capital of Doha, where they pointedly permit their on-air talent to say what other regional news operations are unwilling to allow. Lively debates, provocative hosts,

## LOCAL NEWS FROM AFAR

Satellite television and the Internet in the Middle East allow expatriates living in the West to play an intimate role in their homelands' cultures. Middle East–oriented chat groups and discussion lists abound on the Internet, as does news (in English and Arabic native tongues). Several television stations and many radio stations broadcast over the Internet, and dozens of leading newspapers from throughout the Middle East publish simultaneously on-line (for a sample, see www.sahafa.com). Former Iraqi Ambassador to the United Nations Nizar Hamdoon revealed last year that he was a fan of the Internet while in his official position; he told the *Washington Post* that he liked to read discussions by Iraqi expatriates and keep up with the news through his Internet connection.

On the television side, all the major Middle Eastern stations have a broadcast presence in Washington and London, and the demand is high for native speakers who can bring Western perspectives to an Arab audience. More recently, several Arabic channels have become available on American satellite systems, ensuring that Arabs resident in the United States can follow regional news stories.

Part of this phenomenon is the news itself, which in many cases is produced not in the Middle East, but in the West. The two most important Arabic newspapers, *al-Hayat* and *Asharq al-Awsat,* are published out of London, where the environment is freer than in Saudi Arabia or even Lebanon. The largest Arab magazines are also published abroad. Satellite stations have a substantial European presence as well, with major stations either basing their operations in London or maintaining a presence in the city.

With so many Arab news outlets based in the West, Arabs who choose to live in comparatively freer Western societies are making the decisions about what their compatriots back home are seeing and reading. The effect is a broadening of the bounds of debate, a subtle integration of Western ideas with Arab ideas, and a general bridging of gaps between the Arab world and the West.

J.B.A.

and call-in programs on hot topics are daily fare on al-Jazeera; the titles of its two most popular shows, "The Opposite Direction" and "More Than One Opinion," tell much of the story.

All satellite programming is not heavily news based, however. The Lebanese Broadcasting Corporation (LBC) has a more entertainment-oriented approach, mixing Arabic game shows, light interviews, and reruns of American programs. Hosts on LBC often appear flirtatious, but nothing approaches the notoriety of LBC's most watched program, "Hayfa Is the Only One for You." The show is an exercise program in which a leotard-clad Hayfa exercises on location throughout Lebanon. The afternoon show enjoys extraordinarily high viewership in conservative Arab societies among both men and women.

In addition to the Arab offerings on satellite television, some viewers use their dishes to pick up the transmissions of other regional broadcasters. Israeli and Turkish television is especially prized, the former because of its superior selection of American programming, and the latter for its more liberal portrayal of women. In some countries, movable dishes are pointed toward northern Europe, where satellites show soft-core pornography in addition to their other programming.

A missing link in much of the regional satellite programming is profitability. Television, some have observed, is a medium created to support advertising, but the advertising market in much of the Arab world remains weak. Arab satellite viewers see few advertisements, in part because it is unclear exactly whom those viewers are. While American and European firms can quickly rattle off the age, sex, and income characteristics of consumers of products and media programming in their home markets, the task is far more difficult in the Arab world.

The problem of gathering demographics has several components. One is that the Arab world contains 22 countries, and coordinating data collection over such a large area is quite difficult. Another obstacle is cultural resistance to answering personal questions. A third problem, and perhaps the biggest, is that Arabs simply do not consume very much because of their relative poverty. While pockets of true wealth do exist in the Persian Gulf, the per capita income for the entire region was only $2,050 in 1998. At such levels of income, discretionary spending is low, as is the propensity to spend money on branded products. Some inroads have been made, especially in terms of laundry detergent and tobacco, but for the most part Arab audiences' consumption does not sustain the type of advertising revenue that can support satellite broadcasting long into the future.

It costs in the neighborhood of $40 million a year to operate a satellite station, and most are not close to covering their expenses. Among all the Arabic satellite stations, LBC is perhaps the closest to making money; the others have losses that range from controllable to hemorrhaging. Governments or wealthy individuals with ties to governments pick up the remaining tab, but how long they will be able to cover losses and at what levels is an open question.

## FAX, COPY, REWIND

While satellite television and the Internet, because of their costs, remain beyond the reach of many Arabs, other technological innovations of the last two decades have had a startling effect on the information that residents of the Arab world can receive. Among the most important developments are the photocopier, the fax machine, and the videocassette player.

The photocopier has become so mundane in Western societies that people no longer think of it as a high-tech device. But no single invention has so democratized the wide dissemination of a message at such a low cost. Photocopied leaflets are common throughout the Arab region, as are single-page flyers advocating political and religious positions. Photocopies are inexpensive (often less than three cents per impression), and they do not belie the printer's identity. Equally important, any individual can create a message to be photocopied without involving typesetters or other specialized professionals. While leaflets and broadsheets are not new, what is new is the availability of the technology to individuals even in small villages.

Photocopiers can also intersect with the Internet to widely disseminate web pages or messages previously available only to a few individuals. Under such a scenario, those trying to mobilize a population need only reach a small number with Internet access (who may be far from those trying to do the mobilization), and that small number can then reproduce and distribute the message. The same is true with encrypted messages; only a few people need to understand how to operate the encryption mechanism for it to emerge as a powerful tool to organize people across a vast distance free of surveillance.

Fax machines can be combined with photocopiers as well. Faxes may not enjoy the same security of communication as do encrypted Internet messages, but they remain a popular method to mobilize and spread ideas, used by religious groups and opposition figures alike across borders and within borders. The decline in international telephone tariffs, which will take place in the next few years as a consequence of international trade agreements, may lead to more international faxes being sent. The best-known fax campaigners in recent years have been two Saudi opposition groups: the Committee for the Defense of Legitimate Rights, and the Movement for Islamic Reform in Arabia, both of which operate out of London. There are reports that Islamists in Egypt, anti-Syrian forces in Lebanon, and separatist forces in Sudan are also running fax-based campaigns from Western countries.

Videocassette players were a rarity in the Middle East 10 years ago, but they have become widely disseminated since then. The advantage of videocassettes is that they present compelling images, are relatively inexpensive to copy, and can be viewed many times.

Video rental facilities have spread throughout the Middle East, often offering a combination of popular Hollywood films, action-oriented B-movies never shown on American screens, Indian and Egyptian films, Kung Fu action pictures, and, in some cases, discreetly hidden pornography. The number of video rental stores that carry explicitly religious or political programming is unclear.

Even programming that may appear innocuous in the West may carry powerful messages to Middle Eastern audiences. Films convey attitudes toward gender, class, wealth, religion, and a host of other social issues and, while invisible to Western audiences, they may be the most striking aspect of a film to audiences in the developing world.

Videotapes can carry explicitly religious or political messages, and those messages can take several forms. In 1994 the Egyptian government produced a film entitled *The Terrorist,* which starred the hugely popular comedian in the Arab world, Adel Imam. In a manner that appeared crude and ham-handed to many Western viewers, the film portrayed Islamically-inspired terrorists as venal, corrupt, and misguided, and suggested that much of their anger is only a result of misunderstandings. Among Egyptians, there is a broad perception that this film and others like it helped turn the tide against Islamist political violence in Egypt.

Videotapes can also be used to inspire action against a government for either religious or political purposes. While the content of such films is often harder for outsiders to ascertain, some are certainly used for fundraising, political mobilization, indoctrination, and similar activities. Hamas suicide bombers often have made videotapes before carrying out an attack, explaining their motivations and their expectations of the world to come. Such films are certainly meant to inspire and recruit additional support.

## EVOLUTIONARY OR REVOLUTIONARY?

None of this is wholly new. Regional newspapers have always been available in many countries, albeit at some cost and after several days. Offshore newspapers are not new either—*Abu Nazara Zarqa,* an Egyptian satirical magazine, was published in France in the nineteenth century. Books and pamphlets have circulated throughout the region since the advent of printing presses in the nineteenth century. Regional radio broadcasting also has a long history, dating to Gamal Abdel Nasser's "Voice of the Arabs" in the 1950s and 1960s. Combined with the sudden rise of the transistor radio, Cairo's messages mobilizing the masses in the Arab world had a striking effect and may have contributed to coups in Iraq and Yemen.

Yet changes in the last decade have been revolutionary rather than evolutionary. In only a short time, satellite television has broken out of its narrow elite audience to reach broad segments of the region's population. It now enjoys an audience that far exceeds that of regional radio broadcasts. Inexpensive photocopying, combined with sharply increased rates of literacy, exponentially expands the opportunities for disseminating messages and viewpoints. Videotapes send explicit and implicit messages widely, reaching a far greater audience for a greater variety of programming than films ever could in the past. Although the Internet remains mostly limited to the very rich, Western philanthropic efforts to spread Internet use to civil society organizations puts it in the hands of some who may not be members of the elite.

All this creates a basic shift in the regional information environment. Previously, the emphasis was on accumulating information. Government media outlets dispensed information, and for all but an elite, that was most of what was available. Television was government controlled, and that control was often very tight. While alternative outlets for information always existed (such as through local religious figures), communication between those outlets was often slow and unreliable.

The technological developments of the last two decades, combined with increased literacy, have completely changed this situation. The current information-rich media environment is demand driven rather than supply driven. Viewers switch the channel if they are bored with their government's fare, and they find a panoply of choices. Although most regional television stations have links to some government, the wide variety of choices ensures that stations must present interesting and credible programming to maintain viewership. On the print level, too, far much more is available to read than ever before, and far more people read it.

It may be some time before the Internet becomes firmly entrenched in much of the Middle East. The obstacles to its adoption, especially with the current technology, appear significant. But the information revolution has already arrived in the Middle East, and it poses significant challenges for the status quo. How well individuals, organizations, and governments will cope with the new challenges and take advantage of the new opportunities will be the main engine for change in the Middle East in the next decade.

---

Jon B. Alterman *is a program officer in the research and studies program at the United States Institute of Peace. He is the author of* New Media, New Politics? From Satellite Television to the Internet in the Arab World *(Washington: Washington Institute for Near East Policy, 1998).*

---

*Article 5*                                        *The Observer*, September 23, 2001

# My fatwa on the fanatics

Ziauddin Sardar

The magnitude of the terrorist attack on America has forced Muslims to take a critical look at themselves. Why have we repeatedly turned a blind eye to the evil within our societies? Why have we allowed the sacred terms of Islam, such as fatwa and jihad, to be hijacked by obscurantist, fanatic extremists?

Muslims are quick to note the double standards of America—its support for despotic regimes, its partiality towards Israel, and the covert operations that have undermined democratic movements in the Muslim world. But we seldom question our own double standards. For example, Muslims are proud that Islam is the fastest growing religion in the West. Evangelical Muslims, from Saudi Arabia to Pakistan, happily spread their constricted interpretations of Islam. But Christian missionaries in Muslim countries are another matter. They have to be banned or imprisoned. Those who burn effigies of President Bush will be first in the queue for an American visa.

The psychotic young men, members of such extremist organisations as Al-Muhajiroun and 'Supporters of Sharia', shouting fascist obscenities outside the Pakistan Embassy, are enjoying the fruits of Western freedom of expression. Their declared aim is to establish 'Islamic states'. But in any self-proclaimed Islamic state, they would be ruthlessly silenced.

This is not the first time concerned Muslims have raised such questions. But we have been forced to ignore them for two main reasons. In a world where it is always open season for prejudice and discrimination on Muslims and Islam, our main task has seemed to be to defend Islam.

The other reason concerns Ummah, the global Muslim community. We have to highlight, the argument goes, the despair and suffering of the Muslim people —their poverty and plight as refugees and the horror of war-torn societies.

So, all good and concerned Muslims are implicated in the unchecked rise of fanaticism in Muslim societies. We have given free reign to fascism within our midst, and failed to denounce fanatics who distort the most sacred concepts of our faith. We have been silent as they proclaim themselves martyrs, mangling beyond recognition the most sacred meaning of what it is to be a Muslim.

But the events of 11 September have freed us from any further obligation to this misapplied conscience. The insis-tence by the Muslim Council of Britain that the Islamic cause is best served by the Taliban handing over Osama bin Laden, is indicative of this shift.

The devotion with which so many Muslims, young and old, in Europe and America, are organising meetings and conferences to discuss how to unleash the best intentions, the essential values of Islam, from the rhetoric of jihad, hatred and insularity, is another.

But we have to go further. Muslims are in the best position to take the lead in the common cause against terrorism. The terrorists are among us, the Muslim communities of the world. They are part of our body politic. And it is our duty to stand up against them.

We must also reclaim a more balanced view of Islamic terms like fatwa. A fatwa is simply a legal opinion based on religious reasoning. It is the opinion of one individual and is binding on only the person who gives it. But, since the Rushdie affair, it has come to be associated in the West solely with a death sentence. Now that Islam has become beset with the fatwa culture, it becomes necessary for moderate voices to issue their own fatwas.

So, let me take the first step. To Muslims everywhere I issue this fatwa: any Muslim involved in the planning, financing, training, recruiting, support or harbouring of those who commit acts of indiscriminate violence against persons or the apparatus or infrastructure of states is guilty of terror and no part of the Ummah. It is the duty of every Muslim to spare no effort in hunting down, apprehending and bringing such criminals to justice.

If you see something reprehensible, said the Prophet Muhammad, then change it with your hand; if you are not capable of that then use your tongue (speak out against it); and if you are not capable of that then detest it in your heart.

The silent Muslim majority must now become vocal. The rest of the world could help by adopting a more balanced tone. The rhetoric that paints America as a personification of innocence and goodness, a god-like power that can do no wrong, not only undermines the new shift but threatens to foreclose all our futures.

*Ziauddin Sardar is a leading Muslim writer.*

---

*Article 6*

*Current History*, January 2001

# Iran: Came the Revolution

"Long-time watchers of Iranian politics [believe] Iran is moving away from the politics of Islamic revolution and toward the traditional politics of Iran. . . . [But] authoritarianism is a recurring theme in Iranian history, and some Iranian scholars openly wonder whether the reformists will be any less authoritarian than the conservative clerics."

## JON B. ALTERMAN

The Islamic Republic of Iran defies easy categorization. Although the government is avowedly Islamic and its decisions overseen by a religiously appointed "supreme leader," elections are held regularly, often rewarding candidates opposed to the status quo with victory. Although the forced imposition of veiling and continued disadvantages in family law give precisely the opposite impression, women have made huge strides since the Islamic revolution of 1979. And although it holds the world's fifth-largest proven oil reserves and the second-largest reserves of natural gas, the economy is in a shambles, with no clear route forward. Social tension is also rising as crime, drug use, and divorce rates climb ever higher.

It would be tempting to suggest that the Iranian system is irrevocably broken, run aground on a basic incompatibility between religious governance and democracy. A more rigorous investigation suggests that Iranian society is struggling to mold its own future as it confronts the challenges of the modern world. Much as Ayatollah Ruhollah Khomeini's Islamic revolution proved unique in the modern world, Iran's solution to its current predicaments is also likely to prove distinctly Iranian.

## INTERPRETING IRAN

Two characteristics overwhelmingly dominate Iranian domestic life. The first is the hyperpolitical nature of Iranian society. Political meaning is read into a wide array of actions, from speech and dress to entertainment. Although many reformist newspapers have been shuttered in a recent press crackdown, as late as last spring more than a dozen highly politicized and almost flamboyantly anticlerical publications were flourishing in Tehran, each criticizing the government for various perceived inadequacies. Government offices are politicized as well, with reformist loyalists battling supporters of the clerical leadership for control of policy.

The absence of formal party structures adds to the politicization, since it renders public life in Iran highly improvisational. For example, how should former President Ali Akbar Hashemi Rafsanjani be characterized? Variously described as a moderate, a technocrat, and a conservative, he actively put himself forward in recent parliamentary elections as a compromise candidate who could bridge differences among all sides. His candidacy threw the reformist camp into deep debate as to whether he was a means to keep the reform process alive, or a wolf in sheep's clothing who would destroy that process. Equally important was a heated debate about whether he was an unstoppable force to be appeased and accommodated, or a weakened leader who could be pushed aside. In an environment with so much political uncertainty, politicians' actions are carefully scrutinized for their political import.

The second characteristic of Iranian domestic life is its deep ambiguity. Despite occasionally harsh rhetoric, Iranians have come to look for subtle messages that presage new flexibility or new alliances. Ambiguity helps preserve the governing system despite a high degree of tension, and it also allows the vanquished of one battle to emerge the victors of a future one, or at least maintain the prospect of doing so. The result can be maddening for outsiders, who often must make their decisions based on more rigid organizational models and according to strict timetables. For Iranians, the ambiguity is essential.

These two characteristics—hyperpoliticization and deep ambiguity—are mutually reinforcing. Within the context, much that appears rigid is actually negotiable, from the role of Islam in public life to social môres and outlets for alternative political visions. And much that appears negotiable, such as the limits to speech or political expression, suddenly run up against rigid

constraints. Where the system completely breaks down is not necessarily in its internal functioning but when it interacts with outside systems of power or authority. Multinational corporations respond poorly to systematic uncertainty, and other governments find it difficult to handle intragovernmental processes that require constant bargaining with an ever-changing cast of real and imagined policy actors.

## WHY KHATAMI?

One facet of Iranian political life that has confounded observers is the electoral system. Iran has held regular elections throughout the revolutionary period. The most recent have been truly contested—most important the elections for the presidency in May 1997, for the local councils in February 1999, and for parliament in February 2000. In each, candidates representing reformist trends in Iranian political life have triumphed. "Reformist" in this context refers to those who want to preserve a role for the *Rahbar,* or religious leader, in Iranian political life, but want that role circumscribed and greater personal freedom restored in Iran. Mohammad Khatami emerged almost out of nowhere to lead this tendency. At the time of his election in 1997, he was neither a leading cleric nor a widely popular figure. Khatami has brought a new style and a new language to the presidency. Rather than embrace the highly political approach of his predecessor, Ali Akbar Hashemi Rafsanjani, Khatami has turned to philosophy and intellectualism to disarm his critics. His campaign slogan, "Rule of Law," is elegant in its simplicity and elusive in its true meaning. It has resonated with a population long tired of seemingly arbitrary rule, but it leaves undefined exactly which law will govern Iran.

It would be an oversimplification to suggest that the conservatives allow the reformists to gain electoral office merely because the conservatives retain all the "real" power in Iran.

Khatami has also adopted a strikingly different public style than his predecessor, engaging in banter with reporters and often flashing a wide grin. Thus he has emerged as a startlingly successful politician while lacking an effective political machine or many formed allies. He has proved masterly at generating an image and a mood; while he did not create the reform wave, he has ridden that wave expertly.

Since Khatami's surprise election in 1997, reformists rallying behind him have won convincing victories in each succeeding election. Conservatives, who identify most strongly with the status quo, continue to allow themselves to suffer a drubbing. Led by the *rahbar,* conservatives have been repudiated by overwhelming majorities in election after election. Still, they make few gestures to suspend elections, to alter their results, or to prevent elections from being basically free and fair.

The conservatives have the means to take such steps, but for the most part they do not need to do so. They control key sources of power that are immune from electoral influence. The *rahbar*'s office and the conservative-dominated Guardian Council can check almost any move by the president, his cabinet ministers, or the various elected bodies in the country. Military and paramilitary troops, the police, the judiciary, and the broadcasting authority are all under the authority of the religious leader (although significant reformist sentiment exists in all those organs). In addition, intelligence operatives and thugs can carry out political tasks while allowing deniability to the power structure.

Conservatives also control the process of vetting political candidates, and they have used their power in this arena to restrain popular reformist candidates, although they have been unable to hold back the reformist wave. In the second round of the most recent parliamentary election, conservatives enlisted the judiciary's help to cast doubt on the validity of the voting in Tehran until Khamenei decided that he risked rebellion from openly manipulating election results.

Thus, it would be an oversimplification to suggest that the conservatives allow the reformists to gain electoral office merely because the conservatives retain all the "real" power in Iran. Conservatives are driven both by a desire to preserve the revolution and by a recognized need to allow the public to vent its discontent. Few conservatives have the stomach for the widespread oppression necessary to cement their rule absent concessions to reformist forces. Such oppression would also invite massive resistance. In their calculations, it is far better to share power with their challengers, cooperating where common ground can be found and retaining essential perquisites and prerogatives.

A similar calculation applies to the reformists, who would like to see evolutionary rather than revolutionary change to the Iranian political system. Confident of overwhelming public support and their ultimate success, reformists prefer to make incremental gains rather than hurtle toward insurrection and the uncertainty of revolution. Dysfunctional though their relationship sometimes appears, conservatives and their reformist foes have achieved an uneasy modus vivendi that remains deeply unsatisfying but nonetheless is superior to any apparent alternative.

## POLITICS WITHOUT PARTIES

The seemingly muddled nature of Iranian politics is accentuated by the absence of official political parties; instead, "fronts," associations and societies serve to promote candidates and mobilize popular support. President Khatami's brother, Mohammad Reza Khatami, led the most important of these, the Islamic Iran Participation Front (IIPF). It has emerged as the standard-bearer of the reform movement, although it is by no means the only reformist group. Many reformist organizations have overlapping memberships, and several sought to promote common lists for the parliamentary elections. In the weeks preceding the elections, there was uncertainty about how much collaboration would be possible, with considerable confusion about the number of candidates who would appear on common lists. While reformist candidates captured virtually all the Tehran seats and more than 70 percent of parliamentary seats nationwide, it remains a surprise that such a chaotic system could produce such a clear mandate.

Strikingly, although Iranian society is highly politicized, political machines seem poorly organized. Although former Tehran Mayor Gholamhossein Karbaschi had established an impressive political operation in Tehran, for the most part no strong and direct connection exists between voters and elected officials. Constituencies rarely seem to have been cultivated, and ties between elected officials and their publics are tenuous.

The IIPF coalition is held together by opposition to the status quo. Its candidates support greater personal freedom and a refinement of the role of religious authority in Iranian society. Going much further on common goals is difficult, however, whether they are economic development or relations with the United States. As a group, the IIPF remains united by what it is not rather than what it is; absent a coherent opponent, the IIPF is likely to shatter into smaller groups with competing agendas.

More difficult to categorize is a group called the Servants of Construction, which includes former President Rafsanjani and former Tehran Mayor Karbaschi and which bills itself as a collection of non-ideological technocrats who want to move Iran forward. Although government officials freed the popular and powerful Karbaschi from jail in advance of the parliamentary elections to enlist his support, the former mayor was unable to produce a victory for the group, which won less than 10 percent of the vote. Rafsanjani, quietly touted as a future speaker of parliament who could use his political skills to breach the divides of Iranian politics, faced a humiliating defeat in the Tehran polling and withdrew his candidacy. Rafsanjani retains considerable personal power as the head of the Expediency Council, which arbitrates differences between the parliament and the Guardian Council. Despite its defeat, the Servants of Construction remains a constellation of some of the country's most able politicians who cannot be excluded from future contests. Indeed, some currently serve in Khatami's cabinet.

## DOWN BUT NOT OUT

Conservatives were among the most organized of the forces in last year's parliamentary elections, but they suffered a stunning defeat. Prominent officials lost their seats, and leaders of the faction admitted a need to rethink their approach to the public after the ballots were cast. Many ran under the banner of the Militant Clerics' Society, and they enjoy support among groups like the merchant-based Islamic Coalition Society. While their power base in the parliament has all but dissolved, conservatives retain significant control over many elements of the government. They are unlikely to attempt a frontal assault on the reformists' popularity, although they will seek to maintain a significant role through avenues other than parliamentary representation.

Even in parliament, the conservatives continue to hold many cards. The conservative Guardian Council must approve candidacies for most public offices, and would-be reformist candidates flooded the process in advance of the parliamentary elections to overwhelm and hopefully overcome potential objections. The Guardian Council disqualified a small number of candidates, perhaps hoping that overwhelmed voters would be unable to sort out the mess and thus hand the election to the better-organized conservative forces. Although more than 500 candidates ran for 30 seats in Tehran, and multiple reformist candidates ran in many constituencies, the result was still not a conservative victory. Voters came to polling places armed with lists printed in the newspapers or elsewhere, and although the reformists' political organization was chaotic, it was apparently sufficient to notch a resounding win.

In some cases, conservatives used more heavy-handed tactics. The highly popular reformist candidate and cleric Abdullah Nouri loomed as a likely choice for parliament speaker in the months prior to the election. The former vice president and interior minister was an outspoken advocate of pluralism in religious life, as well as a close ally of President Khatami. In October, a special clerical court handed down a 44-page indictment of Nouri for insulting Islam, dishonoring Ayatollah Khomeini's legacy, fomenting unrest, and a host of other offenses. The Nouri trial became a public circus as the accused turned on his accusers and put forward sophisticated theological arguments to bolster his case. The public avidly followed the trial, and testimony from the proceedings was immediately packaged as a best-selling book. Nouri attracted important clerical support, but he was unable to win his case. The court found him guilty on 15 counts, sentenced him to five years in prison, imposed a substantial fine, and barred him from holding public office. He would not be speaker of parliament regardless of his public support.

## VEILED POWER?

Women have made surprising advances in Iranian life over the last two decades, although their progress has often been obscured by the imposition of veiling and by many women's adoption of *chadors,* or black cloaks, when they go out in public. Women's veiling arouses visceral emotions in the West, where many see it as oppressive to women and menacing to outsiders. Many Iranian women, however, view veiling as giving them a greater ambit in Iranian life. The deprivations of a brutal eight-year war with Iraq in the 1980s and economic collapse drove many middle-class Iranian women out of the home and into the workplace. Veiling allows women to eschew traditional roles while maintaining honor and a degree of distance from new male colleagues. While some would argue that concepts of honor and necessary distance are themselves examples of sexist oppression, others assert that dress restrictions are a small price to pay for a greater role outside the home. In this regard, Iranian women are startlingly better off than women in conservative gulf states. Although the revolution set back Iranian women in many aspects of family law, Iranian women retain the right to work, the right to vote, and widespread access to education. In many ways, Iranian women are among the most emancipated in the Persian Gulf.

One manifestation of their status can be found on university campuses, where women constitute half the student body. Iranian professors avow that many of their best students are females driven by a combination of intellectual curiosity, career ambitions, and the desire to avoid arranged marriages. As more of these educated women file out of the university system, they will change their own society by their demonstration of their abilities and their demands for more equitable treatment.

Women make up an important part of the country's electorate, and they have been reliable supporters of the reformist trend. Through their embrace of reformist politics, they argue for greater autonomy in their personal lives and greater equity from an Islamic court system that is tilted toward males. While women as a group remain disadvantaged through numerous legal encumbrances and remain targeted by enforcers of modesty, they are clearly changing the tide through pressure, persuasion, and politicking rather than direct confrontation.

## CLERICAL BALKANIZATION . . .

The conventional wisdom pits women against the rule of the robed clerics who play a direct role in governing Iran. But positions within the clerical establishment are more complex than they appear. First, many clerics in Iran are not connected with the ruling clerical establishment, and do not wish to be connected with it. The Iranian revolution put into practice the concept of *velayat-e faqih,* or "rule of the jurisprudent," which had been developed by Ayatollah Khomeini during his years of exile. Such a system has a leader or guide (often translated into English as "supreme leader") who ensures that the government's actions conform to the strictures of Muslim law. After the revolution, Khomeini had a chance to implement his system as the first leader. He occupied both a religious role as a "source of emulation" and a political role as a revolutionary leader to develop his own style of charismatic leadership. Khomeini has been succeeded as leader by Ayatollah Ali Khamenei, who lacks Khomeini's religious standing and personal authority. Indeed, he was promoted to the rank of ayatollah only after his appointment as leader, thereby bypassing a number of clerics with higher religious standing. But while Khamenei is not one of the most religiously learned among the politicized clerics, he is among the most politically skilled. His role as a political leader, and his stature among clerics, highlights the tensions of the current Iranian political system. In the words of French scholar Olivier Roy, in Iran the "status and role of religion is . . . defined by political institutions, not religious ones. Politics rule over religion."[1]

In this environment Khamenei faces a not-so-quiet revolt from many leading clerics and their students. Many of them envision a less politicized role for the leader. Some fear that politics will corrupt religion. Others wish to retain their own perqs and prerogatives within the Shiite religious hierarchy without making concessions to politics. The most prominent cleric in opposition is Ayatollah Hossein Ali Montazeri, who had been tapped as Khomeini's successor as leader until a few months before Khomeini's death. Montazeri has been placed under house arrest in the clerical city of Qom and barred from teaching, nevertheless, his views are smuggled out occasionally, and supporters maintain a Farsi-language Internet site devoted to his teachings.

Resistance to the status quo appears to be creating an alliance between older clergy and younger students, who combine to check the activities of those clerics swept along by the revolution. Balkanization among the clerics is given an additional boost by the fact that grand ayatollahs have vast assets and patronage power that can compete with the state. Internal clerical politics, therefore, involve not only issues of faith but also of money and employment. The issues loom large, and no clear resolution is in sight.

## In many ways, Iranian women are among the most emancipated in the Persian Gulf.

### ... AND YOUTH AGITATION

In addition to clerics and women, the other significant bloc in the Iranian polity is the young. Fueled by a baby boom in the years immediately following the Iranian revolution, Iran has a staggeringly young population, 59 percent of whom are under the age of 25 and thus have little or no recollection of pre-revolutionary life. Equally important, fully a third of the electorate is between the ages of 16 and 25 (and this after the voting age was recently raised from 15 to 16 to trim the youth vote). Youth in Iran face sparse job opportunities in a struggling economy, and many chafe against the social restrictions that have characterized post-revolutionary Iran. Some of the wealthy Tehran youth "push the envelope," adapting Western styles, Western tastes in music, and even Western patterns of socializing to flout societal restrictions. One official from the Ministry of Islamic Guidance told a Western reporter that young people "want an end to humiliation. They want an education. They don't want others to make decisions in their names. They want social and cultural opportunities. They want modern things. They want fun."[2] Many in this generation experience Islam in the form of social restrictions, school-led indoctrination, and international isolation. For the majority, it is not an attractive package, and it has fueled calls among the clerics to pull back to prevent the youth from rejecting Islam entirely.

Students played a key role in the 1979 Iranian revolution, both taking to the streets and, in the most symbolic gesture of the year's events, taking over the United States embassy and holding American diplomats hostage. Many of today's students are highly politicized and place their hope in reformist politics. They constitute an important component of President Khatami's support, and in the last several years they have been visible opponents of conservative factions in Iranian politics. Student protests in Tehran turned to riots in July 1999, following the closure of a popular reformist newspaper. Although the riots were brought under control, and although little evidence can be found that Iranian students seek to create a new

revolution, they stand as a reminder of the importance and impatience of Iran's youth in calling for social and economic change.

Youth agitation over social relations and economic concerns point to the difficult problems the Iranian political system must resolve over the next several years. Undoubtedly, many in Iran's conservative establishment fear that greater freedoms will create calls not only for more social liberty but also for a political system less fettered by clerical oversight and intervention. Some Iranians are clearly looking to China for guidance, which has managed to promote dramatic social and economic change while retaining a relatively stable political structure. Pulling off the same feat in Iran would be difficult, although not impossible.

### A RETURN TO TRADITIONAL POLITICS?

While the overall political environment in Iran continues to appear muddled, conservatives seem to be rebounding from their defeats in the polls. The reformist newspapers closed by the conservatives last spring remain shut and appear unlikely to reopen in the near future. While individual newspapers had been closed (both temporarily and permanently) in previous years for individual offenses, eliminating the entire reformist press establishment was clearly an attempt to change the political environment rather than merely set boundaries for future behavior.

Further, the outgoing parliament passed a highly restrictive press law during its lame-duck session, and when the new parliament began debate in August on efforts to overturn the press law, Ayatollah Khamenei wrote a stern letter opposing its efforts. The shot across the bow was effective, and parliament dropped the effort, although not without a good deal of grumbling.

Looking ahead, presidential elections are slated to be held in May. Rumors continue to circulate that Khatami is dispirited by the pounding the reformists have taken and is considering sitting it out. Although another reformist candidate presumably would come to the fore, how Khatami's supporters would respond to their candidate's withdrawal is unclear. Would they too throw up their hands and wait for a more auspicious environment, or would they consider it a sign that the entire system is a failure and must be uprooted? Until now, students and others strongly in the reformist camp have pulled back rather than precipitate unrestrained violence. Khatami, in fact, has been among those counseling restraint. If popular demands and expectations for change through the electoral process are dashed, however, the street could turn away from the ballot box and toward massive resistance.

Long-time watchers of Iranian politics—Iranians and Westerners alike—see the current battles as an indicator that Iran is moving away from the politics of Islamic revolution and toward the traditional politics of Iran. The drama, the intrigue, the power struggles, the maneuvering, and the chaotic nature all hearken back to an earlier age of Iranian politics, although mass literacy and urbanization have made the mix even more volatile. Authoritarianism is a recurring theme in Iranian history, and some Iranian scholars openly wonder whether the reformists will be any less authoritarian than the conservative clerics if they are able to consolidate their control. In this environment, ambiguity and hyperpoliticization hold together a political arena that would otherwise atomize into rancor and division.

Persian culture dates back millennia, and Iran not only has its own history, but also its own language, literature, and art. What may be more important than the outcome of today's political battles is Iran's emergence from revolution and rejection of the outside world to a growing acceptance and interaction with it. Such an outcome would be warmly welcomed in Iran, and in the rest of the world as well.

## Notes

1. Olivier Roy, "The Crisis of Religious Legitimacy in Iran," *Middle East Journal,* vol. 53, no. 2 (Spring 1999), p. 202.

2. Ali-Reza Shiravi, quoted in Elaine Sciolino, *Persian Mirrors: The Elusive Face of Iran* (New York: Free Press, 2000), p. 293. Sciolino's book is an exceptional portrait of social tensions and social realities in Iran.

JON B. ALTERMAN *is a program officer in the research and studies program at the United States Institute of Peace. He recently traveled to Iran to participate in an academic conference.*

---

*Article 7* *The Washington Quarterly,* Autumn 2001

# Iraq after Saddam

## Daniel Byman

The removal of Saddam Hussein from power in Iraq is, correctly, one of the primary goals of the U.S. government for the Persian Gulf region. Since the invasion of Kuwait in August 1990, the United States has viewed Saddam as a second Hitler: aggressive, adventurous, and megalomaniacal. Stability and peace in the region cannot be assured until he is gone. President George W. Bush, former President Bill Clinton, senior U.S. government officials from both parties, and leading congressional and media voices have all called for Saddam's removal. Outside experts share this general opposition to Saddam. Rend Rahim Francke, for example, argues, "[T]he problems that exist in Iraq are inherent in the regime of Saddam Hussein and will not go away as long as he is there. Moreover, the longer he is there, the more they will fester, and the more intractable they will become."[1]

This focus on Saddam drives many aspects of U.S. policy toward Iraq, including sanctions, arms inspections, and support for the Iraqi opposition. Washington has tied its support for lifting sanctions to Saddam's removal. In May 1991, shortly after the Persian Gulf War,

deputy national security advisor Robert Gates declared, "Any easing of sanctions will be considered only when there is a new government."[2] Almost nine years later, in March 2000 Assistant Secretary of State David Welch testified, "[W]e doubt that Iraq will take the sensible steps necessary to obtain the lifting, or the suspension, of sanctions as long as Saddam Hussein remains in power."[3] Although the Bush administration seeks to modify the sanctions, it remains committed to tight restrictions on what Iraq can purchase and to international control over Iraqi spending in general. Arms control experts are especially concerned about the Saddam regime's use of chemical weapons on its own people and against Iran, suggesting possible future use of other weapons of mass destruction (WMD). Because of these fears that Iraq under Saddam will always be aggressive and dangerous, Washington has increased its support for the Iraqi opposition.[4]

The United States is not alone in its focus on Saddam the man. Although many voices in the Arab and Muslim world criticize U.S. policy toward Iraq, Saddam himself has few backers. Islamists distrust Saddam's recent professions of religiosity, recalling his brutal persecution of their cause in Iraq. Arab nationalists at their most forgiving see him as a committed opponent of the United States, Iran, and other *bêtes noires,* but hardly consider him the heir to Egypt's Gamal Nasser. Iran, which seldom sees eye-to-eye with Washington in the Gulf area, shares the U.S. view that Saddam is a dangerous leader.

Saddam takes risks.[5] He is more likely than most possible leaders of Iraq to invade his neighbors, use WMD, repress communities at home, and otherwise destabilize his region. In addition, Saddam bears grudges and will seek to punish Kuwait, Saudi Arabia, the United States, and other foes—even if he must wait years to do so. If he were removed, chances for reconciliation both within the region and with the United States would improve.

Removing Saddam, however, is not a panacea for Iraq's woes. This focus on Saddam overlooks the potential dangers that his successor will pose and understates some fundamental problems that are inherent to Iraq's strategic position, which will make the relationship between Iraq and its neighbors tense for years to come, regardless of its leader.

Saddam's continuation in power also has some surprising benefits. First, Saddam's aggressiveness and outright evil have created a strong and broad consensus that Iraq must be contained to some degree. Any successor to Saddam, even if cast from the same mold, would probably receive control over Iraq's purse strings from the United Nations (UN), a warm welcome in most regional capitals, and the benefit of the doubt most generally. Second, Saddam's incompetence as a general is matched only by his ineptitude as a diplomat. Any likely successor, even including those who share his aggressive ambitions, would likely be more skilled. The United States and its allies should continue to seek Saddam's removal but should prepare for trouble down the road, especially in the event that they succeed incompletely, and a leader from the same power base emerges.

---

## Some problems are inherent to Iraq's strategic position, regardless of its leader

---

### Iraq's Troubling Geopolitics

Iraq cannot escape its neighborhood. Geopolitics shape Iraq's foreign policy almost as much as the regime that rules in Baghdad, limiting the choices that even the most benign ruler could make. Iran and Iraq have an enduring rivalry that predates the 1958 Iraqi revolution and, because of the Iran-Iraq War, is bitterly ingrained in both sides at a popular level. Turkey has conducted repeated incursions into Iraq to quash Turkey's Kurdish movement, the Kurdish Workers Party (PKK), and would continue to do so as long as the movement used Iraqi territory to launch attacks on Turkey. Syria's hostility dates in part from Damascus's and Baghdad's rival claims to leadership of the Ba'th cause, and thus leadership of the Arab nationalist camp. Relations have improved under Syria's new leader, Bashar al-Assad, but

suspicion remains high. Any new regime in Baghdad must manage these difficult challenges.

WMD is perhaps the most problematic issue. Iran, Pakistan, Syria, Turkey, and Israel all possess various types of WMD and missiles. A future Iraqi regime seeking WMD as a deterrent is thus understandable, if not necessarily desirable. Almost any regime would seek to possess a wide range of chemical weapons, in particular. For Iraq, in contrast to most possessors of chemical weapons, these weapons are of proven utility—both to repress at home and to intimidate abroad. The frequent use of chemical weapons during the Iran-Iraq War, and the belief that they played a key role in the victory over Iran, has led to widespread support for their acquisition among Iraq's military and much of Iraqi society.

A post-Saddam regime that is less willing to embrace risks and less aggressive in its intentions is also less likely to seek biological and nuclear weapons. Most leaders would probably recognize the tremendous political and economic price that Iraq might pay—and has already paid—for pursuing biological and nuclear weapons. A new regime, therefore, may be willing to abandon the quest for these weapons if international pressure is high. If not, a key distinction is the possession of WMD—particularly biological and nuclear weapons—as opposed to the use of WMD. A successor regime led by a more cautious individual than Saddam is also more likely to be satisfied with the defensive possession of WMD. Even possession, however, will lead to proliferation in the region and increase the chance of accidental use.

Hostility toward Israel is also likely to remain acute. Saddam gained considerable prestige by his repeated threats against Israel. Any successor might seek to gain similar support by maintaining a hostile policy, or at least rhetoric, toward Israel. This hostility appears to have broad support in much of Iraqi society, particularly among the military. Iraq's track record suggests that hostility toward Israel is independent of regime: Iraq sent more than 10,000 men to fight in the 1948 Arab war with Israel, played a small role in the 1967 war, and de-

ployed roughly 60,000 men to participate in the 1973 war.

As with WMD, however, the true question is one of degree. A regime less dominated by Saddam's power base would probably be less hostile to Israel. Iraq's Shi'a and Kurdish populations probably are less hostile toward Israel than the pan-Arab Sunni core. A successor regime in Baghdad is highly unlikely to be friendlier toward Israel, but it might possibly adopt a policy toward Israel closer to that of more moderate Arab states.

---

## Saddam's continuation in power also has some surprising benefits.

---

Any future Iraqi regime would also face tough choices in its quest for balance among Iraqi unity, domestic peace, and human rights. Iraq's sense of national unity was never strong. In 1933 King Faysal I, Iraq's first ruler, observed, "[T]here is still no Iraqi people, but unimaginable masses of human beings, devoid of any patriotic ideal . . . connected by no common tie, giving ear to evil, prone to anarchy, and perpetually ready to rise against any government whatsoever."[6] Years of misrule, particularly the brutality of Saddam, has only worsened communal relations. In addition to the slaughter of the Kurds and the Shi'a, Saddam has also pitted tribe against tribe and decimated Iraqi civil society. Even if Saddam and his henchmen are removed from power, their bitter legacy will remain strong. Kurds in particular are likely to be highly suspicious of any regime in Baghdad that seeks more than nominal control over their activities. If tribal, ethnic, or sectarian tension grows when Saddam falls, a successor regime will be hard-pressed to end any violence without resorting to significant repression.

Nor will a successor regime likely be free of territorial ambitions. Irredentism has a long history in Iraq. Iraq's leadership before the 1958 revolution sought to persuade the British to include Kuwait in a confederation with Jordan and Iraq. After Kuwait's independence in

1961, 'Abd al-Karim Qasim claimed Kuwait as part of Iraq—even though this declaration isolated Iraq in the Arab world—foreshadowing the claims Saddam would make almost 30 years later. Although a successor regime would not have Saddam's personal honor entangled in Iraq's claim to Kuwait, it would possibly use this claim to shore up its flagging popularity or otherwise distract Iraqis from domestic trouble.

Finally, the dispute over the Shatt al Arab waterway is particularly troublesome and likely to recur. The 1937 agreement over the Shatt al Arab, on the Iranian border, had little support in Iraq. Iraqi rulers before Saddam have claimed sovereignty over disputed parts of the Shatt and have even made claims to the Iranian province of Khuzistan. Moreover, the long and bitter war with Iran has etched itself on the Iraqi consciousness. Even more than Iraq's claim to Kuwait, troubled successor regimes may try to seize on the rivalry with Iran to resuscitate their popularity in the event of economic difficulties or domestic unrest.

## Two Scenarios for Iraq's Future

The transition from Saddam to his successor will almost certainly be chaotic. How Saddam will lose power—from a coup, assassination, insurrection, lucky bomb, or natural causes—is not clear. Iraq has no tradition of peaceful regime change, and civil society has been shattered.

Predicting the why, how, and when of Saddam's removal from power is impossible. Although lacking so many basic skills, the Iraqi dictator has shown a genius for survival. He has survived murderers within his family, would-be military coups, competitors within the Ba'th party, Shi'a revolutionaries, Syrian assassins, the revolutionary zeal of the clerical regime in Iran, and U.S. air strikes. He has weathered these challenges with a combination of ruthlessness and luck, centralizing power in the hands of a trusted few while keeping potential rivals at each other's throats or removing them from power.

In the most obvious terms, a replacement could come either from within Saddam's current power base or from outside it. Saddam's power base consists of military and paramilitary organizations—such as the Republican Guard, the Special Republican Guard, and the Popular Army—intelligence services, several key Sunni tribes (and a smaller number of Shi'a tribes), nontribal elements from or near Saddam's hometown of Tikrit, and Ba'th party hacks. These groups are united by their belief that their survival and prosperity are linked to Saddam's continuation in power.

---

## In war, it is better if your enemy is weak, and Saddam helps keep Iraq isolated.

---

If Saddam took a bullet—and if the assassin did not have the ability to seize power for himself—an individual from these ranks could most easily take power. This individual could be one of Saddam's sons, a close family member, or an uneasy junta that represented various key elements of the regime. In any event, Iraq's security and elite military forces likely will be important actors.

Such an individual would have the network and apparatus for seizing power and could appeal to fellow cronies on the grounds of survival: if an outsider seizes the helm, they will fall together. Any would-be successor who lacked support from security and military forces would have trouble maintaining and consolidating power. A 1995 CIA study contended that Saddam's successor would come from the same "political culture" as Saddam, sharing a commitment to Iraq's hegemony and hostility to the West.[7]

Should Saddam fall, whether one of his cronies will assume power is uncertain. Saddam has preserved power in part by keeping rivals weak, off-balance, and at each other's throat. His fall could lead to bloodletting among the elite, as rival factions seek power but are all too weak to hold it. Thus, a leader could possibly come to the fore from outside Saddam's power base.

The range of plausible contenders from outside Saddam's power base is even wider. Replacements could include a member of a militant Shi'a group, an officer from the regular army, an Iraqi exile with democratic leanings, or—as is most likely—someone whom those outside Iraq do not anticipate or know at all. That individual will act according to his beliefs, personality, and power base—factors that are impossible to weigh given our lack of knowledge about him.

The role the United States or other outside powers play in removing Saddam from power is another important factor. No country likes outsiders to impose a government on it: Iranian nationalists, for example, never forgave the shah for returning to power in a U.S.-backed coup in 1953. Certain segments of Iraqi society are highly nationalistic. The 1958 coup that overthrew the monarchy occurred in part because Arab nationalist officers perceived the regime as too close to the West. By openly backing one candidate for power and helping place him on the throne, the United States and its allies might damage his nationalist credentials, weakening his regime in the long term. Nationalists would inevitably tar him as a U.S. puppet, dismissing any rapprochement he made with the United states or its regional allies as quid pro quo. This disadvantage is not necessarily fatal. Almost all Iraqis would welcome the new leader as a long-awaited replacement for Saddam. Nevertheless, he would have one strike against him in the struggle to consolidate power.

If Saddam fell of his own accord, however, the new leader's nationalist credentials would be far stronger. Even if the United States removed Saddam (for example, through a lucky cruise missile strike) but did not install a replacement regime, the new leader would not be perceived as Washington's quisling.

Any successor to Saddam would probably have a brief honeymoon abroad. If Saddam fell, the international community and the Arab world would likely welcome Iraq back—even if the new leader came from within Saddam's power base. An exception to this probable embrace of a new Iraqi leader would occur if Saddam's sons 'Udayy or Qusayy, or one of his more heinous henchmen, such as 'Ali Hassan al-Majid, took power. A honeymoon would be particularly likely if the United States helped bring about the change of government. Washington would feel compelled to work with the new leader, having worked so hard to bring about a change in regime.

Even though the United States has tried in its official statements to focus on the behavior of the Iraqi regime, all too often it has fallen back on the dangers that Saddam, the individual, poses. This perception is even more widespread outside the United States. France and Russia, already eager to rehabilitate Saddam's Iraq, would likely use his removal as a pretext for normalizing relations, citing the need to work with any successor regime to ensure it does not follow in Saddam's path. In the Arab world, widespread sympathy exists for the suffering of the Iraqi people. If Saddam fell, a call to help restore Iraq and rebuild society would have widespread appeal.

## The Real, but Limited, Benefits of Saddam's Removal

Saddam's removal would yield at least two benefits for the region and for the United States. First, any successor to Saddam would very likely be far more cautious. Saddam, more than most leaders, considers military aggression, the use of WMD, and other dangerous activities to advance his interests.[8] Fearing the threat from Ayatollah Ruhollah Khomeini and the Islamic revolution in the late 1970s, Saddam attacked Iran rather than negotiate. To avoid economic hardship in 1990, Saddam attacked Kuwait rather than focus on economic development. Nor have the recurrent crises in Baghdad since then given any indication that Saddam has learned his lesson: he continues to bully, threaten and provoke. As Amatzia Baram notes, "All the existing evidence points [in] one direction, namely that the Iraqi president is a high-risk gambler not only when it comes to his conventional army, but, also in terms of his nonconventional arsenal."[9] Although a successor to Saddam would possibly be a risk-taker, in Iraq's foreign policy, any replacement—even one who shared Saddam's ambitions—would most likely be far more cautious that Saddam is.

The second benefit would be the possibility of better, though not necessarily warm, relations between Iraq and its neighbors and between Iraq and the United States. Saddam is a vengeful man. He believes that he must maintain his honor, which in turn requires dominating any confrontation. He is willing to wait years to wreak vengeance on his perceived enemies, killing and torturing those he believes have slighted him or his family. With a similar motive in mind, Saddam tried to assassinate former President George Bush, the architect of the military coalition that defeated him. His sense of honor demands that those who shamed or defeated him be punished, a view that makes better relations with Kuwait, Saudi Arabia, or the United States unlikely. Saddam has also played up domestic hostility to the United States and its regional allies, blaming them for the impoverishment and isolation of Iraq. Improving relations at this point would undermine what little credibility he possesses with the Iraqi public. Saddam's replacement would have neither the personal nor political baggage that has arisen from 10 years of confrontation, making moving beyond the past and working with Iraq's former opponents easier.

## The Dangers of a Successor from Within Saddam's Power Base

Saddam's removal from power would not be an unmitigated benefit for Iraq's adversaries. A hostile post-Saddam Iraq will continue to pose significant dangers to the United States and its allies. In war, it is better if your enemy is weak, and Saddam helps keep Iraq isolated. Imagining the survival of sanctions or weapons inspections after Saddam's fall is difficult. His replacement, even if as brutal and as reckless, would not generate the same hostility.

In addition to keeping Iraq isolated, Saddam is a poor strategist and general. Saddam sees the army as a threat to his regime as well as an instrument for domination abroad. He has politicized the Iraqi armed forces—cronies and politically loyal officers advance through the ranks rather than those with demonstrated military skill. Over the years, Saddam's friends, relatives, and cronies have played key roles in Iraq's military, even if they have little or no military experience. In addition, Saddam often

exercised direct control over military operations, stifling innovation at all levels. Saddam regularly rotates senior officers to prevent any of them from building independent authority to his rule and thus posing the risk of leading a coup. He has also appointed commissars to ensure that the military remains in accord with his regime.[10]

Saddam provides poor strategic direction to Iraq's military. In the Iran-Iraq War, he underestimated the strength of Iran's revolution and wrongly believed that terror attacks would induce surrender. After invading Kuwait, he held out for the U.S. ground offensive, believing that the United States and its allies could not stomach the casualties necessary for a ground war. These poor assessments make Saddam a dangerous foe who does not always recognize superior force when he confronts it and uses Iraq's limited resources poorly. Thus, Iraq under Saddam is more likely to be aggressive, but also more likely to blunder when it does so. Iraq under one of Saddam's cronies may be less aggressive, but also less susceptible to failure.

Saddam's diplomatic skills are poor as well. Saddam blusters instead of soothes in his diplomacy, alienating potential friends. As a result, sanctions, inspections, and other methods of keeping Saddam's regime weak have continued for far longer than their creators anticipated. As Pakistan's UN ambassador noted, "Every time lifting the sanctions comes up, the Iraqis do something to ensure that sanctions will not be lifted."[11] This clumsiness may change with new leadership.

## The Bigger Picture

Members of Saddam's power base share many of his most troubling ambitions, suggesting that if a crony replaced Saddam it would still lead to many problems between Iraq and its neighbors. Like Saddam, his cronies are committed to making Iraq the strongest regional and Arab power. They see Iraq as the logical heir to Nasser's Egypt. Moreover, they are hostile to Israel, Iran, the Gulf states, and the United States—although not in the same personal manner as Saddam.

If Saddam's replacement came from outside Saddam's power base, the future would look far brighter. First, the new leader is unlikely to share in the dream of Iraq as the regional hegemon and as the strongest Arab power. Past Iraqi regimes, such as that of Qasim and King Faysal, were far more prudent in their foreign affairs and indeed tried to resist more sweeping revolutionary movements, even as they tried to use their fervor to bolster their own cause. Such prudence is particularly likely if the new leader is a Shi'a or otherwise came from outside the Sunni Arab nationalist core that has long dominated Iraq. Such a leader would have more difficulty donning the mantle of Arab nationalism, which has long been associated with the Sunni school of Islam, forcing him to focus on increasing his appeal within Iraq itself.

A replacement from outside Saddam's power base would also be more likely to concentrate on Iraq's myriad problems at home rather than adventures abroad. Iraq's economy and society are in shambles. What was once a prosperous and advanced nation has, after 10 years of war, sanctions, and isolation, become poor and backward. Saddam's base supported his war with Iran and his attack on Kuwait—and accepted his continued confrontation with the anti-Iraq coalition—despite the resultant prolongation of sanctions and isolation. Any leader who relied more on popular support would have to take measures to improve Iraq's economy and rebuild its society.

A leader from outside Saddam's power base also might be able to restore, or at least improve, domestic harmony in Iraq. Saddam's base shares Saddam's commitment to an Iraq in which Kurds, Shi'a, and other marginalized communities have little voice. They have promoted a pan-Arab identity to strengthen their position in Iraqi society. In this respect, Saddam's base, which disdains and fears Iraq's other communities, fully supports him. It shares his view that a narrow few should rule Iraq and that repression is the most effective tactic for keeping the domestic peace. A leader from outside this core could only be more inclusive.

A new leader who was not a crony of Saddam also would be more likely to improve ties with Iraq's neighbors and the United States. Such a leader could blame Iraq's many problems on Saddam's foolish wars and seek sympathy and support from Iraq's former enemies. Ironically, a leader backed openly by Washington might be less able to moderate Iraq's foreign policy. A leader who came to power with U.S. assistance might have to oppose Washington on several high-profile issues to avoid charges of being a U.S. puppet.

## Implications for U.S. Policy

The above assessment suggests that Saddam's removal is desirable but that considerable risks will remain after his fall. Most worrisome is the possibility that a leader would come to power with the same ambitions as Saddam. This leader not only is likely to be a far more skilled commander and statesman than Saddam but is also likely to be welcomed back into the international community and Arab fold with few reservations. The region could thus face an Iraq that has aggressive intentions but is able to rebuild its conventional forces, acquire WMD, and otherwise strengthen itself for a confrontation.

Such a successor, however, would probably still be preferable to Saddam because he would be more cautious. He would likely recognize that the continued pursuit of nuclear or biological weapons would carry grave risks and could lead to Iraq's isolation anew. Moreover, as long as the United States maintains a robust military presence in the Gulf region, he is likely to be deterred from any adventures, recognizing that a confrontation with the superior U.S. force would be disastrous.

---

### Saddam's removal is desirable but considerable risks will remain after his fall.

---

The greatest benefits for the region and for the United States would come from a change in Iraq's elites, not just Saddam's fall. In addition to installing a more cautious ruler at Iraq's helm, such a change would produce a regime that is far less committed to Sunni hegemony over Iraq and to Iraq's hegemony in the broader Arab world—greatly increasing the possibility of regional and domestic peace.

Managing the transition will be especially important. Although how Saddam will be replaced is unclear, his fall will send shock waves throughout Iraq. The most important role outsiders can play is establishing limits to indicate clearly what behavior is not acceptable. Statements—backed by credible shows of force—that the United States will not tolerate Iraqi troop concentrations near its border with Kuwait, Jordan, Turkey, or Saudi Arabia, or that WMD use will invite international retaliation, will help deter any conflict between Iraq and its neighbors and avoid any accidental escalation in tension.

The United States and its allies also must try to limit outside meddling in Iraq's politics in the event of Saddam's fall—or at least ensure that the meddling is to their advantage. Both Iran and Turkey have strong interests in ensuring that a friendly, or at least not actively hostile, regime takes power in Baghdad. Both are concerned that restive Iraqi minorities might inflame tension within their own countries.

Outside powers can also help prevent or limit civil strife during a transition. If Iraq's communities believe they have been left to their own devices after Saddam falls, they are likely to arm and mobilize in self-defense—actions that have the potential of setting off a dangerous spiral that will lead all communities to take up arms. An outside troop presence might calm some of these fears.

Finally, the United States and its allies must recognize the limits of any success in removing Saddam from power. Even in the unlikely event that Saddam and his entire power base are swept from power, the United States and its allies will still have fundamental clashes with Iraq. Iraq's possession of WMD, particularly chemical weapons, will remain on the top of the list, but so too will Iraq's attitude toward the Middle East peace process, human rights, and continuing territorial ambitions. Even as Washington works to ensure Saddam's fall, it must recognize that his removal from power will not make all these problems disappear.

## Notes

1. Rend Rahim Francke, "Symposium: After Saddam, What Then for Iraq?" *Middle East Policy* 4, no. 3 (February 1999): 13.
2. Andrew and Patrick Cockburn, *Out of the Ashes: The Resurrection of Saddam Hussein* (New York: HarperCollins, 1999), p. 43.
3. C. David Welch, assistant secretary of state for international organization affairs, testimony before the House International Relations Committee, March 23, 2000.
4. See Daniel Byman, "Proceed with Caution: U.S. Support for the Iraqi Opposition," *The Washington Quarterly* 22, no. 3 (Summer 1999): 23–38; and Daniel Byman, Kenneth Pollack, and Gideon Rose, "Can Saddam Be Toppled?" *Foreign Affairs* 78, no. 1 (January/February 1999): 24–41, for more on the motivations behind U.S. support for the opposition and potential problems that lie ahead.
5. Amatzia Baram, "Saddam Husayn Between His Power Base and the International Community," *Middle East Review of International Affairs* 4, no. 3 (December 2000).
6. Hanna Batatu, *The Old Social Classes and the Revolutionary Movements of Iraq: A Study of Iraq's Old Landed and Commercial Classes and of Its Communists, Ba'thists, and Free Officers* (Princeton, N.J.: Princeton University Press, 1978), p. 28.
7. James W. Moore, "Après Saddam, Le Deluge? Speculating on a Post-Saddam Iraq," *Middle East Policy* VI, no. 3 (February 1999), p. 37.
8. For an interesting analysis of Saddam's decisionmaking, see Jerrold M. Post, "The Defining Moment of Saddam's Life: A Political Psychology Perspective on the Leadership and Decision-Making of Saddam Hussein during the Gulf Crisis," in Stanley A. Renshon; ed., *The Political Psychology of the Gulf War: Leaders, Publics, and the Process of Conflict* (Pittsburgh, Pa.: University of Pittsburgh Press, 1993), pp. 49–66.
9. Baram, "Saddam Husayn Between His Power Base."
10. For a review, see Andrew Parasiliti and Sinan Antoon, "Friends in Need, Foes to Heed: The Iraqi Military in Politics," *Middle East Policy,* Vol. VII, no. 4 (October 2000): 130–140.
11. Eric W. Herr, "Operation Vigilant Warrior: Conventional Deterrence Theory, Doctrine, and Practice," (thesis, School of Advanced Airpower Studies, Maxwell Air Force Base, Ala., June 1996), p. 17

Daniel Byman is research director of the RAND Center for Middle East Public Policy.

*Article 8*

*The Economist,* December 23, 2000

A BLUEPRINT OF ISRAEL

# Dreaming of Altneuland

Nearly a century ago, the founder of modern Zionism imagined an "old-new" land much like today's Israel. Much like, but also much unlike

IF ONLY it could have come true. By 1948, many thought it had: after two millennia of exile, the Jewish people had a homeland, in the land where its ancestors had lived. But it was not the homeland dreamed of by Theodor Herzl, the founder of modern Zionism, in his visionary novel "Altneuland", published in 1902. Herzl had made the mistake that many Zionists have made, or chosen to make, after him. His "old-new land" was not "a land without a people for a people without a land". A century ago, Palestine, part of the Turkish empire, was indeed thinly populated. But people there were, and most were not Jews. In Herzl's dream, the existing Arabs welcomed the vigorous newcomers whom he imagined settling there in the 1920s, and the new society they created. Even before that decade, in the real world, was over, he was to be proved bloodily wrong.

His mistake was less obvious in 1902 than it looks now. Europe still believed in its right to colonise the world, and the benefits it brought by doing so; within the past 20 years, the British had taken control of all Egypt, not just a sliver of the Levant. Besides—though it is hard to spot in the book— Herzl's future Altneuland was not independent, but still under Turkish rule, part of an empire in which, in 1902, people of umpteen nationalities and faiths did in fact co-exist. Bulgars, Anatolian Greeks, Armenians, Syrians and sundry other Muslims: they all had their place, not always comfortable, but, on the whole, theirs, and they had learned to live with their different neighbours. Why not a Jewish place, and a people living in harmony with its neighbours, indeed its fellow-citizens? Herzl, after all, had just been trying to negotiate that very thing with the Turks.

## A Jewish land, or just a land of Jews?

At the time, the criticism directed at his book was quite different. To the many non-Zionist Jews, this was just another flight of a fantasy that threatened their position in West European societies. To many others, especially in Eastern Europe, the trouble was that Herzl's place was more new than old, and not especially Jewish. They were half right. Seen from today, Altneuland is essentially a bit of comfortable, cultured, bourgeois 1900-ish Vienna transplanted to the Levant by people who happen to be Jews.

It's true that at a Passover supper Herzl's hero, Friedrich Loewenberg, a Jew who had found that condition in Vienna a curse, not a blessing,

pronounced the *Haggadah* with a penitent's zeal, his throat often tight with emotion. It was almost 30 years ... Then had come "enlightenment", the break with all that was Jewish, and the leap into the void. At this Seder table, he seemed to himself a prodigal son returned to his own people.

But this is not every family's Seder. One guest is Friedrich's friend, the older, wealthy Adalbert Kingscourt (by origin, von Koenigshoff, a German nobleman), with whom he set out 20 years earlier on the travels that brought them to Altneuland. There are three Christian clerics. And, amid the harmony of faiths, the guests listen to an account, on a phonograph roll, of the achievements of the New Society for the Colonisation of Palestine. Altneuland is a land of town planning, engineering, lively commerce, industry, mechanised farming. It has a mixed economy, with many co-operatives. It is run by a benevolent technocracy. There is voting, but little politics: "our courts have repeatedly ruled that the term 'professional politician' is an insult". And Jewish culture, Jewish faith? The common tongue is Yiddish. The Temple has been rebuilt. But the book's most visible rabbi, one Dr Geyer, heads not a synagogue, but a faction within the New Society.

He is hostile to further immigration, and non-Jewish membership in the New Society. The book's second hero—in truth, its real one—David Littwak, son of an ex-peasant street pedlar in Vienna, proclaims, in contrast, that

the New Society rests on ideas that are the common stock of the whole civilised world ... It would be unethical to deny a share in our commonwealth to any man, wherever from, whatever his race or creed.

One of Littwak's friends is Reschid Bey, a Berlin-educated Muslim whose father

was among the first to understand the beneficent character of the Jewish immigration ... Reschid himself is a member of our New Society.

Reschid is very clear about it. "Were not the old inhabitants ruined by the Jewish immigration. Didn't they have to leave?" Kingscourt asks. No, he replies:

It was a great blessing for all of us. Naturally the landowners gained most, because they were able to sell to the Jewish society at high prices ... [But] those who had nothing stood to lose nothing, and could only gain. And they did gain: opportunities to work, prosperity. Nothing could have been more wretched than an Arab village at the end of the 19th century. The peasants' clay hovels were unfit for stables. The children lay naked and neglected. Now everything is different. They benefited from the progressive measures of the New Society whether they joined it or not ... These people are better off than at any time in the past.

"You're queer fellows, you Muslims," Kingscourt goes on. "Don't you regard these Jews as intruders?"

You speak strangely, Christian. Would you call a man a robber who takes nothing from you, but brings something? The Jews have enriched us, why should we be against them?

But do ordinary Arabs think the same?

They more than anyone, Mr Kingscourt. Excuse me, but it was not in the West that I learned tolerance. We Muslims have always got on better with the Jews than you Christians.

As for centuries was true. And the members of the New Society think likewise. In the vote for its congress, the prejudiced Dr Geyer comes nowhere, Littwak triumphs and then becomes the society's new president, the obvious candidate, the older man who built Altneuland, having stood down in his favour.

It's a classic secular-Zionist vision. There were moments in the real 1920s when some serious people believed it possible. But it was always utopian, probably even in the conditions of 1902. Even by the 1930s—long before the anti-colonial upsurge after 1945, or the mass Jewish migration to Israel—the Arab Revolt in British-mandate Palestine was to prove this bit of Herzl's dream a pipe-dream: you can't flood foreigners, however deserving or skilled, into a region and expect that they'll be welcome.

Here is the missing element in "Altneuland": except that the New Society runs a farm penal colony, there's not a hint of force, not even Turkish force. In reality, some Jewish settlers, quite early, had at times to carry guns. And today's Israel, though it doesn't say so too loudly, owes its creation and survival no more to Herzl than to the harsh realists of Zionism, men like Avraham Stern or the young Menachem Begin, who argued that if Jews were to have their state, or indeed a future, they would do so with a rifle at their sides or not at all. In Herzl's dreamland, all is done by worth, thought, skill and civilised decision.

Indeed, having defeated malaria in Palestine, one scientist dreams of doing the same in Africa, thus making "vast areas available for the surplus populations of Europe", and for black Americans too:

I have lived to see the restoration of the Jews, I should like to pave the way for the restoration of the Negroes.

Life should be that simple. Visionary as he was, when Herzl wanders off his main point in this novel, he is a child of his time. He depicts harshly the anti-Jewish hostility that pushed

Friedrich to leave Europe. But, with mass emigration to Altneuland, and thereby less "Jewish competition", that hostility, avers one recent migrant, "has ceased to exist". Still less does Herzl foresee (any more than did others, far later) even a hint of the Nazi horrors that were to come.

## Greening the desert

In some other ways, though, Altneuland is not too far from the real Israel, at least in its early decades.

The first step to it was to buy land, before the New Society's plans became public knowledge; then, having asked the Turks for the time being to maintain controls on immigration, to select suitable immigrants. Prefabricated housing was bought from France, timber from Sweden, iron from Germany, all this, and the shipping, being centrally organised. Supply of the countless everyday items, however, was put out to tender by European department stores, carefully scrutinised for any hint of a cartel. These set up branches, and as the new markets flourished, manufacturing sprang up. Railways were built right and left, with American and (improbably) Russian capital, interest payments being guaranteed by the New Society. And hey presto, at Swiss Family Robinson speed, Altneuland's economy was born.

Not without dispute. Its main organiser

> was reproached for enriching the businessmen. I did not mind . . . If firms made large profits, I was content. Our own cause was served. People will rush to a place where gold grows out of the earth. How it grows does not matter.

Yet, though the economy is mixed, the New Society itself is "a syndicate of co-operative societies, a syndicate that comprises industry and commerce [and] keeps the welfare of the workers in mind." Shades of early Israel's Histadrut. No pure kibbutzim are visible, but farming is mainly done by co-ops.

One may farm for oneself, but actual members of the New Society cannot own land; Reschid Bey has sold his orange groves to it, then leased them back, on the 49-year lease later used by the Jewish National Fund.

And sure enough the newcomers have made the desert bloom. Indeed, they are even smarter than the real Israelis. For a start, they have dug a canal from the Mediterranean to the Dead Sea, and use its final falls for hydro-power, enabling them to employ electric ploughs, instead of the draught cattle that they first planned to import. More than that, from the Dead Sea they draw "great quantities of fresh water" for irrigation—a miracle of chemistry that Herzl wisely (or not noticing, one suspects) does not further explain.

His real lesson, though, was for the Jews of his day. In Altneuland "religion had been excluded from public affairs", and its extremely vigorous cultural life rings more of Vienna than Jerusalem. But there, in the Old City, are two new buildings. One, oh dreams, is the Palace of Peace, the other—site unspecified—the new Temple. Seated in this, Friedrich reflects:

> What a degraded era that was, when Jews had been ashamed of everything Jewish . . . They need not have been surprised at the contempt shown them; they had shown no respect for themselves.

> And out of those depths they had raised themselves. Jews looked different now, because they were no longer ashamed of being Jews. Other nations were grateful to them when they produced some great thing; but the Jewish people asked nothing of its sons except not to be denied.

That part of Herzl's dream has been wholly achieved. One can wonder what he would have thought of another people trying today—albeit by worse methods, because the world paid no attention to good ones—to achieve a land and an identity.

*Article 9*                              *The Chronicle of Higher Education*, September 21, 2001

# The Politics of Holiness in Jerusalem

*By Bernard Wasserstein*

JERUSALEM, we are often told, is a holy city to three world religions. But the holiness of Jerusalem is neither a constant nor an absolute. It may be conceived of as divinely inspired or as a human attribution. What is undeniable is that, considered as a historical phenomenon, the city's sanctity has waxed and waned according to social, economic, and cultural conditions, and, perhaps above all, political influences.

Judaism, Christianity, and Islam claim to venerate Jerusalem as holy—and no doubt the adherents of each make the claim with full sincerity and zeal. But, in the case of the first, religious devotion did not carry with it, until very recently, a demand for restoration of sovereignty. As for the two successor faiths, of each it can be demonstrated that the holiness of Jerusalem was a late historical development rather than present *ab initio*. In all three cases, the dispassionate observer is compelled by the evidence to conclude that the city's sanctity arose as much from political as from purely spiritual sources.

What is at stake here is not merely the destiny of one medium-sized city, nor even the resolution of the Israeli-Palestinian conflict, but nothing less than the future relationship of the Islamic, Christian, and Jewish worlds. Each has invested the Jerusalem question with emotional freight deriving from the attribution of holiness to specific areas of the city. Scholars of all three religions have been mobilized to verify the authenticity of proprietorial claims. As the Palestinian writer Edward Said has conceded, "We must also admit that Jerusalem, in particular, and Palestine, in general, have always provoked extraordinary projections that have combined distant though reverential assertion with rude grabbing."

Thus we find Elie Wiesel, in the summer of 2000, opposing the right of an elected Israeli government to cede Palestinian control over the greater part of the Old City of Jerusalem, which he said was far more central to Jewish identity and consciousness than to Islam. The late A.L. Tibawi, a Palestinian historian who worked in exile in Britain, wrote as if Jerusalem were sacred only to Muslims and Christians, denying Jews any legitimate place there at all.

Such denials continue today. On a recent visit to Jerusalem, I listened to a Palestinian scholar earnestly insisting that any Jewish religious interest in the Temple Mount was bogus, since the ancient Jewish Temple could be proved to have been sited elsewhere. There is nothing new in all this. Under Muslim, Christian, and Jewish rulers, generations of scholars have acted as handmaidens of power, embroidering history to justify exclusive political pretensions.

TWO JEWISH VOICES. The first is that of Ananus, the oldest of the priests of Jerusalem on the eve of the destruction of the Second Temple 70 years after Christ. According to the account of his contemporary Josephus, Ananus, in tears and casting his eyes toward the Temple, which had been seized by the party of Jewish extremists known as Zealots, said: "Certainly it had been good for me to die before seeing the house of God full of so many abominations, or those sacred places that ought not to be trodden upon at random filled with the feet of these blood-shedding villains." The second voice is that of the proto-Zionist Moshe Leib Lilienblum. Writing in 1882 of the future Jewish state in Palestine, he declared: "We do not need the walls of Jerusalem, nor the Jerusalem temple, nor Jerusalem itself."

Two Jewish voices; two Jewish views of Jerusalem.

The Jewish presence in the Holy Land may, as we are often told, have remained continuous throughout the period between the end of the second Jewish Commonwealth and the rise of Zionism. The contention is sometimes extended to an allegedly continuous Jewish presence in Jerusalem. For example, the first president of Israel, Chaim Weizmann, in a speech in Jerusalem in 1948, referred to "the unbroken chain of Jewish settlement in this city." Whatever the truth of such a claim for Palestine in general, the evidence for it in the case of Jerusalem is questionable. Jews were forbidden to live in the city under Roman and Byzantine rule. Although some Jewish pilgrims appear to have visited it, there is no evidence of a Jewish community there between the second and the seventh centuries.

Jews resumed residence in Jerusalem after the first Arab conquest of the city, in 638. A number of documents in the Cairo *Geniza* (a store of old manuscripts uncovered at the end of the 19th century) record financial contributions by Jews in Egypt, Syria, and Sicily toward the support of poor Jews and the maintenance of a synagogue next to the Western ("Wailing") Wall in Jerusalem. When the Crusaders conquered Jerusalem in 1099, Jews were once more thrown out of the city. Only after 1260, under the government of the Mamluk sultans, based in Egypt, did they slowly return, although they came into conflict with Christians, particularly over Mount Zion.

The conquest of the city by the Ottoman Turks, in 1516, created conditions for secure Jewish settlement and slow demographic growth. But in the 17th century, the estimated Jewish population was still only one thousand souls, perhaps 10 percent of the total. In that period, the main center of Jewish life in Palestine, certainly of Jewish intellectual life, was not Jerusalem but Safed. For a long time in the 18th century, Jewish bachelors and persons under 60 were forbidden by the Jewish "Istanbul Committee" to live in Jerusalem. The object of the ban was to limit the size of the Jewish population, which, it was feared, would otherwise be too large to support. The earliest community records of the Jews in Jerusalem, as distinct from records elsewhere about them, date from no earlier than the 18th century. As the Israeli historian Jacob Barnai has written, "the lack of material reflects the lack of organic continuity in these communities during the late Middle Ages and the Ottoman period."

Yet if Jewish settlement in Jerusalem for much of the premodern period was sparse and patchy, Jerusalem has nevertheless always been central to the thought and symbolism of Judaism: the resting place of its holy tabernacle, the site of its Temple, the capital of its monarchy, the subject of lamentation from the year 70 down to our own time. Jews faced Jerusalem when they prayed. They called it "the navel of the earth." Biblical literature, *halakha* (Jewish law), *aggada* (nonlegal rabbinic teaching), *tefilla* (liturgy), *kabbala* (mystical writings), *haskala* (the Hebrew enlightenment of the 18th and 19th centuries), and Jewish folklore all celebrated Jerusalem's ancient glory and mourned its devastation. In medieval Spain, Yehuda Halevi and Shlomo ibn Gvirol wrote poignant verses expressive of yearning for Jerusalem. In Eastern Europe, a picture of Jerusalem traditionally hung on the eastern wall of the Jewish house. In our own day, Shmuel Yosef Agnon rejoiced in the renewal of Jewish creativity in the city whose "hills spread their glory like banners to the sky." Throughout the ages, Jerusalem remained the foremost destination of Jewish pilgrimage. Above all, Jerusalem carried for Jews an overwhelming symbolic significance as the focus of messianic hope and the locus of the imminently expected resurrection.

At the same time, Judaism differentiated between the heavenly Jerusalem (*Yerushalayim shel ma'lah*) and the earthly, or everyday, one (*shel matah*). Religious devotion to the city was not regarded as involving any duty to regain Jewish sovereignty over it. Indeed, when the idea of such a restoration first began to be discussed, in the 19th century, the dominant strain of religious opinion was strongly opposed. That remained true until the destruction of the religious heartland of Jewry, in Eastern Europe, between 1939 and 1945. At least until then, most Orthodox Jewish authorities opposed Zionism as a blasphemous anticipation of the divine eschatological plan. And on this point they found common cause with most early leaders of Reform Judaism—though the two groups would have shrunk with horror from any thought of commonality. Orthodox Zionists were a relatively insignificant stream within the Zionist movement—and equally so within Orthodox Judaism. Zionism, until long after the establishment of the State of Israel, in 1948, remained predominantly and often aggressively secular.

Early Zionist thinkers generally avoided attributing special importance to Jerusalem. The exponent of "spiritual" Zionism, Ahad Ha'am, was repelled by his first encounter with the Jews of Jerusalem, in 1891; later, when he moved to Palestine, he chose to settle in Tel Aviv. The founder of political Zionism, Theodor Herzl, was shocked by Jerusalem's filth and stench when he first visited, in 1898. When Arthur Ruppin set up the Zionist Organization's first Palestine Office, in 1908, he did so in Jaffa, not Jerusalem. The early Zionist settlers in Palestine, from the 1880s onward, and particularly the socialist Zi-

onists, who arrived in large numbers after 1904, looked down on Jerusalem and all it stood for in their eyes—obscurantism, religiosity, and squalor. In particular, they despised what they saw as the parasitism of Jerusalem's Jews and their dependence on the *halukah* (charitable dole) from co-religionists in Europe and North America. David Ben-Gurion, who was later, as Israeli prime minister, to declare Jerusalem the capital of Israel, did not bother to visit it until three years after his own immigration to Palestine.

> The early Zionist settlers in Palestine, particularly the socialist Zionists, looked down on Jerusalem and all it stood for in their eyes—obscurantism, religiosity, and squalor.

Modern Hebrew literature also contained deeply contradictory tendencies regarding Jerusalem: In the last two decades of the 19th century, writers of the *ahavat Zion* (love of Zion) school tended to extol Jerusalem and sing its praises; modernist poets and novelists, from Haim Nahman Bialik onward, took a more harshly realistic view. In the first half of the 20th century, a stream of writing (Yosef Haim Brenner, Nathan Alterman, Avraham Shlonsky, the early Uri Zvi Greenberg) that was hostile to Jerusalem—loathing it, demystifying it, even stressing its irrelevance—shaped a profoundly negative view of the city in the Hebrew literary imagination. Of course, that was only one stream of thought—but, in its time, perhaps the most influential and truly expressive of the Zionist revolution against Jewish traditionalism.

Thus spiritual values exalting Jerusalem competed with, and were overshadowed by, other religious, social, political, and intellectual forces in forming the ambivalent modern Jewish view of Jerusalem.

TWO CHRISTIAN VOICES. First, St. Jerome (c. 342-420), who went on pilgrimage to the Holy Land and spent the last 34 years of his life in a monastery in Bethlehem. He argued that it was part of the Christian faith "to adore where His feet have stood and to see the vestiges of the nativity, of the Cross, and of the passion." The second voice is that of St. Gregory of Nyssa (4th century), who wrote to a disciple, "When the Lord invites the blest to their inheritance in the Kingdom of Heaven, he does not include a pilgrimage to Jerusalem among their good deeds."

Two Christian voices; two Christian views of Jerusalem.

For Christians, the sanctity of Jerusalem derives wholly from the events associated with the life, death, and resurrection of the Savior in that city. Historically speaking, however, there is no evidence of any particular sanctity attached to Jerusalem by Christians until the 4th century, and it is only then that we encounter the first recorded account of a Christian pilgrimage to Jerusalem.

> Squabbling Christian sects were compelled by the Muslim authorities to hand over the keys to the Church of the Holy Sepulchre—the reputed tomb of Jesus—to a Muslim family for safekeeping.

Recent scholarship has focused on the ecclesiastical struggle in 4th-century Christianity between those who affirmed the holiness of Jerusalem and those who tended to play it down. As P.W.L. Walker writes, "Jerusalem and the 'holy places' showed from the outset that, despite their capacity to be focuses for Christian unity, they also had great potential for division." Walker lays stress on the "largely negative and dismissive" views of Eusebius, bishop of Caesarea, in Palestine (c. 260-340), regarding Jerusalem's holiness. Eusebius's opinion may have derived in part from competition between his episcopal see and that of Jerusalem. Beyond that, it has been argued, his view was born of a desire to combat an incorrect emphasis on the physical, earthly Jerusalem—an error he attributed to the Jews.

By contrast, and in opposition to Eusebius, Bishop Cyril of Jerusalem (c. 320-386) maintained that the "prerogative of all good things was in Jerusalem." That became, indeed, a dominant view in the church. Just as Eusebius's somewhat negative view of Jerusalem has been connected to his attitude toward Jews, the more affirmative Christian attitude to Jerusalem in the early Middle Ages was also bound up with hostility to the Jews. According to Amnon Linder, of the Hebrew University of Jerusalem, "The complete destruction of Jewish Jerusalem and its transformation into a Christian city, with the resultant expulsion, dispersion, and subjugation of the Jews, was seen as a Divine punishment and as an essential stage on mankind's road to complete salvation." The triumph of the Christian theological view of Jerusalem's holiness was, however, an outcome not only of debate among the church fathers, but also of the political triumph of the emperor Constantine, who ruled Jerusalem from 324 to his death in 337. The celebrated journey of his mother, Helena, to Jerusalem to identify the sites of the crucifixion and resurrection marked a turning point in the Christian history of the city. The Anastasis (later known as the Church of the Holy Sepulchre), erected over the reputed tomb of Jesus at Constantine's command and dedicated in 335, replaced a temple to Aphrodite at the same location. Like so many other holy places and shrines in Jerusalem, the Anastasis thus, from its very outset, gave physical expression to competitive religious spirit—in this case, between Christianity and paganism.

With Helena's visit, Jerusalem became firmly established as a center of veneration and pilgrimage for Christians. The *Itinerarium Burdigalense*, an account of a pilgrimage to Jerusalem from Bordeaux in 333, is one of the earliest examples of what became a common literary genre. Christian glorifica-

tion of Jerusalem was briefly challenged in 363, when the pagan emperor Julian the Apostate proposed to rebuild the Temple in Jerusalem. But after his death in battle that year, the process resumed with even greater momentum. It was in full flood by the last two decades of the century, when Egeria, probably a Spanish nun, wrote a narrative of her pilgrimage to Jerusalem—still widely read today.

External financial support for Christian institutions in Jerusalem, as for Jewish ones, is a longstanding feature of the city's history, in the case of the Christians extending back to the Byzantine period. During the first period of Muslim rule over the city, non-Muslims almost certainly still formed a majority of the population of the city. At one point in the early Arab period, there is even said to have been a Christian governor of the province. On Christmas Day 800—coronation day of Charlemagne in Rome—the new emperor is reported to have received the key to the Church of the Holy Sepulchre and the flag of the holy city as tokens of respect from the Patriarch of Jerusalem (or, according to another account, from the Muslim Caliph Harun al-Rashid). Charlemagne and his son Louis built a number of new Christian institutions in Jerusalem. That construction work gave rise to some conflict. In 827, for example, Muslims complained that Christians had built a bigger dome over a church than that over the Muslim shrine of the Dome of the Rock. Similarly, competition in pilgrimages, a feature of religious and commercial life in the city throughout the ages and into modern times, is recorded very early. The pilgrimages and the holy days with which they were associated were frequently occasions of communal violence. On Palm Sunday in 937 or 938, a Christian procession was attacked and the Church of the Holy Sepulchre was burned to the ground. On Pentecost in 966, a number of churches were pillaged. And on September 28, 1009, the Holy Sepulchre was again destroyed, by order of the mad Caliph al-Hakim. It was not rebuilt until 1048—and then only partially.

The conquest of Jerusalem by the Crusader forces of Godfrey de Bouillon, on July 15, 1099, inaugurated a new period of terror against Muslims and Jews, all of whom were driven out of the city, their mosques and synagogues destroyed. The Muslim shrines on the Temple Mount were turned into Christian churches. The Crusader kings carved the city into separate districts based on the nationality of the Christian settlers, the knightly orders, and the various eastern Christian communities. The Orthodox Patriarch was packed off to Constantinople, and the Latins (Roman Catholics) assumed the *praedominium* (right of pre-eminence) over the holy places.

After the final ejection of the Crusaders from Jerusalem, in 1244, Christians were compelled to translate their conception of Jerusalem from an earthly to a heavenly sphere. Christian pilgrimages, however, continued: Chaucer's Wife of Bath went to Jerusalem three times. And books of *Laudes Hierosolymitanae* (praises of Jerusalem) were produced in large quantities. The Christian struggle for Jerusalem now assumed a new form. Having lost the war against the Infidel, Christians embarked on a war against each other.

Now began in earnest the great contest between the Eastern and Western churches for control of the holy places, above all the Church of the Holy Sepulchre, in Jerusalem, and the Church of the Nativity, in Bethlehem. Unable to agree among themselves, the squabbling Christian sects were compelled by the Muslim authorities, in or before 1289, to hand over the keys of the Church of the Holy Sepulchre to a Muslim family for safekeeping. When the last Crusader fortress in Palestine, at Acre, fell in 1291, the only remaining Latin institutional presence in Palestine was that of the Franciscans, who had arrived in 1217. In the early 14th century, Pope Clement VI appointed them to the "Custody of the Holy Land" (*Custodia Terrae Sanctae*). That little outpost of Roman Christianity saw as its primary task the battle against the pretensions of the Eastern churches to proprietorship of the holy places. It fought by every means to uphold the enduring rights in Jerusalem of the true Rome. The fight carried on into modern times and, in modified form, endures still. It has colored every aspect of Christian life in Jerusalem, as well as the diplomacy of the Christian powers in relation to the holy city.

Thus for Christians, as for Jews, though in different ways, Jerusalem was both a symbol of unity and a fault line of profound internal schism.

TWO MUSLIM TRADITIONS. The first is a statement attributed to the Prophet Muhammad, according to which he said, "He who performs the pilgrimage to Mecca and visits my grave [in Medina] and goes forth to fight [in a holy war] and prays for me in Jerusalem—God will not ask him about what he [failed to perform of the prescriptions] imposed on him."

The second tradition concerns Umar, the second Muslim caliph, who reigned at the time of the first Muslim conquest of Jerusalem, in 638. Umar, it is said, was in a camel enclosure when two men passed by. He asked where they came from and they said Jerusalem. Umar hit them with his whip and said, "Have you performed a pilgrimage like the pilgrimage to the Kaaba [in Mecca]?" They said, "No, O Commander of the Faithful, we came from such and such a territory and passed [Jerusalem] by and prayed there." To which Umar said, "Then so be it," and let them go.

---

## The Crusaders' conquest of Jerusalem was greeted by Muslim indifference. The heightening of religious fervor for its recapture may be explained largely by political necessity.

---

Two Muslim voices; two Muslim views of Jerusalem.

For Muslims, the holiness of Jerusalem derives primarily from its identification with the "further mosque" (*al-masjid al-aqsa*), mentioned in the Koran as the place to which the Prophet was carried on his "night journey" from Mecca. From Jerusalem he ascended to the seventh heaven.

There is some evidence, however, to suggest that the attribution of sanctity to Jerusalem was, at least in part, connected to the city's central position in the two precursor religions that Islam claimed to supersede. According to Muslim tradition,

Jerusalem was the first *qibla* (the direction of prayer) before it was changed to Mecca in 624. The practice is not attested to in the Koran, but it is ingrained in Muslim tradition—and has survived within living memory in the practice of some elderly worshippers in the Dome of the Rock.

In the earliest period of Islam, there appears to have been a tendency to emphasize the holiness of Mecca and Medina and to stress the importance of pilgrimages to those cities rather than to Jerusalem. There were also, however, some contrary views, and it was not until the second Islamic century (719–816 of the Christian era) that there developed a general acceptance of the holiness of all three cities. A decisive point came during the caliphate of Abd al-Malik b. Marwan (685–705). He was engaged in conflict with a rival caliph, Abd Allah b. al-Zubayr, who was installed at Mecca. Abd al-Malik built Jerusalem's most impressive surviving religious monument, the Dome of the Rock—often wrongly called the "Mosque of Umar": It is, in fact, a shrine, not a mosque, and has nothing to do with Umar. One authority, Richard Ettinghausen, an Islamic-art historian, has argued that the Dome of the Rock was not merely a memorial to the ascension of the Prophet: "Its extensive inscriptions indicate that it is a victory monument commemorating triumph over the Jewish and Christian religions." The great Hungarian orientalist Ignaz Goldziher argued that Abd al-Malik's motive in building the shrine and reaffirming the city's sanctity was to compete with the rival Meccan caliph and divert the pilgrim trade to his own dominions. That view has been widely accepted, although S.D. Goitein, the distinguished scholar of Islamic-Jewish relations, who worked at the Institute for Advanced Study in Princeton, N.J., disagreed, suggesting that Abd al-Malik's object was to create a structure that could match the magnificent churches of Jerusalem and other towns in geographical Syria. What unites all those interpretations is the attribution of an underlying competitive motive to the caliph. The Arabic name of the city, al-Quds ("the Holy"), first appears only in the late 10th century.

Surprisingly, the conquest of Jerusalem by the Crusaders was greeted, at first, by Muslim indifference rather than fervor for its recapture. Even those Muslims who called for a holy war against the invading Franks refrained, with few exceptions, from stressing the sanctity of Jerusalem—which seems in that period to have been neither widely diffused nor deeply implanted in Muslim thought. A change of attitude emerged only in the mid-12th century. As so often in the history of Jerusalem, heightened religious fervor may be explained in large measure by political necessity. In the 1140s, Zenki, ruler of Mosul and Aleppo, with his son and successor Nur al-Din, called for an all-out war against the Crusader state. Their official propagandists consequently placed a sudden emphasis on the holiness of Jerusalem in Islam. That tendency was further accentuated under the leadership of Saladin, who used the sanctity of Jerusalem as a means of cowing potential opponents. In the late 12th century, the idea of the holy city was invoked no less in internal Muslim quarrels than in the external conflict with Christendom. The Muslim reconquest of Jerusalem, on October 2, 1187, was greeted with an outburst of enthusiasm and rejoicing in the Islamic world. Saladin's victory was hailed in letters, poems, and messages of congratulation. During the following years, the literature in praise of Jerusalem

(*Fadail Bayt al-Maqdis*) was hugely amplified and extended. Muslims were encouraged to resettle there or to go on pilgrimage. Returning pilgrims carried to their homes the concept of the sanctity of Jerusalem.

Henceforth, Muslim rule over the city came to be regarded as a veritable act of faith. In 1191, Saladin wrote to Richard the Lion-Hearted, in the course of armistice negotiations, that even if he (Saladin) were personally disposed to yield the city, the crusading English king "should not imagine that its surrender would be possible; I would not dare even to utter the word in front of the Muslims." Jerusalem was nevertheless returned to the Christians by the Treaty of Jaffa in 1229. Under that agreement, Jerusalem, Bethlehem, and Nazareth were handed over to the Holy Roman Emperor, Frederick II, though the Muslims were permitted to retain their holy places there. At the same time, the walls of Jerusalem were demolished so that it would no longer serve as a fortified point. The result was that, for many years, the city was vulnerable to military attack and to raids from nomads. The treaty was to last for 10 years. After that, fighting broke out again, and, in 1244, the city was sacked by invading Kharezmian Tartars. Only after 1260 was order restored under the Mamluks.

Under Mamluk rule, Jerusalem was not a place of any political importance. The division of the city into four quarters—Muslim, Christian, Jewish, and Armenian—had its origins in this period. Islamic institutions were established and the Muslim character of the city enhanced, though, unlike the Christians, Muslims tolerated the presence of other faiths. Religious groups tended to settle around their most important shrines and holy places: Muslims north and west of the Haram al-Sharif (literally "noble sanctuary"—the name given to the Temple Mount); Armenians in the southwest, near their Cathedral of St. James; the other Christians in the northwest, near the Holy Sepulchre; and the Jews in the south, near the Western Wall. By the dawn of the modern era, divided Jerusalem was a geographical as well as a spiritual fact.

S O WE SEE that within Judaism, Christianity, and Islam there have been countervailing positive and negative tendencies regarding Jerusalem—and that, in each case, political considerations have played a significant part in the affirmation or qualification of Jerusalem's holiness. Competition among the faiths has repeatedly focused on Jerusalem. Each has tried to outbid the other two in claiming Jerusalem as a central religious symbol, often by means of hyperbolic special pleading. Yet each religion has been ambivalent or fractured in its relationship to Jerusalem—in how it has seen the city's degree of holiness, its holy places, and its function in this world and the next. These lines of division have determined the history of the earthly city in the modern period.

This cautionary tale should serve as a warning to those who would invoke religious fervor in support of political claims to Jerusalem. Of course, any settlement must make provision for the legitimate spiritual interests of all three faiths. But those can be met without impairing the longstanding principle of the "status quo," traditionally applied to Jerusalem in religious disputes. Muslims already control the Haram al-Sharif. Every Israeli government since 1967 has recognized their right to do so; none has sought to impose direct Israeli control; none has permitted Jewish extremists, hoping to prepare for the rebuilding of the Temple, to establish a foothold. Christians control all of their holy places and no longer seek to use them as stalking-horses for claims of sovereignty over Palestine. Nor does the Vatican any longer seek the internationalization of Jerusalem (a euphemism for what would, in effect, have been Christian control of the city). As for the Jewish holy place, the Western Wall: That is securely in Israeli hands, and Palestinian representatives, in talks with Israelis in recent years, have accepted that it should remain so.

At his final meeting with Israeli and Palestinian negotiators, on December 23, 2000, President Clinton proposed the application to Jerusalem of "the general principle that Arab areas are Palestinian and Jewish ones are Israeli." That, he suggested, should apply to the Old City. In subsequent discussions at the Egyptian Red Sea resort of Taba, the negotiators made significant progress toward agreement on the outstanding issues regarding a permanent settlement both of the Arab-Israeli dispute, in general, and of the problem of Jerusalem, in particular.

That progress has been cast aside as a result of the continuing Palestinian intifada and the Israeli response. But sooner or later, since neither side can totally defeat the other, the two will have to return to the negotiating table. Jerusalem will once more be on the agenda for discussion. Israel has claimed since 1967 to have "unified" the city. Yet no city in the world today is more deeply divided—politically, socially, religiously. Neither side wishes to see a wall re-erected between Jewish and Arab areas, as existed from 1949 to 1967. The population of the city today, including Arab and Jewish areas beyond the city limits but within its sociogeographic region, is approximately half-and-half Jewish and Arab.

Somehow, a way must be found to enable people to live together—but the task is not helped by the *trahison des clercs* of those scholars who help stir up religious emotions to assert political claims. "The religious mind will not easily relinquish its hold on the sacred ground of mystery and miracle," Edward Gibbon warned in a passage on the Crusades in his *Decline and Fall of the Roman Empire*. "But the holy wars which have been waged in every climate of the globe, from Egypt to Livonia, and from Peru to Hindostan, require the support of some more general and flexible tenet." Of course, the tenet to which Gibbon, a child of the Enlightenment, referred was reason. The faithful may scoff. But does not reason's still, small voice, even in this unreasonable age, have some place in the search for a solution to this most intractable of conflicts?

*Bernard Wasserstein is a professor of history at the University of Glasgow and president of the Jewish Historical Society of England. This essay is adapted from* Divided Jerusalem: The Struggle for the Holy City, *being published this month by Yale University Press.*

*Article 10*

*The World & I*, November 2001

# Israeli Dilemmas

*Ariel Sharon's policy of restraint has failed so far to restore security and reverse the consequences of the failed Oslo process.*

MEYRAV WURMSER

Prime Minister Ariel Sharon came to power in February 2001 during one of the most problematic periods in Israel's history, following the failure of the July 2000 Camp David Israeli-Palestinian talks and the subsequent outbreak of Palestinian violence (the al-Aqsa intifada) in autumn. Sharon, who had been considered unelectable because of his hard-line policies as defense minister in the early 1980s, was elected by the largest margin of any Israeli election.

Eight months into his term, however, his policy has yet to become clear, despite the seemingly straightforward signal sent by Israel's electorate. On the one hand, Sharon has embraced a more robust retaliation to Palestinian terrorism. On the other hand, he seems incapable of completely ruling out further deals with the PLO or abandoning the Oslo framework that brought the PLO to direct negotiations with Israel.

Sharon's policy is confused, in part as a result of his need to navigate a number of pressures. He has tried to maintain U.S. support and avoid the threat of international and domestic ostracism (under which he has labored since the 1982 Lebanon war) by responding to massive terrorist attacks in Israeli cities with restraint. Sharon also operates under domestic political constraints, sharing a national unity coalition with the Left that would fall were he to respond more forcefully to terrorism. The eventual aftermath of the September 11 terrorist attacks in New York City and Washington, D.C., has not played out yet.

His measured response to Palestinian violence seems to have prevented Israel from being blamed, at least by President Bush, for the region's deterioration to the brink of war. So far, however, Sharon's policy of restraint has failed to restore security and reverse the consequences of the failed Oslo process. At this point the key question remains: Is Sharon leading or being led? For that matter, it remains unclear whether he has a plan. The latter determines the answer to the former.

## Policy of restraint

Although not doing everything in its power to fight Palestinian terrorism, Israel took measures against the Palestinian Authority (PA) and pursued a policy of targeted killings of Palestinian terrorist leaders. Starting in August, Israeli tanks also destroyed police stations and other key buildings in various Palestinian-controlled cities, but they were quick to leave those cities and did not attempt to take them over. Sharon never crossed the line into an all-out confrontation with the Palestinians, yet he only partially answered terrorist attacks on Israel.

His restraint has been evident not only in military affairs but in diplomacy and public relations. Israel has not embarked on any significant program to delegitimize the PLO beyond mentioning its endorsement of terror. Nor has Israel raised the issues of the PLO's corruption, severe human rights abuses, anti-American rhetoric and behavior, production of anti-Semitic propaganda, cooperation with Iraq, or any other such things.

In fact, all along, Sharon has not excluded the PLO definitively as a negotiating partner. This was the case even in the face of some of the biggest terrorist attacks in Israel's history. While the PA mobilized its population toward a prolonged conflict with Israel, Sharon's government indicated that it still considers a return to the negotiating table viable.

Indeed, Sharon gave the green light to his foreign minister, Shimon Peres, to meet with senior Palestinian officials to discuss ending hostilities even after consecutive terrorist attacks on August 9 and 12, in Jerusalem and Kiryat Motzkin.

Viewing the Palestinian leaders simultaneously as both terrorists and potential peace partners has rendered Israeli policy contradictory and inconsistent. As a result, during Sharon's first six months in office, his government did not effectively defend the Israeli population from terrorism, nor did it modify PLO behavior enough to allow for resumption of negotiations.

Moreover, not only Israelis are confused. Anti-Arafat Palestinians and other Arabs have as yet failed to discern strategic objectives around which to calibrate their hopes and actions. The lack of clarity has also confused Israel's American allies, both in the new administration as well as in the broader community.

While Sharon is clearly putting military pressure on the PA, its purpose remains undefined. Is he putting terrorist leaders on the run to compromise their operational efficacy? Is he pressuring the PLO to return to the negotiating table? Is he destabilizing the PA to bring the PLO down—an objective that a few Israeli leaders privately support but refuse to admit publicly?

# Why Sharon Was Elected

- Prime Minister Ariel Sharon's inconsistent policies are a response to the dilemmas he inherited from former Prime Minister Ehud Barak.

- Barak, who in the 2000 Camp David talks went further than any other Israeli premier in his willingness to make compromises for the sake of peace, lost the elections after the PLO answered his concessions by launching the al-Aqsa intifida.

- Barak's proposed far-reaching compromises placed him outside the Israeli public consensus, which supported compromises for peace but generally opposed Palestinian sovereignty over Jerusalem's holy sites.

- While Israelis kept hoping for peace, most believed that it could not be reached by the Barak regime.

- They elected Sharon with full knowledge of his reputation for decisive, robust pursuit of their country's interests.

## Domestic constraints

Sharon's fluctuations and inconsistency are the consequence of dilemmas that he inherited from his predecessor, Ehud Barak. In the Camp David talks Barak went further than any other Israeli premier in his willingness to make compromises—even in Jerusalem—for the sake of peace, but he lost the election after the PLO answered his proposed concessions with the intifada.

Barak's far-reaching proposals placed him outside the Israeli public consensus, which supported compromises for peace but generally opposed Palestinian sovereignty over Jewish holy sites in the Old City of Jerusalem, particularly the Temple Mount.

The outbreak of violence after the Camp David summit dismayed many Israelis, even some who had previously supported Barak and the peace process. Sharon's election victory reflected Israel's changing mood, namely, a sharp swing to the right.

While Israelis kept hoping for peace, most believed that it could not be reached with the current Palestinian regime. They elected Sharon with full knowledge, if not confidence, of his past reputation for decisive, robust pursuit of Israel's interests.

Sharon, who defeated Barak by an unprecedented 25 points, began office as one of Israel's more popular prime ministers. Yet, before the election he felt he had to prove that his reputation was un-fair, that he could be a man of peace. His election campaign downplayed his military roles and portrayed him as a kind, elderly grandparent.

Despite the hardening public attitude, Sharon immediately invited his Labor Party opponents to join him in forming a national unity government. The alleged rational for this move was that the majority of Israelis wanted a government of national unity, as would be expected of people who suspect they are on the eve of war.

But, as *Washington Post* columnist Charles Krauthammer noted, this was nothing more than "a government of political convenience, a safety net for careerist politicians." Although he had a huge mandate to take a tougher approach toward the Palestinians, Sharon chose to build a government with his left-wing Labor Party opponents to guarantee his stay in power for more than a few months. Without Labor's support he would have had to form a narrow right-wing government. In the current Knesset, such a government would soon collapse, leading to new elections that might bring Sharon's Likud adversary, former Prime Minister Benjamin (Bibi) Netanyahu, back to power.

The unity government has as its foreign minister Labor's Shimon Peres, the architect of the Oslo peace process. It is frequently split over the appropriate policy vis-à-vis the PA. Although Sharon advocated a policy of restraint in the face of Palestinian terrorism, the left wing of his government believed him to be too hard-line and perhaps willing to sabotage future talks with the PA. According to the *Jerusalem Post*, Peres told Sharon in mid-June that he was "not his clerk to take directives from him" after Sharon nixed a three-way meeting between Peres, Yasser Arafat, and UN Secretary-General Kofi Annan.

By early August, the schism had developed a new dimension. The foreign ministry, controlled by Peres, started producing its own assessments of the PA's behavior, which completely contradicted those of the Israeli Defense Forces and various intelligence agencies. The Sharon-Peres relationship reached its low point in August 9, 2001, after Peres opposed taking action against the PA following the terrorist attack in a pizzeria in Jerusalem that claimed 15 lives.

*One source of pressure:* French Foreign Minister Hubert Vedrine has said that "we can't leave the Israelis and Palestinians alone, face to face, in this atmosphere of growing hate and panicky fear."

Then, Sharon took steps to drop his partnership with Labor and form a narrow coalition with like-minded center and right-wing parties. Peres' reaction was to try to form a political front to pressure the prime minister to negotiate with the Palestinians.

Peres was not the only left-wing challenger. Despite the terror wave that was sweeping Israel, a small but vocal group of Israeli activists published a joint declaration on July 27, 2001, with their Palestinian counterparts calling to end the violence and return to negotiations. Largely ignored by both Israelis and Palestinians, it spoke of the Palestinian terrorism and the restricted Israeli response as morally equivalent.

While the Left criticized Sharon for being too hard line, the Right viewed him as overly conciliatory. West Bank and Gaza settlers, the first and most frequent victims of Palestinian terrorism, were his most vocal critics on the right. At the end of June, when Sharon declared that he would "not lead this nation to war," the frustrated heads of the West Bank Settlers Council responded that he was "causing huge damage because he is establishing the view that . . . there is no escaping a political settlement, which we view as a surrender." The chairman of the Samaria Council rhetorically asked a reporter, "What is the amount of blood that [still] needs to spill before Sharon realizes our reality?"

Some settlers have repeatedly threatened that they will take the law into their own hands unless Sharon's government does more to protect them. One warned, "The area is under anarchy, and therefore, Jewish retaliatory actions against Arabs are to be expected." Indeed, in July and August such actions included shooting and killing Palestinians driving on West Bank roads.

Sharon's own party had also criticized his restraint. In a meeting of the party's central committee on July 22, 2001, after Sharon articulated his view that the appropriate response to terrorism is targeted, Israeli surgical strikes, not large-scale military action, other party members attacked him both for his limited reaction to Palestinian violence and his alliance with the Left. In response, Sharon yelled at his critics, "By yelling and screaming no one has of yet defeated anything. It certainly cannot overcome terrorism or defeat me."

Sharon's biggest concern is his Likud rival, former Prime Minister Netanyahu, now the Right's favored candidate for premiership. Netanyahu, who calls for decisive, rapid action against the Palestinians, is so favored by the central committee that one of Likud's members recently told the *Jerusalem Post* that "Sharon evidently has a serious problem in the party." Even Sharon's son and right-hand man, Omri Sharon, admitted to an Israeli reporter,

"Nothing can be done. The central committee loves Bibi."

## International constraints

While having to show sensitivity to his domestic critics, Sharon must also respond to a variety of international (particularly American and European) pressures to return to the negotiating table. At the same time, he is trying to prove his international image as a right-wing extremist wrong.

Europe, which generally supports anti-Israel positions, wants to send its own observer force to the Middle East. French Foreign Minister Hubert Vedrine told the *Washington Post*, "We can't leave the Israelis and Palestinians alone, face to face, in this atmosphere of growing hate and panicky fear." Israel, however, is adamantly opposed to such a force.

Europe has also challenged Sharon on a personal level. A war-crimes lawsuit was brought against him in early summer 2001 in Belgium for atrocities committed under his command nearly 20 years ago. The furor over this old episode comes at a particularly sensitive time, after nine months of violence.

With America, the picture is mixed. President Bush has clearly pinned blame on Arafat for the violence and considers the ball to be in his court. In an August 24 press conference, Bush said the Israelis "have made it very clear that they will not negotiate under terrorist threat. And if Mr. Arafat is interested in having a dialogue that could conceivably lead to the Mitchell process, then I would strongly urge him to urge the terrorists, the Palestinian terrorists, to stop the suicide bombings, to stop the incursions, to stop the threats."

Vice President Cheney has also weighed in, seemingly justifying Israel's assassination of terrorist leaders. He said to *Fox News* on August 2, "If you've got an organization that has plotted or is plotting some kind of suicide bomb attack, for example, and they [the Israelis] have hard evidence of who it is and where they're located, I think there's some justification in their trying to protect themselves by preempting."

Still, the secretary of state remains attached to the concept of "evenhandedness," so much so that the *Wall Street*

*Journal* labeled Colin Powell's position on Israel as "reeking with moral equivalency." A constant flow of sharp criticism emanates from the State Department spokesmen for virtually any Israeli retaliation, no matter how limited or unlethal. For example, when in response to the pizzeria attack Israel seized the Orient House (PLO headquarters) and blew up police and PLO buildings in Jenin, the State Department issued a strong rebuke, saying, "Israeli incursions into Palestinian-controlled areas are provocative, they do not stop the violence and they undermine efforts to defuse the situation."

After Israel killed the terrorist leader Mustafa Zubari, spokesman Richard Boucher, apparently departing from the president's policy, said, "We think Israel needs to understand that targeted killings of Palestinians don't end the violence, but are only inflaming an already volatile situation and making it much harder to restore calm." Washington's mixed message hardly helps to balance the solidly condemnatory language from virtually all other global capitals.

## Conclusions

Sharon's policy of restraint has resulted from the pressures, both domestic and international, he has faced in his first six months in power. While this is in some ways understandable, Israel's broader strategic goals remain blurry and its political endgame is ill-defined.

Instead, Israel continues to leave the initiative in the hands of its enemies, preferring only to react (sometimes ineffectively) to Palestinian provocations. The conflict thus continues to serve the interests of the party that retains the initiative, namely the PLO. Israel has not attempted to reverse any of Oslo's concessions, or to pursue compensation for losses, such as the PLO's assault and capture of Jacob's tomb in Nablus. It has not even tried to enforce PLO compliance with it previous arms-control commitments (which Israel could accomplish by hitting arms depots or illegal weapons-production facilities).

While Sharon has moved to secure sovereignty over Jerusalem by occupying Orient House and shutting down the PLO intelligence operation in Abu Dis, he has done nothing to stop the PLO-run religious authority still controlling the Temple Mount from dismantling, destroying, and dispersing to unmarked dumps the archaeological remains of the ancient Jewish temple—a practice under way since mid-2000, long before the current fighting erupted. Israel has also neither pressed the United States to move its embassy to Jerusalem nor used the complete breakdown of the Oslo process to resume building settlements in key areas.

Historically one of Israel's most imaginative military thinkers, Sharon now displays his creativity by engaging in the sort of impressive surgical strikes that have traditionally won Israel so much international respect, though not necessarily praise. He also has returned Israel to a policy of retaliating against, rather than appeasing, those who draw Jewish blood.

Yet, Sharon seems not to have formulated the key aspect of war strategy: employing force in order to fundamentally undermine the opposing leader and change the politics of the opposing people so they no longer consider war a worthwhile endeavor. This key concept, known as the "Iron Wall," was formulated in the early twentieth century.

For all of its tactical creativity, Israel has never managed to change the nature of its opponents' politics toward it. So far, there is no evidence that this time is any different. Thus, Sharon seems to be led by pressures rather than overcoming them.

*Meyrav Wurmser is director and senior fellow at the Center for Middle East Policy in Washington, D.C.*

*Article 11*

*The World and I*, November 2001

# Palestinian Challenges

*Yasser Arafat stands alone as the undisputed leader of the Palestinian Authority and the Palestinians.*

## DAVID SCHENKER

One year and going strong, the miniwar between Israel and the Palestinian Authority (PA) that has come to be known as the al-Aqsa intifada has shown no signs of abating, at least until the time of the terrorist attack on September 11. Indeed, neither the Palestinians nor the Israelis appear to be on the verge of blinking. Confirming this as-sessment, Israeli Defense Forces planners this August predicted that the violence might last through 2006.

The grim prospect of another five years of violence has fostered a veritable cottage industry of pontification by Washington pundits. Not surprisingly, the most hotly debated issue remains the same one debated 12 months ago: Does PA Chairman Yasser Arafat control the Palestinian street? And perhaps more important, can he stop the violence?

A primary consideration is the fractious nature of Palestinian politics. The political landscape of the PA is littered with dozens of competing factions, only some of which answer directly to Arafat. Still other groups, such as Hamas, operate

*Threatening Israel with "blood and war":* Marching during a rally in a Palestinian refugee camp outside Damascus are (*from left*) Ahmad Jibril, secretary general of the Popular Front for the Liberation of Palestine, Khaled Mashal, head of the Hamas political bureau, and Ramadan Abdullah Shallah, head of the Palestinian Islamic Jihad.

as rivals to the longtime Palestinian leader. Complicating matters, events of the past year have exacerbated (already extant) splits within Fatah, the faction of the PLO that Arafat most directly controls.

These schisms—combined with the growing popularity of Hamas—have contributed to the concern, often voiced behind closed doors at the State Department, that Arafat is in trouble.

The reports of his demise, however, are greatly exaggerated. Today Arafat stands alone as the undisputed leader of the PA and the Palestinians. Despite the authoritarian nature of his regime, he enjoys approval ratings at home nearing 60 percent. After one year of violence, Arafat retains a firm grip on the reins of power in the PA, and Palestinian society has reached an unprecedented level of unity.

Paradoxically, factionalism has proved a source of strength in the confrontation

with Israel. As Islamic Jihad leader Ramadan Abdullah Shallah described it, "The Palestinian people are now in the same trench."

## The political spectrum

Since the PA's establishment in 1994, there have been wide political cleavages in the West Bank and Gaza. Some of this diversity is related to the Palestinian experience under Israeli occupation, where Palestinians were exposed to the workings of Israel's democratic government.

Likewise, the Palestinian population is among the best educated in the region. These factors have contributed, at least in part, to a high level of open political debate. As such, even though Arafat is an authoritarian atop a repressive political system, the political discourse in the PA remains the most vibrant in the Arab world.

The Palestinian political spectrum today comprises diverse nationalist, leftist, and Islamist factions and organizations, only some of which participate in the PA administration. Arafat's Fatah, the largest faction of the PLO, dominates the PA. The Islamic resistance organization Hamas—the next most prominent organization in this arena—is politically active but is not represented in PA government. It is considered part of the "opposition."

Moreover, Fatah itself has been somewhat divided since 1993, when Arafat entered into the Oslo peace process. While its members openly declare allegiance to Arafat, in practice the organization is split between those following Arafat and ostensibly supporting Oslo and those who have never recognized the legitimacy of the peace process.

Since his return to Gaza in 1994, despite differences, Arafat has managed to

# Part of the System

- The Palestinian political spectrum comprises diverse factions, only some of which participate in the PA administration.

- Arafat's Fatah, the largest faction of the PLO, dominates the PA.

- The Islamic resistance organization Hamas—the next most prominent organization in this arena—is politically active but is not represented in PA government. It is considered part of the "opposition."

- While Fatah members openly declare allegiance to Arafat, some follow him and ostensibly support Oslo, while others have never recognized the legitimacy of the peace process.

- Arafat has managed to keep the diverse factions of the PA under the same tent.

keep Fatah—as well as some of the other peace-process rejectionist organizations—under the same tent. Admittedly, the Islamists have proved somewhat more difficult to keep in the fold, particularly given Arafat's Oslo commitment to "fight terror."

Even so, Arafat never attacked the Hamas infrastructure. At the end of the day, this deliberate dereliction of Oslo allowed Arafat to maintain a dialogue

with Hamas, leaving the door open to future cooperation.

## United diversity

National unity emerged as a top priority for Palestinians shortly after the violence started in October 2000. Facing a major conflagration with Israel, Arafat recognized the need to rally the full complement of Palestinian forces under

his command. Cultivating national solidarity was also important to mask the differences among Palestinians regarding the goals of the violence.

Clearly there was broad public support for continuing the intifada. But while nearly 80 percent of Palestinians support the campaign, no popular consensus has emerged as to the goals of the violence.

Rawhi Fatuh, a top official in Arafat's own Fatah faction, posited that the divergence hinges on two popular opinions about the intifada. Whereas the PA and Fatah officially support violence to liberate "1967 Palestine," the Islamists advocate continued violence to liberate all of Palestine.

To reconcile the divergent tactics and goals and maintain the ongoing participation of a broad spectrum of Palestinians in the violence, Arafat encouraged unity among the various political factions from day one of the intifada. As PA Secretary-General Ahmed Abdel Rahman described it, "We are in a state of war. This dictates that all the Palestinian forces rally around the banner of the intifada and the resistance."

To seal the deal, in November 2000 Arafat initiated a full-scale release of Hamas "security" prisoners from PA jails, unleashing a veritable all-star list of terrorists on Israel. Among those released was the person who assembled the bombs carried by suicide bombers onto two buses in Tel Aviv in 1996. Praising Arafat, Gaza Hamas leader Mahmud al Zahar said the release reflected a "wise decision to enable [Hamas] to participate" in the intifada.

Of course, it's not surprising that Hamas and Fatah, rivals in the Palestinian political arena, would cooperate against Israel. The line between Islamists and nationalists was never very firm in Palestinian politics.

Indeed, rather than declaring a single party allegiance, Palestinian family members, particularly siblings, instinctively choose a diversity of political affiliations. A longtime survival strategy, this tactic virtually ensures that a family never bets on the wrong horse. One need not look far to perceive this pattern in Palestinian society. The brother of Khalil Shikaki—a leading (pro-Oslo) political analyst and pollster in the West Bank—was Fathi Shikaki, who was, un-

*Paying his respects:* Hamas political leader Mahmoud al-Zahar (*right*) pays his respects to Palestinian leader Yasser Arafat after opening his office in the Gaza Strip to receive condolences after the death of PFLP leader Abu Ali Mustafa.

til he was assassinated in Malta in 1996, the head of Islamic Jihad. Likewise, the brother of West Bank Preventative Security Head and Fatah stalwart Jibril Rajoub is a high-ranking Hamas cleric. These relations are emblematic of a fluidity of ideological disposition and discourse in Palestinian politics.

One year into the intifada, Arafat's cultivation of national unity has by and large paid off. There have been relatively few clashes between rival Palestinian factions and organizations. What's more, on the operational level, Hamas and Fatah have been cooperating within the framework of an organization called the National and Islamic Forces. According to West Bank Fatah leader Marwan Barghouthi, who also serves as spokesman for the National and Islamic Forces, "We have never witnessed such unity in the past."

## National and Islamic Forces

Established by the PA during the initial weeks of the intifada, the National and Islamic Forces is a coalition of some 13 Palestinian factions including Fatah, Hamas, the Islamic Jihad, and the Popular and Democratic Fronts for the Liberation of Palestine. This organization, through its decision-making body, the Higher Follow-up Committee, serves as the leading coordinator of intifada activities.

In the first months of the violence, representatives of Palestinian factions met on a daily basis to determine the agenda of attacks and coordinate their tactics against Israel. Communiqués issued by the National and Islamic Forces started appearing in the official Palestinian daily *Al Hayat al Jadida* in early October 2000. These documents included schedules of upcoming events (i.e., demonstrations, funeral processions, "days of rage") as well as the organization's policies. The National and Islamic Forces advocate continuing the armed intifada, rejecting negotiations with Israel, denouncing any return to security coordination with Israel, supporting the execution of Palestinian "collaborators," and strengthening Palestinian national unity. In short, the platform represents the consensus positions of the Palestinian factions regarding the intifada.

The institutionalized unity symbolized by the coalition of National and Islamic Forces has proved a great political success. Arafat himself has met with the organization and encouraged its development. During one such meeting this summer, he pledged that he would "preserve and protect" Palestinian national unity, which he described as "baptized on the blood of the martyrs."

Israel has confirmed the Hamas-Fatah connection by the toe tags. On August 1, for example, Israel killed two Palestinians—one Fatah and one Hamas member—near Janin. According to Israeli reports, the men were en route to an attack.

## Trouble in paradise?

No doubt, Arafat's efforts to unite the diverse factions within the PA have paid off. Even so, periodically there are indications that Arafat's hard-won unity is fragile. On several occasions in recent months, Fatah and Hamas have clashed.

Some of these conflicts appear trivial. In August, for example, members of these groups reportedly engaged in an hour-long shootout after a discrepancy broke out at a Gaza funeral. The disagreement centered around which organization the "martyr" belonged to: Hamas or Fatah. According to a surreal UPI report: "The argument degenerated into exchanges of fire, with mourners leaving the dead body draped in a Palestinian flag in the street for an hour.... Hand grenades were hurled as well." More often, though, the discord has reflected fundamental differences between Fatah and Hamas. Essentially, while both groups support killing Israelis and continuing the intifada, Hamas has relatively few constraints in its tactics but Fatah actions are regulated by Arafat himself. Arafat, of course, has more concerns than those of Fatah. As head of a quasi-state, he has diplomatic considerations. As such, he remains marginally concerned with Western public opinion, specifically that of Washington.

Consistent with his public relations interests, Arafat has occasionally or-

## Regional Problem

The Israeli-Palestinain violence of the past year has reverberated throughout the region. Not only do Middle Easterners read about the clashes, they experience the graphic and often gory images nightly in their living rooms, via satellite television. This phenomenon, known as the Jazeera effect—a reference to the leading Arabic-language satellite channel—has stimulated regional support for the Palestinians, in some cases threatening the stability of Middle Eastern regimes.

Most conspicuously, violence in the West Bank and Gaza has shaken the Kingdom of Jordan, which has a Palestinian population widely believed to be at least 60 percent. In the past year, there have been hundreds of demonstrations in the kingdom, some of which have degenerated into violent clashes with Jordanian security services.

The violence has also had an effect in Egypt. In the early days of the intifada, there were several large demonstrations in Cairo. While these popular events have since diminished, in November 2000 Egypt recalled its ambassador to Israel, as an official symbol of protest.

Since then, Egyptian government newspapers have published editorials lavishing praise on Hitler and applauding Hamas suicide bombings. For the better half of 2001, the top song on the pop charts in Egypt was "I Hate Israel (and I Love Amre Moussa)."

In the Gulf, Iraq's Saddam Hussein has capitalized on the violence to further inflame regional sentiments against Israel. During the past year, Saddam has provided families of Palestinian "martyrs," those killed in clashes with Israel, with $10,000 each. During the March Arab Summit, Saddam pledged $980 million (from the UN Oil for Food fund) to support the intifada.

Despite the prevailing negative sentiments and occasional bellicose rhetoric, it bears noting that there has been no indication to date that the Egyptian and Jordanian peace treaties with Israel are at jeopary. If the situation continues to deteriorate, however, radical regional forces, like Saddam, as well as domestic pressures in these states could eventually test the durability of these pacts.

—*D.S.*

dered his security apparatus to curtail specific military activities of Hamas' Iz-zadin al Qassam and Fatah's al-Aqsa Martyrs brigades. Perhaps needless to say, such moves were not well received among these units.

After 10 of its "activists" were arrested by Jibril Rajoub's West Bank security forces in August, Hamas distributed posters accusing Rajoub of "collaborating" with Israel and threatening to kill him if the prisoners were not released immediately. In an incident a month earlier, members of the PA Intelligence Service in Gaza attacked a squad of Hamas and Fatah commandos returning from a mortar attack against Israel, severely injuring some of the men. A joint statement issued by the attacked groups pledged imminent punishment for the PA perpetrators. The next day, 20 armed men from Hamas and Fatah converged on the Gaza home of PA Military Intelligence head Musa Arafat, the nephew of Yasser Arafat, and opened fire.

These clashes between Hamas, Fatah, and the PA suggest that the current amity among Palestinian factions is driven by unity of purpose. Should Arafat ever find himself inclined to pursue a real cease-fire, he may encounter difficulties. Still, if history is any guide, when he feels it is to his best advantage, Arafat has proved that he can crack down on the Islamists and curtail anti-Israel violence.

## Precedent

It has been a long time since Arafat's PA security forces battled the militant Islamic opposition, but there is precedent. In 1994, his forces moved against Islamic militants in Gaza, and the ensuing showdown left 13 Islamists dead. In 1996, after a spate of suicide bombings killed 60 Israelis in nine days, PA security forces arrested nearly 1,000 militants. More recently, following the Wye River summit in 1998, the PA initiated a crackdown on Hamas terrorists that even elicited praise from then Israeli Foreign Minister Ariel Sharon.

None of these actions were sustained. But the very fact that PA security forces remained disciplined during these campaigns suggests that Arafat could once again call on the troops to clamp down.

Given the high level of Palestinian support for the intifada (80 percent) and suicide bombings (70 percent), any PA move against the Islamists will no doubt be unpopular. Yet it's important to keep in mind that Arafat, too, currently enjoys a level of popular support higher than at almost any point since he returned to the PA.

Because much of Arafat's current popularity has derived from his own support for violence, putting the Hamas genie back in the bottle will require the chairman to draw upon his extensive reservoir of political capital. Should he pursue this course of action, Arafat will be compelled to confront both Hamas and a segment of his own Fatah faction. It would be a bruising battle, but Arafat, who controls the purse strings of the Palestinian security forces, would eventually emerge intact.

Pundits might debate this assertion. Regrettably, though, the issue is moot, as a PA crackdown is unforeseeable at any point in the near future. The consensus within the PA on killing Israeli settlers and soldiers in the West Bank and Gaza is too broad. Likewise, the Palestinian belief that the intifada will achieve "liberation" from occupation is too prevalent.

For the time being, then, the pattern of suicide bombings and Israeli retaliatory strikes will continue. While attacks in Tel Aviv pose a diplomatic problem for Arafat, most Palestinians seem willing to tolerate the reprisals. It's a small price to pay, especially when compared to the alternative.

*David Schenker is a research fellow in Arab politics at the Washington Institute for Near East Policy. He is author of* **Palestinian Democracy and Governance** *(Washington Institute, 2001).*

*Article 12*

*Archaeology,* May/June 1997

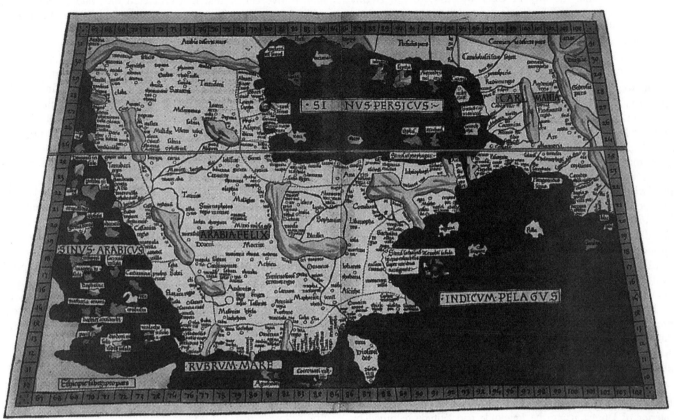

# Atlantis of the Sands

*Southern Oman yields ruins of an ancient city on the fabled frankincense route.*

By Juris Zarins

In 1930 the British explorer Bertram Thomas set out across the Rub al-Khali, or Empty Quarter, in central Arabia. As he approached its southern edge his guide, pointing to the faint outline of a road, remarked, "Look Sahib, there is the way to Ubar. It was a great city, rich in treasure, with date gardens and a fort of red silver. It now lies buried beneath the sands. . . ." Thomas had heard about Ubar on previous journeys through central Arabia, but no one could say where it was. He called it the "Atlantis of the Sands" and speculated that it might have been a trading center in southern Oman's Dhofar province. Herodotus, Pliny the Elder, Strabo, and other ancient authors, though not specifically mentioning Ubar, gave brief accounts of cities in southern Arabia that marketed resins from frankincense and myrrh trees. While it is certain that people of the Dhofar area grew rich trading these commodities, it would appear that the city of Ubar was an *Arabian Nights* fantasy. Arab historians have referred to Ubar as a region, and no city of that name appears on maps of the second-century A.D. Greek geographer Ptolemy. Since 1990 I have been looking for remains of a commercial center splendid enough to inspire such a myth.

The search began with a close study of the classical sources. Herodotus, Pliny, Ptolemy, and Strabo are all fairly clear about maritime trade routes. Myrrh and frankincense resins were brought from inland areas of Dhofar to the coastal towns of Moscha, modern Khor Rohri in southeastern Oman, and Syagrus, modern Ras Fartak in eastern Yemen. Land routes led from Dhofar west to cities such as Shabwah, Timna, and Marib in Yemen, then north through western Arabia to Gaza or east to Wadi Sirhan in northern Saudi Arabia. Ptolemy's maps and the *Periplus,* a collection of anonymous reports by ancient sailors, describe an Omanum Emporium, a trading center located either in Dhofar or as far east as Qatar. Ptolemy mentions frankincense trees near the territory of the Iobaritae tribe in southeastern Oman, and the area may have been named Ubar after this tribe. Other centers on Ptolemy's map such as Iula, Marimatha, and Thabane in the interior of Dhofar may have been settlements within Iobaritae tribal territory. Arab historians say these people lived in a region called Al Akhaf, perhaps modern Dhofar, and that trade cross the Rub al-Khali continued well into the nineteenth century.

Studying Ptolemy's map, Nicholas Clapp and George Hedges, the organizers of our expedition, decided to search the interior of Dhofar using the longitude and latitude recorded by Bertram Thomas for the portion of ancient road system he saw at the edge of the Rub al-Khali as a starting point. They asked for help from the Jet Propulsion Laboratory (JPL) in Pasadena, whose satellite images revealed faint traces of ancient roads. Encouraged by these images, Hedges, Clapp, the JPL's Ron Blom, the explorer Sir Ranulph Fiennes, and I visited the area in the summer of 1990. We traced some 20 miles of road between fields of dunes, but located few archaeological remains.

On subsequent visits to oases in the Dhofar region we discovered red- and black-polished ceramics of the classical period (after 300 B.C.). Based on these finds, we became convinced that the road at the edge of the Rub al-Khali was linked to ancient urban centers mentioned in classical sources and Arab histories. We chose to study Shisur, a ruined city some 90 miles northwest of Salalah on the edge of the desert. A permanent spring there had attracted people since the Neolithic (ca. 5000–2500 B.C.), and a fortress first built during the Bronze Age (2500–1300 B.C.) was in use until A.D. 1500. Bedouin still camp there year-round.

Visitors including the British explorer Wilfred Thesiger (1948) and archaeologists from Harvard University and the Danish Archaeological Survey (1972) had already noted remains of fortifications at the site. Our initial survey revealed the presence of flint materials probably from the Neolithic or Bronze Age. We found red- and black-polished, dot-and-circle, and painted ceramics of a pre-Islamic date (before A.D. 650). We also found several rough-cut stone blocks, partitions along a wall, and remains of a tower described by Thomas and Thesiger.

Between 1992 and 1994 we uncovered a fortress and administrative center that had protected the water supply from raiding bedouin tribes. A seven-and-one-half-foot-high wall surrounded the top of a collapsed cavern leading to the spring. The wall had fallen in places, especially along the western side where a large gate complex once stood. Abutments, or small walls, had been built within it, creating partitions for stalls or rooms. We found the remains of towers in corners inside the wall and just outside it. Debris covered almost the entire wall system. Further excavation revealed irregularities in the wall's height resulting from the removal of stones to build a small fort in 1950. It became clear that the fortress had formed a focal point for people in the region. Small villages that served as camps for caravans moving goods to east Arabia or south to the coast surround the site. These date to the classical or Islamic periods. Thesiger reported evidence of an extensive farming system including plow marks and irrigation channels.

The site was occupied for the first time in the Neolithic, around 5000 B.C.. Because of the construction of the fortress, little remains from this early period. We have found typical Neolithic cores, axes, blades, scrapers, and grinding stones in garbage dumps and built into the fort walls. The recovery of such material links the site with at least 60 other settlement remains concentrated on the ancient river systems in southern Dhofar. Whether or not the site was inhabited continuously after 5000 B.C. is difficult to determine since we do not yet have a clear idea when the earliest ceramics were used in the region. Northern Oman has a ceramic tradition dating back to 4500 B.C., but we know little of its relationship to Dhofar at that date. Comparison with artifacts from sites in Yemen indicate that ceramics could have been brought to the area by 2400 B.C. Some of the simple burnished bowls at Shisur may date to the second millennium B.C. The earliest walls and dwellings at the site were erected sometime after 1000 B.C., and by 500 B.C. Iron Age ceramics such as burnished red wares appear. Dot-and-circle ware is present in great quantities. We first found this type of pottery in 1993 at the site of Al Balid, located in the city of Salalah in southern Oman. Its presence there and at Shisur suggests there was a trade network between interior and coastal Dhofar. Vessels with an overturned, incised rim and constricted neck opening into a larger body are unique to Shisur. A finely burnished red ware introduced by the Parthians in northern Oman ca. 250 B.C. suggests a close tie between the northern and southern parts of the country.

The ceramic material from the Iron Age (1300–300 B.C.) and classical period (300 B.C.–A.D. 500) make it virtually certain that this was a principal city on Ptolemy's map. Ceramic ties with eastern Arabia, such as classical and Hellenistic red wares with incised and appliqué decoration, indicate a long history of trade across the Rub al-Khali, one that originated in the Neolithic with obsidian and seashells as barter items and continued until A.D. 1500. But which city on Ptolemy's map was Shisur? Based on its location within the area of the Iobaritae tribal territory, we believe it is the town of Marimatha. Late nineteenth- and early twentieth-century scholars believed Shisur might have been the Omanum Emporium mentioned in Pliny and the *Periplus,* but this name may have been used for a larger market area, not a permanent settlement. Be that as it may, Shisur was a city with ties to both Parthia in the east and the Hadramaut (modern Yemen) in the west, suggesting that it may have linked all parts of southern Arabia. The frankincense trade declined with the economic collapse of the western Roman Empire during the fifth and sixth centuries A.D. and with the subsequent Christian church prohibition of the use of frankincense for elaborate funeral rites. The Roman collapse resulted in a precipitous economic decline in the entire south Arabian area.

We believe Shisur was a key trading center that linked Dhofar to eastern Arabia and early Mesopotamian civilizations. Classical writers, such as Pliny the Elder and Ptolemy, and early Islamic sources, such as the Omani epic *Kashf al-Gumma,* refer to a people of Ad in Dhofar and describe their involvement in the incense trade. Almost certainly, this is also the period of interaction between the Ad and Arab tribes called the Omani. The Ad may have been the ancestors of modern tribes living in the Dhofar mountains: the Semitic, non-Arabic-speaking Mahra, Shahra, and others. Even today the Mahra and Shahra control much of the frankincense region, and local bedouin harvest the resin for them. One way to identify the ancestors of the modern Dhofaris is to study triliths, small, three-stone monuments set in rows in Mahra tribal territory sometime between 150 B.C. and A.D. 200. Many are inscribed with a south Arabic script that has yet to be deciphered. We think these triliths may have served ritual purposes, possibly connected with Persian-influenced Zoroastrian practices that centered on the harvest. Because many are located along caravan routes, they may have been associated with the frankincense trade. The more we learn from the triliths about the ancestors of the Mahra and Shahra, the more we will learn about Shisur's importance as a trade center.

Shisur was abandoned shortly after the Portuguese navigator Alfonso d'Albuquerque conquered Muscat in 1508, disrupting Omani ocean trade networks. Inland sites bore the brunt of the decline in trade, were gradually deserted, and were in time covered by the sands.

JURIS ZARINS *is a professor of archaeology at Southwest Missouri State University.*

# Credits

Page 178 Article 1. This article appeared in the September 1997 issue and is reprinted with permission from *The World & I,* a publication of The Washington Times Corporation. © 1997.

Page 183 Article 2. Reprinted with permission from *The American Prospect,* Vol. 12, No. 20, November 19, 2001. © 2001 by The American Prospect, 5 Broad Street, Boston, MA 02109. All rights reserved.

Page 187 Article 3. From *The Middle East Journal,* Autumn 2001.

Page 200 Article 4. Reprinted with permission from *Current History* magazine, January 2000. © 2000 by Current History, Inc.

Page 204 Article 5. Reprinted with permission from *The Observer* (Guardian Unlimited), September 3, 2001. © 2001 by Ziauddin Sardar.

Page 205 Article 6. Reprinted with permission from *Current History* magazine, January 2001. © 2001 by Current History, Inc.

Page 210 Article 7. Reprinted with permission from *The Washington Quarterly,* 24:4, Autumn 2001. © 2001 by the Center for Strategic and International Studies (CSIS) and the Massachusetts Institute of Technology.

Page 215 Article 8. From *The Economist,* December 23, 2000. Distributed by The New York Times Special Features.

Page 218 Article 9. Reprinted with permission from *The Chronicle of Higher Education,* September 21, 2001. © 2001 by Yale University Press with permission of the author, Bernard Wasserstein.

Page 223 Article 10. This article appeared in the November 2001 issue and is reprinted with permission from *The World & I,* a publication of The Washington Times Corporation, © 2001.

Page 226 Article 11. This article appeared in the November 2001 issue and is reprinted with permission from *The World & I,* a publication of The Washington Times Corporation, © 2001.

Page 231 Article 12. Reprinted with permission of *Archaeology* magazine, Vol. 50, No. 3. © 1997 by The Archaeological Institute of America.

# Sources for Statistical Reports

U.S. State Department, *Background Notes* (2000–2001).

*The World Factbook* (2001).

*World Statistics in Brief* (2001).

*World Almanac* (2001).

*The Statesman's Yearbook* (2001).

*Demographic Yearbook* (2001).

*Statistical Yearbook* (2001).

*World Bank, World Development Report* (2000–2001).

# Glossary of Terms and Abbreviations

**Abd**—Slave, servant of God (as in Gamal Abdel Nasser: Abd al-Nasir).

**Alawi (Nusayri)**—A minority Muslim community in Syria, currently in power under the Assad family. They are nominally Shia but have separate liturgy and secret rites, with some non-Muslim festivals. The Alevi in Turkey are unrelated but follow some of the same rituals.

**Allah**—God, in Islam.

**Ayatollah**—"Sign of God," the title of highest rank among the Shia religious leaders in Iran.

**Ba'th (Arab Socialist Resurrection Party)**—A Socialist political party that has two main branches, ruling in Syria and Iraq respectively, plus members in other Arab countries.

**Caliph**—In Arabic, *khalifa;* agent, representative, or deputy; in Sunni Islam, the line of successors to Muhammad.

**Chador**—A body covering worn by some Muslim women.

**Colon**—Settler, colonist (French), a term used for the French population in North Africa during the colonial period (1830–1962).

**Dar al-Islam**—"House of Islam," territory ruled under Islam. Conversely, *Dar al-Harb,* "House of War," denotes territory not under Islamic rule.

**Druze (or Druse)**—An offshoot of Islam that has developed its own rituals and practices and a close-knit community structure; Druze populations are found today in Lebanon, Jordan, Syria, and Israel.

**Emir (or Amir)**—A title of rank, denoting either a patriarchal ruler, provincial governor, or military commander. Today it is used exclusively for rulers of certain Arabian Peninsula states.

**Fatwa**—A legal opinion or interpretation delivered by a Muslim religious scholar-jurist; a religious edict.

**Fida'i (plural Fida'iyun, also Fedayeen, cf. Mujahideen)**—Literally, "fighter for the faith"; a warrior who fights for the faith against the enemies of Islam.

**FLN (National Liberation Front)**—The resistance movement against the French in Algeria that succeeded in establishing Algerian independence.

**GCC (Gulf Cooperation Council)**—Established in 1981 as a mutual-defense organization by the Arab Gulf states. Membership: Bahrain, Kuwait, Oman, Qatar, Saudi Arabia, and United Arab Emirates. Headquarters: Riyadh.

**Hadith**—"Traditions" of the Prophet Muhammad, the compilation of sayings and decisions attributed to him that serve as a model and guide to conduct for Muslims.

**Hajj**—Pilgrimage to Mecca, one of the Five Pillars of Islam.

**Hamas**—The arabic acronym for the militant anti-Israeli organization based in the Gaza Strip. Hamas opposes the Oslo and subsequent Palestinian–Israeli agreements and engages in terrorist actions such as suicide bombings and attacks on Jewish settlers.

**Hijrah (Hegira)**—The Prophet Muhammad's emigration from Mecca to Medina in A.D. 622 to escape persecution; the start of the Islamic calendar.

**Ibadi**—A militant early Islamic group that split with the majority (Sunni) over the question of the succession to Muhammad. Their descendants form majorities of the populations in Oman and Yemen.

**Ihram**—The seamless white robe worn by all Muslims making the hajj.

**Imam**—Religious leader, prayer-leader of a congregation. When capitalized it refers to the descendants of Ali who are regarded by Shia Muslims as the rightful successors to Muhammad.

**Intifada**—Literally, "resurgence"; uprising of the Palestinians against Israeli occupation. Intifada II, under way since December 2000, in 2001 became for all practical purposes a civil war.

**Islam**—Submission to the will of God, as revealed in the Koran. The religion of Muslims.

**Jahiliyya**—The "time of ignorance" of the Arabs before Islam. Sometimes used by Islamic fundamentalists today to describe secular Muslim societies, which they regard as sinful.

**Jama'a**—The Friday communal prayer, held in a mosque *(jami')*. By extension, the public assembly held by Muslim rulers for their subjects in traditional Islamic states such as Saudi Arabia.

**Jamahiriyya**—Popular democracy (as in Libya).

**Jihad**—The struggle of Muslims collectively or individually to do right and defend the community; commonly, "holy war."

**Khan**—A title of rank in eastern Islam (Turkey, Iran, etc.) for military or clan leaders.

**Khedive**—Viceroy, the title of rulers of Egypt in the nineteenth and twentieth centuries who ruled as regents of the Ottoman sultan.

**Kibbutz**—A collective settlement in Israel.

**Koran**—In Arabic, *Qur'an;* "Recitation," the book of God's revelations to Muhammad via the Angel Gabriel that form the basis for Islam.

**League of Arab States (Arab League)**—Established in 1945 as a regional organization for newly independent Arab countries. Membership: all the Arab states except Egypt (suspended in 1979) plus the PLO.

**Maghrib**—"West," the hour of the sunset prayer; in Arabic, a geographical term for North Africa.

**Mahdi**—"The Awaited One"; the Messiah, who will appear on earth to reunite the divided Islamic community and announce the Day of Judgment. In Shia Islam he is the Twelfth and Last Imam (al-Mahdi al-Muntazir) who disappeared 12 centuries ago but is believed to be in a state of occultation (suspended between heaven and earth).

**Majlis (Meclis, in Turkish)**—literally, "assembly," used traditionally for a ruler's weekly public meetings with subjects to hear complaints. When capitalized, refers to a national legislature, such as Turkey's Buyuk Millet Meclisior Iran's Majlis.

**Mandates**—An arrangement set up under the League of Nations after World War I for German colonies and territories of the Ottoman Empire inhabited by non-Turkish populations. The purpose was to train these populations for eventual self-government under a temporary occupation by a foreign power, which was either Britain or France.

**Millet**—"Nation," a non-Muslim population group in the Ottoman Empire recognized as a legitimate religious community and allowed self-government in internal affairs under its own religious leaders, who were responsible to the sultan for the group's behavior.

**Muezzin**—A prayer-caller, the person who announces the five daily obligatory prayers from the minaret of a mosque.

**Mufti**—A legal scholar empowered to issue fatwas. Usually one mufti is designated as the Grand Mufti of a particular Islamic state or territory.

**Mujahideen** (*see* **Fida'i**)—A common term for resistance fighters in Afghanistan and opposition militants in Iran.

**Muslim** (*see* **Islam**)—One who submits (to the will of God).

**OAPEC (Organization of Arab Petroleum Exporting Countries)**—Established in 1968 to coordinate oil policies—but not to set prices—and to develop oil-related inter-Arab projects, such as an Arab tanker fleet and dry-dock facilities. Membership: all Arab oil-producing states. Headquarters: Kuwait.

**OIC (Organization of the Islamic Conference)**—Established in 1971 to promote solidarity among Islamic countries, provide humanitarian aid to Muslim communities throughout the world, and provide funds for Islamic education through construction of mosques, theological institutions of Islamic learning, etc. Membership: all states with an Islamic majority or significant minority. Headquarters: Jiddah.

**OPEC (Organization of Petroleum Exporting Countries)**—Established in 1960 to set prices and coordinate global oil policies of members. A majority of its 13 member states are in the Middle East. Headquarters: Vienna.

**PLO (Palestine Liberation Organization)**—Overall PLO authority is vested in the Palestine National Council (PNC). Fatah (the Palestine National Liberation Movement, a guerrilla military group) joined the PLO in 1968, when a charter for Palestinian Arab national independence was issued. The PNC (in theory) supervises the Palestine Liberation Army, a body of 16,000 troops dispersed since 1982 in various Arab states. The PLO holds observer status at the United Nations. Funding comes from annual contributions from the Arab states, mainly Saudi Arabia, plus a 3 to 6 percent tax levied on the incomes of all Palestinians. Headquarters (temporary): Tunis.

**Polisario**—A national resistance movement in the Western Sahara that opposes annexation by Morocco and is fighting to establish an independent Saharan Arab state, the Sahrawi Arab Democratic Republic (SADR).

**PSD (Parti Socialiste Destourien)**—The dominant political party in Tunisia since independence and until recently the only legal party.

**Qaid (Caid, Kaid)**—Particularly in North Africa, a native Muslim official appointed by the French to administer a region or territory during the protectorate period.

**Qanat**—An underground tunnel used for irrigation.

**Quraysh**—The group of clans who made up Muhammad's community in Mecca.

**Shari'a**—"The Way," the corpus of the sacred laws of Islam as revealed to Muhammad in the Koran. The sacred law is derived from three sources, the Koran, Sunna (q.v.), and hadith (q.v.).

**Sharif**—"Holy," a term applied to members of Muhammad's immediate family and descendants through his daughter Fatima and son-in-law Ali.

**Shaykh (Sheikh, Sheik)**—A patriarchal leader of an Islamic community, usually elected for life; also used for certain religious leaders and community elders as a title of honor.

**Shia**—Commonly, but incorrectly, *Shiite*. Originally meant "Party," i.e., of Ali, those Muslims who supported him as Muhammad's rightful and designated successor. Today, broadly, a member of the principal Islamic minority.

**Shura**—an advisory council appointed by a ruler to advise on national issues. Commonly used in the Arab Gulf states.

**Sunna**—Custom or procedure, the code of acceptable behavior for Muslims based on the Koran and hadith. Not to be confused with Sunni, the name for the majority group in Islam.

**Suq (Souk)**—A public weekly market in Islamic rural areas, always held in the same village on the same day of the week, so that the village may have the word incorporated into its name. Also refers to a section of an Islamic city devoted to the wares and work of potters, cloth merchants, wood workers, spice sellers, etc.

**Taliban**—"Students"; originally used for students in Islamic madrasas (schools), the term acquired political significance with the rise to power in Afghanistan of this extreme Islamist movement.

**Taqiyya**—Dissimulation, concealment of one's religious identity or beliefs (as by Shia under Sunni control) in the face of overwhelming power or repression.

**U.A.R. (United Arab Republic)**—The name given to the abortive union of Egypt and Syria (1958–1961).

**Ulema**—The corporate body of Islamic religious leaders, scholars, and jurists.

**Umma**—The worldwide community of Muslims.

**UNHCR (United Nations High Commission for Refugees)**—Established in 1951 to provide international protection and material assistance to refugees worldwide. UNHCR has several refugee projects in the Middle East.

**UNIFIL (United Nations Interim Force in Lebanon)**—Formed in 1978 to ensure Israeli withdrawal from southern

Lebanon. After the 1982 Israeli invasion, UNIFIL was given the added responsibility for protection and humanitarian aid to the people of the area. Headquarters: Naqoura.

**United Nations Peacekeeping Forces**—Various military observer missions formed to supervise disengagement or truce agreements between the Arab states and Israel. They include UNDOF (United Nations Disengagement Observer Force). Formed in 1974 as a result of the October 1973 Arab-Israeli War and continued by successive resolutions. Headquarters: Damascus.

**UNRWA (United Nations Relief and Works Agency for Palestine Refugees)**—Established in 1950 to provide food, housing, and health and education services for Palestinian refugees who fled their homes after the establishment of the State of Israel in Palestine. Headquarters: Vienna. UNRWA maintains refugee camps in Lebanon, Syria, Jordan, the occupied West Bank, and the Gaza Strip. UNRWA has also assumed responsibility for emergency relief for refugees in Lebanon displaced by the Israeli invasion and by the Lebanese Civil War.

# Bibliography

## CRADLE OF ISLAM

Akhtoreddin Ahmad, ed., *Islam and the Environmental Crisis* (London: TaHa Publishers, 1997).

Scott Appleby, ed., *Spokesmen for the Despised: Fundamentalist Leaders of the Middle East* (Chicago: University of Chicago Press, 1997).

Aziz al-Azmeh, *Muslim Kingship* (London: I. B. Tauris, 1997).

Abdelwahab Bouhdiba, *Sexuality in Islam* (London: Saqi Books, 1998); tr. Alan Sheridan.

Paul Cobb, *White Banners: Contention in Abbasid Syria, 750–850* (Albany, NY: State University of New York Press, 2001).

Farhad Daftary, *The Assassin Legends: Myths of the Ismailis* (London: I. B. Tauris, 1997).

Richard C. Foltz, *Religions of the Silk Road* (New York: St. Martin's Press, 2000).

Michael Gilsenan, *Recognizing Islam: Religion and Society in the Modern Middle East* (London: I. B. Tauris, 1996).

Yvonne Y. Haddad and John L. Esposito, *The Islamic Revival Since 1988: A Critical Survey and Bibliography* (Westport, CT: Greenwood Press, 1997).

Heinz Halm, *Shia Islam* from *Religion to Revolution* (Princeton, NJ: Markus Wiener, 1997), tr. Alison Brown.

Anders Jerichow and Jorgen B. Simonsen, *Islam in a Changing World* (Richmond, England: Curzon Publishers, 1997).

Richard K. Khuri, *Freedom, Modernity and Islam* (Syracuse, NY: Syracuse University Press, 1998).

Martin Kramer, *The Islamism Debate* (Syracuse, NY: Syracuse University Press, 1997).

Jacob Lassner, *The Middle East Remembered: Forged Identities, Competing Narratives, Contested Spaces* (Ann Arbor, MI: University of Michigan Press, 2000).

Charles Lindholm, *The Islamic Middle East: An Historical Anthropology* (London: Blackwell, 1996).

F. E. Peters, *Muhammad and the Origins of Islam* (Albany, NY: State University of New York Press, 1994).

Rudolph Peters, ed., *Jihad in Classical and Modern Islam: A Reader* (Princeton, NJ: Markus Weiner, 1996).

James Piscatori and Dale Eickelman, *Muslim Politics* (Princeton, NJ: Princeton University Press, 1996).

Ahmad Rashid, *Taliban: Militant Islam* (New York: New York University Press, 2001).

James Reston Jr., *Warriors of God: Richard the Lionheart and Saladin in the Third Crusade* (New York: Doubleday, 2001).

Olivier Roy, *The Failure of Political Islam.* Trans. Carol Volk (Cambridge, MA: Harvard University Press, 1996).

Armando Salvatore, *Islam and the Political Discourse of Modernity* (Reading, England: Ithaca Press, 1997).

Bassam Tibi, *The Challenge of Fundamentalist Islam* (Berkeley, CA: University of California Press, 1998).

## THEATER OF CONFLICT

Harfiyeh Abdel Haleem, et al., eds.: *The Crescent and the Cross: Muslim and Christian Approaches to War and Peace* (New York: St. Martin's Press, 1998).

Fred Halliday, *Islam and the Myth of Confrontation* (London: I. B. Tauris, 1996).

Michael Hickey, *Gallipoli* (North Pomfret, VT: Trafalgar Square, 1998).

James Jankowski and Israel Gershoni, eds., *Rethinking Nationalism in the Middle East* (New York: Cambridge University Press, 1997).

Leo Kamil, *Fueling the Fire: U.S. Policy and the Western Sahara Conflict* (Lawrenceville, NJ: Red Sea Press, 1996).

Majid Khadduri & Edmund Ghareeb, *War in the Gulf 1990–91: The Iraq–Kuwait Conflict and Its Implications* (New York: Oxford University Press, 2001).

Tim Niblock, *Pariah States and Sanctions in the Middle East: Iraq, Libya, Sudan* (Boulder, CO: Lynne Rienner, 2001).

Itamar Rabinovich, *Waging Peace: Israel and the Arabs at the End of the Century* (New York: Farrar, Strauss & Giroux, 1999).

Tom Segev, *One Palestine Complete: Jews and Arabs Under the British Mandate* (New York: Henry Holt, 1999).

Mary Williams, *The Middle East: Opposing Viewpoints* (San Diego, CA: Greenhaven Press, 2000).

## ALGERIA

Kay Adamson, *Political and Economic Thought and Practice in 19th Century France and the Colonization of Algeria* (New York: Edwin Mellen Press, 2002).

Ali Aissaoui, *Algeria: The Political Economy of Oil and Gas* (New York: Oxford University Press, 2001).

Bradford L. Dillman, *State and Private Sector in Algeria* (Boulder, CO: Westview Press, 2000).

Martin Evans, *The Memory of Resistance: French Opposition to the Algerian War 1954–1962* (Oxford, England: Burg, 1997).

James D. LeSueur, *Uncivil War: Intellectuals and Identity Politics During the Decolonization of Algeria* (Philadelphia, PA: University of Pennsylvania Press, 2002).

## BAHRAIN

Fred H. Lawson, *Bahrain: The Modernization of Autocracy* (Boulder, CO: Westview Press, 1989).

Mahdi A. al-Tajir, *Bahrain, 1920–1945: Britain, The Shaykh and the Administration* (London: Croom Helm, 1987).

## EGYPT

Leila Ahmed, *A Border Passage* (New York: Farrar, Strauss & Giroux, 1999).

Lia Brinjar, *The Society of Muslim Brothers in Egypt* (London: Ithaca Press, 1998).

Joseph Finklestone, *Anwar Sadat: Visionary Who Dared* (London: Frank Cass, 1996).

Boutros Boutros Ghali, *Egypt's Road to Jerusalem* (New York: Random House, 1997).

Saad Eddin Ibrahim, *Egypt, Islam and Democracy* (Cairo: AUC Press, 1996).

Mary Anne Weaver, *A Portrait of Egypt* (New York: Farrar, Strauss & Giroux, 1999).

## IRAN

Ervand Abrahamian, *Khomeinism: Essays on the Islamic Republic* (Berkeley, CA: University of California Press, 1993).

Christine Bird, *Neither East Nor West* (New York: Pocket Books, 2000).

Peter Chelkowski and Hamid Dabashi, *The Art of Persuasion in the Islamic Republic of Iran* (New York: New York University Press, 2000).

Ali Gheissari, *Iranian Intellectuals in the 20th Century* (Austin, TX: University of Texas Press, 1998).

James F. Goode, *The U.S. and Iran: In the Shadow of Musaddiq* (New York: St. Martin's Press, 1997).

Sandra Mackey, *The Iranians: Persia, Islam and the Soul of a Nation* (New York: Penguin Books, 1996).

Abbas Milani, *The Persian Sphinx: Amir Abbas Hoveyda and the Riddle of the Iranian Revolution* (Washington, D.C.: Mage Publications, 2000).

Elaine Sciolino, *Persian Mirrors: The Elusive Face of Iran* (New York: Free Press, 2000).

John Simpson and Tira Shubart, *Lifting the Veil: Life in Revolutionary Iran* (London: Hodder & Stoughton, 1995).

William Spencer, *Iran: Land of the Peacock Throne* (Tarrytown, NY: Marshall Cavendish, 2000).

____, *The United States and Iran: From Friend to Enemy* (Brookfield, CT: Millbrook Press, 2000).

Robin Wright, *The Last Great Revolution: Turmoil and Transformation in Iran* (New York: Knopf, 2000).

Behzad Yaghmaian, *Social Change in Iran* (Albany, NY: State University of New York Press, 2001).

## IRAQ

Said K. Aburish, *Saddam Hussain: The Politics of Revenge* (North Pomfret, VT: Bloomsbury Press, 2001).

Ofra Bengio, *Saddam's Word: Political Discourse in Iraq* (New York: Oxford University Press 2000).

Andrew Cockburn and Patrick Cockburn, *Out of the Ashes: The Resurrection of Saddam Hussain* (New York: HarperCollins, 1999).

Michael Deaver, *Disarming Iraq: Monitoring Power and Resistance* (Westport, CT: Greenwood Press, 2001).

Dilip Hiro, *Neighbors Not Friends: Iraq and Iran After the Gulf War* (New York: Routledge, 2001).

Majid Khadduri and Edmund Ghareeb, *War in the Gulf, 1990–91: The Iraq–Kuwait Conflict and Its Implications* (New York: Oxford University Press, 2001).

Yitzhak Nakash, *The Shi'is of Iraq* (Princeton, NJ: Princeton University Press, 1994).

Rosemary O'Brien, ed., *Gertrude Bell: The Arabian Diaries, 1913–1914* (Syracuse, NY: Syracuse University Press, 2000).

Marion and Peter Sluglett, *Iraq Since 1958: From Revolution to Dictatorship,* rev. ed. (New York: St. Martin's Press, 2001).

William Spencer, *Iraq: Old Land, New Nation* (Brookfield, CT: Millbrook Press, 2000).

Peter Sullivan, *Iraq's Enduring Political Threat* (Washington, D.C.: National Defense University/Institute of National Strategic Studies, 1996).

Hans von Sponeck, *UN Policy in Iraq* (Nicholasville, KY: Anthem Press, 2001).

## ISRAEL

Meron Benvenisti, *Intimate Enemies: Jews and Arabs in a Shared Land* (Berkeley, CA: University of California Press, 1995).

Yossi Berlin, *His Brother's Keeper: Israel and Diaspora Jewry in the 21st Century* (New York: Random House/Schocken Books, 2000).

Aaron Bornstein, *Crossing the Green Line: Between Palestine and Israel* (Philadelphia, PA: University of Pennsylvania Press, 2001).

Avraham Brichta, *Political Reform in Israel* (Portland, OR: Sussex Academic Press, 2001).

Mark Chmiel, *Elie Wiesel and the Politics of Solidarity* (Philadelphia, PA: Temple University Press, 2001).

Yoel Cohen, *The Whistle-blower of Dimona: Israel, Vanunu and the Bomb* (New York: Holmes and Meier, 2001).

Adam Garfinkle, *Politics and Society in Modern Israel: Myths and Realities* (Armonk, NY: M. E. Sharpe, 1997).

Asad Ghanem, *The Palestine–Arab Minority in Israel 1948–2000: A Political Study* (Albany, NY: State University of New York Press, 2001).

Calvin Goldscheider, *Israel's Changing Society: Population, Ethnicity and Development* (Boulder, CO: Westview Press, 1996).

Clive Jones, et al., *Israel: Identity, Challenges to Democracy and the State* (Newark, NJ: Gordon and Breach, 2000).

Efraim Karsh, *Israeli Politics and Society Since 1948* (London: Frank Cass, 2001).

David Kretzmer, *The Occupation of Justice: The Supreme Court of Israel and the Occupied Territories* (Albany, NY: State University of New York Press, 2001).

Moshe Ma'oz, et al., *Parties, Elections and Cleavages: Israel in Comparative and Theoretical Perspective* (London: Frank Cass, 2000).

Joel Migdal, *Through the Lens of Israel: Explorations in State and Society* (Albany, NY: State University of New York Press, 2001).

J. Maxwell Miller, *The History of Israel: An Essential Guide* (Knoxville, TN: Abingdon Press, 2001).

David Nachmias, et al., *Public Policy in Israel* (London: Frank Cass, 2001).

Yitzhak Rabin, *The Rabin Memoirs,* 2nd ed. (Berkeley, CA: University of California Press, 1996).

Nadim Rouhana, *Palestinian Citizens in an Ethnic Jewish State: Identities in Conflict* (New Haven, CT: Yale University Press, 1997).

Alsa Rubin-Peled, *Debating Islam in the Jewish State* (Albany, NY: State University of New York Press, 2001).

Gershon Safir, *New Israel: Peacemaking and Liberalization* (Boulder, CO: Westview Press, 2000).

Ira Sharansky, *Policy Making in Israel* (Pittsburgh, PA: University of Pittsburgh Press, 1997).

Sasson Sofer, *Peacemaking in a Divided Society: Israel After Rabin* (London: Frank Cass, 2000).

Rebecca Torstruck, *The Limits of Coexistence: Identity Politics in Israel* (Ann Arbor, MI: University of Michigan Press, 2000).

Bernard Wasserstein, *Divided Jerusalem: Struggle for the Holy City* (New Haven, CT: Yale University Press, 2001).

## JORDAN

Randy Deshazo and John Sutherlin, *Building Bridges: Diplomacy and Regime Formation in the Jordan River* (Lanham, MD: University Presses of America, 1996).

Eugene Rogan and Tariq Tell, *Village, Steppe and State: The Social Origins of Modern Jordan* (London: British Academic Press, 1994).

Robert B. Satloff, *From Abdullah to Hussein: Jordan in Transition* (New York: Oxford, 1994).

## KUWAIT

Anthony Cordesman, *Kuwait: Recovery and Security After the Gulf War* (Boulder, CO: Westview Press, 1997).

Selwa al-Ghanem, *The Reign of Mubarak al-Sabah, Shaikh of Kuwait, 1898–1915* (New York: St. Martin's Press, 1998).

Miriam Joyce, *Kuwait 1945–1996: An Anglo-American Perspective* (Boston: Woburn Press, 2000).

Mary Ann Tetrault, *Stories of Democracy* (New York: Columbia University Press, 2000).

## LEBANON

Carolyn Gates, *The Making of the Lebanese Merchant Republic* (New York: St. Martin's Press, 1997).

Michael Gilsenan, *Lords of the Lebanese Marches: Violence and Narrative in Arab Society* (Berkeley, CA: University of California Press, 1996).

William Harris, *Faces of Lebanon: Sects, Wars, and Global Expansion* (Princeton, NJ: Markus Wiener, 1997).

Akram Fuad Khater, *Inventing Home: Emigration, Gender and the Middle Class in Lebanon, 1870–1920* (Berkeley, CA: University of California Press, 2001).

Elizabeth Picard, *Lebanon: A Shattered Country* (New York: Holmes & Meier, 2001).

Giandomenico Picco, *Man Without a Gun* (New York: Times Books, 1999).

Magnus Ranstorp, *Hizb'Allah in Lebanon* (New York: St. Martin's Press, 1997).

Kirsten E. Schulze, *The Jews of Lebanon: Between Coexistence and Conflict* (Portland, OR: Sussex Academic Press, 2001).

## LIBYA

Guy Arnold, *The Maverick State: Libya and the New World Order* (London: Cassell Academic Press, 1997).

Ahmad Faqih, ed., *Libyan Stories* (London: Kegan Paul International, 2001).

Judith Gurney, *Libya: The Political Economy of Oil* (New York: Oxford University Press, 1996).

Amar Obeidi, *Political Culture in Libya* (Leonia, NJ: Curzon Press, 2000).

Dirk Vandewalle, *Libya Since Independence* (Ithaca, NY: Cornell University Press, 1998).

## MOROCCO

Rahma Bourqia and Susan Miller, eds., *In the Shadow of the Sultan: Culture, Power and Politics in Morocco* (Cambridge, MA: Harvard University Press, 1999). No. 31, Harvard Middle Eastern Monographs.

Vivian Mann, ed., *Morocco: Jews and Art in a Muslim Land* (New York: Merrell Publishers, 2000).

David A. McMurray, *In and Out of Morocco: Smuggling and Migration in a Frontier Boomtown* (Minneapolis, MN: University of Minnesota Press, 2001).

James Miller and Jerome Bookin-Weiner, *Morocco: The Arab West* (Boulder, CO: Westview Press, 1998).

Kitty Morse, *The Scent of Orange Blossoms: Sephardic Cuisine From Morocco* (Santa Barbara, CA: Ten Speed Press, 2001).

C. R. Pennell, *Morocco Since 1830: A History* (New York: New York University Press, 2001).

Gregory White, *Comparative Political Economy of Tunisia and Morocco* (Albany, NY: State University of New York Press, 2001).

## OMAN

Nicholas Clapp, *The Road to Ubar* (Boston, MA: Houghton Mifflin, 2000).

Isam al-Rawas, *Early Islamic Oman: A Political History* (Chicago: Garnet/Ithaca, 1998).

Carol A. Riphenberg, *Oman: Political Development in a Changing World* (Westport, CT: Greenwood Press, 1998).

Raghid al-Solh, *The Sultanate of Oman, 1914–1918* (Chicago: Garnet/Ithaca, 1999).

## QATAR

Jill Crystal, *Oil and Politics in the Gulf: Rulers and Merchants in Kuwait and Qatar, 2nd ed.* (Cambridge, England: Cambridge University Press, 1995).

Steven Dorr and Bernard Reich, *Qatar, 2nd ed.* (Boulder, CO: Westview Press, 2000).

## SAUDI ARABIA

Said Aburish, *The Rise, Corruption and Coming Fall of the House of Saud* (New York: St. Martin's, Press, 1996).

Anthony Cave Brown, *Oil, God and Gold: The Story of Aramco and the Saudi Kings* (Boston, MA: Houghton Mifflin, 1999).

Anthony Cordesman, *Saudi Arabia: Guarding the Desert Kingdom* (Boulder, CO: Westview Press, 1997).

Joseph Kechichian, *Succession in Saudi Arabia* (New York: St. Martin's Press, 2001).

Robert J. Meadows, *What Price Blood? Murder and Justice in Saudi Arabia* (New York: Robert Reed, 2000).

Alexei Vasiliev, et al., *The History of Saudi Arabia* (New York: New York University Press, 2000).

## SUDAN

Amir Idris, *Sudan's Civil War: Slavery, Race and Formational Identities* (Lewiston, NY: Edwin Mellen Press, 2001).

Jok M. Jok, *War and Slavery in Sudan* (Philadelphia, PA: University of Pennsylvania Press, 2001).

Richard Lobban, Robert S. Kramer, and Carolyn Fluehr-Lobban, *Historical Dictionary of the Sudan.* (Westport, CT: Greenwood Press, 2001). African Historical Dictionaries Series.

Alice Moore-Harrell, *Gordon and the Sudan: Prologue to the Mahdiyya, 1877–1880* (London: Frank Cass, 2001).

Donald Petterson, *Inside Sudan: Political Islam, Conflict and Catastrophe* (Boulder, CO: Westview Press, 1999).

A. H. Abdel Salam and Alexander de Waal, *The Phoenix State: Civil Society and the Future of Sudan* (Lawrenceville, NJ: Red Sea Press, 2001).

## SYRIA

Paul Cobb, *White Banners: Contention in Abbasid Syria, 750–880* (Albany, NY: State University of New York Press, 2001).

Scott Davis, *The Road From Damascus: A Journey Through Syria* (Seattle, WA: Cune Publishing Company, 2001).

Raymond Hinnebusch, *Syria: Revolution From Above* (San Diego, DA: Gordon and Breach, 2000).

Patrick Seale, *Asad of Syria: The Struggle for the Middle East* (Berkeley, CA: University of California Press, 1989).

Ghada Hashem Talhami, *Syria and the Palestinians: The Clash of Nationalisms* (Gainesville, FL: University Presses of Florida, 2001).

Nikolas Van Dam, *The Struggle for Power in Syria* (London: I. B. Tauris, 1996).

Eyal Ziser and Itamar Rabinovitch, *Asad's Legacy, Syria in Transition* (New York: New York University Press, 2000).

## TUNISIA

Derek Hopwood, *Habib Bourguiba of Tunisia: The Tragedy of Longevity* (New York: St. Martin's Press, 1992).

Kenneth J. Perkins, *The Historical Dictionary of Tunisia,* 2nd ed. (Metuchen, NJ: Scarecrow Press, 1997).

Azzam Tamimi, *Rachid Ghannouchi: A Democrat Within Islamism* (New York: Oxford University Press, 2001).

Gregory White, *Comparative Political Economy of Tunisia and Morocco* (Albany, NY: State University of New York Press, 2001).

## TURKEY

Selim Deringil, *The Well-Protected Domain: Ideology and the Legitimation of Power in the Ottoman Empire, 1876–1909* (London: I. B. Tauris, 2000).

Jason Goodwin, *Lords of the Horizon: A History of the Ottoman Empire* (New York: Henry Holt, 1998).

Matthew Gordon, *The Breaking of a Thousand Swords: A History of the Turkish Military of Samarra, 200–275 A.H./815–869 C.E.* (Albany, NY: State University of New York Press, 2001).

Michael Gunter, *The Kurds and the Future of Turkey* (New York: St. Martin's Press, 1997).

Resat Kasaba and Sibel Bozdogan, eds., *Rethinking Modernity and National Identity in Turkey* (Seattle, WA: University of Washington Press, 1997).

Bruce Kuniholm, *The United States and Turkey* (New York: Scribner's, 1998).

Andrew Mango, *Ataturk: The Biography of the Founder of Modern Turkey* (New York: Overlook Publishing, 2000).

Bruce Masters, *Christians and Jews in the Ottoman Arab World: The Roots of Sectarianism* (New York: Cambridge University Press, 2001).

Elizabeth Ozdalga, *The Veiling Issue: Official Secularism and Popular Islam in Modern Turkey* (Leonia, NJ: Curzon Press, 1998).

Hugh Poulton, *The Top Hat, the Grey Wolf, and the Crescent: Turkish Nationalism and the Republic* (New York: New York University Press, 1997).

Libby Rittenberg, ed., *The Political Economy of Turkey in the Post-Soviet Era* (Westport, CT: Greenwood Press, 1997).

## UNITED ARAB EMIRATES

Frank A. Clements, *The United Arab Emirates,* rev. ed. (Santa Barbara, CA: ABC-Clio, 1998).

Joseph Kechichian, ed., *A Century in Thirty Years: The United Arab Emirates* (Washington, D.C.: Middle East Policy Council, 2000).

Peter Lienhardt and Ahmed Al-Shahi, eds., *Shaikhdoms of Eastern Arabia* (New York: St. Martin's Press, 2001).

Farhang Mehr, *A Colonial Legacy: The Dispute Over the Islands of Abu Musa and the Greater and Lesser Tunbs* (Lanham, MD: University Presses of America, 1997).

## YEMEN

William Donaldson, *Sharecropping in the Yemen: A Study of Islamic Theory, Custom and Pragmatism* (Boston, MA: Brill Academic Publishers, 2000).

Ulrike Freitag and William Clarence-Smith, *Hadhrami Traders, Scholars and Statesmen in the Indian Ocean, 1750s to 1960s* (Leiden, the Netherlands: E. J. Brill, 1997).

Mohammed Al-Hamdi, *Competition for Scarce Groundwater in the Sana's Plain, Yemen* (Brookfield, VT: A. A. Balkema, 2000).

Chris D. Handley, *Water Stress: A Case Study of Ta'iz, Yemen* (Brookfield, VT: Ashgate Publishing Company, 2001).

Leila Ingrams, *Yemen Engraved: Foreign Travellers to the Yemen, 1496–1890* (London: Kegan Paul International, 2000).

Tim MacKintosh-Smith, *Yemen: The Unknown Arabia* (New York: Overlook Press, 2001).

## REGIONAL STUDIES

Frederick F. Anscombe, *The Ottoman Gulf: The Creation of Kuwait, Saudi Arabia and Qatar, 1870–1914* (New York: Columbia University Press, 1997).

Bulent Aras, *The New Geopolitics of Asia and Turkey's Position* (London: Frank Cass, 2001).

John P. Entelis, *Islam, Democracy and the State in North Africa* (Bloomington, IN: Indiana University Press, 1997).

Michael Laskier, *North African Jewry in the Twentieth Century: The Jews of Morocco, Tunisia and Algeria* (New York: New York University Press, 1997).

Robert W. Olson, *Turkey's Relations With Iran, Syria, Israel and Russia 1991–2000: The Kurdish and Islamist Questions* (Costa Mesa, CA: Mazda Publishers, 2001).

Rosemarie Said Zahlan, *Making of the Modern Gulf States* (Chicago, IL: Garnet/Ithaca, 1999).

## WOMEN'S STUDIES

Evelyne Accad, *Wounding Words: A Woman's Journal in Tunisia.*. (Portsmouth, NH: Heinemann, 1996), tr. Cynthia Hahn.

Judith Caesar, *Crossing Borders: An American Woman in the Middle East* (Syracuse, NY: Syracuse University Press, 1997).

Maunira M. Charrad, *State and Women's Rights: The Making of Postcolonial Tunisia, Algeria and Morocco* (Berkeley, CA: University of California Press, 2001).

Andra Dworkin, *Scapegoat: The Jews, Israel and Women's Liberation* (Glencoe, NY: Free Press, 2000).

Ayala Emmitt, *Our Sisters' Promised Land: Women, Politics and Israeli-Palestinian Coexistence* (Ann Arbor, MI: University of Michigan Press, 1996).

Kathy Ferguson, *Kibbutz Journal: Reflections on Gender, Race and Militarism in Israel* (Pasadena, CA: Trilogy Books, 1995).

Nilufer Gole, *The Forbidden: Modern Civilization and Veiling* (Ann Arbor, MI: University of Michigan Press, 1996).

Sondra Hale, *Gender Politics in Sudan: Islamism, Socialism and the State* (Boulder, CO: Westview Press, 1996).

Deborah A. Kapchan, *Gender on the Market: Moroccan Women and the Revoicing of Tradition* (Philadelphia, PA: University of Pennsylvania Press, 1996).

Rene Melammed, *Heretics or Daughters of Israel? The Crypto-Jewish Women of Castile* (New York: Oxford University Press, 2002).

Haya al-Mughni, *Women in Kuwait: The Politics of Gender* (London: Al-Saqi, 2001).

Mona Al-Munajjed, *Women in Saudi Arabia Today* (New York: St. Martin's Press, 1997).

Annemarie Schimmel, *My Soul Is a Woman: The Feminine in Islam* (New York: Continuum Publishing, 1997).

Judith E. Tucker, *In the House of the Law: Gender and Islamic Law in Ottoman Syria and Palestine* (Berkeley, CA: University of California Press, 1998).

Madeline C. Zilfi, *Women in the Ottoman Empire: Middle Eastern Women in the Early Modern Era* (Leiden, the Netherlands: Brill Academic Publishers, 1997).

## LITERATURE IN TRANSLATION

Samar Attar, *Lina, Portrait of a Damascene Girl* (Colorado Springs, CO: Three Continents Press, 1994).

*The Intimate Life of an Ottoman Statesman: Melek Ahmed Pasha (1558–1662),* as portrayed in Evliya Celebi's *Book of Travels (Seyahatname)* (Albany, NY: State University of New York Press, 1991). Translated by Robert Dankoff.

Yeshayahu Koren, *Funeral at Noon* (South Royalton, VT: Steerforth Press, 1996). English version of *Levayah batsohorayin.*

Djanet Lachmet, *Lallia (Le Cowboy)* (New York: Carcanet Books, 1986). Translated by Judith Still.

Carol Magun, *Circling Eden: A Novel of Israel in Stories* (Chicago: Academy of Chicago Publishers, 1995).

Hanna Minah, *Fragments of Memory: A Story of a Syrian Family* (Austin, TX: University of Texas Press, 1993).

H. T. Norris, *The Berbers in Arabic Literature* (London: Longman, 1982).

Nicolas Saudray, *The House of the Prophets* (New York: Doubleday, 1985).

Charles G. Tuety, *Classical Arabic Poetry* (London: Kegan Paul International, 1985).

Abdullah al-Udari, *Modern Poetry of the Arab World* (New York: Penguin Books, 1987).

## CURRENT EVENTS

To keep up to date on rapidly changing events in the contemporary Middle East and North Africa, the following materials are especially useful:

*Africa Report*
Bimonthly, with an "African Update" chronology for all regions.

*Africa Research Bulletin* (Exeter, England)
Monthly summaries of political, economic, and social developments in all of Africa, with coverage of North–Northeast Africa.

*Current History, A World Affairs Journal*
At least one issue per year is usually devoted to the Middle Eastern region.

*Middle East Economic Digest* (London, England)
Weekly summary of economic and some political developments in the Middle East–North African region generally and in individual countries. Provides special issues from time to time.

## PERIODICALS

*The Economist*
25 St. James's Street
London, England

*The Middle East and North Africa*
Europa Publications
18 Bedford Square
London, England
A reference work, published annually and updated, with country surveys, regional articles, and documents.

*The Middle East Journal*
1761 N Street, NW
Washington, D.C. 20036
This quarterly periodical, established in 1947, is the oldest one specializing in Middle East affairs, with authoritative articles, book reviews, documents, and chronology.

*Middle Eastern Studies*
Gainsborough House
Gainsborough Road
London, England
A quarterly historical magazine.

*New Outlook*
9 Gordon Street
Tel Aviv, Israel
A bimonthly news magazine, with articles, chronology and documents. Reflects generally Israeli leftist peace-with-the-Arabs views of the movement Peace Now with which it is affiliated.